TAKING ON THE BURDEN OF HISTORY

PRESUMING TO BE A UNITED STATES MARINE

though, and perhaps even more so, is the loss of control over that tiger you're riding. You've passed a critical point, and what happens next is what happens. You're no longer the decider of what's going to happen next. When that was the case earlier has been lost to memory, but it was when you had control and could wave off the whole idea of jumping off that cliff. That you've come to the point where you can't is

TAKING ON
THE
BURDEN
OF
HISTORY

PRESUMING TO BE A
UNITED STATES MARINE

GEORGE M. VAN SANT,
COLONEL, USMCR-RET.

Copyright © 2008 by George M. Van Sant, Colonel, USMCR-Ret.

Library of Congress Control Number: 2008902499
ISBN: Hardcover 978-1-4363-2926-2
Softcover 978-1-4363-2925-5

All rights reserved. No part of this book may be reproduced or transmitted in any form or by any means, electronic or mechanical, including photocopying, recording, or by any information storage and retrieval system, without permission in writing from the copyright owner.

This book was printed in the United States of America.

To order additional copies of this book, contact:
Xlibris Corporation
1-888-795-4274
www.Xlibris.com
Orders@Xlibris.com

Contents

Acknowledgements 9

Preface 11

Chapter 1:   Enlistment And Parris Island (1945) 13
Chapter 2:   Boot Leave, Camp Lejeune, And A Slow Boat (1945) 61
Chapter 3:   China Adventures I (1945-1946) 88
Chapter 4:   China Adventures II (1946) 118
Chapter 5:   Home, Discharge, Between Wars (1946-1950) 149
Chapter 6:   Back To Camp Lejeune (1950-1951) 166
Chapter 7:   Quantico, Becoming An Officer (1951-1952) 182
Chapter 8:   To West Coast And Korea (1952) 204
Chapter 9:   Introduction To Combat 243
Chapter 10: Two Engagements, Things Heat Up (1952) 278
Chapter 11: In Division Reserve (1952) 302
Chapter 12: Stromboli 320
Chapter 13: Bunker Hill I 343
Chapter 14: Bunker Hill II 360
Chapter 15: Final Days With Fox Company, Into Reserve 382
Chapter 16: Winter And Back Online 410
Chapter 17: Back To Reserve And Back To The Lines 429
Chapter 18: Going Home (1953) 448

Postscript 457

Index 461

Dedication

This book is dedicated to the memory of

Edward Dunbar Van Sant
January 18, 1955-December 14, 2007

"He never got to read it."

Acknowledgements

The motivators for writing this book are numerous and go back for many years. Both my son, Edward D. Van Sant, and my daughter, Mary Van Sant Duncan, have been suggesting such an effort since they were children. Twelve years ago, after losing my late wife to cancer two years earlier, I was blessed with my wife, Milena, whose contributions to this book far surpass those of any other person. She also contributed four wonderful stepchildren, with whom I have been able to forge a very close bond. Each one of them, Andrea Micklem, Steve Votta, Nicole Tomiczek and Brandon Votta, as well as their spouses, have also pressed me to "get this thing done."

Milena was absolutely instrumental in producing the book. It was first dictated into a tape recorder and Milena then typed a complete draft of the work. Only she understands how challenging and tedious that job was. Since then she has edited each new version and contributed every step of the way..

One other person has been enormously instrumental in helping me. That is Robert Krick, the Civil War historian. I came to know Bob when he was the Historian with the National Park Service Battlefield Parks in Fredericksburg. Bob has taken up an interest in Marine Corps history and he is now a consultant with the U. S. Marine Corps Heritage Museum in Quantico, Virginia. He has made a great contribution to the installation of the first exhibits in that impressive and fast-growing institution. When the original draft of this work was finished, Bob had just retired and had some free time. He subjected that draft to a meticulous and thorough reading and made many, many positive suggestions and corrections.

Several of the fine people with whom I have served have made significant contributions. Dick Payne, my platoon corpsman in July and August, has contributed pictures and important information. Chuck Lundeen, our 81 Mortar Forward Observer, contributed all the maps. And Major (now Colonel-Ret.) Bob Dominick read and contributed to the account of our serving together. He also contributed several pictures.

Finally, I must thank the staff of Xlibris whose skills and devotion to their work has far exceeded what I had expected.

George M. Van Sant
Colonel USMCR-Ret.
July, 2008

Preface

The news anchor Tom Brokaw has written a book entitled *The Greatest Generation*. This book recounts a number of inspiring stories about the men and women who grew up during the Depression and fought World War II. I was born in 1927 and lived through the Depression, of which I have some painful and vivid memories. I then impatiently endured high school, began college during World War II, and enlisted in the United States Marine Corps in July of 1945. I had almost finished boot camp at Parris Island when the atomic bombs brought an unexpected and abrupt early end to that war. As the reader will see, I was sent overseas anyway, had a number of adventures, returned to college, and was called back for the Korean War.

In the following account, I have tried to recount in plain terms what it was like for an ordinary young man to enter and experience the Marine Corps; its training; and, eventually, combat. In presenting this story, I have endeavored to accomplish several things.

First, I have tried to recapture the responses, the anxieties, the disasters, and the triumphs of this ordinary young man who was probably not particularly well prepared for or conditioned for the military life, especially the military life as practiced in the elite U.S. Marine Corps. Because from the very beginning, I always wondered if I really had the stuff to be a U.S. marine, and because being a U.S. marine has turned out to be a crowning achievement of my life, I have entitled this book *Taking on the Burden of History: Presuming to Be a U.S. Marine*.

Second, I have tried to recall and present, as vividly as I could, some of the extraordinary men and women whom I came to know during that service. Most were persons of exemplary character, and some were funny as hell. But a few were craven cowards or morally degenerate misfits.

And third, I have tried to present both the outrageously hilarious and the poignantly horrifying aspects of my experiences. It is often said that combat veterans really do not like to retell their worst experiences. That is true. When one's memories are of total terror and of witnessing unspeakable sights, sounds, and smells, a recounting of even a portion of these experiences is supremely distasteful. Recalling these memories has been gut- and soul-wrenching for me, and many times, while writing this, I have dissolved into uncontrollable sobbing.

My primary purpose in writing down these stories is to leave a record for younger members of my family, before I forget all these stories or pass on. Maybe other young people can learn something from these stories. They describe the kind of experiences

Taking on the Burden of History

I think few Americans, with the obvious exception of our forces fighting wars and combating terrorism, have ever had. There is perhaps something to be learned from such experiences: the importance of humanity and the glories of being alive, and the depths to which humanity can sink.

A few caveats and cautions must be added at the outset. This is a personal memoir. It is written from a first person point of view. Some readers who were in Korea at the same time may remember certain events differently. In writing this, I have tried to check facts as well as I could from sources available. But as von Clausewitz said, "War is accompanied by a 'fog.'" This makes every individual's recollections of a war different from that of every other individual's. Inevitably, there are a very few persons the reader will encounter in these stories who, *from my point of view*, behaved very badly in a rich variety of ways. In some cases, I have gone to some lengths to conceal their identities. I do not want to gratuitously offend anyone. Also, there are a very few individuals whose identities cannot be concealed but who, I believe, have all passed on to street-guarding duty in heaven.

One last personal perspective must be shared. An enduring memory of life during World War II, and the half dozen or so years following it, was how often one heard variations on the word "service." One went into the "service." One was "in the service." The term "serviceman" produced instant respect. We were millions of young people who were called "to serve," and every American, civilian or military, respected that.

At Parris Island, I was merging my tiny, "maggoty" little self into a mass of literally millions of other people who were "serving" the rest of our nation. I was nothing—a mere number—but what I was doing was "serving" my fellow countrymen, and humanity in general. This feeling of service was palpable for the Greatest Generation. One can still see and feel it at any gathering of old vets from WWII. The loss of this omnipresent attitude toward service is perhaps the greatest loss of our modern era.

Chapter 1

ENLISTMENT AND PARRIS ISLAND (1945)

I can remember the exact moment when I decided to become a United States marine as if I were living it now. The day was a Sunday afternoon in late March of 1944, and these were the circumstances.

When I had been admitted to St. John's College in Annapolis, Maryland, in July of 1943, I was not quite sixteen years old. Although I lacked a credit for senior high school English, St. John's had admitted me as they did many other fifteen-, sixteen-, and seventeen-year-old males during the war. I had been able to finish my freshman year of college by the middle of March 1944 because the war was on and I could attend classes on a year-round basis. But now I was enjoying a two-week break until classes resumed for my sophomore year at St. John's in April.

My family had moved to the Maryland/DC area at the beginning of the Second World War, in 1941, but on that March day two years later, I returned to the place of my birth—State College, Pennsylvania. I still had many friends there from my childhood, reaching clear back to my beginnings.

It was my destiny to return to State College. I stayed in the big old house of a close friend of my parents, Mrs. Boucke, the widow of one of the great figures in the history of Penn State—so great, in fact, that today there is a very large academic building at Penn State called the Boucke Building.

It was the middle of the war, and Penn State was on a full wartime status. There were practically no male civilian students present. Most of the students were enrolled in various kinds of military programs, and they wore the uniforms of all the services. There were military students from the army, navy, and the Marine Corps, and these students marched to class and marched back to their billets, which were often the old fraternity houses turned into military housing. The small town had very much a wartime atmosphere about it.

I had managed to have some nice reunions with a few of my old friends, whom I had not seen since the time of Pearl Harbor, and on this particular Sunday afternoon, somebody said, "Hey, let's go out to Autoport."

Taking on the Burden of History

Now Autoport, built in 1936 and flourishing to this day, was the first modern motel established in Pennsylvania, and eight years later, we still thought it represented the height of elegance. Even before I had left State College, it had become a kind of hangout for upper-grade high school and college students. It boasted a restaurant and a beer bar.

"Let's go out to Autoport," one of my friends said; I think it may have been Douglas Mead. "A lot of guys hang out there on Sundays." Somehow, and I don't remember how, the two of us managed to get ourselves to our destination. We must have caught a ride with somebody because transportation was hard to come by during the war, and we certainly could not have walked there because in those days, it was outside of the town of State College.

We arrived at Autoport, and lo and behold, in walked my old friend Dan Stearns, resplendent in the uniform of a United States marine. During the thirties, my parents and I had lived on a small farm outside State College, and I had attended one of the last one-room, one-teacher-for-eight-grades schools in Pennsylvania. Dan had been a year ahead of me and was two years older, but living in the country, you take your friends where you can find them, and we had been pretty good buddies as children.

Dan had graduated from high school the previous June and had worked through that summer and fall on his father's farm. His family prevailed upon him to stay with them almost until Christmastime, but in December of 1943, he had enlisted in the marines.

By now, he had been in the Corps about twelve weeks and was on boot leave. Since Dan's father had been a marine in World War I, and something of a hero, Dan's choice was not surprising.

For several of the half dozen or so guys gathered together that Sunday afternoon at Autoport, this was going to be their last fling before going into service. As soon as Dan entered, everybody flocked around him, and with not too much prompting from us, Dan began telling us about Parris Island.

Dan was a good storyteller. He told the most horrendous, horrible, hair-raising stories about how harshly he had been treated at Parris Island and how hard the program was and how awful it was and how rough it was at boot camp. He made it all come alive, and you could just tell he was pleased as Punch that he had made it all the way through.

While he talked, I could feel the Marine Corps seeds slowly dropping into me and rapidly germinating. The challenge the Marine Corps posed, and still poses, for young men, and nowadays for young women as well, is this: "If others can endure and make it through the program, then why can't I?"

The more horrible he made the program sound, the more attractive it became to me. He looked dazzling in his uniform, and I might add that Dan Stearns is someone with whom I have had some contact since that fateful afternoon. He was sent overseas and fought all the way through the Battle of Okinawa, and we both ended up in China at the same time, although our paths never crossed there. Dan left the Corps after World

Presuming to be a United States Marine

War II and, just as I did when I got out, joined the reserves. We both were called up in 1950, and as luck would have it, Dan and I ended up in the same battalion at Camp Lejeune in 1950. Our careers up to that point had been somewhat parallel, although mine had started much later than his.

Once the Marine Corps seed was planted in me, and fertilized by Dan, it became firmly rooted although in March of 1944, I was not yet seventeen and could not even legally enlist in the Marine Corps. In order to get in at the age of seventeen, a parent's signature was required, as my parents, very forcefully, reminded me. Later that year, my father would be going overseas, and his impending departure loomed over us all. I remember my mother plaintively asking me, "If Daddy goes overseas, you are surely not going to leave me here all alone?" But in my mind and in my heart, I firmly knew that when the time came and the opportunity presented itself, I would become a marine.

Months passed. My father went abroad, and my mother was left alone with my young sister. She rented out a room in our house to a woman physical education teacher from my old high school so that she would have someone staying with her. My sister at that time was only five years old and had not even started school yet. I came home fairly frequently from Annapolis to visit.

We got through 1944 and the last Christmas of the war, and although I think that it was very clear to everybody that the United States and our allies were going to prevail in the end, even then it still looked like a long, long haul to reach that goal. Christmas of 1944 was still a somber time. The largest battle U.S. forces engaged in in the entire European theatre was being fought around Bastogne. The two largest battles of the Pacific war were yet to be fought in February and March of 1945 at Iwo Jima, and in April, May, and June of 1945 at Okinawa. It had become abundantly clear that the Japanese were not going to give up easily.

It was an interesting home front in those months, and I remember it well. First of all, there were practically no young men without a uniform to be seen anywhere. Everybody was in the service. Because I was tall and looked older than my years, I was periodically accosted by middle-aged ladies who sternly asked me why I was not serving. The buildup to get into the service was getting bigger and bigger. At St. John's College, the student body dropped below one hundred during the winter and spring terms of 1945, and a great many of my classmates and friends were already in the service. There were people leaving almost every day.

At St. John's, the tradition was that anyone leaving for the service was given a suitable farewell party, and since people were leaving so constantly, the parties went on almost continuously. Not surprisingly, my academic performance during those two terms, the winter and spring of 1945, slid right down the tubes. As you will see later on in this story, when I returned to St. John's after the war, my record for that period of time would be mercifully obliterated.

The outside pressure on me to enlist was building all that winter and spring of 1944-45, but of course, my mother remained the biggest obstacle to my enlistment in the marines. As spring turned into summer, in June of 1945, I took myself down to

Taking on the Burden of History

the Marine Corps recruiting station in Washington DC. It was explained to me what I would have to do in order to enlist at my age, and I picked up the necessary papers. That enlistment station, by the way, was a temporary building on Pennsylvania Avenue, between Fourteenth and Fifteenth streets. It is now a small park.

I took the papers home to my mother, and she prevaricated and delayed and piddled along until I finally got her to set a deadline sometime in July for her signature authorizing me to enlist. In early July, she relented.

In July of 1945, the war in Europe was over, and the full weight and strength of the French, the English, and, of course, the Americans was turning on Japan. Although Japan was embattled, there were ample signs that the Japanese were going to make us pay for every inch of their homeland.

The Sunday before my long-awaited enlistment, my girlfriend, Margaret Bolgiano, whom I had been dating since the previous Christmas, and I decided to take a long bike ride up through northern Prince George's County and into Howard County, Maryland. We packed a light picnic lunch and took a couple of soft drinks along. It was a warm July day, and our liquids were soon depleted. Way out in what was then a very remote and rural part of the Maryland countryside, we decided to stop at a lonely little farmhouse and ask for a drink of water. We cycled along a long lane, walked up to the front porch, and knocked on the door. A wizened old lady came out and, in response to our thirsty request, came back out of her house with two tall glasses of ice water. We stood in her front yard sipping the cool water while she talked with us.

She asked me the universal question: "Are you in the service?"

I proudly told her, "I am going to enlist in the marines tomorrow." And Margaret added that we were on our last bike ride together.

And then the lady said something that some weeks later I was to recall with considerable amazement. She told us in her shaky, querulous voice, "I don't think you really have to worry about the war, young man. I feel that we have developed some kind of a special weapon or bomb that's going to end the war soon. You will never even have to get involved in it."

Margaret and I finished sipping our water, returned the empty glasses to her with profuse thanks, and began the long cycle home. As we rode down the road out of the old lady's sight, Margaret rolled her eyes and rotated her finger at the side of her head, looking back toward the old lady's house.

The next day, I returned to the recruiting station to take my physical. First of all, as soon as I arrived, my height was measured. As I did not attain my full six-foot-five height until I was nineteen years old, I drew myself up and was measured to be six feet and three and one-half inches. My slender weight was 178 pounds. The recruiting sergeant told me, "Son, you know, you are just too tall for the Marine Corps. Can't you slouch a little bit?"

"What?" I said, and he explained that because I was enlisting as a seventeen-year-old, I had to conform to all the physical standards of the regular Marine Corps. Although I was enlisting in the Marine Corps Reserve, I was still subject to regular standards. At that time, the height limitations in the regular Marine Corps were between five feet six and six feet two, so I was one and one-half inches too tall. Crestfallen, I watched my dream evaporating and asked the sergeant, "My god! What are you saying? You are not going to take me?"

He replied, "No, we can get you a waiver, but you will have to go before a medical board for evaluation to make sure that you are capable of meeting the standards."

Had I waited until I turned eighteen years old that fall, and had I been drafted and then volunteered for the Marine Corps, there would not have been any problem with my height, which would have been acceptable up to six feet six or even six feet seven. But of course, I was too young to be patient. The fall seemed too far away. I was eager to become a marine now. I wanted to get in right then, and not anytime later.

Next, my blood pressure was taken, blood for testing was drawn, and a corpsman took my pulse. And *tung, tung, tung,* my pulse raced. By this time, having been told about the height waiver, I guess my pulse rate had shot up to ninety-two, and the corpsman said, "My god, you have a fast pulse. You can't get into the Marine Corps with that kind of a pulse rate!" And that was certainly another less-than-calming statement for me to hear.

The corpsman looked at me intently and said, "You really want to get into the Marine Corps, don't you?"

I answered him, truthfully, "Yes, I do."

"I'll tell you what, you go off into that little room over there and just lie down for a few minutes and try to calm yourself, and I'll take your pulse rate again later," he told me. I lay down on a gurney for a few minutes, making an enormous effort to relax. I must have been successful because when the corpsman retook my pulse, it had dropped to an acceptable seventy.

Next came the medical board for the height waiver, consisting of one single doctor, and it turned out to be a very curious experience. The doctor sat behind a desk in a barren office, a sparsely furnished room with blank walls. He had all my papers spread out in front of him and told me to take off all my clothes.

I stood there, stark naked, and he said, "What we are going to do is give you some coordination tests because you are pretty tall and gangly. But I think you know that already."

I remember the tests precisely. In the first test, I had to stand with my back, the back of my legs, and my heels flush against a bare wall, and my arms extended clear out to the sides against the wall. I was instructed to do a deep knee-bend, all the way down to the floor, keeping my back against the wall, simultaneously bringing my arms forward and touching my two forefingers together. Naked, I had to bob up and down in deep knee-bends three or four times, but I managed to get my fingers together every time and never fell away from the wall and was told, "Okay, that's all right."

Next, he came over with a triangular ruler, the kind used by engineers. He held it in front of me, parallel to the floor, between the palms of his hands. He had me spread my hands side by side with palms down over top of the ruler. Without giving me a clue as to when he was going to do it, he would spread his hands apart at indeterminate intervals so that the ruler would begin to drop. My task was to catch it before it hit the floor, which meant that I had to make a sudden sweeping motion down. It was a test of reflexes.

I just chortled to myself as we were doing this because some of my friends and I had, in our spare time, been working on this exact maneuver for years. I had become an expert in catching triangular rulers, and the doctor seemed quite impressed that I was able to easily catch it every time.

Next, he tested all my other reflexes. He tested the reflexes in my feet, in my knees, in my hands, and in my arms. Naked as I was, he swarmed over me like a pack of ants and finally said, "Son, you seem to be very well coordinated, and you have good reflexes. You pass."

There were three other guys being examined and tested on the day I enlisted. We ended up in boot camp together. And so we progressed through processing. After all of us had passed the physical, signed our papers, and everything was deemed to be in order, we were ushered into a captain's office. At this point, I was utterly naive about ranks in the Corps. Although I had heard about corporals and sergeants and knew that there were officers and enlisted men, I did not have a grasp on the technicalities and the finer points of ranks. We were, I now understand, actually ushered into the relatively exalted presence of a captain.

The sergeant took us in and introduced us and asked us to line up in front of the captain's desk, and we were asked to raise our right hand and to swear allegiance to the Constitution and to obey the orders of our officers, and I can't remember the exact words of the oath, but they were formidable ones.

The most interesting thing about this procedure was that up to the point when we were taken into the captain's office, the sergeants, the navy corpsmen who were giving us our physicals, and the clerks who dealt with us were extremely polite, pleasant, even respectful to us. One could almost be reminded of a bank, where the customer opening a new account is always right. "Mr. Van Sant, please step over here," the sergeant had asked me politely just a short time ago.

Our oath, though, seemed to have caused a complete personality transformation in our sergeant. From being simply the most obliging guy in the world when we entered the captain's office, he was suddenly converted into a terse, bellowing creature, yelling, "All right, you guys, line up, these are your orders. You will report to Union Station at 1800 hours for boarding train number so-and-so, and don't you even think of giving me any shit." Holy Moses, once they had you after that oath, they had you by the throat, and the contrast was simply amazing. Three gentle but eager civilians had walked into that office. Three utterly shaken would-be-marines emerged.

I was sworn in, I would guess, at about one o'clock in the afternoon. I dashed back out to Hyattsville to say good-bye to my mother and my sister. I called up my girlfriend, Margaret, and she was excited and said she would come to see me off at Union Station. Our instructions called for bringing only the clothes we were wearing on our bodies, which eliminated the necessity of packing a suitcase. But we had to bring our orders, and I clutched them in a big brown envelope, together with other official papers and documents and my train ticket.

Margaret and I went to Union Station together, found the train, and enjoyed a lingering, bittersweet farewell kiss. She waved me off as the train started moving. The train, as it turned out, was completely filled with military personnel. I would say that two-thirds of the people on the train were marines who were returning from their boot leave to go on to Camp Lejeune, North Carolina.

The Marine Corps has a great tradition. When you have finished boot camp and have officially become a marine, you are sent home for ten days to brag about it. And in that process, of course, the marine seed gets further disseminated and planted, as it had been planted in me by Dan Stearns.

These guys were now traveling back to Camp Lejeune, where they were going to begin advanced infantry training at what in those days was called Tent Camp. And they were in abundance. The other people on the train were young men like myself who were still in civilian clothes and completely green and were destined to arrive at Parris Island sometime the next afternoon.

The train must have started in Boston because there were new marine enlistees from Boston, New York, Philadelphia, Baltimore, and Washington. Almost everybody on the train had either just finished boot camp or was on their way to it, so that it was really a troop train. A couple of sergeants rode with us and checked our orders and checked our tickets and made sure we were all in the right places.

The train first stopped in Fredericksburg, Virginia. On the platform at the train station stood some older ladies and gentlemen with hot coffee, which they served us through the windows of our coaches. We were not allowed to leave the train, but these nice people made sure that we had some hot coffee inside us. And that was my introduction to Fredericksburg. Before my father left to go overseas in 1944, I had taken care of my sister for a long weekend while my parents visited Fredericksburg. They had returned enthralled with the beauty of the city, which was later to become my home. After living there for forty-eight years, I still have an abiding fondness for Fredericksburg.

The train continued on to Richmond, Virginia, where we encountered the same generous coffee treatment. We must have reached the station at about ten or eleven o'clock at night, but there were people serving coffee to us even at that late hour of the night.

As I tried to open my window to reach out for some more coffee, I realized that it was stuck and would not open. I began hitting the frame with the heel of my hand, and suddenly my hand slipped, and the window broke and cut the palm of my hand. It was not a very deep cut, but it bled. The conductor, who was clearly not happy about my busting a window in his train, came with a first-aid kit and grudgingly bandaged my hand. I can truthfully report that after my arrival at Parris Island, with all its rigorous training, I never once thought about that cut, or even noticed it. That cut simply ceased to exist.

Taking on the Burden of History

The train had two destinations. First, it went to Rocky Mount, North Carolina, where all the marines headed for Tent Camp at Camp Lejeune got off and streamed into acres of buses waiting for them. After that stop, minus a number of cars, the train continued on down to Yemassee, South Carolina, a tiny village almost to the Georgia border. There we transferred to a little pokey train, which took us through the bowels of the universe to Port Royal, South Carolina. One of the many carefully planned features of boot camp for the recruits was the loss of a full night's sleep en route to it. We had departed from Washington at six in the evening and arrived at Parris Island early the next afternoon, having sat up in our coaches all night.

Between Washington DC and Rocky Mount, we civilians had to listen to some more horrendous sea stories, told to us with some relish by the recent graduates, about what was going to happen to us once we arrived at Parris Island. Dan Stearns's stories paled to insignificance compared to some of the accounts I heard on that train, and I am sure the Marine Corps planned all this quite deliberately and thoughtfully, because by the time we arrived, we were not only tired, but we were in a state of shock.

At Yemassee, late the next morning, we were pulled off the train. Yemassee intersected with the little local rail line that snaked down to the tiny town of Port Royal. Throughout my life, the name "Port Royal" has, with some regularity, escaped me for reasons that will become clear in a minute, when you will fully understand why I am apt to block it from my memory.

This second train was really ancient. The seats were not upholstered; I remember they were simple wooden benches. That creaky railroad car had to have been at least sixty years old. The train moved very slowly, never more than at most thirty miles per hour, through a semijungle, with very heavy, succulent tropical vegetation. What I remember most distinctly on that trip of about forty miles is that the train was moving through what had to be the backwater of the South. Here and there, farms had been hacked out of the jungle, but what was most profoundly memorable to me was the enormous number of Negroes, living in shacks along the railroad tracks. As the train crept along, stopping about twenty times, a crowd of little boys, the oldest one being probably eight years old, would come out and start dancing for us. And what they were dancing for was money to be thrown to them. Most of the guys on the train got into the spirit of things and, as these boys were dancing, threw nickels, dimes, and quarters, which the boys would scramble to catch.

It was very sad, and I remember looking at the shacks these people were living in, and the conditions under which they existed and their obvious and deep poverty. The children were dressed in nothing more than dirty rags. There did not seem to be any obvious industry to support these people, not even much farming. I remember thinking at the time that this was a face of America I had never quite seen as starkly as on that day on that train from Yemassee to Port Royal. As long as it seemed, the ride finally bumped to a close, and now the excitement was going to begin.

We arrived in Port Royal into the waiting arms of dozens of marine corporals and sergeants, all very sharp-looking in their immaculate uniforms and panama hats. As soon as the train stopped, they swarmed onto every car and pulled us off the train in about two minutes. Once off the cars, they got us lined up into what, to a civilian, might have looked like a military formation. When we finally stood at some semblance of attention, these sergeants began briskly walking up and down the lines.

I remember that a couple of guys reported in wearing a zoot suit coat. During World War II, zoot suits had long tapered coats with very heavily padded shoulders, worn with pants pegged in at the ankles. Oh Lord! The sergeants just had a ball with them. They made these guys take their coats off, spread them out on the ground, jump on them, and then leave the mangled coats behind. The coats were gone; they were finished forever, left behind in the dust. Then there was a guy who brought his tennis racket to Parris Island. Man, that thing went flying off into the boondocks. You wondered what that misguided young man had been thinking of. That poor fellow must have thought that, surely, there would be some time for recreation provided for him at Parris Island.

I was a little better prepared. Once I had firmed up my intention to go into the Marine Corps, I made it a point to talk to Dan Stearns and some other marines. Having learned that the physical aspect of boot camp was going to be very rough, I had embarked on a conditioning program during the weeks and months before I had enlisted. Two features of the program were a good deal of running and push-ups to build upper-body strength. My push-up routine every night before going to bed was to add one push-up to the number of push-ups I had performed the day before. By the time I left for Parris Island, I had reached fifty-nine, which for athletic fellows these days is perhaps not a whole lot. But when I arrived at Parris Island, I was at least not completely soft, though as we will see, even after my very careful preparations, I was still not completely ready for the rigors awaiting me.

After jumping on the zoot suits, the tennis racket, and on all of us on general principles, our sergeants had us all thoroughly terrorized. I must say that I had never been more frightened in my life. On the other side of the train yard were lined up a number of stake body trucks—great, big eighteen-wheelers. The flatbed of this kind of truck was fenced in by vertical and horizontal slats about five feet high. We were herded aboard these trucks, and the speed with which we scrambled up just completely dissatisfied the sergeants. They stood at the end of the stake bed, bang-bang-banging with sticks. "Get on, get on, get on!"

Once you got on and stood up on the flatbed, you saw that the first guys who had made it up were able to get a place to hold on to the stakes around the perimeter of the big rectangular truck bed. But the sergeants and corporals must have packed a couple hundred people on each truck, and most of us had nothing to hold on to except each other. It soon became obvious that the drivers had been carefully instructed to drive as vigorously and erratically as possible, and being good marines, they strictly followed their orders. The ride to Parris Island quickly developed into one of the scariest truck rides imaginable. While humanity was packed solidly enough to force us to stand up, we were forever losing our balance and swaying back and forth wildly as the truck whirled around every curve, with the drivers slamming on their brakes at inappropriate and most unexpected moments, then quickly accelerating. The ride could not have been more than, at the most, three or four miles, but it was four miles of pure terror.

Parris Island, for those who have never been there, is a rather large island. In World War I, it was used as a marine training spot only to be reached by a boat, but between the two world wars, the government had built a causeway between the island and the shore.

We now drove out across the causeway and entered a large formal gate guarded by very sharp sentries. The driver of each stake body truck poured his vehicle crisply through the gates, slammed on the brakes, threw everybody toward the front of the flatbed, and took off again. As soon as we cleared the gate and arrived inside the base, which completely covered the entire island, we were surrounded by all kinds of marine activity. We began passing marine pedestrians, and as they saw the trucks driving by, the immortal call went ringing up to the skies, "You'll be sorry!" And drawn out, "You'll be sooorry!" If you weren't fully demoralized already, by this time, you were quickly approaching the last stages of deep melancholy.

We finally slammed to a stop in front of a complex of long, low buildings, which, I later found out, carried the wonderful name of Sanitary Unit. At the time I arrived at Parris Island, the Sanitary Unit was commanded by a Marine Corps legend, Master Gunnery Sergeant Lou Diamond, and we had somebody in our group who knew him by his reputation. It was Master Gunnery Sergeant Lou Diamond's job to welcome us to Parris Island.

Diamond had been in the Corps in both World War I and World War II. He had been a hero at Guadalcanal and had reached the status of a legendary figure. He did not deal with us directly, of course. He just oversaw our reception and periodically issued enormously loud and intense commands to his enormously attentive and intense subordinates.

We were herded into long rooms and ordered to take off all our clothes. We stripped. We were given baggage tags to fill out with our home address, and we had to fold up our clothes and put them in a cardboard box, along with our watches. Our underwear and socks were thrown away, compliments of the Marine Corps. The label we had written out was put on each box to be sent back to our mothers. We were received into the Marine Corps, so to speak, as we had been born, stark naked and defenseless.

After we had showered our naked bodies, we moved from the shower unit to the barber shop. There were long lines of barbers. I use the word "barber" loosely since these guys appeared to have absolutely no training, although this in no way prevented them from manning very fine clippers with which they sheared off all our hair, turning us into what was then affectionately known in the Marine Corps as "skinheads." This term has received some bad connotations in recent years, but in those days, a skinhead was a boot.

After the barbershop experience, we found ourselves in another room, where people behind long counters threw six pairs of underwear or drawers, as they were called, and six T-shirts at us. In those days, all of this underclothing was dyed green, I guess for jungle warfare. At the next counter, we were asked our shoe size and given two pairs of boondockers, the field shoes at that time. We were given socks and a seabag. We put on our underwear, first, and then received our utility or field uniform, our dungarees.

Next, we were given what was known in the "nice" parlance as a fore-and-aft cap, more familiarly known as a "piss-cutter." This was the hat for boot camp in those days, although very soon after I finished boot camp, the policy changed, and boots began wearing utility caps made from the same material as the dungarees. We were given belts and buckles and some little thin pieces of rope, which were a complete mystery to us. It turned out that those were tie-ties used to tie laundry to clotheslines when it was hung to dry. All these items we were told to place in our seabags. The next room equipped us with soap, toothbrush, toothpaste, shaving cream, a razor, and all the provisions necessary for personal care because, by golly, the Marine Corps was not going to let you be without these articles of personal hygiene. The interesting thing, though, was that all these toiletries were deducted from our first paycheck. We had to pay for them, and that was the procedure for such luxuries.

We were run through this course as quickly as we could be made to run, and there were any number of people constantly yelling at us, "Move over here, move, move, move! Pick up this, pick up that, MOVE!" We were under constant pressure to get everything we were supposed to get as quickly as we could get it, but with the clear understanding that we were never, under any circumstances, quick enough.

We were finally disgorged from the end of this building complex, and as we went out, we passed by sergeants standing there with clipboards and rosters, who checked our names and pointed us in various directions. On the day I entered the Marine Corps, I think something like ten platoons were organized. There were 75 men in a recruit platoon, so there must have been about 750 of us going through this initial processing.

The only word I can use to describe the foregoing process is "traumatic." By the time you emerged from that building, everything that you thought of as you, the person, or yours, as any personal belongings, were gone. Your watch was gone. Your clothes were gone. Your hair was gone. You had been broken down to the basic human being. And the brutal process of turning a maggoty, low-life, absolutely worthless "shit-bird" into a marine was about to begin. There were two corporals and a sergeant waiting for the group in which I ended up, and as soon as we came out, with a good deal of yelling and screaming, they got us lined up. We were all carrying a seabag full of stuff and had just put on our not-always-well-fitting brand-new utility uniforms. Mine was a bit too large for me in the chest, and as I remember, we all looked a little like scared and ridiculous misfits. But here we were. Too late to run.

When all seventy-five of us were lined up, the senior drill instructor, Sergeant Hendricks, got out in front of us and introduced himself. Next, he introduced the two junior drill instructors, who were Corporal Bonin and Corporal Bartell. Bonin took us all the way through, and Bonin was the man who probably had the greatest impact on us all. God, he was a mean little son of a gun, and he was a terror! Sergeant Hendricks was a relatively quiet man. He was a Southerner, with a soft drawl to his accent, and for the most part, of the three—but only relatively speaking, mind you—seemed to be the most gentle. I learned quite by accident that Bartell had taken some college courses at Cornell before coming into the Marine Corps, but this was not evident when we first met. All in all, he was pretty mean too.

The first thing we were taught was our platoon number. We were Platoon 467. That meant that in 1945, that July, we were the 467th platoon, because platoon number one started each January 1. The year was about half over, about 190 days had gone by; and by that time, the Corps had already ingested 467 platoons, or an average of 3 or 4 a day. Parris Island was packed with recruits at that point. We were told to never forget our platoon number. Next, we were told to look at our orders. Our orders had our serial number on it. I looked at mine and found that my serial number was 584645. I will never forget this number as long as I live because Corporal Bonin told me that I would go directly to hell if I ever forgot it.

Now I had my platoon number and my serial number, and that was all I needed. We were given the command for right face and marched off to our barracks. Untrained as we were, we did not march very well and, therefore, had to listen to a great number of negative comments about our marching skills. You would have thought that these three guys had just collected the most miserable assortment of humanity that could possibly be scraped up from the bowels of this earth, and they steadily reminded us of that fact all the way to our barracks.

Our barracks was in a long row of barracks the rear sides of which backed up on a fifty-yard-wide open area that sloped down to the sea. There was land visible way across that water from where our barracks stood. In front of the barracks was the drill field, an enormous roughly triangular asphalt-covered plain, which must have encompassed at least thirty acres. I think it was almost one mile long in its longest dimension and at least a half mile wide. Literally, dozens of platoons could drill on that big expanse simultaneously.

Getting settled into the barracks was a total fiasco. We peeled off, lined up, and took whatever bunk popped up as we arrived at it. The bunk had a mattress, a pillow, and a locker box. That was it. We were issued sheets and were immediately taught how to make a bed the only correct way, which was the Marine Corps way. Of course, everybody screwed it up, and if that was possible, we were at once demolished some more with criticism about being "the stupidest bunch of idiots" our drill instructors had ever had the personal misfortune to encounter. The bunk was made up with a lower sheet and an upper sheet. We had been issued two blankets and had to learn how to put one blanket, with proper corners, as tightly as possible over the upper sheet. The other blanket had to be folded in a very precise way. Eventually, we stenciled our names on that blanket so that our name showed on the fold. And so we made our beds, which took a good deal of time because every single one of us was visibly and obviously incompetent for the task.

Our seventy-five people were to live in one big room with double-decker bunks on both sides; this was our squad bay. Whenever we were in the squad bay, we had to stand at attention at the end of our bunk, the upper-bunk man on the left, and the lower-bunk man on the right. There was a space of a couple of feet between the bunks.

Now the sergeant came in and bellowed, "467, OUTSIDE!" We proceeded to tumble over each other as quickly as we could to get outside. We were on the second deck, or second floor, of the barracks. We had to go out through a door at the end of the squad bay to a small porch and an exterior wooden stairway, or ladder, leading with a 180-degree bend to a landing, and then down the rest of the way.

And we went up and down that stairway, I don't remember how many times, because we were not exiting fast enough in our abysmal incompetence. I remember one of our drill instructors, whether it was Hendricks or Bonin I couldn't be sure, shouting, "When I say 467, OUTSIDE, by the time I say 'SIDE,' you should be standing at attention out in front of the building." We practiced over and over again until we got pretty good at it. We could get seventy-five people down that staircase in about two seconds. Phoom, and we were down, standing at attention. Next, we were taught the proper position of attention, although the exact sequence of events during those first few days is somewhat hazy in my memory. I have tried to recapture and recall it as best I can, but I am never sure whether I can remember it all in the proper order.

There was a lot of processing and administration to be accomplished. We were given another complete physical exam, which I will tell you about in a minute. We were issued rifles. We were measured and fitted for our uniform, the Marine Corps greens, and these were tailor-fitted. We had to sign up for pay purposes, and we had to sign up for allotments, if we wanted to make them; this was money taken out of our pay and sent home. We had to sign up for savings bonds as everybody had to buy defense bonds. At the time I enlisted, the monthly pay was $50. Of course, there was nothing to spend our money on at Parris Island; we were just saving it up in the bank. We had to sign up for our National Service life insurance, and all of the preceding involved taking the platoon to some administrative office, passing out forms, and being instructed on how to fill them out. During these administrative activities, even the clerks in these offices treated us like maggots. Everybody was yelling at us at all times, and that was part of the program of keeping us, literally, off-balance and under constant stress.

We also had to be tested. During the first few days, everybody took what was called the General Classification Test, a form of IQ test. We took something called the Eddy test, which checked our capacity for electronics. We also took a couple of language aptitude tests. And every one of these tests meant that the whole platoon had to stumble down those stairs, line up at attention, and be marched or double-timed, which is running in step, to these various places and be herded through these various processes, with our drill instructors harassing us every step of the way.

Taking on the Burden of History

Not only did we have a complete medical examination, we also received a complete dental examination. The Marine Corps fixed up everybody who came in, and when you came out of Parris Island, your person was fixed, and your teeth were fixed. Although I had always taken care of my teeth, I apparently needed two fillings. At this point, the thought of having my teeth drilled and filled seemed like a wonderful break, because I would be able to go to the dentist by myself without any harassment from my DI. And there is another story to be told later.

I recall that all this processing began on the very first day. The first day, remember, is just the day after the evening before, when I left DC. I had had no real sleep, and we had not eaten yet. It was about five in the afternoon when we had the first part of our physical exam. The dispensary we were marched to was clear at the other end of the long dimension of the asphalt drill field. Our drill instructors took us out on the drill field, and then we double-timed; we ran from our barracks to the dispensary. I guess they wanted us to arrive for our physical out of breath. As you know, I had been doing some exercises before I left home, so I was merely exhausted at the end of the run, but I made it. A number of my fellow boots in the platoon were not so lucky. They fell down or fell out, and oh my god, the drill instructors just climbed all over them. Most of them got kicked or punched until they managed to get themselves down to the dispensary in one way or another.

And there was a tragedy in that particular run. One of my fellow boots, somebody I had not even really met and only vaguely remember seeing as we were going through the evolution in the reception center, and later in our squad bay making up our bunks, died on that double-time march. I was to learn later that a significant portion of our Platoon 467 consisted of a levy of people who had volunteered for the Marine Corps through the Holland, Michigan, Selective Service. They had been drafted, and the bulk of them were eighteen or nineteen years old. But some of them apparently went up to twenty-three or twenty-four years of age, and believe me, a person at the age of twenty-four going through Parris Island really has problems—it is that rough.

One of the gentlemen from Holland, Michigan, who had volunteered, was twenty-seven, and he had been a little soft and pudgy. We subsequently learned that he was a man who had spent his life sitting at a shoemaking machine, and as we started running from the barracks to the dispensary, this guy started double-timing along with the rest of us but soon fell out and fell down. The drill instructors went over to him and were about to begin harassing him when they realized that he was unconscious. He was, in fact, dead. He had died right there, on that run.

That put the fear of God into us, as you can imagine. We had sustained a fatal casualty our first day in our training, and I have often remembered that poor fellow whom I never got to know. He must not have thought through properly his idea of volunteering for the Marine Corps when he was drafted. He would certainly have benefited by preparing for the program and getting into better physical shape.

After we completed the first part of our physical, we were marched back out of the dispensary. Although we still looked awful, at least we moved like a platoon, and were rewarded by, finally, being taken to our first meal—dinner. I want to say, for the record, that throughout recruit training, we were well fed. The food was plain and simple, but good and abundant. I had weighed about 178 pounds when I enlisted. When I left Parris Island, I weighed 193 pounds. In spite of all the horrendous physical exercise and constant harassment, I had miraculously put on 15 pounds, most of which was muscle. Our dining hall was only about one hundred yards from our barracks, so that while we were being harassed a good deal on the way to our first meal, at least we did not have a long distance to go. And I must say that once we got into that dining hall, there was absolutely nobody yelling at us. We were allowed to eat in peace. I did not realize that on the first day, but I came to appreciate it in the days to follow. Having talked to subsequent generations of marines, I am told that this is no longer true, and I think that is a mistake. After our peaceful meal, we were allowed to straggle, individually, back to our barracks from the dining hall. We were marched to our meals, but were not marched back to our barracks. During that little stroll, we were allowed to smoke a cigarette. That first day at Parris Island was the day I started smoking seriously, a habit I had to break off, with great difficulty, much later on in life.

Once we got back to the barracks, the training began again. We trained until it got dark. The first things we learned, in addition to the position of attention, were how to make a facing movement, an about-face, and the principles of marching and flanking movements and oblique movements, and how to salute; and all of this was accomplished under the constant attention of the drill instructors, who were jumping all over us at all times, because we simply, and lamentably, never did it right.

On the third day, we were marched to the quartermaster to be fitted for our good service uniforms. Naturally, we had to stand at rigid attention in front of the building where the uniforms were stored and the tailoring people worked. We were called off singly from our platoon formation to go in and begin the measuring process to be fitted. On the next day, the fourth day, the platoon was rearranged, and we were graduated by height, which meant that I was a squad leader, as I was one of the tallest men in the platoon. At the time of uniform fitting, though, I was still somewhere in the middle of the platoon. The drill instructor stood in front of us, calling off our names. By this time, we knew that when called, we never walked—we ran from the formation, not breaking through the ranks. We had to run down the rank and down around the end of the platoon, and run into the quartermaster's building to be fitted.

I had soon learned the technique of looking as if I were at rigid attention while at the same time relaxing. I must confess that I was not paying the strictest attention to what was going on around me since we were obviously just going to be standing there until our names were called. At that point, we were under Corporal Bonin's charge.

Corporal Bonin yelled out, "Sant!" And that did not register with me at all. "SANT!" I saw that the blood had begun rising up his neck, because Bonin had a temper that could go off like a roman candle. "SANT, WHERE IN HELL ARE YOU?" bellowed Bonin, and finally, a guy behind me whispered, "Hey, Van Sant, I think he means you."

So I leapt out from the formation and stated, "Sir, *Van* Sant, sir."

Taking on the Burden of History

"What's that?" roared Bonin.

"Sir, my name's Van Sant, sir."

And Bonin said, "Goddamn it, if I want to call you Sant, I WILL call you SANT. Now get up there." But Bonin did call my name out correctly the next time, and for the rest of boot camp.

Corporal Bonin was a man for whom I still have enormous respect. We remained in touch with each other throughout our military careers, and he retired as a colonel too. Corporal Bonin was a tough bird. He was from Louisiana, had enlisted in the Corps at the age of seventeen, and had gone overseas immediately. He had fought in the battles of Bougainville, Guam, and Iwo Jima. He had just returned from Iwo Jima and had only taken through one other platoon before ours as a drill instructor. He had been the lightweight boxing champion of the Third Marine Division. He was tough, and he let us know it right away. Bonin was a very athletic-looking man, but he could not have been much taller than five feet four or five feet five.

You will remember my telling you that my dungaree uniform was a little big in the chest. This was because in order to achieve a good fit of my long arms in the sleeves, the girth around my torso had to be much too roomy. On one of those first days, Bonin came up to me, gathered the excess material from my uniform in his hands, and rocked me back and forth a couple of times.

"Van Sant," he yelled up into my face, "you think you can beat me up? DO YOU?"

I was still generally scared, although I had perhaps begun to harden up a little bit. Looking down on him, since I was about a foot taller, I had a fleeting but powerful vision of balling up my fist, bringing it down on top of his head, and driving him right into the ground. Immediately following that thought came the realization that this would hardly be a prudent thing for me to do under the circumstances.

In fact, one of the first stories the drill instructors told us as they were organizing our platoon was about a certain platoon at Parris Island that had started training in January. They told us that the platoon still remained at Parris Island for the reason that one of the members of that platoon had been hit by a drill instructor and had hit the DI back. A court-martial was declared, and the entire platoon was being held as witnesses for that court-martial, except that the court-martial, to date, had never been convened. The message to us was clear: don't mess with us, or you will be here forever—a thought too horrible to contemplate.

And now drill instructor Bonin continued rocking me back and forth, yelling, "Do you think you can beat me up?"

"Sir, no, sir!"

"Damn it, I can't hear you, Van Sant."

"SIR, NO, SIR!"

"Damn right you can't!" roared drill instructor Bonin. He let go of me and, satisfied about having shaken me up, went on his way.

That very first night, before we were finally allowed to go to sleep, we received some more instructions. Going to bed and getting up in Platoon 467 had a ritual all its

Presuming to be a United States Marine

own, as we were to learn. First of all, we were lined up at attention by the ends of our bunks. By the end of that first night, we all knew how to stand at attention, at least in principle, although our drill instructors continued in their opinion that our execution of that maneuver was undoubtedly the least satisfactory in the entire history of Parris Island, if not the entire military history of the world.

Our locker boxes were under our bunks, and at the end of our bunks was an open aisle space about fifteen to eighteen feet wide, which ran the whole length of the squad bay down the center of that long room. When we were all lined up and at attention, at 2200 hours, or ten in the evening, the drill instructor would yell, "Hit the sack!" And as soon as he said "hit," we were all expected to jump into our beds. The idea was that this would be performed simultaneously, by all of us, down to seventy-four boots by now, and all seventy-four bedsprings were to groan at the same time.

Needless to say, the first couple of times we tried this, we produced a cacophony of bedspring groans, extending over several seconds. We had to jump out again, stand at attention again, and perform the entire exercise again. The people occupying the top bunks were faced with a much more awkward and extensive leap. On the one hand, I was glad not to have occupied a bottom bunk, because the guys on the bottom bunk often bumped their heads on the top bunk in their efforts at increased speed. On the other hand, there was always a chance that the guy on the upper bunk would plummet right through his bunk and land on top of the guy underneath. There were clear advantages and disadvantages in both cases. After practicing hitting the sack three, four, five, six, seven, eight, ten times, we were, finally, hitting our bunks in absolute unison.

From the very beginning of our training, the drill instructors used a certain tactic to further demoralize their boots. In each platoon, there are always one or two guys who don't get it, who are too slow. The full wrath of the drill instructors will come down on them, but the full wrath of the rest of the platoon will come down on them also, because it is their screwing up that was keeping the rest from getting into bed to stay. While there is a little bit of divide-and-conquer on the part of the drill instructors, I hasten to add that the great virtue of the Marine Corps, based on its boot camp training and any subsequent training, is that it builds teamwork in the most excellent and solid kind of way. In order to build a team, you have to have a group of adequate individuals to start with, and the Corps makes absolutely sure that they have made more than one of every boot. Some of the platoon knuckleheads were already beginning to get exposed by the first day, but I am happy to say that I don't think I was ever a platoon knucklehead. Frequently, I was singled out for very severe criticism, everybody was, but I don't think my screwups caused others to suffer.

One of my fondest and most nostalgic memories of my very first night was that after having played "hit the sack" numerous times, and having finally, very grudgingly, met the drill instructors' lowest standards, the lights were finally turned out. And just after the lights went out, we heard taps. The bugler stood clear across the drill field, in a location that was apparently central to all of the barracks and tents, and blew his bugle into a huge megaphone. The solemn tune wafted out all over the island. It was

Taking on the Burden of History

a beautiful, pure sound, and we knew then with gratitude that, at least for the next few hours, the drill instructors could not get to us.

Arising in the morning entailed another elaborate procedure. While we were still sound asleep, perhaps catching the last part of a wonderful dream, suddenly the lights would come on with "HIT THE DECK!" roared by a drill instructor, and before he completed sounding out that brief sentence, we had to be standing at rigid attention at the end of our bunks. Again, that was the theory. In fact, that too sounded like a cacophony of bumps the first time. We practiced many times over, and for the rest of boot camp, every morning, we would jump out of our bunks and, as they say in the Olympics, "stick it." We would all leap to rigid attention in unison, all seventy-four pairs of feet landing at the same time. And so our day at Parris Island would begin, a day that invariably stretched out into eternity.

After we were issued our rifles, we had to learn the code of the rifleman, and we also had to learn the manual of arms with the rifle. We were taught very carefully and painstakingly how to take the rifle apart, how to clean it, and how to care for it. There were many repetitions in this training too, and we had our rifles inspected two or three times daily. The rifle was inspected in a military formation, with inspection arms and all of the rituals associated with it.

The interesting thing was that nobody's rifle was ever found to be clean. It was always dirty. We could spend hours cleaning it, and darned if the DI did not find the minutest speck of dirt somewhere on it. He would immediately go into paroxysms of anger and distaste. "Your rifle is FILTHY!" There might merely be one microscopic grain of dust hiding in some obscure portion of the rifle, but the drill instructor would inevitably search it out.

We learned how to take care of our uniforms. We had to stencil our names on every item, since we were never trusted to be competent enough not to lose it somewhere. Every minute of each day was packed with some kind of instruction or drill or exercise. At least, to begin with, there were no breaks, literally, during the day. Never. We were just always on the go.

In July of 1945, it was hot on Parris Island, and we perspired profusely. Fortunately, we were allowed to drink as much water as we wanted. There were water fountains in every barrack, and by each water fountain was placed a dispenser of salt tablets. We were encouraged to take these tablets, and I would bet that I was taking about twenty salt tablets a day. The ingestion of these salt tablets produced an interesting effect because the salt in our sweat spread in a white stain over our glistening new green dungarees and soon became so embedded in the fabric that even the strong fiber scrub brushes we were issued could not remove it.

The morning of our second day, we were all lined up and marched to physical exercises. If you have watched any newsreels from World War II, you will have seen large groups of men doing exercises together all over the world. On Parris Island, we stayed together as a platoon in this formation, but we were in with many, many other platoons as we performed these workouts. A physical drill instructor stood up on a platform holding a megaphone, giving us our commands, and we counted by the numbers while performing various exercises. I clearly remember the first time we fell out for the physical training exercise with at least ten other platoons, each one of which was supervised by its three drill instructors. One of the exercises was pushups. My advance training in pushups really saved the day for me, because the drill instructors went up and down the ranks of the platoons, with all of us on our stomachs on the asphalt doing pushups by the numbers. At boot camp, we started at sixty, one more than where I had left off at home, and so I was one of the few recruits in our platoon who had no problem with pushups. But the poor bastards who had not previously practiced their pushups got kicked in the butt and were harassed mercilessly for being no-good weaklings. As I was bobbing up and down on the asphalt, I was thanking the good Lord that I had been advised to get ready.

The war had been going on for some years now, and the army had made a number of, looking back on it, excellent training films on many military subjects. All the rudiments of map reading and compass reading were taught by movies. I must say that for me, anyway, the movies were very instructional and have stuck in my memory. These films had a little bit of a plot too. You would see young private so-and-so learning how to use a compass and being taken out on the ground for a demonstration on how to read it. The films were well paced; they were repetitive in their instructions; and at the end of the film, all the instructions were reviewed.

The subjects we learned by film, in addition to map and compass reading, were patrolling with compass and field sanitation. The field sanitation and several other health-related movies were quite funny, and there is one that particularly sticks in my mind. In it, all the principles of sanitation were taught around a mythical company, Company B. This army company goes into the field, and everything about sanitation is done wrong. They do not dig their latrines, as they were called in the army (in the navy and the Corps they are called heads), in the right place, and they do not dig them properly. They do not clean their mess gear, they do not keep their area clean, and they do not take care of rainwater runoff. Everything this Company B does is wrong. As the movie progresses, the entire Company B comes down with various forms of illness, all because of their lack of sanitation, so that at the end of the movie, it becomes the "late" Company B. For all the good it does me, I can remember to this day how to purify water and wash mess gear and keep my person and my surroundings clean in the field.

While the entire presentation was very sensible, and even interesting, there was one big drawback to all of the training films, not in any way the fault of the makers of these movies. The films had to be shown in a completely dark and windowless room, and to this end, a sort of field-expedient movie theater was built, called a Butler hut. These huts would hold about five or ten platoons sitting on the floor. There were no seats or windows, just 16 mm film projectors manned by marine projectionists, and a big screen on which to project these films.

It was July and hot as Hades, and I don't think anybody on Parris Island had heard the words "air conditioning" at that point, although I am sure that there were fans circulating the heavy, humid air around as we were all sealed inside these huts. Coming off the drill field, hot and sweaty, we would be put in platoon formation and lined up and herded into the Butler huts to view a training film. Having just had lunch a couple of hours ago, and with a temperature inside these huts rising to maybe 110 degrees, we would find that sleep became our greatest enemy. Naturally, the drill instructors were all equipped with flashlights. From time to time, they would run the beams from their flashlights across the platoon, just to make sure that everybody was still wide awake. And if you ever made the mistake of falling asleep while viewing one of those films, the wrath of the gods fell directly and decisively upon you.

A typical day in that period of recruit training began at 0530, when we were forcefully awakened. At 0530 that is, if we had a normal night, and I will explain that a little later on, because we undeniably experienced several abnormal nights. You first took care of yourself, and that meant that you shaved; showered, if you had not showered the dirt off the night before; and brushed your teeth. And speaking of shaving—the very first day at Parris Island, the DI had ordered us to shave every day, "whether you need to or not!" At that age, I still had nothing but a light peach fuzz on my face, but I mostly obeyed the order anyway, with the exception, that is, of one certain morning. That morning, and it must have been ten days or so into the program, I was in a terrible hurry and behind schedule. I looked at myself in the mirror and could not detect any fuzz. I decided that I would chance it and skip shaving that morning.

During the meticulous inspection of our rifle and person, which he conducted every day, Corporal Bonin examined me very carefully in the bright sunshine. After swelling up in the characteristic way when his temper was about to go ballistic, he yelled, "Van Sant, did you shave this morning?"

Realizing that telling the truth to Corporal Bonin was absolutely the only right thing to do, I said, "SIR, NO, SIR!"

He then went ballistic all the way and gave me a warning that was very much in vogue in those days. He said, "After inspection, report to me and stand by for a ram."

Bonin subsequently found another poor soul in the platoon who had also tried to finesse shaving, and after inspection, the two of us were ordered to go to our locker boxes and get our razors. He then lined up the platoon in the open area in the center of the squad bay where they were to be the spectators to our humiliation. He ordered us to exchange razors and to dry-shave each other—that is, I shaved him with his razor, and he shaved me with my razor, and we performed this task on each other simultaneously. But Corporal Bonin added one more requirement. We were to continue to dry-shave each other until there was a visible drop of blood on the squad bay deck between our feet. One drop each, that is. It was a very strange and painful punishment. After this experience, I shaved every day, without fail.

Continuing with our daily routine, after our persons were clean, we made our bunks, fell out, usually by 0600 hours, and marched to breakfast. As soon as we returned into the squad bay, everybody turned to and scrubbed, swept, and cleaned the squad bay. It had to be immaculate by the time we fell out at 0730, when our training day usually started. We would almost invariably have a color ceremony at 0800; we were always in formation at 0800, and usually, we would already have had a rifle inspection or be in the midst of one. Somebody would yell, "Colors!" The drill instructor would bring us to attention, and we would go to present arms. Then, coming out over the amplification system were the sounds of the bugle blowing to the colors. And that constituted the official beginning of the day. During the first week, we had to pass swimming qualification, which was no problem for me. In order to qualify, we had to jump into a fifty-meter pool with our uniform on and swim the length of the pool and back. There must have been about ten people in our platoon who could not do it, and those poor guys had to give up the hour of free time we eventually got in the evenings. While the rest of us spent that time writing long lamenting letters back home about how horribly we were being treated, these miserable men had to go back to the pool for swimming instruction. One could not graduate from boot camp without knowing how to swim.

My recollection of boot camp is that we were never allowed to sit down between our many activities, and the standard orders were to be at attention for most of the time, but if we were not at attention, we were at ease. In the position of at ease, the right foot is kept in the place it was when in the position of attention, but the left foot can be moved off and around. One is not allowed to talk to one's fellow boot while at ease. Very occasionally in the beginning, but slightly more often as boot camp progressed, we were commanded to "Rest." At the position of rest, we had to keep at least one foot, and it could be the left or the right, in the place it had been when at attention, and we could talk. Oh, rest was a big, wonderful break!

Usually, though, we were being punished for somebody's screwup, and the punishments were varied. In retrospect, some of these punishments seem pretty awful. I remember that once, we screwed up in some sort of drill formation. We were ordered to stand at attention in platoon formation out on the drill field in the middle of the day under the blazing sun, and the drill instructor periodically commanded us to assume the position half right face so that we would always face into the sun. And we just had to stand there, at attention, blinded and blistered by the sun.

When we had first arrived at Port Royal, one of the guys had been wearing dark glasses. Sunglasses were to a drill instructor an instrument of the devil. Clearly, any candy-ass, stupid, sissy, softie idiot who had to wear sunglasses would never make a marine, unless he became a "Hollywood marine." Nobody in our platoon ever made the mistake of wearing sunglasses after that terse interpretation by our drill instructors. And so we stood at attention for a couple of hours, facing the sun, with temperatures close to one hundred, and several people passed out in the process.

Occasionally, the wrath of the drill instructors would fall upon one particular individual who had really screwed up. On some such occasions, they would decide not to punish everybody but focus only on that individual. I remember one guy who received that kind of punishment, and I even remember his name—Boyer, from Pennsylvania. With the large group of recruits from Holland, Michigan, another large group came from Harrisburg, Pennsylvania. There were four of us from Washington DC in our platoon. All of us came from fairly homogeneous backgrounds, although there were several areas of the United States represented. I am sure that at least some of Boyer's ancestry was Germanic; he had a little bit of an accent. He was a tough guy, had grown up on a farm, and we later saw on the rifle range that he was an excellent shot, having hunted all his life.

But Boyer had screwed up somehow, and one of the drill instructors latched on to him after dinner. While we were doing something in the barracks that night, the DI told Boyer, "You see those two telephone poles, recruit?" The two poles were on the edge of our drill field in front of our squad bay. And the DI said, "I want you to run back and forth between those two telephone poles until you drop."

And whatever we were doing in the squad bay allowed us to keep track of Boyer through our window, and we saw Boyer running back and forth between those two telephone poles for a long, long time because Boyer was a tough guy, and he was not going to drop anytime soon. After it had turned completely dark outside, the drill instructor came in, grabbed two guys, and told them to go out and bring Private Boyer back. He had finally dropped to the ground where they found him. Boyer was a good guy and became a tough marine. Five years later, when I got called back to go into the Korean War, Boyer and I ended up in the same battalion at Camp Lejeune. He had made PFC and still loved the Marine Corps.

One time, several weeks into the program, we were mass-punished. The platoon, at least in the eyes of the drill instructor, had screwed up badly. And so after dinner, we were marched to a one-acre spot where the ground was covered with piles of gravel about five feet high. These very small stones were being used as aggregate for concrete to be used for a new outdoor movie theater screen, which was being built at that corner of the drill field. At that point, construction on it had just begun, and it was not quite finished by the time I left Parris Island. Our drill instructors took us out and marched us through that gravel pile. The Marine Corps shoe in those days was the low-cut boondocker, which came up over the ankles, but was not a boot. After boot camp, we wore leggings with the boondockers, and these were put around the bottom of the trousers. But we wore no leggings in boot camp. The boondockers, which tended to flare open at the top, created little funnels around the ankles, and as we marched around in the gravel, sinking into it quite deeply, the tops of our boondockers were funneling small pieces of gravel into our shoes.

We were doing "to the rear, MARCHes," spinning around on one foot, and we did all that in the deep gravel. After the drill instructors were damn sure that every man had two shoes full of gravel, they marched us back over to a big concrete sidewalk platform. There we were marched back and forth, doing small flanking movements since the concrete pad was big enough to accommodate such movements. Darkness was settling when we finally stopped marching on that concrete pad.

This was several weeks into the program, and we were getting to be pretty sharp and good marchers by this time, doing everything in unison. The DI would sometimes call out the cadence, "One, two, three, four," or sing cadence, "Hey-Lomp, Hey-Lomp" when we were on a hard surface to keep us in perfect step. But sometimes they would yell, "All right! Now listen up! DIG!" And "dig" meant that you brought your foot down with the heel, very sharply against the hard surface. A platoon of marines digging sounded very much like a German storm trooper outfit—*clunk, clunk, clunk,* like that.

Well, we dug on this concrete pad with our shoes full of gravel. It was a mass punishment, and it was brutal, and when we were finally released back into the barracks, every single man had bloody socks because everybody's feet were cut and shredded. Some of the men's feet hurt so badly that I remember four or five tough guys in the platoon quietly crying. Back in 1945, men did not cry. It was awful. It was brutal, but whatever mistake we had made, we surely never made it again.

After dinner, we would usually have school in the squad bay. The main subjects, history and traditions, were taught in the squad bay by the drill instructors themselves. This is where we learned the language of the Corps, which was, of course, the language of the navy. I look back on these instructions fondly because the drill instructors, for the most part, were really trying to put over the traditions of the Corps, which they themselves clearly cherished, and they only turned nasty, momentarily, when a recruit did not immediately give the right answer to their questions.

We found out why we are called leathernecks, and why we have the quatrefoil on top of the hats for officers. Both these expressions date back to the early days of the republic when marines were often placed in the rigging of sailing ships as snipers. The quatrefoil on officers' hats enabled the troops in the rigging to distinguish their officers from the enemy in case hand-to-hand combat was taking place, either on the enemy ship alongside or on their own vessel. The leather neck collars were presumably protection against saber blows.

We learned about all the various ranks in the Corps and their significance and what their various responsibilities were. We learned the whole structure of the Corps, how it went from fire teams to squads to platoons to companies to battalions to regiments to divisions to corps, and who commanded each one and what their responsibilities were; and we learned all that in squad bay from the drill instructors. It was a comprehensive and thorough course, and we had written examinations on it.

By the time we left Parris Island, we knew the name and the date of every battle the Marine Corps had ever fought, including all the battles of World War II. We had to learn who the first marines were, and that they were enlisted at Tun Tavern, Philadelphia, Pennsylvania in 1775. We learned the names of the commandants, and we also learned the chain of command.

I can still hear my drill instructor saying, "Every marine at every moment must always know the name, rank, and position of every person between him and the president of the United States." Of course, we knew the names of our drill instructors. Those names, by the way, are never forgotten by a marine no matter how long one may live. They are branded into the memory forever.

Taking on the Burden of History

There was a warrant officer who was actually our platoon leader, but he had about ten platoons, and we only saw him once at our two-week inspection. We had to know his name, which I have since forgotten.

Then we had a company commander, who must have commanded dozens of platoons, and we had to know his name, which I do not remember.

And then we had a battalion commander who, as I recall, was a major. Parris Island at that time had six training battalions, and we were in the Third Battalion. I do not recall his name.

Finally, there was the commander of the base of Parris Island, who at the time was Major General Pedro Del Valle.

We had to know the name of the commandant of the Marine Corps, of course, who at that time was General Archibald Alexander Vandegrift, a man whom I came to know reasonably well many years later when he retired in Charlottesville, where I attended graduate school. General Vandegrift was the marine commander at Guadalcanal and was a legend in both World War I and World War II.

We had to know the secretary of the navy, who was then James B. Forrestal, and the president of the United States, Harry S. Truman. And that was my chain of command at Parris Island.

The history, traditions, and chain of command were all taught in the evenings in the squad bay. In those classes, we would sit on the deck, or floor, and the drill instructors would prepare the classes and rotate as teachers. Periodically, we would be given written tests.

Usually at about 2030 or 2045, we finally had some free time to ourselves. But even during that period, there were many things we had to do. For one thing, we had to start shining our shoes. In the Corps, enlisted men used to spend probably 5 percent of their total time shining shoes, at least until the wonderful invention of Corfam some twenty years later, which makes the shoes automatically shiny. But in those days, we had to take what were really dull-looking shoes and polish them, and polish them, and polish them, and polish them until they were shiny, so shiny that we could see ourselves in them but, much more importantly, so that our DI could see himself in them.

And we were polishing brass all the time. If our belt buckle wasn't glistening bright, we were designated as being even more worthless than had been expected of us at first sight, and in addition, we were filthy, dirty, no-good, rotten worms. At night, we also cleaned our rifles for the morning's inspection, trying desperately not to let any dust settle on them overnight.

But after all that, if we still had a little time, we would write our very colorful and pitiful letters home, which dramatically illustrated all the unspeakable things that were being inflicted upon us each and every day. And, of course, we talked. Talking among the recruits, particularly during the early weeks of boot camp, I am sure, is standard. I have checked with other people, and they all agree with me that everybody who has ever enlisted in the Marine Corps, on about the third day on Parris Island, regardless of the circumstances and no matter what the original motivation for joining may have been—but on about the third day at Parris Island, just about everybody is deeply flooded with regret, and this regret becomes palpable and universal.

Everybody looks at each other and says, "My god! Why did I do this?" And I particularly remember some of the draft recruits who had volunteered for the Corps saying, "Oh God, what a mistake! I could have been living it up now. I would probably be going to the PX in army basic training." PX? What PX? On Parris Island, I never even got close to a post exchange, where they have things to buy and goodies to eat. Never.

Whenever you have a large group of young men thrown together, the topic of conversation inevitably comes down to sex, not excluding some tall stories and even outright lies. There was a good deal of discussion on the subject of sex in general and, in particular, with thick clouds of testosterone swirling around us. Early in my boot camp career, I had made a crucial mistake. Somehow or other, it became publicly known that I was still a virgin. If you went back and reassembled 467 today, or those of us who are still alive, one of the things they would undoubtedly remember about me would be, "Oh yeah, he was the virgin." Now, I am morally certain that there were many other virgins present in our platoon, but being the only one stupid enough to admit it, I took an enormous amount of static and was teased mercilessly. All the rest of the members of the platoon, by their own testimony, were, of course, enormously experienced swordsmen. And my goodness, since there was quite a leavening of men who were twenty-three, twenty-four, and twenty-five years old, of whom several were married, I would say that a majority of the platoon were not virgins. Nevertheless, I feel sure that there were more virgins among us other than that one single, solitary pathetic figure—me.

One day, one of the guys came running up and, within my earshot stage-whispered to the other guys, "Hey, did you hear?"

"No, what?"

"Van Sant entered flesh today."

"What?"

"Yeah, the toilet paper broke." This was followed by great guffaws.

Another feature of life was, as I had mentioned before, that our teeth were brought up to shape. We all had dental inspections, and those of us who had flaws had to go back to have their teeth filled and fixed up. And now follows one of the most terrifying experiences I had on Parris Island. It started out quite well. One of the drill instructors called me down to the office, said, "Here," and shoved a paper at me, which authorized me to proceed out of formation. You remember, recruits were not allowed to walk around on Parris Island, except in marching formation. I had to have something like the hall pass you got in high school, a slip of paper allowing me to go from the barracks, and only from the barracks, to the dental dispensary, and only to the dental dispensary.

Now, the dental dispensary at Parris Island was fairly elaborate for that era. I remember hearing later, and it may be from my good friend George Oliver who was

Taking on the Burden of History

a navy corpsman down there at the time, that the large frame building held sixty navy dentists. These were men who had been recruited into the medical/dental corps to be dentists. In addition, there was a flock of medical corpsmen acting as dental assistants.

After breakfast, I reported over to the dental dispensary, as ordered, and sat in a waiting room for a brief time until a corpsman came in to call me out. These guys treated lowly recruits the same way drill instructors treated us—as nothing more than a maggot, and with bad teeth at that. I followed the corpsman up some steps and down a long hall and into a little dental room with a dentist's chair and a lot of equipment, including an assortment of the usual drills. The corpsman sat me down, draped me with a dentist's apron to keep the debris expected to come out of my mouth off my dungarees, got me all set up, and left me.

I sat there in a kind of reclining position, and sat there, and waited, and waited. Finally, I heard a noise at the door, and in came a young dentist, a lieutenant junior grade. He was one of the first officers with whom I had ever had any contact since I had arrived, with the exception of the captain who had sworn me in.

The lieutenant did not treat me the way the drill instructors did. He greeted me with, "Your name's Van Sant?" Then he leaned over the chair in which I sat with a probe and a mirror in his hands. As his face hovered over mine, I was assaulted by a tremendous puff of alcohol fumes. It almost took my breath away. He was quite chatty and chummy, saying, "Man, did I have a liberty last night! We all went up to Savannah, and boy, I got blasted! Didn't get home until four o'clock this morning, and to tell the truth, I don't feel too good."

It immediately became evident to me that he was still drunk, perhaps from having had a morning shot of the hair of the dog that had bit him the night before. And in the face of the large assortment of various dental drills, my dentist's erratic behavior certainly alarmed me. But I obediently opened my mouth, and he looked at my teeth, and he looked at the chart that had been prepared for him.

Then he whipped out the drill. As he brought his hand with the drill in it up to my mouth, I realized that his hand was shaking violently and I became, suddenly, petrified. He managed to insert that drill into my mouth and started drilling on my tooth, and the drill lingered on the tooth for a second, and then the drill slipped off into my gum. He was now drilling my gum. My mouth was filling up with blood while my dentist articulated something like, "Oh shit!"

I was scared stiff, and what presence of mind I still possessed caused me to jump out of the chair with the dentist's apron still around my neck and beat a hasty retreat. I ran down the hall to a desk with a corpsman behind it. With blood filtering out of the corner of my mouth and dribbling down to my chest, I reported to him that "the dentist seems not to be feeling very well."

"Just have a seat here, for a minute," the corpsman told me, having looked me over sharply, and I sat down for a while. Around the corner, I caught a glimpse of a couple of other corpsmen and, later, a couple of officers, presumably investigating the intoxicated dentist. I don't know what eventually happened to that fellow, but after about ten or fifteen minutes, I was sent to another room with another dentist. By that time, I had stopped bleeding, and the new dentist very efficiently filled my tooth and sent me on my way. A drunken dentist with a drill in his shaking hand has to be one of the scariest things one can ever encounter. I am reasonably sure that this was not, at least officially, a part of my Parris Island prescribed boot camp training.

We conducted training six days a week. On Saturdays, we had the end-of-the-week inspection by an officer. At the end of the first week, we had the end of the first-week inspection; at the end of the second week, the end-of-the-second-week inspection; and at the end of the third week, the end-of-the-third-week inspection. At each one of these inspections, we were expected to have advanced tremendously in all military skills—drilling, cleaning our rifles, and keeping our gear and our uniforms squared away; and we were to be really sharp in all these things by the end of the third week. After each of these inspections, we continued training for the rest of the day.

And then there were Sundays. On Sundays we did not get up until 0630. We were granted an extra hour of sleep and were marched to breakfast as usual. We straggled back to squad bay with the ever-present cigarette, and at 1000 hours, in a military manner, we fell out for church.

The Marine Corps' views on religion and church at that time were pretty interesting. During one of the many segments of processing on our first days in boot camp, we were issued our dog tags. The dog tag, that familiar little metal tag, showed our name, our serial number, our blood type, and our church affiliation. As we were filling out a form with information for engraving on the dog tag, it was made very clear that completing the question of our religious affiliation was obligatory. We had to declare ourselves to be either Roman Catholic, Protestant, or Judaist; and those were the only choices given.

As the dog tags were being issued, probably on the second day when we were still stupid enough to ask questions, I remember one recruit saying, "Sir, I don't really have any religious faith." And the drill instructor told him in no uncertain terms, "You are a Protestant!" Clearly, if you had any questions about your religion at all, you put down *P* for Protestant.

On Sunday mornings, this whole drill was repeated. You had your three choices, but you went to church. You were allowed to make the decision whether you wanted to go to a Catholic church, a Protestant church, or a Jewish temple, but you had to make your selection. You could not stay in the barracks; you were required to attend one of the three religious services.

As I remember, there were a couple of Jews in our platoon, and one of the drill instructors was assigned the task of marching these two men across the base to the synagogue. The rest of the platoon were either in the Protestant/atheist/other or the Roman Catholic contingent. I would assume that if there were persons of any other religious persuasion whatsoever, they were promptly classified as Protestant and marched off to church under that category.

Taking on the Burden of History

I must say that I attended church every Sunday, partly because I had no choice, but also because this gave me the gift of at least one hour when nobody was yelling at me for being a no-good maggot and ordering me to get squared away. The tenor of the sermons demonstrated a clear recognition on the part of the chaplains that each one of their congregants was presently going through his own personal hell trying to get through boot camp, which, the chaplains obviously felt, made us especially vulnerable to receiving the Christian message. I remember at least one of the prayers led by the chaplains in which we all appealed to the Almighty to give us the strength and courage to persevere through our trials and tribulations. I thought this prayer to be reassuring, refreshing, and helpful, although I am not sure what the professed atheists got out of it except, perhaps, a semi snooze. As for me, I sang the good old Protestant hymns lustily and without regard to waking up any of my fellow boots.

What I discovered in the Corps, even in boot camp, was that the Protestant church services—which were attended by Episcopalians, Presbyterians, Methodists, Baptists, Reformed, and others—were serviced by chaplains selected from all these churches. The orders of services in our combined prayer book and hymnal were fairly liturgical; they were very much like the morning prayer service in an Episcopal church. As an Episcopalian, I found chapel, as it was called, familiar and reassuring.

After the prayer service, we had to form up by platoons, which caused a veritable cacophony of sound because there might have been guys from fifty different platoons attending service. A drill instructor or, as boot camp progressed, a boot charged with marching the church detail, would be yelling out various numbers: "328, over here!" "394, over here!" "367, over here!" And there was a bedlam of clamor as the herd of service attendees was being reorganized into platoons again to be marched back to the barracks.

Every Sunday at noon, we had a really fine meal, usually consisting of some kind of beef with gravy and potatoes. We thought of it as a sort of celebratory meal and looked forward to it all week long.

And then Sunday afternoon's activities began. We were not allowed to do anything personal or go anywhere, so what we did was to launder our clothes. After a week, if you followed any kind of sanitary rules, all your clothes would be filthy. The way we washed clothes was interesting. At Parris Island, the Corps had built long concrete tables, which slightly sloped down to the center, and there were cold water spigots at either end of these tables. We had, of course, no hot water. Each table had a slightly raised edge around it, so that any water on the table would collect there and drain off into a drainage system of some sort. We were issued buckets, and the "recruit's bucket" is famed in song and legend, because if we really screwed up at something, we would have to march with the buckets over our heads so that we could not see where we were going. Several times, while I was at Parris Island, I saw other platoons marching with buckets over their heads, looking quite ridiculous, getting out of step, running into each other, and clanking the buckets against each other in the process. Naturally, the more out of step they got, the more the DI yelled at them. Our platoon actually had the honor of performing this exercise a couple of times too.

But the bucket's primary function was for soaking our clothes. We were issued laundry soap for which, as I found out when I received my first paycheck, along with articles of personal hygiene, I had paid for myself. We were also issued a very stiff fiber scrub brush. We would soap up our clothes, put them on the long concrete tables, scrub them vigorously, rinse them, and hang them up. We tied up our clothes with the mysterious little tie-ties to clotheslines running parallel to the concrete tables. There was enough table space, so everybody in our platoon, working for several hours on a Sunday afternoon, could get their clothes scrubbed, rinsed, and hung up to dry. After my first laundry experience, I thought, *Ah! now I can relax.* But no, absolutely not.

After doing our laundry, we had boxing matches, which were considered to be a recreational activity. The order was that everybody in our platoon had to box at least one match by the end of boot camp. The drill instructors issued us two sets of gloves, and that was the only equipment we were given. The ring was created by the rest of the platoon in the shape of a square. All boots stood facing inward, thus becoming both ring and spectators. We were allowed to arrange the matches ourselves, after which we got our name ticked off a list as proof that we had boxed at least once. I don't think that anybody boxed more than once, because while we were in boot camp, we probably only had four Sundays within which to accomplish this kind of recreation in the time allotted us. We provided our own timekeeping and refereeing, and the drill instructor would check on us periodically to ensure that he had the names of the people who had boxed marked off.

In the stress and strain of the entire boot camp experience, several people had developed some enmities with their fellow platoon members, and one of the purposes of the Sunday afternoon boxing match was to allow these people to work out their little difficulties. We witnessed a couple of memorable fights between pairs of guys who had gotten into each other's hair, as they stood there, facing each other like two bulls, and whaling the daylights out of each other.

But the majority of us just sought out and made our own matches in a competitive but amicable way. That first Sunday, after I had washed my clothes and had hung them all up to dry, we had boxing call. The DI brought out the gloves, and I think we had seven or eight matches that day. Between then and the next Sunday, a great deal of voluntary matchmaking went on in our platoon. There was a guy from one of the Pennsylvania contingents, somewhere close to Philadelphia, and I still remember his name. Porter was a man probably not quite as tall as I was, so he must have been at least six feet one. But he was a little heavier than I was in those days and must have weighed about 190 pounds. When I finished boot camp, of course, that became my weight as well, but at this point, I probably weighed no more than 180 pounds. For some reason, Porter, although he was a reasonably well-built guy, did not look very muscular. He, in fact, looked soft. And Porter came up to me one day before the second Sunday of boxing and said, "Hey, you and I are about the same size, why don't we have a match?"

Hell, I thought, *Porter does not look very dangerous.* And so I said, "Sure, okay, we'll do it."

And as the matches were being arranged, Porter and I volunteered that we were ready to fight. At the prescribed time, somebody tied our gloves on, and we had a couple of guys acting as our "seconds." If I remember correctly, we did not box rounds, but instead, we just boxed on until somebody gave up or was knocked out.

When Porter and I were ready for our fight, somebody called out, "DING!" And that was our signal to start.

I turned around. The whole platoon was gathered in a four-sided square of spectators, and as soon as Porter came out of his corner, he put his fists up and began bobbing and weaving around. As I watched him, something told me that this guy was not without experience. We met in the center and flicked out some jabs at each other. The next thing I knew, from nowhere, in a flash came a fist and landed flat on my face. Boom! And the back of my head was hitting the ground. I don't believe I ever saw it coming, and although I was not out, I had indisputably been knocked down.

Everybody was yelling and screaming, and my friends were urging me to get up and keep fighting, and so I did. But I had to call upon all my skills to retreat with honor, backpedaling and backpedaling. Some of you may recall that Muhammad Ali, when he was in his prime, had something called Rope-a-Dope, and when he wanted to take a rest, he would get his elbows out, his arms up, and protect his face while the other fellow flailed away at him.

Porter flicked a few more on me, but I actually landed a couple of blows on him as well, and he never knocked me down again after the first five seconds into our fight. We both landed some blows, although he probably landed more than I did, but he really did not hurt me except for that first blow, of which I was still feeling the effects when the fight was over.

As our gloves were being removed, I asked Porter, "Now, Porter, admit it, you have boxed before, haven't you?"

And he said very casually, "Well yes, I have."

"Where did you box? What did you do?"

And he said, "Well, I was in the Golden Gloves in Philadelphia."

"How well did you do?" I asked him.

"I lost the finals in the light heavyweight division," he confided modestly. He had reached all the way to the finals in the biggest amateur boxing tournament held all over the country! And he almost won in Philadelphia, which, in those days, had the reputation for being a pretty tough town. Well, when I heard that, I started feeling pretty good about managing to stay in the ring for at least five minutes after that first blow from a Golden Glove almost-champion had landed on my face. We had eight scheduled training weeks. We spent the first three weeks in the barracks at main side and in the drill field. The next four weeks we went to the rifle range. The last part was to be one week, originally, back at the barracks, but it stretched out to two weeks before graduation because the end of the war brought with it much reorganization

Presuming to be a United States Marine

and shifting. In those nine weeks, three times, and I think it was usually on a Sunday evening and without any warning at all, the drill instructors would make us fall out with our buckets as darkness fell over Parris Island.

In addition to the two uses already described, the bucket could mean some kind of field day; for example, when we would have to turn to and scrub something. Or the bucket could mean a movie.

At the risk of making the Marine Corps of those days sound extremely soft and easy by offering varied recreational facilities, in addition to the boxing, I must tell you that on some Sundays we were marched way off into the distance, carrying our buckets, for a hike of at least one and a half miles to what was then the outdoor theater.

You will remember that the gravel we were marched through was to be used for the new outdoor theater to be built on the parade field. The old theater was down in a kind of sandy woods, where enough trees had been chopped down so that you could put your bucket upside-down in the sand and sit on it for the viewing of a movie projected on a giant screen with a huge, loud sound system. We were never told in advance that we would be watching a movie. It always came as a surprise, but what a pleasant surprise! No matter how bad the movie might be, the experience was thrilling.

I have mentioned the various punishments inflicted upon us, such as standing in the sun and being marched through gravel. There was another favorite punishment, but one that had a point. We had to take our M1 rifle, which weighed close to eleven pounds, and hold it straight in front of us with both hands extended. One hand was around the narrow part of the stock, and the other hand was around the upper hand guard, which was made of wood. We had to stand in this position indefinitely. And woe betide the boot who let his rifle begin to droop! Our arms were to be parallel to the deck as we held our rifle straight out.

The fatigue and pain of holding one's weighted arms out in this manner for a long period of time can be considerable. As an exercise, though, it did a lot for our upper-arm strength, our biceps, and triceps. When I returned home from my boot leave and visited St. John's, my friend Archer Jones came running up to me to greet me. He extended his right hand to shake mine and, with his left hand, grabbed my upper right arm, which, he told me with some surprise, felt like a drainpipe.

I might say a word about the world situation at this point. Periodically, from the first day we arrived, the drill instructors, and many of the other people with whom we had contact as we went through the various forms of processing and other activities, followed a common and often-repeated theme in what they were telling us. Particularly, the drill instructors would endlessly tell us, "You men know what you are going to be doing. When you finish here, you will go to Camp Lejeune for six weeks of advanced infantry training. After that you will be put aboard ship and sent as a replacement for the landings on Japan. And 'replacement' is spelled C-A-N-N-O-N F-O-D-D-E-R. Six to nine months from now, one-half of you will be dead. Pay attention to what we are teaching you, and you might be in the lucky half."

Taking on the Burden of History

And that was our motivator. We believed the message and had every reason to believe it. In subsequent years, in the advanced stages of my career, I have had the privilege of examining the operation plans for the landing on Japan, which may be found in several good museums and military libraries. There were two Marine Corps operation plans, one for the landing on the southern island of Kyushu, and one for the landing on the main island of Honshu.

The first landing was to be in November of 1945, and I would certainly have missed that. But the second landing was to take place in February of 1946, and by the summer of 1945, the Marine Corps planners had already listed and named the replacement drafts that were going to be involved in supporting these landings. And that second landing was where we brand-new boots would all end up.

I well remember that during the second or third week at Parris Island, after supper, when our platoon was scheduled to go off to some other training and we were falling out into platoon formation, our drill instructor, probably Bonin, who was a very smart man and abreast of world affairs, told us, "I have an announcement to make. The United States has dropped an atomic bomb on the city of Hiroshima in Japan, and it has wiped out the city. Also, the Soviet Union has entered the war against Japan. Both of these events have happened almost simultaneously. There is heavy fighting in Manchuria." And Bonin added, "This is good news for us."

The effect of this announcement was electrifying and was followed, three days later, by a similar announcement that we had dropped an atomic bomb on Nagasaki. We had no newspapers, we had no radios, we had no connections to the outside world. At that point, we belonged to the drill instructors—lock, stock, and barrel. Our entire world began and ended with them, and that barracks and that mess hall and that drill field, and we appreciated any information they gave us.

On what must have been August 15, one of the drill instructors announced that Japan had surrendered. This produced a spasm of pure joy on the part of everybody, and we even then could imagine how the rest of America felt. I subsequently learned of some of the many celebrations going on in every city and town in America, with sailors kissing strange ladies in the streets and such. I will tell you about the heartfelt thanks we gave at our own celebration on Parris Island later on in this story.

Meanwhile, our drill instructors made it very clear to us that "there will always be a need for marines, and we will not let up with your training. Just don't even think about not doing your best at all times!" Once again, they strongly implied that our best was not good enough under any circumstances, anyway.

I admired Bonin because he never, not for a minute, ever let down or relaxed. Now Bartell, the Cornell student, took off the night of V-J Day and went to the slop chute. We were, needless to say, not allowed to go to the slop chute, the slop chute being the beer garden. Corporal Bartell, a veteran of at least two or three island campaigns, went over to the slop chute where he must have really caroused. He did not actually come back into the barracks, and it may be that Bonin had stopped him from doing so; but he stood under our windows and, in a very loud voice, simultaneously celebrated the end of the war and cursed us out as miserable maggots, worms, and miscellaneous other forms of lowlifes. It was probably a good thing that he did not come in to show us, instead of telling us, exactly what forms of lowlife we really were.

And speaking of punishments, there were two other things the drill instructors did to us to remind us of the total absurdity and stupidity of war.

One of these was something called over-and-under. Now this drill and the next about which I will tell you were both conducted at night. We were awakened to these, which made them singularly horrible and made us inwardly really angry, although obviously, we could not in any way complain even though we were seething with pent-up frustration and fury. In the over-and-under, we would be popped out of our bunks at eleven or twelve o'clock at night, when all of us were sound asleep, and it was hot as blazes at the end of July or in early August. We were ordered to put on all our clothes. By this time, we had been issued our green uniforms and a long green overcoat.

We were ordered to put on two pairs of heavy wool trousers; a blouse, which is the jacket; and the undershirt and shirt under the blouse, topped off with the heavy green overcoat. Thus clad, we looked like overstuffed dummies, padded and stiff with clothing. We were lined up at the end of the squad bay and had to climb over a top bunk, then fall down under the bottom bunk, skinny on the floor under the bottom bunk, then climb up over the next top bunk, and so on, over and under.

That may sound fairly reasonable, except, remember, under the bottom bunk, at each end of it, stood a locker box belonging to the two residents of that double-bunk, and hanging from tie-ties, were our rifles. The rifles were very carefully hung only about five inches above the deck. This meant that as you slithered under the bottom bunk, it was easy to dislodge the rifle out of its tie-ties, and if it hit the deck, you were in deep trouble for damaging somebody else's weapon. This was a dreadful exercise. We were wearing too many clothes, which took away any mobility and flexibility. Hampered by these many layers of apparel, we had to make a complete circuit of the squad bay and found ourselves enormously exhausted at the end of the exercise. It was one nightly drill we had to perform twice, with both times being equally memorable.

The other drill, which, mercifully, we only did once was called locker box drill. Our locker boxes were locked, and we each were issued a combination lock. In the locker box drill, we were popped out of bed in the middle of the night, we were each ordered to pick up our locker box, and to fall out and fall in a platoon formation. The drill instructor yelled, "I want you at ORDER locker boxes." Well, the "order arms" command with your rifle means that the butt of your rifle is on the ground and you are holding it by the upper hand guard just to your right, with the muzzle pointed up in the air.

The "order locker boxes" must mean, then, that our locker box had to be placed just to our right, standing up vertically. So far so good. Then, however, we were given the command PORT locker boxes, which meant that we had to pick up our entire locker box, throw it across the front of our body, and then grab it with two hands, holding it in place. And these locker boxes were by no means light; they were heavy as hell.

Taking on the Burden of History

But then the command came, "LEFT SHOULDER locker boxes," which meant that we had to put our locker box up on our left shoulder. And when we got them to left shoulder locker boxes, we were given the command, "right face." And so we marched with our locker boxes at left shoulder locker boxes. This exercise created total chaos. There were some guys in the platoon who, literally, could not lift up their locker boxes; they had too much in them. They tried to drag them and pick them up, and people's locker boxes were banging into each other. Hopeless confusion reigned, giving further proof to the drill instructors of our complete general ineptitude. One must remember, though, that by the end of the second week of boot camp, we had begun looking like a pretty sharp platoon. We marched well, we could do the manual of arms flawlessly, we could perform pretty complicated drills and flanking movements. But our attempt at performing with a locker box, instead of a rifle, made us appear to be considerably less than sharp again, undoubtedly the reason for the exercise.

And here is another little game the drill instructors used to play. The two-story barracks we lived in were made in the shape of an *H*. Each of the wings of the *H*, each story, would hold one platoon, so that the entire barracks could hold four platoons, two on the first deck and two on the second. There was a long, connecting bar between the two sides of the *H*, and in there were contained the shower rooms, bunches of basins for shaving in the morning, and the urinals and commodes for life's functions. At certain times of the day, particularly after breakfast, there was a considerable demand for these things, and we often had to line up and await our turn.

In addition, in the center section connecting the wings were the drill instructors' offices, where they kept their gear. When you are a boot, you are probably far from sensitive to this, but looking back, and particularly after having spent many years in the Corps and having talked to the many, many noncommissioned officers who had been drill instructors, it has become clear to me that a drill instructor's life is far from easy. A DI carries an enormous amount of responsibility. Almost all the time, even at night, one of the three drill instructors had to be with us. The drill instructors, after all, are entrusted with the awesome task of creating the next generation of marines, and they take their responsibility very seriously. Drill instructors, in fact, never have much time off. It was, and probably still is, a legend in the Marine Corps that family problems for drill instructors are of great and continuing concern because of the enormous stresses and daily demands of time and energy on them. I must confess that it would be an understatement to say that as a new recruit, I wasn't much worried about any personal problems my drill instructors might experience, although in later years, I have come to appreciate just how difficult a DI's life is.

There was a good deal of horseplay between the drill instructors, and sometimes they would concoct little games to play, which would pit one platoon against another. The barracks themselves were made out of wood, and in that particular climate, and because they stood on a low island, they were placed on spaced cinder block piers, so that they were raised off the ground, probably about three feet. If you looked underneath one side of one of these barracks, you could, although the ground was sandy and unevenly bumpy, see all the way under, or at least get glimpses of light from the other side.

Once, thankfully during the day, one of our drill instructors had a great idea. He lined us up as a platoon, shoulder to shoulder, flat on our stomachs on the ground outside one side of the barracks. Another drill instructor then took his platoon and lined the men up in the same manner on the ground on the other side. The order was given to each platoon to get through to the other side, which meant that the two platoons commenced crawling on their bellies toward each other from opposite sides, under the barracks, with the objective of getting all the way through the oncoming, creeping platoon to the other side of the barracks. We were all told by our respective drill instructors to not "let anybody hold you up, just shove them out of your way any way you can! You understand?"

As one can imagine, around the center underneath the barracks, as the two platoons met, pure bedlam reigned. People were trying to whale away at each other, but we were so confined that we really could not take a poke at anybody very much. It became an immense, titanic struggle of surging bodies, like two swarms of ants meeting in the sand. I suddenly came face-to-face with a boot from the other platoon, and we both silently, with a quick look, agreed to let the other by, and so waded through. But some of the other guys got into some real brawls under that barracks, as cramped as it was. The drill instructors, finally, had to send some people back under the building to retrieve the rest of the stuck guys from their platoon.

In another platoon competition game, I learned a very important lesson in life. At lunchtime, we were always marched in platoon formation to the mess hall. Facing forward, we would halt, the drill instructor would shout, "Column of files from the left, MARCH!" And the first squad, the leftmost squad, facing forward, would take off; and as soon as the last man in the first squad passed, the squad leader in the second squad would do a half-left and a half-right and fall in behind, and this created a single file of boots.

Well, it happened that one day I was the squad leader of the first squad when we were given the command of column of files from the left. I headed for the doorway entrance to the mess hall, leading the whole platoon. The Parris Island mess halls at the time were not very elaborate buildings, and the entrance to them was simply a reasonably wide single door, with a closed screen door behind it. As soon as we entered the mess hall, we would pick up our metal tray and the silverware off a table, and start down through the mess line.

On this particular day, one of our drill instructor's buddies' platoons was approaching from the other direction, had halted, and he had given the "column of files" command from the right. As I turned onto the sidewalk to the entrance door to the mess hall, I realized that on my right was a boot from the other platoon, and our lines were exactly parallel, in a column of twos, but from two different outfits. The two drill instructors were both shouting, "Don't let those guys get ahead of you!", thus assuring a struggle between the two men leading their respective platoons.

Taking on the Burden of History

We reached the door at the same time, and fortunately for me, the guy from the other platoon was not very large, so that when we got up to the door, I threw him aside and growled, "Get out of the way, you son of a bitch!" Just like that, and I pushed him aside and led my platoon into the mess hall. Grabbing my tray, I started to go down the mess line for my lunch when I felt a little tug on my sleeve, and here was the boot from the other platoon, whom I had just shoved out of the way.

He said with earnest seriousness, "I am sure that if you and I had a fight, you would probably beat me. But don't ever call anybody a son of a bitch because, you should realize, you are talking about somebody's mother."

This was a moment, and I had several of those in the Marine Corps, when I was reminded of my humanity and, at the same time, found a need to caution myself against turning into a completely gross animal, which is how I had just behaved. All the aggressiveness drained out of me, and I apologized to the guy, and we had a tender moment in the midst of many harsh moments. Since that day, I have never called a fellow human being a son of a bitch no matter what the circumstances.

Our drill instructors, and I gave them credit even then, were keeping us informed and repeated over and over again that there was still an enormous demand for marines, and that if any of us thought about getting discharged and getting out, we should immediately forget about it. I was soon to see the truth to that statement. They explained to us that all the armed services had a point system with a point given for every month of service, an extra point for every month of overseas service, five points for every combat engagement, and five points for every personal decoration. There were many men, particularly some of the older noncommissioned officers at Parris Island, who had hundreds of points; and word was that these men were going to be discharged as soon as possible, and that they were going to be quickly reduced in numbers and phased out. Different requirements applied for marines overseas because they still had operational responsibilities and missions even though the war was coming to an end.

If you will remember, the official end to World War II, the official V-J Day, the day on which the Japanese actually surrendered on board the USS *Missouri*, came on September 2, 1945. That was when General MacArthur, Fleet Admiral Chester Nimitz, and other Allied military officers met on deck of the *Missouri*, anchored in the harbor of Tokyo Bay, and the premier of Japan signed Japan's unconditional surrender. That day was celebrated all over the world as the day that ended the war. I have a very vivid memory of that day, of marching from the rifle range back to main side, a distance of several miles, and then marching to the outdoor theater. We did not have our buckets on that day. We were in our regular utility uniforms, but they were clean, and we wore our fore-and-aft caps and carried our weapons; but as I recall it, we were carrying them at sling arms, so that we did not perform the manual of arms as we marched. We just carried our rifles along.

As we converged on the outdoor theater, I suddenly realized that every recruit on Parris Island was there. I think that twenty-five thousand men were marched to the outdoor theater on that day, September 2, and for many of us, it was the occasion when we first encountered a general. General Del Valle was there, on a big stage with a huge sound system all around it. So many marines and recruits were present that some of us were pushed clear back into the woods. But we could still see, and certainly hear, surrounded as we were by the powerful loudspeakers.

The commandant of the Marine Corps, General Vandegrift, had issued an order for the day, and that order was read. General Del Valle made a few remarks and introduced the guest of honor for this occasion, the brand-new congressman from that area of South Carolina. I believe he had been in the service in the war, had been discharged because he had suffered injuries, and had been appointed to Congress only recently.

Anybody familiar with modern American history will remember his name, and I think that we heard one of the earliest ceremonial speeches he ever made. He was Mendel Rivers. Rivers eventually became chairman of the House Armed Services Committee and also became one of the leading powers of the segregation forces. A conservative opponent to school integration in the fifties and sixties, he became known as one of the real bad-ass curmudgeons in the United States Congress. But in 1945, he was still a young man, just starting out his career, and we detected no trace of prejudice in him.

I can't remember what he said, but we were all so filled with the emotion of the reality that we were not going to get killed, at least for now, that we all listened carefully to all the speeches given on that day. When the speeches were over, and they were mercifully short, the colors were presented, and the National Anthem was played. Then General Del Valle asked us to sing the Marine Corps Hymn. The Marine Corps Hymn, sung by twenty-five thousand marines with a new lease on life, was pretty moving. It was moving then, and it remains so in my memory to this day.

I have read that as troops from Australia and New Zealand were sailing in a large convoy of ships on their way to the Dardanelles in 1915 during World War I, suddenly, some of the Australians began cheering loudly. They did so because they were sure that they were going on to victory, and the people on the other ships in the convoy, one by one, picked up their cheer until there was a mighty noise; and everybody who had been there later said that they had never heard anything like it and did not expect they would, ever again. Of course, that cheer was the prelude to the tragedy at Gallipoli, but I would imagine that our marine voices on September 2, raised in unison and in gratitude, might invite a comparison, at least in the magnitude of the volume. It was beautiful.

By the time all that was happening, we had been moved from instruction in the barracks to the rifle range. The rifle range was an interesting experience. Quite abruptly, everything changed for us, and we were thrown into a very different set of circumstances, which, I am sure, was again the result of a very conscious effort on the part of the Corps. Up to that point, we had been living in the barracks, where we had to scrub the floor with toothbrushes, and our entire life had been consumed with physical exercises, drills, and studies of Marine Corps history and military subjects.

Taking on the Burden of History

Suddenly, we packed up all our gear; our locker boxes were marked with our names, put aboard trucks, and hauled out separately to the range. We put on field marching packs, a pack arrangement worn on long marches for lengthy stays in the field, and we marched from the main post out to the rifle range. On the rifle range, we were billeted in tents. Each tent contained six bunks, and while I don't remember any of the guys I tented with, I do remember that we all got along well and were friendly with each other. We still kept our drill instructors, and for them, the rifle range was a pretty good deal. They did not have to worry about us for most of the training day. They got us up for breakfast and picked us up at the end of the day; but for almost all the daylight hours, we belonged to our coaches. Each platoon was assigned two rifle instructor/coaches, and it was their job to teach us how to fire all the small arms used by the Corps at that time.

We had four weeks at the rifle range. The first week was spent "snapping in." "Snapping in" was a variation of Oriental torture in which the leather shoulder sling is taken from the rifle and put into a whole complicated new setup. Then we learned the four positions of shooting. The first position is standing, or, as it was called, offhand. The second is kneeling on one knee and sitting on the foot attached to that knee, with the other knee put forward and the elbow resting on that knee. The third position is sitting with both feet on the ground, arms hooked over the knees, and leaning way down to fire the weapon. This is a very stable position. Finally, there is the prone position on the ground, propped up on both elbows and on the rifle. This is the best position for shooting, and the position from which, probably, 90 percent of the shots in combat are fired. There are several reasons for this. For one thing, in a prone position, one presents a much less visible target, and secondly, propped up on the elbows as well as the rifle steadies one as a rock, so that the marksmanship is much improved over firing from any of the other positions.

We practiced these positions over and over and over again, getting down into them, getting up from them, getting back down into them, and snapping off, learning how to squeeze the trigger. The trigger is never pulled, it is squeezed. We learned how to keep score on the rifle range. We learned how to blacken the sights on our rifles to get a good picture as we looked down these sights, and then we learned to adjust the sights for the peculiarity of our rifle and our own eyes, and that process is called zeroing the rifle.

Near the end of that first week of snapping in, we all practiced shooting .22 caliber rifles, which were similar in size to the M1 and gave us the experience on how to shoot bullets. The second week at the rifle range, we practiced with the rifle and practiced with the carbine, the carbine being a smaller version of the rifle. At the end of the second week, we fired the carbine for our marksmanship records. The third week, we again practiced with the rifle, with live fire, and on the last day of that week, we fired the rifle for record. I must confess that the first time I fired a .22 was the first time I had ever fired a weapon of any kind. I had never before touched a weapon, so that this was an entirely new experience for me, and I am grateful to the Marine Corps to have taught me to fire the right way.

Presuming to be a United States Marine

The rifle range was hard work. There were fifty targets on each range, and at that time the Corps had a carbine range, three M1 ranges, and a Browning automatic rifle (BAR) range. Each relay of marines was fifty strong. We fired from different positions on the range. We started out offhand and kneeling at two hundred yards, then sat at three hundred yards, then did our prone rapid-fire firing, and finally at five hundred yards away from the target, we took slow carefully aimed shots from the prone position. Each relay would work its way back, firing at these different ranges and would then be marched off down to the butts, or earthworks, in front of the targets.

Working the butts was the other part of the process. First we shot the rifle. Then because each shot on a target had to be recorded with a marker over the hole so the persons back in the line could record where the shot had gone, other marines had to work behind the earthworks from which the targets were erected. As soon as we were finished with one shooter, we had to pull the target down. We used little paste-covered squares over all the holes the bullets had made so that we could see where the next shots hit. Yanking those targets up and down was a lot of work.

We were also getting the additional benefit of finding out what it feels like to get shot at. The bullets were flying right over our heads when we were down in the butts as we were pulling the targets up and down, and what a wonderful experience that was! Two or three times when I have been on the rifle range, some idiot would miss badly and hit one of the steel stanchions of the target, the chain-and-wheels system that works them up and down, with a stray shot; and occasionally somebody would get hit by a ricochet, although I never saw anyone get seriously injured. But there were noncommissioned officers down in the butts too, yelling and giving orders all the time, and nobody wanted to hit any of them, of course. I would have been one of the few men tall enough to be able to look over the butts toward the line if I had pulled myself up and straightened myself out, which would have meant that I would have been looking right down the muzzles of the firing rifles. Understandably, I was never tempted to do this.

Our coaches took us all the way through these exercises, and they worked with each one of us individually. I am left-handed, so I suggested to one of the coaches as they came around that, maybe, I should shoot left-handed.

"Nope," he said. "You can't do that, and I am going to make you shoot right-handed." And I have always been grateful to him. As I subsequently learned, my right eye, which is the eye you sight through when you shoot right-handed, is much better than my left, so that I had a far clearer picture of the target. In addition, when shooting an M1 rifle left-handed, and I tried it once, the bolt handle comes back right in the direction of the face; and while it does not hit it, one will inadvertently flinch, thinking it is going to land on the face. This kind of training was very intensive and quite different from anything we had done before and had its own stresses. Everybody wanted to excel and become a good shot, and some were better at it than others. I barely qualified as a boot and never got any marksmanship medals. Finally, later in my career, I managed to work up to sharpshooter but have never been an expert rifleman.

Taking on the Burden of History

The last day of the last week on the rifle range, we fired the Browning automatic rifle, a little bigger weapon, for the record. All the Browning automatic rifle fire was done from the distance of three hundred yards, which is pretty far, when you think about it. It is three football fields long. But the BAR is an extremely accurate weapon, and I did very well on it. In fact, I made sharpshooter on the Browning automatic rifle, right from the start. We were also given practice firing on the machine gun, and next, everybody had to throw a real hand grenade.

On the hand grenade, understandably, we were given considerable training. We descended into a pit, were handed a live grenade, and were thankful the coach was there with us, as hand grenades have a tendency to reduce people to panic. Looking down on that pineapple and reflecting on all the explosives contained in it can, no doubt, produce some anxiety. The coaches told us that on that boot range, about once a week, some idiot boot would drop his grenade. If you dropped the grenade at your feet and the spoon flew off, the clock would start ticking. You had about four and a half seconds before that pineapple would explode, and that was why the coach always remained close by. If necessary, the coach would reach down, grab the grenade, and throw it out before it could do any harm. I have read some statistics on training with hand grenades, and I think that in the seventy-five years that Parris Island has been in existence, about three or four people have been killed on the hand grenade range, invariably because a boot panicked, or because a boot did not throw the grenade very accurately. In the pit, you were behind a big sand bag wall, and you threw the grenade out over the wall into a large crater excavated by the thousands of grenades boots had thrown into it over time. I found that throwing a live grenade was a fascinating experience, and many years later, in Korea, the training I received in throwing grenades probably saved my life.

At the end of each day at the rifle range, we were lined up, and everybody had to draw back the bolt on their rifles and inspect the chamber in their rifle to make sure there weren't any bullets left in it, then let the bolt go home and pull the trigger. Once, when we did that, some guy in our platoon pulled the trigger and—*bang!* The rifle went off. He still had a round in it. One can only imagine the apoplexy of Corporal Bonin when he heard this. Safety dictated that we not be allowed to take ammunition off the line at the range. The reason for this will be seen in a moment.

At the range, we had a kind of platoon street of tents. One row of tents stood on one side, and another row down the other. Since there were six persons per tent, there must have been about six tents on each side of our platoon street. By this time, we had lost some people because of injuries or other attrition. There was some kind of respiratory infection people got at Parris Island, something called cat fever, which, if you got it, completely wiped you out with a temperature of a hundred and six, so that you had to be taken to the hospital. Several people in our platoon got cat fever, and by the time we went to the rifle range, we were down to maybe sixty or sixty-five people left in Platoon 467.

Presuming to be a United States Marine

The rear of our tents backed up to the rear of the next platoon's tents and their platoon street. One day a man in the tent, which backed up to our tent, apparently, either got a Dear John letter from home, or the stress and strain of trying to become a marine finally got to him, and he somehow contrived to smuggle a round off the line. While his tent mates were not looking, or were outside, he placed the muzzle of his rifle in his mouth and pulled the trigger. There was not much distance between the rows of tents. We heard the shot as we were sitting around inside ours, and then we heard screams from the other tent, and soon after that, the sound of an ambulance. We were not allowed to leave our platoon area when we were not training, so that we had to remain in our tents, but we found out almost immediately what had happened.

Then there was a man who, after he had been injured in some exercise, had been transferred from another platoon to our platoon in order to finish boot camp. But the guys who lost their platoon and were thrown in with a platoon of strangers had a tough time adjusting. We were all issued bore cleaner to clean out the bore of our rifle after it had been fired. The bore cleaner was a very toxic liquid material. In the middle of the night, this poor soul, who had just been transferred into our platoon, went to the great, big community head at the rifle range, a huge wooden building that contained showers and johns and basins. He had to walk past several other platoons to get to it. He took his can of bore cleaner with him, went into the head, and drank down the liquid. He was found dead the next morning in the head. Parris Island was not without death and suffering, and yet, life on the range offered an interesting reprieve from life on the drill field, and most people enjoyed the four weeks we spent there.

We had a post exchange on the range, which sold food of various sorts, but of course, we were absolutely forbidden to go there, and the clerks at the PX were absolutely forbidden to sell anything of whatever kind to any boot. We were not allowed to buy anything because, after all, we were not yet marines; we were only scummy, undeserving boot-maggots. One guy in our platoon, though, found out from somebody that there was ice cream to be had at the PX. We were allowed some time off at the rifle range after dark, although we had to spend large amounts of time with our rifle every night, cleaning it and taking care of it. But this crazy fool crept away and somehow finagled it so that he did not look like a boot, wearing a hat to look like a drill instructor, and he got himself to the post exchange, where he managed to buy four pints of ice cream. His plan was to take the ice cream booty back to his tent mates for a feast.

Well, poor misguided fellow! As luck would have it, on the way back from the PX to our platoon tent area, he ran right into the drill instructor.

"What you got there, boot?"

"Sir, nothing, sir!" the hapless boot replied, but the DI had already grabbed the bag with the four pints of ice cream in it and the four wooden spoons.

"Well now, isn't that nice! You like ice cream, boot?"

"Sir, yes, sir!"

"WHAT DID YOU SAY?"

Taking on the Burden of History

"SIR, YES, SIR!"

"EAT IT," came the command. We heard this dialogue because it occurred right outside our tent in the platoon street, and the DI's volume was turned up, way up. A couple of us sneaked a peek around the tent flap to see what was happening.

And there sat the boot, with the drill instructor towering over him; and with a little wooden spoon, he ate four pints of ice cream, tiny spoonful after tiny spoonful, while the DI harassed him with, "Faster, boot, FASTER! Get a move on! You are too SLOW!"

Well, needless to say, by and by the ice cream was beginning to stick in the boot's throat; and when he was finished, he became quite sick. After that, nobody else tried to sneak off to the PX for anything at all, ever again—at least in my time.

I haven't mentioned yet that I had a couple of minor medical problems myself at Parris Island, fortunately not of a sufficiently serious nature for me to lose my platoon. Early in the second week of boot camp, as I was shaving one morning, I noticed a swelling under one of my upper eyelids. By the evening, I realized that I had a pus sack the size of a small marble under my lid. When I came back from dinner that night, I went to the drill instructor's office, the only time I had ever done that voluntarily. You realize that to get to see the drill instructor was in itself an odyssey.

I banged on the door, and, as everything you did in boot camp, I was not doing it right. I was not banging loud enough. On the other side of the door, the DI kept yelling after each one of my bangs, "For God's sake, wimp, just hit the damn door RIGHT!"

Finally there came a grudging "All right, what is it?"

"Sir, Private Van Sant requests permission to speak to the drill instructor, SIR!" I yelled from outside.

"I can't hear you!"

And I yelled my name and request a few more times, as crisply and with as much resonance as I could muster and finally received permission to enter the DI's sanctum.

By the time I had reached the drill instructor himself, it was obvious that something unseemly was swelling under my eyelid. He ordered me to lift the eyelid, gazed at my pus sack, and growled, "You better go to sick bay." And so I was allowed, all by myself, to walk from the barracks to the sick bay. It was almost worth it.

In the sick bay, the corpsman was halfway decent, although he still leaned on me a little bit from sheer habit. After one look at my eye, though, he said, "You'd better see the doctor." And having waited for some time, I was called into the doctor's presence. He said, "Oh my goodness, that's a chalazion. I have not seen one of those in months! Gee, that's a beautiful one!" He continued raving to me about my splendid pus sack until I interrupted him with my question of what could be done about it.

"Oh, we'll take care of it. Now you just sit there. It's going to hurt a little bit." And he whipped out a sterile lance, nicked that beautiful chalazion, and produced a geyser of pus from my eye. He cleaned everything out and washed out my eye and disinfected it, and I remember admiring his deftness. He certainly inspired more confidence in me than the dentist had.

Presuming to be a United States Marine

Next, he gave me an eye patch and told me, "If you keep the eye patch on through the night, I think that by tomorrow morning, you will not have to worry about your eye."

I returned to the platoon and reported back to the drill instructor. The platoon was just falling out for some evening drill. I had a slip with me from the doctor saying that I was to be on "light duty," and made the mistake of showing it to the DI.

"Oh hell," he said. "That means that you can drill." And there I was, drilling with an eye patch over one eye, and I must say that I became the object of much interest on the part of my fellow boots. But while I was able to enjoy my few fleeting moments of fame, it did not get me out of anything, and one-eyed, I drilled right along with my platoon that night.

The other medical problem I had was actually more serious, as far as shooting and marching were concerned, even though I never went to sick bay about it. I had grown a very lively ingrown nail on my big toe, which produced excruciating pain, particularly on the rifle range. Deciding to treat it myself, I sterilized a razor, cut the ingrown toenail out myself, sprinkled it with some disinfectant, and bandaged it up. It hurt like Hades! Unfortunately, it was on my right big toe, the toe that gets bent back when you get down on it in the kneeling position on the rifle range, so that the kneeling position was always a struggle for me, just because my toe hurt so much. But all things will come to an end. My self-administered treatment worked, and by the time we got off the rifle range, my toe had healed up fine, and I have never had any trouble with it since, except for the scar tissue that eventually formed around the toe and had to be cut off as well.

After we had fired all the weapons and fired the rifle and thrown the hand grenade and had our fun on the rifle range, we were marched back to the main side and back to a different squad bay in the same building we had come from. There we remained for what was the eighth week of our training, but because the war had just ended, our training got stretched out a little bit, as I have told you, so that we ended up doing almost nine weeks of boot camp. After that, we were to be held up for another week or ten days before being allowed to go on our boot leave. The administrative burden on the Marine Corps carrying on its training missions, while demobilizing and discharging thousands of marine veterans was so great that it delayed our departure.

We never really felt the delay, and the last week and a half went by in a blur. We completed something called the confidence course, which had us swinging on ropes across streams and climbing over obstacle courses while carrying all our equipment. After these exercises, we were drilled again to sharpen up our manual of arms and were given a final inspection by the company commander. We had to lay out every piece of gear, all our equipment, and our rifle in an absolute prescribed manner on our bunk, affectionately known as junk on the bunk, and stand at attention to answer questions from the inspecting officer. Everything had to be stamped or labeled with our name, and it took an enormous amount of time getting ready for that final inspection.

And then our day of glory arrived. Finally, we were prepared for our graduation parade. The graduation parade is a very emotional and marvelous capstone to the boot camp experience. We marched as platoons by the reviewing stand, and after we had successfully completed our parade, we received our Marine Corps emblems—the beloved eagle, globe, and anchor.

It is hard to describe, after all the horrors we had been through, how triumphant we felt after receiving that precious emblem and being called a marine for the first time. As we passed in review, eyes right, we beheld old General Del Valle, saluting back to us, and it was a thrilling and brilliant moment. We were now marines. There is no question in my mind that the experience of getting that emblem goes to the very core, the very heart of one's being. That emblem gets stamped on the soul forever. The moment of succeeding in becoming a marine is a very proud moment indeed.

When I first went to Parris Island, men marched through the parade, got their emblems, became marines, and were immediately processed through for their boot leave. Unfortunately for us, and incidental to the demobilization, we did not get our boot leave. We were moved out of the barracks and into a tent area along the seashore, where we remained.

After our graduation, we lost Corporal Bonin, although he was still with us through our parade. Sergeant Hendricks, the senior drill instructor, was one of the first people to leave. Before leaving, he came out to say good-bye to us on the firing range. Bonin returned to Louisiana and eventually graduated from Louisiana State University. In 1950, he volunteered to go back into the Marine Corps, and because he had been a noncommissioned officer and a drill instructor, and had graduated from college, he was commissioned as a second lieutenant during the Korean War about a month ahead of my commissioning, so that he was always slightly senior to me. I am glad that I was able to tell him, as our paths crossed, that he had been, far-and-away, the leading influence on our platoon all the way through boot camp. Louis A. Bonin, obviously of French extraction, was a character and an excellent marine.

After we were moved, Corporal Nelson, who had been assigned to us after Sergeant Hendricks left, was put in charge. Each day, a few more of our guys got their orders for boot leave, but most of us were kept behind and assigned to work details overseen by Corporal Nelson.

It was at this point that I had one of the funniest experiences of my Marine Corps career. In the processing, when I had first arrived at boot camp, not only did I have to take the General Classification Test, but I had to fill out a very complicated questionnaire about myself, my life, my experiences, and my education. Of course, I noted that I had attended St. John's College (and you will remember, that school was located in Annapolis, Maryland). Another question asked concerned my general interests and any sports activities I had engaged in, and so I put down that I had played basketball at St. John's.

In 1945, St. John's University (then called St. John's College) on Long Island, New York, was a preeminent basketball college in America. They had won the NCAA several times during the war and had a fantastic team, which achieved some prominence even after the war. The New York St. John's College was well known as a basketball school.

Presuming to be a United States Marine

Somebody in the records and classifications office on Parris Island, rifling through Van Sant's records, suddenly saw a red flag—aha! St. John's College! Interest: basketball. Height: six feet four inches (I grew another inch later on). And that person, with his thumb action, put two and two together and got five, and on my first day on the work detail, a message came through that Private Van Sant was to report immediately to the base special services officer for assignment to the Parris Island basketball squad.

During the war, and for several years after the war, each Marine Corps base kept a full panoply of teams, especially football, baseball, basketball, and usually wrestling and boxing; and this full complement of teams engaged in athletic competition on the intercollegiate level. In fact, back in those days, several times teams of marines and other services took intercollegiate championships in various sports. During the war, the North Carolina preflight school, which was a navy school, had the best college football team in America, and as a matter of fact, right after the war, many of the Cleveland Browns players were drafted from that school. Parris Island had a basketball team, and now the powers that be assigned me to that basketball team, and I reported in. My emblem was brand new, and I was not used to being called a marine, nor was I used to being spoken to as if I were a bona fide human being. For nine weeks, I had been nothing but a low-life worm, after all; and suddenly people were not only talking to me, but talking to me nicely and asking me questions in a friendly tone of voice, and a very congenial sergeant asked me rather politely, "Son, can you type?"

"Sir," I told him, "I don't know how to touch-type, but I can type pretty fast."

"Okay," he said with much enthusiasm. "What we will probably do is we'll assign you as clerk here in headquarters, but your main job is going to be playing basketball. You go pick up your equipment and report to the basketball team." By now, it was mid-September, and since basketball season starts near the end of October or early November, the Parris Island post basketball team had already begun practicing. I went to the gymnasium, drew a uniform for the Parris Island team, and drew a jockstrap. I was assigned a locker, and then I dressed and went out onto the floor of the gymnasium. There was a captain in summer uniform but with sneakers on. He was the coach. I reported to him, and I was sent to a group of about a dozen or so marines who were shooting baskets. After a few minutes of warming up, we began some drills, throwing and catching and dribbling, and the pace was fast, intense, and quiet. There was very little of the shouting one often encounters in basketball practice. After running drills for some time, the coach blew a whistle and dismissed us for the day with instructions to report back in the morning. I returned to my tent and to the tender ministrations of Corporal Nelson, who took us to meals and made work assignments for us.

The next day, I reported back to basketball practice. This time, we did fast breaks, one-on-one, and practiced some set plays. I threw myself into this work with a passion, but in all honesty, I realized that most, if not all, of my teammates were far better ballplayers than I. In fact, I learned later that two of them went on to the NBA. Finally, in the afternoon of the second day, the coach scheduled a full-team scrimmage. I was assigned as a center and paired off with a center for the other team, a guy who was at least three inches taller. We began playing, and I had a terrible time. I think my opponent scored at least five baskets over me, although I am very proud of the one I scored. As luck would have it, while we were scrimmaging, a photographer from the base newspaper came by and took a beautiful picture of me fully extended, blocking a shot from my nemesis. It was the one shot of his that I had managed to block. The next day, the picture appeared on the front page of the Parris Island newspaper. But alas, that next day also marked the day my basketball career screeched to a halt. After practice that afternoon, the coach said, "Van Sant, I want to see you before you shower." He told me, "Your records show you played basketball at St. John's College. Is that true?" And I replied, "Sir, I think there may have been a misunderstanding. The St. John's I went to is in Annapolis, Maryland. I am not from the basketball school."

He then said, "I don't think I have to tell you, you must realize that your skills are not up to some of these other guys here." I said, "Of course I see that, sir. So I guess I won't be on the Parris Island team?" He said, "That's right, but I do give you credit for effort. Try to build your basketball skills, but I'm afraid we can't use you now." Thus ended my dream of big-time basketball in the Marine Corps.

I returned to my buddies in the tents, who were all excited because the paper had just come out with my picture and my name on the front page. Unfortunately, I had to tell them that my moment of basketball fame had flared up only to burn itself out all too quickly. The next day, I reported back to Corporal Nelson for work assignment.

I think I was on work details for about five or six more days. The first two were spent at the Parris Island dump. My job there was to keep the landfill even and to direct the trucks bringing in the trash. The place where I worked was located where the dump trucks full of empty beer bottles from the slop chutes came to dump their load. In those days, all beer was sold in bottles, and the bottles were simply thrown away. Recycling had not yet been thought of. I must have placed a dozen or more dump truck loads of empty beer bottles on each of my two days. Many of the bottles had been broken in the process of being put in the trucks, and the dumping finished the breakage job, so that I was working in a vast sea of broken glass. It was not entirely unpleasant, though, because the fumes of leftover beer swirling around me were mildly intoxicating.

My last three or four days of work details turned out to be the most interesting. I was assigned to the base bakery. In those days, the Marine Corps baked all of its own bread and other baked goods. The bakery was inside a massive brick building with large rooms several stories high. The main product, of course, was the white bread to feed twenty-five to thirty thousand marines, and there were separate rooms where cakes and pies were prepared. Finally, in solitary splendor, sat an automatic doughnut-making machine.

The first day I reported to the bakery, I was taken aside and assigned to a corporal who spent about ten minutes explaining to me how the doughnut-making machine worked and how its one operator could turn out thousands of doughnuts a day. The batter for the doughnuts was created in another room and placed in large vats. The first phase of my job was to take a trolley, go to the mixing room and pick up a vat, wheel it to the machine, and raise it up and pour its contents into a hopper. I would throw a switch, and the machine would take over. Automatically, the batter was measured out, shaped into doughnuts on a conveyor belt, and transported into an automatic oven, which baked them to perfection for the prescribed time. They emerged on another long conveyor belt completely formed, baked, and sugared. My job then was to take the doughnuts off the belt and put them in boxes, which were stacked at the end of the machine in great quantities. Each repetition of this cycle took over an hour so that I could produce five or six batches of several thousand doughnuts a day.

When the corporal had finished explaining the machine, he leaned over and whispered confidentially, "You'll probably want to sample your product. It's okay to eat one or two, but don't let the sergeant or anybody else see you."

That first morning, I set about producing doughnuts. I had been busily working away for a couple of hours when a sergeant came by to watch me. He asked, "How are things going?" I truthfully replied that things were going great. By this time, I had already sampled a couple of my wares and found them to be delicious.

The sergeant leaned over secretively and said in a hushed voice, "You'll probably be tempted to sample some of 'em. It's okay to take one or two, but just be sure the master sergeant doesn't see you."

Sometime during the morning of my second day on the doughnut machine, the awesome large and revered master sergeant came by to check on me. He asked me how it was going, picked up a sample of my doughnuts, ate it, took me aside privately, and said, "It's okay for you to try a couple of these. Just be sure you don't ever let the mess officer see you."

And then that afternoon, as I was busily filling my machine with batter, there was a loud call of "ATTENTION!" I put down my vat and sprang to attention. "Carry on, men," said the tall slender captain who had entered our building. He proceeded to move around the edifice and disappeared into several of the other rooms. I later found out that he was the base mess officer.

I "carried on" with my preparations, started the machine, and as I was about to finish boxing the last of the previous batch I had baked, I noticed the captain standing there, watching me. Marines do not salute indoors, but they do snap to attention in the presence of an officer. He again told me to carry on and continued watching me. Then he asked me, "Private, how long have you been making doughnuts?"

"Since yesterday morning, sir," I replied.

"D'you ever eat any of them yourself?" he asked.

Old honesty, the best policy, prevailed, and I said, "Yes, sir."

Then he told me quietly, "That's fine, but just be careful, son. Don't let any of the sergeants see you."

Thus was I introduced to the inner workings of the chain of command, and how marines always take care of each other.

When I returned to our tent area after my third or fourth day in the bakery, Corporal Nelson called me in to tell me that my orders had come in, and I was being transferred to Schools Regiment at Camp Lejeune. I was to take ten days of boot leave before reporting in, and the leave was to start the next morning. By the time I left our little tent camp, there were only a half dozen or so members of Platoon 467 left, although other marines from later platoons kept filling the place up. I spent the evening getting my uniform slicked up, shining shoes, packing, and doing all I could to get ready for the trip. I had to pick up tickets for the train and my orders, but all of that was accomplished expeditiously in true Marine Corps fashion.

Chapter 2

BOOT LEAVE, CAMP LEJEUNE, AND A SLOW BOAT (1945)

I don't remember exactly what time of day it was when I finally climbed on the bus from Parris Island to Port Royal, but I was on my way. As had been the case on my trip down, when I made the transfer at Yemassee, the train again seemed to be mostly filled with marines. The majority of the marines on the train, however, were being discharged; only a handful of us were boot leavers. These other guys were salty old veterans, and although they treated us with respect, they pretty much kept to themselves.

A number of them had managed to get hold of some booze, and as we proceeded northward through South Carolina, and later North Carolina, the level of intoxication on the train increased noticeably. None of my fellow 467ers had been put on leave on that day, so I knew absolutely no one on the train. But that didn't bother me. I felt like a million bucks. I was a marine; don't mess with me, or I'll clean your clock. No more cocky, arrogant, full-of-himself seventeen-year-old marine existed than Private George M. Van Sant 584645 USMCR, riding on that train from Parris Island to Washington DC.

As we proceeded northward, I finally got into conversations with some of the quieter dischargees and listened to their tales of Pacific battles, wild liberties on the West Coast, and encounters with legendary marine heroes. As time went by, even some of them got pretty drunk and rambunctious. At some point during the trip, the men's head (bathroom to you, civilians) on our railroad coach ran out of toilet paper. One of the more drunk dischargees, feeling a call of nature from the bowel region, went into the head to relieve the pressure. Only after he finished his business did he realize that there was no paper. At first he let out a howl that was heard all over the car, but when he emerged he proudly told us that he had found no problems with the lack of paper because, fortunately, he had carried his orders and discharge packet in with him and had used his discharge to perform the wiping function, then flushed it down onto the track. I remember being awestruck by the cool initiative and devil-may-care attitude this marine demonstrated but have often wondered since how much red tape he had to go through later in life to replace that precious piece of paper.

Taking on the Burden of History

I arrived back in Union Station sometime in the evening of a beautiful early October day, took a taxicab back to Hyattsville, and had a pleasant reunion with my mother and six-year-old sister. They were quite excited about my return, and my sister was awestruck by her big brother in his splendid uniform. My mother, who obviously still had serious reservations about my being in the Marine Corps, had written to me at boot camp about her relief that the war had ended, and she told me now how happy she was to know that I would no longer be cannon fodder. It was clear, though, that she was still anxious about my father, who had spent the last year of the war in Chongqing, the wartime capital of China, and was, apparently, experiencing some difficulty in being able to return to the States. My father had worked with the Lend-Lease Program, but after World War II ended in September of 1945, the Lend-Lease effort to China, and everywhere else in the world, was terminated as of the thirty-first of December of that year.

In the hierarchy of officials in Chongqing, my father was somewhere down on the ladder. The more senior officials returned to the States immediately, but since there was still work to be done in China and money disbursed, my father remained behind. He eventually ended up being in charge of the China Lend-Lease Program himself for the last couple of months of 1945 and worked from an office in Shanghai. He finally left, as the last member of the staff, in mid-December of 1945, so that I missed seeing him.

My mother really outdid herself in the preparation of meals for the returning, conquering, cocky hero. My first order of business was to get together with Margaret, my girlfriend, and we were able to accomplish that on my very first evening, briefly, when, as I remember, she came over to our house. My mother liked Margaret, but was old-fashioned about having girls calling boys on the telephone. A couple of times, before I had left for Parris Island, Margaret had called me, which had slightly upset my mother.

Margaret and I immediately made plans for a number of dates. In fact, the duration of my boot leave of nine evenings remains a blur. Margaret, who had worked as a hostess and on the staff of the USO at nearby Fort Meade since she was a senior in high school and during her first two years at the University of Maryland, had apparently talked about her Van, the marine, and she now wanted to show me off in my uniform. This was a little awkward because everybody in the USO wore army uniforms, and since I was suffering from a vast superiority complex, I had to constantly stifle the temptation to break out into the sounds of *arf-arf*, which is what we more than mildly insolent marines liked to do in the presence of soldiers back in those days. Certainly being as outnumbered as I was by strapping young soldiers helped me to hold my peace. I remember double-dating with Margaret's sister and her fiancé, an Army Air Corps B-17 pilot on leave from flying bombers out of England. Of course, I also returned to St. John's College to see my friends, who were beginning their fall semester. St. John's had changed with the ending of the war, and the student body had mushroomed into a very lively, vibrant, and academically fertile atmosphere. I spent at least one evening with my friends there, honing my storytelling skills and holding them all spellbound with dreadful and hair-raising accounts of Parris Island. My leave passed in a blur and all too quickly, and I remember my mother, not surprisingly, being saddened by the fact that she had not been able to see more of me during my leave.

Margaret, again, took me down to Union Station to bid me a tender farewell, and I took off on the same train I had taken down to Parris Island the first time. Just as on that previous trip, the passengers on this one were marines. Most of us were going to Camp Lejeune, but there were some people in civilian clothes who were boots on their way to Parris Island. The Marine Corps was still recruiting and enlisting people, although not at the same pace as when I had enlisted a few short months earlier.

I remember several things about this train trip. For one thing, we did not get served any coffee from the platform in either Fredericksburg or Richmond. I guess that when the war ended, those wonderful and dedicated volunteers just felt that their job was done. The train was so crowded that I never got a seat and had to stand all the way from Washington DC to Rocky Mount, North Carolina. Since I had not had any supper yet, and since there was a dining car, I decided to stand in line there, thinking that I might as well stand up waiting for a reward at the end. It seemed to me that I had been standing for hours. Ahead of me in the line stood a woman, probably in her late twenties, who was talking about her work in Washington with someone she clearly knew. As the train progressed, we struck up a conversation, and I found out that she was working for the Foreign Economic Administration. I told her that before going to China, my father too had worked in Washington with the Foreign Economic Administration.

"What is your father's name?" she asked, and after I had told her, it turned out that she had been my father's secretary, and so we had a glimpse of our small world together.

We arrived at Rocky Mount in the darkness, and as before, there were acres of buses waiting for us. We climbed on a bus, which took us about another ninety miles to Camp Lejeune, where we arrived at dawn. When I got off the bus, it became clear that this was not quite like Parris Island, as there were no people jumping all over us. Instead, the people waiting for us had information about what to do and where to go. I went through a check-in process and was told that I had been assigned to Schools Regiment, which, fortunately, was not very far from the bus station; and I took my seabag and walked to the barracks.

I reported to a corporal, who signed me in and assigned me a bunk. By this time, it was midmorning, and since the Marine Corps never allows you to sleep except for specifically designated times of their own choosing, I spent the rest of the day being processed into the regiment. By the end of the day, I had already been processed out of the barracks first assigned to me and into another barracks near the mess hall, where the messmen were housed. It turned out that, as soon as I had arrived at Camp Lejeune, I was placed on mess duty.

Back in those days, if you were a private or private first class, the Marine Corps could assign you up to a month per year of mess duty, unlike the army, which rotated

KPs through day by day. It was quite simply luck of the draw. We could be assigned a month of mess duty, or a month of guard duty; but not both, and the duty to which we had been assigned was entered in our record book. I owed the Marine Corps one month of mess duty and learned that one of the joys of being promoted to corporal would be that one was no longer eligible for mess duty.

After being assigned to my duty and given my new bunk, I was allowed to sleep—however, with the knowledge that I would have to get up at three thirty the next morning. While on mess duty at Camp Lejeune, I got up at three thirty each and every morning. I must say that mess duty was hard work. Breakfast was served at five thirty or six each morning. Our mess hall was huge and must have fed at least one thousand people, if not more. We were assigned to various duties, and the organizational structure was quite interesting. Some people were assigned to assist the cooks back in the galley by helping to break out the various ingredients, loading vegetables into the huge six-foot-high steamer pots, or working on the grills. Then there were people with general duties who ran up and down the mess hall itself, providing more food and iced tea or water or coffee to the tables; and their job description included cleaning everything up after each meal and resetting the tables for the next meal. The Camp Lejeune mess hall did not have a chow line in which one went down and had food slopped on his mess tray. We ate family style, in a fairly civilized fashion. We had silverware; we had big heavy-duty plates rather than metal trays, and we drank coffee out of cups rather than metal mugs as we had at Parris Island.

All in all, my messman's job turned out to be a pretty good deal. After a crash course of instruction, I was assigned to preparing coffee. There was a center wing behind which were the kitchens, refrigerators, and storerooms. On either side of this center wing containing a number of tables and benches were side wings also filled with tables and benches. At each of the corners, where the wings intersected the center section, there sat a gigantic coffeepot built back into a hollow space in the corner wall. This pot was about eight to ten feet high, and I had to climb up a ladder in order to be able to reach the top of it. These two colossal percolators were five feet in diameter and made of stainless steel. The process of percolating the coffee, and this is where the skill came in, was in the operation of two valves, the water valve and the steam valve. I had to adjust the flow of water between the water and the steam valves by gauging the big thermometer to about two hundred degrees Fahrenheit. Just as in an ordinary percolator, the water and steam combination was piped up through a center pipe inside the big tank, and it then flowed down through a huge heavy-duty cloth bag. One of my jobs was to take the bag out after each pot was made, dispose of the coffee grounds, wash out the bag, and fill it again with seventy or eighty pounds of freshly ground coffee. That tank must have produced at least two hundred gallons of coffee.

There were gigantic spigots all around the bottom of the two big coffee tanks. The messmen serving would bring big metal pitchers up and fill them with hot coffee. And it was pretty good coffee too, if I may say so myself. My main job was to make coffee

Presuming to be a United States Marine

twice a day. I filled the pots completely for breakfast and for lunch and used the leftover coffee from the midday meal for dinner, as not everybody drank coffee in the evening. But for breakfast, I had to fill both pots to their maximum capacity, and from three thirty in the morning until breakfast was served, I did nothing but work on the tanks making coffee, which would take two and a half hours to get ready.

When breakfast was over, I had to mount the ladder; lift out the bag with the wet grounds, which by now must have weighed about one hundred pounds; dispose of the grounds in a dumpster; then climb down into the interior of the coffeepot, clean and scrub it inside, and follow that up by climbing out of the pot again in order to scrub and polish its outside. The pot had to look polished on the outside at all times. This job took me most of the morning, and after that, I would have to get started on putting together the lunchtime coffee, which would also get us through dinner. In the evenings, sometimes I had general cleanup jobs. And I don't mind telling you that all of this was hard work. While I worked diligently and never had a moment off in the morning, it always seemed to me that I lagged a little behind schedule. On the other hand, because I did not have to clean the pot in the afternoons, I would have a few enjoyable hours off each day. After the evening cleanup, I would usually not be able to leave the mess hall before 1900 hours, or seven o'clock in the evening, although about three times, while on mess duty assignment, I was given liberty.

One of the first Saturdays I was on duty in the mess hall in mid-October, a couple of us found our lunch duty to be lighter than usual, as many people were off on liberty, and we were able to finish up quickly. We had heard that there was a football game scheduled in the stadium right in the center of the base, so we put on our service uniforms and walked to the stadium. It turned out that the Camp Lejeune football team was playing one of the other marine base teams, perhaps Quantico; and it was a big game, and the stadium was packed. We found seats as close to the fifty-yard line as we could get, and while we were waiting for the game to start, and people were still filing in to fill up the seats, we noticed a special platform clearly reserved for senior officers. Soon a bantam-rooster-like man appeared, not very tall, but very erect, along with an exquisitely elegant lady, whom I presumed to be his wife; and I heard a buzz up and down the lines of marines in the stadium. "Look, there is Chesty, there is Chesty!"

I must confess that at that point, while I had heard of Chesty Puller in a lecture about Marine Corps history given by one of our drill instructors at Parris Island, I was not familiar with the full legend of the man. But the reaction from the marines when they saw him was so palpable that it all gradually fell into place with me. I knew that the commander of Schools Regiment at Camp Lejeune at that time was a Colonel Lewis B. Puller, and I suddenly realized that I was in Chesty Puller's outfit, and now in Chesty Puller's presence. I had never seen him before that football game, but there he was. At that moment, I could not have foreseen that I was to come to know this legendary man well in later years.

Taking on the Burden of History

A DIGRESSIVE SKETCH OF CHESTY

Chesty Puller was born in West Point, Virginia, and grew up in the quiet little town of Saluda, Virginia, not too far down the river from Fredericksburg. After graduating from high school, he enrolled in the Virginia Military Institute in Lexington and attended VMI for one year, from 1917 to 1918. By this time, Chesty had already developed into a pretty warlike individual and, after finishing his first year at VMI, found it impossible not to become involved in fighting wars. In the summer of 1918, he enlisted in the Marine Corps as a private. He was sent through boot camp with somewhat the same timing I had been; both of us finished at the end of a war—he, at the end of World War I, and I, at the end of World War II.

He missed the war in France but was sent overseas to Haiti. After his return, because of his attendance at VMI and the fact that he had already established a good record as an enlisted man, he began the process of becoming an officer—a process that took him several tries over the next few postwar years. In 1925 he finally succeeded, attended officer training, and was eventually sent to the Marine Corps as a second lieutenant.

Chesty began making a name for himself in the old so-called Banana Wars in Nicaragua, Haiti, and El Salvador. By the time he ended his service in Central America, he was a captain and had picked up two Navy Crosses, the second highest decoration for valor a marine can be awarded. There are some legendary stories about Puller's patrols and Puller's ambushes and his capture of one of the bandit leaders in Nicaragua. After these distinguished pursuits, he was sent to China. As a Virginian, he was an outstanding horseback rider and was assigned to head up the Horse Marines in Beijing.

He was rotated back to the United States in 1937 and became an instructor in the Philadelphia Officers School. During that period of time spent in civilization, he met and married Mrs. Puller. This was followed by another tour in Shanghai, China, where he was allowed to be accompanied by his new wife. Fortunately, his outfit was withdrawn from China in time to escape imprisonment by the Japanese after Pearl Harbor.

With World War II looming on the horizon, he became one of the original members of the First Marine Division in its formative stages at the brand-new base at Camp Lejeune. As a new lieutenant colonel, he became commanding officer of the First Battalion, Seventh Marine Regiment, and sailed with them in the spring of 1942 to the American Samoan Islands. Here the Seventh Regiment trained while the rest of the First Marine Division was landing on Guadalcanal on the eighth of August 1942. Chesty was distressed at missing this initial offensive action by the United States in the Pacific but in mid-September, he landed with his battalion on Guadalcanal and was soon in heavy combat with his battalion, notably in the Second Battle of Matanikau, one of the decisive engagements of the entire campaign. Chesty picked up another Navy Cross.

After Guadalcanal, the First Battalion marines were sent to Australia, refitted with replacements, and went on to Cape Gloucester, a landing on New Britain island. Chesty fought with distinction there but, for this battle, was executive officer of the Seventh

Presuming to be a United States Marine

Regiment. After the Gloucester campaign, the First Marine Division was refitted at Pavuvu Island. Casualties had not been nearly as heavy at Gloucester as they had been at Guadalcanal, but it had still been a nasty little battle. At Pavuvu, Chesty was promoted to colonel and became the commanding officer of the First Marine Regiment as it geared up for the Battle of Peleliu. At Peleliu the First Battalion marines were the critical regiment in that particular campaign, the most famous battle of which was the one fought at the Bloody Nose Ridge.

Chesty had developed a reputation by then for being extremely aggressive, and throughout the Marine Corps, there were some people who thought that he was too aggressive and that in some cases, he unnecessarily wasted lives. These accusations infuriated him. It was his opinion, as he said, that "you have to seize the initiative. If you have the initiative, you save men's lives."

But the one thing everybody agreed on was that Chesty, perhaps more than any other marine officer, had the ability of relating to and looking after his troops. His popularity was thoroughly established in World War II and was really based on the fact that with Chesty, his troops always came first. He was, and still is, a hero to every young enlisted marine.

Peleliu was secured in the fall of 1944, and he was rotated home. After an extensive leave, he came to Camp Lejeune to take over the Infantry Training Regiment, the so-called tent camp, which was busy preparing replacements for the impending battles of Iwo Jima and Okinawa. With the end of the war, he was transferred to command the special training or schools regiment into which I had been ordered.

But Chesty had one more chapter of bravery in him, and that chapter was written in the Inchon landing, the retaking of Seoul, and at the Chosin Reservoir in Korea. When the First Marine Division was forming up for Korea, he had insisted that he be given his First Regiment again and became its commander. At the Reservoir, the Puller legend deepened. There are two famous and familiar, although undocumented, Chesty quotes from that campaign. When the division was completely surrounded by an enormous Chinese force, Chesty is said to have exclaimed, "All right, they're on our left, they're on our right, they're in front of us, they're behind us . . . they can't get away this time." And when somebody asked him, "How do you account for your retreat?" Puller blew a fuse and said, "Retreat, hell! We were just advancing in a different direction!"

Chesty received five Navy Crosses in his career, and there was always a good deal of banter between him and the other senior officers in the Marine Corps about whether he would trade them all in for one Congressional Medal of Honor. He indicated several times that he never did anything for the sake of a medal but that, yes, it would have been nice to have received the Congressional.

I will end this little thumbnail sketch of Chesty Puller with a couple of stories of my own interaction with him later on in my life.

In 1955, when I was a graduate student at the University of Virginia, I spent the three months of my academic summer vacation on active duty in the Marine Corps Reserve, as I did during all the summers between 1953 and 1977. I had just received

Taking on the Burden of History

my master's degree, was starting on my PhD, and was assigned to the Reserve Liaison Unit at Camp Lejeune. We were set up as a cadre to organize and coordinate the training of approximately seventy Marine Corps Reserve units coming for their two weeks of annual training duty. They would arrive in two-week increments, and in the twelve weeks I was on active duty, we would assist in the training of six increments of reserve units.

I had just been promoted to captain the year before, so that I was still fairly junior and was assigned duty as a training assistant. This meant that I was assigned as liaison to an individual unit for the entire two weeks of their training. Before they arrived, I made sure that all their billeting was squared away and that their meals were accounted for and that all the transportation needed to move them around the base was provided for. I also had to ensure that the unit training them was fully prepared with instruction, problems to work through, and field exercises set up so that they would receive proper training. In addition to that, for three days out of every two weeks, every reserve unit would go to the rifle range to fire the rifle for record and to requalify.

The job of a training assistant was a busy job. We had to become licensed as Marine Corps drivers in order to be able to drive ourselves to our various assignments. This was an exception to the customary practice of officers having assigned drivers for their jeeps. During August of 1955, my assigned reserve unit was a communications unit from somewhere just north of New York City, a unit commanded by a fairly senior major, a veteran of World War II. For the first week, after I had bedded them down, they were to be trained by the Communications Battalion of what was then called Force Troops.

On the Tuesday of their first training week, Camp Lejeune went on a hurricane alert. Hurricane Connie paid us a call, and by late Tuesday, the base was closed, and all training was suspended. I was sent back to quarters, as we all were. The barracks where the reserve unit was bedded down had to be tightened up, and everybody had to sit inside while the hurricane hit Camp Lejeune with enormous force. The quarters where I was living with my late wife and my son, Ned, who was then about seven months old, flooded, and the water came up higher and higher until it finally stopped rising a mere six inches before it would have poured all over the floor of our little apartment. I had never before seen so much water, nor had I heard the howling of such wild winds. After three days of closure, we resumed training, and the Communications Company was able to get in another Friday of training. On Saturday, we were able to pull off some kind of a parade, dodging a good deal of debris all around the base.

Then we went out on the rifle range, but as luck would have it, on Monday of this second week of training, the entire base went on a new hurricane alert, this time for Hurricane Diane. As it turned out, Diane did not hit Camp Lejeune as hard as Connie had, but it still scored a hit, slamming into New England on its way up the East Coast and turning into one of the worst hurricanes in history. And Diane's rising wrath was powerful enough to disrupt our training again. I don't think the poor members of that communications unit ever were able to fire for record, because their last day at the range was wiped out by this second hurricane attack. I finally got the unit moved

Presuming to be a United States Marine

to Camp Geiger, an outpost of Camp Lejeune, where they were going to spend their last few days. The barracks assigned to them, as luck would have it, were completely swamped by one or the other of the two hurricanes. Everything was ruined, and the bedding was soaked. I had to do a good deal of scratching around to find alternative accommodations for this entire company of reserve marines so that they could be billeted for their final three days.

At this point, their commanding officer, a major, perhaps understandably, snapped at the fact that his unit had been unable to engage in any meaningful training in the two weeks they had spent at Camp Lejeune. The enforced idleness was just too much for him, and the fact that the barracks, to which I was finally able to move his unit, was dry but turned out not to be quite ready, in no way helped to restore his equilibrium. He decided that the entire mess was all expressly my fault, apparently bestowing on me the ability to attract, or deflect, any and all hurricanes from their designated path. In his anger, the major suddenly pulled his trump card.

"Let's see," he said. "General Puller is the commanding general of this base now, isn't he?"

"Yes, sir," I said. This was just before Chesty had suffered his stroke, and Puller was now a major general.

The major advised me that he had been Puller's communications officer at Peleliu, and again at the Chosin Reservoir in Korea, so that he knew the general quite well.

And the major said, "I don't like to do this, but I am going to call up the general, and by golly, we are going to get this thing squared away right now."

He got out the base telephone book and put in the call, and he wanted me right there, at his elbow, while he was calling up the general. He got through by telling the clerk who answered the telephone that he was Major So-and-so, an old friend of General Puller's, and that he wanted to speak to him.

"Oh, General," said the major and rattled off the places where they had served together. Next, he took off on a tirade, not quite personally directed at me, at how screwed up the entire reserve training business seemed to be, and how it seemed that there had not been any preparation for dealing with hurricanes, and he went on and on, unloading on General Puller. Finally, after throwing a few barbs at me for not being as cooperative as I should be, he became quiet for a minute, listening to the general's response. Then he handed the receiver to me, saying triumphantly, "Here, Captain, General Puller wants to speak with you."

Oh God! It had been ten years since I had seen Chesty Puller at my first Marine Corps birthday celebration at Camp Lejeune. In the intervening years, I had become more familiar with the legends surrounding this larger-than-life figure. It would be an understatement to say that I was filled with foreboding and apprehension as I took that telephone receiver into my hand. I knew that I was about to receive the greatest chewing out of my Marine Corps career.

"Captain Van Sant here, sir," I said into the receiver, bracing myself. And this is what Chesty Puller told me.

"Captain Van Sant, I feel sorry for you. That goddamn major always was a whiner! Now, you and I have got to put our heads together and figure out a way to keep him happy."

I don't have to tell you that at that instant, Chesty Puller had earned my undying loyalty.

"You just tell him that I said . . . ," And he proceeded to think out aloud about some of the things that could be done "to keep the major happy."

I deliberately kept my face in a very serious and attentive expression during our conversation because I did not want the major to know that I was being stroked with great sympathy by Chesty over the telephone.

"I will do that, sir. Yes, sir. Yes, sir," I said and hung up the phone. I don't remember just how we worked things out, but we did, and we were finally able to get the major and his unit loaded on the train back to Yonkers, or to whatever place in the state of New York he had come from.

It was during that summer that Chesty Puller suffered his stroke, which resulted in an involuntary retirement from the Marine Corps for medical reasons. He was promoted to a three-star general, a lieutenant general, and returned to his home in Saluda, Virginia.

Our paths did not cross again until 1963. By that time, I was a professor of philosophy at Mary Washington College in Fredericksburg, where I taught all my life. As I was greeting an incoming class of freshman students, I noticed the name of Martha Puller on my list. Puller is a fairly unusual name, and I had never had a student by that name before. When the class was over, I stopped her to ask, "You are not any relation to General Puller, are you?"

"Yes, he is my father," she said and asked me whether I had been in the Marine Corps. When I told her that I was still in the Marine reserves, and that on a couple of occasions I had served under her father, she said he would be glad to know that at least one of her teachers was a marine. As it turned out, Martha Puller became a student in several of my classes, and for a brief period, I was her faculty advisor. Soon after this first meeting, she came to my office and asked me if there were any other marines on the faculty. The only other marine was Mike Houston, the director of admissions. He had been a noncommissioned officer at the Chosin Reservoir, where he had been badly wounded. Mike and I remained good friends until he died tragically a few years later.

Several months into that first class, Martha came up to me and said, "Daddy is coming up to visit me tomorrow, and he would like to have lunch with you." I expressed my delight at his command.

The next day, we met in the College Shop, which was the college's restaurant in those days, and he took me to lunch. That established a routine, and since Saluda is less than a two-hour drive, Chesty would come up to see Martha at least a couple of times a semester. Sometimes he would come up with Mrs. Puller, and sometimes he would come up alone, but almost every time he came, he would first call up Martha

Presuming to be a United States Marine

to say, "Tell Van Sant I want to have lunch." I am sure that he enjoyed these lunches because it gave him an opportunity to talk about his beloved Marine Corps with someone who loved it also.

For me, the lunches were delightful interludes, and I soon got into the habit of asking him leading questions about particular phases of his career, because once you got him started, he would take off fast and furious. What was so great about the man, though, was that he always expressed interest in my career, as well. He wanted to know where I had been and who my commanding officers were and whom I knew in the Corps. He was never a blowhard. He was a genuine human being.

We used to talk about China. He wanted to know all about my experiences there, which I will pass on to you also later, and he told me many stories about his own China experiences. He listened to my recounting of the events I had witnessed in Korea, and of my company commander, Griff Moody, whom you will also meet down the road in this accounting. Chesty knew Griff, thought highly of him, and was glad that I had served under such a good man. During this period of the 1960s Griff suffered his heart attack, and this upset General Puller greatly.

One of the features of these very pleasant lunch occasions was that Mrs. Puller would sometimes join us, although Martha never came, as it was always deemed to be strictly a lunch for "adults." After participating in this ritual a number of times, I was struck by the fact that when Mrs. Puller graced us with her presence, Chesty was every inch the gentleman. Mrs. Puller was a very distinguished Southern lady, and Chesty was obviously very proud that she had deigned to marry him. He invariably treated her deferentially and with respect, and his language was always immaculate and irreproachable in her presence. On the other hand, Chesty had always had the reputation for being a, shall we say, garbage mouth. Although it does not seem fitting to use this old Marine Corps term in connection with the exalted General Puller, he was a pretty profane speaker among the troops. When Mrs. Puller was not lunching with us, the contrast in his approach to a conversation with me was vividly noticeable.

The general had been medically retired from the Marine Corps in the fifties. During the years his daughter Martha was in college, Vietnam was beginning to crank up, and as the war began escalating, Chesty had formally written a letter to the commandant of the Marine Corps, General Wallace Greene, asking to be brought back on active duty. He simply could not stomach the idea of his Marine Corps fighting a war without him in it. Of course, General Greene turned him down, and there is not a person in the Corps who does not understand the reason for the rejection. Puller, mad as hell, griped and said some pretty unflattering, although undeserved, things about General Greene. I subsequently got to know General Greene. Greene knew, admired, and understood Chesty and was never bothered by any unkind comments from him.

One day at lunch, I made the mistake of asking Chesty, "General, what do you think of the state of the Marine Corps now, generally speaking?"

The answer was articulated in his best parade ground voice, which was considerable, and drawn out into three syllables: "Shi-i-it!" Just like that. We were sitting in the College

Shop, and it was crowded, with every table occupied, and by the time the general had arrived at the *t*, there was dead silence in the room. Every single person in that lunchroom was looking at him. At that time, you must remember, this particular word was almost never heard in public. It was clear that, in his retirement, the general's voice had not lost one iota of its command volume.

Poor General Puller! He looked around among the hushed lunch crowd, and this is the only time I saw something of a sheepish expression of "Ah, maybe I should not have said that" on his face. Obviously, Mrs. Puller was not lunching with us on that particular occasion.

One of Martha's best friends and classmates at Mary Washington College, Toddy, eventually married Martha's twin brother, Lewis B. Puller Jr., whom I subsequently met. Lewis Junior graduated from the College of William and Mary, followed in his father's footsteps by going through Officer Candidate School at Marine Base Quantico, and was sent to Vietnam as a lieutenant. He was very badly wounded there, losing both legs and one hand. Lewis Puller Jr. wrote a book about his relationship with his father but, discouraged by his crippling wounds, eventually committed suicide. Toddy, his widow, later became a state senator from Virginia.

Martha married a Marine Corps officer, whom I took through Officer Candidate School at Quantico and who retired as a general. The eldest Puller daughter, Virginia, married another Marine Corps officer, whom I had also taken through both the junior and senior Platoon Leaders Class program when I worked in Quantico as a company commander, so that both of Chesty Puller's daughters married men whom I had trained in the Marine Corps. When I drove to Saluda in more recent years, I was welcomed into the Puller home, and this association was a very moving experience for me. Chesty remains unforgettable not only in my memory, but in the memories of all the men who knew him.

And as I am writing this memoir, we continue to make the pilgrimage on the Marine Corps birthday to Saluda, Virginia, for a memorial service for General Puller. On my first celebration in 1945 at Camp Lejeune, I celebrated the Marine Corps' 170th Birthday with Chesty Puller, and fifty-five years later, I attended the 225th Birthday in Saluda, with Chesty's spirit still strongly palpable among us.

Many years ago, and I think this was initiated by some drill instructors at Parris Island, young marines were taught to say before going to sleep, "Good night, Chesty, wherever you are!" And that tribute continues to this day.

END OF DIGRESSION

Everyone who has ever known a marine knows that no matter where you are in the world, the Marine Corps Birthday on November 10 will be celebrated, even in combat. There is a prescribed ceremony of reading the commandant's message, a reading of the Marine Corps Manual is given, and the birthday cake is presented with fanfare, accompanied by the Marine Corps Hymn. The cake is cut by the senior dignitary, and it is cut with a sword. The first piece of cake is presented to the oldest marine present, and the second piece is presented to the youngest marine present. The celebration of the Marine Corps Birthday dates back to November 10, 1775, when the first marine in history was recruited at Tun Tavern in Philadelphia, Pennsylvania. With considerable ceremony, at least throughout the twentieth century to the present time, this date has been observed wherever marines are present.

Of course, on November 10, 1945, at Camp Lejeune, I did not yet know what my future as a marine would bring. I simply knew that the Marine Corps Birthday was a very special annual celebration. There was a good deal of stir in the mess hall at Camp Lejeune. The mess sergeant got us all lined up and told us about the special ceremony to be held in front of the mess hall involving a Marine Corps birthday cake. The observance was to take place in the afternoon before dinner while it was still light outside. As soon as our lunchtime work was finished, all the messmen quickly changed into sharper uniforms to be fallen in to form two sides of a square. The third side of that square was made up of all of the other troops in the regiment, and the fourth side of the square was made up of a long table with a huge and impressive cake reposing on it and some chairs for the senior officers.

After we had put on our uniforms to try to look reasonably military, we ran back to help make up our two sides of the hollow square around the ceremony. On that occasion, I saw Chesty Puller for the second time because he himself arrived to preside and read the greeting from the commandant. Another officer read the passage from the Marine Corps Manual, and then we sang the Marine Corps Hymn. Although there was no band on this occasion and we just had ourselves, we sang the Marine Corps Hymn lustily. Colonel Puller made a few remarks, and I don't remember what he said, but I do remember that by that time, I had heard enough about the Puller legend to realize what an honor it was to be in his presence. He cut the first piece of cake with his sword, and that was in 1945.

One evening, in early November of 1945, some of our details of messmen were declared eligible for liberty at about 1800 hours (6:00 p.m. civilian time). We rushed back to the barracks and slipped into our little-used uniforms of the day and rushed down to the Lejeune bus station for the twenty-five-minute bus trip into the great metropolis of Jacksonville, North Carolina. At that time, there was very little of any interest to see between the main gate to Camp Lejeune and the town itself, so that the trip was fast but boring.

Jacksonville at that time was a seedy little town with a few bars, jewelry stores, and pawnshops. We piled into the first bar we encountered, and I had the first beer I had tasted in some time. After a couple of beers, three or four of us left to look for a decent restaurant. We wandered around a good deal until we finally found an adequate-looking place where we had a meal and lots more beer. It could not have been a very memorable evening, because I don't remember what I ate, who my companions were, or even where the restaurant was located. The town was full of lonely Marine Corps privates milling about looking for action, which poor little Jacksonville could not provide.

Taking on the Burden of History

There were absolutely NO, but NO young females to be seen, only pretty hard-looking waitresses well on their way to middle age. My one abiding memory of this particular Jacksonville liberty is that at about 2230, or half past ten in the evening, one member of the party, whose speech had slowly taken on a new and fuzzy dimension, said to the rest of us, "Lesh get tattooed!"

"An eggshellent idea," we all agreed. We asked our waitress where the nearest tattoo parlor was, and as I recall, our party of three or four had to cross a bridge to get to it. Eight or nine marines were already lined up outside. Apparently, there were only two "artists" at work inside, and each tattoo took some considerable time to create and execute.

By half past eleven, three or four of the marines in line had gone inside for the desired embellishments on their bodies, but there were still four or five people including my colleagues ahead of me. As time went by, I began sobering up by degrees, until my head had cleared sufficiently to realize that it would probably be one o'clock in the morning before a tattoo artist could reasonably be expected to begin his artwork on me. In addition, I would have to figure in the time for the bus ride back to the main base at Camp Lejeune. Suddenly, the 3:30 a.m. reveille inexorably stared me in the face, and so I and one of my companions bade farewell to the other two, who remained undeterred in their decision to stick it out. The two of us deserters went back to the base to three short hours of sleep. Thus I was prevented from fully enjoying the Jacksonville tattoo experience.

I remained on mess duty through the balance of the month of October and into November, and then word came down that all of us recent graduates of boot camp, who were now in the Schools Regiment, were being placed into the Ninety-fourth Replacement Draft. In the space of about five days, we were issued new rifles, and we got all our gear, weapons, and uniforms up to snuff. We were sent through the medical dispensary and given what I like to recount as eight shots. To be quite honest, it was only seven shots, plus one vaccination administered simultaneously—two in the forearm and two in the upper part of each arm. As I found out later, we were destined for China, although we did not know that yet, and the shots were for every disease known to that country at that time. We then made up field transport packs, the largest pack the Marine Corps had, and wearing our overcoats, we were marched across the base of Camp Lejeune to the railhead and loaded aboard trains like cattle.

It was the fall of 1945, and I was eighteen years old. I later learned that this particular movement involved ultimately, when the ship was loaded in Norfolk, I think, nine thousand men. Of those nine thousand men, about six or seven thousand of us must have been loaded at Camp Lejeune.

We completed roll call in the Camp Lejeune industrial area and climbed aboard the train around midnight. It was a dismal night with bursts of rain showers. We spent most of the night on the train, and by the time we arrived in Norfolk, it was light outside. The trip was not long in terms of miles, but the train itself was once again very slow, very old, and very dreary. It took us right onto a dock in Norfolk, and we were herded off the train aboard the USS *Wakefield*.

Presuming to be a United States Marine

In its glory days, the *Wakefield* had been a transatlantic liner known as the SS *Manhattan*. She was built during the late twenties and, for a period of time in the late twenties and early thirties, was the largest American flagship in the North Atlantic trade. The *Wakefield* displaced 24,289 tons, and boasted three large smokestacks. Throughout World War II, she had been used to ferry army replacements across the Atlantic to the European theater. After the end of the war in Europe, she had carried a number of loads of GIs from Europe but now had been sent down to Norfolk to reprovision and was ready to pick up our enormous draft of marines. We loaded aboard, and off we went. Our life aboard this ship can easily be summarized in one word—"dreadful."

We slept on a steel rectangle inside of which was laced a smaller rectangular piece of canvas. There was no mattress, just the piece of canvas. The steel rectangles could be folded up against the bulkhead, where they could be let down on chains; and they were stacked, depending upon the height of the compartment, either four or five high. The distance between each rectangle with its canvas and the guy on the rectangle directly above was probably between eighteen inches and two feet. If you turned over as you lay on this thing, your shoulder hit the bottom of the canvas of the guy above you, and that's how cramped the quarters were. We had, in our tiny little compartment, 280 marines, and we were just one compartment back in the stern of the ship on the next to the bottom deck, well below the waterline.

We were served two meals a day. In the morning, we had breakfast, which was not very good. We stood up to eat from a metal tray with some oatmeal and a couple of moldy pieces of toast slapped on it and some coffee and some kind of fruit. We stood up during the entire meal as we gulped down the food, and that was our first meal of the day. At lunchtime no meal was served, although we could sometimes get soup and sometimes fruit. That was all. The best description of the evening meal is that it did not significantly lag behind the morning meal in quality, taste, or appearance.

We took off from Norfolk, sailed out around the Virginia and the North Carolina capes, and headed south for the Caribbean. The weather was good, and everybody was up and looking around. In the distance, we could see the Atlantic coastline. Once we got into the Gulf Stream, although the weather was still nice, the sea began swelling and rolling. On about the second day out, seasickness attacked the troops. I have always thanked my genes and the good Lord that I have never been seasick, and having witnessed mass seasickness at various times in my life, I certainly hope that I never will be. I was surrounded by seasick marines. We had a small town, a small city of nine thousand people on this ship, and that's a lot of people! It took two and a half hours just to run everybody through the mess deck to get their stand-up meals. To reach the mess deck, we had to climb down ladders for several decks and climb up them again after the meals. On the second day, not too many people partook of the evening meal because seasickness was so rampant. I followed the old advice that in order to prevent seasickness, one should eat because on an empty stomach, one would get even more sick. So I went down and ate a full meal, and it wasn't too bad, only as bad as usual. As I started to climb the long ladder up two decks to get up and out of the mess hall, suddenly, the guy above me on the ladder got sick and bombarded me, and I think that description is graphic enough. It was so awful that I immediately wanted to get off that ladder. I turned around to start down, and hell, the guy below me on the ladder was also sick. I found myself trapped between two guys, one below me and one above me on the same ladder, all the time wishing to be somewhere else, anywhere else.

On about the third day out, and incidentally, I am not going to go through this day by day because it was a monthlong trip, word came out on the loudspeaker that we were going to have a "field day," which means a massive cleanup in all the troop berthing compartments. It was announced over the PA system that everybody was to turn to and first sweep fore and aft, then scrub with mops and scour and clean out all the toilets, or heads as we call them, and get it all done without delay.

It must be said that the disciplinary structure in our 280-person compartment was not too strong. We had a corporal in charge, and he was a so-called brig rat. He had been a master sergeant but got busted down, sent to Portsmouth Naval Prison, and was put on this draft as a probationer in order to salvage his career and at least allow him to get an honorable discharge. He was an older guy, and I would not call him one of the most inspiring leaders I had ever encountered in the Marine Corps. Although we had some officers on board, we almost never saw them. We listened to the communication over the PA as we were all lying on our little old racks, trying to read or to entertain ourselves shooting the breeze, while the message about the field day was being repeated regularly. Obediently, I found a broom and swept up all around our little area, and then I got a mop and was preparing to use it when I suddenly realized that I was the only guy doing anything at all. Nobody else was turning to. I thought, *This is stupid!* and put away all my cleaning implements because by this time, I had the place pretty clean anyway. I reached into my little pack and grabbed a book. Behind the bunks back in the corner of the compartment, at the back of a large ventilator pipe, was a quiet little place, a tiny little cubbyhole. I crawled into it with my book. For better or for worse, once I started reading, I became so absorbed that I completely ignored what was going on around me.

Suddenly there was a noise of someone clearing his throat, and I looked out around the ventilator pipe and saw that everybody was scrubbing with mops, and there were people brandishing brooms, and there were people climbing up the overhead, wiping up, and everybody was working like demons. In stark contrast, I was sacked out and reading, with a young lieutenant looking down on me intently.

He said, "What do you think you are doing, marine?"

And, stupid me, I said, "Sir, I had already done a lot of cleaning, sir."

"Yea," he said, "I can see that. You are working real hard," he said. This lieutenant wasn't much older than nineteen, but, "Young man," he told me, "I got a brand-new little notebook here." And he added, "I am going to make you the number one man on my shit list." He asked me, "What is your name, marine?"

And I gave him, "Sir, Private George M. Van Sant, sir."

Presuming to be a United States Marine

He said, "Serial number?" And I gave him, "Sir, 584645, sir."

And he said, "Okay, you are now on my list. You turn to, and you will be hearing from me."

Oh God! I was scared. I had really screwed up now, what a terrible thing! So I turned to and swept everything again and mopped everything again and went in and worked on the head and scrubbed and scrubbed everywhere else, and we did get the place nice and clean, I must say. I waited with apprehension, and the next day, over the PA system throughout the ship, there sounded, "Private George M. Van Sant, 584645, lay down to the troop sergeant major's office. Private George M. Van Sant, 584645, lay down to the troop sergeant major's office."

Of course, I had no idea where the troop sergeant major's office was, but I went up on the main deck, stopped and asked a couple of people for directions, and finally found somebody who knew where it was. I walked into the sergeant major's office and said, "Private Van Sant reporting as ordered, sir."

"Oh yeah," he growled. "Yes," he said. "You are the guy who was corking off on field day, eh?" And I answered him, "Yes, sir."

He said, "All right. Now here is what you do." He then instructed me that I had been assigned to the ship's laundry. And thus began one of the most wonderful breaks I ever had in my Marine Corps career. One might think that service in the ship's laundry sounds pretty onerous, doesn't it? But the ship's laundry assignment turned out to be the greatest thing that could have happened to me on this trip. In fact, it made the whole trip tolerable for me.

The skipper and all the permanent crew on the *Wakefield* were coastguardsmen. The coast guard crew maintained a pretty high standard of spit and polish. All the officers aboard ship wore starched white shirts, the enlisted guardsmen wore the blue dungaree costume, and the senior petty officers wore starched tan shirts, so there was a lot of laundry to be done on the ship, just servicing the crew.

The marine passengers, most of whom were privates, did not get any laundry service. You will remember that at boot camp, we were issued tie-ties, the very heavy pieces of cord used to tie clothes to a clothesline. To wash *their* clothes, the marine passengers on board ship first had to scrounge a long piece of rope. They would thread this long rope through the sleeves and trouser legs of their clothing. Using the little issue tie-ties, they would attach their clothes to the long rope. The rope was thrown over the side of the ship until the clothes got well down into the salt water, where they were vigorously dragged as the ship steamed ahead. This procedure would soak the clothes, and they would get beaten by the water and bleached by the salt. It was an expedient way of doing laundry. The clothes would dangle in the water for ten or fifteen minutes, and after that, the rope was pulled up so that the clothes were completely out of the water. The ship, moving at 20 to 25 knots, created quite a wind, and in this wind, the clothes would flap and dry, usually in less than an hour. A transport carrying marines in the middle of the ocean could look pretty grungy with its hundreds of ropes of clothing hanging off the side of the ship, aflutter in the breeze. Some of the more knowledgeable and physics-trained friends of mine and I attempted to calculate as to how much drag this laundering method put on the ship in its forward progress.

Unfortunately, there were several hazards associated with this method of laundering. The heads on the ship at sea had a stream of salt water pumped through troughs in the various compartments. These troughs picked up all varieties of human waste and piped it to the outside of the ship. Flowing out of the ship, the waste would pass impelled by gravity out into the ocean—Mother Nature's sewage system. The problem was that once you had your clothes down in the water, sometimes you would pick up in your baggy pockets undesirable little "gifts" from this sewage system. And that was only one of the hazards of using this technique of laundering.

Another problem was that on a sunny, clear day, as the ship steamed along, there would be literally hundreds of ropes with clothes hanging over the side, and these ropes would inevitably get tangled in the wind. This would precipitate occasional confrontations among the marines, which could sometimes turn a little bit nasty. In addition, from time to time, people lost clothes that were not tied down securely enough to stand the beating of the big drag through the ocean.

The coast guard crew, on the other hand, had excellent laundry facilities with huge washing machines, dryers, and a large variety of pressing machines. As it turned out, the laundry crew was shorthanded, and the ship's captain had asked the troop sergeant major if he could make available a marine to fill out the complement of the coast guard laundry crew. Since the lieutenant had put me on his infamous list, when the request was received by the sergeant major, he decided to nail me with the laundry job, thereby inadvertently bestowing on me a great gift. I was instructed in the rudiments on how to run the washing machines and the dryers, although I was never entrusted with the art of ironing shirts. The officers' sheets, by the way, had to be laundered and pressed also.

One of the immediate fringe benefits I achieved as a member of the laundry force, after making good friends with several of the coastguardsmen who worked there, was that my new friends outfitted me with the blue dungarees of a coast guard crewman from surplus clothing. I shudder to confess this, but for most of that trip of over thirty days, I had my meals in the crew's mess. The enlisted crew on the ship had a very nice mess hall, and more importantly, they sat down to some very lovely food, which I enjoyed eating with them. I was always in a little bit of danger of discovery, though, because coastguardsmen wore black low quarter boots in those days, with heavy, thick rubber soles. Marines wore boondockers, the heavy low boots. This boot was bigger than low quarter shoes, and it was fairly distinctive in appearance. It had a composition, not a rubber, sole and was brown in color. I had to continue wearing my Marine Corps boondockers, and if one of the senior petty officers had noticed my shoes, I would undoubtedly have been in big trouble. Fortunately, I got away with it, and for the entire trip, I mostly feasted in the crew's mess, all the time feeling a touch disloyal, I must say, for not roughing it with my fellow marines. While working in the laundry, I received days off, although this did not happen very often, and on my day off,

Presuming to be a United States Marine

I had to return to eat in the passenger troop marine mess, which remained a horrible experience to be avoided at all cost.

We sailed down the East Coast and continued on through the Caribbean, saw Cuba from a distance, and crossed over to the Panama Canal. We did not stop at the Atlantic end of the canal but sailed right through, stopping at the town of Balboa. The Panama Canal is an awesome example of human ingenuity at the time it was built. It defied imagination. Almost more awesome than the locks and the ability they have to use large engines to pull huge ships through, were some of the cuts through the mountains excavated with steam shovels in the early twentieth century. The steam shovels dug a river through a mountain, and while I don't want to exaggerate, the sides of some of these cuts must be close to five hundred feet high.

If you have seen the Monument in Washington DC, and imagine that as one side of a trench, and then envision a corresponding trench side of equal height on the other side, that's what it was like to sail through the narrow Galliard Cut on a ship. The angle of the cut was so steep that there were lots of rocks left along the wall of it, and if you were on deck, it would seem that you were passing them within ten or fifteen feet. On the rocks basked the most amazing variety of fauna I had ever seen—birds and lizards of all different kinds. Our ship passed at very low speed, so that I almost felt I could reach out my hand and touch them. It remains one of the most spectacular sights I have ever seen.

We reached Balboa on the Pacific end of the canal, and lo and behold, the authorities commanding the troop passengers and the skipper decided to give everybody on the ship what was in those days called base liberty. That meant that you could get off the ship and explore the sizeable Balboa Navy Base. I took advantage of this opportunity to go ashore. Thanks to my laundry work, I boasted a nicely starched uniform, unlike any of the other troop passengers. There were a number of stores in the bazaar on the base, a great big warehouse structure with lots of booths in it. It was early December of 1945, and Christmas was fast approaching.

I knew that I was going to be away from home for Christmas, and I thought of my poor mother, who would be all alone at home with my little sister, as my father remained overseas. What I did not know, at this point, was that my father was just starting out on his way home from China. And of course, neither did I know yet that I myself was on my way to China.

In the bazaar, I found a shop selling silk stockings. I remembered my mother's foot size and bought three pairs of silk stockings for her. This may not make much of an impression on any woman who did not live through World War II, but at that time, silk stockings were the most exciting gift you could possibly have bought your mother. Women on the home front during World War II could only get cheap rayon stockings, which, they always said, seemed to last about five minutes. All silk went to the war effort, and nylon, although it had been invented by that time, had not yet been released to the civilian market. I was thrilled that I could buy something so great as silk stockings for my mother.

Taking on the Burden of History

Unfortunately, I had forgotten how tall my mother was for a woman. She measured about five feet nine inches and had long legs. I bought what I thought were the most elegant silk stockings, managed to get them wrapped, and immediately mailed them off to my mother from a post office in Balboa. Many years later, long after she had sent me a letter to China thanking me profusely for the wonderful stockings, she finally admitted that they had barely reached up to her knees. Even then, she assured me that although she had never been able to wear the stockings, she had been very happy to get such a lovely and thoughtful Christmas present from me.

We poked around the base and bought some of the goodies one was able to get ashore, like hamburgers and milk shakes. As we straggled back to our ship, we saw that a USO show had been brought down and set up on the dock near our ship, with entertainers and music, a band with a female singer who, I still remember, was very attractive. She sang, "I'm Dreaming of a White Christmas" for us. It was beautiful but also tough because here we were, a whole shipload of guys who were not going to be at home on Christmas. Instead, we were in the tropics, not too far away from the equator. It was a lonely moment, as I recall.

We loaded back aboard the ship and took off west again. A couple of days after our Panama stop, probably the worst crisis of the whole trip occurred. The passenger troop mess provided as the midday food some grapefruit taken aboard, I guess, at Panama and a kind of a bean soup. I did not eat any of it, probably because I had feasted royally with the coast guard crew, but many of the hungry passengers had eaten all the food available to them on that day.

Being two days west of the Panama Canal placed us the closest we were to come to the equator, which was probably only one hundred miles or so south of our position, and it was extremely hot. In fact, we were in the area visited by El Nino in 1998. On deck, the temperature easily reached one hundred degrees. Unfortunately, the grapefruit had rotted, or were spoiled enough to cause violent intestinal disorders. Not too long after the first people had eaten the grapefruit, they began feeling sick. I have never seen illness to match what I saw on that ship on that day, not even the seasickness. It was quite frightening.

In our troop compartment, for example, where I went right after lunch, there was a big head with troughs you could sit on and other troughs where you could stand and do your business in. As I mentioned before, the troughs had salt water running continuously through them. Those troughs were filled with diarrhea and vomit, to the point where they all overflowed. The head had these products to a depth of three or four inches all over the deck. And that's hell.

Those of us who were able-bodied spent our time carrying unconscious and semiconscious marines to emergency sick bays, where liquids were being administered intravenously to counteract dehydration. I saw people literally go into catatonic states. One of the marines whom we carried out of our compartment was a little bit older than the rest of us—a brig rat about whom I will tell you more later on. He was probably twenty-five years old and very ill. He passed out and went into a completely rigid state.

Presuming to be a United States Marine

In order to get him to sick bay, we had to carry him up ladders. He was so stiff that we handed him up like a board. We were sure he was going to die. We got him to sick bay, and a corpsman and a doctor, who had been pressed into service, spotted him and began treating him at once. He survived, although he was in the ship's hospital for a couple of days. It was a nightmare. We heard later that about two thousand passengers had suffered from food poisoning. Of course, once people started getting sick, the grapefruit was not served anymore, so that those who were farther back in the food line never became ill. There were enough people who had eaten the fruit, including many of my friends and those in my compartment, to create a real crisis.

From very early on in the trip, I had made contact or established friendships with several guys who were pretty interesting, and what brought us together was the game of bridge. Even though I worked an eight-hour day in the laundry, I still found myself with at least some free time. Three other guys and I used to get together just about every night and play bridge for hours. One of them was a very interesting fellow from Alabama, and I remember his name, Kemmerling. He was Jewish, had attended the University of Alabama as an English major, and was interested in journalism. A couple of months after we got to North China, while he was still a private first class, he became the editor of the *North China Marine*, the newspaper for all marines in China. He'd already had a good deal of newspaper experience. As partners, we eventually reached the point where we could read each other's mind. We seemed to always know exactly what the other fellow held in his hand.

The people we played against were two Ivy Leaguers. One, and I remember his name also, Taylor, had been to Princeton for a year. Taylor's family was included in the *New York Social Register*. His father worked on Wall Street, and his mother was a socialite. Taylor, a nice guy, was born with a silver spoon in his mouth and had never sweated a dollar in his life, I am sure. In the early part of his marine career, right after he got out of boot camp, he had himself tattooed, probably in circumstances similar to my near miss at the tattoo parlor in Jacksonville. It was a very tiny tattoo of an anchor, but positioned as it was on the back of his hand, it was easily visible. When he went home for leave before we took off for China, Taylor's parents saw the tattoo and apparently went ballistic. His mother immediately started investigating with plastic surgeons about removing the tattoo, but back in 1945, I am not sure that plastic surgery had advanced to the point where tattoos could easily be obliterated. Taylor was a good bridge player. His partner, I remember, had gone to Dartmouth, but I can't remember his name. We played some monumental matches. If we had kept score, I think Kemmerling and I would have been well ahead because we had really clicked as partners. The games whiled away some of the time, and we all wanted to stay away from our crowded, hot, and generally depressing compartments as much as possible. All this time, I continued being grateful that I had screwed up sufficiently to be put into the ship's laundry. It really paid off in the next story I am going to tell.

We made our way from Panama to Pearl Harbor. It was only four years after the bombing, and there was still quite a bit of visible evidence of the Japanese attack present, including wrecks of ships' hulls, which had not yet been dragged away. We were informed over the PA system that we would remain in Pearl Harbor for two days, and that we would be given base liberty. But in order to go off the huge fenced-in naval base to Honolulu or to the rest of the island of Oahu, we would have to obtain special liberty passes from the troop office.

My father's two youngest sisters lived in Honolulu. The older one, Anne, had settled there in 1936, and Betty followed her in '39. Aunt Anne and Aunt Betty had both cared for me frequently when I was little and living in Pennsylvania. By 1945, both of them had married and started families in Oahu. Although I did not have any proof with me that I had relatives in Honolulu, I ventured down to the troop office anyway to see if I could get any liberty. Of course, I encountered the same sergeant major who had assigned me to the ship's laundry, and he, unfortunately, remembered me quite well. One of the great disadvantages of being as tall as I am is that people don't forget you very easily.

I said, "Sergeant, Private Van Sant requests permission to get liberty at Pearl Harbor."

"Ye-ees?" he drawled, and I said, "Sir, I have two married aunts who live in Honolulu, sir."

And he said, "I'll just bet! You got any proof? You got a letter from them, for example?"

"Sir, no, I don't. You've got to take my word for it, Sergeant," I pleaded and tried to tell him the story about my aunts.

The sergeant said, "Son, you cooked up a pretty convincing story there." But then he added, "I have been around a long time, and you are not fooling me, and you are not going anywhere." And that certainly kind of ticked me off a little bit, as you can imagine.

Sailing into Pearl Harbor from the open ocean is a wonderful experience. The whole island of Oahu is a magnificent jewel as it rises out of the sea. The vision of the harbor was spectacular.

Thanks to my hard and diligent work in the laundry, I was probably the only marine passenger dressed in an immaculately starched khaki uniform. I myself had pressed my shirt and trousers and looked sharp. The liberty uniform at Pearl Harbor, even for base liberty, was khaki. You can imagine how grungy our troop passengers looked, whose khakis had been rolled up in seabags for many weeks. When they unrolled their uniforms and put them on, their attire looked all limp and wrinkled. But man, I looked sharp as a tack. Since I was allowed to leave the ship, at least for base liberty, I got off and went to the clubhouse right inside the main gate.

I looked up my aunts in the phone book, called them, and got Aunt Betty. Oh, they had no idea that I was coming, and they were very excited because my father had passed through on his way home from China only a week or so before, and we were obviously crossing paths.

Presuming to be a United States Marine

Betty said, "I am going to come right down to the base." Then I explained to her that I would need some kind of proof that she was my aunt before I could go home with her. I stood by the gate noticing great swarms of mostly sailors, because it was a naval base, flashing a liberty card as they were leaving the base, and the liberty card looked almost exactly like our Marine Corps ID card in those days. There were no standardized ID cards then. I decided to chance it. When the next big mob of sailors came along, I fell right in with them. I walked by the guard, flashed my ID card, and was out.

Within five minutes, my aunt Betty drove up, and it was about five o'clock in the afternoon then. She said, "Oh, you got out after all."

And I said, "Yes," without explaining how I had managed it. I was actually "over the hill!" you see. I jumped into her car, and she took me back with her. She and her husband had two little children at that point, and the youngest had just been born a few months earlier. Their oldest son was only four years old. And Aunt Betty was really excited as she drove me to her house. As I walked up to the porch, the front door flew open, and there was my Uncle Jack. This was the first time I had ever met him because Betty had married him just before the war. My Uncle Jack's right hand came out to shake mine, and then his left hand came out, with a whisky highball in it. And I was impressed! Jack was a very exuberant, wonderful guy. He was a salesman, and later in life, he became a big office machinery distributor on the Hawaiian Islands. He had a pair of shiny shoes and a smooth line, and he could sell anything to anybody. His was a great personality.

Aunt Betty fed me a big dinner, and I played with the babies. I spent the night there, and the next morning, we drove out to Kaneohe, on the other side of the island of Oahu, where my Aunt Anne lived in a beautiful house with a dock right on Kaneohe Bay. I went swimming with my Uncle Charlie, who was only about forty years old then and looked like a Polynesian god. He was a big, tall broad-shouldered brown-skinned man, the son of an English sea captain. His mother was one of the seventy-nine daughters of the last king of Hawaii and so, actually, my Uncle Charlie had royal blood in his veins. Aunt Anne and Uncle Charlie's oldest son was seven years old and interested in the Marine Corps. We swam out from a beautiful beach, past some coral reefs, and were surrounded by a wonderland.

Our ship was going to sail out that afternoon, I think at five o'clock, and I knew I had to get back to it. Right after lunch, both aunts returned me to the main gate at Pearl Harbor. It was a lot easier to get in, as a matter of fact, than it was to get out because I was in uniform. I whooped through with my ID card again; climbed the ladder up the ship, which, fortunately, was still there; and climbed down to my compartment. In my compartment, the guy I had come to know best was a fellow named Larsen from Wisconsin, who bunked in the rack just above mine. Larsen liked to talk endlessly about the mink farm he was going to start back home when he got out of the Marine Corps.

As soon as I came in, Larsen asked me, "Where were you last night?" Because he had heard all about my initial problems with obtaining a pass to see my aunts.

Taking on the Burden of History

I said, "Oh, I had a wonderful visit." And then I asked him a little apprehensively, "Am I in any trouble?"

"Well," he said, "no. You aren't. You really lucked out!" The brig rat corporal who, you remember, was going over to China to rehabilitate himself, was in charge of our compartment. He had taken base liberty and, having been in the Corps a long time, had run into some old buddies. They all went out together to the slop chute on the Pearl Harbor base, where our corporal, apparently, had poured himself a real snootful. It seems that everybody had been rounded up on the base at eleven o'clock that night. Even in the town of Honolulu, there had been MP jeeps circling around and sirens blowing because a lot of people from the ship had gone ashore. But while the MPs were rounding up the miscreants, I had been safely ensconced in my Aunt Betty's house.

At about eleven fifteen the previous night, Larsen told me, word came over the ship's PA system that all compartment commanders were to take muster of their compartment. After that, they were to report all absentees to the troop sergeant major's office. Our corporal, not being in the best of shape, decided, rather than reading and checking off each name on his list, to make everybody get into their bunk. He then went around and counted every single body in every single bunk, and although he must have noticed that my bunk was empty, this did not register with him. Larsen said that he simply kept on counting and, in the end, managed to come up with four extra people. Not one to bother with a recount, Larsen told me, he had turned in a report of, "All present and accounted for, sir." And I was saved. But in some of the other compartments, some guys were caught as absent during that particular roundup and were subsequently court-martialed.

When I look back on that experience, I realize how lucky I was to get away with it, because in terms of Marine Corps order and discipline, what I did was clearly wrong. I quite simply went over the hill, and had I been caught, I would have been punished. My whole subsequent marine career could never have happened because the Corps would never have commissioned a former enlisted man who had a court-martial on his record, at least not in those days. I was very lucky, and I thank God that our corporal had run into those old buddies of his, and that they apparently helped to mess up his arithmetic.

We bid farewell to beautiful Pearl Harbor and sailed on. It was an interesting trip because of the course we took. We sailed fairly close to Midway Island, the scene of a famous battle early in World War II, and we sailed past Iwo Jima, where I could see that celebrated scene in our history: Mount Suribachi, the site of the famous flag raising. Our course from there took us right through the chain of the Ryukyu Islands. The home islands of Japan are fairly large, but they trail off into little volcanic islands that lead all the way to the bottom island, which is large, and that is Okinawa. While Okinawa is not really a home island, it is connected by this string of volcanic islands to the home islands of Japan. We passed pretty far north of Okinawa, right through this chain of quiescent volcanoes, a chain that marks the boundary between the Pacific Ocean and the North China Sea to the west.

Presuming to be a United States Marine

I was still left with certain responsibilities in the troop compartment, although I continued working in the ship's laundry. One morning, I got the trash detail. The standard procedure in the navy and coast guard in those days was that the trash was always dumped off the fantail of the ship, the stern of the ship, right after dawn. I don't know the reason for that very early hour in the morning. Maybe it was so that the trash had all day to sink and, polluting the Pacific Ocean, become invisible. I was carrying a big garbage can full of trash to the fantail of the ship, and when I got there, I had what can only be described as an aesthetic experience, an epiphany, a vision. I realized that there were many other guys from all the other compartments on the ship also on trash detail. Everybody was absolutely quiet, standing still with a look of awe on their faces. I looked in the same direction and saw one of the most beautiful vistas I have ever seen, and it moves me intensely even now, as I am remembering it.

The sea was calm and smooth. The ship's course was absolutely straight, and on the mirror-sea, the ship's wake cut all the way from our ship eastward to the horizon, exactly bisecting a gap between two volcano islands. That in itself was impressive and interesting. But beyond the volcanoes was the most fantastic cloud bank formation I had ever seen, and rising out of these clouds was the morning sun. It was breathtakingly beautiful. There must have been thirty marines—callous, tough guys—all clearly awestruck by this vision, and it looked like heaven to us.

In the North China Sea, we sailed along what had been the route between the Chinese mainland and Japan throughout World War II. Japan imported a number of commodities from China even before the war, and the support of close to 2 million Japanese in China created a tremendous trade back and forth. It was not until the very end of the war that any of our planes bombed the Japanese supply ships. Earlier in the war, we had sent some long-range mine-laying planes to drop mines all over the North China Sea to block off the Japanese shipping lanes. In addition to the mines we had sown, the mines sown by the Japanese themselves helped to create probably one of the most heavily mined stretches of ocean in the world by the end of the war. We dropped our mines at random in what we thought were Japanese shipping lanes, so that any ship sailing through the North China Sea in those days had to be preceded by minesweepers. We had two criss-crossing in front of us.

A minesweeper had a floater plane attached to a long cable, and it swept as it rushed through the water. Sea lane mines usually dropped an anchor to the bottom, from which automatically a cable released the mine upward, keeping the mine underwater but fairly close to the surface and in place to hit the hull of a moving ship. In the mine-clearing operation, the minesweeper's plane on its long cable would intersect the cable attached to the mine. Because the cable was trailing from the minesweeper, the mine would slide back along the minesweeper's cable until it reached the plane. A sawtooth knife blade would cut the cable holding the mine, and the mine would float up to the surface of the water so that it could be clearly seen and destroyed.

One of the minesweepers in front of us caught a mine, snagged it on the cable, and cut it loose. The mine bobbed up, a great dangerous big round black mine, and drifted in the currents on the starboard side of the ship, somewhat forward. The minesweeper had done its job with the mine, and now the crew of our ship was expected to take care of it.

A mine had horns, and each horn was an impact point so that if anything hit it, the mine exploded. The way these floating mines were disposed of was by shooting one of its horns, or fuses, to explode the mine. The average sea mine probably had ten horns all around it.

I saw a coastguardsman running down to the forecastle, the high part in the bow of the ship, carrying an M1 rifle. Well, this poor guy banged away at that mine, using up a whole clip of eight rounds. I think he may have glanced one round off the body of the mine, which, of course, did not explode it. The rest of the shots did no good at all, except for kicking up splashes around the bobbing mine. By this time, the hapless coastguardsman must have had a thousand spectators, all U.S. Marines—all crack shots, and all giving him a whole lot of gratuitous advice. They were really having a field day with remarks like, "Don't they teach you how to shoot, Coast Guard swabbie?"

The poor young coastguardsman emptied another clip. By this time, the mine was beginning to float a little closer to the ship. The ship itself had been slowed to a stop and was not moving as the captain, understandably, did not want to run into the mine at full speed. Finally, a marine sergeant from the group of spectators on the deck ducked under a rope, which separated the forecastle where we marines were not allowed to go, walked over to the coastguardsman, and said, "Here, son, let me have that rifle." And with the first round, he took out the mine. There was a huge explosion. An enormous cheer went up from the marines.

We safely crossed the North China Sea. First, we landed in a port called Qingdao (then Tsingtao), near the bottom of a peninsula projecting into the North China Sea. Qingdao, still known for its beer, was the headquarters of the Sixth Marine Division, which at that time was commanded by Major General Lemuel Shepherd. Shepherd became commandant of the Marine Corps some years later and, in fact, was commandant when I went to Korea. General Shepherd and his Sixth Division were controlling the whole area where the Yellow River enters the North China Sea and the Shandong Peninsula, which, interestingly enough, in the nineteenth and the early twentieth century was pretty well completely occupied by Germany.

Nearly half of our troop passengers were taken off ship in Qingdao. We sailed around the peninsula up to Taku, a port about twenty miles below Tianjin (then Tientsin). Tianjin sits on a river that flows into the North China Sea, but its port was then just a small beachlike area. As we approached China, we were all given assignments and told to which organization we would be going. I learned that I was assigned to the First Marine Regiment. We were issued a rolled-up mattress, and we had our seabag, filled with our belongings. In addition, we put on our old friend, the field transport pack, our rifles, and cartridge belts.

It is very cold in North China in the winter months. As we arrived in December, we wore our heavy green uniforms, and over them, we draped our large green monster

Presuming to be a United States Marine

overcoat. The field transport pack consisted of two bags, a blanket, and a shelter half. Every marine had a shelter half, with a set of buttons on it. Two marines would put their shelter halves together to make a pup tent. The tent half was wrapped around the blanket roll, which was then wrapped around the two bags of the pack. It was a huge pack with suspenders to help hold it.

In addition, we had a cartridge belt, a rifle, a helmet, the seabag, and the rolled-up mattress. I am a pretty big guy and was able to carry all this baggage, but only barely.

Unfortunately, our schedule went askew, and we were late getting off the big ship into the landing ship. This was a Landing Ship Infantry, which was really a small ship with a very shallow draft. The landing ship had a ramp in front that was let down onto a wooden wharf on the beach, so that we did not get wet while disembarking.

We were in the middle of winter, and it was dark by the time we got off the ramp onto the wharf. I was now in China. I was also in the direct path of an unseen hole in the wooden surface of the wharf. I stepped into the hole and fell flat on my face with my seabag, my mattress, my helmet, and my rifle flying independently in every direction. It was a most ignominious entry into China, I must say, and I was embarrassed, although, fortunately, it was pitch-dark; and I had reason to hope that nobody had seen my fall.

Chapter 3

CHINA ADVENTURES I
(1945-1946)

We were herded in the dark to a train and put aboard. I had my first ride on a Chinese train, with many more to follow. It was freezing cold. Although we were enveloped in many layers of warm clothing, and gloves, we were still chilled, and it was cold even inside the train. We fumbled around for what must have been a couple of hours during which roll call was taken, and we were divided up and herded around some more, since a number of us had ended up in the wrong places. It was all a big hassle. At about midnight, we pulled out from the beach in the train for the twenty-mile trip to Tianjin, and that trip took at least an hour, if not more.

We pulled into Tianjin at about two o'clock in the morning, got off, and were rounded up again in the dark. The Fifth Marines were returned to the train to be taken to Beijing, which we then called Peking. There were many other organizations to which other men were assigned, although these made up smaller groups.

The First Marine Regiment group finally got marched off the platform in the downtown Tianjin railroad station, where we continued our wait until, eventually, some trucks arrived. We climbed on the trucks and were taken out to what we were told was called *Ingwo Yung Pa*, which is Chinese for "English barracks." *Ingwo* was the Chinese word for "English," and these barracks were to be my home for the entire time I was in China.

It must have been about three or four o'clock in the morning by the time we arrived at the barracks. We were unloaded and divided up into the First, Second, and Third Battalion. The Second Battalion had to load back aboard the trucks because they were being taken to some other place in Tianjin. Thank God I was in the First Battalion!

We were lined up and divided into replacements for the various companies. I was sent to the third company in the battalion, Charlie Company. By this time, we were down to about twenty or twenty-five of us who were all going to Charlie Company. We were lined up alphabetically, and people with names beginning from A to E went to the first platoon, and so on. But the last big platoon was the machine gun platoon, and because my name begins with *V*, I became a machine gunner. We were pointed to our barracks and squad bay. I ended up as the only replacement for that particular machine gun platoon squad bay.

I came blundering into the barracks at around four in the morning, and the temperature was probably close to zero, and of course, I woke everybody up with my grand entrance, laced as it was with a blast of cold air. I thought that this started me off really well, being the guy who wakes everybody up in the middle of a frigid night. But a friendly voice spoke up, "There is an empty bunk over here." And it turned out that the voice belonged to Bill Boatsman, about whom I will tell you much more later.

Before I continue my stories about my experiences in China, it might be helpful to give some overview and background on why we were there and the tasks we were facing.

When World War II ended in August of 1945, the Japanese had approximately 2 million elite, experienced troops under arms on the mainland of China. We knew before the war ended that the Japanese had made elaborate plans to transport large numbers of these crack troops back across the China Sea to the home islands in order to help in the defense against the American invasion. Our military commanders' best estimates at the time were that the war was probably going to be prolonged until late 1946 or even early 1947.

These Japanese troops in China were fully equipped, supplied, and in good shape. When the war ended, there were a number of steps that had to be taken. From the Marine Corps, the Second and the Fifth Marine divisions were sent into Japan in September of 1945 to participate in the occupation of the home islands. The Tenth Army Corps went into South Korea, north to the capital of Seoul, and up to an arbitrary line, which had been decided on at Yalta between the Soviets and the United Nations. The American forces were to occupy up to the 38th Parallel, and the Russian forces were to come down to the 38th Parallel from the north. I will talk more about Korea later in this story.

Students of World War II history know that on the fourth of August 1945, exactly eleven days before the end of the war, the Soviet Union entered the war against Japan by attacking Manchuria. The Japanese tried to defend Manchuria for those ten or eleven days but were overwhelmed by the enormous strength of the Soviet Army. Once the war in Europe was over, the Russians immediately moved huge numbers of troops and materiel to the Orient in order to participate in the defeat of Japan. Those Russians had occupied all of Manchuria by the time the marines first entered North China in early October 1945, before I got there.

The First Marine Division occupied the northern sector, which included Beijing, the old capital, and Tianjin, the other major city. The Sixth Marine Division occupied Qingdao on the Shandong Peninsula farther south on the Yellow River. The mission of the marines in the subsequent weeks after their landing, which was still in progress when I arrived, was to round up the Japanese army, disarm it, receive its surrender, and begin preparations for repatriating the Japanese soldiers back to their home islands. We had the additional mission of finding any internment or prison camps established by the Japanese in North China, evacuating those camps, and shipping the internees and other nationals back to their own countries.

In addition, there was a quieter, less discussed mission for the occupying marines. As soon as World War II ended, the Chinese civil war, which had been fought in the thirties and which simmered throughout World War II, erupted again, and the Chinese communists moved in and took over great tracts of Manchuria from their Soviet communist friends as the latter pulled out.

Chiang Kai-shek, the leader of the Nationalists, had been driven far inland by the Japanese, mainly to the south and west. He now wanted to move quickly to get his troops north and east to the coast. His capital was Chongquin, where my father had spent the last part of the war.

North China was up for grabs. Because the Chinese communist headquarters was in Jinan, about seven hundred miles west of Beijing, and they were pretty much entrenched in many parts, the Nationalists had to move large numbers of troops quickly to North China. There is an interesting sidelight from the end of World War II in this Asian arena. Since the great mass of the organized Chinese Nationalist Army was in Southwest China at the end of the war and had to be moved quickly, many were moved down through what we now know as North Vietnam to Haiphong harbor and loaded aboard a large number of LSTs (landing ship tanks) the United States had made available to the Nationalists. Each LST could hold about one thousand troops. This aid on the United States' part enabled Chiang Kai-shek to move hundreds of thousands of troops from Southwest China out of Haiphong, landing them up in North China where our marine units were located.

One of the great ironies of this whole maneuver was that the person who helped to facilitate this movement of Chinese Nationalist troops was Chiang Kai-shek's old friend, Ho Chi Minh. He smoothed the way for the Chinese to move through North Vietnam to the Haiphong harbor. Years later, as the leader of the communist North Vietnamese, Ho Chi Minh achieved infamy, but in 1945, he was still cooperating with the Nationalists, as were the Russians. The marines who came to China became spectators to a developing civil war.

A few more words about geopolitics. Tianjin was occupied by us marines and the Chinese Nationalists, but the Soviet Union kept a large consulate there, ostensibly as an ally of the Chinese Nationalists. As time went on, it became clear that the Soviet consulate was playing a two-sided game. They were a very visible presence, with big black Russian ZiS limousines floating around and flying the hammer-and-sickle flags of the Soviet Union from their front fenders.

In addition, there was a detachment of Soviet troops in Tianjin, and when we had our big United Nations parades, they paraded with us as if we were all great buddies. It was a very strange situation. We generally begin dating the cold war from Winston Churchill's famous speech in Missouri in January of 1946 when he said, "There is an iron curtain descending across Europe."

Presuming to be a United States Marine

In late January of 1946, when I was sent all the way to the Manchurian border, we reached the Great Wall of China as it sweeps down to the sea. There was a gate in the wall, and on the other side of that gate was Manchuria, still considered to be a separate province of China. We had marines posted at the south side of the wall in North China proper, while the Manchurian side of the wall was guarded by Soviet troops. There was no friendliness lost between these two sets of sentries. The Russian sentries had clearly been instructed to display a grim face, along with a generally noncommunicative demeanor.

President Truman and the U.S. State Department were trying desperately to resolve the Chinese civil war in some way and to get the two sides to sit down and reach some kind of compromise, and for that reason, General George C. Marshall was sent out to China in early January of 1946 soon after I arrived. He remained in China for six or seven months without being able to achieve much success.

As you will see in subsequent stories I will tell, the communists had the upper hand—they had the initiative, and they were clearly better organized than the Nationalists. By the end of World War II, many of the Nationalist government officials and senior military officers were, to one degree or another, corrupt. The whole structure was so riddled with "kum shaw"—the Chinese word for a kind of tip, consideration, or bribe—that many parts of the Nationalist structure were rotting.

We gave the Nationalists a lot of help; in fact, it can safely be said that the rail lines and the highways in North China, insofar as they were usable, were kept open by marines. We guarded the trains, we had guard posts set up on all the bridges across the rivers, and the whole city of Tianjin was covered with marine guards of one sort or another. Tianjin was secure, and the Nationalists were in good shape there.

So now I had stumbled and sprawled into China, and what an experience it was to become! I spent my first few days getting oriented and trying to get used to the cold. The temperatures went down to zero most nights in late December, January, and February. We were issued cold-weather gear. We had a kind of boot with an insulated liner, and while it was not as efficient as the cold-weather boot developed during the Korean War, it was serviceable, and our feet were usually fairly warm and comfortable, at least as long as the outside of the boot was in good shape.

The kind of duty we performed in *Ingwo Yung Pa* (which was really a kind of fort) required us to be highly visible to the local population. This meant that no matter how cold it was, we fell out at eight o'clock every morning, we had our morning formation and inspection on the parade ground, and then we'd right face, right shoulder arms, forward march, and off we went marching out of the fort and across the city through its various streets. We would march to some of the athletic fields and soccer fields, which were frozen and as solid as concrete, and we would drill there for thirty to forty-five minutes, and then we would march back to the fort.

These were pretty colorful marches. The regiment had a drum-and-bugle corps to accompany us, and we must have looked pretty impressive to the local Chinese because we marched so much and drilled so much that we really looked sharp. A marine infantry battalion marching, four abreast, down the middle of the street presents a very formidable picture. It was a formation of over one thousand men stretching for block after block, marching to accompanying band music. As impressive as we appeared, we always knew, looking forward to see the other troops of our formation, that everybody was collectively freezing their butt off. Nevertheless, we marched every day without fail, looking very sharp while shivering. Several times during that winter of '45-'46, our regiment participated in a grand parade of the whole division. This parade took place on the Race Course—a huge, lavish, and elegant monument to the British colonial empire. It had an enormous concrete grandstand topped off by glass-encased luxury boxes. The infield of the race track was about the size of four football fields so that it made a splendid place to have a division-sized parade marching by the reviewing stand, "passing in review."

One of the high points of these division parades was the playing of the various national anthems of the United Nations by the First Marine Division Band. It is customary for the troop formations to be at present arms during the playing of any national anthem. At this parade we had, we sang anthems in the following order: "The Song of Marseillaise," "God Save the King," the Soviet National Anthem, the Nationalist Chinese ("San Min Chu Ai") national anthem (which was, incidentally, almost funereal in sound), and finally "The Star-Spangled Banner."

In the position of present arms, the rifle is held vertically in front of and about four inches away from the body with the butt of the rifle pointed toward the ground and the muzzle toward the sky. In a correct present arms position, we were expected to stare through the stacking swivel, a flat metal loop about six to eight inches away from the muzzle of the M1 rifle. As we stood there at attention for the interminable playing of all these stirring anthems for a combined total of about twenty-five minutes, the weight of the rifle seemed to slowly increase until at the end we were all staring down the muzzles of our rifles instead of at the stacking swivels.

In April we had a second division parade at the race course with the same format, only this time the geniuses at division headquarters had decided that the tanks, Amtracks and artillery would "pass in review" first, ahead of the infantry. The parade took place right after a huge rainstorm (which will produce another story later), which had turned the race course infield into a sea of mountains and valleys of mud. Fifty-some tanks and close to a hundred trucks and cannons had so mucked up the ground that by the time we came marching in, it was almost impossible to stand up, let alone march in step. It was too bad because our battalion had really become a very sharp marching unit, having had so much practice. Incidentally, in this April mud parade, we also had to stand at attention for the five national anthems.

I immediately developed an affection for the Chinese, partly perhaps because of all the stories my parents had told me when I was growing up of their missionary work in China during the early twenties. Now I had a chance to meet Chinese for myself. I became fond of them because they were always smiling. They were extremely good-natured. They were not a nasty or a petty people, and they had an enormous ability to cooperate with each other in order to achieve something, as well as an enormous capacity for suffering. I observed these poor people throughout their first winter after World War II, after having suffered tremendous hardships and deprivations for years. And yet they were digging in and trying to pull together.

My new friend, Boatsman, had taken me under his wing since that very first night when I had stumbled into the barracks. Boatsman had a number one boy, as these Chinese personal servants were called, a young boy he called Sambo, whom he gladly shared with me. He said that a number one boy could take care of two marines pretty easily. I must confess that the connotation of the name "Sambo" bothered me in subsequent years.

Sambo was a marvelous young man. I'd say he was about twelve or thirteen years old. He really took good care of us, shined our shoes, cared for our clothes, made up our bunks. We had a kind of box in which we concealed him at night behind our bunks, and he slept there. We brought food from the mess hall to feed him.

The Marine Corps later tried very hard to eliminate number one boys, but at the time of my arrival, there was no absolute rule against them. Just after I left China the next fall, Sambo had somebody write to Boatsman that all the Chinese personal servants had been driven out from the barracks and out of the fort.

Boatsman returned to the United States in June, and I had by that time been promoted to sergeant and lived in different quarters. I could not have had a number one boy at that point, and I really did not need one, but for the first five or six months I was in China, I was grateful for the care Sambo gave to us. He had an official pass that enabled him to get through the gate in and out of the fort, so that we could send him on errands. Sometimes late at night, when we were huddled around the stove against the cold, Sambo would go out for hot sandwiches. His service was the one luxury among the hardships, particularly the freezing temperatures.

At this point, I was still a private, and there was machine gun school going on all the time. In fact, I soon became an instructor myself, to whose humble beginning I can trace my subsequent teaching career. One day, a few days after I arrived, our platoon sergeant, Staff Sergeant Petrocelli, had looked up my record book and had seen that I had been to college. He came by the barracks one afternoon and said, "Van Sant, you're a college boy, you can teach." He handed me the machine gun manual and said, "I want you to teach the first three phases of machine gun functioning at 1000 hours tomorrow." So I took a gun apart by myself with the help of the book, learned how it functioned, and taught functioning the next day. It was the first time I had ever taught a class in anything, and it turned out to be an exciting and enjoyable experience for me.

In addition to the almost constant training, we spent a good deal of time guarding Japanese prisoners. This often was a boring job, but sometimes it had its moments. I would be given a detail of Japanese soldiers assigned to do some menial task like picking up the trash around the fort. We would guard them the same way you see a convict gang on the highways in America watched over by an armed guard. I would be assigned six or seven Japanese soldiers and told to police up the parade ground and all areas around regimental headquarters.

My relations with the Japanese soldiers were usually very pleasant. They were impressed with my size, and when I wore my winter parka and winter hat, I must have looked like a mountain to them. They would come up to me, look way up, and say, "Tok san, tok san." Which can be translated as "a lot." They were all anxious to get home, and we knew that. It is a tribute to the Japanese that, when the Emperor Hirohito and the Japanese government surrendered at the end of World War II, to my knowledge, there were practically no incidents of any loony Japanese officers trying to keep on fighting the war. In fact, the commanding general of all the Japanese armies in China made it a point to personally turn over his sword to General Rockey, the senior marine in China. General Rockey received the sword at an elaborate surrender ceremony in Tianjin. We disarmed the Japanese, stored their weapons, and kept them in compounds guarded by marines. The Second Battalion of our regiment was responsible for a couple of large prisoner-of-war compounds in Tianjin. I never had to guard the compounds, but we did get called out one night. The Chinese civilians in that area of North China had suffered at the hands of the Japanese for almost ten years and had stored up a great deal of bitterness. One night, this hatred erupted. A group of Chinese broke into the back entrance of one of the prisoner-of-war compounds and started dragging out Japanese soldiers and tearing them apart, limb from limb. A general riot ensued, and our unit was mobilized. We were taken over to the compound by trucks to help put down the uprising.

The irony was that a majority of the men in my machine gun platoon and in Charlie Company then were veterans of not only Okinawa but also of Peleliu, where they had been fighting the Japanese for two or three years. Now, suddenly, these same marines were ordered to save the lives of the Japanese against a Chinese mob. But as commanded, order was restored by our well-trained marines, and the Chinese calmed down.

The Marine Corps began expediting the Japanese repatriation process, and some marines from our unit were assigned as guards aboard the repatriation ships to the mainland of Japan. I volunteered for this duty but never got a chance to go. Many of my friends did, however, and they would herd one thousand Japanese soldiers, many accompanied by their wives, onto a landing ship tank deck, seal it up, and sail them across the North China Sea as fast as possible to the mainland. The trip would take about twenty-four to thirty-six hours. If the weather was bad, that vintage of LST notoriously rolled. Then of course, everybody would get seasick, and there were some pretty horrendous experiences people had guarding the ships returning the Japanese to their homeland. I think that the last Japanese were repatriated to the mainland in April of 1946, and because they were quite anxious to get home, they were very cooperative. There were no disciplinary problems. The war was over, and the Japanese wanted nothing more than to return home.

Presuming to be a United States Marine

From time to time, we had special assignments. One of our first assignments after I joined Charlie Company was to assist in the repatriation of a large group of internees who had been held in the Kalgan prison camp north of Beijing. The Japanese had interned there a number of Europeans, mostly English, Belgians, and French, including a large number of priests and nuns. Another marine unit had brought these distinguished prisoners from the Kalgan camp down as far as Tianjin, where we put them on a train for the trip to the harbor at Qinhuangdao (then Chinwangtao). Our entire company, Charlie Company, and that's over two hundred marines, was assigned to guard the large passenger train.

We were carried in trucks down to the main Tianjin railroad station. We disembarked from the trucks and lined up—company online, platoons online—on the main platform of the station. When the company was in this formation, the machine gun platoon was the leftmost unit of the company. Our platoons in those days lined up in accordance with our table of organization billet. I was the fifth ammo man in the second squad of the first section of the platoon. This meant that I was not only the leftmost person in the platoon, I was the leftmost person in the company.

We had been formed up at attention, and contrary to his usual practice, our then company commander, First Lieutenant German, forgot to give us the command, "At ease" or "Rest." So we all remained at rigid attention. While we were in this position, another smaller unit wheeled up, halted, and did left face to our left. I could hear them, but since I was at attention, I could not turn and look at the unit. The unit's first man could not have been more than three or four feet away from me. Finally, our company commander gave us the order to Rest, and I immediately turned to my left to look at the people who had joined us on the platform. To my amazement, my eyes were fixed on a belt buckle instead of a face. I began to raise my head and found myself looking up at one of the tallest men I have ever seen. It is not very often that I encounter someone I have to really look up to.

When I engaged this giant in conversation, it turned out that he was in a group of newly arrived navy medical corpsmen. As our two units were lined up together for about ten minutes, this six-foot-eleven corpsman and I had a chance to converse. He noted that I was fairly tall too and asked me, "Do people often ask you 'how's the weather up there?'" I replied in the affirmative. He said, "Let me tell you a good response: 'There's a telephone in my ass, why don't you call up and find out?'" He told me that it had been necessary for him to get a waiver to join the navy, but he was proud of being a corpsman. Lieutenant German suddenly called us to attention and gave us our orders, and we went to work.

We met and escorted the released internees to the train, loaded them on board, and then the machine gunners were sent to create machine gun nests with sandbags on several flat cars. Qinhuangdao, our destination, is next to the Manchurian border, which meant that we would have to travel along a route potentially under fire from the ongoing skirmishes between Nationalist forces and the communists, and it was felt that the train and its precious cargo needed to be carefully guarded.

Taking on the Burden of History

It was an interesting trip. Because of all the uncertainties along the route, it took several days, although the distance was only about two hundred or so miles. We stopped at several cities, including Tangshan and Linsi, which were both nearly destroyed by an earthquake in the 1970s. Some distance north of Tangshan, someplace in the Jehol province in a very mountainous, barred, and forbidding area, our train stopped briefly in a tiny little village station. As we approached the station, I noticed that there were people swarming like ants all over the wooden station platform. They appeared to be literally tearing it to pieces. We stopped to inquire what they were doing and received a chilling answer. It was now near the end of January in the first winter after the war. Apparently there was no food left in the village, and we were told that these people were taking the splinters of wood home to try to boil them up for food.

Our final destination, Qinhuangdao, was the only port on the North China coast where oceangoing ships could actually dock at wharves. All the other ports had to use intermediate ships, or lighters, to carry cargo and passengers from anchored deep-sea oceangoing vessels to shore, but Qinhuangdao had a deep-water harbor, and so the United Nations Relief and Rehabilitation Administration (UNRRA) had sent a ship there for the people from the Kalgan prison camp.

During the train trip, I had a chance to talk to a few of the internees and listened to their grim stories. Some of them had been interned since 1937. They wore shabby clothes, patched and then patched over again. They were all very slender, none of them obviously having eaten well for years as this was now January of 1946.

It was a long trip, and it continued to be very cold. When we arrived in Qinhuangdao late in the afternoon, we witnessed a very moving scene. The relief workers from UNRRA came aboard the train. One of the UNRRA men addressed the internees, "We understand what you have been through. Aboard ship we have a wonderful steak dinner waiting for you. But first you may want to have a shower and put on some new clothes. After supper we will tell you about your trip back home." There were many tears of relief shed as these poor people finally were able to leave China. We got the train emptied in a surprisingly short time.

But then it turned out that there was no billeting for us, the marine train guards, in Qinhuangdao. We found ourselves with nowhere to sleep. Our company commander, Ken German, had been a great football star at Columbia University back in the early years of the war. He was somebody I had heard of before I joined Charlie Company. He checked with the marine authorities at the small marine headquarters in Qinhuangdao, a unit of the Seventh Marines, our fellow regiment from the First Division, and yes, somebody had screwed up, and there was no billeting for us. We still had to get off the train, of course, because it was continuing on into Manchuria. We would have to spend the night in Qinhuangdao and pick up another train the next morning to ride south and back to Tianjin.

We had our mountain sleeping bags, lined for winter use, with us, and we wore winter clothing. We were taken out to what had formerly been a small girls' school that had either been bombed or blown up, and all that was left of it was a portion of the roof and the pillars holding it up, with a concrete courtyard under it. Some of us, but not I, got to sleep under that bit of the roof. The rest of us were laid out in the open courtyard, without any mattresses or pads, just in our sleeping bags, directly on the concrete. It was the twenty-ninth of January 1946. I remember that it was the twenty-ninth for reasons that will become clear in a minute. It was, and still is, the coldest night in my memory. In fact, it was the second coldest temperature I have ever experienced.

I crawled completely inside the sleeping bag and zipped it all the way up, leaving a hole of about two inches wide above my nose for breathing. Oh, it was cold! I tossed around all night until, finally, reveille sounded in the morning. We got up. Our first sergeant, a wonderful old marine character named Bennett, was always well equipped and prepared for everything. He had brought a thermometer with him, and it showed twenty-nine degrees Fahrenheit below zero. Twenty-nine below on the twenty-ninth. Being enlightened by that knowledge actually did not help any, and I was quite sorry to have found out just how cold it was.

We rustled up a nice cold C-ration breakfast and got ourselves formed up and back down to the train station. Sometime that morning, the train came through, and that's when we had our distant encounter with the Russian troops occupying Manchuria.

The Soviets pulled out of Manchuria in April 1946, but in January, they were still a very visible presence. That spring, Chiang Kai-shek fought a very difficult and ultimately unsuccessful war trying to keep control of Manchuria. By the summer of '46, large areas of Manchuria were in Chinese communist hands. For the Nationalists, this was unfortunate because Manchuria was the industrial base for all of China at that time. The Japanese had occupied Manchuria since 1931 and had developed a large heavy industry there. Manchuria had coal mines, iron mines, and steel plants. But the Chinese communists could not immediately take advantage of this industrial wealth because the Soviet Russians, as they were leaving, had stripped everything almost completely. Anything that moved—all of the heavy, well-made Japanese machinery—was taken back to the Soviet Union. Once the Chinese communists began taking over in 1946, they commenced restoring the heavy industry, and Manchuria today is, you might say, an enormous Pittsburgh of China.

After our distant, unfriendly, glimpsing encounter with the Soviet guards at the Wall, we boarded the train for the relatively uneventful trip back to Tianjin. Most of the time, when traveling the road from Qinhuangdao to Tianjin, or from Tianjin up to the Manchurian border at Qinhuangdao, our progress would be interrupted by one disaster or another. Oftentimes, for example, the track would get blown up in front of the train. Train trips tended to be pretty hairy at that time in China, and I had several such experiences.

We returned to Tianjin, back to our English Barracks, on January 30, really tired. For one thing, we were hungry. We had been on C-rations for about four or five days, and in addition, we were bone cold. The cold was penetrating, and it was with us all the time, even in the barracks. The squad bays in the barracks we lived in would each hold about twenty-five to thirty bunks, and we double-decked some of the bunks to get more people into them. The barracks had windows along both sides. There was a passageway down the center, and the bunks stood at right angles to the outside walls. The ceilings were vaulted, high-peaked plaster ceilings.

The barracks were heated by potbellied stoves, which sat in the center of each squad bay or area and had a smokestack that extended all the way up and out through the top of the ceiling. The potbellied stove could burn either coal or wood. In addition, we were issued some kerosene space heaters, but when we had the potbellied stoves fired up right, they were much more effective in keeping our squad bay warm.

There was one absolute rule. Even though we had fire watches or sentries that marched through the barracks at night all the time, the rule was that there could not be anything burning in the stove at night. So every night, which of course is the coldest time, the temperature inside would drop down to what it was outside.

In our squad bay, we had a system of rotating duty, which some of the more senior corporals and sergeants had devised. When you had the duty, you had to be the first person up in the morning. As soon as the first reveille sound was heard, you had to immediately jump up into the icy-cold air. The fire had already been laid out in the stove the night before but was unlit. In order to light the fire, newspapers soaked in kerosene were placed over the coals. To accomplish this, we had a long pole with a nail on the end of it. We would open the door of the potbellied stove, set fire to the newspaper at the end of the long pole, and quickly jam that flaming newspaper inside the door of the stove. The kerosene would just explode, and, in fact, the whole stove would almost explode, but it certainly started the fire. The sudden blast of flame emanating from the stove when we lit it in this way required the use of that long stick so that we would not also get charred in the process. This method really worked because the morning explosion in the belly of the stove almost instantly heated up the squad bay, so that everybody else could safely get up. Before we went to sleep each night, we would get everything set up for the next morning, and each day one of us would have to get up first in the bitter cold and light the paper torch.

One more "cold story." Back in those delightful days in the Corps, we were permitted to purchase beer by the case, and we could keep it in the barracks. There were strict orders against drinking beer during working hours, but when our day was over, after dinner, we used to sit on our bunks in the barracks and have a couple of beers. And that was very pleasant. But it got so cold in that barracks that several times the beer ration under my bunk, froze. The beer just simply turned to ice. Now remember, this was indoors, and that will give you some idea of the cold. It takes a pretty cold temperature to freeze beer, certainly well below zero.

The routine established very soon after I got to China was that unless we were on special assignment of some sort, and we were on many of those, we would operate on a three-day cycle. Every third day, our whole company, all of Charlie Company, was assigned the interior and exterior guard for Tianjin. This meant that we had sentries posted all around our fort and all around the city of Tianjin at strategic places. There were about sixty posts on this guard, so that it took 180 sentries just to man these posts, with three reliefs of each guard.

The way this worked, and I am sure anybody who is familiar with the military will understand, was to have watches from twelve to four, four to eight, and eight to twelve. The company would take over the guard at noon on any given day, and then we would stand it until noon of the next day. Each one of us sentries would have two four-hour watches on a post during those twenty-four hours. The other sixteen hours were spent in the guardhouse, trying to sleep or to read. But we always had to be available for duty because whenever there was any emergency, the off-duty reliefs of the guard were called out first.

If we got off duty at noon, we had that afternoon to clean up and recover. We would usually go off on liberty the day after our guard day, normally at four o'clock in the afternoon, and we had to be back in the barracks at eleven at night. That was our liberty day.

On the morning after a night of liberty, we had a training day. We would spend the entire day training, from eight o'clock in the morning until five o'clock in the afternoon. We would engage in training of one sort or another—that is, if we did not have a special assignment.

As instituted by our illustrious regimental commander, we had formal guard mount each day at noon, when the incoming guard would relieve the outgoing guard in a formal ceremony on the parade ground, with drum-and-bugle corps and flags and the whole ball of wax. Like the British colonial army, we were very colorful, indeed.

We fell into the rhythm of having about a day and a half of training; a full day of guard duty; and, every three days, an afternoon and an evening off. One fell into this rhythm, and it was not at all bad.

I could fill many pages with stories of liberty in Tianjin. For one thing, everything was cheap. When we were on liberty in the city, we had to pay with Chinese money, and the exchange rate was so favorable that it was very hard to spend as much as a dollar anywhere at any given time. Because we had to pay for everything with Chinese currency, the first thing we would do on liberty was to exchange our money. As soon as we left the fort, we would be surrounded by money changers anxious to give us Chinese money for our precious American dollars. One of the saddest aspects of my stay in China was the runaway inflation. When I first arrived, we were using Chinese dollars that had actually been printed by the Japanese. These were soon exchanged for new Nationalist currency as the Nationalists consolidated their grip on North China. Each dollar of the new money was worth $5 of the old Japanese currency. The new currency rapidly inflated. When I arrived, C$100 could be purchased for US$1. When I left China in September, the rate was about eighteen thousand to one. With this marvelous currency, you could get drunk for 50¢. You could get a steak dinner for 50¢. The standard rate in Chinese brothels was 50¢ (short time), US$1 (long time). For most of the time I was in China, I drank mainly the local vodka because it seemed safe. A small bottle cost no more than US$1. We hoped that the alcohol would kill any germs the vodka might have acquired.

We had movies from the United States shown in our fort several times a week, and they were usually the latest thing, but it was much more exciting to attend the movie theaters in downtown Tianjin, of which there must have been a half a dozen. Two things stand out about the movies in Tianjin. They were multilingual. The film might be French, so the sound would be French, and it would have English subtitles, but the dialogue would be projected simultaneously in Chinese onto a smaller screen beside the main screen.

Another feature of the Chinese movie houses was that most of them had been built by the Japanese during their eight-year occupation. The Japanese tend to be a small people, so that there was very little legroom between the narrow rows of seats. This became a real barrier to my movie enjoyment because I literally found it impossible to sit in my seat and accommodate my legs. After a couple of unfortunate attempts, I found a solution to the problem. I would buy two tickets, each costing the equivalent of 5¢, for the same show and sit in one seat, with my legs draped over the back of the seat in the row ahead of me. If anybody came along and asked to sit in the seat where my legs were located, I would whip out my two tickets. Most of the Chinese accepted this, although a few of my fellow marines grumbled about it. It is hard to describe how cramped those theaters were, and it is depressing to find that some American airlines have adopted the Japanese standard for legroom.

Officers had clubs almost from the beginnings of the marine occupation in October, and the staff noncommissioned officers had a staff NCO club. In April of '46, a "sergeants and below" club for our regiment was finally organized in a lovely big old mansion in downtown Tianjin. This club was for privates, privates first class, corporals, and sergeants.

In June of 1946, I was promoted to sergeant and promptly put on the board of the club, so that I got to know it intimately and found it to be a grand institution. It had a restaurant and a lovely bar, and in those days, even privates could go into the bar and get a shot of whisky for 10¢. The restaurant had good food, and there was a dance floor. Sometimes we had what we called a DJ day, or some small local band would get organized, and at least once a week, we would have a dance with live music and Chinese hostesses to dance with and to buy drinks for.

From the very beginning of my duty in China, the American Red Cross had a beautiful club in downtown Tianjin. This club was staffed by young American women, which made it a wonderful place to go to, and as an enlisted man, I found it very pleasant to talk to young women from back home. But off duty, these women would only date officers. The Red Cross Club had lounges, pool, and Ping-Pong tables, nooks for letter writing, an excellent restaurant, and a soft drink bar. And that reminds me of a story.

One of the guys in our outfit fell madly in love with one of the American hostesses in the American Red Cross Club. These young women were not forbidden to date enlisted men, but they simply chose not to go out with them. Well, this guy kept after this young woman, and he kept asking her, "Why can't I take you out sometime? We can go out and have dinner and go dancing and really have a ball." And she kept putting him off, and putting him off. I knew this guy pretty well. He was a corporal in Headquarters Company, and he just had to have a date with this woman; he simply had to go out with her.

Finally she said to him, "Well, look, when I go out on dates with officers, they always have a vehicle. They have a jeep, or some kind of vehicle to carry me in. I am not going to ride around in a rickshaw in Tianjin. I want to ride in a car."

Now this dumb, smitten idiot fooled and finagled and managed to liberate, without authorization, from the regimental motor pool a command car. It was a completely open-top car, without any doors. It had scalloped-out places on the sides for climbing in and out of the vehicle, and it had roomy front and back seats. It was quite a nice vehicle, the kind of vehicle that colonels and generals ride in when they are in combat.

This darned guy managed to work up some kind of fake paperwork to get the vehicle through the main gate, and he had managed to make a date with his Red Cross lady, and he took that command car down to the club to pick her up.

The Red Cross Club had a driveway that looped around in front of a veranda, where people sat and where cars loaded and unloaded members and visitors at the bottom of the steps. A bunch of us were lounging on the veranda when my friend drove up in his hijacked command car. He jumped out and ran up the steps to the veranda. As he approached the doorway, his Red Cross date came out. But just as she emerged, a jeep driven by a captain pulled up, and she swept right by my friend, shouting, "Oh, Captain, so you were able to come after all!" And she fluttered down the steps to the jeep, jumped in with the captain, and off they went together.

My friend, with his "stolen" command car, was left in the dust, without a date. Needless to say, he did not pursue her favors after that. In fact, he got into a lot of trouble over the vehicle and was lucky not to get busted. He did not lose his stripe over it, but he got fined and restricted for unauthorized use of a military vehicle. It would have been worth it if he had managed to have his date, but he did not even have that to remember, the poor fellow.

By early 1946, I was back in mail communication with my father. As I have indicated, he was flying back from Shanghai as I was sailing to China on the *Wakefield*. In fact, he had just visited my aunts a few days before I did when I went "over the hill" at Pearl Harbor. His job with Lend-Lease in Chunking had involved a lot of work with people in intelligence, and one of his coworkers was a man named Hiram Hodes. Somehow or other, through his U.S. government connections, my father was able to mail me Mr. Hodes's address in Tianjin. It seems that when the war ended and his services were no longer needed by the U.S. government, Hodes had gone back to his expatriate life as a fur trader in North China. One late afternoon in March, when I was on liberty, I went around to the address of Mr. Hodes that my father had sent me. His apartment was in a modern building in the nicest part of the old British concession, facing Victoria

Taking on the Burden of History

Park, which was itself a little bit of Anglia with a bandstand and formal English gardens. The first two floors of the building housed the Belgian consulate, I think, and the top three or four floors were obviously lush apartments.

The building had one of the few operating elevators in Tianjin. I found Mr. Hodes's name on the directory and rode up to his apartment. A Chinese servant answered the door, and I gave my name. The servant returned a few minutes later and asked me to come in and sit down in a kind of foyer. I could just make out a man's and woman's voices in discussion and some scurrying sounds. A few minutes later, Mr. Hodes appeared, obviously having just completed dressing. He greeted me most warmly as I apologized for intruding on him so unexpectedly.

He waved this off and insisted that I stay for drinks and dinner. What followed was surely the most elegant banquet and conversation I had in China. We drank good scotch and sat down to a sumptuous meal formally served by servants. The conversation flowed easily as I brought him up to date on my father's activities. By this time, my father had connected with the State Department in Washington DC. Hodes entertained me with stories about some of the times my father and he had experienced in Chungking during the war. He clearly thought that my father was a really splendid and witty fellow, especially after a couple of drinks.

Mr. Hodes told me that he was in the process of moving up to either Harbin or Mukden in Manchuria. He said he was waiting for the Russians to pull out, and then he planned to reestablish his fur-buying business in Manchuria. Several weeks later, I checked by his apartment, only to find that he had moved out. I have often wondered what happened to him. Manchuria in the spring and summer of 1946, and especially in 1947, was an active battleground in the ongoing Chinese civil war. Hodes was either a true expatriate or engaged in some undercover activities. Three years after our elegant dinner meeting, when I was living in Manhattan, I went down into the fur section in the garment district of the city and found somebody who knew Hodes. I was told that Hodes had disappeared in Manchuria without a trace, and no one had heard from or of him.

Liberty in Tianjin was a splendid thing. Of all the places we could have been stationed, Tianjin was by far preferable. Since my experience there, I have talked to a number of other China marines who were stationed out in the boondocks. Their memories of China are not quite as pleasant as mine. Many marines patronized the plentiful houses of prostitution. This carried with it some dangers because the venereal diseases of gonorrhea and syphilis were universal. I kept my participation in these activities to a minimum because of my fear of venereal disease. However, I did rectify the situation that had produced such merriment for my boot camp platoon. My guide for this activity was Boatsman, who had gone all the way through the Iwo Jima campaign worrying about dying as a virgin. He too had rectified his situation on his first liberty in Tianjin.

I must say, we did drink a lot on those liberties when we went ashore, mostly vodka when we were in the local economy and whisky or beer in the clubs. Looking back on it,

Presuming to be a United States Marine

I think that I got drinking out of my system in China and have never really drunk heavily since then. But a couple of times in China, I certainly drank very heavily and invariably found that it was not the smartest thing to do, considering the aftereffects.

There is one story I do tell, and it deals with the Great Drinking Contest. The whole time I was there, replacement drafts were continuously arriving in China. The American government tried very hard to demobilize quickly and also to rotate back to the United States the veterans who had actually fought through the hell of the Pacific war. I would say that most of the combat veterans of World War II got sent home by June or July. Poor old Boatsman, my buddy, was one of the last to go back, and Boatsman had been through hell in Iwo Jima. As the veterans were being sent back to the United States, they were being replaced by new recruits who were put into replacement drafts, as I had been.

We received a new draft with a guy who became our company clerk, the man doing all the typing in the company office and keeping the records. I remember him well. His name was Posey. Posey was from Texas. He had a big mouth, and he was somewhat boastful. I can't remember all the details about how the contest between Posey and me got started, but it happened in April 1946 soon after our club was opened, while I was still a private first class. The contest had already been established and was governed by very precise rules.

We were first to line our stomachs with a good Red Cross Club steak-and-egg dinner. Then we were to walk from the Red Cross Club to our First Marines Club, a distance of about not more than five or six blocks. To give you a better idea of the challenges that lay ahead, though, there were at that time twenty-three local Chinese or White Russian bars (run by refugees from Communist, or Red, Russia) between the Red Cross Club and the First Marines Club. The idea was to go into each and every one of the twenty-three bars, order a shot of vodka, drink it down, and then leave and go to the next bar and have a shot of vodka, and so on. If and when one finally arrived at the First Marines Club, one was supposed to drink a double shot of whisky to complete the course.

Although several people had tried this before, I don't believe that anybody had succeeded in actually completing the Great Drinking Contest. Twenty-three shots of vodka is about a fifth, and that's a lot of booze! Granted, you are taking it a little bit at a time, and you are getting fresh air between each shot, but it is certainly a very dangerous game.

Anyway, Posey had heard about this challenge, and Posey was swaggering and mouthing off about how good a drinker he was, and somehow or other, I rose to the challenge. I said, "Damn it, Posey. Let's you and I do this thing." And this was just fine with Posey.

We went out to the Red Cross Club together and had a huge steak with eggs on top, got our stomachs all greased up, and started out. Posey too was a fairly large man, not quite as tall as I was, perhaps, but probably a little beefier. As we entered each bar, we had our shot of vodka and threw it down, usually with a chaser of some sort. The last local bar was right across the street from the First Marines Club. By the time we got there, we were pretty much staggering. Anybody who looked at us would have known that we were deep in our cups.

My recollection of all this is getting a little fuzzy by this time, but it seems to me that Posey fell down a couple of times. We both had a hard time getting across the street to the First Marines Club, but we finally managed to stagger into the bar and, "Two double shotsh of whishky," we ordered from the bartender.

The First Marines Club bar was something that had been installed rather hastily. The bar itself was made out of a fairly wide piece of plywood. If you sat on a stool on one side of the bar, there was about four feet of plywood between you and the bartender, with his bottles all stacked up behind him.

The bartender put a double shot of whisky in the bottom of a tumbler, poured out another, and set them both up on the back edge of the bar so that we would have to reach across the bar for them. I think I was on the right, and Posey was on the left. When you have had that much to drink, your vision gets very narrow, like a tunnel. At that point, I was looking out of my eyes through a very narrow cone of vision. But within this cone, looking left, I saw a right hand creeping across the bar to pick up the tumbler with the double shot of whisky from the far side of the bar. Posey and I were both still standing.

I will never forget that hand sliding across the bar. I was fully concentrated on that hand. The hand reached a point about five inches from the tumbler and then, by degrees, slowly began to recede. With an enormous amount of effort, I turned my head and looked to the left to see Posey slowly descending into a heap on the floor. He had passed out, and he had not drunk his double whisky yet.

I said to myself, *I have won! All I have to do is to drink that double shot of whisky, and I have won.* So, I reached across the bar, slowly, and clutched that double shot. And I was being very deliberate now and very careful as one is when one gets this drunk. I grabbed the glass, and I brought it up to my mouth slowly, and I was concentrating on the glass, and I was looking down into it, and I saw the golden triangle of whisky flowing down from the bottom of the glass toward my mouth. And I glimpsed the bottom of my glass.

After that, everything went black. I had passed out. I had won, and luckily, I did not die. I woke up the next morning in my bunk, and how I got there, I did not know. But the unit spirit of the marines was very high, and we always took care of each other so that obviously, a couple of my fellow marines had picked both of us up, carried us back, and put us to bed.

In Tianjin, the political situation and the feuding between the Nationalists and the communists was always the background to everything that happened and how we reacted. There was always trouble brewing. For example, several times our sentries were attacked while walking their posts. In fact, on a post I walked regularly, a sentry was killed, stabbed by an "unknown." We always assumed this was done by agitators who did not like the marines being there and got us for it. The death of that sentry

Presuming to be a United States Marine

gave me an eerie feeling, I recall, because it happened on exactly the same post I had walked just the night before.

Against this background, we, the enlisted men, sergeants, and below and to begin with, even staff noncommissioned officers, were not allowed on liberty overnight. We had to be back at eleven o'clock in the evening, or 2300 hours in military time. But the regiment was having a lot of problems enforcing this rule, and guys continued coming back well after eleven o'clock.

In those days, the Corps still published orders to troops in formation. The order was published by reading it out at a company formation for three days in succession, to be sure that everybody had heard and absorbed it. One day, when we were lined up in company formation, a new order was published stating that "henceforth any member of the First Marine Regiment who comes through the main gate at the English barracks after 2300 hours will be punished, as follows: for every minute he is late, he will be sentenced to one day of solitary confinement on bread and water." It was a very effective punishment the Corps could administer in those days. For each minute, mind you, for each late minute, a tardy marine would receive one day's confinement on bread and water. When the order became effective, it also required that the regimental officer of the day was to stand at the main gate and log people in after eleven o'clock at night.

Another thing done at company formations was to read out punishments imposed by courts-martial. Seven or eight days after this new order mandating punishment for lateness became effective, we were all lined up, and a punishment was read that "Private So-and-so from Baker Company had arrived at the main gate three minutes after eleven (2303) and is sentenced to three days in solitary confinement on bread and water." Then a couple of days later, "PFC Joe Blow from some other company in the Third Battalion had come in five minutes late and is sentenced to five days in solitary confinement on bread and water."

After that, nobody came in late. Thereafter, it never occurred that a member of the First Marines returned late from liberty. One way or another, everyone got back on time and sometimes, as was true in my case after the drinking contest, rather miraculously. That one order, probably, did much to strengthen unit spirit. If you were on liberty, rushing back to the English barracks, which were pretty far out from the center of town, and you saw a poor, drunk, or passed-out marine, the first thing you did was to ask if he was from the First Marines. And if he was, you picked him up, threw him in a rickshaw, and carried him back through the main gate so that he would not be in trouble. It was a marvelous application of a very severe punishment, and while coming in from liberty late may not sound like a serious offense, the Marine Corps did not want marines running around, or weaving about as the case might be, late at night all over the city under the circumstances; and we all understood the point.

Most people who had ever been on bread and water in solitary confinement never stepped out of line after this harsh punishment. Solitary confinement meant that you were put in a box. (In the Camp Lejeune brig, the boxes were reported to be three feet by four feet by five feet.) Inside the box, it was pitch-dark, and you could not read, you could not move, you could not do anything. You were allowed to come out and go to the head so many times a day, and the rules were that you could have all the bread and water you wanted, and every third day, you were given a full meal. I guess some softies decided that a full meal every three days was the correct humane action.

Solitary confinement was tough, but once the punishment was announced, people got back on time. And clearly, after the drinking contest, I had been brought back by some guys who said to each other, "He is in the First Marines, and we've got to get him back!" And so they did.

There are one or two more stories of adventurous train trips I want to tell. It was April of 1946. In late March, I had written a letter home, and my mother still had it years later. In this letter, I wrote, "Dear Mother and Dad, I have been very successful in most of the things I have set out to accomplish, but for a variety of reasons, it looks like I am never going to be promoted above private in the Marine Corps."

Because of the tremendous flux the armed services went into after the war, promotions shut down almost completely. In those days, no one made private first class out of boot camp; everybody came out a private. As I have indicated, I was first sent to Camp Lejeune and put on mess duty, and then into the replacement draft and shipped over to China. I had never had the chance to create a record in any place but was pushed around from pillar to post instead.

And then suddenly, on the first of April, I, along with a number of other privates in C Company, was promoted to private first class, which came as a wonderful shock and surprise. I rushed right out and got chevrons and the single stripe of a private first class to sew on all of my uniforms. As it turned out, I was actually a private first class for only three weeks, and then I was promoted to corporal, and by early June, I was promoted to sergeant. But that's another story.

Suddenly my dreams had been realized. I was promoted and, right after the promotion, was assigned, along with fifteen other machine gunners and about forty riflemen, to a guard detail, guarding the new commanding general of the First Marine Division, our overall organization in the northernmost portion of the Marine Corps' China responsibility.

We had to report down to the railroad station, and this was about the first week in April. The weather was beginning to warm up some by this time. It was getting to be spring, although spring in North China was by no means a particularly glorious season.

General Peck, the commanding general of the First Marine Division, was going on an inspection tour of all of the First Marine Division units in all of North China. When we picked him up, he had already completed his examination of the Fifth Marines in Beijing and was now prepared to inspect all the marines strung out along the railroad tracks between Tianjin and Taku, and Taku and Linsi, and Linsi and Tangshan, and Tangshan and Beidaihe Junction (then Peitaiho Junction), and Beidaihe Junction and Qinhuangdao. Although a number of marine units were located some distance away from the rail line, it was the general's intention to inspect them all.

Presuming to be a United States Marine

It turned out to be about a five-day expedition. The general himself rode in a magnificent railroad car, which had been left over, I guess, from the luxurious days of the Peking-Mukden Railroad before World War II. This was an observation car, a car designed to be hooked onto the tail end of a train. The observation deck on the back of the car was a large glass-enclosed bubble through which passengers could watch the scenery as it receded into the distance. But in our expedition, this car was turned around and placed at the front of the train, with the glass bubble pointing forward for observation. The rest of the car was luxuriously made up with a sitting/dining room, a kitchen, a bedroom for the general, and other rooms for the general's aides and staff. Behind the observation car was a flat car on which my machine gun section built sandbag bunkers and mounted two water-cooled machine guns facing in each outboard direction to cover the train. Behind the flat car were, I think, two Pullman cars where we slept. Behind that was a kind of a freight car, which held our food. Most of the time, we ate C-rations, but a couple of times on this expedition, we received a hot meal. Behind all of this was the engine that pushed the entire train, led by the glass bubble, through the North China countryside.

The general arrived at the railroad station with much fanfare, and we gave him a present arms. He inspected us, and we climbed on the train. We had not even left the station yet when word came that all of us in the company who were six feet two or taller were to report immediately to the platform. As it turned out, there were six of us over six feet two among the forty riflemen and fifteen machine gunners assigned to this detail. We six were divided up into three reliefs and were told that we were to sharpen ourselves up as much as possible, polish our brass, and get everything looking good. We were going to be the general's personal guards, and this seemed like a great honor. I had my brand-new private first class stripes on my uniform, and I thought that I was really hot stuff.

For the bulk of the trip, then, I spent my time two hours at a stretch standing with the other member of my guard relief in the glass bubble, facing forward at a forty-five-degree angle from the train, at parade rest. Parade rest is not as demanding as the position of attention. It is a position where one stands with feet about eighteen inches apart and the left arm across the small of the back. The rifle is held in the right hand at order arms with the butt on the ground. One is not allowed to talk at the position of parade rest, and normally, one is not permitted to move head or eyes. On this particular guard post, though, we were ordered to constantly scan the tracks for anything suspicious. We must have looked rather terrifying to the Chinese in the small railroad stations along the track, who had probably never seen giant men standing at parade rest in a moving glass bubble.

I spent the next several days during the daylight hours, only standing at parade rest, two hours on, four hours off, crossing the countryside of North China and looking out over the landscape from my glass bubble. I must say, it was a very interesting way to travel, and I did see an awful lot of North China.

Taking on the Burden of History

By this time, there had already been a number of instances when communist guerrillas had blown up parts of the Peking-Mukden Railway track. I took the admonition to guard the train quite seriously, including the order to scan the horizon, as well as close in, to make sure that nobody had been tampering with the tracks themselves and that there were no explosives planted on the tracks. I am happy to say that, as I am still here, the communists, obviously, let us go. Had the train run over some pressure-sensitive mine on the tracks, my fellow sentry and I standing at parade rest in our bubble probably would have been the first and main casualties. We tried not to spend too much time thinking about that.

The routine, once we got started, was that after spending my allotted two hours on duty, I would go back to the railway car, where the rest of our troops and our bunks were, for my four hours off duty.

We got a detailed tour of every place where there were marines in North China. The entire Seventh Marine Regiment was strung out from Tianjin to Qinhuangdao, a distance of 180 to 200 miles, and they were subdivided into very small units in some places. We would cross over a bridge, and there would be a squad guarding it with a sergeant and, maybe, ten men.

General Peck, bless his heart, wanted to visit every one of these squads, platoons, and companies, and it was a remarkable achievement that he managed to do so. Apparently, the general's staff officers in the nice observation car had direct radio or telephone contact with the engineer. We would be whooping along the railroad tracks, although never too fast, glimpse what looked like a marine unit, and sure enough, the train would stop. The instant the train stopped, if I was on duty in my parade rest formation, I would jump down off the train along with my fellow sentry, face inboard at present arms, and the general and his party would come down the steps. We would then precede the general wherever he went, making sure that we looked fierce and formidable in our sharpened-up uniforms, and this tableau was repeated often.

Most of the time, when we came to a town, a bridge, or someplace where there was a detail of marines, they had been alerted and were all decked out and standing ready to be inspected, and their quarters were groomed. But in a couple of places, we caught a marine unit by surprise. They had clearly either not received the word or they had forgotten or something had intervened, and they were in disarray. These kinds of visits upset the general deeply because he wanted to see tip-top efficiency on the part of every single unit spread out in that region.

One of the locations the general visited was Tangshan, a large coal mining city. Tangshan was built by the English and had something of an English quality of architecture and layout of streets and gardens. It was the headquarters of one of the battalions of the Seventh Marines, so that there were quite a few marines stationed in the city. We spent the night in Tangshan. Those of us who were on guard detail on the train were given a hot meal by the Seventh Marines, and that was very pleasant, indeed.

Presuming to be a United States Marine

The general also inspected Beidaihe Beach (then Peitaiho Beach), a resort by the North China Sea, established in the late nineteenth century by a consortium of all the Christian denominations with missionaries in China. The architecture was purely European, and the town was built as a spa for the families of missionaries, who would come from most of China north of the Yangtze River during the summer vacation months. It was a lovely town with many trees and a beautiful beach. As it was such an elegant place, naturally, one of the battalions of the Seventh Marines had set up headquarters there.

Beidaihe Beach was not on the railroad line, being located about four or five miles from the railroad station. It was accessible from Beidaihe Junction by truck, or by sedan in the case of the general. This was another welcome stop and respite on our trip. A later visit to Beidaihe Junction looms very large in my memories of China.

On General Peck's inspection tour, we had to go overland one other time to visit a unit west of the railroad in Jehol province, but once we reached Qinhuangdao, the general's inspection tour was complete. Our magnificent train was turned around back to the front, and I stood guard once again in the glass bubble, at parade rest. I think we made the trip back in about a day, and I remember seeing other trains on the track. There I was, back in the bubble, zooming down the track and asking myself, *My god, if we run into anything, who goes first?* And answering myself once again, *The two poor sentries standing in the glass dome.*

We returned to Tianjin unharmed. The general was very gracious to the whole unit, giving special praise to his personal guards, whom by that time he knew by name. General Peck could not have been more than five feet six inches tall, with a little forward curve to his body, and we, his personal guards, loomed over him; we towered over him when we escorted him on his inspection tours. We were given some liberty before being sent back to guard duty.

There are a few other vignettes of life in Tianjin and in the English barracks worth recounting. The English fort was well wired with electricity, but the wiring itself was, unsurprisingly, pretty primitive. Every week or two, at some time in the evening, suddenly all the lights would go out in the entire fort. We were naturally curious as to the cause of this. Eventually we learned that the coal-powered plant at the edge of Tianjin, which provided electricity for the entire metropolitan area, was located relatively close to a communist-controlled region.

Apparently, the communists would arrive periodically, sabotage the power plant, and cut off the power. As a result, the marines decided to put a unit there, and the Nationalists added a big force as well in order to protect the power plant from communist infiltrators.

One night, when we were sitting around the barracks playing cards, *boom!* The lights went out for a minute or so and then came on again. The light stayed on for several minutes and then went out again. One could not help seeing a mental picture of communist guerrillas and Nationalist engineers fighting over a master switch,

Taking on the Burden of History

taking turns pulling and tugging at it. And that was just one of the vagaries of life in Tianjin.

The months of January, February, March, and April when I was still a private and walking sentry posts all the time were the really cold months. I must say that there is nothing worse in this world than being outside at 2:00 a.m., when it is about ten degrees below zero, guarding something as a sentry. It was a pretty miserable life and yet, occasionally, even this misery was brightened by lighter moments.

We assumed guard for the city of Tianjin on every third day. We had about ten sentry posts in and around our own fort, with another forty-five posts scattered around throughout the city. When I was a private, I managed to walk almost all of these posts at one time or another. Some of the posts around our home fort were quite interesting.

The fort must have covered the equivalent of about four average American city blocks. There were two sentries whose job was simply to walk in opposite directions around the external perimeter of the wall of the fort. This wall impinged on streets all the way around. It took at least twenty or twenty-five minutes to completely walk around that outer wall in a military manner.

A sentry guarded the main entrance gate, a huge Gunga Din-like medieval wooden portal, at all times. About fifty yards away from the main entrance, the fort intruded into a civilian commercial district at a street intersection. Three corners of this intersection contained Chinese civilian businesses. There were several restaurants, a bar, a laundry, a grocery, and several other commercial establishments. The fourth corner of this intersection was, of course, the corner of our fort. We maintained a permanent sentry at this intersection. The job of this sentry was to assist marines coming back from liberty to direct traffic as necessary, and to otherwise interact with the civilians in this very public place.

About fifty yards down from the intersection, along one of the side walls of the fort in the other direction from the main gate, was a side gate to the fort, and there was a sentry posted at that gate. The sentry at the intersection had a sentry box, a wooden shack with a door and one acetate paper window at the back of it. That sentry was allowed to stand inside the shack with the door open. We were not allowed to close the door because once closed, there was no way to look out, except for the back window through which the only thing to be seen was a wall. It so happened that I had that corner post one bitter-cold night, on duty from 4:00 a.m. until 8:00 a.m. I was spending most of my time inside the box, as it was well below zero, and I was all bundled up.

Pretty soon one of the rotating sentries, whose duty it was to walk all the way around the perimeter of the fort in a clockwise direction, came by. We greeted each other. "God, it's cold!" he said. "Can I get into your box for a little while?"

"Sure," I said, and he got into the box.

A few minutes later, the sentry who walked in the counterclockwise direction around the fort arrived and said, "Man, it's cold. Can I get in your box?" And he got in.

The sentry on duty at the smaller side gate was taking all of this in and slid up along the wall to join us in the box. Pretty soon the main gate sentry joined us too. It was about 5:00 a.m. and pitch black outside. By this time, it was getting pretty crowded in my little sentry box with five of us squeezed inside.

We were all standing in the elevator-sized box, getting warm, comfortable, and cozy, with the door closed. Somebody got an idea and said, "Hey, why don't we send out for sandwiches?" Because even at 5:00 a.m., there would be some enterprising Chinese civilian ready to fetch food for us. We found such a guy, and he returned within a few minutes with some delicious piping-hot beef-and-onion sandwiches.

And so all five of us stood inside that sentry box with the door shut, munching away on our sandwiches, all warm and happy, when there was a knock on the door. The sentry closest to the door turned the little keeper that held the door shut, opened the door a crack, and immediately slammed it shut again.

"Jeeeesuz!" he said. "It's the officer of the day!" And the fool had closed the door right in the officer's face! Well, as luck would have it, the officer on duty that day was our company mortar officer, a very nice lieutenant. He was a reserve officer, gung-ho, and a good marine but, most importantly, possessed of a sense of humor. There is a ritual, or ceremony, when the officer of the day checks marines manning guard posts: the prescribed formula for reporting a post is to salute and say, "Private So-and-so reports post number 38 all secure, sir. Post and orders remain the same."

And after the door of our sentry box was opened again, we were told by the officer of the day, "All right, gentlemen, I want you to come out, one at a time, and report your posts." And each guard came out in turn, reported his post, and then returned into the warmth of the sentry box. When all five of us had reported our posts, the lieutenant said to us, "Now, men, I realize it is real cold, but," he said, "actually, Private Van Sant is the only one who is on his post, so I suggest that you return to your posts immediately, men." Which they all did, carrying their sandwiches with them.

There is one other sentry story I love. It must have been early in April, during one of the last times I actually walked post as a sentry. That post was a supply dump at the edge of the city and pretty far away from our fort. The supply dump itself covered an area about the equivalent of one-half to two-thirds of a city block. It had a high wall of at least ten to fifteen feet of heavy brick and stone around it, surrounding an open concrete base, or floor, without a roof over it. A unit of the Third Amphibious Corps, our parent unit, had appropriated this site as a location for storage of jeeps and large waterproof cartons of various military pieces of equipment and military and building supplies. I don't know what else was stored there, but it was jam-packed with extra materials and supplies of a great variety.

The orders for the sentry were that once every half hour, he was to close the entrance gate and walk around the inside of the wall. There was a kind of a pathway all the way around the inside perimeter with no material stacked up against the wall, so that a complete circuit could be made, with a visual inspection of the entire contents of the supply dump. After the tour was completed, the sentry returned to the entrance gate until the next tour. At the completion of the circuit, the entrance gate would be reopened, and the sentry assumed his position in it. In case of inclement weather, there was a sentry box by the gate. During the daytime, the sentry checked people coming in and out.

I had the twelve-to-four watch, which, of course, meant that I stood the watch there from noon until four o'clock in the afternoon, 1600 hours in military time. During my afternoon tour, a couple of drivers with trucks came, and I checked their papers to see whether they were legitimate.

That afternoon it started raining. I went off the watch at four o'clock in the afternoon for a bit of sleep until my return to the post at midnight. In my absence, it had been raining hard, and when I returned, the weather was quite miserable, with a deluge of rain. Fortunately, I could find shelter from the rain inside the sentry box. There were three weak floodlights back in the dump. A small lightbulb cast a circle of dim light on the concrete driveway through the gate that connected the dump with the Tianjin street outside. Because it had been raining so heavily and for a long time, the entire supply dump, with its walls and concrete deck, had turned into a big bathtub. And because the wall continued all the way around the concrete floor, the only place the water could get out was through the entrance gate, where it gushed out in a torrent into the street and into the primitive storm water drainage system of Tianjin.

As the night wore on, I did my tours around the entire dump, getting my feet wet. At the end of each of my tours, I hastened back into my sentry box as quickly as I could, leaving the door open, and stood my watch in the faint light of the single lightbulb over the entrance gate. Sometime around 0300 hours (3:00 a.m.), I was standing in the sentry box in a kind of somnambulant state, while being wide awake, as every marine sentry always is, of course. I had noticed that from time to time, assorted flotsam and jetsam, sticks, small planks, and other objects would come floating by in the torrent, or a piece of crating from the stored supplies. I could not always identify each piece of debris, but on it would float in the raging stream out into the street.

Suddenly, I noticed in the innermost portion of the circular lighted space something being swept along, and I could not tell what it was. It suddenly stopped floating. My curiosity aroused, I began watching it. It did not seem to be floating regularly with the current. Its movement in the torrent was erratic, stop and go. I must confess that I had no idea if it was an animal, vegetable, or mineral. But it provoked my curiosity enough for me to step out of my dry little sentry box into the rain. The mysterious object was about five or six inches in diameter and somewhat oval-shaped. It extended up out of the water about three inches, but it seemed to occasionally resist being pushed along in the stream. I bent over to pick it up, and as I reached out to touch it, a list of possible things it could be was running rapidly through my mind. Just as I got my hand on the thing, the running list in my head came up with "porcupine." And that's what it was!

What a porcupine was doing there, and how he got swept up in this torrent, I don't know, but there he was. It was a porcupine, and I had grabbed him right by his back. It is said that porcupines shoot quills. While they don't really shoot them, they can certainly release them vigorously. My porcupine stuck three needles right into the palm of my hand. The needles, on the business end away from the porcupine's body, are equipped with a barbed hook. One of those hooks stuck in my hand. Then another, and another. I looked down to see three spikes sticking out of my hand, and they were by no means short, being five or six inches long.

I was curious about this fellow who, meanwhile, found himself back in the torrent because, of course, I had let go of him as soon as he let me have it with the needles. I grabbed a bucket that was in the sentry box and held it so that the water would wash the porcupine into it. It was being drowned in the stream, poor thing. I managed to get him into the bucket, poured all the water out, and placed him, still in the bucket, in my sentry box to dry out.

When I got relieved at four o'clock, I took the bucket with the porcupine in it back to the guardhouse and then, after we were relieved at noon, back to my barracks. Without having any idea of what porcupines eat, I went to the mess hall and got some leftover chow for him. The assortment of foods must have pleased him because he went right to it and ate it all. I guess he was pretty hungry from his ordeal.

All the guys in my barracks were entranced by this animal, and we decided to keep him as a pet. What about the quills in my hand? Well, I pulled them out. And of course, when I pulled them out, I pulled out a little bit of my hand too, where each one of them had gone in. As a matter of fact, I was fooling around with Band-Aids and medications for a couple of weeks afterward. It is never pleasant to get struck by a porcupine. But my discomfort is not really an important part of the story.

We kept the porcupine in our barracks, and he settled in. He made a little nest for himself under my bunk, and he would wander around in the barracks. You do not pet a porcupine, obviously, but he was curious about us, and we were curious about him. He liked to go out and sun himself on a porch outside our squad bay. At that time, there were many dogs living in our fort. These stray dogs had attached themselves to various units of the regiment, and marines were a good source of food for them.

A couple of times, when we were out drilling, or doing formations on the parade ground, we would hear the sounds of howling and squealing. A little while later, a dog would slink by with a couple of porcupine quills stuck in his nose. Eventually, the dogs learned not to mess with our barbed pet. He remained with us for several weeks, and then one day, he disappeared, and I'll never know what happened to our barbed friend, the porcupine.

Subsequently, in my years of teaching philosophy, when talking about the theory of knowledge and epistemology, I used to maintain to my students that most of us, when we see something, know what we are looking at, and the way we know what we are looking at, the key to our understanding of it is that we have a name for it, we have a label for it. I used to point out to the class that there are relatively few occasions in life when one actually encounters something without having any idea at all of what it is, and we have no label to apply to it. I told my porcupine story as an example of one moment in my life when I saw a lump being pushed along in a current of water but had absolutely no name for that object. And so the porcupine provided me with a useful philosophical story as well.

Taking on the Burden of History

Another episode in our life in China was the celebration of the Chinese New Year. Anyone who knows anything about China knows that the Chinese love fireworks. In fact, they are generally credited with having invented them. Chinese New Year, which came, in the year I was there, at the end of February, was a big time of celebration for the Chinese. Even though these poor people had been destitute during the war, and even though there was not enough food to go around, they still celebrated the New Year in style. Somehow, fireworks appeared out of nowhere, and there was a great street party for all.

When you get a bunch of young marines around a bunch of fireworks, you will find that the two naturally go together. We managed to get hold of a great many fireworks ourselves. For two or three days, there was an almost continuous *bang-bang-bang*, with firecrackers and rockets going off in all directions.

While Boatsman and I were on liberty during this period, we bought something similar to what we call a roman candle in the United States. It was a cardboard tube, maybe an inch in diameter and about ten inches long. On the bottom, protruding from the side, was a wick. When that wick was lit, a projectile would fly out of the tube, way up into the air, and explode like a rocket. We had bought a number of these in downtown Tianjin and were leaning the tubes up against a curb in the street, lighting the wick, and *phoom!* The thing would go up forty or fifty feet in the air and explode.

A Chinese policeman came along. He watched us with great interest, smiling, and quite taken with the fact that we were enjoying this Chinese roman candle-like firework. After a while, he indicated to us that we were not doing it the right way. He pointed to himself and then to the firework, and we understood that he wanted to show us how to set it off properly.

He showed us with gestures that the way the Chinese did it was to take the roman candle, hold it in the hand, light the wick, and let it go off from the hand. Well, we had not tried that because it did not look all that safe. But he insisted that he wanted to show us how to do it the right way, the Chinese way; and so we gave him one of the roman candles, and he lit the wick with one of our cigarettes.

He positioned himself with his arm and hand fully extended to the side, with a big smile on his face, in full uniform, with heavy gloves on his hands, and an expression of *See, I told you, this is more fun when you do it right.* He was looking at us, grinning, when there suddenly was a tremendous explosion, and we realized right away that the roman candle had not performed as expected and had, instead, blown up in his hand.

The picture is indelibly impressed in my memory. The policeman, a man of authority, smiling broadly and so proud of himself, showing the stupid young Americans how to shoot off Chinese fireworks. His smile slowly faded, and his head slowly turned to the right to look at his hand, which was still fully extended. He shook off the remnants of the roman candle, and the bits of his heavy glove, and, finally, bits of skin from the palm of his hand. I don't think he was too badly hurt, except for his pride, but there were some burn marks and some blood on the palm of his hand. He went slinking off with another policeman, his demonstration not having worked out too well in the end. We continued with our own safer method of shooting off Chinese roman candles.

During that New Year's season, and it really is almost a season as it lasts for several days, while on liberty, a friend of mine and I invented a game. In their old concession in downtown Tianjin, the British had built a very broad, wide boulevard through the center. There were, of course, practically no automobiles then, and the main traffic on the boulevard consisted of Chinese pedicabs, vehicles with a bicycle in front and a passenger seat on two wheels in the rear.

Our game, played at night, consisted of obtaining a big supply of cannon firecrackers and paying our pedicab drivers extra to get them into the spirit of things. Their task was to maneuver us around on the boulevard while we tried to bombard each other with the firecrackers. What a night we had, roaring up and down the boulevard, pelting each other with the firecrackers; and the pedicab drivers, especially the younger ones, readily joined in our game. They would go careening around, maneuvering for position, and we would try to sneak up and surprise people with our bombardment. It was a great sport and a lot of fun, and I am happy to say that nobody got seriously hurt.

Early in my stay in China, I had my first experience of a Chinese funeral. I was in the British concession, not too far from the Red Cross Club, when I heard a great clanging and beating of many drums and the blowing of numerous whistles. I looked down the street and saw a not-very-well-organized procession of Chinese coming up the middle of the street. They were dressed in very colorful costumes, and in the lead was a ragtag band of musicians playing their tambourines and drums and vigorously blowing on whistles and flutes. The band was followed by a group of wailing and keening men and women swinging banners. At the rear of the procession, drawn by a very spindly horse, came a rather elegantly polished wood and glass hearse, with a coffin resting inside.

As the procession passed by my spot on the sidewalk, where I stood respectfully saluting, I was horrified to see that one of the processing men and one of the women were pulling their eyeballs out of their sockets, letting them dangle by the optic nerve on their cheeks, and then returning them to their sockets. Accompanied by crying and wailing, they repeated this horrible exercise. I later inquired about this phenomenon and found that I had witnessed professional mourners, who made a good living by working for Chinese undertakers. I was told that the deceased must have been quite wealthy to afford such a splendid funeral with not one but two eyeball pluckers.

Another story from that winter and spring in China deals with my foot problems. At boot camp, I had been issued the boondocker boots with composition soles. They had fit perfectly. When we were in formation, marching, or training, we wore canvas leggings with our boondockers, tucking our trousers tightly into the leggings. But by the time I got to China, my old boondockers were pretty well worn with all the marching and hiking I had done. Soon after my arrival, first one sole, then the other wore all the way through until I had a fifty-cent-sized hole in the bottom of each boot.

Taking on the Burden of History

I went to the quartermaster, the supply sergeant of the company, and asked him if he had any shoes my size. Since he did not have any, he tried battalion, and they went to regiment, and regiment went to division, all without any positive results. Clearly, the big supply chain and buildup was not yet in place. The supply sergeant next put through an emergency order that Private Van Sant needed new boondockers. I waited and waited and waited, but the boots never came.

Meanwhile, many of my fellow marines were experiencing the same kind of problem, and many of them were wearing through their own boondockers. Our outfit began to look like a bunch of hoboes, going around with cardboard in the bottom of our boots. When it is chilly and you have to cover up a big hole in the bottom of your shoe, cardboard certainly does not provide you with the necessary warmth.

One day, word came over that "Hey, Van Sant, the supply room's got in a pair of shoes for you." I gratefully rushed over to the supply sergeant, who had traveled over to China with me. He was Private H. B. Gray, a hero of Guadalcanal and a Staff Sergeant. Then he had gone over the hill and was sent to prison. He was one of the "brig rats" being given a chance to rehabilitate himself. He proudly pulled out a pair of shoes for me—size 16, the biggest darned shoes I had ever seen.

I said, "Gray, those are much too large for me, I take a size 13." And he said, "Sorry, this is all I could get. Jam some paper in the toes." He gave me the shoes, and I took them back to barracks, jammed some newspaper down in the toes, and put them on.

These boots were undoubtedly responsible for my getting the nickname Foot. When I brought them into the barracks, my friends bestowed on me that name, which stuck for the rest of my time in China. Guys would say, "Hey, Foot, what's up?" And several people thoughtfully advised me that "Foot, you can just row back home in those, you don't have to wait for ship transportation back to the States."

Walking around in a pair of shoes that are much too big isn't easy. Marching in them is much harder. You are trying to look sharp, and you are commanded to halt, and you come to a full stop. The boot is firmly planted on the ground, but unfortunately, it will take a little bit longer for your foot and the rest of your body to slide all the way up to the inside of the boot's toe. There is no question that it was hard for me to be a squared-away, sharp-looking marine in the size 16 boots. And so the nickname stuck.

Two of my many friends in the machine gun platoon were Francis Xavier Nicoletti, who was a great burly fellow, and Joseph Bianco. Both were Italian Americans from New York City, sons of immigrants, with only one goal in life, and that was to be New York City policemen. As Nicoletti once told me, "You know, Foot, if you grow up in New York and you are Italian, you have two choices. You are either in the Mafia or in a business that cooperates with them, or you are a cop." Nicoletti wanted to be a cop.

Several years later, in 1948, when I lived in New York, a big New York City cop went roaring by on a motor scooter on Fifth Avenue. I looked, and by God, I saw it was Nick. I shouted, "Hey, Nick!" And the cop slammed on the brakes and turned, and it was Nicoletti. As soon as he saw me, he bellowed, across all the pedestrians, "Hey, Foot! What are you doing here, Foot?"

Presuming to be a United States Marine

Nick taught me a very important lesson about Italian Americans of that time. Once, he and I were verbally sparring around in the barracks, arguing about something. I told Nick, "You damned Wop, you can't say that to me!" And he got mad as hell, gathered me up in my utility jacket, and slammed me up against the wall.

He told me, "Now, Foot, let me tell you something. You can call me a Guinea, and you can call me a Dago, but don't you ever call me a Wop!" Chastised, I said, "Sure, Nick, I didn't mean it." And then I asked, "But why is 'Wop' so insulting?"

Then he explained to me that when the great masses of Italians began immigrating into America at the turn of the twentieth century, some had papers/passports, and some didn't. If they did not have papers, the immigration officials at Ellis Island would hang a big sign around their neck that read "WOP"—meaning "without papers." If you wanted to call somebody second class, or, possibly, an illegal alien in the United States, you would call him a Wop. Nick was pretty firm about that, and for me, it was an interesting piece of information, which I could, and always did, respect.

CHAPTER 4

CHINA ADVENTURES II (1946)

I have already mentioned my friend Bill Boatsman, the man who greeted me on my first night in China. Boatsman was a member of the under-thirty-five-point rotation group. He had thirty-three points.

DIGRESSIVE SKETCH OF BILL BOATSMAN

From the moment of that first meeting when I checked in during the middle of the night, Boats became my closest friend in China. In the months between January 1946 and his final rotation home in June 1946, I came to learn a lot about, and much more from, him. He had enlisted in the Marine Corps in the spring of 1944 after finishing high school in Kelso, Washington. He had gone through boot camp at San Diego and through infantry training at Camp Pendleton, California. Like thousands of other marines he was assigned to a replacement draft and had sailed from California to Guam late in 1944.

His draft off-loaded at Guam, but the men were never assigned to units and were reembarked, still in the replacement draft structure, on a troopship that set sail for Iwo Jima. Those men not having been assigned to a unit were kept in a kind of strategic "replacement reserve" of warm bodies to be used to replace casualties at Iwo in one of the three divisions making the landing and invasion. Boats's draft, which was the twenty-eighth, I believe, was assigned to the Third Marine Division. Some troop transports containing drafts were off-loaded almost as soon as they arrived off the beach at Iwo. Other drafts lucked out and remained aboard their transports throughout the entire operation with a ringside seat for the bloodiest battle in Marine Corps history. There were literally thousands of marines, including my aforementioned friends, Nicoletti and Bianco, taking part in the Iwo Jima campaign who never went ashore.

No such luck for Boats. His draft was off-loaded on the second day of the operation, when fighting was at its heaviest. Things were mighty confused when his group arrived on the beach. Boats, along with about one hundred other strong bodies, was assigned to the medical battalion and given the task, along with a partner, to go to the front and carry back the wounded. The two of them, for the next twenty-five days, operated almost independently as a team, cruising the Third Division battle area, picking up the wounded and carrying them back to the rear.

They were often under fire and, on several occasions, became involved in close-up combat with the Japanese. Boats said he lost track of the number of wounded marines he had carried back to aid stations, but it had to have been in the hundreds. He and his partner, who also escaped the battle without a scratch, would occasionally curl up in a hole and try to sleep; but most of the time, they moved around in a zombielike state, picking up wounded, hauling them back, and returning to the front lines for more.

Boats took up smoking for the first and last time in his life. He and his partner managed to get a daily carton of cigarettes from the supply sergeant, and between them, he swore, they would smoke the entire carton each and every day. The day the campaign ended, Boats stopped smoking, and I don't think that he ever smoked again. In fact, Boats was the first person I ever knew, over sixty years ago, who was adamant that smoking was an evil and unhealthy habit, although he admitted that it might have helped him survive the horrors of Iwo Jima.

After the battle for Iwo, Boats was shipped back to Guam and assigned to a rifle company in the Third Division. From April until September of 1945, his company in the Ninth Marines trained heavily in the hills of Guam. All attention was being focused on the preparation for the landings on Japan, although, thanks to the atom bombs, those landings were never necessary. In September, demobilization began. The fall of 1945 was a difficult and unlucky time for Boats. First, Guam was hit by a monstrous typhoon, which caused enormous destruction. Then the Third Division began its preparations for redeployment back to the United States, with Boats just missing the cut.

While the men in the Third Division with thirty-five or more points were put to work preparing the gear to be sent, along with themselves, home to the States, the lower-point men were assigned the task of preparing to be transferred to the First Marine Division in China. During that demobilization autumn, while repairing typhoon damage, packing, and working hard, Boats took up boxing as a way of keeping himself occupied. He had a natural aptitude and began winning bouts at the perennial Marine Corps "smokers," which were unit boxing matches held by every outfit in the Corps. He ultimately became light heavyweight champion of the Third Marine Division.

Boats came to North China only a few days before my arrival with the *Wakefield* replacement draft. I think what threw us together, initially, was that neither of us knew anybody. I was the only *Wakefield* replacement put in the machine gun platoon. On that miserable cold early morning when I stumbled into his squad bay, Boats's warm greeting had to have been at least partially motivated by the fact that he had a good idea of what it was like to join a strange outfit in the middle of a cold night.

In effect, we were both "new boys" thrown into a pretty salty outfit. The machine gun platoon of Charlie Company, First Battalion, First Marine Regiment, First Marine Division was an elite and experienced group. Some of the oldest timers had been together since Cape Gloucester (1943), Peleliu (1944), and Okinawa (1945). They were seasoned veterans, and by now, some of those who had accumulated over one hundred points were turning bitter about continuing to be stuck overseas. Although they respected Boats for his service on Iwo Jima, he was, to them, a "low-point man." I, with my three points, was out of sight and beneath contempt.

Boats was almost two years older than me and vastly more experienced in the ways of the Corps, and of life in general. Because he had already been in China for several days, and had gone on liberty, he insisted on taking me out on my own first liberty. He showed me the mysteries of exchanging money, buying booze, and finding decent restaurants and local houses of ill repute. Boats, like me, had come to boot camp in a virginal state, but unlike me, he had never been foolish enough to share this information with any of his boot camp fellows. Although by this time, I had learned enough to conceal my own pure state from him, he made sure on this, his second liberty and my first, to provide me with the opportunity to correct any possible deficiencies in that area.

Boats had a natural ability for finding his way around in a strange city, discovering the most exotic places, and, most of all, bargaining with the Chinese. Boats was a natural-born and shrewd bargainer and haggler, and he loved to engage Chinese merchants in trade. He was one of the few Americans I observed who could beat the Chinese at their own bargaining game and, as a result of this talent, was able to make a number of wise purchases of valuable items like jade and furs.

From that first time in January throughout the winter and spring, we often went on liberty together, sometimes with another marine from our platoon, who hailed from Cleveland, David Skyrm. David had been with the machine gun platoon from Pavuvu, through the Okinawa campaign, to China. He had more points than Boatsman and was able to return home in April. We would sometimes meet up and have dinner with some of Boats's old boxing buddies from Guam, who had also been transferred to China and were now assigned to other outfits in Tianjin. One of these friends, Rocky Castellani, a middleweight, went on after the war to become a perennial contender for the middleweight championship. I believe he had only a few losses, but because he could never beat Sugar Ray Robinson, he never won the championship. You can still see some autographed action photos of Castellani at Minetta's restaurant in Greenwich Village in New York.

Because we were in the same squad, Boats and I often worked together. We were deployed several times that winter and spring of 1946, and Boats came along on both the war detainee repatriation trip and the General Peck train escort.

For recreation in the barracks, Boats taught me cribbage, a game that he played better than anyone else. We also played pinochle. This required four people with two pairs of partners, and under Boats's tutelage as my partner, I became fairly proficient at the game.

There were two somewhat unsavory characters in our outfit, who kept badgering us to play pinochle with them. We set up a game with them, which Boats and I lost badly, losing money in the process. Several days later, these two characters inveigled us into another game, and again, we lost badly.

Presuming to be a United States Marine

After the second game, Boats took me aside and said, "Foot, do you notice how A always hits B with the right suit every time and vice versa, depending on who is bidding? They must be signaling. Let's play them again and see if we can pick up on something."

A few days later, we had another opportunity to play, and this time Boats and I didn't care whether we won or lost. Our objective was to discreetly listen and watch. Naturally, we lost again, and by this time, A and B were having a hard time concealing their glee over regularly "waxing" the best pinochle players in the platoon. But their triumph was short-lived because Boats had been able to detect their system. They were using foot taps under the table to signal their best suit. It was a ridiculously simple system: one tap meant clubs, two taps diamonds, three hearts, and four spades.

We played them again, and this time Boats had a strategy. One of us would deal, and when we heard A or B tapping his foot, Boats would carefully add one or two more taps, always trying to signal to me his own best suit. Soon we were clobbering them, and as we continued to play, you could see the anger and frustration begin to mount between the two of them until, like all moral defectives, they began to fight with one another. Finally we could see from their faces that they understood that we had smoked them out, but because they had initiated the cheating, they could hardly accuse us of cheating them back. Needless to say, the four of us never played pinochle together again, although nothing was ever said about it.

During the cold winter months, Boats spent a lot of his spare time in boxing training. The regimental special services officer had picked up on his boxing record from Guam, and beginning around the end of January, Boats was often driven to the division gymnasium to spar and work out on the bags. We had very primitive training facilities in our own fort at the English barracks. When Boats could not get over to division, I would work out with him, although we were a decided mismatch. Boats generally weighed about 175 to 180 and boxed at 175. He was five feet eleven, or so, but in superb condition, very strong and heavily muscled. I was about 190 to 195, tall and rangy at six feet four-plus, and not nearly as strong. He taught me a lot about boxing, and several times later in my life, I have been grateful for his instruction, although I always wished I had known him before I boxed Porter in boot camp at Parris Island.

When I say Boats was strong, I mean he was one of the strongest people I have ever known. Special Services, in their zeal to give us things to do, issued some weights for our platoon squad bay. We were all awestruck watching Boats picking up two separate one-hundred-pound weights, one in each hand. He simultaneously raised them to each shoulder, pressing them slowly over his head.

Because Boats was so good, he began to box around North China. He won the regimental light heavyweight championship first; then he won the First Marine Division championship; and, finally, he won the Third Amphibious Corps championship late in February or early in March of 1946. After this, we bid Boats farewell for a while. He was flown down to Shanghai where he won the All China-All Service Light Heavyweight Championship, but he lost in the final bout for the All Far East Light Heavyweight

Championship. He came back from his trip to Shanghai a little frustrated, because he had lost on a decision and thought he should have won. His successes boxing in the Marine Corps led Boats to try a professional boxing career after his discharge in 1946. We stayed in touch for the first few years after the war. Boats wrote me that he had won all his fights on the West Coast but had broken some bones in his hand and had become disgusted with some of the nefarious practices surrounding professional boxing. In 1948, he retired, undefeated.

Boats was the epitome of a good marine. He was reliable at all times, always did his job, never goofed off, and yet never tried to apple-polish or work deals. He had a wonderful sense of humor and never let things get him down. He was a solid, wonderful guy to have in a military outfit. And yet, as loyal a marine as he was, he felt that the Marine Corps had not done right by him.

During the last six months of the war in 1945 and the next nine months of the demobilization chaos, the promotions situation in the Corps was in a considerable state of turmoil. In the summer of 1945, the last authorization for promotions to marines serving in the Pacific came through. Having come off Iwo Jima as an unassigned stretcher bearer from a replacement draft, Boats had only recently left this somewhat orphaned status and had eventually been assigned to a machine gun platoon in the Ninth Regiment. Because of the slaughter on Iwo, many of the noncommissioned officers and officers were either dead and buried or in hospitals somewhere, so that no one really knew Boats. He was quite simply overlooked when the promotions came out. The war ended, and the division was split in two. Typhoon damage repair, packing up gear, and preparing for the move to China filled the days for Boats and his colleagues. There were no promotions anywhere in the Pacific after that one opportunity in the early summer of 1945.

The first week in April 1946, the log jam broke up. The First Marine Division headquarters published an order with a roster of new privates first class and both Boatsman's and my name were on the list. I eagerly accepted my stripe, picked up the order, and began sewing on the new stripes on my uniforms. But Boats took a different tack. He told the powers that be that "the Marine Corps has seen fit to keep me in for almost two years as a private. I came in as a private, and I shall go out as a private."

This unprecedented response produced a real problem for the company headquarters. First Sergeant Bennett called Boats in and advised him to take the promotion. Boats refused. Bennett, normally something of a lovable father figure to us all, lost his temper. Boats stood fast. The first sergeant then "ran him up" to the company commander.

Lieutenant McCulloch argued with Boats for at least twenty minutes. He was aware of Boats's outstanding record and told Boats there was simply no procedure for someone not to accept a promotion. Boats stood fast. I think that even if the commandant himself had ordered Boats to accept the promotion, Boats would have declined, respectfully.

To Lieutenant McCulloch's credit, he realized that he was in the presence of a strong man. He decided to accept Boats's rejection of the promotion, and the matter was dropped. After Boats was finally rotated home, he wrote back to me in China that he was once again offered a promotion before he was discharged, and that he had again refused to another irascible first sergeant, this time almost risking a delay in his discharge. William F. Boatsman walked away from the Marine Corps in late July 1946 as Private Boatsman, with head held high.

My own second promotion to corporal in late April, probably because of my work as an instructor in the machine gun school, could have created real problems for our friendship. As luck would have it, I was placed in charge of the section that included Private Boatsman. By this time, we were really close friends and a lesser man than Boats could have resented me for my promotion, or could have been tempted to take advantage of this new situation. To his everlasting credit, he was always loyal and supportive—hell, I owed him most of my practical knowledge about the Marine Corps—he never let on in front of others and never tried to take advantage of our friendship.

In early June (thank heavens, several days before my promotion to sergeant), Boats's rotation orders came through. Although fraternization between corporals and privates was somewhat discouraged, we went out and pitched one hell of a last liberty together. The next day, I had my final vision of Boats waving from the back of the truck that was taking him to the railroad station to begin the journey home. I never saw him again.

In truth, I can say that Boats had a profound and lasting effect on me. He had come from humble origins, from a family that helped settle the southwestern corner of Washington State. He was a man of absolute integrity. He was straightforward, honest, gentle, and kind. He was smart, even shrewd (witness his bargaining), and he always tried to improve himself. Physically, he was probably the most capable man I have ever known. In addition to developing his boxing skills, he had learned some judo on Guam. With these capabilities, he was fearless, and I once saw him singlehandedly demolish three white marines who were hassling and tormenting a young black marine. When I knew him, he was twenty years old, but he was already a wise, and even learned, man.

In my thirty-two years of active association with the Marine Corps between 1945 and 1977, there were four men, all dead now, with whom I served, who have always epitomized what it means to be a marine—four men to whom I shall always look up. We have already met the first one of these men—Chesty Puller. The second one was Bill Boatsman. It is ironic that Boats, though proud of being a marine, always felt that the Marine Corps had not done right by him. He was right.

END OF DIGRESSION

In addition to Boatsman, there were other marines in our company who were veterans of Iwo Jima. Our unit, Charlie Company, First Battalion, First Marines, had fought on Okinawa. Sometimes the Third Division Iwo veterans, who had moved into the unit from Guam, and the old-time First Division guys would start trading sea stories about how tough Okinawa was compared to Iwo, and vice versa. The fact is, they had both been pretty terrible battles.

One of these Third Division guys was a gentle young man named Rattunde, from somewhere in the Midwest, maybe Wisconsin or Minnesota. Rattunde was a very blond, almost white-haired, fellow, and he had a high, squeaky voice, which was his most memorable characteristic. Rattunde almost seemed too delicate to be a marine, but he was a good marine. He worked hard and had been through some horrible fighting on Iwo Jima.

Rattunde was the principal character in a story that I read many years later in *Reader's Digest*, a famous story about five marines on Iwo Jima. One night Rattunde and four other marines were patrolling around their positions to make sure that the Japanese were not infiltrating. They were moving down a little trail in a draw, or small valley. It was pitch-dark, and they remained pretty close together so that they would not lose contact with each other. They were creeping along when Rattunde, who was the fifth man in a file of five men, heard footsteps behind him. He moved forward, nudged the guy in front of him, and whispered, "Hey, how many people are on this patrol?"

The guy ahead of Rattunde whispered back, "Five." Rattunde whispered again, "We seem to have six!" The reply, in a low voice, was, "No, we only have five." So without any further comment, Rattunde just turned around and shot—*brratatat*—with his Browning automatic rifle. And sure enough, a Japanese soldier had fallen in right behind them, creeping along on this patrol in the dark, as if he were just another marine. Rattunde was the man who shot that enemy.

In February, soon after we returned from the trip with the internees, our company commander, Lieutenant German, was relieved by another senior first lieutenant named Bill McCulloch. McCulloch was my commander from February of '46 until I came home in September. As this is written, Bill McCulloch, a 1944 graduate of the Naval Academy, has retired as a brigadier general. He had been sent from the Marine Corps Base in Quantico to Okinawa and had fought all the way through the Okinawa campaign where, apparently, he did a good job. He came to us from the billet of battalion adjutant but had not liked that type of work. He was given our company as commander and had kept the job. Even as a noncommissioned officer, I got to know him fairly well. I gather that he had noticed my instructional work with machine guns, which I did so constantly that I had become a scholar on the subject. I had studied everything I could get my hands on and, by April, was giving most of the machine gun instruction for the whole platoon, even as a private. Apparently, word of that scholarly pursuit had reached Lieutenant McCulloch, and he had seen that I had gone to college, although I don't know whether he knew that I had gone to school right across the street from his alma mater, the Naval Academy. I did not realize it at the time, but I think now that he helped me to get promoted.

I have already mentioned in my digression on Boatsman my April promotion to corporal. To make corporal is a great achievement in the Marine Corps because, from then on, you don't have to stand guard duty on sentry posts. You become a corporal of the guard, which means that you post the guards, go around, and inspect them, but you never walk the post yourself as a sentry. You don't have to do mess duty if you are a corporal, either, because you are now a noncommissioned officer, and it was this exalted position I had been striving for at Camp Lejeune.

As soon as I found out about my promotion, I rushed over to the quartermaster, got a whole new set of stripes, tore all the private first class stripes off, and sewed on the corporal stripes. As a corporal, I was eligible to become the duty noncommissioned officer (Duty NCO) for the whole company, a job which would bring me much closer to the heartbeat of the operation. In the absence of officers and noncommissioned officers, I would be in charge of the company for approximately ten to twelve hours a day, sitting in the company headquarters office. People had to check out with me, and after I issued them their liberty card, they signed the liberty list, and off they went. I also assisted the company first sergeant with some of his paperwork duties and signed for all incoming correspondence and deliveries. Even in those days, we would get deliveries of orders, reports, and articles like that at any time during any given twenty-four-hour period. Somebody would ride up in a jeep and hand you some new document, and you were responsible for accepting and logging it in. In a separate log, the company duty noncommissioned officer recorded every incident that had occurred in the company during the twenty-four hours he was on duty. It was an interesting and responsible job.

Another duty was breaking out the troops and marching the company from their barracks to the mess hall for breakfast and for the evening meal. The Marine Corps, at least in those days, just somehow did not believe that a man could make it from his living quarters to the mess hall on his own, without being marched there. So I marched the unit to the mess hall.

But the new job immediately presented a number of leadership challenges, as will be seen. My dizzying rise to corporal in that brief period was a surprise even to me, and I was probably the youngest corporal in the division, if not in the entire Corps. I was barely eighteen and a half years old and certainly one of the least experienced marines in all of Charlie Company.

Here is a story that happened in early May, shortly after I had made corporal. I was called up to the company office and told that I had been assigned the mission of leading a train guard. The first sergeant briefed me on it and told me that I was to take six men from the machine gun platoon and report down to the Tianjin railroad station, where I would be given further orders. Thus began one of the great adventures and the first great leadership challenge of my Marine Corps career.

I did not personally select the six men, but five of them were good guys, men whom I had come to know and with whom I got along well. The sixth man was a fellow from Kentucky, whose first name was Virgil. In college I had read the poet Virgil, and I thought this Marine had a truly noble name. Virgil knew that he had been named after the poet too. I am trying to think of a nice way to say this, but Virgil presented

Taking on the Burden of History

a leadership challenge to anyone in charge of him. He was a brawny, big man with a very high opinion of himself, who constantly complained because the Marine Corps did not seem to share this opinion. He was bitter that he had not been promoted to corporal, and I had. To make things worse, even though he had been in the Corps longer than I, he was now under my command. He was older than me too, and that made it tougher for him all around. Fortunately, Virgil came across as so obnoxious that the other five guys in my little detail always silently showed me their support. I was glad for it because, as you will see, we were about to face some critical times on this mission together.

We loaded into a truck with rations, ammunition, and supplies to last for a number of days and were driven down to the railroad station. I reported to a sergeant and signed some papers. I was given two boxcars filled with nonperishable foods and a refrigerator boxcar filled with perishables—fruit juices, lots of fresh fruit, fresh vegetables, milk, and other fresh staples. As I was signing for the cars, workers were just finishing icing up the refrigerator car from the big ice plant at the freight yard. Refrigerator cars in those days had two large, hollow columns extending through the roof and reaching down to the floor of the car. These columns were probably four feet square, and they would be filled and topped off clear to their crown from the roof with ice. After I got my six guys together, we loaded our rifles and ammunition on the boxcars, and I asked the sergeant where we should position ourselves on the train. He answered that we were to ride on top of the boxcars and the refrigerator car. I was to guard the three railroad cars with my six men. We were going to the Second Battalion, Seventh Marines in Beidaihe Beach, probably 180 miles from Tianjin. I was to guard the three railroad cars under all circumstances and deliver their contents safely to the supply officer of the Second Battalion, Seventh Marines.

After some palaver with the Chinese railroad authorities, we, finally, had the three cars hooked on to a trainload of empty coal cars returning to Tangshan to be refilled for Beijing. We departed for what was going to become an odyssey. Our train had about fifty or sixty Chinese Nationalist troops aboard, and they had their own passenger car to travel in, unlike us. They were guarding the empty coal cars, while we were guarding our food supplies for the Seventh Marines.

The train crept along but moved, even during the night. The top of the refrigerator car and the boxcars had flat catwalks, probably about three feet wide. We unrolled our sleeping bags on that catwalk, tied them to it, tied ourselves on with ropes, and tried to get some sleep.

We got through the first night unscathed and arrived in Tangshan the next morning, where the coal cars were detached. Our supply cars got hooked onto another loaded coal train going north to Manchuria. We shuffled around in Tangshan most of the day and started out again in the evening. Again there were fifty or so Nationalist Chinese soldiers guarding the train. They even had an artillery battle car with them. It looked like the Civil War Monitor with sloping sides and about four ancient cannons protruding out each side through square openings. Once again, we traveled all night, tied securely to the boxcars.

Early the next morning, I had one of the most horrifying experiences of my life. I can see it vividly to this day. It was morning, and I was still tied to the top of the boxcar in my sleeping bag, lying on my stomach, just barely waking up. I lifted up my head, and about three feet in front of me, I saw the bottom girder of a little bridge across the tracks.

Had I raised myself up a second or two later, I would probably have been decapitated. Even after pressing myself down and flattening myself out as much as I could on top of my boxcar, I just barely cleared that bridge. It was as close a fit as you can imagine, and to this day, I shudder when I think that a part of me was very nearly scraped off my body on top of that train.

It was late the next afternoon when we pulled into Beidaihe Junction. I began negotiating with my Chinese army counterparts and the engineer to unhook our cars before the train proceeded on to Manchuria. We finally got them detached and placed on a siding way down, away from the station, near a mud fort the Nationalists were occupying on the edge of the junction village. Beidaihe Junction was not even a town, it was just a railroad terminus. Other than the road to Beidaihe Beach, there were no other overland roads connecting Beidaihe Junction with anything.

I saw a marine outside the small railroad station with a field telephone and a jeep. I reported to him and told him that I had food to be delivered to the Seventh Marines. He informed me that he himself was going to get out of Beidaihe Junction immediately.

I asked him why, and he replied, "Well, I am only supposed to be here until five thirty, and then I am driving back to Beidaihe Beach." I asked him if I could use his phone. I got on the phone, managed to get hold of the supply officer of the Second Battalion, Seventh Marines and told him that I had brought two boxcars and a refrigerator car of food supplies.

He said, "Oh, that's fine. You stay with them and guard them, and we will be down there first thing in the morning to pick the food up." Well, I said, "Aye, aye, sir."

As soon as I hung up the phone, the marine disconnected the phone from the line and ran to his jeep. I asked him, "Why are you getting out of here in such a hurry?"

He replied ominously, "There's going to be some trouble here tonight." And he took off, and that was the last I saw of him that night.

Our boxcars were sitting all by themselves, sticking out like sore thumbs, and just beyond them was the little fort. I looked around and saw a Nationalist Chinese officer. I tried to hook up with him to find out what was going to happen and realized that he really looked panic-stricken. He did not know any English, of course, and my Chinese was pretty slender, but I finally understood that the word was the communists were going to attack Beidaihe Junction that night, and that the Nationalists were now preparing for the attack.

Taking on the Burden of History

I could see that many sandbags had already been filled, and the Nationalist soldiers were running all around the fort. They had a big fieldpiece mounted up on the fort, an old cannon they were preparing to fix up to fire. But the most disturbing aspect of this hustling and bustling was that every one of these soldiers looked scared as hell.

I contemplated my duty. My duty, I thought, clearly was to guard the two boxcars and the refrigerator car. I went back and gathered my six-man detail and gave them what little information I had been able to extract from the marine before he took off with his telephone and the Chinese Nationalist officer after that.

"Instead of sleeping on top of the cars," I said, "we will dig in." And I added, "I want us to arrange ourselves in a perimeter around the three cars. We will dig fighting positions so that we will be prepared in case there is trouble here tonight."

Most of the men thought it was a good idea, because they could see that the Nationalist soldiers looked shaken and that there was a lot of tension and anxiety in the air. But Virgil thought it was a stupid idea, and he wasn't afraid to say so. I replied, "Private, it is my considered opinion the prudent thing to do here is to prepare for any eventuality, to protect ourselves, and to protect what we have been assigned to protect—namely, these cars—and I am ordering you to dig yourself a fighting position."

And he said, "Supposing I don't?"

I said, "I am going to shoot you."

I must have convinced him that I would, although I certainly don't know if I would have had the nerve to shoot him. It helped me to know that the other five guys were with me on this. And in the end, Virgil dug himself a nice position.

Unquestionably, this was a defining moment in my life. I had found myself in charge of six people, completely cut off from the rest of the Marine Corps, all by myself in a little railroad junction in the middle of nowhere in northeastern China, not too far away from the Manchurian border, and my authority had been challenged. And it had been challenged directly. If Virgil and I'd had to settle our differences physically, he probably would have prevailed. He was that big and strong a gentleman.

We were now well dug in. We had a nice perimeter around our boxcars as nightfall began to settle. The one pleasant aspect of guarding the food-filled cars was that we could treat ourselves to some pretty nice chow, which, I hasten to add, I had been given to understand by the supply sergeant in Tianjin was all right for us to do. We were guarding the food, but we were also able to partake of it a little bit. I remember that we found some canned pineapple juice, and we put it down in the ice. The pineapple juice was really good and cold and something we had not been able to savor in a long time.

Night fell, and very jumpy Nationalist soldiers were everywhere, although most of them had fallen back into the fort. It must have been around eleven or eleven thirty that night when suddenly a flare went off in the field in front of the fort, and there was a hail of rifle fire all around. I heard a few of the bullets clanking through the boxcars above us, because the railroad siding we were on was slightly elevated. But we were nestled down in our positions in the ditch beneath the ballasted rails. Although the fire from the field was concentrated on the fort, it was not surprising that some of the bullets had strayed over to our boxcars.

This was the first time I had been shot at in my life, even though it was indirectly, and my emotions were pretty intense. Later, in Korea, it was confirmed to me that combat often produces great chaos.

The Chinese Nationalists reacted with a tremendous volume of small arms fire punctuated by an occasional shot from the cannon mounted on the platform inside their little mud fort. It was an ancient cannon, probably a relic from World War I, but they were booming away with it. The communists laid down a hail of fire too, and I expected to see them come charging up at the fort and at us. But they never did. I had strict fire discipline over my own men. They were under orders not to fire until we had a target we could shoot at, and that target would clearly have to be a target hostile to us.

I said, "This is not really our fight. This is a Chinese civil war, and we are only the spectators. But if the boxcars are in any jeopardy, why, we will shoot."

Fortunately, the communists were just executing a probing but clearly successful attack to shake up the Nationalists. The return fire from the Nationalists was overwhelming, and the whole thing was probably over in ten or fifteen minutes. I divided us into watches, and we tried to sleep the rest of that night, although with varying degrees of success.

The next morning, a marine lieutenant from Beidaihe Beach, five miles away, arrived with a convoy of about twelve or fifteen six-by-six trucks and a large detail of troops from the Seventh Marines. I reported to him, and he said, "It sounded like there was some trouble down here last night, Corporal." I was being very cool and offhanded when I assured him it had been nothing. But when he found the bullet holes in the boxcars and saw that some of the cartons of food had been damaged by the bullets, he was a little bit upset. I told him, "We had stuck by our posts and had protected those cars, sir, with our lives!"

The cars were completely emptied. I had to sign some papers, and the lieutenant told me to report back to my unit in Tianjin.

"Aye, aye, sir," I told him and returned to the railroad station, where I found my old friend, the telephone man, back at his post.

He asked, "Was it rough here last night?" Then he added, "Geez, we could hear it all the way up at the beach." And by this time, some of the tales told by my guys were already getting taller and nastier about what a horrible night we'd had fighting off the communists.

With the help of the telephone operator, I got the Chinese stationmaster, and he explained what we had to do next, and I signed a whole stack of papers. We were issued very large and elaborate train tickets, consisting of several pages written in Chinese. I was made to understand that the railroad would bill the United States Marine Corps for our fares.

Taking on the Burden of History

For a pleasant change, a relatively nice passenger train arrived soon. We settled down in our seats and got back to Tianjin in time for supper. The trip up had taken much longer, but we got back in one day.

It was nice to return to what, under the circumstances, seemed like civilization. I felt good about doing the right thing and digging in because, quite frankly, if we had spent the night on top of the boxcars, some of us might have been hit in the hail of bullets. My first big leadership challenge as a corporal was behind me.

Another new duty for me was that of corporal of the guard, the noncommissioned officer in charge of a whole relief of sentries. Since our guard duty in China at that time consisted of the many posts scattered throughout Tianjin, being the corporal of the guard meant being responsible for a total of forty-six or forty-seven men. The corporal's responsibilities included waking up the relief sentries, making sure that they were ready to go on post, and that the sentries being relieved were picked up and taken back to barracks. The Tianjin guards were distributed by truck. The whole relief would get aboard a big truck driven to their various posts and dropped off, as the old sentry climbed back up on that same truck. The corporal would ride around in that truck to make sure that all the posts were posted. Sometimes the corporal would be asked by the officer of the day to accompany him as he inspected the guard, which in those days, and I guess still is, was done frequently. The officer of the day is responsible for making sure that the sentries are doing their job.

At one point, I was assigned by the sergeant of the guard, my superior, to conduct the color ceremony. At the main gate to the English barracks flew the regimental colors of the First Marine Regiment. The reason for that was that the First and Third battalions were stationed inside the barracks, and the regimental commander, Colonel A. T. Mason, our commanding officer, kept his headquarters there. The regimental colors were flown from a large flagpole mounted on the tower over the main gate. This presented a picturesque and colorful scene, and I regret that I don't have a photograph of it among the few pictures I brought back with me. Even then, it looked like something out of another century. I was assigned to get two privates of the guard to take down these regimental colors. The regimental drum-and-bugle corps always sent a bugler up to blow "colors" for the lowering of the flag.

Some of the protocol surrounding the American flag in those days was that colors were raised at 8:00 a.m., or 0800 hours in military time, and they were raised as rapidly as possible. The flag was yanked right up to the top of the flagpole. In the evening, colors were lowered exactly at sunset by the astronomical clock. The weather bureau gives the precise time of sunset, and at exactly that time, the flag was lowered in such a way that when the bugler began playing the colors tune, the guards started lowering the flag. They had to be finished lowering the flag just as the bugler finished blowing colors. It is a precise and solemn moment at the end of the day, as the sun sets.

My privates of the guard had been instructed, and they knew the procedure exactly. On this particular day, we went out to lower the flag, and one of the sentries took one of the two halyards or lines, and the other one took the other. As the flag was coming down slowly, the color guard privates were accurately gathering it in with their free hand and pulling it together to be folded up, or cased, properly.

As the corporal of the guard in charge of this flag-lowering detail, I was standing at attention, saluting the flag as it came down, while the bugler was blowing colors. Just before the ceremony began, as luck would have it, the regimental commander, Colonel Mason, drove in. He got out of his command car and, standing at rigid attention, saluted, swelling with pride, and solemnly watching his regimental colors coming down.

My privates of the guard continued lowering the very large flag, and they were keeping in time with the bugler so that they would all end up neatly together at the appropriate moment. But it happened to be a very windy day. The private gathering the flag in had a big mass of it gathered up in his arms when a strong gust of wind suddenly blew the flag right out of his arms. Just as "colors" were finished, the whole flag flopped out of this private's arms and sank down to the ground. Oh Lord!

Colonel Mason roared, "Corporal, get me the officer of the day!" I ran into the guardhouse and found Lieutenant McCulloch, the officer of the day. He came out, and the colonel bellowed, "This color detail has dragged MY colors on the ground. You will have them burned instantly!" Oh God, poor Lieutenant McCulloch! I was standing there, just quivering, and this has now become one of the worst moments of my Marine Corps career, because I have just desecrated Colonel Mason's flag, the regimental flag, the American flag!

I took the two yardbirds who had been pulling the colors for me, and the flag, to a big furnace back in one of the supply areas of the regiment, and we put the regimental colors in there and set fire to them and burned them. To this day, no matter how large or small it is, cloth, paper, or plastic, if I ever see the American flag touch the ground, I become upset. Some days after the desecration of Colonel Mason's flag, the new regimental colors of the First Marines that somebody had been able to dig up somewhere, were raised. Alas, it was a smaller flag that now flew at the main gate.

There is another wonderful story about Colonel Mason. He was not a large man, but he was one of the most erect men I have ever known, as if he tried to stretch himself out as much as was possible. He had relieved Chesty Puller after Peleliu and commanded the regiment through the Okinawa campaign. He was a tough nut, who had earned the respect of the regiment, but he did not seem overly endowed with a sense of humor.

I have told you about my own problems with shoes. Shoes, in fact, became a pretty serious problem for other marines in China, as well. In the first months we were over there, it was hard to get anything out of the supply chain; but shoes, of course, were critical. The bane of a marine's life is inspections. You are always in some sort of inspection cycle. You are always being inspected by either the platoon leader or by the company commander or by the battalion commander. You have a battalion inspection, or you have a regimental inspection, and the various levels of command contrive to keep you constantly off guard with inspections.

Taking on the Burden of History

It so happened that we were having a regimental inspection by Colonel Mason himself. We had the whole company online, all the platoons online. Each platoon was three ranks, but the three ranks were all facing, so that the platoon front was thirteen or fourteen men wide and had the second and third rank behind it. That was the formation for inspection. The first platoon was on the right-hand flank of the company, facing in one direction, and the next platoon faced in the same direction, and so on, down to the machine gun platoon. Colonel Mason came wheeling up in front of the whole company, and the company commander reported the company ready for inspection. Colonel Mason went down to the first squad of the first platoon. He took a couple of rifles and inspected them. The rest of the company was positioned off to the left of the first platoon, and we were all standing at ease, waiting to be called to attention for our inspections. Clearly, this was gearing up to be a thorough inspection.

Colonel Mason finished inspecting the rifles of the first squad, first platoon, and that meant that he had inspected all the way down to the end of a line of thirteen or fourteen men. Then he marched back to the beginning of the rank, going down behind the men standing rigidly at attention. He was looking at the fit of the uniforms and their appearance, to see if they were squared away and clean. And when he got back up to the head, up to the squad leader's position at the right flank of the platoon, he said, "All right, men of the first squad, I want you to listen very carefully to my command. I am going to say, 'raise RIGHT foot, RAISE!'." And when I say 'RAISE,' lift up your right foot with the sole of your shoe pointing toward the rear, and hold your lower calf parallel to the deck.

He called out, "Raise RIGHT foot, RAISE!" And all the men in the first squad of the first platoon raised their right foot, so that the calves of their legs were parallel to the deck and the soles of their shoes were pointing backward. Colonel Mason went down the rank and inspected the bottoms of each man's right shoe.

All the rest of us in the company were listening very carefully, because we could see something coming. When Colonel Mason reached the end of the squad, the command came, "All right, now listen carefully, men. Raise LEFT foot, RAISE!"

But the colonel had neglected to get the troops to put their right feet back down on the ground. You could just see it coming; you could see it coming! The first squad, bless their hearts, who could see it coming too, fell flat on their face as one man in perfect unison. It was beautiful! That ended Colonel Mason's foot inspections for the rest of his general inspection of our company, and I don't think that he ever tried that maneuver again.

Here are a couple of liberty stories. One of them took place when I was still a private first class, and the other one when I was a corporal. My life changed in June when I became a sergeant, but in the early liberty days, I managed to have some pretty fun times.

The first story, and this could become R-rated, is the story of a young woman I met when I was on liberty alone in a little Russian bar in downtown Tianjin. It was a nice little place, and it sometimes had a small orchestra, and there was dancing and drinks, and you could eat there too. Prices being what they were, you could have a lovely evening for about a dollar.

I was in this place one night when I met a very attractive young woman with dark hair and sparkling eyes, as I recall. I wish I could remember her name, but I think it began with an *N*, and since she was a White Russian, it was probably either Natasha or Nadia.

We struck up a conversation in a way people will in a bar, having a drink. I immediately became very interested in her because she was so different from the usual girls who floated around the bars in Tianjin. She was a little older than I. She had been born in Harbin, the big city in Manchuria, in 1925, and she confided that her parents had been members of the nobility in Old Russia. They had left on an odyssey on the Trans-Siberian Railway, before she was born, and had ended up in Manchuria. Her father, apparently a prudent and resourceful man, had managed to create a good life for his family in Manchuria in one of the heavy industries, which had begun to flourish there in the twenties.

After the Japanese occupation of Manchuria, her family had left and moved down to Tianjin. In the trauma of this move, both her parents had died, and she was left with only her older sister. She was a woman of some education and discernment. She could talk about Dostoevsky, for example, and was familiar with classical music. She had a fairly good singing voice too, and one of my great memories of her is when she sang "Ochi chernyja," ("Brown Eyes"), a gypsy song, for me. We spent a wonderful evening together. Before she left, she invited me to visit her some afternoon in her apartment. I made a date to see her the next Sunday afternoon.

That Sunday, with a great deal of excitement, I spruced myself up very carefully for liberty. I walked over to her apartment, which was on the second floor of a fairly commodious building in the old Russian concession. The apartment building surrounded a courtyard, to which there was a gated entrance. N. lived with her sister—or her sister lived with her, I don't know which. It was a humble enough apartment, but probably better than most people in China at that time were able to obtain.

After some conversation with her sister, we went into a bedroom and began—how do I say it discreetly?—necking, and she was really beautiful, and I was really excited; and so some clothes started coming off. And then, suddenly, there was a knock on the door of the bedroom. It was her sister knocking. The sister's voice was filled with panic as she called out, "Look out the window!"

We looked out the window, and there was a very large, burly very angry-looking somewhat older man striding purposefully across the courtyard of the compound. My lovely date looked at me with great panic, sadness, and sorrow and quickly confided, "There is one thing I did not tell you. That is my husband out there."

Oh, he looked very angry to me, this Russian bear, and I quickly gathered up what clothing I had already shed, ran out of the bedroom, out of the apartment, and down the hall. I found a narrow broom closet; squeezed myself in; closed the door; and, with considerable difficulty, completed dressing inside it, all the time listening very carefully for any sounds.

Taking on the Burden of History

Apparently, somehow, word had reached this man that his young wife was entertaining a marine. First, I could hear him noisily stamping up the stairs, then I heard him banging on the door of the apartment, and finally, I guess the sister let him in. He closed the apartment door, and, in my tight closet from the distance, I could hear an enormous amount of shouting in Russian.

As soon as the apartment door was shut and I had my clothes on in some semblance of order, I quickly exited the closet, crept down the steps and out of the apartment building, and, alas, never saw my lovely White Russian again. Being an incurable idealist, I thought that perhaps she was forced to marry this older man, who might have been a friend, or even a distant relative, because her parents had died when she was still very young. It was clear that theirs was not a marriage made in heaven. And so I conjured up all kinds of dismal but romantic scenarios for her life.

In this recent story, I mentioned that my lovely White Russian's sister's apartment was in the Russian concession. Elsewhere in this account, I have mentioned various concessions. The term "concession" was still in use right after World War II as a way of referring to neighborhoods, but the extraterritorial significance of these areas had been eliminated. They are one of the sad reminders of a time when China was shamelessly exploited by the European powers. During the nineteenth century, in the major cities of China, different countries appropriated for themselves areas of cities that were considered part of the sovereign territory of the appropriating country. These so-called concessions were extracted from a succession of Chinese emperors by threats, manipulation, and pure purchase. It is to the everlasting credit of the United States that our country participated very little in this game—a fact that in 1945 and 1946 was gratefully acknowledged by the Chinese themselves.

Most of the members of the United Nations during World War II renounced their extraterritorial concessions. In that first postwar year when I was there, Tianjin had identifiable Russian, German, Japanese, Italian, French, Belgian, and British concessions. The greatest number of the main buildings, attractions, hotels, stores, banks, and so on was either in the French concession or in the British concession. In all the concessions, there were buildings that architecturally reflected their country of origin. In each concession, you could find vistas, streets, or neighborhoods that made you think you were back in the homeland.

Between the world wars, many countries also maintained a military presence within their concessions. Our British barracks were once the home of various regiments rotated through during the twenties and thirties. Their coats of arms were displayed in the base theater, a beautiful old building, which burned to the ground in January when our company was away taking the internees to Qinhuangdao. After the Japanese occupied Tianjin in 1937, these military units were allowed to remain, but their moves were restricted. After Pearl Harbor, the English units were made prisoners of war by the Japanese. I don't believe that either the Italians or the Germans maintained much in the way of military organization in their concessions. Of course, by the late thirties, there was an understanding between the Japanese, the Germans, and the Italians. By

1940, their relationship was formalized in the Rome-Berlin-Tokyo axis. That left the French.

At the time of France's surrender to Germany in June of 1940, the French government maintained a full battalion of the French Colonial Army in Tianjin's French concession. Since Japan and France were not at war with each other then, the Japanese permitted the French battalion to continue to maintain order within their concession, subject to some restrictions. However, over the next year, the lieutenant colonel commanding the battalion apparently convinced the Japanese that his sympathies lay with the Vichy government and Nazi Germany. After the United States and Britain declared war on the Japanese in 1941, and de Gaulle's Free French movement had identified itself as an ally of Britain and the United States, the wisdom of the French battalion's commanding officer was vindicated. His battalion was allowed by the Japanese to remain in their concession, and although they were surely restricted in their movements, they maintained a facade of continuing to be a French presence in China.

One can imagine the consternation the French lieutenant colonel must have felt when Japan surrendered unconditionally, and the United Nations, in the form of the U.S. Marine Corps, were going to occupy Tianjin in early October of 1945. He apparently convinced General Rockey, the USMC commander, that his most deep sympathies all along had been with the Free French under the valiant leadership of the great General de Gaulle. So the French battalion was tolerated and not interfered with. But they were a sad lot. I came to know some of the men in that battalion, and they were truly tragic figures. All of them had been stuck in Tianjin for at least eight or nine years. They were completely cut off from their homeland, and in that first year after the war, their homeland had forgotten them.

Some of our officers indicated that the colonel became something of a pest as he attempted to ingratiate himself with the Americans. At the same time, he was very prickly and sensitive about our respecting their status as independent Frenchmen. These men became something of comic opera figures. Their commander would ride around in his huge old convertible sedan with its top down, driven by a uniformed French soldier. I believe the car was a Hispano-Suiza, probably of early thirties vintage, polished to a dazzling shine.

The French, too, loved to parade and march through the streets, even in their pitiful appearance. They were all old for soldiers—the youngest must have been thirty—and their average age was well into the forties. Their uniforms were a bit shabby, and they all looked pudgy. In spite of the harsh conditions during the war, they managed to maintain self-sufficiency by keeping large farms across the river. I must confess that we found them amusing, almost comic; but at the same time, they *were* survivors, and their French pride remained palpable. They could be described as men without a country.

Here is another story. I must confess that there was one instance when I can say that I was engaged in a barroom brawl while I was still a private or a PFC. A few times,

Taking on the Burden of History

I went out on liberty with a fellow named Weber, who was from Michigan. Weber was a big man, about my size, and strong as an ox, but a very genial, gentle giant. He could not wait to get out of the Corps and go back to his chosen profession of driving a great, big eighteen-wheeler truck. He was good company and a lot of fun, and we liked to explore the Tianjin clubs and bars. Of course, all of these places liked to scrape a little money off the marines who were stationed there.

Down in the English concession, along Victoria Road, among some nice established bars, a new one had just opened, boasting music and dancing.

Weber said, "Let's go down and try this place." And we decided to go. We sat down, drinking our usual vodka, and surveying what kinds of females were coming into the place and what our prospects might be with them. I had to go to the men's room, and in order to do that, I had to walk past the end of the bar through a door to a dark hallway.

When I reentered the bar, I realized that the whole atmosphere inside had changed. Suddenly, there was palpable tension.

I had noticed, as I had been sitting down earlier, a navy first class petty officer. He was a machinist mate, and you could tell that because they wear a propeller in their insignia. He was very sharply dressed in his sailor's uniform and had come in with a very attractive White Russian girl. These two young people were just sitting there, minding their own business.

When I returned to the bar, the machinist mate, who was a pretty husky fellow, was standing about ten feet in front of me, with his back to me, facing the dance floor. On the other corner of the dance floor stood a little skinny marine, who looked like he might weigh one hundred pounds, soaking wet. He was on his feet, making fists and gesticulating around in his corner of the dance floor. He had obviously had far too much to drink. And so he stood there bobbing and weaving and declaring, "All swabbies eat shit!"

Understandably, the machinist took offense at this, but, I could tell, he did not want to get involved. Weber was sitting just beyond the marine.

I motioned over to Weber to calm the marine down and to take care of the situation. After all, the sailor had a nice date. Weber smiled, and I thought he had understood me. I approached the machinist's mate behind his back. We were now both standing in front of the bar. I tapped him on the back of his shoulder, intending to say to him, "Please, sir, just sit down, we will take care of this matter." And I opened my mouth to say just that.

But the poor sailor was so tense by this time that he did not wait for any explanation. Man, he just turned around and delivered a tremendous right-handed blow. I think he expected to hit me in the face, but since I am taller than most people, he struck me right in the breastbone. It was one of the hardest blows I had ever been dealt. He was a tough guy. The blow lifted me up and sent me, literally, flying, backward.

Now this little nightclub was fairly new, and for a bar, they had vertical pieces of plywood that provided the uprights for it with the usual longer piece of plywood across the top. And that was all there was to the flimsy bar. When I came flying backward, spread-eagled, the bar just disintegrated under my weight, and I completely cleaned out the bottles and glassware on the shelves behind the bar. It was a mess!

By this time, understandably, I was pretty angry. I had never been hit so hard in my life. I came flying out of the debris halfway across the dance floor and, with a roundhouse punch, hit the sailor pretty hard right on the jaw. I don't know what happened to him because we could suddenly hear whistles being blown outside. Tianjin had a very efficient marine military police company, which kept strict order, and it was clear that they were on their way to restore it.

Weber grabbed me and said, "Come on, Foot!" And we took off through the back door near the bar and back toward the men's room and into the men's room, where we crawled out through a window into an alley behind the building.

Sirens were shrieking everywhere. Once that sailor had hit me, all hell had broken loose in the bar. Although I was a little upset with Weber that he had not intervened sooner, he had managed to extricate me from the general brawl. Had we not managed our escape, I am sure the owners of that restaurant would have remembered the person who had messed up their new bar. We took off running down that dark alley and down some other dark alleys and got to the barracks safely without getting caught. That was my one and only genuine barroom brawl experience in China.

One more feature of life in Tianjin and in North China that spring of 1946 and into the summer was quite serious. We became exposed to Japanese encephalitis, a kind of sleeping sickness carried by mosquitoes. Sometime in the early summer of 1946, an epidemic hit the First Marine Division full-force. And this is a very sad story.

The exact details and dates may have clouded over in my memory a little bit, but my recollection is that a number of marines throughout the division came down with encephalitis, all at the same time, and that in one day, nineteen of them died. It was a terrible tragedy.

The American military never takes things like this lying down, and immediate and stringent measures were taken. First of all, almost overnight, and I don't know how they did it, since they could never seem to find any shoes that would fit me, every single marine in North China was issued a mosquito net, racks, and pegs. Our wooden cots already had holes for the pegs of these mosquito net racks. A division order was promulgated that every marine, regardless of rank or station, would sleep under a mosquito net every night, no matter what his circumstances were.

If you were on guard duty, you had to take your mosquito net with you because if you were going to sleep in the guardhouse, you had to erect a mosquito net and sleep under it. Every duty NCO and every sentry was given strict orders to ensure that every marine slept under a mosquito net.

There was also a massive campaign under way to exterminate mosquitoes. Of course, this was back in the good old days before we worried about DDT. So, man, we had the life squirted out of us by spray trucks in order to kill any mosquito foolish enough to be sitting on us.

Taking on the Burden of History

The third measure taken was that every man in the division had to be inoculated against Japanese encephalitis. All these steps were taken within forty-eight hours of the outbreak of the disease. I am always amazed at the efficiency the Marine Corps can display when it wants to.

Even though everything had happened very quickly, the reputation of the inoculations preceded the actual administration of them, because there were a couple of older men in our outfit who had been given them before. They assured us that this was the worst shot known to mankind, and that it would really knock us out, so that by the time we lined up to be inoculated, why, we were pretty apprehensive about the whole matter.

The whole company fell out, and Lieutenant McCulloch had all his officers there, and he stood out in front of us. Lieutenant McCulloch said, "Now, men, you have probably heard that this shot is bad, but I am here to tell you that this is not true. The shot is perfectly harmless."

The whole company formed into one single file at a small medical building in the corner of the parade field. Lieutenant McCulloch and the other officers moved right to the head of the company to lead us in file, and Lieutenant McCulloch said to us, "Men, the officers are going to get their shots first."

The officers went in the door at the far end of the building filled with corpsmen holding needles and vaccines at the ready to mass-administer. In a few moments, Lieutenant McCulloch reemerged from the end of the building nearest us, smiling at the rest of us lined up waiting to get our shots, and he said, "Now see, men, there was nothing to it!" Having taken about seven steps in the direction of the company office, he fell flat on his face.

And then the other officers began to come out. Some of them got as far as about thirty or forty feet before they fell, but some of them did not even get as far as Lieutenant McCulloch.

Here we were now, all lined up, waiting for our shots, watching this massacre, and, I must say, it did not inspire a whole lot of confidence in us. Pretty soon, we were taking bets on how far the next guy would make it before he keeled over. We had orders that once the shot was administered, we were to go straight to our barracks and to bed.

The little medical building was at the corner of the parade ground, and next to it was a large concrete apron in front of the barracks occupied by the machine gun platoon.

I can truthfully tell you that not one man made it all the way back to the barracks. The shot simply zapped one unconscious momentarily, and we would all fall down. After regaining consciousness, most of us crawled or limped from the spot where we had fallen back into the barracks and into our bunk. But not a single one of us made it straight to the barracks, not one single soul.

The machine gun platoon was always near the end of the column, so we had the privilege of witnessing over a hundred horror stories, and I must confess that it became

Presuming to be a United States Marine

increasingly more difficult to give credence to Lieutenant McCulloch's offhanded assessment of the shot.

Finally, my group entered the medical building, and I remember that after I got my shot, I began to understand what had happened to Lieutenant McCulloch and the others. The shot itself did not hurt much. But suddenly, wham! It hit you like a blow. I actually managed to get pretty far on my pilgrimage back to my barracks but eventually fell to my knees and, by degrees, gratefully crawled into my bunk. After spending two or three hours in our bunks, we were all fully recovered.

Having been promoted to corporal, I remained at that rank until June. In June, a new round of promotions came down through the division. Each company was given the option of appointing a certain number of people to the next rank. Our machine gun platoon was a good platoon, but we still had a fair number of experienced machine gunners who were PFCs. We had about four corporals, of whom I was one, and we had a staff sergeant, who was our platoon sergeant. Our staff sergeant was a marksmanship expert. He had been on the Marine Corps rifle team and, in June, got yanked out and detailed to be put in charge of a new rifle range up in Beijing, set up so that everybody in the division could requalify with the M1 rifle.

The machine gun platoon had to have a sergeant. And as luck would have it, on about the fifteenth of June, I was promoted. By this time, I was already conducting most of the platoon's training. I was taking advantage of the knowledge of some of the older men in our company, who knew something about machine guns, in addition to my thorough and detailed analysis of all training manuals and books on machine guns that I could get my hands on.

We did have an officer, of course, whom I will call Lieutenant T. In the annals of my Marine Corps history, Lieutenant T goes down into the ranks of the very few second-rate officers I ever knew. Lieutenant T was not an evil man. He was not nasty or vicious or any of those things. Lieutenant T just really did not give a damn. He was lazy. He was our platoon leader from about March of 1946 until he went home in late July or early August. I can honestly say that other than for inspections, when either the battalion commander or the regimental commander were coming around to look at us, I saw Lieutenant T, maybe, only four times. He was just never present.

That June, about the time I got promoted to sergeant, the situation in North China was beginning to get a little more tense. In April a map-making group from one of the division units was out in some jeeps when they were ambushed, and a couple of marines were killed. Then early that summer, the Seventh Marines had a supply dump attacked, and a couple of marines were killed there as well. In addition, some marines were kidnapped and hauled off, and there was a big hoop-de-la about getting them back, which was eventually successful.

As a consequence, our training became a lot more intense and serious, and for some time that summer, our First Battalion, First Marines, was relieved of the responsibility of guarding all posts. That job was assigned to another organization, and we were put on a very rigorous training cycle.

Taking on the Burden of History

A machine gunner first has to know how his gun works by taking it apart and putting it back together. There were several adjustments to be made in something called the head space, and these adjustments had to be made accurately, or the guns we used at that time would not fire.

Next, shooting the gun has to be taught properly. The main vehicle for teaching machine gunners how to shoot a machine gun accurately is what is called a thousand-inch range. A thousand inches, if you think about it, is not very far. It is eighty-some feet. The companies were given the order that all machine gun platoons had to set up one-thousand-inch ranges.

We had to go through a big hassle to get the right kind of targets. These targets are little sets of one-inch squares set horizontally in rows or vertically in rows or diagonally in rows. A machine gunner turned two wheels, which controlled the gun as it went up and down, to the right and left, and up on a diagonal. A good machine gunner had to be able to fire three round bursts and take out each one of those little squares. It was a fairly tricky and technical matter to learn to do.

After the order came down that we were to set up this training, Lieutenant T appeared with a wad of papers. He always called me Van, real friendly, not Sergeant, but Van, which I resented. He handed me the big sheaf of papers and said, "These are my notes from Basic School. I want you to go and set up a thousand-inch range."

We found an area on the outskirts of Tianjin, beyond the edge of the city, where the topography was right, with a big overhanging cliff we could use for the bullets to bound into so that they would not go careening all over the civilized creation. Next, we set up a thousand-inch machine gun range from scratch and qualified everybody in the platoon on the machine gun. By now, we were getting to be pretty good marksmen. Word came down next that we were to conduct some studies on the tactics of machine guns. With no other materials than Lieutenant T's Basic School notes—which he always generously provided to me just before taking off for parts unknown—and the many manuals I managed to collect, I gave a great deal of instruction on the subject.

As I have already said, this experience is what kindled in me the desire to become a teacher later in life. With nobody looking over my shoulder, I had our machine gun platoon really whipped into great shape. We put on gun drill demonstrations for the whole battalion a couple of times, and that was something we learned to do well. A gun drill is practice in deploying a machine gun. The number one gunner runs out with a tripod and throws it down in the correct place. The number two gunner carries the machine gun itself, sets it down on the tripod, and clamps down all the turning knobs. The number one ammo man runs out with a box of ammunition and loads the gun. Then the gunner commences firing.

The troops are trained to "fall out one," and that means that the gunner becomes a "casualty" in this drill. Then everybody else moves up one and has to complete the next job above them.

It was good training, and we used to do this on the double, running all the time, up hill and down dale, pretending to deploy the machine gun under combat conditions.

Presuming to be a United States Marine

Later, when I was leading a rifle platoon with a machine gun section attached in Korea, I saw that in real combat, those gunners will do it just the way they learned it in gun drill.

It was a busy time in China that summer, bringing with it new responsibilities all the time. Occasionally, something would happen with the guard, and our company would have to assume their responsibility. We only had about seven or eight sergeants in the whole company, so that I used to have to stand as sergeant of the guard fairly often. And that was an interesting experience, because the sergeant of the guard went around with the officer of the day checking posts.

Several times I was sergeant of the guard when the officer of the day was Lieutenant McCulloch. As much as a sergeant and a first lieutenant, who is almost a captain, can converse with each other, we had some interesting talks while driving around at night, checking the sentries all over Tianjin.

A couple of years ago, at the dedication of our Korean War Memorial in Washington DC, I had lunch with now General McCulloch who too had ended up in Korea. As I indicated earlier, my career undoubtedly owed a lot to his oversight.

One of our sentry posts in Tianjin was the Third Amphibious Corps Headquarters, the highest headquarters for all marines in North China. These headquarters were in a former French bank, a beautiful great big building in downtown Tianjin featuring a large safe. In those days, marines were paid in cash, in American currency. If you can imagine, we had one hundred thousand marines for a while in North China, and that constituted an awful lot of dollars being brought in on a regular basis to pay out. The old bank safe was inside a locked room on the second floor, which had a very heavy door with a glass window in it. A sentry was posted there at all times, with orders to stand in front of that door and to sacrifice his life, if necessary, in order to keep anyone unauthorized from entering the room containing the safe. Every minute, he was to look through the glass panel to make sure that the safe was closed and secure and that there was nobody unauthorized near the safe. These instructions were in the orders for that particular post.

Late one night, Lieutenant McCulloch and I were checking posts, including the Third Amphibious Corps Headquarters. The outside sentry at the front entrance, one of our guys, reported his post, "Post number 38 all secure, sir." He saluted sharply. We climbed up the beautiful marble staircase, went down a hall, and arrived in an antechamber leading to the door with the glass panel, and into the room with the safe.

There was a bench in the antechamber and on it lay our sentry, curled up and sound asleep, with several million dollars of American cash under his presumed surveillance. Lieutenant McCulloch reached over carefully and lifted up the guard's rifle. Ammunition was carried to most of our posts in Tianjin, and the guards were expected to shoot if anything happened. Lieutenant McCulloch handed the rifle over to me and said, "Here, Sergeant, take this rifle back to the jeep."

When I returned, Lieutenant McCulloch was still quietly leaning over the sleeping marine. We continued standing there together for some time, and the marine was

Taking on the Burden of History

out—man, he was gone. Lieutenant McCulloch finally cleared his throat, harrumph, and the kid suddenly woke up.

While sleeping on post was a pretty serious offense on his part, you had to feel a little bit sorry for him. What a terrible way to wake up, with the officer of the day and the sergeant of the guard standing over you.

As soon as he woke up, the hapless sentry started looking around desperately for his rifle, which, of course, he couldn't find because it was now in the jeep. So he jumped to attention, saluted Lieutenant McCulloch, and said, "Post number 93 all secure, sir."

Lieutenant McCulloch said something like, "Get serious, man!" He placed the guard under arrest and took him out to the jeep. Then Lieutenant McCulloch gave me the sentry's rifle and posted me on that post. The young man was confined to the guardhouse and eventually got what in those days was called a deck court-martial. Sleeping on watch is a pretty serious offense in itself, particularly when there is something of importance being guarded.

The emphasis shifted that summer from dealing with the Japanese and eventually repatriating them, to keeping the communications lines open and, in effect, supporting the efforts of the Chinese Nationalists to consolidate control in North China. As it turned out, this was a rather hopeless task, but we continued trying, and that produced some amusing and, a couple of times, tragic consequences.

By the summer of 1946, the demobilization of the American forces had set in, and the size and strength of the First Division and its other units was being drawn down. As the marine units began reducing in size, some of their equipment was being turned over directly to the Chinese Nationalists. A tank battalion in those days had a total of fifty-four tanks and was divided into three companies. The companies each had three platoons, and each platoon had five tanks. As the First Tank Battalion was reduced in size and strength, the Sherman medium tanks, which were in those days the state-of-the-art tank in America, were being turned over to the Chinese Nationalists, a platoon at a time, or five tanks at a time. The tank company in Tianjin was reduced by one platoon, and the tanks were turned over in a little ceremony. The Chinese Nationalists were certainly excited because a Sherman tank was a pretty awesome and formidable-looking object rumbling down a dusty road in China.

It seems that the Chinese Nationalist commander at the time thought it would be great to shake up the communists in the surrounding countryside some. The railroad tracks, the rail lines, and the cities and towns were still occupied by Nationalist soldiers and marines. Of course, there were many more Nationalists, maybe a half million men in that area, than marines. On the other hand, it was clear that the countryside was pretty well controlled by communists. We were always under strict orders not to venture farther than one thousand meters beyond the city limits of Tianjin, unless we were in a tactically deployed formation. The few times I did go out to the edge of the city, there was always evidence that the communists were ensconced there. The civilians were obviously frightened and did not look as self-possessed as they did in the downtown areas.

Presuming to be a United States Marine

This Chinese Nationalist commander was naturally well aware of this situation and decided that "the thing to do is to take my five tanks and do a big sweep around Tianjin and show these people that we mean business."

Yes, a tank is a very formidable thing, but a tank all by itself is useless. The Nationalists had sent two men per tank to our tank battalion for training. One man learned how to operate the weapons, the other one how to drive the tank. A regular tank crew in those days was five men, but the Nationalists only had two specialists per tank.

After the ten Chinese got trained as tank drivers and gunners, a column of five tanks, flying the Nationalist flag, was dispatched from Tianjin on a long, sweeping tour around the south and southwest perimeter of the city.

It was a hot summer day, and they were cruising through villages, but the communists, wasting no time, immediately began tracking them. The tanks arrived at a village about twenty-five miles from Tianjin. It was noon, and the Nationalist officer in charge of the tanks saw a nice well. He pulled all the tanks into the village square, and everybody climbed out and went to get a refreshing cool drink of water, leaving the tanks parked and unattended.

On their return, communists hidden in each tank proceeded to dispatch them, one by one. The communists turned out to have enough experienced people to drive the five tanks away into the mountains.

Understandably, our operations people became a little bit leery after this incident. Up until that time, the operation of tanks was not a capability that the communists were thought to have. As a result of this incident, the balance of power in North China shifted slightly.

In July of 1946, the marines were hit by what came to be known as the Anping incident. Anping was a village outside Beijing. In those days, there was a highway between Tianjin and Beijing. The highway would have been a one-lane concrete highway in America, but it was considered to be two lanes in China. Periodically, several of the communications outfits in both Tianjin and Beijing used to tour back and forth on this highway to check the telephone lines we had strung between those two cities, and to make sure that everything was in good order. These were normally relatively peaceful trips.

On July 28, a convoy of three jeeps from the communications battalion and one jeepload of people from the artillery regiment made the trip from Tianjin to Beijing. They were nearing Beijing when they came to a barricade across the road. They stopped, and the communists opened fire. It was an ambush. Four marines were killed, and the rest were wounded. It was a debacle in which the marines did not even have time to return fire.

That incident happened probably at one or two o'clock in the afternoon and threw everybody into big consternation. By four that afternoon, our whole company was broken out, we were all issued ammunition, and we were ready to mount up and go out on a punitive expedition. A lot of our guys were pretty angry about this ambush. Although from the point of view of the communists, we were certainly being supportive

Taking on the Burden of History

of Chiang Kai-shek, we were not oppressive in any way. If anything, we were trying to help in any way we could.

We started out on a relief expedition, but Division Headquarters, realizing that nothing could be achieved by it, stopped us and turned us around. The First Division then established the policy that every three days, a mechanized sweep of the entire area, not just the highway, would be conducted between the two cities. The force appointed was a reinforced rifle company from our regiment, the First Marines, accompanied by tanks and weapons carriers and covered from the air by Corsair fighter bombers, all in all a pretty awesome display of power.

For the rest of my time in China, from late July until early September 1946, every three days, I went out on this road patrol from Tianjin to Beijing. We took a whole day to make a sweep. Although the two cities are only about one hundred miles apart, in order to achieve the complicated sweep up and back again, we got up early in the morning and returned well after dinner.

After the freezing cold temperatures in the winter, it was now extremely hot and dry in North China, with temperatures often well over one hundred degrees. The first time our company went out, we were allotted one canteen of water. In this extreme heat, one canteen of water lasted about ten minutes. By the time we returned to the barracks from our first patrol, I was so dehydrated that there was a deep dry crack running all the way down the center of my tongue. I remember trying to put salve on it to keep it moist, but the crack remained dried out like a riverbed in Death Valley for some time.

After this experience, the medical powers-that-be prevailed, and it was decided that the old Marine Corps principle of water discipline did not apply to the desertlike heat of North China, and from then on, we were allowed to take four canteens, buckled around our waist. In addition, two five-gallon cans of water were brought along on each truck.

A marine six-by-six truck, stripped down, could be used as a fighting weapon. It carried us to combat, and we could disembark from it very quickly and set up machine guns. We practiced deploying machine guns from these trucks over and over again.

We would load up our guns and our ammunition and our C-rations and water on these trucks, and when the tanks and the planes were coordinated, we would take off. We must have impressed the heck out of the communists, because they never messed with us.

We would deploy ourselves and investigate any suspicious activity. As machine gunners, we were always a kind of base of fire for the company, and once that base was established, the riflemen would go out on little patrols, sweeping the areas away from the highway. One day, as we were returning from Beijing, we came to a village situated on a knoll, with a long sloping hill on the far side dipping down into a valley. There at the bottom of the hill, across the road, was a barricade. We immediately thought of Anping.

Our column halted. We brought up the machine guns and set them up along the top of the hill, facing down toward the barricade. Lo and behold, suddenly there appeared in the distance a bunch of the rattiest, grungiest, most patched-up-looking people I have ever seen.

Over the centuries in China, there were warlords, and the designation of "warlord" was often a synonym for "crook." Even after World War II, there were many people in China who commanded private armies. Some of these private armies were nomadic, moving around constantly. They were, in effect, independent and neither part of the Nationalists nor the communists. They tried to capture whatever they could obtain for themselves, whenever and from whomever they could get it. They would loot cities and villages. While this phenomenon was, by 1946, on the decline, nevertheless it appeared that we had stumbled into some stubborn warlord's ambush.

I have to give our commanders credit. They quickly realized that these troops, deployed across the valley at the bottom of the hill and blocking our way, were not communists and ultimately no threat to us. The ragtag assemblage blocking our way at the bottom of the hill had, in fact, seriously underestimated our strength, obviously thinking that we were some kind of a little caravan coming down the road they could stop and loot. Immediately after we had seen the barricade, I got word to deploy my machine guns, and man, I had them lined up, and we were going to lay a base of fire that would blow away an entire army. But next, I got word that when the signal "commence fire" came, we were to fire well over the heads of the raggedy group. The officer who gave me that order told me that I was personally to check each gun to make sure that it was laid in such a way that the bullets would fly well over our adversaries' heads. Under no circumstances were we to hurt anybody. At this point, our tanks were not yet visible from the road block. Our mock attack was beautifully coordinated. The tanks suddenly appeared over the brow of the hill and started thundering down the long sloping road while we held our fire until they reached the bottom of the valley. At that point, the tanks opened fire with blanks from their cannons. Then the machine gunners were given the order to fire, and man, we just creamed the Chinese air with precisely placed fire. The noise was deafening.

Well, those poor guys took one look at this magnificent display of military prowess coming down the slope at them, and they scattered to the hills in total disorder, running in every possible direction to escape. Not a soul was hurt in the process. It was really beautiful.

My tour in China was coming to an end. There are a couple of observations I would like to make about my life that summer, particularly during the months of July and August when I was, for all intents and purposes, the platoon leader of the machine gun platoon.

Life had changed for me in many ways. For one thing, a lot of the people I had been closest to in China had rotated home for demobilization, and there was a great deal of turnover in the unit. In addition, because of my elevation to the exalted position of sergeant, I had become a little bit more distant from the troops. Soon after I made corporal, this was further accelerated by the regiment's insistence that corporals and sergeants could not live in the squad bay with the troops, that they had to be billeted separately.

Taking on the Burden of History

And so, for my last few months in China, I inhabited a small room with another sergeant and a couple of corporals. We had a little more space to spread out, which was pleasant, and those guys became good friends as well. But it wasn't the same as it had been when I was down with the troops, so to speak.

There was a steady stream of departures now. By June, anybody who had been overseas and had fought on either Iwo Jima or Okinawa, the last big battles of the war, had been rotated home. In July, the people who had been overseas but had not actually had to fight in the battles were being rotated back to the States, and so the whole makeup of the unit changed.

I have already introduced Lieutenant T, our platoon leader in name only. He was a marine officer who had been sent overseas in a replacement draft sometime in the last six months of the war. Because he had not been committed to combat, and therefore did not have very many points, he was finally rotated home in July.

Lieutenant T's most notable characteristic was that he only turned up for battalion and regimental inspections. When our main focus had been removed from standing sentry duty and we had begun our patrols, or sweeps, between Tianjin and Beijing on a three-day schedule, we were still training intensively the rest of the time.

One evening, when we were all in the barracks at about eight or nine o'clock, one of the privates in my platoon knocked on the door of the sergeants' quarters and said, "Sarge, I think you'd better come over to the squad bay. The lieutenant is there." I could not imagine why he would be with the troops and, with some trepidation, went to the squad bay.

Since nobody was on liberty, all the troops were sitting around, writing letters, and doing what they normally did. It was immediately apparent that Lieutenant T had had a great deal to drink. He was going from bunk to bunk, saying his good-byes. Had Lieutenant T been any kind of leader, and had any of the troops ever seen him prior to this time, it could have been a deep and sentimental moment for all.

The lieutenant had received his orders to leave the next morning for the United States when he was suddenly struck with a need to say adieu to his troops. As he did not know who most of the troops were and as they barely knew him, and, in addition, as he was drunk, the tender moment he had envisioned turned out to be quite awkward.

I mustered my courage and approached him. He was in a deep one-sided conversation with one of the troopers, and I said, "Excuse me, Lieutenant, sir."

He turned around and looked up, "Hey, Van! I got my orders to go home, so I just had to come over and say good-bye to everybody, and I especially want to say good-bye to you." And he fell all over me.

"Lieutenant," I said, "if you are leaving in the morning, are you packed yet?"

"Well, no," he replied.

"Sir, don't you think you'd better go home and get a good night's sleep for the trip?"

"Well, maybe that's a pretty good idea," said Lieutenant T, who, at this point, could barely walk. Thank God he had brought a jeep and driver, and never mind how he had finagled that jeep and driver. I escorted him to his jeep, got him inside, and we commenced having a prolonged emotional farewell. "Man, it's been great knowing you, keep in touch," Lieutenant T said, tearfully.

This man, who had heretofore been totally and utterly uninterested in his troops, his job, or his command, suddenly, the night before he went home, suffered a deep and abiding sorrow over his separation from the men. Fortunately, he was drunk enough to be relatively pliable and maneuverable, but he left behind some very embarrassed troops.

Margaret, the young woman I had known since high school in Hyattsville, Maryland, and whom I had dated from December of 1944, and who had seen me off to both Parris Island and to Camp Lejeune, had kept up a vigorous correspondence with me in China. The winter of '44-'45, my last months in college in the spring and then in the early summer, we had spent an awful lot of time together. While we did not have any kind of serious understanding, we had written to each other faithfully the whole time I was in China.

But sometime in the early part of July, I received a letter from Margaret, in which she confessed that she had met another man, a pilot who, fortunately I thought, was a marine also. Margaret wrote that they'd had an intensive courtship and that they were going to get married in February of 1947. This classic Dear John letter absolutely crushed me. I was heartbroken. Suddenly China looked good to me, and the Marine Corps looked good to me. I felt desolate and rejected and had all the emotions anyone feels when he gets such a letter.

For a while, this shocking blow seemed to support a decision to enlist in the regular Marine Corps. I talked to several old sergeants and to the battalion adjutant. They all said the same thing: my rapid rise in rank and the fact that I already had over two years of college almost guaranteed that, if I enlisted as a regular marine, I would soon be promoted to staff sergeant, and probably be sent to Officer Candidate School. In fact, Lieutenant McCulloch wanted me to apply to the Naval Academy. He thought it would be great to have a St. Johnny graduate from the academy.

I decided to go ahead with the enlistment in the regular Marine Corps. To their credit, both the battalion sergeant major and the adjutant told me that my stay in China would be extended indefinitely if I became a regular. But when I thought about going back to a United States without Margaret, China began to look better and better. So I told them to fill out the papers and made an appointment to be sworn in to the regular Marine Corps by Lieutenant Colonel Meyerhoff, our battalion commander, at 1100 hours on September 4, 1946, at the battalion headquarters building.

About 1030 hours that morning, I reported to the adjutant, a man whose name I no longer remember, but to whom I shall always owe a debt of gratitude. He told me, "Sergeant Van Sant, an order just came in from division that I would like to show you." The order listed the names of the men who were to report to the Tianjin railroad station at 1000 hours on September 5 for transportation to the coast, to board ship, to be rotated back to CONUS (Continental United States) for discharge from the United

States Marine Corps. As one of the relatively few sergeants eligible for rotation left in the division, my name was near the top of the list.

He informed me that I could always enlist in the regular Marine Corps after I returned to the States. He told me I would have ninety days after my discharge to reenlist without losing rank or any seniority. By this time, it was twenty-five minutes to 1100 hours and my appointment with the colonel. I asked if I could step outside to think. I went out and walked slowly around the outer perimeter of the parade ground, weighing my options. On the *one* hand, I was miserable over Margaret; I was having a great time running the machine gun platoon; the duty in China was adventurous and interesting; the Marine Corps seemed to appreciate my talents, such as they were; and I seemed to have a promising future in an organization I had come to love. Why not make a formal and permanent commitment?

But as Tevye says in *Fiddler on the Roof*, "on the *other* hand," I had not seen my father in two years; I had not seen my mother and sister in almost a year; I could always still do the enlistment after I had had a chance to visit at home. It was one of those life-determining decisions, and as I walked around that parade ground on this pleasant September morning, I agonized. Finally, I decided to accept the orders home and postpone my enlistment until after I had returned to the United States. I went into the adjutant's office and cancelled my appointment with the colonel. The adjutant was very understanding and sympathetic and told me he thought I had made the right decision.

And I started packing my seabag and my gear and getting ready to leave the next day, I must say that I left China with some sadness, because I'd really had such an extraordinary time there. That poor country was in terrible shape. I had been presented with new challenges and felt that my stint there had been a positive experience for me.

Chapter 5

HOME, DISCHARGE, BETWEEN WARS (1946-1950)

I boarded the train to Taku Bar, the same place where I had landed almost one year earlier. An LSU took us through the shallow water to a regular navy transport, the USS *General J. C. Breckinridge*. This was to be my home for close to four weeks.

In contrast to the *Wakefield*, this ship had been constructed as a troop transport and launched in 1945. She was named after a Marine Corps general still living at that time. Somewhat later in my Marine Corps career, I met his eldest son, James C. Breckinridge Jr. He and I were almost contemporaries although he was a little older and a rank ahead of me as an officer. The troop-carrying capacity of the *Breckinridge* was 5,650. I was assigned quarters as a sergeant and placed in a smaller and much less crowded compartment than the one I had been crammed into on the *Wakefield*. As I remember, there were about twenty of us, all corporals and sergeants.

I had not been on board for more than ten minutes when a message came over the loudspeaker system: "All passengers of the rank of sergeant and above, sergeant and above, report immediately to the troop office."

In response to this command, I dispatched myself to the troop office, where a sergeant major had a roster of us and called the roll. Out of the more than five thousand marines on board, there were only seventy sergeants. We were taken to the crew's mess hall, along with an even smaller number of marine staff noncommissioned officers, and were asked to sit down in rows. The captain of the ship himself arrived, addressing us as "gentlemen." I had rarely been called a gentleman before. He advised us that the ship required a crew of 524 officers and men, but because of the demobilization and the mustering out of so many sailors, there were only 183 officers and men available. He said, "That is not enough men to run this ship, and that is the crisis we now face. Each of you will be assigned a responsible petty officer's job. You will have additional marine privates, PFCs, or corporals to help you carry out your missions." On a purely random basis, we were divided into the various working divisions of the ship. As luck would have it, I became the noncommissioned officer in charge of the ship's refrigerators and freezers.

Taking on the Burden of History

Perhaps some explanation of the navy's rank structure and organization is in order. In those days, the bottom ranks were apprentice seamen, seamen, and seamen first class. A seaman first class began what was called "striking." A "striker" was a person trying to get rated as a petty officer in a specialty. A seaman first class was the equivalent of a corporal in the Marine Corps. A person who has decided on a specialty might pursue electronics or communications or become a boatswain's mate or a quartermaster, or any of the other jobs available in the navy. Seamen first class go through preliminary training before becoming strikers. A striker, really, was an apprentice.

The *Breckinridge* table of organization called for a chief petty officer as the highest-ranking enlisted man to be in charge of the ship's refrigerators, assisted by perhaps a first, second, and third class petty officer, along with five or six seamen, or seamen first class as laborers. As we went aboard the *Breckinridge*, the ship's refrigerator department had one (!) seaman first class, a refrigerator man striker.

The ship's refrigerators/freezers were quite an elaborate installation. There were eight large refrigerator compartments (several were freezers) on two decks in the bottom holds of the ship, four on one deck, two on each side of the ship with a passage between, and four similarly laid out on the deck right above them. Each one of these eight compartments was approximately twenty-five feet by twenty-five feet wide and about eight or ten feet high. The two refrigerator decks were connected by an elevator shaft between the lower and the upper levels. This shaft continued up through the hull of the ship to the kitchen (galley) space, the mess hall, and, finally up to the officers' mess. This five-story elevator serviced the entire mess installation, with the refrigerators being the foundation almost at the bottom of the ship.

The person rated as refrigerator man would have an understanding of how refrigerators operated, including, I would assume, some knowledge of air compressors, Freon gas, and such. As we have seen, on this trip, the *Breckinridge* had just one seaman first class even partially rated as a refrigerator man. Fortunately, he was a very fine sailor, a smart young man who knew his job. I am sure that within months of our trip, he deservedly got his rating as a third class petty officer refrigerator man.

When I became the noncommissioned officer in charge of refrigerators, I was really filling a chief petty officer's billet, with the young sailor as my assistant and technical adviser. In addition, I was given two corporals and some thirty marines. These men were divided up into two watches, with one day on and one day off duty. I was in charge of both watches, and the corporal in charge of each relay reported to me. One of my jobs entailed the signing for every disbursal of food from any refrigerator to the galley, where the food was prepared.

There were probably forty naval officers and a couple hundred marine officers to be fed in the officers' mess. The elevator reached all the way up to the officers' mess galley. In addition, we had five thousand troop passengers on the ship, who had to be fed three meals a day.

The job was not without some magnitude.

Presuming to be a United States Marine

With each day's relay of marine laborers, I reported for duty, and by that time, the galley would have sent down their requests, or breakouts, for the day to be removed from the refrigerators or freezers. There were refrigerators filled with huge sides of beef, whole pigs, avalanches of hot dogs, and other kinds of meat. The freezers had frozen ground beef and milk (which had to be thawed out) in mind-boggling quantities. We had enormous quantities of oranges and apples, and at least one of the eight reefers was filled with nothing but huge cans of juice.

I would get an order for quantities of these items to be broken out. My fifteen-man marine work detail would actually perform the physical labor of hauling these items, placing it on dollies, and wheeling it to the large elevator to be lifted up to the kitchen.

When I was assigned this job, I was not quite nineteen yet. In spite of my tough experiences in China, the refrigerator work was a bit overwhelming for me. Suddenly, I was responsible for an immense amount of paperwork, and any number of other related details. I will always remember one of the papers I had to sign. It was a strange form, requesting acknowledgment of receipt of a deceased commander's body. The mess officer explained to me the sad story in connection with this document. A regular navy commander, stationed at Qingdao, was permitted, in the late summer of 1946, to have his wife join him on his tour of duty, as had other higher-ranking enlisted men and officers stationed in China. Troop transports coming to Asia at that point in time were not usually completely filled, so that a number of wives could be brought over on these ships.

The commander had been overseas for most of the war and had not seen his wife in about four years. In early September, he stood on the quay, anxiously awaiting the arrival of his wife on a shallow draft boat from the *Breckenridge*. As he waited, he suffered a heart attack, which instantly killed him. The distraught widow returned to the ship and prepared to escort her husband's body back to the United States. The commander's body had been embalmed and placed, first, in a casket, then into a metal liner, which was sealed and nailed up into a very large heavy wooden crate with casters.

One of the eight refrigerator compartments was completely empty. We placed the huge crate with the casket inside it and tied it down to the duckboards in the center for cold storage. The commander's crate will surface again later.

In addition to the military passengers we had on board, there were also about twenty or more recently married wives of marines, most of whom were White Russians, with a sprinkling of Chinese wives among them. These women had married marines and, by the laws of those days, were entitled to transportation back to the United States, along with their husbands. Unfortunately, these ladies were kept on the uppermost stateroom deck on the top of the ship in absolute quarantine. Husbands and wives traveled in total segregation. For those of us who were troop passengers, it was pleasant when, in our time off, we could look up to the top decks and behold visions of lovely ladies walking around or lying in deck chairs looking elegant and mysterious.

Taking on the Burden of History

After we sailed through the North China Sea, we were on the great circle route across the northern Pacific. We came to within one hundred miles or so of the Aleutian Islands and continued from there all the way down the coast of Canada and the western United States. We came so close to the United States that we could listen to radio stations from California. We proceeded down the coast of Mexico to the Panama Canal and continued on to Norfolk.

Since the *Breckinridge* took the northern route, the trip was a little faster. The ship got us home in about twenty-six days. On this particular rotation back to CONUS, there was practically nobody from either Charlie Company or the First Battalion, which meant that most of my fellow passengers were strangers.

By three or four days out, we had left the Japanese home waters and were heading northeast toward the Aleutians. At the northernmost point of our trip, we ran into a dreadful storm, the worst storm I have ever experienced at sea. At times, the bow of our huge ship must have risen up in the air fifty or sixty feet. In its downward passage, the waves would break up against the bridge, the highest point on the ship. The ship tossed about like a small toy. The waves were so dangerous that at times the marine passengers were not allowed to go up on the deck. Lines were rigged up, and we had to walk holding on to a line so as not to be swept overboard.

In the middle of the night, while the storm was at its greatest intensity, I was awakened by an enormous thump, which made me think we had hit an iceberg. About two minutes later, over the loudspeaker came a message. "Sergeant Van Sant, Sergeant Van Sant, lay down to the ship's refrigerators immediately." Gulp. I quickly threw on some clothes and, via a circuitous route through the ship, managed to find my way down to the refrigerators, where I met a highly excited group, who had also been summoned. There was the officer of the deck, a number of sailors, my trusty seaman first class refrigerator striker, and a number of my marines standing by outside the refrigerator compartment where the commander's casket was stored.

It did not take me long to figure out what had happened. The ship was rolling so badly that the commander's casket on its casters had broken loose from the ropes tying it to the duckboards and was careening around the compartment. From time to time, it would slam into the bulkhead or an interior wall of the refrigerator compartment. At other times, it would slam into the outer wall of the compartment, or the ship's hull, about twenty-five feet below sea level. The sound that had awakened me was the casket hitting the side hull of the ship after it had busted loose. Since the refrigerator compartment was so far below the waterline, it would have been a disaster to have the commander's casket bash a hole in the side of the ship, risking the sinking of the entire ship. The officer of the deck made it perfectly clear to me that he was not going to have his ship sunk by a runaway casket.

He commanded me, "Sergeant Van Sant, secure that casket!" I looked at my troops. The danger of being in that compartment on a rolling ship with a casket weighing several tons and lurching about on casters was considerable.

Presuming to be a United States Marine

We were all quite uncomfortably aware of the fact that it could easily flatten any one of us on contact. The sailors, having obtained several lengths of strong rope, turned into interested spectators because, of course, it was the marines who were expected to secure the casket. I gathered six of my trustiest and huskiest marines around me to discuss the tactics of capturing the runaway casket. They were to remain on high alert and, for God's sake, stay away from that dangerous missile.

The floor of the refrigerator compartment was made of duckboards, or boards set on vertical risers with spaces between them, to allow moisture to drain to the deck floor. This makes for a rough and bumpy surface, but that meant that the runaway casket was not completely free to whiz from one side of the refrigerator to the other. Our task was clear. We had to get the casket lashed down to the duckboards.

In the process of this exercise, we had a couple of really close calls. For a gut-wrenching moment, I was sure that one of my guys was going to get mashed to a pulp. He barely leapt free of the hurtling casket. With the enormous rolling of the ship, the casket would careen across the unexpectedly steep angles the compartment deck took.

With great quantities of rope and the exercise of extreme caution at all times, we got the commander lashed down. There must have been thirty or forty interlocking ropes applied in every possible direction when we finished, but the casket was secured and could no longer move. The officer of the deck was clearly happy that his ship was not going to be sunk by a friendly, albeit dead and dangerous, navy commander.

One of the features of my job as the noncommissioned officer in charge of the ship's refrigerators was my ability to barter because, sooner or later on a troop transport out at sea for a long time, everybody gets hungry. I myself was able to eat an apple almost every day from the enormous apple stock. It should be understood that this was by no means called stealing. We called it, simply, scrounging. One day I was approached by one of the few marines from Charlie Company, whose job was in the sick bay. He had been able to make contact with the small handful of other guys from our First Battalion in China and thought we really ought to have some kind of reunion party. He said, "I have access to some 190 proof sick bay alcohol. If you will get us some fruit juice, we could have a party with the old crowd." For some reason, he also wanted some apples.

While none of the people I was going to party with were close friends, they were people from the same outfit in Tianjin. We agreed that I would bring apples and fruit juice, and he would contribute the sick bay alcohol. Another First Battalion guy, working in the dry stores, added his resources of crackers and such. We found a small out-of-the-way compartment down in the storage section of the ship, and the half dozen of us who met there and drank our elegant cocktails out of coffee mugs. It should never be tried at home, but here is how we prepared a cocktail with sick bay alcohol. We covered the bottom of a mug with about a quarter inch of alcohol, then topped it off with pineapple or grapefruit juice. I can't remember what we did with the apples, if anything.

Taking on the Burden of History

Earlier, I mentioned the large freight elevator connecting the lowest deck in the hold of the ship all the way up to the officers' mess on one of the top decks. The elevator was used primarily for transporting goods, although personnel rode in it to accompany whatever food was being shipped. My troops would load up with, say, about four or five sides of beef and fit one marine into the elevator at one time. Thank God the ship still had a qualified butcher.

For some reason, I decided to ride up once myself with some big cartons of something or another. The elevator started up but only reached between the upper level of refrigerators and the lower level of the galley, where it stopped. I have heard stories of claustrophobic people panicking inside a stuck elevator. While the experience was not too bad for me, although the elevator was immobilized for a fairly long time, the people in the galley were getting increasingly upset because they were in need of the food they had ordered. Unfortunately, one of the missing specialists on the crew was the man rated for the maintenance and repair of elevators. I was trapped, although kindly souls kept calling out to me the progress of the ongoing search for a qualified repairman. At long last, somebody from the engineering department arrived, fiddled around, found the problem, and fixed it. This episode tended to make us all rather nervous about what we would do if he had to hand-carry all supplies up to the galley for a big food breakout.

You may remember that in my excitement of sailing through the Panama Canal the first time, I had spent the entire time out on the deck, carefully observing every piece of scenery and memorizing every view. On the way home, however, I was pretty blasé. I had been there, seen it all.

If you look at a map of the Panama Canal, you will see that the way the Isthmus of Panama curves from the Pacific to the Atlantic makes the canal almost run east to west. On the first trip, we had floated through the canal, stopping at the far end in the town of Balboa. Coming back, we sailed through the canal first and stopped at Cristobal at the Atlantic or Caribbean end.

The morning we arrived in Cristobal, we were given a number of instructions over the loudspeaker that all marine passengers who did not otherwise have ship's duties would be given liberty from 1300 hours (one o'clock in the afternoon) until midnight. We knew that Cristobal boasted USO clubs, dance halls, and other interesting places.

We had not even arrived yet when I got called down by the mess officer for a staff meeting. It was explained to us that we were going to take on a large amount of provisions, as we had begun running out of supplies and the refrigerators were emptying fast. We had finished the entire stock of ice cream, which was obviously a disaster, although we still had some apples left. I clearly remember that we never ran out of apples.

I personally was told by the mess officer that he had arranged for a shipment of bananas to be taken on board, which he thought would be a nice break from our constant diet of apples. In addition to the mess officer giving orders, the staff meeting was attended by the chief petty officer in charge of the entire mess operation; by the chief in charge of the galley, the food preparation, and the butcher shop; and the navy rated man, a first class, in charge of the dry stores. I was, of course, in charge of the refrigerators, but although I was the only marine sergeant, it would soon become painfully apparent that I was the lowest-ranking of all the staff.

The mess officer told us, "All of your divisions will be expected to keep your troops aboard the ship with no liberty until provisioning has been fully completed." This officer was efficient and a pretty nice guy, and he added, "Now I want to stress that we have arranged to have the material here as soon as we arrive, and this entire operation should not take more than a couple of hours. As soon as it is completed, your men can go on liberty."

We tied up at a huge dock in Cristobal, long enough to accommodate three or four big ships in an end-to-end row. The day, I remember, was one of those beautiful days that can bless you in the tropics. It was sunny and hot, but breezy and pleasant. Instead of the flora and fauna that amazed me on my way to China, this time I was astounded by the various kinds of equipment—the cranes, pulleys, and metal carts with rollers on them used to move provisions when taking on cargo. This was called getting the ship rigged for loading. There must have been about forty-five marines from all the various divisions in the mess operation.

Promptly at 1300 hours, word came out over the loudspeakers, "All marine passengers otherwise not engaged in ship-loading procedures are hereby authorized liberty." And man, within a minute, the gangplanks were filled with slicked-up marines hitting the town of Cristobal. But those of us with our labor details, who had to stay aboard ship, were watching those boys enviously. As is human nature, the poor stuck marines were bitching. There is no other way to put it, they were griping, and for that matter, I was mad myself. I wanted to go on liberty too. Instead we were bound by duty to remain on board.

We waited. Fifteen, then twenty minutes passed. A couple of trucks came roaring up with some dry stores. Some happy marines got off. About a half hour later, the ice cream arrived in huge refrigerator trucks, and we quickly stowed it away in the freezers. More happy marines disembarked for their liberty.

It was about two o'clock by now. I saw the mess officer talking to the mess chief. The officer said, "Well, we've got pretty much everything we ordered. The only thing we don't have yet are the bananas. So I think I am going to go on. I have an old friend here, and I think, Chief, that you can handle this." The last instruction he left, as all of us left on duty heard, was, "Now, one thing about the bananas. They are bulky, so there will probably be several truckloads of them. We are going to put them in a warm refrigerator space. But the important thing is," he emphasized, "those bananas are to be ripe. If they are green, don't take them. We are taking on ripe yellow bananas only."

And that was the order to the chief. And the old chief, he hung around for fifteen or twenty minutes longer. No bananas. He called the junior chief to come to him and said, "Look, I'd really like to go fishing. You can handle this. The only thing we are waiting for is for the bananas to go to Sergeant Van Sant's place, and he is all ready for them with the warm refrigerator space." Before he took off, he added, "We are not to take the bananas on if they are green. Refuse them if they are green. They were ordered ripe."

Ah, me! You can see what's coming now. That chief, after waiting for some time, called the first class over, the dry goods guy, and said, "You can handle this, just give the bananas to Van Sant." And off he went. It was about three o'clock now.

And the first class hangs around to close to three thirty, and still no bananas. He approached me and said, "Sergeant Van Sant, you know where the bananas go, and you know that the only thing you've got to remember the lieutenant said was that if they are green, don't take them. I am going to go ahead and shove off on liberty."

In the meantime, I still had my work detail of marines, impatient to get off. After all, everybody else was leaving ship and going on liberty. In good old marine tradition, we settled down. We hurried up and waited.

Then at about four fifteen, we heard the rumbling of trucks in the distance. As the sound got louder and louder, we saw in the distance a convoy of battleship-gray navy trucks. Five or six trucks, stacked with bananas, drove down inside the warehouse. But the bananas were the greenest, most unripe bananas imaginable. It was a Saturday afternoon when this drama took place. It must have taken a big work detail of sailors to load these trucks, and two or three sailors from the work detail were sitting on each truck with the bananas, and a petty officer sat in the cab with the driver. In the lead truck sat a lieutenant senior grade, the equivalent to a captain in the Marine Corps, obviously in charge of the detail.

He ran his convoy right to the ramps we had set up for loading. I broke out my grumbling marines but could not help noticing how green the bananas were. Emerald green. Grass green. Not a speck of yellow on them.

Walking up to the lieutenant, saluting him in my best manner, I said, "Sir, I am sorry we cannot take on these bananas. They are green."

"I have hauled fifteen people off liberty to pick up these damn things," the lieutenant replied, "and you are not going to take them? Who in hell are you?"

I showed him all my paperwork documenting that I was official and in charge, but he said, "No damn marine sergeant is going to tell me what color these bananas are!" And you could see that the sailors sitting on the trucks, listening to our conversation, were getting upset too. The lieutenant was about to issue a command to his men to carry the bananas on board the ship. Meanwhile, my guys, who had been held off liberty to wait for these bananas, quickly sized up the situation and realized that maybe they would not have to work after all since the bananas were clearly anything but ripe and might, therefore, not have to be unloaded. We were suddenly faced with one of those wonderful conflicts you occasionally encounter in the military. I continued to hold my ground while the lieutenant became more and more apoplectic. At last he demanded to talk to somebody with more authority than I had. At that moment on the USS *Breckinridge*, the only officer on duty was the officer of the deck, who, when a ship is docked, is usually a low-ranking ensign or, at most, a lieutenant junior grade. We dug him up, and I reported to him the orders I had from the mess officer.

What saved me from his full wrath was the fact that on the requisition, which the lieutenant in charge himself had in hand, was the specific notation that the bananas had to be ripe. That notation was in place because our mess officer had thought there was no way that in the remaining days of sailing between Cristobal and Norfolk green bananas would ripen enough to eat. He probably had in mind to have a big banana-fest on soft golden bananas as soon as we left Cristobal.

Fortunately, since the memo about ripe bananas was clearly written on the requisition, the *Breckinridge* officer of the deck fully backed me up, and the entire banana convoy had to turn around and rumble back, which, of course, meant that the poor, hapless sailors had to eventually unload all the bananas they had just loaded onto the trucks. My marines, on the other hand, bid the departing trucks a fond adieu. As soon as I had secured all the other items we had taken on board the ship, man, I declared liberty call for all hands. By that time, it was probably close to five o'clock, but we still had liberty until midnight.

A humorous addendum to that story deals with that old and very senior chief in charge of all mess operations who wanted to go fishing. When he went to get his fishing equipment after leaving the ship, he must have encountered some whisky somewhere. Just as I, dressed up for liberty, was leaving ship, here came the old chief, well equipped with his fishing pole and a pail with some bait in it, staggering down to the wharf. He was so intoxicated that he could not walk a straight line, and he wobbled back and forth from side to side, lurching to the edge of the dock. I don't think he fell in, but I don't think he caught any fish, either.

I went ashore to a big dance at the USO with lots of lovely young ladies, our hostesses, and had a great time in Cristobal. We were all feeling good because now we were only a few days from home. Those days passed quickly.

We arrived on the thirtieth of September or the first of October 1946, sailing through the mouth of the Chesapeake Bay into the Norfolk harbor. Through a flurry of activity, we cruised through that beautiful point where the Chesapeake Bay enters the Atlantic Ocean. It became readily apparent that the reason why our ship had sailed through the Panama Canal to the East Coast was that most of the passengers on this ship were marines from the East Coast.

We landed in Norfolk, probably at the same dock from which we had sailed on the *Wakefield* almost a year earlier. Our docking was not very elegant or efficient and almost produced a disaster. In retrospect, I think that the problems were likely caused by the lack of qualified sailors aboard the navy tugs guiding us into the wharf.

We turned into the dock from the river bow first. As we rotated, one of the tugs at the stern continued pushing us around the turn, so that we ended up between the wharf where we were going to tie up and the wide body of water, almost coming in sideways. That would have been bad enough in itself, but what that meant was that the stern of the *Breckinridge* began bearing down rapidly on a small destroyer escort tied up at the adjoining wharf. There was panic all around. The skipper of the destroyer escort had been alerted, and he emerged screaming and yelling and gesticulating wildly. The sailors on the *Breckinridge* manning the lines to the tugs, in preparation to manning the lines to tie up at the dock, were yelling and screaming and gesticulating at the tugboat captain to stop pushing us. It was a fiasco of the first order, with all hell breaking loose. At long last, the tug stopped and reversed engines to slow us down. The *Breckinridge* swung all the way around, gently tapping the destroyer escort, at which point the tugs got us straightened out, and we eventually came in parallel to the wharf and tied up. This may have been an even more ignominious way to return to the United States than my falling on my face as I entered China.

We were divided up into groups to Philadelphia, Camp Lejeune, or Quantico Marine Corps Base. We had to find our name on a roster to determine where we were being sent. I hoped it would be Quantico for me. No such luck. I was going back to beautiful Camp Lejeune, the place to which I would be returning for many years thereafter.

There was a cluster of maybe several hundred civilians waiting on the dock, waving and greeting us as we arrived. Even though I knew that my own family would not be waiting for me, it was nice to see the welcoming crowd.

We gathered up all our gear and filed out, were mustered several times, and then roll was called. The train came right onto the dock, and we walked off the ship onto the train to Lejeune. It was the same line I had taken on my way up to China. In broad daylight, the troop train proceeded right down the center of the main street of Washington, North Carolina, where strolling civilians waved us on.

We arrived at Camp Lejeune to more roll calls and the division of people into various groups. Along with about four hundred of us, I was marched, carrying all my gear, including the seabag and field transport pack, to barracks close to the center of the main base, then called the Second Area. All Camp Lejeune brick barracks in those days were set up in the H form. In the center of the H lived all senior noncommissioned officers. In the wings were two floors of long squad bays, each holding about one hundred men. As soon as we arrived, a staff sergeant called my name, and it turned out that I was to be his right-hand man and troop handler for a four-hundred-person detail of privates and PFCs being processed for discharge. We had to get medical exams and had to get our uniforms checked by the supply center in the industrial area of the camp to make sure that they were up to snuff. Next, we had to go through the inevitable mustering-out administrative paperwork procedure, climaxed by the payment of whatever the government owed each marine, along with the official presentation of our honorable discharge and the freedom to go wherever we wished to go. My main task was to call the roll and march the troops, as no marines were to move around the base, except in marching formation.

Experienced military persons will understand that a unit of four hundred men, marching four abreast and a hundred men long, is not an easy-sized unit to march. The guys in front will march to cadence. But by the time the speed of sound carries the cadence along a long line of people to the back row, the delay will likely create a wavy line. We marched to breakfast, lunch, and supper, and we had to march from the barracks to each of the stations for the discharge process. It was a good hike, and I was able to acquire further experience in marching troops.

It had been explained to me by the staff sergeant that I would go all the way through the process and then get myself processed for discharge too. That sounded pretty good to me, as the process took only about four days.

I immediately plunged into leading my first group. I called roll every morning; marched the men to breakfast; called the roll; marched them through the various phases in the industrial area, the medical exam, and, finally, the administrative offices where their discharges were prepared and their mustering-out pay was calculated for their final payoff.

It was a pleasant task. In a discharge center, senior noncommissioned officers rarely had any disciplinary problems. Naturally, every one of the men was quite ready to get out, and in no way did anyone wish to mess up his discharge. Nobody ever questioned anything I said, and that was a most delightful experience in itself.

Only once did I have a minor problem. We were falling out in the morning in preparation for marching for breakfast, and I was calling the roll. Suddenly a guy, so overcome with joy about getting out of the Marine Corps, ran to a tree, climbed up on it like a monkey, and whooped out, "I'm getting out, I'm getting out!" It was during morning hours, so I don't think he was drunk.

I approached the tree and looked up at him, and he shouted down to me, "Sergeant, I am so happy I am leaving!"

I told him sternly, "Now look, if you don't get out of that tree now, then you are not going to get discharged." And he scrambled down that tree trunk, quick as a flash, with unsurpassed exuberance and agility.

One of the phases of the discharge process was the shakedown. Each man was required to take everything he had brought with him from China out to a paved old unused tennis court and empty out his seabag on his blanket to be carefully examined by an officer. At the same time, the barracks were also very carefully examined to make sure that nothing had been hidden there. The Marine Corps did not want us to leave the service with any contraband articles, particularly weapons.

On one of my details being shaken down, a lieutenant had just finished with one guy, telling him to pack everything back up again. Before packing the heavy canvas seabag, it was customary to bang it on the ground in order to flatten the bottom so that the bag would stand upright and be ready to receive the items to be placed inside.

Having passed inspection, a marine, with apparent relief, bounced his seabag on the cement surface of the court, which produced a sharp clinking sound. The lieutenant had already turned around and stepped away to inspect the next fellow, but the sound caught his attention.

"What was that?" the lieutenant asked our hapless guy. It became quickly apparent that he had, in his spare hours in Tianjin or on board ship, done some tricky tailoring work on his seabag. He had inserted one bag inside another. Between the two bags, he had very carefully quilt-stitched a detail-stripped Japanese Nambu machine gun. It must have taken him days to sew the two seabags together. He carefully quilted around each machine gun part so that they would not be hitting against each other. After that, he had packed the inner seabag with his regular gear, being careful not to overstuff it so that the outline of the parts did not create a bulge on the outside. He dealt with the problem of camouflaging the barrel of the gun so that the bulge was on the inside of his bag. In spite of the magnificent piece of sewing work, he must have missed a stitch somewhere, which produced the unfortunate sound of two pieces of gun metal hitting against each other when the seabag was plopped on the hard surface of the ground.

Naturally, the lieutenant made our marine rip out all the beautiful stitchery connecting the two bags and place on the blanket each gleaming piece of the Japanese Nambu gun. This full machine gun was a beautiful weapon in mint condition, except for a missing stock, which could have been easily made in the United States. It is hard to describe the look of utter desolation on that marine's face. The system proved to be too good.

After my group was processed, I got myself dressed in my best uniform, all slicked up, for my honorable discharge and payoff. Behind a long table in the discharge center sat a lieutenant with some sergeants, surrounded by stacks of beautiful, suitable-for-framing honorable discharge diplomas from the United States Marine Corps.

A sergeant major looked up at me. "Oh yes, Van Sant," he said. "Now here is your discharge." And he picked it up, held it up, and, just as I reached for it, he snatched it back and tore it up.

"What are you doing, Sergeant Major? That's my discharge!" I said, distressed.

"Sergeant," he said calmly, "we have a tremendous shortage of qualified noncommissioned officers. You are being held in the Marine Corps COG."

"Sergeant," I asked, completely mystified, "what is COG?"

"Convenience of the Government," he replied. "It's perfectly legal, and there is nothing you can do about it. Go back to your barracks. We will give you a call in a little while and give you new orders."

When I returned to the barracks, I found myself in charge. It had become my barracks. Soon I was told to go down to the bus station in the morning to meet a whole new convoy of buses. I was to pick up the men, march them to my barracks, and, "You know the process, take them through the procedure and, maybe, at the end of this group, we might be able to discharge you with them," I was informed.

Since I had notified my parents of my discharge, they and my sister were excited to hear that George was coming home. Only, now I had to call them back and tell them there had been a change in plans because the Marine Corps was keeping me, COG.

The group I picked up next morning was not too large, probably about a couple of hundred people. I took them through the four-day processing.

When it came time for me to pick up my discharge, it was torn up again, though with perhaps the mildest hint of sympathy on the part of the sergeant major. I called home again and told my family, "I'll tell you what. I won't call you again until I know I am out, COG."

Presuming to be a United States Marine

I picked up a third group, and this time I managed to get myself discharged with them. When I walked out, the precious paper clutched tightly in my hand, a young taxi driver walked up to me, asking if I knew anybody going to Union Station in Washington DC.

I found some other marines, in addition to myself, who needed a ride there. The taxi driver told us, "I have a brand-new Ford here. I'll take five of you to DC for $15 apiece. I will only stop for gas, and you can run to get something to eat and go to the john. We will not stop for anything else, and I will guarantee to get you there in six hours, by 9:30 p.m." That sounded awfully good to us, although I had no time to call home first. The vehicle must have been one of the first Fords off the assembly line after the war. Five of us piled in, having first stuffed our seabags and packages into the trunk of the big car.

Not surprisingly, this six-hour trip to DC became one of the most amazing automobile trips I have ever taken in my life. While our taxi man was a good, observant driver, who never speeded recklessly, he preferred driving at one hundred miles per hour, whenever he deemed it to be safe. His car could do it, held down nicely by the driver, five marines, and all our seabags. That vehicle must have been about four inches above the ground. And speaking of ground, we did cover it!

For those of you who were not around then, or are not familiar with the area, in 1946 there were no interstate highways, or even four-lane highways in Eastern North Carolina. There really was not even a good state highway system. The two-lane roads were actually pretty awful, although not winding much on the relatively flat landscape, and with very little traffic.

We flew across Carolina, up the route to Scotland Neck, over to Route 301, and up Route 301, and on to Petersburg and Richmond, Virginia, from where we took Route 1 North.

We stopped about halfway through the trip to gas up and were given exactly three minutes to relieve any calls of nature, including those for food. This regimen worked well with us, as we were very much accustomed to being pushed.

It had become pitch-dark and we had crossed the Virginia/North Carolina border when, from a side road on the left, an ambulance with blaring siren and flashing lights approached. Our driver became ecstatic. "Boy," he said, "now we can really start making some time by getting behind him!"

Politely, our driver slowed down to let the ambulance precede him, and then pulled in behind it. The ambulance passed everything in the road, and we stayed right behind it. But the ambulance settled down to a nice, steady eighty miles per hour. Our cabdriver, I could tell, was getting frustrated. After several miles of this progress at a mere eighty, our foiled driver pulled around it and passed it. Well ahead of the rescue vehicle, we settled back into our regular one-hundred-miles-per-hour routine, pulling into Union Station at precisely 9:30 p.m. by the big clock at the station. Within a minute or two, we had all dispersed in different directions. At home, I was received with great joy, particularly by my father, whom I had not seen in over two years. After a few days,

Taking on the Burden of History

I was able to brag about being a marine at some of my old high school hangouts, ever conscious of the pall hanging over all my joy. There was no Margaret in my life this time, because she planned to get married that coming February.

I returned to Annapolis to visit my friends at St. John's College, which I found in a state of some considerable change. The founders of the New Program, Stringfellow Barr and Scott Buchanan, were both gone, which was a shock to the institution. I had a meeting with the new dean, Jack Neustadt, who asked me, "Well, are you coming back?" I could only tell him that I was still debating it. He said, "Then let's get out your records."

In those days, the official records were kept in a gigantic ledger. During the formal convocation, after I had enrolled in July of 1943, I had placed my signature at the very top of the first page of my record. The registrar had then very carefully lined out and written in by hand all the courses I had taken under the program with the grades I had received. I sat beside the dean as we looked through the ledger together. When we reached, particularly, my last term before leaving for the Marine Corps, it appeared that my academic achievement was something of a disaster.

Dean Neustadt looked at me and asked, "What happened here?" My record through my freshman and my sophomore years had been pretty good. When I started on the junior year work, not only were so many students leaving for the service, but I knew that I would be leaving myself. No doubt, the constant parties were not conducive to serious studying, either.

The dean said, "When you return in January, why don't you pick up in the second term of your junior year? If you do that, we'll expunge the term you have allegedly already taken from your record." I thought that was pretty generous of him and promised I would think about it.

There was another new factor in my decision-making process. While in China, my father had become a good friend of a Chinese college president. Not only did this man offer my father the job as chairman of the economics department of Huachung University (now in Wuhan, a combination of the cities of WuChang and Hankow), but he laid the groundwork with the National Council of the Episcopal Church to have both my parents return to China. My mother was to teach English at St. Hilda's, an Episcopal girl's school connected with Huachung. This joint appointment was very exciting for them, and they had already signed their contracts. They were preparing to sail to China, a country they both loved, in the summer of 1947.

After serious consideration about a career in the Marine Corps, I decided in the end that I needed to finish my education at St. John's after the Christmas break. I remembered the arguments raised in the discharge center that I should at least enlist in the Marine Corps Reserve to preserve my sergeant's stripes. An old administrative captain at the center had told me, "I haven't got the time to look it up, but I really believe that you may be the youngest sergeant in the Marine Corps. You ought to preserve those stripes, son!" He had added, "You are nineteen years old. If you don't enlist in the reserve, you will probably be eligible for the draft, if there is another war. In that case, of course, you would have to go through Parris Island again."

Presuming to be a United States Marine

That did it! The thought of having to endure Parris Island once more was entirely unthinkable, utterly out of the question. After all, it was now November of 1946. Winston Churchill had already made his iron curtain speech, and it was clear that the world was far from being at peace.

I celebrated Thanksgiving and Christmas with my family. It was a special and wonderful time for me, and I had a great deal of fun with my sister. She was older now, and we could embark on all kinds of different little adventures together.

Right after Christmas, I went to the same recruiting station in Washington DC where I had first enlisted eighteen months before, and reenlisted in the U.S. Marine Corps Reserve for four more years as a sergeant. In those days, there were two kinds of reserves. To be in the organized reserve, I would have to join a unit somewhere and participate in a drill one night a week, as well as two full weeks in the summer. In the volunteer reserve, all I had to do was, without fail, to keep the Marine Corps informed as to my exact whereabouts. In return, the Corps would preserve my rank and seniority. My name would be placed on the mailing list for several publications so that I would be kept abreast and informed of all opportunities in the Marine Corps. I had the option of transferring from the volunteer reserve to the organized reserve at any time.

Remembering the academic demands placed on a student at St. John's, I knew there was no way I could be going to a drill one night a week and taking two weeks off in the summer. That just was not in the cards. I decided to enlist in the volunteer reserve. On January 3, 1947, a captain swore me into the Marine Corps for four more years, until January of 1951. This was my last immediate contact with the Marine Corps for some time, although I kept them steadfastly informed about my many places of residence during the next few years. Since the draft was still in effect, I also had to register with the Hyattsville, Maryland, Draft Board, who eventually hounded me all the way to Korea.

We might call my return to St. John's "the education of George Van Sant," a series of stories perhaps saved for another time.

Time moves forward approximately three and a half years after my return from China. The date is June 25, 1950. I find myself driving north on U.S. Route 301, just over the border of Caroline and Hanover counties in Virginia. I am driving a brand-new Plymouth convertible, the top is down, it is a bright day, a great day to be driving a convertible.

By this time, I had graduated from college in 1948 and had spent almost a year and a half in New York, where I met and married Shirley, a lovely, luminescent young woman with blond hair, blue eyes, and a droll sense of humor. After almost eighteen months of financial struggles in New York, St. John's offered me a job in the college's administration, and Shirley and I had rented an apartment in Annapolis. I had become the manager of the college's bookstore and the director of the print shop at the very beginning of what was later to become the St. John's College Press. While I was low on the administrative totem pole, my earnings kept body and soul together.

Taking on the Burden of History

On this day in 1950, I was just returning from Richmond, where I had taken a man named Harvey Poe. Harvey, whose life had been turned upside down by the war, was a tutor and assistant dean at St. John's. He had been awarded a Rhodes Scholarship when he graduated from the University of Virginia before the outbreak of World War II but had been unable to take it as he immediately joined the navy. He had a distinguished career fighting in the Pacific. After the war, he had come to St. John's for a year, sharing an apartment with a man named Winfrey Smith, who ultimately became dean at St. John's. It was Winfrey's big car I had used to drive Harvey Poe, a collateral descendant of Edgar Alan Poe, to Richmond, on his way to Oxford, England, to begin his Rhodes Scholarship work.

Now I was driving the car back to its owner. The time was a little after twelve noon. I was on a stretch of Route 301 running from the Hanover County border to a point just south of Bowling Green in Caroline County. The road was absolutely straight for a number of miles, although it gently dipped and rose from time to time as it progressed through deep woods, with very little civilization in evidence in those days.

With great pleasure, I listened to lovely music on the radio. The sun was brilliant, the air was soft, and a light breeze ruffled my hair.

This idyll was suddenly interrupted by a voice over the broadcasting system. "We are sorry to interrupt this program. North Korea has invaded South Korea, crossing the 38th Parallel line. Heavy fighting is taking place north of Seoul. President Truman has been advised. We are awaiting further developments."

The air around me abruptly turned harsh. The bright sunlight dimmed. Come the following January, I was slated to get my final discharge from the Marine Corps. Oh, I still loved the Corps, as I always will, being proud of serving in it. Now, though, other good things beckoned. I had, at that point, begun thinking of continuing my education in graduate school.

I will apologize for the language I used after the announcement. I simply said to nobody in particular, "Oh shit!" because I could see what was coming. I returned to Annapolis in a somber and subdued state.

My wife, Shirley, was not in good health by that time. In fact, she had been in and out of a couple of hospitals and was being attended by several doctors in Annapolis, who were trying to come up with a diagnosis of her illness. Now a new worry had been added to my worries about her.

In the subsequent weeks, the Marine Corps called up all their organized reserve units and announced that the entire volunteer reserve was going to be called up. That meant me.

It was decided that Shirley, with her health problems, would best be served by returning to her home in Pittsburgh to stay with her parents, until it became clear what was to happen to me in the military.

In the meantime, the Marine Corps, bless their hearts, were keeping me steadily informed about all kinds of things, but primarily the fact that I needed to stand by for orders. I was also sent information about a program instituted in 1950. Anybody who had been discharged as a noncommissioned marine officer, a corporal or above, and had graduated from college after the war, could apply for a direct commission as a second lieutenant. The reasoning, I would assume, was that if you made it to the rank of a noncommissioned officer, you must have met Marine Corps standards, and by obtaining a college diploma, you had also met its education standards.

I immediately sent off my application for the program. Time went by, without my hearing anything from the Marine Corps. Years later, I learned why that had been the case. Long before the New Program came in at St. John's in 1937, the college had fallen on such rocky financial times that accrediting agencies had taken away its accreditation. St. John's decided the priority was to first get the New Program well established. By 1950, the application for re-accreditation was in, and it was granted a year or so later. The college, with its unique academic program, has been a fully accredited institution ever since. The unusual record of its graduates and their successes in various graduate and professional programs has been so enormous that accrediting agencies would look rather silly if they ever decided to withhold accreditation from this exceptional school.

But in the summer of 1950, all I knew was that I wanted to get a commission, and the Marine Corps, without any explanation, would not give it to me.

When I received my orders to report in early September, I found out that, having been a noncommissioned officer in World War II, I could take two steps. First, I could take the Graduate Record Examination, which would serve to establish the equivalency of a college diploma; and, second, if recommended by my unit, I could be sent through Officer Candidate Screening.

But I was called back as Sergeant Van Sant. My MOS, or military occupational specialty, was machine gun noncommissioned officer, 0335.

Chapter 6

BACK TO CAMP LEJEUNE (1950-1951)

I got myself down to Union Station to once again board a train bound for Camp Lejeune. Before reporting there, my cousin Marjorie, a newly married registered nurse working in Washington at the time, invited me to a lovely dinner to bid adieu to my civilian life. My sister and parents were trapped in communist China, and I had not heard from them directly since early 1949.

I had put a very sick Shirley on a plane at the Washington National Airport to fly back to Pittsburgh. She hemorrhaged during that flight and had an ambulance waiting for her at the Pittsburgh airport. Our Annapolis doctors, who had been floundering around trying to come up with a diagnosis, had overlooked the obvious. Shirley had tuberculosis. By the time it was diagnosed in Pittsburgh, she was very seriously ill. She was immediately hospitalized and subsequently placed in a sanatorium.

On my last day of civilian life, I was making arrangements about how to pay for the sanatorium. Shirley took up residence in late September of 1950 and remained there until her death a year later, on October 2, 1951.

The scene at Camp Lejeune was a familiar one to all of us—literally thousands of recalled reserves. We were taken into barracks, given physical exams, and taken to the quartermaster to be issued new uniforms. Next, we went to classification and assignment. In classification, we sat down with a thoughtful young corporal or sergeant, who wanted to know everything there was to know about our civilian skills. Subsequently, he would make elaborate recommendations about our assignments in keeping with our impressive qualifications. After that, we walked through a door to the assignment room, where we sat down with a gnarled old gunnery sergeant making the actual assignment.

I was trying to dope the system out as I was talking to the classification guy, and he was such a nice young man, very well educated, you could tell. I was wracking my brains about how I could contribute to the welfare of the Marine Corps by utilizing all my skills. I came up with, "Look, I have managed a bookstore. I have had experience in the retail trade, and I think that work in the post exchange would be just the thing for me."

Presuming to be a United States Marine

At this stage of my emotional and Marine Corps development, I wasn't really that gung-ho for action. I was, first of all, worried about Shirley's health. I did not really want to go to Korea, to tell the unvarnished truth.

That fine classification guy had filled an entire sheet with notes, had checked off a great number of boxes, and had managed to convince me that, surely, I would ride out my period of military service working in the PX, and no question about that.

I took my record book with all the handwritten notations inside it to the gunnery sergeant in the Assignment Office. He never looked beyond the cover, which had "Sergeant George M. Van Sant, MOS 0335, machine gun noncommissioned officer" clearly written on it. He never cracked the record book open.

The gunny looked at the cover and said, "Second Division needs people like you. Sixth Marines." I tried to say, "Sergeant, look at all the notes in the book—," but he interrupted. "Nah! We need machine gun NCOs." And that was that. I returned to my barracks for one more night to be sorted out the next morning.

Periodically in my Marine Corps career, I have been awestruck with admiration at the efficiency of the Corps. When things are working right and everybody does their job right, the Marine Corps can pull off feats of organization that boggle the mind. This day at Camp Lejeune, I was a witness to one such feat. I want to emphasize that there were literally thousands of marines, all just recalled from civilian life, who had to be sorted through various points, put in trucks, and hauled hither, thither, and yon with their gear. This was the age before computers, remember.

I found myself at a barracks with 220 other enlisted men and seven officers. Although there were some people who must have known each other, since the Marine Corps is relatively small, most of us had never seen each other. One by one, each squad of each rifle platoon was laid out.

The Marine Corps has something called the Table of Organization, or structure for setting up a unit. For every job in the Marine Corps, there has to be a military occupation specialty, and there has to be a rank.

A perfect rifle company was formed with those of us who had been recalled. We had every man a rifle company should have. Everybody was in the right billet, with the right rank and with the right experience and military occupation specialty, right down to the last man.

A machine gun sergeant in the Marine Corps Table of Organization at that time was a squad leader. There were two squads in each machine gun section, and the machine gun section was commanded by a staff sergeant. There were three sections, so there was a total of six squads. The six squads were commanded by buck sergeants, and the three sections by staff sergeants. The machine gun platoon sergeant was a gunnery sergeant, a five-striper. The number one gunner, the man who actually fired the gun, was a corporal, and the number two gunner was a private first class. There were five ammunition carriers in each machine gun squad, either privates or PFCs, and they were number one, two, three, four, and five. As time passed, they worked their way up from last ammo carrier to first.

167

Taking on the Burden of History

In China, we never had the requisite number of corporals, sergeants, and staff sergeants, but as this particular unit of the Sixth Marines was organized in 1950, we had a perfect rifle company, right down to the last gnat's eyebrow. That meant that as a sergeant, I was now a squad leader.

We were billeted by unit in pretty crowded squad bays and marched off to chow. The food was terrible. In fact, that whole fall of 1950, when the Marine Corps mobilized its entire reserve, I have to say that the food in the mess halls was unspeakably bad. Once, when I took a work detail into the mess hall, I was able to gain some insight into the poor quality of the food. The meat we broke out of the freezer, as the date stamp on it clearly showed, had been frozen in 1944. To make matters worse, some of the butchers and cooks called in from the reserve had clearly lost their finer culinary skills in the interim.

All the meats, in fact, were mystery meats. We were given meat every night, but while chewing on it, we gained no significant insight into the species from which it had been butchered. One day, word came out from the mess hall that we were going to have steak that night. I slapped my tray down eagerly to receive my steak. I found myself gazing at a sphere not unlike a flying saucer with a gently tapering fringe all around its perimeter. While the center was possibly still alive, the tiny fringes on the outside were cooked to a crisp and had the consistency of old shoe leather. But I digress.

We immediately began rigorous training in our various specialties, and thanks to my scholarly work as a machine gun noncommissioned officer in China, I was probably among the most academically knowledgeable machine gunners in the platoon. We had guys who had fired machine guns on Guadalcanal, but I had the book learning, at least.

My unit was F Company, Second Battalion, Sixth Marines. The Sixth Marines had been completely reorganized from scratch. Our regimental commander was Colonel Buse, a name I recognized from China. Our paths would cross a number of times in future years.

There were some interesting marines in my machine gun squad. My number one gunner, Corporal Nadeau, from Messina, New York, was of French Canadian extraction. He was a lively and witty fellow who often raised our morale with his stories. The number two gunner, Flanagan, was a real veteran. He had gone through the entire Okinawa campaign as a machine gunner. Unfortunately, he had been caught up in the same promotion drought that had caught my friend Boatsman. Flanagan's rank upon recall was as a private first class. Flanagan was from Poughkeepsie, New York, where he had held down a good job as a machinist with IBM for the five previous years. We were all most impressed with IBM's policies with respect to their employees recalled for Korea by the armed services. For starters, the company immediately assumed all the costs of Flanagan's mortgage. In addition, for the duration of his service, IBM made up the difference between his military pay and the pay Flanagan had been earning at IBM. Since he was only a PFC and had received much higher pay during the five years he had worked for IBM, this difference was considerable. It meant that he did not have to worry about his wife and young children back home. This policy was in sharp contrast with the situations of many of the other low-ranking men who had been called up. Many of them were relative newlyweds who had taken on large obligations, such as mortgages and car loans, and now found themselves with a paycheck of $100 per month. As I was married, I could draw my quarters allowance, but all of it, and a healthy chunk of the rest of my pay, had been placed in an allotment to Shirley's TB sanatorium. This situation called for various coping skills.

One young lad by the name of Cooper, a rifleman in our squad bay, had been married three days before reporting to the Marine Corps for duty. He spent a good deal of his pay on long and, at least in our collective considered opinion, moony and drippy collect calls to his new bride. He must have spent an hour a day writing to her and relentlessly hounded the mail clerk for incoming letters from her.

There was a very clear split between the married men in the outfit and the unmarried when it came to liberty practices. For the single marine there were a number of colleges in Eastern North Carolina where they could take their chances on meeting suitable young women. For the more earthily inclined, there were numerous fleshpots within about an hour's drive around Camp Lejeune. Many of the single marines and, alas, a very few of the married ones, especially the ones who were a little older, often visited these hot spots. The great majority of us married marines, I am happy to say, spent our liberties looking for good food and, perhaps, a few good drinks.

One day Cooper, our newlywed, along with some of his married buddies, decided to have his picture taken by a professional photographer in Jacksonville. This particular photo man had a stock of Marine Corps dress blues of various sizes in his studio, and Cooper proudly had his formal portrait taken in dress blues. He selected the best shot and shipped it off to his loving wife as a present from her ever-loving husband. Unfortunately, the photographer, in the final printing, had reversed the negative. Cooper still looked fine and resplendent in his blues, but in the reverse print, his wedding ring appeared to be on the ring finger of his right hand. Mrs. Cooper, the sweet young thing, immediately noticed it and jumped to the conclusion that Cooper, out on a wild liberty picking up girls, had switched his wedding ring in order to appear single. She wrote him an accusatory letter; hung up when he tried to call her; and, in general, carried on furiously. Cooper was in despair. In order to appease his wife, I remember, poor old Cooper had to get a notarized statement from the photographer admitting his mistake.

As vigorously as we trained in that long fall of 1950, we were given fairly frequent liberty, even during the week. I established the habit of going out with two other sergeants. One of these was Sergeant McCauley, a bus driver from Scranton, Pennsylvania. McCauley was older and wiser than most of us. He had enlisted in the Marine Corps in 1938 and had been a machine gunner at Guadalcanal, New Britain, and Peleliu. He had been wounded once, but not badly. After Peleliu, he had been sent back to the States and had been a drill instructor at Parris Island from late 1944 until he got out in the early fall of 1945. McCauley was devoted to his wife and not interested in any fleshpots.

The other sergeant was John Sclavas, who was of Greek parentage. His father owned an elegant restaurant south of Wilmington, Delaware. Sclavas was younger than McCauley but had seen a couple of years service during World War II, most of it stateside and in the Caribbean. He was a good machine gunner who, like me, had never fired a machine gun in anger. John had become engaged before returning to duty and he too was not interested in any fleshpots.

I recently looked John up. The engagement had culminated in a very happy marriage and produced seven children. John and his wife were about to celebrate their fiftieth wedding anniversary. After inheriting the restaurant, John kept it going for many years. Having taken up portrait painting as a young man, he kept up his art with great success.

We three sergeants explored Jacksonville and Wilmington, North Carolina, as well as other surrounding communities, looking for good food. In those days, there was not an abundance of decent restaurants, but we managed to find what there was to find in culinary pleasure.

On several occasions, when the news from Shirley's doctors was not good, these sergeants provided me with much appreciated and stalwart support. We had many laughs and, as a rule, drank only moderately, although on one occasion, Sclavas overindulged on a weekend visit back to Delaware. He fell out on Monday morning for inspection in his full dungaree field uniform, paired with the shiny black pumps he had worn the night before. He had apparently driven back all night from a lively weekend with his fiancee. While this getup troubled Lieutenant Quirk, our platoon leader, Sclavas managed to survive the debacle.

Sometime late in November, or early in December 1950, we had our regimental inspection performed by our regimental commander, Colonel Robert Buse. Our company was lined up in the typical formation, company online, platoons online, at open ranks. Just before the colonel arrived, Lieutenant Quirk had conceived a brilliant idea. He had us all take off our duty belts, the canvas belt that carried our carbine magazine pouches, our first-aid packets, and our canteens. Then we were ordered to take up our belts by one notch. This exercise, in Lieutenant Quirk's mind, was intended to cinch in our guts by two inches, thus throwing out our chests, and considerably sharpening up our appearance for Colonel Buse's inspection.

The colonel, accompanied by our company commander, arrived, completed his inspection of all the rifle platoons, and approached the machine gun platoon. Lieutenant Quirk, standing in front of us, reported the platoon ready for inspection, and was asked by the colonel to accompany him. The inspection party formed with the lieutenant preceding the colonel, followed by Captain McNulty, the company commander. The trio wheeled up in front of our platoon guide, who sharply presented his carbine for inspection. The colonel declined to take the weapon and rapidly moved in front of the next man to the guide's left, our section staff sergeant, not taking his weapon either. As the squad leader of the first squad of the first section, I was next in line. Unprepared, because of the colonel's unexpected speed, I was a bit hurried in my performance of Inspection Arms. This maneuver with a WWII-Korea vintage carbine was a pretty awkward maneuver at best. The magazine had to be removed from the weapon and smartly stuffed behind the duty belt. The carbine's bolt was to be slid back and locked into the open position, the magazine retrieved from the belt, and the weapon, held by the small of the stock in the right hand with the magazine flat in the palm of the left hand, was presented to the inspecting officer.

As I hastily went through the procedure, and no thanks to Lieutenant Quirk's misguided attempt at sharpening us up, the magazine, stuff it in as hard as I might, would not fit behind my super tight belt. With a last desperate effort, I at last managed to stick it in partially, hastily slid back my bolt—by this time, the colonel was already standing before me—and reached for my magazine. Alas, with a *pop!* the magazine, powerfully squeezed by my cinched belt, catapulted out and landed on the ground in front of me.

What followed next would rival any well-directed, well-rehearsed circus clown, Three Stooges or Marx Brothers routine. At precisely the same time, Colonel Buse and Captain McNulty both swiftly leaned over to pick up my magazine. Their heads clashed together with a loud crack, which sent them both staggering back, knocking off their hats, and producing involuntary but audible grunts of pain from both.

I stood at a horrified position of attention, as did Lieutenant Quirk, the root cause of this disaster, while the colonel and the captain tried to reassemble their dignity. The colonel had won the retrieval contest and handed me my magazine back. He took my carbine and subjected it to an unusually thorough inspection, while Captain McNulty resumed the position of attention, staring daggers through me. I don't think there were many more times in my life when I so desperately wanted to disappear into thin air.

Through the fall of 1950, my unit was F Company, Second Battalion, Sixth Marine Regiment, a regiment boasting an illustrious history. Along with the Fifth Regiment, it was part of the marine unit that forever earned the title Devil Dogs from the Germans, as a result of a slashing marine attack and occupation of Belleau Wood near Paris in 1918. In 1919 the two regiments were awarded the French fourragere, a corded rope looped over the shoulder of the uniform to be worn by members of the Fifth and Sixth Marines forever.

We in the Sixth Marines were part of the Second Marine Division headquartered at Camp Lejeune. The Second, Eighth, and Tenth regiments did not have fourrageres, so they often greeted us with cries of "Pogey Rope Marines" when we were on liberty. The term "pogey" evolved from a derisive Marine Corps term "pogue." A pogue is a marine who is a slacker, a candy-ass, soft, greedy, and a danger avoider. The greedy part of being a pogue dates back to World War II, when the Sixth Marines managed to get their fourrageres designated as a pogey rope. They had been put on a troopship for transport to the forward jump-off island for the assault on Tarawa, and they are reported to have bought out the entire ship's store supply of candy in a few hours—the only time during the Pacific campaign when a unit managed such a feat.

Taking on the Burden of History

During my service in the Second Battalion, I found out that Dan Stearns was a sergeant in the Third Battalion. I managed a brief reunion with Dan, and we realized that we had both been in China in 1945 and 1946, although in different outfits. It will be remembered that it was Dan's lurid tales of boot camp that had first kindled in me the desire to become a marine.

There were three other Third Battalion lieutenants whom I did not meet at that time. The first was the colorful Lieutenant George Morrison, who will loom large later in this account. The second was Lieutenant Jack Nichols, whom I came to know well when we served together five years later. Nichols was an all-American basketball player from Seattle University. He went on to a stellar career as a member of the old Boston Celtics under Red Auerbach, and held the Celtics rebound record for a number of years.

The last person of note from the Third Battalion, another reserve lieutenant called back for the Korean War, was the gifted, well-known author William Styron. Although I never met him, I must have seen him many times when the two battalions performed functions together. His second major book, *The Long March*, is based on an actual episode in the history of his battalion.

Sometime in November, I was called before a battalion screening board to be interviewed for a determination on whether or not I was fit to be sent to Quantico for Officer Candidate Screening. After these boards, I got hauled out and, over a period of several days, was given the Graduate Record Exam of that time, a comprehensive examination of mathematical and verbal reasoning skills. As I was taking it, I realized that the education I had received at St. John's had given me the very best preparation possible for the successful passing of this exam. Some of my fellow applicants found that various parts of the exam were just Greek to them, but there was nothing in it I had not encountered in my studies at St. John's. An administrative officer (the same one who many years later explained that St. John's at the time of my graduating had not been an accredited college) at Headquarters, Marine Corps, informed me that I had received the second highest marks on the exam of all the marines on the East Coast. Several years later, when I applied to graduate school at the University of Virginia, I did not have to retake the exam. I felt then, and will always feel, an enormous gratitude to the program of St. John's College and its excellent tutors for giving me this advantage. As the various hurdles for Officer Candidate Screening were successfully passed, I was informed that, at some point in the future, I would receive orders to Quantico.

Our unit was sent for Christmas leave in December in two increments. My visit to Pittsburgh was memorable. Shirley had now been in the sanatorium for three months and, for those first months, had seemed to make some progress against the TB. I spent most of my ten-day leave in her private room. We talked, read, and listened to music on her record player. Various good-hearted local citizens came out to the sanatorium and serenaded the patients with Christmas carols. All the wards and hallways were nicely decorated, and we had many tender moments anticipating Christmas. It was to be her last.

Presuming to be a United States Marine

Events in Korea had a strong impact on my situation, both before I went on leave and after I returned. Before my departure, it had been determined that our Second Battalion was to be the Mediterranean float battalion for six months beginning in January or February. For my friends in the company, this was both good and bad news. Since our unit was almost completely composed of recalled reserves, it meant that none of them would be exposed to Korea. That would be good. The bad news was that all the men would be separated from their families for seven to eight months. Because I was already caught up in the Officer Candidate Screening process, and because of the compassion the Corps had for my situation with a wife in a sanatorium, it was determined that I would be transferred to the First Battalion when the Second Battalion shipped out.

When I returned on December 28, all the privates, PFCs, and corporals in the Second Battalion were ordered to pack and report for a flight replacement draft to Korea. The First Division had sustained so many casualties and frostbite victims at the Chosin Reservoir in Korea that fresh marine bodies were needed immediately. Men from our company were loaded aboard buses and transferred to Cherry Point, the nearby marine air base, where they loaded aboard transports and were flown directly to Korea. Sergeants and above and all officers were to remain at Camp Lejeune. New levies of privates were to be sent to the Sixth Marines from the Camp Geiger Infantry Training Unit to be integrated into the float battalion and rapidly trained. The Second Battalion was still slated to go to the Mediterranean sometime in late January, but while its officers and senior noncommissioned officers would be experienced, its troopers were to be raw recruits.

The day after my return from Christmas leave, all the lower ranks left. The barracks were empty as we awaited the new trainees. The chilling word came down that taking the lowest three grades had not produced enough bodies. All sergeants were ordered to pack and report out to the drill field immediately. I wasn't sure about my status but obeyed the order and fell out with the rest of the sergeants. Conflicting emotions filled me. I certainly wanted to do my duty to help the Marine Corps in a tough situation, even if that meant going to Korea. On the other hand, going through Officer Candidate Screening in Quantico would bring me closer to Shirley. I stood there with all my gear and uniforms and waited to see what would happen to me. Over a loudspeaker, a lieutenant began reading off the names of sergeants alphabetically. About a dozen sergeants from the battalion with names beginning from *A* to *C* were called up, loaded aboard trucks at once, and sent to Cherry Point for their flight to Korea. Some minutes later, the lieutenant emerged again and pulled out another couple of dozen of sergeants with names up to the letter *H*. After that there was a long wait. At last the lieutenant returned to tell us that enough bodies had been culled, and we were to go back to our barracks and unpack.

When our large contingent of sergeants had returned to the barracks, we were informed that at 0800 hours the day after the morrow, we were to pick up approximately two hundred men who had completed advanced infantry training after boot camp. We

Taking on the Burden of History

could not go on liberty, and for lack of something better to do, a bunch of us sergeants and staff sergeants started a marathon blackjack game. It began at four o'clock that afternoon and lasted until about eight the next evening, for a total of twenty-eight straight hours of blackjack. I had about $35 on my person when the game began. The stakes were kept relatively low. The maximum bet, I think, was $2. There were six or seven of us playing, and at one point during that time, I may have held as much as several hundred dollars in winnings, although at another point, I was down to the princely sum of 75¢ in the form of three quarters. When we quit, I counted my money. I believe I had netted about $5 for my twenty-eight-hour marathon efforts.

We picked up our new troops, quickly organized them, and a new accelerated training cycle began. This training only lasted about two and a half weeks until mid-January. Then F Company packed up and left for Morehead City, North Carolina, to be loaded out for the Mediterranean. I was transferred to B Company, First Battalion, Sixth Marines. While I was sorry to see my old buddies of over four months go, I was happy not to be cut off from Shirley for the next seven to eight months.

My new outfit—B Company, First Battalion, Sixth Marines—had different policies. The company had created sergeants' quarters by using lockers as a wall in the barracks, so that sergeants lived a relatively segregated life. I had actually enjoyed living with the troops in the Second Battalion. I had the upper bunk, my corporal was in the bunk under me, and my assistant gunner and the ammo man were scattered on the bunks right beside us. We had lived together companionably, communicating freely with one another.

As a section leader in B Company, I had a staff sergeant's job with two squads in an intensive training program. We worked like slaves. One of the sergeants with whom I bunked was a fellow named Shine from a distinguished New York family. His younger brother, G. David Shine, eventually achieved some notoriety working as an assistant to the relentless communist-hunting Senator Joseph McCarthy. When G. David Shine was drafted into the army, Senator McCarthy became disturbed because, as he claimed, Shine was not being treated right by the army. As a consequence, the senator pronounced "all those army people" to be communists who were trying to get back at him personally by taking it out on Shine. But that's another story. Our marine sergeant Shine was a nice fellow.

One day, after we had been sent out to the rifle range to requalify on the rifle, a large tract of pine trees south of the base in Eastern North Carolina was hit by a bad forest fire. Our whole company and another company from the rifle range were mobilized as firefighters. We were loaded up into a convoy of trucks with firefighting tools. We battled the fire for a whole day, and it became a pretty exciting experience, although there is nothing on earth dirtier than firefighting; it is filthy and frightening. My whole section of two squads was designated as an underbrush team for this job. We were dropped off in a sector of the scrub pine forest that had a lot of undergrowth. The tallest trees had not caught fire yet, but the flames were rapidly moving through the dry undergrowth. It was late January or early February, and the ground was covered with dry leaves from the deciduous brushwood. We were equipped with shovels, picks, and forks, as well as beaters the size of welcome mats, made of very heavy flexible rubber, to smother the ground fire.

We formed up a front and charged into the fire. From the back, I was giving heroic commands, "Forward, men! Into the fire!" Then one of my troops said, "Sarge, look over there!"

I looked to the right where he was pointing and saw that the fire was beside us and moving in behind us. Then I looked to the left and saw the fire sneaking up on us from that side. In one awful moment, I realized that we were enveloped on both sides by flames. We beat our way out at the narrowest point of the fire encirclement and lost some of our cockiness about firefighting in the process.

From the time I arrived at Camp Lejeune in late September until March, when I left, I would travel to Pittsburgh on weekends to see Shirley whenever I had the opportunity. We were given liberty on Friday afternoons, usually at 4:30 p.m., and with any luck, I could get a ride to Washington with somebody by helping him pay for the gas.

From DC I would try to get a bus to Pittsburgh. I could make it there by early Saturday morning, spend all my time with Shirley, and leave on Sunday at noon in order to get back to Camp Lejeune. My financial situation at that time was not too grand. After payment to the sanatorium for Shirley's care, what was left to me would be all of about $40 a month. Even in those days, you could not travel with any regularity from Camp Lejeune to Pittsburgh and back on that amount of money.

There were, by necessity, two other expedients I used. One was developing my skills in blackjack. In Baker Company, we organized a small blackjack casino, where "fish" from other units, particularly sailors from the Naval Hospital right next to us, could sometimes be cleaned out. Two things need to be stressed here. First of all, it is hard to cheat at blackjack, and I never cheated; and, with one exception, none of the other men in our group ever cheated. But if you have a good memory, and if you can develop a systematic approach to the game, you can pretty consistently win, particularly playing with people who do not really understand the game. I am not inordinately proud of it, but I think that between October of 1950 and March of 1951, I probably won at least several hundred dollars, which enabled me to continue my frequent trips to the Pittsburgh sanatorium.

The other expedient was hitchhiking. This method of transportation provided me with some very interesting experiences. But by whatever method, these trips were well worth any effort I could muster.

Shirley and I had wonderful weekends together. Her father had bought her a nice record player. Shirley loved music, and we'd listen to it together while we talked. As Shirley was becoming a shadow of her former luminous self, I was all too aware that her illness was progressive.

Some hitchhiking adventures stand out, even now. Once, on my way back to Washington, I was picked up by a soldier, who was giving a ride to a sailor. We were at the edge of Pittsburgh where the Pennsylvania Turnpike turned off. Representing the three services, we had a nice time talking. As we emerged from a tunnel and rounded a curve, we suddenly came upon an upside down battered car blocking both lanes. We were the first vehicle to arrive upon the scene.

Our driver was able to pull his car around the wreck and onto the shoulder. All three of us jumped out, and the soldier walked behind the car to slow down oncoming traffic. The navy man and I ran to the vehicle and were confronted with a most heart-wrenching scene.

The driver, when we finally found him tangled up in a blanket, was a young man. His passengers were obviously his wife and an infant child. They were clearly not people with much money. When the car had rolled over, possibly a number of times, some food supplies had scattered around the inside of the vehicle. A great, big glass jar of milk had shattered, sending lethal flying glass shards all over the inside of the car. The woman and the baby were bleeding. There was blood everywhere. We were able to get the woman out through the broken rear window. Although she had probably been sitting in the front seat, she must have been thrown back in the revolution of the car.

The front seat had no seat covers. A blanket had been used to cover the bare seat. The driver had become so completely entangled in this coverlet that we could only find him by his moans for help. He turned out to be the least hurt. But that poor baby! I'll never know whether the baby pulled through. One of the larger pieces of glass from the bottle had cut off the back of its head, and it was completely covered with blood. The mother was panic-stricken, while the father repeated over and over again, "I don't know what happened!" Neither did we, of course, since we had not seen how the accident had happened. A crowd, mostly of westbound travelers, immediately gathered.

I noticed the heavily dripping stream of gasoline flowing from the gas tank of the overturned car. A lady covered with furs and jewelry waltzed up, wailing "Oh my goodness!" waving a burning cigarette in a long holder near the gas tank. "Lady, put out that cigarette!" I yelled, knocking it out of her hand. She appeared to be quite offended.

The casualties were being taken care of by a doctor from one of the cars stopped behind us. Our army driver told us that he had to get back to his post, indicating that he knew we had to get back as well. I have often wondered how the folks in the overturned vehicle had fared.

On another of my hitchhiking trips, I did not arrive in Washington until suppertime Sunday and had to be back at Camp Lejeune before the final roll call went off at seven o'clock on Monday morning. Again, with no visible means of transportation other than my thumb, I got out on the highway, and people stopped to pick me up. On this particular trip, though, I was never able to get a ride for more than ten or fifteen miles. The entire trip progressed in tiny little increments. While it took time to get out of the car each time, get my thumb back up, and wait for the next driver to stop, I was certainly offered a concatenation of amusing experiences during that one trip.

It was getting pretty late at night, and I was still in Southside, Virginia, with my thumb out, when a guy stopped, saying, "I'm only going a few miles down the road." I assured him that I was grateful for the ride.

Presuming to be a United States Marine

He asked me, "You're in the marines?" When I confirmed this, he said, "Well, I was in the army myself." I asked him, "Were you in the Pacific or in Europe?"

He says, "I was in Europe. I was a truck driver. Did you ever hear about the Remagen bridge?" And that I had. The Remagen bridge was the first bridge across the Rhine River captured by the American forces in the winter of 1944-45. The Germans had wired it to blow up, but something had gone awry, and it did not completely detonate. The Americans were able to get trucks and people across it for almost a week before the bridge finally collapsed.

And my driver told me that he was in such and such a motor transport outfit, and he added, "I drove the first truck across the Remagen bridge." I must say I was really impressed. And the guy let me out, and I was back in the darkness of the road, with my thumb in the air, and finally another guy came along and picked me up.

And, so help me, this is the truth. Our conversation was almost identical to the first one. "You are in the Marine Corps? I was in the army, myself." And he had been in Europe in the war, and he had been a truck driver. Had I ever heard of the Remagen bridge, he asked?

He proudly confided, "Well, I drove the first truck over the Remagen bridge."

"That's interesting," I replied, frankly not as impressed this time around as I had been the time before.

A third guy picked me up, took me about ten more miles. Before setting me down on the road, he revealed to me that he had been a truck driver in the army, and it was he who had driven the first truck over the Remagen bridge.

Separately, I encountered three people in a row, with no intervening vehicles, who had allegedly all driven the first truck across the Remagen bridge. That partially damaged bridge must have been pretty crowded when three trucks drove over it, all abreast. This time I was completely unimpressed.

It was getting to be close to 2:30 a.m. I had barely reached North Carolina and stood in a desolate and lonely spot, worried whether I would be able to make it back in time. After a while, a car stopped. When I approached it, the driver turned on the dome light and handed me a card with information that he was deaf and unable to talk. He gave me a map and pointed to a place about ten miles north of Jacksonville. As this was almost home to Camp Lejeune, I indicated that I would be happy for the ride. We drove on in silence. The man was a good driver in a nice Pontiac. As he drove along, gradually, his speed would increase, and he would drive faster and faster. The wind rushed by as the speedometer showed seventy, eighty, eighty-five miles per hour, and the car began to vibrate. Then he would look down on his speedometer and either take his foot off the accelerator or hit his brakes. He would proceed driving in a more sedate fashion for a while. Invariably, though, the speed would begin creeping up until the vibrations set in. The driver would look startled and slow down again, and so we both survived the trip very well. After a last ride with the driver of another car, I arrived at my company office at Baker (now Bravo) Company. As I walked through the door, the duty noncommissioned officer had just picked up the receiver to call me in late. And that was the narrowest escape I ever had. Because I was being held out for Officer Candidate Screening, I was in a very vulnerable position. That status could be revoked for any infraction. Coming back late from a liberty weekend, in those days, was a pretty serious offense. I might very well have lost a stripe and been demoted to corporal. It was a very close shave.

Most vivid of the seven weeks of service in Baker Company are the memories of field training from Monday morning until Thursday morning or Friday noon. That meant that we slept on the ground most of the time. We had many night tactical problems and slept in foxholes. The reward for all the hard work was that if we returned from the field in the late afternoon on Thursday, we would have evening liberty, followed by liberty from early Friday afternoon until 0700 hours on Monday. This schedule made it possible for me to spend even more time with Shirley.

The combination of the intensive field work and sleeping on the ground meant that I probably did not sleep in my bunk in the sergeants' quarters more than eight times in those seven weeks. A noteworthy fact about the time span of February-March 1951 is that this was one of the rainiest periods ever experienced in East Carolina to that date. It was, of course, a good thing because the early winter had been dry enough to produce the forest fire we had encountered earlier.

During the field training, we accomplished many things. Perhaps most notably how to carry on when miserable, which later stood me in good stead in Korea. My machine gun teaching experience in China began to pay off. The mortar men and the machine gunners, the operators of crew-served weapons, were often split off from the rest of the company to carry on our own training. Our platoon sergeant was a nice gunnery sergeant named Manthey, who joined my battalion a year or so later in Korea. Sergeant Manthey had me explaining the intricacies of advanced gun drill to the whole platoon one morning in the woods. Manthey had marched the platoon off into a little clearing. There, he had ordered us to remove our field marching packs and lay them on the ground in platoon formation. Next, he ordered us to lay our carbines across the packs. Men armed with the M1 Garand rifle, when getting instruction in the woods, normally stacked arms, forming those little triangular clusters of rifles one often sees in pictures. But stacking arms is not possible with the carbine because it has no metal stacking swivel. The sergeant's expedient of placing packs in platoon formation and resting the carbines atop them was often used by experienced NCOs.

I was holding forth enthusiastically, using troops to demonstrate some of the variations on gun drill and, as usual, was completely immersed in my teaching. Then I noticed two new figures approaching from the woods and taking position beside the other NCOs to the rear of my rapt audience of machine gun platoon marines sitting on the ground.

One of the newcomers wore the unmistakable star of a brigadier general, and the other man had a general's aide fourragere. When my lecture/instruction was finished, I directed the men to break down into squads for a practical application run-through in a larger part of the clearing. But first I gave them a ten-minute break. This accomplished,

Presuming to be a United States Marine

I walked back to the gathering of the NCOs and the general's party. In the best DI's tradition from Parris Island about having a firm grasp on the chain of command, I knew the name of the visiting general. Standing beside Gunnery Sergeant Manthey, I saluted smartly. The general greeted me warmly and said, "Fine job of instruction there, Sergeant." I thanked him smartly.

The general addressed two questions to both of us, which, to this day, have somewhat negatively colored my appreciation of him. He first asked what unit we were. Manthey replied, "Machine Gun Platoon, Baker Company, Sixth Marines, sir."

"What battalion is that, Sergeant?" asked the general.

In its 226-year history, and especially after regiments were formed around 1900, companies A, B, and C have always been in the First Battalion, no matter what the regiment. From time to time, there have been D companies in Marine First battalions, but there had never been a B Company in any battalion other than the first. Poor Sergeant Manthey struggled to keep from laughing, but replied briskly, "That's the First Battalion, sir."

I, too, was appalled at the ignorance that lay behind the question and made a great effort to maintain my military demeanor, and then the general dropped his second dumpling of ignorance. This time, his voice contained unmistakable tones of criticism and command displeasure. "Why aren't these weapons at stack arms, Sergeant?"

Any marine of the time, who had been in the Corps even for a few weeks, would have known the difference between the M1 rifle and a carbine. With an admirably straight face, Sergeant Manthey explained the lack of a metal stacking swivel on a carbine. He diplomatically indicated that when troops were armed with carbines, as we were, they were also equipped with field marching packs, and arranging the packs in a platoon formation with the carbine laid across the pack was a widely used expedient throughout the Marine Corps. By this time, the general may have begun to grasp the stupidity of his questions, because he grunted, "Carry on." And, with his faithful aide trotting behind, he disappeared into the woods. When we were sure he was out of earshot, Sergeant Manthey and the other platoon NCOs dissolved into derisive laughter.

On those weeks, when we came out of our foxholes on Thursdays, there was often a good deal of rambunctious behavior in all three rifle companies of the battalion. We really did not have time to pitch a liberty in town, so most of our troops went to the slop chute instead. Privates, PFCs, corporals, and sergeants went to the Sixth Marines Club. Staff sergeants and above went to the base Staff Noncommissioned Officers Club. The Sixth Marines Club was a very nice spacious brick building where about three varieties of one item could be ordered. The single item was ice cold canned beer. Cokes were available for the eight people in the battalion who did not drink beer. Sometime late in February, after a shower and a meal in the mess hall, hundreds of us descended on the club on an early Thursday evening tending, as was usual, to gather in accordance with our unit structure. We Baker Company troops congregated in one corner of the large hall. There were several tables of riflemen from the various platoons, but we the machine gunners, had our own collection of tables.

Taking on the Burden of History

Some guys from one of our company's rifle platoons began creating a large pyramid of empty beer cans. The pyramid grew and grew as we consumed more and more beer, and afterward, the other platoons from Baker were invited to join in the intricate construction.

I don't want to exaggerate, but as the evening wore on, we had to move tables away in order to expand the base of our pyramid. The top of it rose almost to what must have been at least a fifteen-foot ceiling. Marines began to erect human pyramids to permit the little guys in the outfit to place the topmost cans on our extraordinary Baker Company creation. Needless to say, we continued with a ready source of raw material. Men from the other companies in the battalion began noticing our soaring production, and several of them began trying to duplicate our feat. We stood supreme, at least for the time being.

It must be remembered that a beer can pyramid is an inherently unstable structure, and the inevitable happened. Some drunken lout from one of the other companies, probably consumed with jealousy, spontaneously assembled a detail of his fellow unit members, approached our architectural marvel, and kicked a big hunk out of the bottom of it. What ensued was bedlam.

First, the collapse of the pyramid itself was spectacularly noisy and drawn out. Second, the offended members of Baker Company, to a man, rose up and charged the culprits, who had meantime assembled behind their infamous leader. There followed a most violent riot. While about three or four hundred of us were in some stage or another of beer-induced stupor, and aspirations often exceeded actual performance, by my estimation, at least forty fistfights broke out. Chairs, beer cans, and an occasional body went flying through the air, accompanied by lusty cheers, screams, and grunts.

The club was located next to the Regimental Headquarters building. The officer of the day was either called by the club manager, or he may have heard the deafening noise on his own. Through the door appeared a lieutenant with OD armband and duty belt, accompanied by the sergeant of the guard and a couple of scared-looking sentries carrying rifles. The lieutenant shouted "ATTENTION" at the top of his lungs, but the noise level completely overwhelmed his voice. He jumped up on a table, aimed his .45 caliber pistol at the ceiling, and fired—in slow, deliberate style—four shots. By the third shot, the room had become totally hushed and silent. He announced that we were all confined to our barracks. He quickly separated us by unit and had us marched off into the night to our barracks. It was an impressive performance. Later, when I returned to the club, I inspected the ceiling. Sure enough, there were four .45 caliber slugs buried in it. I wonder if they are still there.

Three of us had been pulled from Fox Company, Sixth Marines, and sent to Baker Company for officer screening. One of these two was a rifleman, Corporal Goldstein from New York. The other was Staff Sergeant Matson from Texas, section leader of the 60 mm mortars. In late March, the three of us were given orders and transferred from Camp Lejeune to Quantico to attend the First Officer Candidate Screening course. Those of us who passed the screening were scheduled to become the Fifth Special Basic

Presuming to be a United States Marine

Class of student officers. Goldstein had a car and invited us to split expenses and drive up with him. Matson, who was married, had his whole family to transport to Quantico and declined Goldstein's offer, but I was glad to ride up with him.

Quantico was, and is, a legendary base. I had never been there before. The base had always been the ne plus ultra of the Marine Corps, first of all, because all the officer candidate training and officer schools were there, and secondly, because the enlisted men who went there seemed to have a kind of elitist attitude. To be stationed in Quantico, it seemed to me, was very special. In addition, I would now be in much closer proximity to Shirley.

We reported in at Quantico and got processed in. Until noon the following day, there was nothing for us to do, so Goldstein and I decided to jump back into his car and investigate whatever city was nearest. That, of course, was Fredericksburg. We drove down Route 1 to this lovely old Virginia city, which held my fond memories of civilians serving us hot coffee in the train station during the war. We looked around the town and found what I think was then the Wakefield (now the Colonial Inn). We got ourselves cleaned up and went out to explore the nightlife of Fredericksburg. We had a hard time finding a place to eat downtown, and I must confess that at least on a weekday night, there did not seem to be too much to do in Fredericksburg at that time. This turned out to be my first night in the city where I would live for forty-seven years, and where I would subsequently find plenty of things to do.

Chapter 7

QUANTICO, BECOMING AN OFFICER (1951-1952)

Officer Candidate Screening was a challenging program the Marine Corps decided to carry out at the beginning of the Korean buildup, because of a need for officers. The Corps has always thought that noncommissioned officers were good officer material, provided they'd also had some education. Even by that time, the Corps had recognized the importance of some formal education beyond the high school level for an officer. The days of the pure old Mustang who got out of high school and worked his way up through the ranks were quite simply over. In some sense, this is sad, but it is clear that the Marine Corps understood the value of a good education.

Somebody in the Marine Corps hierarchy had become quite excited about methods for assessing people developed by the new federal agency known as the CIA. The Marine Corps set out to assess people in the same way the CIA did, and we became the first guinea pigs to go through this new program. The program has been modified and changed numerous times since, and I know this because in subsequent years, I kept coming back as a staff person in the program.

The screening process itself took a total of five weeks. First, sixty psychiatrists, psychologists, and other clinical types were brought in, who administered to us every psychological test developed at that time. We were put through that testing first for a couple of weeks, and then through the screening program based on the CIA's system for three weeks. In the psychological phase, we were given the Stanford-Binet intelligence test, analogy tests, the Rorschach test, and all kinds of association tests. The flood of testing was almost ludicrous. In addition, we were interviewed by psychiatrists and given a thorough physical examination.

Throughout the psycho part of this testing period, our officers, the people who, after this testing, were going to be our screeners, remained extremely remote and detached. They never chewed us out, but we felt their eyes on us at any given moment all the time. It is my understanding that the psychological tests were administered in this intensive and comprehensive fashion to our class and to one more class after us. After this, the tests were consolidated, condensed, and completely standardized, so that the need to hire enormous numbers of expensive help to come to Quantico for screening had been eliminated. A psychological profile was made up on each one of us. The teams of evaluators were apparently instructed to prepare for each one of us a prediction: a) whether we would pass the CIA type screening course and b) how successful we were going to be as Marine Corps officers. Those results were compiled but not passed on to the marine officers who later screened us. They were sent to the Navy Bureau of Medicine, and it is my understanding that these psychological test results and predictions are still there, and, moreover, that if I wished, I could see for myself how well I had been expected to perform as a Marine Corps officer. Apparently, the Corps wanted to determine if it could economically screen potential officers by means of psychological testing, rather than the manpower-expensive screening course. I must say that I have never had the nerve to look up my psychological profile. A couple of my classmates have dug into it and, fifty years later, have examined their records. Frankly, I've been kind of afraid to do that because, supposing they had found something? Supposing you were found to be unsuitable in some way, with a question of "What is he doing in the Marine Corps?" appended to their finding? Or the comment of "This man will never amount to a hill of beans," or something like that?

During my several psychiatric interviews in the course of the testing, there was a great deal of exploration about my responses to Shirley's illness, including any degree to which I might feel responsible for it. I am sure that whatever responses I gave figured in some way in my evaluation.

After the two weeks of psychological testing, we were turned over to our screeners. The rank level of our screeners was quite high. We were in platoons, and each platoon had a major as the platoon commander, and at least a captain as a squad leader. Each week the squad leader would change, so that three different squad leaders observed each one of us, while the platoon leader saw all three squads the entire time. There were, I think, only twelve of us in each squad, or just thirty-six people in the platoon. By the end of the four-week program, four different people had examined each one of us most thoroughly.

We were often taken out to various places in the field and broken down into, usually, four- or five-person teams. We were given a task, but only some of the materials necessary to accomplish it, and we found that several of the tasks were literally impossible to complete by a mere mortal in the assigned time.

There would be three of four guys with clipboards standing nearby, watching our every move. We were never told how we were expected to do anything. We had to organize ourselves as to who would take charge and who could be expected to come up with good ideas and how these ideas would best be implemented by the group.

Among the tasks assigned was to get a body across a stream, I recall and, something which we could have accomplished had we been given more time, to change all four wheels on a jeep. After we were thrown into a task, we were observed as to how we responded, how we reacted, and how we got along with the other team members.

Taking on the Burden of History

When you are a marine in training, of course, there is somebody yelling at you constantly and without letup, and you learn to expect that kind of in-your-face attitude on the part of the people training you. But suddenly, nobody raised a voice, only watchful eyes. In fact, the way we were being methodically stressed out was by not ever being told anything at all, so that we remained in constant quandary as to what was expected of us.

From time to time, though, during this low-key, silent, nondirective screening treatment, the people doing the screening would calmly and quietly say something to us that would really shake us up, without in any way clarifying what was required of us.

When I returned from Korea two years later, many aspects of the screening had changed. The basic curriculum remained the same, but the attitude of the assessors had, strangely, become much more involved; it now resembled that of drill instructors on Parris Island, with a barrage of constant but familiar stress on the candidates trying to get through the screening. But in this first Officer Candidate Screening course, the emphasis clearly was on subtlety and detachment, which quite thoroughly confused, and even frightened, most of us.

I was promoted to staff sergeant during the screening process. Along with all the other sergeants at Camp Lejeune, I had taken the examination for staff sergeant, and when the wheels had finally ground through, I was, briefly, promoted. I only held that rank for about three weeks.

There is a great dividing line in the enlisted ranks between private through sergeant, and staff sergeant, gunnery sergeant and master sergeant, the latter three being the staff noncommissioned officers.

The promotion to staff sergeant was presented to me and about four other men in our company, and one man was promoted to gunnery sergeant. The company had a couple of administrative officers, as well as the assessors who were with us all the time. The administrative officers were responsible for company functions, and they made sure that all our gear and records were up-to-date.

The promotion ceremony had to be held after hours. After the evening meal, one day, the whole company was lined up in company formation, and the five of us being promoted were called up front and center, and we marched out; and the administrative officer of the company, who was an Irish captain by the name, I think, of Reilly, called out the promotions and presented each one of us with our certificates. And that was pretty exciting, even though by that time, I wanted to be a second lieutenant.

The ceremony broke up at about eight o'clock in the evening, and I went directly back to the barracks, devoting myself to one or more of the usual menial tasks of cleaning my rifle, shining my shoes, or polishing something in order to present the right appearance the next day at formation. I went to bed by about nine o'clock that night, got up the next morning, and had breakfast. We fell out at 0800 hours and had our first inspection of the day by our assessors.

My uniform was as sharp as could be. An assessor, a major, came up and said, "Van Sant, what is your rank?"

Presuming to be a United States Marine

"Staff sergeant, sir," I replied.

"Well, then, why are you wearing sergeant's stripes?"

Of course, I could not say to him that I had just been promoted the evening before. I knew better than to try to make an excuse. I just said, "No excuse, sir." He got out his clipboard and made a notation, and I knew I had screwed up! And that is how it was; there was a lot of note taking, without anybody ever making any comments. By golly, as soon as I got loose at eleven thirty, I gave up lunch, which all who knew me then would recognize as a big sacrifice, no matter what the quality of food.

I ran down to the quartermaster and got a whole bunch of staff sergeant stripes, ran back to my bunk, got out my sewing kit; and when we fell out for the one o'clock formation, there I was with my new staff sergeant's stripes. I'd had no lunch, but I was now an official staff sergeant in the U.S. Marine Corps. I stayed home that evening and sewed on my staff sergeant's stripes on the rest of my shirts.

Near the end of the program came an exercise which, particularly in looking back on it, but even at the time, amazed me by its ingenuity. Something like it has been adapted and is still being used by the Marine Corps. This was an exercise called a competitive hike. All of us were divided up into about twelve, thirteen, or fourteen marine squads. There were three squads to a platoon, and three or four platoons to a company, in a couple of companies. We had a total of, I think, 560-some people in the screening course. Almost all the noncommissioned officers had fought in World War II at least to some extent, and all had some college, or had graduated from a non-accredited college, as I had.

Each squad became a team on this hike. We were given a map with a route marked out on it, and we were to organize ourselves using any tactic we wanted to. However, our team could never spread out more than one hundred yards from the first person to the last person. In other words, if you had a really strong hiker or runner, you could not stick him out in front because we had to all remain together as a unit. Hiking as fast as we could on this course, we were to get as far as we were able. The course took us clear across Route 1 and up on the other side of Route 1, beyond what is now Interstate 95. We left at 7:00 p.m.

There was no limit as to how far out we could go, but we had to be back from our farthest point of advance and across the finish line in front of the barracks on the main base of Quantico by 11:00 p.m. For every minute we were late coming back, we were penalized one hundred yards from the total distance. But get this, for every minute we got back earlier than the designated time, we were penalized also.

The idea was that we would fan out on the hike as a group so that there would not ever be a distance of more than one hundred yards between the first and the last person. We would reach some point on the prescribed course, turn around and come back, and the winning team would be the group of people who hiked out the farthest distance and who received no penalties for arriving too early or too late. We were each given a boat marker, which was a big, long wooden pole put on landing craft for amphibious landings. We planted our boat marker at the farthest point of our advance so that our referees could measure our distance. We were, incidentally, in full combat gear, with helmets, rifles, and packs. We were not dressed as athletes, we were dressed as marines.

Many subtle things happened during this hike. For one thing, the best hikers and runners instinctively wanted to take off fast, go as far as they could, and come back as quickly as possible in order to win. But every squad had people who were physically not quite up to the shape of the rest. One team with an exceptionally fine group of hikers had one guy among them who happened to be someone I knew and saw many times later. Bill, quite simply said, was somewhat overweight. Throughout screening, he was always the last man for everything. He was his team's big liability, and it was later said that Bill actually came back in on the point of a bayonet. He desperately wanted to stop for a rest throughout the hike, but you see, once a person stopped, the whole team would be penalized, because the entire team had to stay together in order to complete the hike.

I carried the boat marker all the way to the farthest point, and when we finally reached as far as we figured we could go in order to get back in time, not too soon and not too late, I sprinted one hundred yards ahead and planted the marker while the rest of my teammates took a brief rest. That was my contribution to the team. As soon as I got back, we began the return trip. Our team did not win, but we came in twelfth of thirty-six teams, and I was pretty proud of that. We had walked some nineteen miles in just four hours. We had timed it pretty well coming in, and we had no penalties either way.

Our assessors, bless their hearts, walked with us all the way. I think that the suggestions I made on that hike about how to get organized, how far we should go, and what we could realistically hope to accomplish may have contributed to my overall scores for screening. And we did quite well, finishing ahead of twenty-four other teams. The winning team hiked for something like twenty-one miles, which was only a couple of miles farther than we had gone. What this exercise brought out was that each team was only as strong as its weakest link. As you can imagine, this was a fairly stressful experience, because we knew from the beginning that a lot rode on the individual and team effort on this competition.

We completed the Officer Candidate Screening course near the end of May 1951. Those who were successful would be commissioned as second lieutenants in the United States Marine Corps. Those who were not successful would return to their former units at the same rank they had held when they entered the screening class. There were 560 of us, as I recall, and 289 were commissioned, so that it was almost fifty-fifty up or down.

The great day came when we were to find out whether we had passed or not. We were placed out in front of the barracks in company formation. One of the senior officers came out, called roll from a list of names, and told all those people to fall out and fall in at one location. And then he called another list of names to fall out and fall in at another area. As people were being called out and put in one group or another in alphabetical order and while I awaited my turn, as always, in the Marine Corps, I tried to figure out from the two groups which one was which. I thought I'd had a pretty good idea of who the successful candidates were, but I saw a couple of people placed into what I thought was the successful group, of whom I could not believe that they would have made it. By the same token, there were a couple of people put into what I thought was the unsuccessful group, whom I had thought of as outstanding. The tension mounted. My name was finally called, and I was directed to the group which I thought, overall, might be the successful one, without, of course, being sure about whether my assessment was in any way correct.

We were at attention. We could not speak to one another, although we were able to furtively exchange some significant glances. One of the senior officers came, fell us in, and marched us down several hundred yards to one of the classrooms. We went in, lined up, stood at attention, and were told, "Seats, gentlemen." We sat down.

Into the profound silence a lieutenant colonel said, "Congratulations, gentlemen!" It was a great moment. We had made it.

We were told that every effort was being made to get our list of names through Congress before the first of June. This effort turned out to be successful because Congress passed our commissions on the twenty-ninth of May, which meant that our dates of rank were always ahead of all of the class of 1951 from the Naval Academy, the platoon leaders course, and the Naval Reserve Officer Training Corps. All these other officers were given a date of rank of 1 June 1951, and so we were always two days senior to that large class of officers. There were a couple of instances in the future when this seniority became very helpful to me, although that was not always the case.

We were told to pack up our gear and were moved out to Camp Barrett, way out on the other side of what is now I-95 and Route 1, in what was then a large rural area of Quantico. As it turned out, we were moved from fairly comfortable brick barracks into simple Quonset huts. We were second lieutenants now, but our living quarters went down a peg or two. While we waited for Congress to pass our commissions, which happened within a day or two, we were issued gear, books, and other materials. We were also given orientation about how to comport ourselves as officers and were reminded to return salutes.

After the strange ordeal of the screening, when we never knew what was going to happen next, but with the understanding that we were being observed all the time, this was a nice break. On May 29, on a gravelly, dusty field at Camp Barrett, we lined up and took our oaths as second lieutenants, USMC.

I have subsequently felt guilty about something that happened, or rather did not happen, after that ceremony. There is a long-standing tradition in the Marine Corps that a newly commissioned lieutenant gives a dollar to the first enlisted man who salutes him or her. The day I was commissioned as an officer, I was flat broke, without a dollar to my name. The enlisted men who worked at Camp Barrett, of course, were very familiar with the tradition and were standing all around the perimeter of the field, waiting for us to swear our oaths.

Taking on the Burden of History

Our commissioning was pretty barren. Nowadays this ceremony often takes place in more civilized surroundings, with mothers, wives, or sweethearts pinning the gold bars on. But there were no families present for us, and so we simply pinned our own bars to our collars and were dismissed into the saluting arms of the waiting young troopers, who were picking up dollar bills by the bushel.

I hung back and slunk around and tried to pretend that I had already given my dollar to somebody else, but I have always felt guilty about not observing this time-honored tradition, and I will carry this guilt to my grave.

Almost immediately, our class plunged into the Basic School training, and that was a pretty rough go too. It was carefully explained to us that we would be ranked based on our performance. Our performance was measured on two dimensions, one of them academic. We went through extremely intensive instructions in what amounted to twenty-five different military subjects, and we took a final examination on each of those, so that we had a total of twenty-five examinations. The cumulative score on these exams determined one-half of our class ranking.

The other half was a somewhat nebulous category called leadership. The platoon and section officers observed us under all conditions and measured the way we had performed—how well disciplined we were, how sharp we were, what kind of an attitude we brought to any given task, and our general ability to perform that task.

All through Basic School, we were constantly put in positions where we were drilling the other officers and giving commands. We were often asked to inspect the other officers. At the same time, our officer-like qualities were very carefully weighed and assessed.

Our class was called special basic class for two reasons. For one, we were given a special abbreviated course. As former noncommissioned officers the Marine Corps, I think rightly, felt that there was not much basic military instruction we had not already received. The concern prevailed that the war was still in full swing, and the Marine Corps was anxious to get the new lieutenants over to Korea as soon as possible.

We actually only had a little over thirteen weeks of Basic School. In those days, the standard special basic class lasted twenty weeks, and a regular basic class was thirty weeks long. Because of these circumstances, our training week lasted from Monday morning until noon Saturday, with no long weekends off.

Throughout our training, we would be handed little slips of paper called chits. We would get the original, a copy would go into our record, and a copy was maintained by our platoon commander. The chits could be good chits or bad chits. If you screwed something up, you would get a bad chit, which would go straight into your record. If you did well at something, you were awarded a good chit, and you hoped it would go into your record as well. The unfortunate platoon commander would have to write chits about each person's progress continuously for each one of the thirty-five or forty people in his platoon. In the course of the whole summer, I got probably six or seven chits, and these were, fortunately, all good chits.

Presuming to be a United States Marine

Two "chits" prepared by my Platoon Commander, 1st Lieutenant Faust. Note that the second one is dated July 31 and reflects my newly developed skills in inspecting rifles.

I still remember what a few of these were for. On something called the bayonet course, carrying our rifle with the bayonet on it and running all the time, we had to climb over obstacles. Strategically placed, we would encounter dummies we had to either spear with our bayonet or give a vertical or horizontal stroke with the butt-end of our rifle. The situations were made quite realistic, with an occasional dummy "jumping" out at us from behind a tree.

The officers running the program would congregate to watch us at one particular obstacle, where we had to climb over a wall with bayonet at the ready. Just on the other side of the wall, we would come upon a trench line with enemy soldier dummies lying in it. Our task was to jump down into the trench line and bayonet them. We were expected to put a lot of ourselves into this bayonet course, such as yelling "Die!" to the dummy enemy as we proceeded to slash him.

And I came tearing up the wall, hard-charging. I leapt over it and jumped down into the trench full speed, jabbing my bayonet into the dummy, roaring "DIE!" I was so carried away with the program that I actually bent my bayonet, driving it right through the dummy into the hard ground. But my platoon commander who happened to be watching—man, he must have been really impressed by this display of extraordinary valor on my part.

We would have a little spare time in the late afternoons and evenings, and when I was not traveling to Pittsburgh, and later to Alexandria, I would sometimes hang around with the guys in the Quonset hut. In those days, the areas surrounding Quantico were largely rural and, occasionally, farm boys would sneak in with watermelons. We used to buy these watermelons and were able to refrigerate them. When we came in from the field at five o'clock, we would sit down before dinner and eat a big hunk of luscious ice cold watermelon.

One of the things we had to learn to do as junior officers was to inspect the troops. That may not sound very hard, but there are things you have to look for in a marine to tell whether he or she is up to snuff, and of these, the most important one is to inspect the rifle. Over the years marines have evolved some pretty fancy and distinctive ways of inspecting a rifle. As a young marine I had had my rifle inspected by some very colorful and flamboyant inspecting officers. The inspection procedure itself was not prescribed, but what the inspector was to look for on the rifle was prescribed. The act of taking the rifle and handing it back could be as elaborate, or as simple, as one wanted it to be. The inspecting officer could just reach up and take the rifle, look down the bore, examine the face of the bolt, look at the screw heads, look at the condition of the chamber, check the butt plate, and then hand the gun gently back to the marine. That would be a simple, straightforward inspection. But what some of us were doing while we were Basic School officers was to develop more elaborate and colorful schemes for inspecting, and we avidly drilled on those schemes. A few of us in the platoon spent a lot of time practicing inspecting.

I developed a fairly elaborate technique myself. The marine would stand in front of me, and instead of taking the rifle, I would reach up and hit the upper end of it. The rifle would fly out of the marine's hands, because he knew that the minute I touched his rifle he had to let go of it. At that moment, the rifle had become my rifle. I would flip it all the way over, and I would spin it. With a flourish, I would raise the rifle up in the air and start examining the barrel to check if there was any dried powder in it, then swish it back down, spin it around, look at the butt plate, and hand it back to the marine. I practiced this routine while one of my friends practiced his own routine, and we would take turns taking each other's rifle and inspecting it. A few days later, I had perfected my system, and I must say with some degree of immodesty that my procedure was quite distinctive.

We always had morning formation at eight o'clock, and the platoon commander would say, "Lieutenant Gratz, inspect the first squad." And, "Lieutenant Van Sant, inspect the second squad." We would fall out and pretend to be the inspecting officer, go down the line, and inspect all the other lieutenants. When my flip of the rifle was down to perfection, I went all the way down the line, whipped up all the rifles, inspected them carefully, handed them back in a very military manner, and got a good chit for my trouble. I have recently found this chit among my papers.

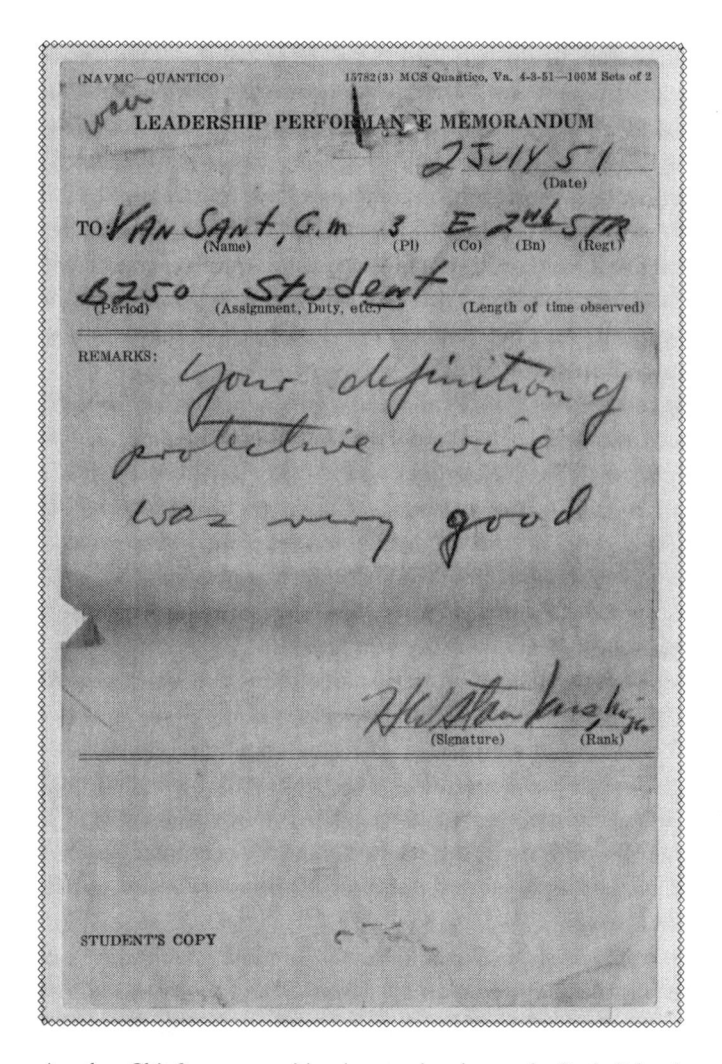

Another Chit for a recognition in a tactics class at the Basic School

The only other good chit I remember getting was for being the point man on night scouting and patrolling. I had extraordinarily good luck that night in finding all the booby traps that had been placed, disarming them, and leading all my men to safety. We were competing for the most successful night patrol, and I got a good chit for that. All of that helped to give me my final class ranking.

Quantico, of course, is a lot closer to Pittsburgh than Camp Lejeune was, so that I was able to get to Shirley's sanatorium just about every weekend to see her. By the summer of 1951, Shirley's health was very poor, and it was becoming ever more important for me to see her as often as possible. On the twenty-fourth of June, about four weeks into the training, I got a cable message through the Red Cross about my mother, father, and sister, with whom I had been unable to directly communicate for over two years (although I'd had some messages from the National Council of the Episcopal Church about them.). I had previously received a message that they had all been successful in getting out of China, where they had been detained for over two years, and that they had now arrived in Hong Kong. This second message, which came on a Friday morning, informed me that my parents and sister were landing in Boston on a ship that same Friday afternoon. I went to my company commander, a good and fine marine but tough as nails, and requested permission to take Friday afternoon and Saturday morning off. I explained that I needed to travel to Boston to meet my parents and my sister, whom I had not seen in four years, because they had just managed to escape from the Chinese communists.

The commander looked at me and said, "Van Sant, that means that you will miss this afternoon's training and all of tomorrow morning. So no dice." This was one of the very few times in my entire Marine Corps career when I really was a little bit ticked off. I thought that, under the circumstances, whatever training I received that afternoon and next morning could not be as important as my being in Boston to see my family. But that was the verdict, and I had to abide by it. It brought back memories of my experience at Pearl Harbor in 1945 when I wanted to visit my two aunts, although this time, I had no intentions of taking my own leave.

I got off on Saturday at noon, found a ride to National Airport, arrived in Boston late that afternoon, and was able to talk to my family by phone as soon as I had landed. They came into the city and picked me up at a hotel in downtown Boston. The four of us had dinner together and spent Saturday night in the house of my parents' friends, where they were staying. The following morning, I had a chance to spend some time with my sister, whom I barely recognized. She had been eight years old when I had last seen her, and now she was twelve and sporting a "veddy" clipped British accent.

I asked her, "When was the last time you had a milkshake, Peggy?" And found out that she did not remember what a milk shake was. So I took her out for a good thick milk shake, realizing how much a child can grow up in four years. When my sister Peggy had left for China in 1947, I was myself a kid going back to college. Now I was in my uniform, with my ribbons on, and probably looking pretty awesome to her. It was wonderful seeing my family again even though, before long, I had to get back to Logan Airport for my return flight to Washington DC.

My parents did not quite know what to do upon their return to the States. They had unloaded just about everything they owned before their trip to China, except for some furniture they had taken with them, most of which they'd had to leave behind. They had been able to bring out of China a number of trunks with some of their possessions. My father told me once that, at that point, all he had was $5,000 in savings, most of which had come from the 1947 sale of their house in Hyattsville. But my parents still had good friends in the States, notably Reverend Jack Ambler, who had become the rector of Emmanuel Church in Alexandria, Virginia. Both of the Ambler children were away at school, and the rectory was a beautiful sprawling brick building, including an apartment over the garage. The Amblers invited my parents to move in with them until such a time as they could find their own accommodations.

My father set about diligently to find a job. He would have preferred to stay in academia; that preference, after all, had been the reason for his leaving government in 1947 to go back to college teaching in China. He now received a couple of teaching job offers, but the pay was so pitiful that he did not feel it was possible for him to accept either one of them. Eventually, he was offered a job in the Pentagon with the International Security Administration. At that time, the ISA performed economic intelligence, which was what my father had done during the war in China. The federal government snapped up a trained economist with a PhD, who had just spent four years in Communist China, even though almost half of it had been under house arrest, and made him a GS-14 right away. Within a year or two, he was promoted to GS-15, and in those days, that was about as high as a nonpolitical person could advance in government.

My mother found a job as an English teacher at St. Agnes School in Alexandria, and within a year or two, she was head of the English Department and senior adviser. By August of 1951, both my parents had rented a decent little house in Alexandria; both had jobs and had enrolled my sister in St. Agnes School as a student. After an ordeal of four years, they were able to begin making a good life for themselves.

One of the first things my dad did was to buy a car. But since he took the bus to work all the time, I was allowed to use this family car at various times that summer while finishing Basic School in Quantico. My mother did not drive, my sister was too young to drive, and you can imagine how convenient it was for me to suddenly have a vehicle.

Almost every weekend that summer, I would drive up on Saturday afternoon for dinner with my family, then take an overnight bus from Washington, which would arrive in Pittsburgh at 6:00 a.m. I would sleep on the bus and spend the entire day with Shirley. When I did not have use of my family's car, I would leave Pittsburgh on a Greyhound bus at about eight or nine o'clock Sunday evening. In Washington, I would catch another bus to Richmond and get the driver to let me off at an intersection not too far from Camp Barrett. The bus would get there at about five o'clock in the morning, and I would run the three or four miles to Camp Barrett and arrive just in time to clean up for the day's activities. I realize now that during that period in my life, on weekends, I seldom had a regular night's sleep. I slept on buses both nights, then plunged into the vigorous Basic School training very early Monday morning, performing as well as I could on bayonet courses and obstacle courses and strenuous hikes and runs through the woods. But I was young and in great shape in those days and ever mindful that Shirley's health was steadily declining.

When we graduated from Basic School, my class ranking out of the 287 was 26th. I have always felt very good about that because there were some outstanding people in my class, including several who later made general and several who subsequently performed with heroism in Korea and Vietnam. Almost half of my basic class sought regular commissions and made careers out of the Marine Corps. These men were a fine group of people, and it was a wonderful experience for me to be promoted along with them.

My leave after graduation was for ten days. I had arranged with the sanatorium and with Shirley's parents to take her to her family home in Mount Lebanon outside Pittsburgh. There she and I had our own room, and we spent a wonderful time together, and with many of her old friends who came by to see her.

Shirley was dying. She was twenty-four years old. She knew that she was dying, and she knew that I knew it as well. But we were together, we listened to music, we read, and we talked. It was a tender and beautiful, and at the same time, a profoundly sad time.

When my leave ended, I returned her to the sanatorium, where I had spent so many hours in her room with a nice view, and reported back to Schools Demonstration Troops (SDT) in Quantico on about the twentieth of September 1951. Most of my class had been sent to the West Coast and on to Korea. The Marine Corps, in their sensitivity, knew about Shirley's situation, and would not send me overseas but kept me at Quantico so that I could remain close to her.

Schools Demonstration Troops was a unit in those days, whose task was to put on demonstrations and act as enemy aggressors for student officers. There are three levels of officers' schools in Quantico. Basic School is for lieutenants, Amphibious Warfare School (then called Junior School) for captains and junior majors, and Command and Staff College (then called Senior School) for senior majors and lieutenant colonels. At all three of these levels of schooling, there were occasional demonstrations for the student officers.

More commonly, we were expected to provide enemy forces when the student officers, particularly in the Basic School, were engaged in any kind of platoon or company tactical instruction. This instruction was done against an enemy, and Schools Demonstration Troops became the enemy. In the process, we were issued crazy helmets that looked something like the old Greek helmets, with a big ridgeline down the middle, thus clearly showing us to be the foe. Donning these helmets, we would lie in wait to ambush the student officers, or we would counterattack them on tactical instruction. As a platoon commander, I found that this was a wonderful way for a brand-new second lieutenant to learn how to lead troops in the field.

On the night of the twenty-ninth of September, I received a Red Cross message that I should come to Pittsburgh immediately. I knew what that message meant and was able to leave at once. Shirley died on the second of October. I was with her when she died. This was a very hard time.

Shirley had converted to Roman Catholicism several years before we married. She had never discussed with us how she wished to be buried, but we thought she would want to be buried as a Catholic. Shirley's brother, a student at Washington and Jefferson College about thirty miles south of Pittsburgh, belonged to a fraternity. There were about a half dozen PLC marine officer candidates in his fraternity, and they all came out to be Shirley's pallbearers.

Presuming to be a United States Marine

When all was over, I rode back to Washington with my mother, father, and sister and began preparing for life without Shirley. Shirley had been a beautiful, loving, caring, and sensitive person. She had a kind of translucent beauty and had always seemed a little bit detached from life. Her stay on earth was brief; at the time of her death, she was a little over two months past her twenty-fourth birthday. She died exactly three weeks short of our third wedding anniversary. Her last words were expressions of concern for my comfort, because I had been sitting by her bed for almost forty-eight hours. A crowning irony was that she was one of the last people in America to die of tuberculosis. It had been a race between death and the availability on the market of a new drug her doctors told me all about. Death had won.

I returned to my duties at Schools Demonstration Troops in a pretty depressed state, but I threw myself into my work. My financial situation was grim. Beginning in 1949, I had run up a number of debts to doctors and hospitals and had made some personal loans. Because of my forlorn state, emotionally and financially, the best course of action, it seemed to me, was to volunteer to go to Korea. I would not need any money in Korea because I would be in combat, and that would allow me to get out of debt. There was also a darker side to my desire for combat. I felt so miserable without Shirley that I fantasized about sacrificing myself in some final great heroic act, because I had nothing left to live for.

With that decided, I submitted an official personnel request form for assignment to the First Marine Division. In my request, I expressed gratitude to the Marine Corps for keeping me stationed close to my wife during her illness and explained that since she was now dead, my presence here was no longer required. Furthermore, all my Basic School classmates had by this time been sent over to Korea, and one of the most popular members of our class had already been killed. I felt like a slacker. Headquarters, Marine Corps, replied in their best bureaucratese (paraphrased) something like this:

"Subject request is appreciated. The commandant would be glad to accede to your request. However, because of the provisions of Public Law (umpty-ump) your period of service as a recalled reserve is scheduled to terminate in February 1952. If you will extend your active duty period by at least twelve months, on form (umpty-ump), we would be happy to issue you orders to Korea sometime in January, detaching you from Quantico sometime in early February."

I submitted the form requested, extending my active duty to August 1953. My thinking was that if I survived Korea, I might still like to go to graduate school, and the period of service for which I had signed up would let me out just before the beginning of an academic year. At the same time, the old yen to become a regular marine, which had first appeared in China, was still present, and I also wanted to keep that option open. All of this agonizing and correspondence took place during October of 1951. I submitted form umpty-ump and, by early November, was officially informed by Headquarters, Marine Corps, that I would receive orders in January.

I talked it over with my father and, on his advice, made out a detailed list of all my debts and obligations. I had a power of attorney prepared for him and arranged to have my Marine Corps pay deposited in a special account in Alexandria to which only he and I had access. Bless his now-departed heart, he searched out every one of my creditors during my fourteen months of absence, paid them off, and still managed to create a small nest egg for me when I returned home from Korea.

My service in Schools Demonstration Troops (SDT) during the fall of 1951 and early 1952 was, indeed, valuable experience. I performed a wide variety of duties and learned much about being a lieutenant in the Marine Corps. In fact, when I left the unit, my MOS was changed from 0301 to 0302. For the uninitiated, MOS stands for Military Occupational Specialty. All numbers that begin with 03 are infantry. Remember, my MOS as a machine gun noncommissioned officer was 0335. The number 0301 means a basic infantry officer. For basic here, read, "inexperienced, doesn't know anything, but wants to be in the infantry." The number 0302, on the other hand, means "trained, experienced infantry officer." MOS's are not tied to rank. Although most 0301s are lieutenants, I have seen lieutenant colonels who have an 0301 MOS. In fact, I met up with one in Korea.

Because I was part of the so-called permanent personnel at the base at Quantico, I was given a number of additional duties. I found myself assigned to the audit committee for the Staff Noncommissioned Officers Club. This meant that, once a month, I spent a good part of the day counting up all the cash and auditing the records of that club. We even checked bar receipts against the liquor consumption. On a monthly basis, for every bottle of liquor in the bar's stock, we had to measure the amount in the bottle to the nearest quarter bottle.

Schools Demonstration Troops had a quasi-regimental structure. We had an infantry battalion but were structured as a Marine Expeditionary Unit with a battery of artillery and platoons of tanks, engineers, amphibious tractors, motor transport, etc. The unit was commanded by a full colonel, Colonel Missar, with whom I had several somewhat tense confrontations. The colonel had the authority to convene general and special courts-martial, and as a young bachelor lieutenant, I got appointed to both. Fortunately, we never had to convene a general court-martial, but the special court-martial must have met three or four times in the period between September, 1951, when I joined SDT, and February 11, 1952, when I departed for the West Coast.

Students of military legal history will remember that the Uniform Code of Military Justice (UCMJ) took effect on September 1, 1951. This was the complete revision of military law that took place after World War II. Legal scholars and authorities felt that the old Articles of War and Articles for the Governance of the Navy were out of date. The UCMJ incorporated many constitutional principles such as presumption of innocence, right to fair trial, right to representation, no cruel and excessive punishments (e.g., bread-and-water solitary confinement), right to enlisted jurors, etc. The good old days of the absolute authority of the commanding officer had come to an end.

We had some pretty juicy special courts-martial. The president of our court and presiding officer was Major Sullivan, who commanded our Weapons Company. There were a couple of captains and one other lieutenant on the court besides me. In early

Presuming to be a United States Marine

October, we convened the very first special court-martial under the UCMJ ever held in SDT, and we had to have the new UCMJ manual open in front of us as we proceeded. I don't remember the details of the case, but when we removed ourselves from the courtroom and retired to make our finding of guilty or not guilty and decide on a sentence, we quickly found the accused guilty. That decision seemed easy, but then we had to come up with a sentence, or punishment. Both the captains, the major, and I had all come into the Marine Corps during World War II and had served under the old Articles of the Navy (Rocks and Shoals as they were affectionately known). It turned out that all four of us had a deep and abiding belief in the virtues and efficacy of solitary confinement on bread and water (also known as piss and punk). The advantage of solitary was that when you sent a young miscreant off to this kind of punishment, he would enter the brig, serve his sentence quickly, and return to his outfit without ever having had any contact with the other garbage (brig rats, as they were known) in the brig.

As we were struggling with the new code and how to determine a punishment, I happened to stumble across an appendix to the first edition of the UCMJ manual, which had something called Table of Equivalent Punishments. The charge for which the accused had been tried, as I remember it, if found guilty, carried with it, according to the main text of the manual, confinement for up to three months, a fine up to $250, and reduction in rank of up to two ranks. In the main text of the manual, there was no mention of solitary confinement on bread and water. But in this obscure appendix I had managed to unearth, a court could substitute one day of solitary confinement on bread and water for each five days of ordinary confinement. Our group leapt on this provision. We took the ninety days of ordinary confinement we were allowed to give as set out in the main text of the manual and converted it to a very reasonable twelve days of solitary confinement on bread and water. Brilliant!

We had three or four more special courts that autumn and liberally used the same Table of Equivalent Punishments on all, zapping our guilty with our sure, swift, and efficacious punishment and sending them back to their duties without delay and without any corruption by contact with other brig rats. Alas, if we had only read the fine print, we would have discovered an asterisk with a footnote that these equivalent punishments could only be applied under very specific field conditions and, mainly, aboard ship.

As a result, the findings and sentences from the first four special court-martials held by Schools Demonstration Troops, after the Uniform Code of Military Justice took effect, were bounced back with some pretty nasty letters from the U.S. Navy Judge Advocate General to our commanding officer, Colonel Missar. My role as discoverer of the Table of Equivalent Punishments in the UCMJ fiasco was fortunately never disclosed, but I subsequently had a couple of other interactions with Colonel Missar.

First, the negative one. My interest in basketball was a matter of record in my official record book. This had led to my all-too-brief membership on the Parris Island Base basketball squad back in 1945. In early November of 1951, the CO of Weapons

Taking on the Burden of History

Company (who was also president of the special court) stopped me one day and said, "Hey, Van, you are coming out for the regimental basketball team, aren't you?"

"I don't think so, Major Sullivan," I replied.

"Gee, Van, we could really use you," he said.

I have already talked about the base teams of the WWII-Korea era. As a matter of fact, a number of basketball and football stars were designated as officers in Schools Demonstration Troops. We never saw them because they spent their time in conditioning and practices. Occasionally, they would appear in our barracks for some battalion ceremony, or they would volunteer to pay the troops. (All marines were still being paid in cash by an officer in 1951.) But the primary focus for these athletes was their role on their base teams. Even then, this practice of the Marine Corps of fielding competitive base teams at an intercollegiate level was producing a lot of internal criticism and friction. The nonathletes felt they were being forced to work harder to make up for an athlete who was a nonproducer in the outfit, and I am happy to say that the Marine Corps abandoned this practice many years ago.

In addition to the teams that represented the base, the Marine Corps also ran a strong intramural program. Each unit on the base had a baseball team; a basketball team; and, in several instances, a football team. These intramural unit teams also competed with club teams in the civilian world. It was this intramural unit team that I was being asked to join.

A few days after my conversation with Major Sullivan, I received a message in our company office that Colonel Missar wished to see me in his office. I immediately dashed the several hundred yards separating our company office from the SDT Headquarters and reported to the adjutant, who escorted me to the colonel's office.

"Come in, Lieutenant Van Sant," said Missar, the imposing marine colonel, genially. "You just recently completed Basic School, didn't you?"

"Yes, sir, about two months ago," I said. (This conversation took place in early November.)

The colonel then went off on some other topics, beating around the bush about the weather, the war news from Korea, and other unrelated topics. He mentioned that he had heard I had been promised orders to Korea in February. Then he finally worked himself up to his point. "In your Basic School instruction, did they tell you about a commanding officer's wishes or desires?"

I quickly remembered the principle that had been pounded into us that a commanding officer's expressed wishes or desires have exactly the same status as a direct order, and I promptly replied, "Yes, sir."

Sighing deeply, Colonel Missar said, "Well, it is my desire that you play on the Schools Demonstration Troops' basketball team." He followed this statement with a sharp, direct, and commanding look into my eyes.

His expressed wish aroused a variety of conflicting emotions in me. On the one hand, I was, by 1951, an absolutely committed and obedient marine, with the lessons of Parris Island and Basic School deeply emblazoned on my soul. On the other

Presuming to be a United States Marine

hand, I was aware of my rising resentment of the way the Marine Corps handled athletes, coupled with the realization that, despite the Basic School instruction about a commander's wishes, Colonel Missar knew he was on pretty shaky ground appealing to this principle in order to strengthen his basketball team. I indicated my acquiescence to his desires, but added that the discipline of training for and playing basketball, in addition to my regular duties, which would not be reduced for my last ten weeks or so prior to going overseas, might be difficult to maintain. He dismissed me with a positive expression of satisfaction and appreciation for my willingness to support the unit.

And so, once again, I drew my athletic gear and basketball uniform and reported for additional duty as a member of a Marine Corps basketball team. By the end of the first practice, several things had been established. In addition to Major Sullivan, who was the non-playing coach, I was the only other officer on the squad. After we had played several games in the season, and after a couple of weeks of practice, I realized that Major Sullivan must have been anxious to get me on the team, not for my basketball-playing ability, but because, as an officer, I could be responsible for the team when he had to be elsewhere.

I was ostensibly a center, but it was soon established that a very lanky and graceful African American corporal of similar height was a much better player than I. Firmly established as the second string center, I played about ten to fifteen minutes a game to give my corporal friend brief rests. Our team was actually pretty good and did well in the base tournament, after I left them in midseason to go to Korea. My other function on the team was to act as Major Sullivan's second in command and, several times, taking the team on the road and acting as coach. The upshot of this additional duty, however, was that it really cut into my precious time with my family in Alexandria.

My other interaction with Colonel Missar had a happier outcome. The officer complement of Schools Demonstration Troops consisted of a colonel, a lieutenant colonel, a couple of majors, half a dozen captains, and probably thirty-five lieutenants. Of this group of officers, perhaps eight or ten, mostly lieutenants, were athletes and did not perform many duties. The unit had an officer of the day on duty every night and all day on weekends. The OD's main task was to supervise about eight sentries on the equipment parks and ammo dumps, the duty noncommissioned officers in each company, and a small emergency guard detail to handle contingencies. Only lieutenants stood this duty. As luck would have it, there were only three bachelor lieutenants in the whole outfit, and one of them was a very senior first lieutenant.

By the end of October, I began to realize that I was the OD every other Saturday. When the November duty list came out, I had two Saturdays as well as the Marine Corps Birthday, November 10, and Thanksgiving Day. With twenty-five or more officers eligible to stand the duty, four times a month seemed to me to be a bit too many—especially when they were all Saturdays and special occasions. Very humbly, hat in hand, I went to see the adjutant, First Lieutenant (selected for captain) Daskalakis, a formidable presence, who was the man responsible for preparing the duty roster.

Taking on the Burden of History

I tried to show him, with a calendar in hand, how unfairly I was being treated. Most officers had the duty only once in a month, a few had it twice; but four times seemed excessive. First off, he tried to make me feel that I was being too whiney—good marines take their medicine and like it. When I refused to back down from this ploy, he went over to a cupboard, and with a conspiratorial look, as if he were revealing to me some top-secret document, he reached up on a shelf and took down a big chart board. He said, "I don't usually share this, but this is my duty officer matrix." He then, speaking very rapidly, launched into the most complicated and devious argument I have ever heard, the gist of which was that I was being absolutely fairly treated. He made frequent but vague gestures toward the chart, his voice rising and falling dramatically. I ended up not understanding a word of it. There were mentions of shaky marriages, seniority, etc.

I finally just said, "Thank you, sir. I hope you remember my concerns when you prepare the December roster." Then I did an about-face and walked out, completed my November duties, and awaited the December duty roster.

In due course, near the end of November, the December assignments came out. There I was, plainly signed up for the second Saturday in December, and for both Christmas and New Year's Eve. Fuming, I sat down and listed the five Saturdays in October, November, and December, plus the Marine Corps Birthday, Thanksgiving, Christmas, and New Year's Eve on a piece of paper.

I stormed into Lieutenant Daskalakis's office and told him how upset I was. He purred that he had cut me back to only three duties, after all. Of course, no other officer in the unit had more than two in any one month. I told him that his system was monstrously unfair. Then he said, "Well, if you don't like the way I'm doing my job, let's go see the colonel."

Now I think that he made a serious miscalculation with this offer. First of all, I think he mistakenly thought that, inexperienced officer that I was, I would never dare to appeal such an assignment to the colonel. Secondly, he had been present the month before when Colonel Missar had instructed me on commanding officers' wishes and desires. I believe he thought that Colonel Missar would back him up and quickly throw me out of his office. But I replied to his threat, "Yes, sir, let's go see the colonel." We went in together.

The adjutant began by saying, "Colonel, Lieutenant Van Sant doesn't like the way I am assigning officers of the day and has asked to see you."

I quickly produced my little list, refreshed the colonel's memory on the number of officers eligible to stand the duty and pointed out the number of times I had been assigned (Of course, I knew better than to bring up the athletes.). Colonel Missar carefully studied my list and turned to Lieutenant Daskalakis. "Is this true, Mr. Daskalakis, that he has had duty on all these occasions?"

Brusquely, Lieutenant Daskalakis said, "Yes, sir, those dates are correct."

The colonel studied my list for another twenty seconds and then said, "Well, I think the lieutenant has a point. He has never had a weekday duty, only Saturdays and holidays."

Presuming to be a United States Marine

Daskalakis's face was beginning to fall. Then the colonel added, "Either Christmas or New Year's Eve, but not both, and only two duties in December." I had triumphed. With a smiling face, I about-faced and left the office. Of course, for the moment at least, I had made an enemy; Lieutenant Daskalakis was livid. But when our paths crossed again, a year or so later in Korea, we made up our differences and laughed about them.

As a platoon commander in SDT, I had to perform many exotic tasks. In December or January, I was appointed a convoy commander to take a mixed assortment of large trucks, lowboys carrying tanks and amphibious tractors, and some other large specialized vehicles. They had all been brought into the main base at Quantico for overhaul and repair and were now to be taken out into the field and returned to duty. In those days, to reach the maneuver areas west of U.S. Route 1, one had to drive off the base at Quantico to the town of Triangle, get on U.S. 1 South for about three miles, and then turn west on a narrow concrete road into the large maneuver and training area. I was senior to the other lieutenant assigned to this duty (remember that May 29 date of rank), which put me in front of the convoy of this assortment of large vehicles, while the other lieutenant brought up the rear in another jeep. We both had radios.

We drove out of the base all right and, with the help of military policemen, stopped the traffic on U.S. 1 so that we could turn the convoy south on to the highway. Any traffic turning south out of Quantico immediately starts up a long and very steep hill. As my driver almost reached its top, I turned around and saw the last vehicle in our convoy, the other lieutenant's jeep, just making the turn and starting up the hill.

I turned my attention forward again, when over the radio came, "Lieutenant Van Sant, Lieutenant Van Sant, we have a problem." My driver kept on driving, but we heard the other lieutenant saying, "Please stop, Lieutenant! Stop!"

So we stopped and backed up. Our convoy was in the right lane of the four-lane undivided highway, Route 1. We had the right lane to ourselves, but the left lane was filled with civilian cars trying to get around our elaborate convoy with some pretty wide vehicles in it.

I jumped out of the jeep, started walking back down the hill, and saw the nature of the problem. One of the large trucks was equipped with a strange contraption consisting of continuously jointed heavy wire chain-link matting normally folded up, accordion-like, on a rack over the truck bed. It was designed, when activated by the driver, to lay down the chain-link matting on a beach. In effect, it could create its own road through the sand. A little motor on top of the rig pushed forward this chain-link mat and laid it out on tracks, which extended forward over the cab and hood. The matting draped itself over the hood of the truck and down under the front wheels, which grabbed on to it. Next, the mat was fed under the truck to the wheels in the rear, which grabbed on to it with some fervor, and it laid a matted road behind the truck. The lever to activate this elaborate mechanism was on the cab floor right beside the low-range gearshift. The less-than-experienced driver, wishing to slip into the low-gear range to climb the steep hill, had inadvertently hit the lever that put everything in action with the mat-laying rig. In this manner, having activated the enormously well-thought-out mechanism, our driver had laid about fifty yards of chain-link matting, not on a sandy beach, but on the well-paved and highly traveled Route 1.

Oh God! Well, what can you do? It became what is all too well known as a real leadership challenge. Here we were, stuck, already impeding the flow of traffic on what was at the time the main north-south route in the entire eastern United States. It was clear that the only way we could extricate ourselves was to put the truck in reverse, somehow pick the matting up, and have it fold itself up neatly into the truck bed again for another dormant period.

To our relief, it turned out that the little motor on the rig moved in both directions and was fully capable of picking up the matting. But in order to pick it up, the truck had to be driven in reverse back over all the matting on the ground. Easy enough in theory. The problem, though, was that right behind the truck sat a couple of big, long trailer lowboys with tanks on them, which now were right on top of the newly laid matting. In order for the truck to back up and gather up its mat, the trailers had to back up first. And, quite frankly, the level of driving expertise on the part of the drivers of most of the vehicles in this convoy did not seem to be quite up to snuff, hence my leadership challenge.

The other lieutenant and I, after examining the damage, stopped all civilian traffic. It was the only thing we could do, although by that time, word of our problems must have reached the state police, because Virginia state troopers had begun to swarm to our rescue, keeping all traffic stopped, waiting for us to disentangle the dilemma.

We were able to back up the whole convoy about fifty or sixty yards, which left enough space for the mat-laying truck to back up over his appendage and gather it all up again. The entire operation must have taken about an hour and a half, by which time we had probably gummed up Route 1 all the way back to Washington DC. What a disaster!

The calm, understated voice of the other lieutenant over the radio—"Lieutenant Van Sant, we have a problem"—had held the right inflection for a good marine under pressure. On the other hand, the driver of the truck with the matting, poor soul, was really shaken up and absolutely convinced that his career in the Marine Corps was for all time over, finished, and done with.

In the spring of 1952, the Defense Department planned to conduct some extensive atomic tests in Nevada. Representative bodies of troops from the army and the Marine Corps were sent out and placed in fairly close proximity to these sites in order to test the various types of fortification, and also to get troops to overcome some of their fears about the atom bomb. The plan was announced in 1951, when the atom bomb was only six years old.

Our Schools Demonstration Troops was one of the service organizations asked for volunteers to participate in these atomic bomb tests. At that time in my life, and at my age, this really appealed to me; and I submitted a volunteering request to the

Headquarters Marine Corps, as did another of the unmarried lieutenants in our organization, Lieutenant Butler.

In response to my request, I received a call from somebody from headquarters. "I thought you wanted to go to Korea? Well, you can't go to Korea, if you are going to the atomic bomb tests." And since my first priority, of course, was to go to Korea, I cancelled my request. In view of the fact that I survived Korea, I believe I was very lucky. Some of the people who participated in the atomic bomb testing subsequently developed problems with cancer from radiation. The Atomic Energy Commission had seriously underestimated the danger of nuclear blasts and their effects on people's health, and so I am really quite happy that I decided to abstain from that adventure.

As I was beginning to wind up my activities with Schools Demonstration Troops, I spent as much time as I could with my parents and my sister that fall and winter. I was beginning, rather somberly, to look forward to going to war, although my mother was even more somber about my decision, perhaps because she, my father, and my sister had been through quite an ordeal themselves during their four years in China. My parents were understanding, but I could tell they were not happy. My mother insisted that I find a photo studio in downtown Washington to get an official portrait in uniform taken so that she would have something to remember me by. That portrait hangs on my wall now.

My mother's macabre feelings were pretty much in tune with my own feelings at the time. I was still so dejected and despondent about Shirley's death that I felt if I went into combat, I surely would not give a damn whether I lived or not.

Chapter 8

TO WEST COAST AND KOREA (1952)

In those days, every officer in the Marine Corps traveled to the West Coast on his way to Korea. If he so chose, he could drive his own private vehicle. The Marine Corps paid 6¢ a mile, and for three thousand miles, that came to $180. As an officer, I was given that amount of money to get myself to the West Coast in any manner I wished.

After investigating different train schedules, I bought an interesting assortment of tickets, all of them very cheap. First, I took a train from Washington to Pittsburgh and stopped off to see Shirley's parents. I also visited Shirley's grave and the tombstone we had erected there.

Next, I rode the train from Pittsburgh to Chicago, with a layover of about thirty-six hours. From there, I was to catch a train with some sleeper cars, leaving Chicago at about eight o'clock in the evening. The cost for the train ticket from Washington to Los Angeles had only been $140, and I will explain in a minute why this transcontinental train trip turned out to be so cheap.

When I arrived at the Chicago railroad station, I hailed a cabdriver. "Look," I told him, "I have to stay here this afternoon, overnight, and all day tomorrow, and I will be leaving by train tomorrow evening. Can you take me to a nice hotel that's decent but not too expensive?"

He took me to such a place, and I soon realized that it was primarily a navy hotel, mostly for enlisted personnel. As soon as I had settled down, I went to the nice big bar off the main lobby. In the bar was a mob of women, all in civilian clothes. Standing in the doorway, I listened in a little bit to their conversation and determined that they were all recruits from the boot camp for women at the Great Lakes Naval Base basic training program in Wisconsin. I slipped out to change from my uniform into a sports coat and tie, which was at that time a perfectly legal thing to do, although for the first year of the Korean War, we had to wear uniforms at all times, even off duty. I went back down to the bar, which was still jumping.

Presuming to be a United States Marine

One of the young women, in the uniform of a third class petty officer in the WAVES (the female branch of the U.S. Navy), struck up a conversation with me. She asked me, "Hey, Lieutenant, what are you doing in Chicago?"

"What do you mean by 'lieutenant?'" I asked her.

"I noticed you before when you were standing in the door in your uniform," she replied, and I realized, once again, that sometimes being big and tall is not all it's cracked up to be. I certainly had not wanted her to know that I was an officer, because in those days, as is still true, for an officer to fraternize socially in any way with enlisted personnel in the military was against regulations.

She told me a wonderful story of what all these young women recruits were doing in the bar of the hotel. They were near completion of their WAVES boot camp and had been given their very first shore liberty on the previous weekend. But one of the new sailors had been so fed up with boot camp and all its strict regulations that she had decided simply not to return from her first liberty in Chicago. Her female commanding officer, not wanting her to get into any trouble, had dispatched a second recruit to Chicago on Monday to find and retrieve the missing first recruit.

In the meantime, the first recruit had found the bar in this hotel with some guys in it, and she was able to talk the second recruit into staying on as well. And now they were, as we say, both "over the hill." Finally, a third young woman recruit was sent out to locate the other two and bring them back. When this recruit did not return immediately, either alone or with the two others in tow, the navy decided to expend a member of the staff—the petty officer third class with whom I was talking—to travel to Chicago and gather up and return all of the errant recruits. Although she had laid down the law to the recruits, she had allowed them one last night, informing them that she had arranged for transportation and that they were all going back to the base very early the next morning. She was a very pleasant young woman, and we had an early breakfast and coffee before I returned her to the bar so that she could continue to oversee her charges.

At the appointed time on the following evening, I arrived at the Acheson, Topeka, and Santa Fe railroad station in Chicago to board my transcontinental train. I must tell you that the train was not very impressive, and once I got on it, I realized why it had been so cheap.

The first night, the train traveled through some very nice but barely visible scenery. During the day, the panorama was more monotonous, mostly Kansas, and as we began approaching the Rockies, night fell again and obliterated any glorious vistas. In addition, because it was such a cheap train traveling during bad hours, I soon realized that I was probably one of the few paying customers or, at least, customers paying full fare. Most of the passengers were either: railroad employees, retired railroad employees, or clergymen.

As a matter of fact, I have never seen a greater concentration of clergymen of all faiths than were to be found on this train. Apparently, clergymen were able to obtain a dirt-cheap rate, and most of the railroad employees were on vacation and probably paid nothing. I realized that I was riding the economy train to the West Coast, but I rode on it only from Chicago to Albuquerque, New Mexico, where I had made arrangements to get off.

The train had both a club car and a dining car. I ate a little meal and then went back to the club car, where I participated, with two other gentlemen, in one of the most illuminating conversations I have ever had. One of these gentlemen was a Roman Catholic priest, and the other was a Baptist minister, and the three of us plunged into a heavy theological discussion.

During this most fascinating conversation, the Baptist was steadily drinking ginger ale, while the Catholic priest and I were knocking down whiskeys. I acted as something of an impromptu moderator. Both men were older than I, but they seemed to have some interest in me, perhaps because they realized that I had acquired some education at St. John's. From my knowledge of St. Thomas Aquinas, St. Augustine, Calvin, and others, I kept throwing out questions to these two men, trying to determine where they disagreed and where they could agree. It turned out to be a most pleasant, interesting, and profound discourse, with a kind of grudging mutual respect developing between these two clergymen, and it continued on for hours. One often finds highly educated Catholic priests, but the Baptist pastor easily held his own and was one of the most intellectual Baptist ministers I have ever encountered.

This conversation made such an impression on me that, many years later, when I had to write a term paper for a graduate medieval philosophy course at the University of Virginia, I used the format of that discussion as the basis for my paper. The Catholic priest became a Thomist professor, and I changed the Baptist into a Wittgensteinian. Professor Hammond, under whom I was studying this course, was delighted with the paper and gave me an A, but my work had simply consisted of setting the stage as I had experienced it during my trip, and then assembling the arguments.

I got off at Albuquerque to visit with my father's younger sister, my Aunt Louisa, a doctor, in Socorro, New Mexico about ninety miles south of Albuquerque. She and her doctor husband practiced medicine together. My father's mother, who had been widowed in 1944, lived with them, and I wanted to stop off to visit all three. My Aunt Louisa who, I had always thought, was a very dignified and serious lady, met me at the railroad station in Albuquerque. I had not seen her in some years.

In those days, a two-lane highway ran south of Albuquerque straight to Socorro. And when I say straight, I mean straight as an arrow. The road went on for about forty miles, bending just once for a bridge across a dry riverbed. As soon as we crossed that riverbed, the road straightened out again and continued right into Socorro.

What alarmed me, after my Aunt Louisa got us out of the city of Albuquerque and onto that straight road, was that she began to speed. She got her speed up to ninety miles per hour. We remained at that speed. And we only slowed down to make the little turn across that bridge, and for the last forty-five miles, again, we sped along at ninety miles per hour all the way. We made it from Albuquerque to Socorro in a little over

Presuming to be a United States Marine

one hour, although I must say in my aunt's defense that, in early 1952, we probably only encountered two other cars on the entire trip. Having always regarded my Aunt Louisa as being a mature lady of great gentility, I was utterly surprised to find in her a streak of that legendary racecar driver of previous times, Barney Oldfield.

I had a nice reunion with my grandmother; met my little cousin, Nancy, who was then only about five years old; had a good meal and a good time. I did not spend the night in Socorro but boarded another train from Albuquerque in the evening, which took us through the rest of New Mexico, Arizona, and on to Southern California. This train turned out to be a much nicer train, even boasting roomettes.

As soon as I had settled into my little roomette, I found the club car. There were not very many people in it. I ordered a drink and was just sitting down on a nice sofa when an attractive young woman came in. She looked around the car and the many open seats in it, but she spied the other end of the sofa I was sitting on. She halted in midcourse of her entrance, made a sharp turn, and plopped herself down at the other end of the sofa. We struck up a conversation, and I found out that her name was Lorraine. She was older than I, in her early thirties. She was leaving an eight- or nine-year career as a radio personality in a little town in Illinois because she had managed to get a job as a script writer for a documentary film company in Hollywood. We sat together for most of the trip to Los Angeles; and I enjoyed our talks, thinking Lorraine to be a very fine woman.

We arrived in Los Angeles, I think, on the twelfth of February 1952, and after getting Lorraine's address and telephone number in Los Angeles, I bid her good-bye and immediately caught another train down to Camp Pendleton. I reported in with all my gear, my footlocker, my seabag, and uniforms, and was assigned to the Twentieth Replacement Draft.

The Twentieth Replacement Draft was, at that time, way up at the north end of the base, in what was called Tent Camp. Everybody lived in tents while going through advanced infantry training. The way the Marine Corps organized things in those days was to set up the draft structure into the equivalent of a couple of battalions, and each battalion had three or four companies, and the companies had platoons. Lieutenant members of the replacement draft were assigned to the training companies as platoon commanders. The company commander, the first sergeant, and the senior noncommissioned officers were all stationed at the base permanently. They would take a set of draft companies through advanced infantry training, see them into their last processing, put them on board ship, and send them off to Korea. These permanent personnel would then go back and pick up another company.

The company structure had corporals and sergeants and staff noncommissioned officers, who were regular marines being rotated over to Korea, and they held all the different positions in the training company. But the mass of the company, the privates, were all recruits just out of boot camp, being sent up to Camp Pendleton for advanced infantry training and assignment to a draft. It was an efficient system, and we accomplished an enormous amount of training; Camp Pendleton is a wonderful base for that, with its long open grassy vistas and an abundance of hills to climb. It is easy to train troops to maneuver at Camp Pendleton.

Our Tent Camp, as I said, was at the north end of the base, and within a half a mile or a mile from our camp, a gate lead out onto Route 101 and into the town of San Clemente. San Clemente, of course, is the city that, many years later, gained great notoriety as the refuge of President Nixon after he had resigned from office. San Clemente was even then a nice town. It lies on the coast and, like all California coastal towns, I thought, had a certain opulent look about it.

After being assigned to the Twentieth Replacement Draft in Tent Camp, I was next assigned to a company and then was billeted in a tent with three other officers. The four of us lived there for the next five weeks as we went through training. For the last two plus weeks before shipping out to Korea, we were moved south to the main base at Camp Pendleton, where the troops lived in barracks, and the officers lived in a bachelor officers quarters.

The four of us became good friends in our little tent. Two of the lieutenants were junior to me (remember May 29), but our fourth tent mate was George Morrison, a first lieutenant. For the next six months, George and I became good friends, and our paths crossed frequently. He deserves another digressive sketch.

A DIGRESSIVE SKETCH OF GEORGE MORRISON

George was born and grew up in Pittsburgh, where his father owned a very successful restaurant in the Squirrel Hill neighborhood. George was of Greek descent; his father had come to the United States just after the First World War, changing his name from something like Masteropoulos to Morrison. George was a graduate of the University of Pittsburgh, where he had been a football star. With his height of six feet three and weight of about 240 pounds, he had been a muscled mountain of a football tackle. George was a tough guy and had, when I met him, already accumulated a wealth of life experience. Although he was not physically very handsome, he had a way with women. He was a big, beefy fellow with a hooked, beaky nose, and a massive chin that tilted up so that, in profile, George's nose and chin seemed to be pointed at each other defiantly.

George was a great gambler who had spent many hours perfecting his art in various illegal casinos around Pittsburgh during his college years and after he had graduated. He knew his way around a pack of cards and a pair of dice. But he was a man who had a penchant for getting into trouble. After George graduated from the University of Pittsburgh NROTC program as a Marine Option student in 1950, he became a member of a very famous basic class at Quantico, destined to produce a commandant and more generals, I believe, than any other class in history. It was the Seventh Regular Basic Class, composed of 1950 college, Naval Academy, and ROTC graduates. When the Korean War started, the members of that basic class were accelerated through and left Basic School in January. Many of them went on to great and memorable things.

Presuming to be a United States Marine

George had come down to Camp Lejeune in January of 1951, and as it turned out, when I was an enlisted man in Baker Company, he had been in the Third Battalion of the Sixth Marines as well. While we did not know each other then, we now found that we had overlapped in the Sixth Marines for at least a month.

At Camp Lejeune, George had a couple of pretty serious problems. One occurred when his battalion was sent up to Norfolk for amphibious training at the Little Creek Amphibious Base. After completion of their exercise, the battalion was given liberty, and George went out with a group of other officers into the town of Norfolk. What subsequently happened has always been a little unclear to me, even though I later discussed it with a number of other officers who knew about the episode, but it seems that there developed some kind of altercation in a bar in downtown Norfolk. The shore patrol, the military police, arrived, and George ended up in the hoosegow, which is not exactly a worthy place for a second lieutenant to find himself in. The authorities certainly frowned on second lieutenants getting arrested in barroom brawls. George managed to extricate himself from the jail and return to his unit, but in his officer's record book was now a letter of reprimand, and this clearly bothered George a good deal.

As if he was not already in enough trouble, after George returned to Camp Lejeune, his love for gambling produced an episode that brought him further grief. He and some other officers in the BOQ, the bachelor officers' quarters, had a big poker game going on one night, and they had a bottle or two of whisky with them in order to keep their senses oiled and alert. George and his fellow officers were having a high old time playing poker, and as sometimes happens under these circumstances, it all got just a little noisy. Suddenly there was a knock on the door, and a man in a bathrobe came striding in. He told the card sharks in a fairly imperious way, which—as it later turned out—he had every right of manifesting since he was a major, to "knock it off and keep quiet."

Well, George somehow just did not like the tone of voice this fellow was using. And so George gathered up the front of the fellow's bathrobe unceremoniously and slammed him against the wall, barking right in his face, "We'll make as much noise as we please!" After all the dust had settled from this unfortunate encounter with the major, George had a second letter of reprimand in his file jacket.

One of the first things I learned about George, when I met him in that tent, was that George saw the war in Korea as his only chance to salvage his career. He had a regular commission and wanted to be a career marine, but even he had to be mindful of the fact that he had already screwed up twice. So he said to himself with great resolve, "The only way I am ever going to get out of this whole mess is to get the Congressional Medal of Honor." George was hot to trot, and as we will see, trot he did; and I could tell George stories effortlessly and for a long time. He was a very shrewd man, but everything was a gamble with George.

We eventually moved out of our tent for the last several weeks before we sailed, and lived in a building in the BOQ, at the main base at Camp Pendleton. And that was a pretty barren BOQ. It had a little lounge with a pool table and a Coke machine, and that was about it.

One night, after evening chow, as George and I were walking back to the BOQ, he asked me, "Do you want to shoot some pool?"

"Sure," I said. I am not a pool shark, although I have played it on and off all my life.

But George said, "Let's play for something. How about a Coke?"

So we played rotation, which, I was to learn later, was a game that lent itself best to the George tactic. And man, it was a close game! I stayed right in that game, but George had a lucky shot at the very end and said, "You owe me a Coke!" Okay. "Do you want to play one more?" George asked me.

In that second game, the same thing happened. He did not beat me overwhelmingly, but came through in the nick of time at the end to win. So now I owed him two Cokes. As we continued, we would play for the whole number of Cokes I owed George. Well, as every schoolboy knows, the powers of two go up in rapid succession. We played many pool games, each one close, but without my ever winning, and this went on until I owed him 512 Cokes. I think Cokes were a dime then, and at 10¢ a clip, my debt was $51.20. By that time, of course, I had realized that, in a very friendly way, I had been had; and I immediately adopted the resolution that I would never play pool with George Morrison again for money. George and I subsequently played several other gambling games, poker and blackjack. I was able to beat him a few times just because in those games, if you are lucky and get the right cards, you are in good shape. But George was sharp, and I had learned my lesson. More stories about George and his gambling are coming.

People often refer to Southern California as "sunny Southern California." I arrived there on the thirteenth or fourteenth of February and sailed for Korea on about the sixteenth or seventeenth of April, so that I was in sunny Southern California for about eight weeks. I would venture to say, though, that for at least one-half of those weeks, it rained. I had never seen so much rain in my life! Of course, all the local people would constantly assure us that it usually never rained, that the weather was almost always beautiful, and that they had lovely, sunshiny days just about every single day, as a rule. Except not when I was there. It rained. The incessant rain created, I thought, a certain characteristic California mud, which seemed to be unlike any mud I had encountered anywhere else, although I was destined to encounter even more abundant mud later in Korea. And it was chilly in sunny Southern California too, but without any snow, of course, since Camp Pendleton is just above San Diego.

We were released for liberty at noon on Saturdays, and after my first week at Camp Pendleton, I managed to bum a ride with another officer to Los Angeles. After my arrival in Los Angeles, I called Lorraine, my friend from the train, who was staying

Presuming to be a United States Marine

with her aunt there. As it turned out, for the seven weekends or so while I was at Camp Pendleton, on what little liberty we got, I always went to Los Angeles. We would get off at noon on Saturday, as we had at Basic School, and had to be back at midnight on Sunday. This gave us only a day and a half of liberty, but I spent every one of those weekends in Los Angeles.

Lorraine, of course, was just settling into a new job and learning about the area herself, asking many questions and getting suggestions about sightseeing from her coworkers. Every weekend I would hitch a ride to Los Angeles with somebody and check in with her. She would have had the whole week to plan what we would explore next. Although we never saw a film studio, Lorraine was able to obtain tickets to a television production and a radio show.

We ate wonderful dinners on Saturday night and at noon on Sunday. Los Angeles had a pretty extensive streetcar system in those days, and we explored that. I learned all about Long Beach and Santa Monica by traveling there and to Beverly Hills, Hollywood, and North Hollywood; and we saw many of the movie stars' homes. We visited a number of nightclubs and had some pretty amusing experiences.

Lorraine lived with her aunt for her first three weeks in California, and then found a small apartment. It was really not much more than a room with a kitchen and a bath, although the one room was fairly large. After she moved into the apartment, Lorraine prepared a couple of dinners for us and turned out to be a pretty good cook.

Her aunt had moved out to California as a very young woman. She and her husband had lived in one of the old, early-twenties vintage subdivisions fairly close to Hollywood. The houses were modest and plain and stood in rows. It was not in any way an upper-crusty or, as my daughter would say, la-di-dah neighborhood. Lorraine's aunt was a widow, and Lorraine had warned me about her. "You know," she said, "you may find my aunt a little eccentric, maybe." But she did not go into any specifics.

On the second weekend I went up to tour Los Angeles with Lorraine, her aunt had very kindly arranged to cook dinner for us both on Saturday night. It was an excellent meal, and I enjoyed it very much. After the table was cleared off, Lorraine's aunt sat down, folded her hands in her lap, and said, "Now let's talk about metaphysics."

Apparently, Lorraine had told her aunt that I was a graduate of St. John's and interested in philosophy. And this lovely lady went to get a set of tracts published by some Southern California organization, and God! It was the weirdest stuff I had ever seen. But she was really into what would probably be called New Age writing now, and she clearly expected me to be an authority on the subject.

I tried to tell her that my interest lay in the history of philosophy, like Plato and Aristotle. In a kind but patronizing way, she said, "Oh yes, those were some of the fine old ones." Clearly indicating that she was far more interested in the "fine new ones." But she was a splendid, hospitable old lady, and I had a good time with her.

One of my favorite stories, and this happened on one of the last weekends before I left for Korea, came about when Lorraine and I decided to put on the dog at the Mocambo Club. In 1952, the Sunset Strip was the nightclub center for all of Los Angeles and Hollywood, and the Mocambo Club was the place to go on the Sunset Strip. There I had one of the most curious but exciting experiences of my life.

I had called ahead for reservations, and at the appointed time, Lorraine and I checked in with the maitre d' at his little desk. "Oh yes," he said. "Lieutenant Van Sant." And he beckoned us to follow him. The route took us through an elegant long barroom. And there, with an elbow hooked over the bar, stood Groucho Marx. And Groucho Marx looked just like Groucho Marx, there was no mistaking him. While I would not say that Lorraine was beautiful, she was a handsome woman—fairly tall, brunette, and shapely, with an all-American kind of face. As we approached the bar behind the maitre d', with Lorraine to my left and closest to the bar, Groucho, in a very exaggerated and elaborate fashion, looked Lorraine up and down, from the floor to the top. He then, with his right hand, launched himself from the bar and, walking in the distinctive deep, bent-knee Groucho walk, propelled himself toward us. He very elaborately wheeled around and hooked his right arm under Lorraine's left arm.

And there we were, Lorraine in the middle, with Groucho Marx holding on to her left arm, and me suddenly clutching her right arm—and all three of us followed the maitre d'. When we subsequently talked about this, Lorraine told me that she had been absolutely petrified and struck speechless. I, on the other hand, became the victim of one of the greatest emotional conflicts of my life. On the one hand, I was meeting, in the flesh, somebody who as a comedian was one of my undisputed heroes. On the other hand, he was trying to steal my date, which put me in a rather conflicted state of mind, I will tell you.

Then I said something really inane like "You better watch it, Groucho!" in my best deep marine voice. He leaned forward from the waist, glancing at me around Lorraine, and looked me up and down. I was in uniform and had my World War II and China ribbons on and, once again, he looked me up and down carefully, then wheeled away from Lorraine and slouched back to his location at the bar. I would guess that he did not want to fool with me, and so I had managed successfully to save Lorraine from Groucho Marx.

Subsequently, I read in a biography of Groucho that in that spring of 1952, he was experiencing a very low and difficult period in his personal life. The previous December, after many years together, he and his first wife had dissolved their marriage, and he was not in good shape, apparently spending a lot of time in bars. Subsequently, he got his act back together and soon started his famous quiz show on television, and remarried.

The Mocambo looked like the kind of nightclub you see in 1940s and '50s movies, with terraced balconies of dining tables, all leading down to a big dance floor, with a huge bandstand at one end. It no longer exists, but in those days it was quite posh and expensive, with well-known orchestras playing dance music. Since I was going to Korea to be killed in a week or two anyway, the expense be damned, I thought. I was going to try to have a good time first.

Presuming to be a United States Marine

For me and for Lorraine seeing movie stars: Victor Mature and a date were seated at the table next to us, and in this elegant setting, it was an awesome experience, and we happily ate our dinner; observed all that was taking place around us; danced; and, as they say, put on the dog.

Meanwhile, back at Camp Pendleton, our instruction continued. We were given a number of final tests before going on board ship. One of those was the live fire experience. The way the Marine Corps conducted this exercise in those days was pretty interesting, and you could not help getting some idea of what it was like to be shot at in combat. The drill took place on a big field covered with barbed wire and little trails leading through under the interlaced barbed wire. Along the sides of this barbed wire field was a concrete platform with large water-cooled machine guns, very carefully bolted down and very carefully laid in with steel bars underneath so that they could never drop below a certain point. During the exercise, these machine guns fired continuously, raking the bullets back and forth over the barbed wire. And the guns were set up so that no bullet would reach below three feet above the ground as it sailed over you, but you certainly got the feel of what it sounds and feels like to have real bullets flying overhead, while you slither along on your stomach desperately trying not to get hit. The instructors who put us through this test told us to remember, no matter what, not to raise our head up, not to elevate an arm or a leg under any circumstances. They would then regale us with stories about the guys whose extremities had flown up and were hit by a bullet, and other similar horror tales.

For this exercise, we started out in a trench line. Then we climbed out of the trench and started sliding on the various tracks through the barbed wire, while the machine guns opened up and began sweeping back and forth over us. To spice things up a bit, the instructors were also setting off TNT charges around the field that simulated incoming mortar and artillery fire. It was quite a large installation, which could accommodate about twenty-five men on the little tracks at one time. The tradition called for the platoon leaders, the officers, to lead their platoons through this exercise, and it so happened that my platoon and George Morrison's platoon were the first two to line up.

Our troops, but particularly George's troops who appeared to have taken on George's inveterate gambling habits, began a parlay as to which lieutenant was going to finish first. And there was some real money at stake, mind you, between George's and my platoons. George and I had become good friends by this time, but we suddenly found ourselves under a good deal of competitive pressure. Being a lot thinner than George, I had some natural advantages, while burly George had the unfortunate tendency of getting hung up on the barbed wire. I was also very lucky to have chosen a track across that field, which had turned into some of that slick and smooth mud from all the rain we had been having. Of course, I was willing to sacrifice one of my dungaree utility uniforms for speed. And man, I was able to slither along like a snake and must have beaten George by four lengths, which left my platoon really happy with their winnings.

Taking on the Burden of History

When you get ready to go overseas to war, the training you undergo takes on added significance. You really do pay attention, and you want to make sure that you learn to do things right, even if, as was the case with me, you do not think your own life to be of overly much value. The psychological aspect of preparing to go into combat begins to play a role. I still sharply remember a moment, at the time we were still in Tent Camp by San Clemente, when the two other second lieutenants, George, and I were all sitting around in our tent, just before going to sleep one night, and one of the guys said, "You know, this is kind of a solemn thought, but probably six months from now, one of us is going to be dead."

And unfortunately, it was a good prophecy. The two second lieutenants were badly wounded; I was wounded, but not badly; and George was killed. At the time, we all jumped on the guy who had said it with, "What in hell are you saying something like that for?" Because we were all too uncomfortably aware that he had spoken out loud what we all had been thinking privately.

Two more stories of life in Los Angeles and at Pendleton, and of life with George Morrison. The last weekend before we sailed to Korea was Easter weekend. On Easter Sunday, Lorraine and I attended a sunrise service in the Hollywood Bowl. The Los Angeles symphony orchestra played, and the main speaker was the international commander of the Salvation Army, an Englishman who, as I recall, delivered a rousing sermon. It was a strange feeling to be attending church surrounded by about thirty or forty thousand people. At a very critical point at the recollection of the resurrection, the sun rose above the Hollywood Bowl and shined over the famous sign, which is still there, the big HOLLYWOOD sign on top of the cliff. Inside the Bowl, we looked up at that sign illuminated by the rising sun. Maybe it was a little bit hokey, and maybe it was a lot hokey; but for me, it was an impressive sight and, as the sun continued to rise, a proper spiritual event to attend just before going to war.

I spent that entire last weekend, except for the Easter sunrise service at the Hollywood Bowl, with Lorraine in her apartment. She had cooked up some delicacies for me. George had come to Los Angeles in the same car with me, and George had set for himself the goal that he was going to bed as many women as possible that weekend. Please keep in mind the circumstances under which we were living at that point in our lives. George had Lorraine's telephone number, where he knew that he could reach me. As soon as we arrived in Los Angeles, George went to the Beverly Hills Hotel, and within about ten minutes, he had picked up an attractive young woman in the lounge. He took her out for a couple of drinks, and mercifully, the details of this rendezvous escape me; but essentially, his goal was to take her to her place, which happened to be nearby. As soon as they had completed their horizontal mambo exercise and she had left the bedroom for some reason, George quickly called me to give me the telephone number where he was. I received my first call at Lorraine's at about five o'clock that Saturday afternoon; George had worked fast.

"Okay," he said, "here is her phone number, do the deal." The deal was that I would call the young woman's number, and when she answered, I would say, "This is

Presuming to be a United States Marine

Major Schmitz from Camp Pendleton. Is Lieutenant George Morrison there?" And she would tell me that he was. Then I would say in an important voice, "Well, may I speak to him?" And George would pick up the phone, and I would say, "There has been a change in plans with the draft. You must report back to Camp Pendleton immediately." And I would say it loud enough, and he would hold the telephone so that she could hear it too.

And "Oh God, I've got to go," I heard him say before he hung up. George got up quickly, got dressed, and took off for the lobby of another hotel. Literally, we pulled this drama off three times from Saturday noon to Sunday afternoon, each time enabling George to escape from his latest bedding down. And it worked all three times.

I remember the last one with the third lady on Sunday afternoon, when George said, "I have to go right away, I can't stay." And she actually started crying. This cruel deception! I certainly felt very bad about my role as George's agent in this infamy.

The last George Morrison at Camp Pendleton story is one that illustrates, you might say, George's appetite for fun and alcohol. It was, I think, the Wednesday night before our big Easter weekend. By this time, we were all fitted out and less than a week from loading on board the ship. We only had one more training exercise to complete, and that was combat in built-up areas and towns, which was going to take place on Thursday. We would clean up from that, have liberty for Easter weekend, complete our final packing up, and then move to our ship in San Diego on Tuesday.

That Wednesday night before the combat-in-built-up-areas exercise, somebody came by the BOQ and said, "Hey, there is a restaurant in Oceanside that is having a special on martinis. You want to go?" Oceanside was the small city right at the entrance to Camp Pendleton.

We had finished our training fairly early, it was probably four o'clock or four thirty in the afternoon, and a bunch of us got cleaned up, including George and me. One of the fellows had a car, and in it we all whipped into Oceanside and found the restaurant. It was a nice place serving, at half price, a double martini, poured into a great, big martini glass with a flared top. My recollection is that I had several of those, along with a steak dinner, and everybody else was knocking them down too.

We had polished off the martinis and our steak dinner, and it was still only about 9:00 p.m. As we were headed back to the base, George said, "Let's go out some more, I want to have a little more fun." But neither one of us had a car.

My roommate in the BOQ was a fine man by the name of Bill Hildebrandt. Hildebrandt had a master's degree and received his PhD after the war. He was a biologist, a scholarly fellow, who spent his working life teaching at one of the branches of the University of California. But more to the point, in those days, Bill Hildebrandt also had the distinction of owning a prewar Pontiac. After we returned from our martini expedition, and as Bill was getting ready to go to bed, I asked him if I could borrow his car. Bill responded with, "Oh sure," gave me the keys, and I gathered up George, who lived down the hall. We put on civilian clothes, which may have been good, I don't know, and off we went. The original plan was to drive to Tijuana, Mexico, below San

Diego. But after we got on Route 101 on our way to San Diego, George began feeling awfully thirsty.

"Why don't we find some place here in San Diego before we go on to Tijuana?" he said.

By this time, it must have been close to midnight. Down by the harbor, we spied a nightclub called the Blue Note Cafe. I still have the large neon sign with a big blue neon musical note as its motif indelibly imprinted on my memory.

George and I entered this place, and it was a really jumping kind of place with a dance floor, music, and people drinking. I guess you could get something to eat, if you were really desperate for food. We looked the place over, and it seemed to be pleasant enough. Most of the men in it were naval officers, and the women in it looked nicely put together, and so it seemed to be an agreeable spot.

Two naval officers—lieutenants j.g., or lieutenants—with two quite elegantly dressed young women came in just after we did and immediately moved over to a large table. And George said to me, "Let's move in on these guys!" So we each grabbed a chair and sat down at the table with them. George, who'd already had quite a bit to drink, was trying to be charming but wasn't necessarily pulling it off too well. The two lieutenants looked somewhat terrified, and the young women seemed kind of scared too, because George was being pretty aggressive. I tried to soften our image as much as possible by being exquisitely polite and asking the young lady next to me some innocuous questions.

Finally, George slips in that he said, "You know, we are marine officers." You remember, we were in civilian clothes, and I could see the poor navy lieutenants looking even more uncomfortable. In those days, I was probably in the best condition of my life—muscular, lean, and weighing 213 pounds, while George was a muscular mountain of a guy. As a pair, we must have looked pretty formidable. And, "We are marine officers, you know," repeated George, thumping his chest like Tarzan.

We danced with the girls, while the unfortunate lieutenants stewed, but I could see that George began to feel sorry about our behavior. Perhaps the two letters of reprimand he already had in his folder may have had something to do with it, but George said to me, "Aw hell, why don't we leave these guys alone?" And so we did. You never saw two more relieved naval officers and, most likely, two young women as well.

We went back to sit at the bar of the Blue Note Cafe, where George got down to some really serious drinking. Hours and hours had passed by this time, and it must have been two o'clock in the morning when George got sleepy. So George just climbed up onto the bar, stretched out full-length, and simply went to sleep. A few people were still sitting and drinking at the bar, but there was George, on top of it, and presenting a frightening appearance with his beaked nose, his pointed chin, and his beefy body. I sat on my barstool, continuing to drink quietly, and much more slowly than George had. He remained curled up on the bar, his head resting on his arm, snoring away, sound asleep. None of the bartenders had the courage to wake him and make him get down. They clearly felt it was more prudent to let this huge sleeping dog lie.

Presuming to be a United States Marine

About the time George had snuggled up for his nap on the bar, a young woman came into the bar alone and sat down near me. We struck up a conversation, and when the bar closed at three o'clock, the young lady helped me get George out of the bar. We woke George up, a risky thing to do, given his condition. George was pretty unsteady on his feet, and it took the two of us to carry him out, George not being a very light person. We got him out to the street and pushed him in through the back door of my roommate's car. He lurched all the way across the backseat and became violently sick. This disturbed me a little bit since I had borrowed the car, and I began thinking of the condition in which I would be returning it. We locked George up inside the car. My new friend suggested that we continue our conversation in her car, and we drove off to her place, not very far from the Blue Note. We pulled up in front of the house where she lived, but since her roommate was at home, and since it was so late, we decided to remain in the car and continue our talk there. When I happened to look at my watch, I saw that it was a quarter to five by this time, and I was to fall out at Camp Pendleton at 6:30 a.m. for combat in towns. So the young woman took me back to my roommate's car, where George was still snoring away on the now somewhat less-than-pristine backseat. After saying my good-byes to the young lady, I jumped into the driver's seat and took off with George.

The distance between San Diego and Camp Pendleton in those days was approximately sixty miles on old Route 101. There were no interstates, so, driving like hell, in those days you might be able to make it in an hour. By the time I had started off from the Blue Note Cafe, it was after five o'clock, and I realized that I had a tough task ahead of me. At that hour in the morning, that stretch of the coast is often draped in very heavy sheets of fog, and that particular morning was no exception.

Fortunately, the good Lord was watching over me, because I sailed along at seventy on Route 101 in dense fog, without hitting anything or anybody. I pulled up in front of our BOQ at approximately ten minutes after six.

I told George, "George, we have to go!"

"Uhh!"

"George, come on!"

"Unh!" And he went back to sleep again.

So I said, "To hell with it," and ran up to my room. I explained to my roommate that his car was still occupied and slightly worse for the wear, but that I would make sure George would clean it up for him. I returned the car keys, quickly changed into uniform, and fell out at six thirty, having had no sleep at all and being the not-so-proud possessor of one of the monumental hangovers of all time. I made one more attempt to wake George. No luck, he was out cold.

I said, "Well, George, here comes your third letter of reprimand." But he did not hear me. I fell out, and a vehicle came around to pick us up and took us to join the rest of the troops in the company for combat in towns.

I remember that day only in snatches. It was a hot day, as I recall, bright and finally sunny. Combat in towns started with a briefing and a lecture. We then had to run up to some buildings, which had been permanently erected for this exercise. We had to throw a kind of big fishhook with a rope on it up the building, climb the rope up into the second- and third-story windows, followed by a sweeping out of the house from the top down; and that was the technique we were being taught.

We were using blanks and dummy hand grenades and a lot of smoke grenades. Smoke grenades, when you are in top physical form, are obnoxious. When you are feeling like I was feeling, they were pure hell.

This exercise took all day. We went charging through a problem in the town, climbing ropes, with exploding dummy grenades and smoke grenades going off all around us all the time, while we were shooting blanks; and this cacophony of sounds and smells from all that gunpowder, mixed with the turbulence in my stomach, made for a truly terrible day.

But I got through the morning exercises, and we broke for lunch, although I must say that I had no appetite for any food. Since the place used for combat in towns was still under construction, there were piles of building supplies and lumber scattered all around. I found a cubbyhole inside a pile of lumber, where nobody could see me. I crawled into that cubbyhole and went sound asleep.

I was awakened as troops were mustered back for the afternoon problem, and beheld George among them. The son of a gun was all slicked up and looked fine, because, hell, he had been sleeping since about two o'clock the night before. George sidled over to me and told me he had completely cleaned up the car, and I was glad to hear that.

George asked, "Do you think anybody noticed I wasn't here this morning?" And I said, "Well, I didn't tell anybody you weren't." And so George got away with his latest escapade. He looked fresh and energetic, which was no wonder since he was very well rested, while I probably looked like I felt, simply suffering. There is no other word to describe my condition, and I certainly will never forget that afternoon as long as I live. I walked like a zombie through all of the exercises we had to do, climbed in and out of windows, and assaulted the "enemy" inside these houses in a most pitiful personal condition of disrepair.

At long last, the day came to an end, and I gratefully crawled back to my BOQ room and into bed; collapsed; and, I think, slept for twelve hours. Thus passed one of the last days left to us in the United States. The next morning, Friday, we packed, stenciled our footlockers, so we could go on liberty that afternoon. We were told that when we arrived in Japan, we were to divide up all our gear, so that the only thing we took to Korea was our field pack with our underwear, socks, a couple of changes of field uniform, and whatever personal items we wanted to bring with us into combat. All the rest of our uniforms, clothing, and gear were to be stored in our footlockers and left in Japan. We were instructed to keep our good uniforms out, because we would have liberty in Japan before going over to Korea. On Tuesday the trucks came, and the troops got mustered, and we moved from Camp Pendleton down to the San Diego Naval Base, and from there loaded onto the troopship.

Presuming to be a United States Marine

We were the Twentieth Replacement Draft. The Marine Corps tried to send a replacement draft to Korea every month. There were almost three thousand of us in the draft. The ship carrying us was not as big as either of the transports on which I had traveled across the Pacific to China and back, but it was a comfortable ship.

Our departure from San Diego was fairly dramatic. The Korean War was not fought under the very strict secrecy of World War II, so that when replacement drafts left San Diego, the marines' families could see them off at the dock; and this became a colorful occasion. The Camp Pendleton Base Marine Band played as we loaded aboard the ship up the gangplank with all our gear. I remember a funny episode about the crowd packed onto the dock, as they witnessed our departure. There had been a change in company commanders near the end of our training in the replacement draft at Camp Pendleton, and our new commander, who went to Korea with us, was an older man. He had been enlisted for a long time and had been commissioned near the end of World War II, rising to the rank of captain by 1952. By that time, he was nearing his thirty years of service. This captain was a nice-enough man but, unfortunately, absolutely devoted to the bottle. He was, as we could soon see, really one of the most pitiful alcoholics I have ever encountered in life. This condition, however, in no way prevented him from being something of a Romeo; and it may have even encouraged this passion in him.

We were all leaning over the railing, waving good-bye to the mob of people on the dock. It was a big crowd of people, a throng of relatives and friends of the guys shipping out. To begin with, our captain stood in our group, and he was waving and blowing kisses at a somewhat blowzy-looking woman standing on the dock, dabbing her eyes. Somebody asked him, "Oh, is that your wife down there?"

"No, no," he said. "My wife is at the other end of the dock." And he continued blowing kisses to this woman, who was sobbing miserably. Finally, he indicated to her that he had duties to attend to and disappeared from the rail. We next observed him slinking away from the crowds of troops at the rail. He ran toward the stern behind the troops and took up a position at the stern, emerging at the front of the troops right on the rail, where he began waving and blowing kisses to his wailing wife, who was well separated by the crowd of people on the dock from the other woman. Both women were obviously completely unaware of each other. Our captain was obviously a real operator who knew how to keep them apart.

The ropes were pulled off, the tugs began pulling the ship away from the dock, and the ship began moving under its own power. The end of the dock was cleared for the band, which marched very smartly clear to the end of the dock, and played the Marine Corps Hymn, as we sailed out of the harbor of San Diego. And it moves me even now when I remember that scene, our last glimpse of the United States before sailing for Korea.

We found our bunks in our staterooms, and I must say, traveling across the Pacific as a second lieutenant was a little more pleasant than my previous transits had been. The bunks were only double, with a top and a bottom bunk. There were about a dozen, but no more than fifteen, officers in the compartment, and captains got a compartment with only six bunks. We all ate in the officers' mess, which was very comfortable, as we could sit down to eat and were privileged with all kinds of other little niceties like that.

The trip over to Japan and Korea was much shorter than my previous crossings. It only took us about two weeks. We did not stop anywhere but sailed from San Diego straight to Kobe, Japan. Several interesting things happened along the way.

First of all, George, my good old friend, was very much a part of my life in those days. George saw the crossing of the Pacific as a chance to indulge in some very serious gambling. Unfortunately, our rather intensive liberty exercises the last weeks we were in California had caused George to become almost broke. I think he had about $4 with him when he boarded the ship, but he got into some kind of a game and lost it all.

George approached me and said, "Van, I need twenty bucks. Have you got twenty bucks?"

I said, "Sure, I have it."

He said, "Well, could I borrow it?"

"Well, sure, George," I told him.

He said, "I'll tell you what. I will give you two choices. I'll either pay the $20 back as soon as I win, or I will split fifty-fifty with you everything I make on this trip with this twenty."

I then and there made a very stupid decision. I said, "George, just pay me back the twenty. I don't want to make any kind of deals."

"No," he told me. "I'm serious. I would, you know. I would do that. I am flat broke, and I need the money, and I am willing to split everything with you fifty-fifty."

I said, "No, George, just pay me back the twenty when you have it and can spare it."

"Okay," said George.

He took that twenty, and George got into a variety of games. First of all, he was very skilled at gin rummy for money. He found a couple of fish on the ship and took them out. He shot a lot of crap and dice, and even sometimes crossed over into enlisted country for crap games, of which there were many. He played blackjack and poker. George could play anything, and he played everything well. To go to the end of this story, a replacement draft shipload of marines, heading out from California probably did not have too much loose money on it because most of the guys had spent everything they had in their final days in California. But there is always what you might call "loose and available gambling money" present. By the time we landed in Kobe, I think George had collected just about all the loose and available gambling money on that ship, because he got off with a total of $8,800 and sent three or four money orders back home into his banking account. Needless to say, within a few days of borrowing the $20 from me, he had repaid his debt. When I saw the $8,800, I was forced to contemplate that $4,400 of that amount of money could have been mine! I was never upset about my decision, though, and always recognized George as a superb gambler.

Presuming to be a United States Marine

Another interesting observation was on the reaction of some men to the lack of alcohol on board. The United States Navy, since sometime before the Civil War, has absolutely banned alcohol from its ships. There is no consumption of alcohol whatsoever. There are naval officers and naval enlisted men, of course, who are alcoholics. Although officially they were, and are, not permitted to bring any alcohol on board ship, the fact of the matter was that some people did sneak alcohol aboard. The navy lieutenant commander, the chief liaison from the ship's crew to the replacement draft, became firm friends with our marine captain, and it was clear that the basis of their friendship was mainly their mutual interest in booze. But the lieutenant commander probably realized several days out from Kobe that he had made a mistake befriending our captain, because our captain had finished off his own supplies and had begun dipping into the stock the lieutenant commander had brought along. Several days out from Japan, they both found themselves out of booze, and I have never seen two more desperate individuals than these two men.

Our captain first approached us, his officers, and, with an absolutely frantic look in his eyes, said, "Guys, have you got any whisky, or any booze at all?" I did not have a drop, personally; I had not had a drop since I got on board ship, and I had to tell him no, I did not. Then he asked, "Well, jeez, do you know anybody who has any?"

"No, I don't, Captain," I answered. Quite frankly, of all the rest of the officers in our crowd, the ones who were in our company and with whom we had trained, including George, no one was so dependent on booze that they had to have it around them all the time. I think our two alcoholics must have had to tide themselves over with the last desperate refuge for a boozer in those days, and that was Aqua Velva. Aqua Velva, an aftershave lotion, contained a significant amount of alcohol. Most people got sick from drinking it, and it left an unmistakable odor on the breath.

In my previous trans-Pacific crossings, I had been assigned specific jobs. As a second lieutenant, aside from looking in on my troops every day to see if everybody in the draft was getting along all right, I had no real responsibilities. In addition to perfecting my bridge game, I also participated in some really memorable Monopoly games, a fun game for a crowd. One of the most colorful participants in this game was the man who lived in the upper bunk above me. He was a young lieutenant named Dee-Dee Shepherd. Now Dee-Dee, and that was his nickname, was a man of some distinction because it so happened that his father was the commandant of the Marine Corps at that time, the very famous, heroic, and colorful General Lemuel C. Shepherd. But you would never hear from Dee-Dee that his father was the commandant. Dee-Dee was a graduate of Washington and Lee University in Virginia and a really fun guy. He had a wonderful sense of humor and was a passionate Monopoly player. He had a great collection of sayings, which he used as he rolled the dice. "Ah, the last of the big spenders is about to take the plunge and build hotels on the Boardwalk," he commented, and he would always have a running line of palaver when it was his turn to play.

But at one point, Dee-Dee almost got into a great deal of trouble. Dee-Dee had a friend, a lieutenant named Tougas. When officers were being assigned to the staterooms

Taking on the Burden of History

on our draft, there turned out not to be enough space for lieutenants, but there was a commodious six-space compartment that had only three captains in it, so that there were three extra bunks left. As a consequence, Lieutenant Tougas was put in with the captains in that compartment. I never knew Tougas very well, but he was a good friend of Dee-Dee's, and Dee-Dee liked nothing better than to play tricks on Tougas.

When we had almost reached Japan and were probably about two days out from Kobe, word came down that we ought to get our good uniforms out of our footlockers and get them squared away so that we could go on liberty in Japan. Everybody began fussing with their uniforms and their shirts, trying to get them in as good a shape as one could aboard a ship. The three captains, too, had taken their uniforms out and had hung them on the bulkhead to air out the wrinkles so that they would all look sharp on liberty in Kobe in a couple of days.

Well, Tougas had been working hard all day, and Tougas lay down in his bunk and fell fast asleep right after supper. And that gave Dee-Dee a bright idea. There were fire extinguishers hanging all over the ship. Dee-Dee crept into the compartment Tougas shared with the three captains, first making sure that they were all out and that Tougas was completely alone and fast asleep on his bunk in the compartment. Dee-Dee took the fire extinguisher off the bulkhead inside the compartment and very gently and softly laid it down in the bunk, right beside Tougas. Then Dee-Dee silently stole away, never waking Tougas.

Disaster struck. Tougas apparently thrashed about in his sleep a good deal. Rolling over on his side, he collided with the fire extinguisher and panicked, pushing it out of the bunk. The decks on the ship were all steel. The fire extinguisher landed on the deck in an upside-down position and hit with enough force to set it off. And it was a big heavy metal tank extinguisher with a rubber hose to direct the flow of the liquid carbon dioxide to the flames. With nobody holding on to the rubber hose, it just whipped about in the compartment, spreading a layer of white foam over everything, including all the captains' uniforms, which became completely covered and coated with foam.

By this time, of course, Tougas was wide awake. He grabbed the fire extinguisher and turned it off. But just about that time, one of the captains returned to the compartment. As might be expected, he was less than pleased when he saw the damage inflicted by the errant fire extinguisher.

Of course, the incident was immediately reported to the officer of the deck, who was the acting commander of the ship at that time. Within minutes, shore patrolmen and ship's officers appeared at the scene of the crime. They cordoned off the stateroom and began grilling Tougas who, of course, had no idea what had happened. He must have finally managed to convince them that he was innocent, and they started questioning people all around as to who might have observed what had happened. Meanwhile, Dee-Dee had been hanging around on the fringes of all this activity, and of course, Dee-Dee was the man who had done the deed.

As the captains were trying to home in on the perpetrator, Dee-Dee confessed and arranged for the captains' uniforms and the stateroom to be cleaned. You could tell that once both the captains and the officer of the deck became aware that the culprit was the son of the commandant of the Marine Corps, they began to exhibit a certain reluctance to push too hard for punishment. Dee-Dee proved himself to be a gentleman and made everything right again, all the time entertaining us thoroughly with descriptions of what Tougas looked like waking up and finding himself in bed with a fire extinguisher. And that was part of our diversion on the way over to Japan.

We arrived in Kobe in late April of 1952. As a consequence of its industry, Kobe had been heavily bombed in World War II. There was still a lot of evidence of the destruction caused by the bombing, but it was a vibrant and lively city and remains the jumping-off point to some interesting places to visit in Japan.

I went ashore with my old roommate, Hildebrandt, from BOQ days at Camp Pendleton and another friend of ours, and one or two others who had already been to Japan and knew the country pretty well. We caught a train for Kyoto, the jewel of Japan. It is the traditional capital, filled with Buddhist temples and palaces and wonderful landscaping. Most notably, thanks to the intervention of a former U.S. ambassador to Japan, Kyoto was never bombed during World War II by the Allied forces, and consequently, the city was even then its luminous self.

I had my first trip on a very fast and efficient Japanese train. The train arrived at the platform, very much like a New York subway. The doors opened. There was a lot of shouting over the loudspeaker and from the conductors on the train, all just as unintelligible as on a New York subway. We were herded into a car, and then—wham! The doors shut, and off the train went. In my several visits to Japan, I probably only had a seat once, and for the rest of the time, I stood up. Standing on a Japanese train, at least in those days, I soon discovered, was not too difficult for me because the ceiling of the railroad car was about two and a half inches lower than my height, so that I didn't even have to hold on to anything. I simply planted my feet on the floor, wedged my head against the ceiling, and braced myself in that position.

We disembarked from the train in Kyoto, got a map, and explored. We saw the emperor's summer palace, where all the coronations of Japanese emperors take place. When you travel to England and visit Buckingham Palace, you see that everything there is designed on an imposing and royally large scale. In Japan, the sacred or ceremonial spots are not created on a grand scale at all. The buildings and grounds are small, delicate, and extremely carefully and artistically designed and constructed. Even the emperor's summer palace and the coronation yard were not imposing in size, but exquisite in design with carefully trimmed trees, little fountains and brooks babbling along, all presenting a marvelously put together experience.

We visited some temples and saw some of the great, big gongs that were beaten with what looked like a telephone pole swinging on a rope, producing a deep, heavy sound calling the monks to worship. We found a nice Japanese restaurant, had a very fine dinner, and got back on the train for Kobe to prepare for our departure to Korea the next day.

Taking on the Burden of History

On the train back to Kobe, I had an interesting experience. I was standing inside the carriage, braced in the usual manner, but holding on to a vertical pole for extra steadiness. A smiling Japanese man wearing thick glasses rushed on to the train, grabbed the same pole I was holding, looked at me, and smiled even more broadly, flashing big blobs of gold in his teeth. Being an extra amiable chap, he engaged me in a sort of conversation.

"Ah, you Amelican?"

"Yes, I am."

"Ah, you, me, have English convelsation!"

"Oh good. Let's have an English conversation."

"Ah yes, yes, yes, we have English convelsation?" And each time he repeated this sentence, his inflection changed slightly, so that sometimes there was an exclamation point at the end and sometimes a question mark, and sometimes he just asserted it as a statement. After about four or five repeats of this, it became apparent that the only English this gentleman knew was "you," "me," "have," and "English convelsation." He had a book tucked under his arm, and I saw that the title on the cover was *The Collected Works of William Shakespeare* in English. I pointed to the book.

"Ah, yes, yes, yes," he said and handed me the book. I opened the book. And the word "Shakespeare" on the cover was the last word in English I saw, for the whole book inside was written in Japanese. I indicated to him, as best I could, that I thought he would really enjoy reading the plays and sonnets. And thus we had reached the limit of our English conversation. But we smiled at each other periodically, were very congenial with each other all the way back to Kobe, and at least several more times he told me, hopefully, "You, me have English convelsation?" And he certainly was a most pleasant gentleman.

We got back to Kobe, returned aboard our ship, took care of our gear, got ourselves fitted out for going on to Korea, packed our footlockers with our good uniforms, stacked them up, and bade them farewell. They were to be stored in Kobe. We spent the night on the ship. The officers, up to this point, had not received their arms, although the troops had boarded in San Diego with their rifles, including bayonets. The standard weapon for a lieutenant in those days, and it was to change while I was in Korea, was a carbine. The next morning, we were issued our carbines and some ammunition. Being armed added a certain somber significance to our approach to Korea.

We sailed away from Kobe and took the relatively short trip over to the North China Sea and up the west coast of Korea to Inchon, our point of landing.

L to R: David Skyrm, the author, Bill Boatsman, unknown.
This must have been our first outdoor pinochle game in April, 1946, because Skyrm was returned to the U.S. in late April or early May.

The two men in the back row are the author on the left and our company supply sergeant, Private H.B. Gray. The other two men in foreground were members of the C Company Machine Gun Platoon whose names I have forgotten. This picture was taken in late spring of 1946.

The author with Chinese Nationalist Lieutenant who commanded the Chinese Army detachment guarding the coal train, to which our provisions cars were attached, on the trip from Lin Si to Beidahe Junction, May, 1946 (Note the brand new stenciled corporal's stripes.)

Three members of my train guard detachment on the way to Beidahe Junction. Note the sleeping bags and the fact that they are tied on. The other two cars of our little convoy are to the right and left of this car.

A small market and R.R. station along the tracks between Lin Si and Beidahe Junction. This was on the same trip with the Nationalist officer.

A picture of my first wife, Shirley (1927-1951). The man to her left is Richard Miller, her father. This was taken in the early spring of 1949 when we visited her family cottage in Bethany Beach, DE.

My mother insisted on having this photo made at a fancy studio in Washington, D.C. before I left for Korea. She made it clear that she thought I might not return and she wanted something to remember me by.

The Easter, 1952, Sunrise Service I attended with Lorraine two days before sailing to Korea.

Lt. Vincello (left) and Lt. Vick, the other two officers who joined 2nd Battalion, 1st Marines with me in May of 1952.

This is the battalion commander's tent in the camp for the reserve battalion of the right regiment of the 1st Marine Division in Sangkorangpo. Picture was taken in late November, but the patio above the C.O.'s jeep is the same one where Colonel Quilici interviewed us in May.

My platoon runner helping with the new command post, built in May after I was evicted from my former command post by a rat. We incorporated the cave into the structure. Where he is standing was eventually covered over with timbers strong enough to support a tank.

This Maxim gun was captured by the 2nd Battalion, 1st Marines and adorned the Battalion Headquarters tent wherever we went. I often had the privilege of serving as the target for one of these.

Some men from Fox Company. This was taken in June of 1952 when we were in reserve at the "Rock Pile." On our next stretch on line from July 27 to October 15, many of these men were either killed or wounded.

The Honor Guard Platoon: drilling at the "Rock Pile." I am at the extreme left of the picture and the non-commissioned officer facing me is Gunnery Sergeant Kelly.

The author. This was taken during the Beach Party I authorized on the 4th of July. The can in my hand is a well known beverage. Note the sergeant's stripes on my dungarees, issued to me at the shower point. The troops called these "shower promotions."

The Beach Party continues with a swim in the Imjin River just below the Widgeon Bridge. Note author to the left, still clutching can.

The officers of Fox Company taken about the 1st of September after we had pulled off Bunker Hill after the Battle of Aug 25-26. Standing (L to R): Lt. Janelle, Lt. Burhans, Captain Moody, the author. Kneeling are the newly joined Lt. Hill to the left, and Lt. Haebel. The word was that the battered old sign had been with the company since the Inchon landing

My last formation with Fox Company. I am Receiving the Purple Heart from Captain Tom Barrow.

No November 10, the Marine Corps birthday, can go unobserved. Fortunately we were in reserve. The gentleman seated in the camp chair is Col. Warren.

Replacements being flown in. Taken either late November or early December, 1952.

The range of hills in the mid-distance is the reverse slope of our MLR (Main Line of Resistance) in the sector of the flank regiment of the 1st Marine Division. Taken in December when Sgt. Sullivan and I reconnoitered blocking positions.

Private First Class Greer, our S-3, Operations jeep driver from most of my tour from November to April, 1953.

Major Robert L. Dominick USMC, Operations Officer of the 2nd Battalion, and my boss, from November until I left in early April of 1953. Retired as a Colonel in early 70's and assisted in preparation of this book.

The big bend of the Imjin River at Sangkorangpo. We were here as regimental reserve battalion until mid December when this picture was taken.

Corporal O'Brien. Operations Assistant. He was the hero of the story of liberty in Inchon when he masqueraded as a Lieutenant

The flamethrower firing in the practice course that Colonel Gilliland had us set up in January and early February of 1953.

Headquarters, Ascom city Transient Center. I stopped here on my way to R & R in Japan, and also in April on my way home.

The de-lousing in which we were all compelled to participate before going aboard ship. This picture taken at Ascom City near Inchon in April of 1953.

The Author in Ascom City the day before boarding ship for return home. I look anorexic. They gave us a physical examination and I weighed in at 187. I arrived in Korea weighing 213.

Chapter 9

Introduction to Combat

As we approached our anchorage off Inchon, we could hear the deep rumble of artillery in the distance off to our northeast. I remember a fine young marine sergeant who had been in the same training company as me all the way through our draft training at Camp Pendleton, standing near the bow for some time, then turning and starting to walk aft. I was going forward to the bow, and as he passed me, he saluted and said, "You know, Lieutenant, there was a funny look on a lot of the men's faces when they first heard those artillery shells going off."

Even though I was now an exalted lieutenant, at this point, I was no more than a body that had to be put ashore, and I was aware of the fact that, no matter when the ship arrived at Inchon, it had to be unloaded. At Inchon, there was no dock. All the ships coming to Inchon anchored in the harbor, and smaller boats were sent out to take us ashore. We had to climb over the side of our ship and descend on cargo nets into a small landing craft, a pretty tricky maneuver under the best of circumstances. In the darkness, it became even more complicated, although there were searchlights trained on the ship, so that we could dimly see our craft in the shadows, down at the bottom of the net, bobbing around in the murkiness. As it turned out, during my year in Korea, I would climb up and down nets in the Inchon harbor a number of times. I remember that the water was never calm. The landing craft would bounce up and down, and we would climb down the net, and just as we were ready to step off, the boat would lurch away three or four feet, or else it would come slamming up against us and bang us off the net into the boat. It was not a very pleasant or elegant way to arrive in Korea, but then we knew that what was to face us there would not be pleasant or elegant either.

Once the boat was loaded, we were taken ashore and lined up along a railroad track. We had all been broken down and organized several days before we even arrived in Japan. All the officers were allowed to select the regiment in which they wished to serve. Of course, artillery officers would have to serve in the Eleventh Marines because that was the artillery regiment of the First Division, and the other specialty officers, like tanks and engineers, would automatically be sent to their respective units. But infantry officers had their choice between the First, Fifth, and Seventh regiments. Having been in the First Marines in China, I figured that I was a First Marine all the way, and therefore selected the First Marines. It turned out, as luck would have it, that a fair number of the troops I had trained with in California ended up going into the First Marines also, and at least fifteen were assigned to the same company with me. And that was quite nice because I already knew them and they knew me.

Now all of this activity on shore was carried out in the pitch-dark along a railroad track, where we got organized, mustered, and divided up. Our train arrived, loaded with all of the people from, probably, the Eighth, Ninth, and Tenth replacement drafts, who had come over ten, eleven, or twelve months earlier and were now being rotated home; and all the veterans of these many months in Korea were getting off the train and marched down to the landing craft that had brought us ashore to board the ship for home.

And suddenly, I heard, out of the jet black night, from the guys going home that same wonderful shout that I had first heard on my arrival at Parris Island. "You'll be sorry!" And it was drawn out in the same ominous way: "You'll . . . be . . . soooorry!" And I guess you could say that this refrain sounded a kind of a homecoming to us.

When all the marines were cleared off the train, we climbed aboard. The train went up the Inchon peninsula, and we crossed the Han River to Seoul. The train stopped, and some of the people got off, but most of us remained on the train because the railhead of Munsan-ni, north of Seoul, was quite close to the headquarters of the First Marine Division.

By the time we got off the train, it had to have been two o'clock in the morning. The trucks arrived, finally, and all of us joining the First Marines were sent to the far right flank of the division for the longest trip in the big bouncing old truck, the standard six-by-six used by both the U.S. Army and the Marine Corps from 1940 to 1970. We were brought to the headquarters of the Second Battalion, First Marines, and the troops got billeted down in their tents. There were three of us officers joining that battalion, and we were taken to an officer's tent. By this time, it must have been about four o'clock in the morning, and it was still dark outside.

I had just started to move into the empty officers' tent with my two fellow arrivals when a shadow appeared in the doorway, and a voice called out, "Lieutenant Van Sant?" The voice turned out to belong to Marion Etheridge, who had been a classmate of mine in Officer Candidate Screening and Basic School. He was the adjutant of the Second Battalion, First Marines, and had seen my name on the list as one of the new incoming officers. He got up in the middle of the night to welcome me, and I found that to be a most unexpected and kind greeting.

The other two officers were Lieutenant Vick and Lieutenant Vincello, so that we became known as the Three Vs. We sat together, companionably, and I remember that Lieutenant Etheridge talked with us for at least an hour. First of all, he told me what had happened to all my Basic School classmates. If you will remember, most of my classmates from Basic School were sent immediately to the West Coast and on to Korea, while I was held back for "humanitarian reasons," because of Shirley's terminal illness. It was now early May, and many of my classmates had been in Korea since November or December of the previous year.

Presuming to be a United States Marine

Etheridge did a nice job of filling me in on what had happened to everybody we knew, what was happening to our marines in general, where they were, and what they were doing. The Second Battalion was in regimental reserve and, therefore, responsible for welcoming in all the replacements for the entire regiment. The campsite was on a lovely bluff on a sharp curve of the Imjin River, a U-turn the river takes at this bend, at a place called Sangkorangpo. Just across the river from us, and to the south, was a Marine 155-artillery battery, so that our little conversation was periodically punctuated by great volleys of artillery shells flying right over our tent. I could hear the shells passing over us and heading toward the Chinese. While this was a nice introduction to the noise of war, thank God, that night the Chinese did not see fit to shoot back at us, so that the shells were at least coming from only one direction.

We finally had a little sleep, got up, had some breakfast, and started into what I found to be a very worthwhile program the Marine Corps had for arriving replacements. We were not immediately sent to our units but were, for five days, put through a fairly extensive conditioning, orientation, and training program.

First of all, we went out and hiked in order to stretch out some of the kinks that had set in after two weeks aboard ship. Next, we got to zero in on our weapons and shoot them, making sure they were working properly and were sighted properly. We were given some on-the-ground and on-the-map orientation on the exact situations we were going to face. We had two intensive days of countermine warfare training in order to be able to deal with the mines, which were ever present in our area. Mines were a constant threat, and I am sad to say that many of my marines and friends were wounded or killed by mines, some of them horribly.

We were given a good overall view of the situation before we received our assignments, and this was done not just for the officers, but also for the enlisted men, who participated in all aspects of this training and were given a lot of pointers on how to survive in field conditions in Korea.

As a background for all of the subsequent stories, let me give a brief summary of the Korean War. It began with an invasion of South Korea by North Korean forces on June 25, 1950. The North Koreans practically rolled up the South Korean army, such as it was, with their own much more powerful and better-equipped forces. Seoul was taken immediately since it is located close to the border in the northern part of South Korea. The handful of American troops sent over from the occupation forces in Japan during July were pushed south and, along with the South Korean divisions that had survived the initial North Korean onslaught, were eventually penned up in a perimeter called the Pusan Perimeter at the very southern end of South Korea. At this point, and here I must speak admiringly of my fellow marines, the Fifth Regiment, was thrown into the fray. It had sailed from the West Coast as soon as the war had begun. This regiment became a regimental combat team and was thrown into the perimeter where, in early August 1950, it fought the decisive battle of Naktong River, stopping the North Korean advance and saving the Pusan Perimeter. The Naktong ran roughly north to south along the western side of the perimeter and became the line of contact

Taking on the Burden of History

between the North Korean forces and the Americans. By that time, there were not too many organized South Korean fighting forces left.

The Americans, as a result of the Fifth Marines' victory, threw back the North Koreans and broke out of the Pusan encirclement. Simultaneously, the First and Seventh Marines, along with all the supporting forces of the division, were loaded aboard ship and were taken up the west coast of Korea. At the last minute, the Fifth Marines were pulled off the lines at Naktong and sent aboard other ships to Inchon to join their fellow regiments. The entire First Marine Division landed on September 15, 1950, making an end run around the North Koreans. They landed at Inchon, retook Seoul within eleven days, and completely cut off the North Koreans in the southern part of South Korea.

What started out as simply an encirclement ended up with a rout, and many North Koreans were taken prisoner. The South Korean army found itself again, became reconstituted, and joined the effort. After the taking of Seoul, by the fifth of October, there were no North Koreans left in South Korea. This had been a very decisive victory. The First Marine Division was brought back down to Inchon and loaded aboard ships, which sailed clear around South Korea and north along the east coast. They landed at a port called Hungnam, from which they attacked northward.

Elements of the Tenth Corps, including the First Marine Division; a British Commando, which was really a battalion of British Marines; and one army division, penetrated all the way up into the northeast corner of North Korea to a huge reservoir, the Chosen Reservoir, the scene of the famous battle, and to the Yalu River, the border between China and North Korea.

To the west of the Tenth Corps was the Eighth Army, the bulk of the U.S. Army's forces in Korea, and they had been attacking northward after the fall of Seoul. Following the retaking of Seoul, five or six U.S. Army divisions and an equal number of South Korean army divisions pushed as hard as they could north. They took the North Korean capital of Pyongyang, and a few of those units almost reached the Yalu. Things began looking really great.

At this point, and this was in early November, about a million and a half so-called volunteers from the Communist People's Republic of China, which was then only about a year old, crossed the Yalu River and came south to help their North Korean comrades. Under the assault, the Eighth Army on the flank of the Tenth Corps to its west almost disintegrated. In fact, the official army history of that period, near the end of November 1950, notes that for thirty-four days, the Eighth Army was out of contact with the enemy. That means that the soldiers were either being captured or were retreating before the huge assaulting force. Next, the Chinese turned the full attention of their enormous military power to the east against the one army division, the one marine division, and the British Royal Commando around the Chosen Reservoir.

The Chinese completely surrounded this force. The marines, in an epic struggle, broke out of the encirclement and came back down to their port at Hungnam, bringing with them all their dead and wounded and, in the course of this struggle, destroying about four Chinese divisions. It was a monumental battle, about which we immediately heard a great deal when I was still a sergeant at Camp Lejeune. The reader will remember that had my name begun with *H* or lower, I would have been sent as a replacement after that battle because the marines had suffered such enormous casualties, both from enemy action and the cold weather.

But the surviving marines had returned, bringing with them their equipment and their dead and wounded. They were backloaded aboard ships at Hungnam and sailed down to South Korea. There they were put ashore and marched back up almost to the 38th Parallel, the original border between North and South Korea. In the spring of 1951, the Chinese and the reconstituted North Koreans mounted an all-out offensive. They were able to push the line south, in most places, by twenty or thirty miles, and in the process almost retook Seoul. In the late spring of 1951, American forces counterattacked and, by July of 1951, had returned the line, roughly and approximately, to where it remains now.

At that point, truce talks began at Panmunjom. These talks periodically broke down, stopped altogether, and then resumed. Meanwhile, unremitting seesaw action on the front line continued. That action consisted of giving up or taking a hill here and a rice paddy there, constant patrolling, and little skirmishes this way and that, but the basic, general line of division between the two forces remained roughly the same from the summer of 1951 until the war ended two years later.

In comparing casualties for that two-year period, there were more marine lives lost as a result of fighting along static positions in the trench warfare, and I think there were also more army casualties than in the entire first year of the war when our forces were moving up and down the peninsula in a war of maneuver. At the end of the Korean War, nearly 55,000 Americans were dead, and more than 120,000 wounded.

The Marine Corps was positioned on the east coast of the peninsula from January of 1951 until February of 1952. For over a year, the marines were in their positions on the east coast, usually fairly close to the eastern end of the line. Marines were sometimes shifted around slightly in that zone farther inland, but their main battles were fought around a huge valley they called the Punch Bowl, and under that name, several marine legends were born.

In February of 1952, the First Marine Division was pulled off the line on the east coast, brought over to the west coast in a massive truck convoy, and placed in position just north of Seoul. The reason for this was that by the winter of 1951-52, there was considerable Allied intelligence that the North Koreans and the Chinese were most likely to mount an all-out offensive in the spring. The concern was the South Korean divisions' ability to protect the capital. These divisions were replaced by the First Marine Division and the Korean Marine Corps, a unit that had been founded after World War II and had been trained and brought up along with the U.S. Marine Corps. The two organizations were very closely knit together, and the Korean Marines had adopted most of the U.S. Marines' traditions. As will be seen, I worked with the Korean Marines a couple of times and found them to be tough.

The Koreans and the First Marine Division were given the responsibility of protecting the main corridor that led down from North Korea to Seoul on the western

Taking on the Burden of History

side of the peninsula. We also had in our zone of action Panmunjom, with its truce talks. General Mark Clark, who by this time was the chief of the Allied forces in Korea, wanted to have people on whom he could rely protecting the truce site. There was a very elaborate plan for an extraction force to stand ready to act in case the truce talks collapsed and any skirmishes broke out. The truce talks were held one thousand yards north of our positions and one thousand yards south of the Chinese positions. We were always on the alert and prepared for any rescue missions necessary.

And that was the situation. By the time of my arrival, the division had been moved to the western front. The First Marines and the Seventh Marines were online when we arrived, and the Fifth Marines were in reserve. However, the front was spread out so much that the First Marines had seven companies online to man the Regimental Front. A regiment in those days had nine companies, so that there were only two companies of the Second Battalion in reserve, and one company online attached to the Third Battalion.

Our five-day orientation included, in addition to the hiking and other training, a couple of reverse slope reconnaissances of the front lines, with continued briefings on mine warfare. On the fifth day, in the middle of the afternoon (it must have been May 10), we three officers, Vick, Vincello, and Van Sant, were informed by the adjutant, Lieutenant Etheridge, that we were to see the colonel, our battalion commander.

This was the first time we were to meet Lieutenant Colonel Quilici, who turned out to be a good man. I will be making evaluative comments about the four lieutenant colonels under whom I served in Korea; and of the four, Quilici was the second best.

He had a rather nice headquarters tent, set up on what looked like the ruined foundation of some sort of a temple or monastery up on a hillside, looking out over the great big bend of the Imjin River at Sangkorangpo. Colonel Quilici's tent faced south onto this beautiful vista, and another ridge line rose behind us, separating us from the front.

The colonel explained to us that he had most of his Weapons Company; D Company, or Dog Company; and E Company, or Easy Company, here with him in his headquarters in reserve. He said that Fox Company was online and attached to the Third Battalion. The colonel told us that he had three openings. "I have an opening for a platoon commander in the heavy machine gun platoon of Weapons Company. I have an opening for a platoon commander in Easy Company, which is back here in reserve. And I have an opening for a platoon commander in Fox Company up on the lines."

As we had been escorted to his tent and had sat down on the veranda with the view in front, the first person he turned to, as luck would have it, was Vincello. I did not know Vincello very well, but I knew something about his background. Vincello was a second lieutenant who had just graduated from college in June of 1951, had gone through OCS, graduated successfully with a commission, gone to Basic School, and come out to Korea. Other than his candidate training and officer training, he had no experience in the Marine Corps.

Well, Vincello now said, "I have always been interested in machine guns." And my heart sagged just a little because when I had heard that the machine gun platoon was available,

Presuming to be a United States Marine

I was tempted to volunteer to lead it. On the one hand, after all the training we'd had in Basic School, which was primarily designed to shape us into rifle platoon commanders, I wanted to be a rifle platoon commander. But on the other hand, the opportunity to be back with my old machine guns, as I had been in China, held a temptation for me.

But Vincello said, "I have always been interested in machine guns." And looking back over his seven- or eight-month career in the Marine Corps, I'd just bet he had always been interested in machine guns! By his own admission, he didn't know much about 'em but had always been "interested."

Colonel Quilici said, "Well, fine, you have got the heavy machine gun platoon." And then he turned to Vick next, saying, "Lieutenant, that leaves two rifle platoons. Which one would you like?" And Vick, of course, said, "Well, I would sure like to get to know my men before I go up on the lines with them."

And Quilici told him, "Well, fine, you are going to be with Easy Company." And then he turned to me and said, "Well, Lieutenant Van Sant, I guess that leaves you with the Fox Company Rifle Platoon."

"Yes, sir," I replied. And he said, "We'll get the adjutant to get one of the jeeps, and we will get you right up to your company." So I drew myself up, "Yes, sir!" rushed back to my tent, and gathered up my gear. A driver and a jeep arrived, I threw my gear into the vehicle, and we took off for the lines.

I must say that even though I had come to Korea fully prepared to have my life come to an end, I now seemed to experience conflicting emotions as I reflected on Vick back there, meeting his men in the tent, and getting to know them "really well." As it turned out, though, they came up online about ten days later.

I was riding up to the lines, and it was probably about five o'clock in the afternoon by this time. As we approached the lines, I could hear occasional shells going off. Every once in a while, I heard a big boom, and that would be an artillery shell, or a small boom, and that would be somebody throwing a grenade or a mortar shell. But there was not a whole lot of noise or activity. It was late afternoon, and things usually quieted down during that time of the day in this war.

The jeep pulled up behind a big ridge line, which constituted the main line of resistance (MLR) or, as we called it, Line Jamestown. It was the reverse slope on the forward slope of which were our main line and battle positions with all our trench lines and dug-in installations. There was a big tent erected on this reverse slope of the hill, and this was clearly a mess tent.

At that time, the policy of the First Marine Division was to try to give people one hot meal a day, even though they were online. The troops would filter over the top of the ridge line and come down to the mess tent all day in little relays to eat a hot meal. The rest of the time, the meals were supplemented with C-rations. Apparently, though, the hot meal tent had been shelled, and the couple of dozen troops eating inside the tent were digging into C-rations.

A big wooden box was being used for a table, with some smaller boxes around it, and I could see four officers sitting there. I assumed that one of them was the company commander. I had been told by the adjutant, my friend at the headquarters of the battalion, that First Lieutenant Moody had just taken over the company and had been assigned as company commander. I did notice that one of the officers had silver bars on and determined that this must be Lieutenant Moody sitting there with three second lieutenants.

I climbed out of my jeep, pulled my gear out and my carbine, threw them down on the ground, and walked up to the tent. I saluted the first lieutenant, "Lieutenant Moody?" And he said, "Yes." And I said, "Lieutenant Van Sant reporting for duty."

Lieutenant Moody graciously said, "Grab a C-ration, Lieutenant Van Sant. Sit down and join us, we are having dinner." Then they went on with what they had been doing before I showed up. And what they had been doing was, as I learned later, what they did at five o'clock in the afternoon every day. At that time of the day, all the platoon commanders assembled with the company commander, wherever he might be, either in his headquarters bunker farther up on the hill or down in the mess tent. They would all have their daily meeting, and at the end of that meeting, at six o'clock, the password and countersign for the next twenty-four hours would be disseminated.

The password would be given to the platoon commanders by the company commander, and the platoon commanders would return to their platoons, call in their sergeants, and convey the password for the next twenty-four-hour period to them.

Now, anytime in combat, there always is a password and a countersign. When you are challenging anybody, the person being challenged gives the password. The challenger then gives the countersign so that the person who has just given the password is sure that the person asking for the password is legitimate. There have been some funny Marine Corps stories over the years, when this smooth-working system had not quite worked out properly.

Lieutenant Moody made a game out of publishing the password by playing Twenty Questions. The lieutenants were supposed to guess the password. So they went round and round, and, as it turned out, and I shall never forget it, the password on my first day of attendance was "wheel," and the countersign was "chair." I did not enter into the game because I was so new, but I caught on fairly early what the combination was to be.

As soon as that business was all taken care of, everybody turned to me with, "Hi, where are you from?" About the third question after that was, "Where did you go to college?"

I said, "St. John's," and everybody stared at me, startled, and I added, "In Annapolis." And the man sitting right across from me dropped his C-ration can. His name was Bill Holmberg. As it turned out, I was looking at five officers, four of whom, including Lieutenant Moody, had gone to the Naval Academy. The fifth was a Princeton graduate.

I saw them exchanging glances when I told them I had graduated from St. John's, which they knew to be a highly academic institution but probably considered to be pretty nerdy, and I reflected to myself that I seemed to be off to a great start with these guys!

Presuming to be a United States Marine

Lieutenant Moody courteously asked me to come to his command post later so that we could talk. I exchanged some more small talk with the other guys. One of the officers I was talking to was Cal Killeen, our artillery forward observer, and then there was Lieutenant Clark Wozencraft, both of whom had graduated from the Naval Academy. Byron Hollingshead, who was the machine gun platoon officer, had gone to Princeton. Having exchanged some pleasantries, I managed to let Hollingshead know that my father was a Princeton graduate as well, hoping that this would raise me in his estimation.

I walked back from the mess tent, carrying my gear up to the command post, Lieutenant Moody's bunker on the nose of the hill. Climbing out of the bunker and around a little hill, Lieutenant Moody and I arrived at another fortified position, an observation point from which we could see the entire company front. Lieutenant Moody gave me a briefing, and by this time, it must have been close to seven o'clock in the evening, but it was still light outside.

Lieutenant Moody pointed out to me that in front of us, we had on the right flank of the sector, facing north toward the Chinese enemy, a hill called OP-3 (Outpost 3), which vaguely resembled a big pyramid sitting along the right side of the sector between us and the enemy. To the left of that, and at a much greater distance, was something called the OPLR, or outpost line of resistance. Our main position was the MLR.

The OPLR was approximately a mile in front of us. It was a fairly substantial hill, although by this time, most of the top of it had been denuded of all vegetation. It had turned into a brownish red-colored bald mass from the shelling; and OP-3, which was directly in front of us, had become pretty barren too.

OP-3, when I first arrived, was neither occupied by the Chinese, nor by us. Just to the right (or east) of it, in the next company sector, was a hill that some months later was named Reno and became the scene of a fairly famous battle. But since Reno was occupied by the marine company to our right and dominated OP-3, neither side occupied OP-3. From the OPLR back toward our positions, there was a ridge line pointing roughly at us, with a barren stripe on top of it, which, I later found out, was called the "old tank road," because it had been used to take tanks up north.

To the left (or west) of that, and still farther away, was a great hill mass called Kumgok. Portions of Kumgok continued to have some vegetation clinging to them, and that made it somewhat unusual. Lieutenant Moody explained to me that at the time of my arrival, the OPLR was occupied during the daytime by two squads of riflemen and a machine gun section from our company that went out at dawn and spent the day there, mainly to protect the artillery forward observer who could call fire deep into the Chinese area from this position. North of the OPLR, you could see for miles into North Korea. At night, we pulled off the OPLR, and our men returned to their positions on the main line of resistance.

We also maintained on the forward slope of Kumgok a sniping position aimed at several large Chinese positions. From Kumgok a good, accurate sniper could pick off the Chinese as they moved about their own positions.

Taking on the Burden of History

Lieutenant Moody now said, "What I intend to do with you, Lieutenant Van Sant, is to send you back for tonight to sleep behind the third platoon command post. I want you to spend tomorrow familiarizing yourself with the men of your platoon who are not out on the OPLR, and then, the next day, I want you to go out to the OPLR with Lieutenant Wozencraft, and I want you to spend at least two days there with him. His second platoon has the OPLR duty this week for three more days. When the second platoon comes off the OPLR for the last time, I want you to take over the platoon, and I will make Lieutenant Wozencraft the company executive officer."

It so happened that I had, by this time, ascertained that Wozencraft was a member of the Naval Academy class of 1951. As I mentioned earlier, the Naval Academy class of 1951 had dates of rank of June 1, 1951, while our Fifth SBC had the date of rank of May 29, 1951, so that I was senior to Lieutenant Wozencraft. I made the big mistake of pointing this out to Lieutenant Moody.

"Yes, sir," I said, but unwisely added, "I hope it will not create a problem that I am senior to Lieutenant Wozencraft."

I remember that Moody looked at me with great disdain and simply said, "I don't think that will be a problem, Lieutenant." He must have told Wozencraft and Holmberg, both members of the Naval Academy Class of 1951, about my observation, because both of them, during the next few days, told me of the time-honored Marine Corps principle: "Seniority among second lieutenants is like virginity among whores."

Lieutenant Griff Moody subsequently became my lifelong friend. He had graduated from the Naval Academy in 1945, and the people who were commissioned right at the end of the war spent three years as second lieutenants, and four years as first lieutenants. As we will see, in the next month after this all took place, Lieutenant Moody was promoted to captain. He was a very senior first lieutenant when I met him.

I found a place to bunk in with the third platoon, and spent a rather restless night there. I met Lieutenant Wozencraft, who had spent all day on the OPLR with most of his platoon. Wooz was a genuine character. He was a kind of scrawny, wizened—and old-looking man although, as it turned out, at that point, Wozencraft was only twenty-seven or twenty-eight years old. He had enlisted in the navy near the beginning of World War II and had been a tail gunner on a torpedo bomber all through that war. He had seen a lot of action in a couple of big naval battles, including the Battle of the Philippine Sea. The torpedo bomber, by the way, was the largest airplane the navy flew from aircraft carriers. I had seen them taking off, right after World War II, before there were catapults, and these bombers would take off into the air in a kind of flutter as they came off the end of the carrier, almost hitting the water first. Wooz must have had a pretty exciting time in his little tail gun bubble on takeoff.

When the war ended, Wooz, together with other young enlisted men who showed promise of being officer material, had been sent to Bainbridge, the Naval Academy prep school, and from there, in 1947, to the Naval Academy. While at the Naval Academy, he got all gung-ho about the Marine Corps, and when he got his commission, he took it in the Marine Corps. He subsequently found himself in Korea, fighting his second war in six or seven years, only this time planted firmly on the ground.

Wooz was a good officer. He told me about some of the people in the platoon, who the good ones were, and who the not-so-good ones were; and we made arrangements for me to go out with him the next morning to take over the platoon at the OPLR. I spent that day familiarizing myself with the terrain and the situation and getting to know some of the troops in the second platoon who were not on the OPLR.

That afternoon I was again up at Lieutenant Moody's command post, the bunker with the observation post, and we watched as the OPLR was shelled pretty heavily by the Chinese. That was certainly anxiety producing. I was standing back on the main line, relatively safe, watching the explosions from incoming shells on the hill. Through binoculars, occasionally, you could see some of our troops running around, and a couple of people were wounded on that day and had to be evacuated back. *Gee, I thought, tomorrow I myself will be out there!* I was girding myself and getting myself steeled, but I must confess that I was suddenly scared as hell; my disdain for life had considerably weakened, if it had not completely evaporated.

I tried to sleep that night, but did not get a whole lot of slumber. I lay there with thoughts swarming through my head, and at about four o'clock, somebody came to wake me up. I gathered my stuff and joined Wozencraft and the rest of the detail.

The hike out to the OPLR was pretty rough and took a long time. We were trying to reach the OPLR just as the sun came up, or soon thereafter. We walked down a road, then forked off onto another road, and then climbed up a hillside through an abundance of underbrush. The troops were telling me, "This is the old Easy Company mortar position." And that was the way they identified this place. It was located down below the tank road I mentioned earlier.

Finally, we got up on a little ridge line, with a saddle connecting it to the much bigger hill mass of the OPLR. This saddle had been nicknamed by the troops the One-Hundred-Yard Dash. The Chinese held the areas both to the west and particularly to the east of the saddle, which meant that the saddle itself, running roughly north and south, was always under enemy observation. Anybody trying to reach the OPLR was forced to race across the One-Hundred-Yard Dash in order to reach safety.

We got up to the ridge line on the friendly side of the One-Hundred-Yard Dash, and just as we arrived and Wozencraft and his point men were starting to proceed down across it, there was suddenly a blast of small arms fire from the OPLR directed at us. And this was the precise moment when I joined that select fraternity of those who have seen the little flower that grows from the end of an enemy rifle being aimed at them. Then three or four rounds of mortar fire landed around us and in among us. Fortunately, no one was hit.

Somebody said, "Well, I guess they don't want to let us have the hill back this morning!" There had been ample evidence for the past week or so that the Chinese had been coming up onto the hill at night from their side.

Taking on the Burden of History

Wozencraft, cool as a cucumber, got on his radio and called in variable time fuse artillery fire. There are fuses on the end of these artillery shells, and when the shell gets to about ten feet above ground, it explodes, showering the ground with fragments. It does not hit the ground in one piece before exploding, as ordinary shells do. And our artillery laid down this fire, and the next thing we saw was the Chinese turning tail and running.

But I must tell you the story of what happened to me when we first came up over the ridge line to the One-Hundred-Yard Dash. I was up fairly close to Wozencraft when that fusillade of fire came raining down from the hill across the Dash, less than a hundred yards away. I could hear the bullets and see them hitting the ground, and I, together with everybody else, hit the deck quickly.

As I lay on my stomach, I remember very distinctly becoming aware of the fact that my lower jaw was trembling uncontrollably, and I suddenly realized that I was terrified. I put my arms up around my head with my face buried into the ground so that people would not see me quivering. This uncontrollable trembling had hit me completely unexpectedly. I could not have foreseen being so frightened that I would start shaking, and I realized, *My god, if I am going to be a lieutenant in command of these people, I can't show them my fear!* Lying prone about five yards farther up on the hillside above me was a private in what was to become my platoon, and Lindsay was his name. Still lying down, as was everybody else, I looked up at him and saw that he was smiling at me.

He said, "Gee, Lieutenant, It looks like they want to keep the hill this morning!" And he was laughing about it. And I thought to myself, *Damn it, if he can be that casual, I can be too!* And for the rest of the almost twelve months I spent in Korea, I remained grateful to Lindsay. He was the only person who could possibly have seen my quivering chin, but his sense of humor prevailed and helped to calm me down. I don't think I ever again showed, at least to my troops, the kind of fear that had so forcefully permeated me at that moment. And I looked at Wozencraft, unaffected and calm, calling in artillery fire, and I realized, *By God, that is how you are supposed to be in battle!* I also realized something else. When I had been negotiating with Headquarters, Marine Corps, to volunteer for Korea, one of my underlying thoughts, as you know, had been that since Shirley was dead, I really did not give a damn about living anymore. At that moment, after my chin stopped shaking, I thought that yes, I did give a damn; and I knew then that my life was still enormously worth living.

The Chinese pulled off. We started across the ridge line to the One-Hundred-Yard Dash, but the Chinese were not through with us yet. We had a total of about thirty-five men, and I must have been about the seventh or eighth across the Dash. By the time I ran across, the Chinese were lobbing mortars, so that I was running with mortar shells landing all around me. The sides of the ridge line were very steep, and of course, as I ran along the top of the Dash, I was very visible. The mortars landed mostly down on the sides as I was sprinting along, but they were still too close for comfort. I got across and got in, and the whole crew got in, and everybody got set up in their positions. Our fighting positions were on the forward slope of the OPLR, facing the enemy.

Presuming to be a United States Marine

I must explain that in Fox Company, the going nickname for the enemy at that time was Gooney. I know it is politically incorrect to use such terms now, and I think you understand by now my love for the Chinese, and I have never ceased to respect and revere them, even while I was fighting them; but while I was fighting them, they became Goonies, and their territory was Goonieland. I apologize to anybody who is offended by that, but that is just the way it was. It is; after all, always best to try to depersonalize the person at whom you have to shoot to kill.

We had a good view. Near the center of our position was the artillery forward observer (FO) position. Lieutenant Killeen set up there with his radioman and his crew. He had three enlisted men with him. The rest of our two squads of riflemen and the section of machine gunners were spread across the front of the hill and around its flanks. I told Wozencraft that I would like to go around and visit all the men in their positions, if I could, to get to know them a little bit and to get keyed in to what was going on.

So I worked my way across the front of the hill, with a number of permanent Chinese fortifications within two hundred yards of our position. Our OPLR had a trench line about four to five feet deep, and while it did not completely cover me, if I bent over running along it, I would be fairly safe.

The troops were grouped in little two- or three-men cluster positions, and as I came upon them, I would stop and introduce myself. I worked my way down toward the end of the position, which was the left or western end, when I realized that another group of marines from our company were coming up behind our left rear by a different route from the main line. They were the sniper team moving out onto the forward slope of Kumgok. As they came into sight, I saw that the man in charge of the team was a gunnery sergeant who had come over on the ship with me, and that he too was going into his first day of combat in Korea, and I waved to him.

The sniper team were coming up a little valley, and they were going to turn left (west) up to Kumgok, where their position was. Suddenly, a Chinese concealed in some shrubs up at the head of this little valley started shooting at them. From where I was standing on the hillside, I looked right down at the Chinese, so I whipped out my carbine, and these were the first shots I fired at an enemy. I don't think I got him. From the movement of the heavy undergrowth, I could see that he was running away. I kept firing, but by this time, he was 150 yards away, and 150 yards with a carbine is a pretty long range. Once we got rid of him, the sniper team came on up the valley and got into their positions.

I asked Wozencraft if I could pick up a man and move over to the sniper position to explore Kumgok. He assigned me a man, and we went back down through the valley and climbed up onto the forward slope of Kumgok. We got into the sniper position in a deep trench line on the forward face of Kumgok, and I met all the guys there. The trench line had been dug by the South Koreans, probably about six months earlier, and it ran in a northwesterly direction all the way across the face of Kumgok right up toward some very heavily fortified Chinese positions. When I told the other officers in the company what I had done, they thought I was nuts. But with a trooper, hell, I felt we could go down that trench line to see what we could find.

And so we did, and walked all the way across the face of Kumgok in the trench line to a wonderful viewpoint, where I could see a well-known hill called Tumae-ri, and in the distance TaeDocSan, which you will hear about much more in this memoir, and we had a great vision of the Chinese positions from there. Fortunately, we did not encounter any Chinese, and nobody shot at us.

In light of subsequent events that took place over the next few days, the trooper and I had to have been the last Americans to stand on that forward point of Kumgok, because our forces were never that far out again. We were probably about a mile and a half in front of our lines at that point, with a front-row seat to an American air strike on Tumae-ri, a very heavily fortified hill with tunnels the Chinese had dug all through it.

U.S. Navy planes were bombing the heck out of this hill, and right in the middle of the raid, we saw a poor Chinese run out of a hole on the side of the hill, throw himself down, and just pound his fists on the ground. I guess he could not stand remaining down in his position any longer, and one could certainly feel empathy with him. I soon began to understand better what he must have felt after I worked my way back to the OPLR and to Lieutenant Wozencraft's little command post. We were sitting there when, suddenly, there was a fairly large explosion from what must have been a large artillery shell behind us on the reverse slope of the OPLR. A minute or so later, there was another explosion forward of us. I worked my way back down to the artillery FO, but could not talk to him because he was busy calling his own mission. Way in the rear of the Chinese territory, that we could observe, was a very large set of holes in the face of a mountain, and the FO, Lieutenant Killeen, was trying to stick an eight-inch shell, our precision mission weapon, into one of the holes.

A precision mission consists of an observer with one big gun assigned to him. The observer orders a round to be fired, watches it land, and then lets the gun position know whether it was over or under, right, or left of the target. Now right or left corrections are pretty easy to make. But over or under, at a distance, are more difficult to adjust. The FO would split the difference between the over and the under, and then have another round fired. Theoretically, within fifteen to eighteen rounds, one ought to be able to hit any target. The eight-inch gun, which was being used for this mission, was a U.S. Army gun in support of the marines. It was an extremely accurate gun and, if properly observed and brought in, would hit the target.

It was Killeen who had called the precision mission, and now a Chinese artillery FO, from the little hillside across from us, had figured out from where our mission was being called and proceeded to call a precision mission on us. On my first day of real combat, I found myself among the intended victims of a Chinese precision artillery mission. In this case, judging by the magnitude of the enemy shells when they landed, the Chinese were using a 152 mm gun, which was about the largest and most accurate field artillery piece they had.

Presuming to be a United States Marine

We soon caught on to what the Chinese were doing—over and under. The next round would come much closer, but if it was over, then we would know that the next round was going to be under, and even closer. And then the Chinese would split the difference. You could feel it, and you could see it, and it was quite unnerving.

Wozencraft had crawled into his bunker because the shells were really coming close now. I had moved toward the left front of the OPLR but found that the shells were coming pretty close there too, and so I got back up near the artillery observation post with a machine gun position right beside it.

After my arrival on the line, I had talked to the machine gunner a little bit and found out that his name was Ridenhour and that he was from Silver Spring, Maryland, part of the Washington DC metropolitan area where my parents now lived. We exchanged a few words, and then I moved away, because he was pretty close to the observation post, and I had realized by now that the OP was what the Chinese wanted to hit.

I moved back on the reverse slope, and just as I moved away, a shell landed. It did not land right in the OP but dropped down in the trench line just between the observation post and Ridenhour's machine gun position. In fact, Ridenhour had climbed out of his position and moved toward the OP for some reason. The shell, shot from the 152 heavy gun, achieved a direct hit on Ridenhour.

The corpsman and Wozencraft started out right away to get him, but all they found of Ridenhour were his feet and the top of his head in his helmet. And I had just been talking to him not more than five minutes earlier. One of the artillery FO team members was wounded, and the other two were buried alive in a little carved-out hole they had moved into. The explosion had buried them, but Lieutenant Killeen immediately had them dug out.

I came to find out later that Fox Company had not had much contact with the enemy in recent weeks, although they'd had a number of men wounded online during this period in the week or two before I arrived. Part of this relative lack of heavy combat experience was due to the fact, as I have said, that the division had been pulled off-line on the east coast had made the move to the west coast, and that the First Marines had been in reserve when they first arrived on the west coast.

Ridenhour was the first man in Fox Company to be killed since February, and it was now May 12 or 13. I felt some sense of guilt about this. It seemed to me that no sooner had Lieutenant Van Sant arrived on the scene than we got somebody killed. But we were all pretty shaken, and Wozencraft confided to me later that he was glad I was taking over his platoon, because he did not think he could have taken it much longer. I remember that he said another thing, as we tried to hole up together, when not much was happening. During that lull, Wozencraft came forth with an all-time great piece of wisdom, and that was, "There are no ideologies on the OPLR." We were out on a hill, surrounded by other hills with our enemy on them, and we were shooting at each other and shelling each other, trying to kill each other, and you really could not be thinking about any higher principles being defended at that point.

Taking on the Burden of History

The shell had not hurt Ridenhour's machine gun, and so I carried it back to the main line that night. Coming off that hill gave me an awfully nice feeling, after having spent the day in much too close camaraderie with the enemy. But I went to sleep that night with the full knowledge that on the following day, I would have to return to the OPLR. The next day, Wozencraft went out with me again, and I carried Ridenhour's machine gun. His assistant gunner and a couple of his ammo men were there, but I carried the gun for him. Ridenhour's assistants, of course, were capable of setting it up and firing it.

The second day was not nearly as eventful as the first day had been, although we were shelled a couple of times, and Killeen called in a few more good strikes. An air strike we called on a different part of Tumae-ri, I think, did some damage.

On that second day, when I went out on the OPLR in the process of relieving Lieutenant Wozencraft of command of the second platoon after the air strike about midafternoon, Wooz and I were sitting in our little command post bunker when who should walk up but Lieutenant Moody, our company commander. He was armed with his carbine but looked like somebody out for a pleasant Sunday afternoon stroll. We jumped up, and Lieutenant Moody said, "Lieutenant Van Sant, I want you to take me on a tour of all your positions here." I realized that Griff, as I called him later, but that Lieutenant Moody, as I called him then, was checking up on me to see if I had learned my stuff.

I immediately started down the trench line connecting all our positions on the forward slope of the OPLR, and by this time, I knew intimately what the responsibility of each position was. We had two machine gun positions and several Browning automatic rifle positions, each one accompanied by a rifleman. We had the artillery observation post fairly high up on the hill, and I took Lieutenant Moody to all these places, realizing that he certainly knew what and where they were already but wanting to show him that I, too, had learned what they were. I planned on taking him around clear across the face of the hill and then down through the little valley at the end of the OPLR to visit the sniper team.

We started out and visited a couple of positions, and Griff talked to the men there, and I talked to them also. There was one place fairly high up on the hill, with a long stretch of trench line between two positions, and the trench line was only about three or four feet deep in this sector. We were strolling along, with part of the upper halves of our bodies exposed. Across the little valley in front of the OPLR was another ridge line, almost as high as the OPLR, occupied by a number of Chinese. And so we were walking along the trench line when suddenly a Chinese sniper cut loose. *Bang, bang, bang*, about three or four rounds, and you could tell he was shooting at us because you could hear the bullets whistling by, and they were kicking up the dust right beside the upper slope of the hill above our trench line. Several of our marines thought they had spotted him and fired back.

Well, as soon as those first Chinese rounds whistled by, I threw myself down, cowering in the bottom of that shallow trench line. When I looked up again, I saw two boots. I looked up the boots, and I followed all the way up the legs, and the upper body, and there was Lieutenant Moody, standing fully erect, looking down at me coolly, with a face that expressed, *What in hell are you doing down there on the ground?* His look further expressed, *A Fox Company officer never ducks for snipers!* And I felt like two cents as I scrambled back up on my feet. Even though the sniper had not succeeded in his mission at that point, if looks could kill, I would have been a dead man. But you have to remember now that Lieutenant Moody was probably about six or seven inches shorter than I, and this certainly crossed my mind at the time. In fact, the trench line provided him with a good deal more coverage than it was providing to me.

I quickly stood up, and we continued our little stroll, while Old Joe Gooney, across the way, banged away at us. Griff did not say anything, but he continued to project an air of invincibility. And by golly, as you will see, it was well founded. We walked around the nose, and the sniper could not see us any more, but he must have fired a total of about twenty-five rounds at us. Some of these rounds had come awfully close, and I walked along, thinking how fortunate it was that Chinese marksmanship training at that time was pretty lousy, or else the rifle the sniper was using was not very good. I could not believe he wasn't hitting us, but he never did, and so we continued on our round. Later on in my year in Korea, I was sniped at several more times, and I must say that Chinese sniper training never appeared to be that thorough, because I am still here to tell the story.

We made a detailed inspection tour of the whole outpost, including our sniper position. Lieutenant Moody seemed to be pretty pleased, overall, and I detected that he might have been a little bit scared of that sniper too, but he wasn't about to show me any fear. He then strolled back to the MLR about a mile away. We pulled off the hill that night, and I was still carrying Ridenhour's machine gun. The Chinese threw a few rounds at us, but we made it back.

As soon as we returned, the second platoon was relieved by the third platoon of OPLR duty, and I formally took over the second platoon of Fox Company, Second Battalion, First Marine Regiment. Wozencraft packed up his gear and went back up to the command post to become the company executive officer.

I moved with my platoon into our new and permanent position on the main line we had taken over from the third platoon. We were the very left flank platoon of Fox Company, and Fox Company was the left flank company of the First Marines. My left squad, on a little knoll overlooking a road, was tied in with the Seventh Marines, who were the left regiment. We were the right regiment. I made a complete reconnaissance of my platoon front and became a bit discouraged.

Looking back at the terrain for which I was responsible, I find it hard to believe just what we were expected to defend with a single rifle platoon, which, under normal circumstances, has forty-four men and one officer. True, we were reinforced by a machine gun section of fifteen men with a staff sergeant, and additionally, I had in my sector a couple of Weapons Company people manning 3.5 rocket launchers, so that in total, I must have had about seventy men. But these seventy men were spread across a front three quarters of a mile long, and that was how thinly we were spread out. We had a continuous trench line all the way across, and with the exception of a rice paddy where it was more shallow, our trench line was a good six or seven feet deep

Taking on the Burden of History

and connected by a very carefully designed set of interlocking fighting positions. The main positions had machine guns, and we also had extra machine guns.

Now, normally, a section of machine guns would have two guns, but we had four just in my platoon, and we also had nine Browning automatic rifles, and each one of them was in the center of a cluster of defenders, so that the front was, we hoped, very well covered. I honestly believed there would be no way the Chinese could ever have broken through us, and it turned out they never did, at least not through our main line.

As I became familiar with the front I had to defend, I realized that I needed to have a command post. Wozencraft had actually never been in this position, so that there was no designated command post. One of my sergeants suggested a nice old bunker right up on the top of the hill, which actually had been built, probably before 1950, by the South Koreans. We could tell this, because South Korean sandbags had a different design from ours. The bunker was pretty small and not very tall, but I thought that it would do.

Here was our routine. When a rifle platoon was online at that point of the war in Korea, we would sometimes have a team of men in what was called a listening post, in front of the main line of resistance in order to intercept any enemy advance early. But in our particular case, since we had quite a vista in front of the company, having a listening post did not really seem necessary. We conducted patrols with some regularity but, of course, did not want to patrol too regularly, or the Chinese would catch on. I will tell some patrol stories later on.

In a normal day, when they did not have any of those extra duties, the men would spend the day cleaning up, squaring things away, and preparing for the night, because most events took place in the darkness. At night, we had what was called a 50 percent watch, and that was achieved by pairing everybody up; nobody was on the front lines alone, everybody was with at least one other person. The deal was that at night, one person would be awake and the other asleep. The two men would work it out among themselves as to how they would trade off their watch during the night, whether it would be one hour or two hours or four hours. It was left up to the discretion of the individual marines how they wanted to plan their watch.

The lines were set up so that all night, every twenty or thirty yards, there was a wide-awake marine on duty, alert and watching. When I joined Fox Company, there was a division order that, on an irregular basis, every rifle platoon commander was to check all his lines twice a night during the hours of darkness to make sure that everybody who had to be wide awake, actually was.

This was a rule that I always scrupulously obeyed. Sometimes I would make my first tour fairly early, maybe at ten o'clock at night, not too long after it had gotten dark, and the next time I would not come through until three in the morning. Sometimes I would wait until one o'clock for my first tour, and then start right over again one and a half hours later.

I'd be climbing along in the darkness and going through password and countersign with each fighting position. I would come up and stop to talk to each one of the troopers, so that the process of checking lines took at least an hour with all the challenging and back-and-forth, because we were spread from here to kingdom come. The rest of the time, I would go back to the bunker and try to get some sleep.

My headquarters consisted of my platoon sergeant and some additional noncommissioned officers, which meant that, in addition to the platoon sergeant, I had an assistant platoon leader, who was a master sergeant. I also had a gunnery sergeant, whom I used for additional duties; a guide, who was a buck sergeant; a platoon runner, who was a PFC; and the platoon medical corpsman. In our impressive headquarters, we always had at least one person awake and on watch. When you were on watch in headquarters, you were monitoring both the radio and the sound power telephone. We were linked by telephone and radio to the company commander, and somebody had to be on watch and listening at all times. After I returned from my check of the lines, I would leave instructions on when I wanted to be awakened. My old Korean bunker was too small to accommodate more than one person, so that for the rest of my headquarters party, we used another bunker next door, and that bunker was not very comfortable, either.

After returning from checking lines the first night to my new platoon headquarters bunker, I crawled into my sleeping bag and began drifting off to sleep. Then I heard some scratching noises up in the overhead among all the timbers, where the South Korean sandbags were piled up on the roof. I did not pay any attention to it and fell fast asleep. On my second night in the bunker, lying on my back and just falling asleep, I heard more scratching in the overhead. Again, I did not pay any attention but sank into a deep, exhausted sleep. Suddenly, four little feet landed squarely on my face. The four little feet scampered right down my chest, down my unzipped sleeping bag, down my stomach, and down the whole length of my body to my feet, before they darted out of the little entranceway into the bunker. There was no mistaking it, those little feet belonged to a big rat. Wide awake, I gathered up my sleeping bag, took it outside, and went to sleep under the stars for the rest of the night. I told myself I would never go back into that horrible bunker to sleep again.

The next morning, I called my headquarters together and said, "Men, I am going to establish a new command post. Let's look for one." We went over the top and down the forward slope of our hill. The main trench line ran all along the forward slope of the ridge line but about a hundred yards down from the top. From the top of the hill, there was a nice deep trench line that ran back up over to the reverse slope of the hill and forward down to the main trench, connecting with it in a *T*. As I walked down this connecting trench line, I saw a fairly substantial cave off to the right. I called my sergeants together and, "By golly, why don't we dig out that cave, put a reinforced roof over it, and build a command post that is big enough to accommodate all of us?" I said to them, thinking to myself, *All of us minus the rat*. My sergeants thought that was a good idea. I called up to the company headquarters and received permission to proceed.

Behind the company headquarters on the reverse slope of the main line hill, there was a camp manned by what was known as the Korean Service Corps. The Korean Service Corps was a group of South Korean men who were a little too old to be fighting in regular infantry units, but who had volunteered to help with the war effort. When we were in heavy combat with casualties, the Korean Service Corpsmen often carried the stretchers and did a wonderful job, because they tended to be mature men, and they were very gentle and concerned and caring about the wounded. They were really fine men. When they were not needed as stretcher bearers, they were to be used as labor for digging and construction of fortifications. The Korean Service Corps was commanded by regular South Korean army sergeants and lieutenants, but the troops doing the hard work were all volunteers. It was from these fine people that I came to have an appreciation of the devotion of the South Koreans to their cause.

Lieutenant Moody now assigned me a whole squad of Korean Service Corpsmen, who came over with picks and shovels, hauling great masses of the heavy beams we used in the construction of bunkers and carrying sandbags, and the whole ball of wax. They were marched over to my new headquarters position by a South Korean army sergeant. We turned to vigorously. My own sergeants and I all chipped in with the labor of digging, and together we constructed what became one of the most magnificent places I ever lived in during my stay in Korea. We assembled that thing in two days and one night. Because it had been a cave, we took the top off the cave and inserted our structure into the hillside. We built a heavily reinforced roof the top of which was flush with the surface of the hillside. We reinforced all the walls, put up the beams overhead, with layer after layer after layer of sandbags on top, and then camouflaged it. It was dug in so deep that on the surface, it looked like flat ground on the hillside, and in fact, we cut sods and planted them over the roof. The bunker had a beautifully concealed and well-covered entrance, and it was big enough to accommodate us all. Inside we had a big day room, where we kept the radio and the communications equipment. We created a bedroom that could accommodate four sleeping people at any one time. We even carved bunks along the walls right out of the ground, and the entire interior was simply luxurious.

While we were working on the bunker, and I was digging away with my sergeants, I noticed that the South Korean sergeant remained squatting up above our deep hole and outside of it, supervising all of us.

So I called out to him, "Come on down here and dig too!" And we had a wonderful dialogue. He said, "No, no!" And he pointed to the three stripes on his sleeve to indicate that he was a sergeant, and sergeants did not work. I pointed to my collar and said, "I am a lieutenant, and you come down here and dig!" I shamed him into coming down, and all the Korean servicemen thought that was really great, and I became a hero to them for making their exalted sergeant work. I will say that once he started digging, he was a really dedicated worker.

We now had a great command post. I will tell more about life online during that period, and I do want to tell about what happened on the OPLR. When my platoon's responsibility for the OPLR ended and I relieved Lieutenant Wozencraft, the third platoon, commanded by Lieutenant Holmberg, took over the OPLR responsibility. They went out the first day without any problems, and on the second day, there were no problems. But on the third day, problems arose, and I will come to that in a moment.

Presuming to be a United States Marine

In the meantime, there was a rather sad episode involving a young gunnery sergeant in charge of the sniper team under Holmberg. This marine had volunteered for the duty because his regular billet was as gunnery sergeant of the machine gun platoon of the company. Since the machine guns were all assigned out to rifle platoons, he had attached himself to Holmberg's platoon and was available for all kinds of duties that required a knowledgeable and hardworking sergeant. The sergeant's name was John Francis Kelly who, as I write these memoirs, remains a friend of mine and actually does not live too far from us in Virginia. He had been in Korea since August 1951 and was one of the most experienced noncommissioned officers in the company.

John Francis was a great expert on demolitions and booby traps. Booby traps are explosive devices concealed in a great variety of ways and set up in hopes that the enemy will make a mistake and investigate the booby trap, set it off, and be killed. John Francis had been a regular visitor to our sniper position and set booby traps for the Chinese who visited the position every night. Every evening, as his sniper detail pulled off, John Francis would set up a booby trap of some sort. He had made something of a career setting up these traps and never repeated the same method twice. The next morning, there would usually be evidence of bloodstains, proof that John Francis's booby trap had been sprung.

The third morning Holmberg's platoon went out to take over the OPLR, John Francis came along to examine the success of his booby trap. My recollection is that the booby trap he had set had been sprung but that there was something wrong with the setup of this little position in the trench line, and as a consequence, John Francis went up to investigate. He picked up something and, click *boom!* The Chinese had booby-trapped John Francis. What they had done was to conceal a so-called bouncing Betty, a small antipersonnel mine on a small explosive charge that blows it up into the air about six to eight feet, and then shatters into a whole lot of fragments that shower the area below.

This bouncing Betty went off right behind John Francis and gave him a whole flock of fragments in the back. He was wearing a flak jacket, as all of us did, reinforced with leaves of armor plate. But one of the fragments from that bouncing Betty was big enough and had sufficient strength behind it to penetrate between two armor leaves of John Francis's flak jacket, lodging itself in his back. And John Francis was mad as hell. The corpsman told him he had to be evacuated, but John Francis would not allow anybody to take him out on a stretcher. He insisted on walking back. And it was a good mile, but John Francis walked from the sniper position all the way to our lines, wounded, but unaided and unescorted.

It just so happened that we had heard about this incident back online. Since the trail out to the sniper position went through my platoon's position, I went down to the front line and waited. Soon I saw ole John Francis plowing along, and on first sight, you would have thought he was out for a vigorous afternoon hike, except that his whole back was covered with blood. But what I remember most is that he was just as mad as hell that the Chinese had outwitted him. I used all my powers of persuasion to stop him, and we brought a jeep ambulance up and convinced him to get in it so that he could be taken back to the battalion aid station and on to the hospital. This happened, I think, around the seventeenth or eighteenth of May, and on the night of the twelfth and thirteenth of June, John Francis went AWOL from the hospital, as I will describe later. By that time, he had been a patient for over three weeks. We subsequently heard that a shell fragment had come to rest in a vertebra about one-eighths of an inch from his spinal cord. It was in such a delicate position that the doctors decided, after opening him up, to leave it where it was. To this day, John Francis walks around with a big hunk of a Chinese bouncing Betty in his back.

We had a sergeant, Sergeant Drinkard, in Lieutenant Holmberg's platoon who was very badly wounded out on the OPLR that same day by a shell. He was bleeding profusely and had gone into shock. The corpsman who was taking care of him said that the sergeant would have to be evacuated by helicopter. Up to that point, marines had never taken a Medevac helicopter out to the OPLR, but there was a little reverse slope with a pretty deep little ravine beside the One-Hundred-Yard Dash to the west, relatively well protected from enemy observation and from observed fire.

The forward air controller, who was assigned to our company as liaison from the aviators, called the Medevac outfit and told them that we had a case to be evacuated from the OPLR. The squadron commander of the helicopters decided to make this a volunteer exercise and asked his pilots for a volunteer. One of the helicopter pilots volunteered for the mission, and we got word that our wounded sergeant would be picked up.

Almost everybody has seen the Medevac copters on television in the immensely popular *M*A*S*H* series. Well, the helicopter sent out to our OPLR was exactly the same model. The pilot sat in a big glass bubble, and there were outside stretchers attached to either side of the bubble, where the casualties were placed. The helicopter itself was small and very maneuverable.

Our sergeant was really in bad shape, and I think he had lost consciousness. While the corpsman was working feverishly in order to stabilize him, the helicopter came over the horizon—these little helicopters could fly just above the ground so that you could barely see them, although you could hear them. *Chunk-chunk-chunk*, the helicopter came up over our main line positions, and *chunk-chunk-chunk*, sneaked on out across the rice paddies in front of us, up over the old tank road; and the forward air controller brought it in beautifully, and the pilot came right in and landed his helicopter in the depression to which the casualty, Sergeant Drinkard, had been carried.

But the corpsman, bless his heart, and I even remember his name, Mahannah—well, Doc Mahannah was not quite ready for Drinkard to be put on the helicopter yet. He was a very careful, meticulous corpsman, and his concern always paid off. I would say that over the time I was with Fox Company, Mahannah probably saved many men's lives just by the attention he brought to his job. And now Mahannah motioned to the helicopter pilot that he was not ready. He was trying to stop the bleeding, getting his patient warm, giving him morphine, and doing all the things a good corpsman does when his patient goes into shock. And all of that, of course, takes time.

Suddenly, the pilot started to take off, because by this time, the Chinese had commenced to lob mortar shells into the little ravine. But just as the helicopter began to rise, Holmberg and his men, who were watching the evacuation in progress, grabbed hold of the little skid runners on its bottom, and they held down the entire helicopter, so that the pilot did not have enough power in the rotor to take off. Holmberg and his men just held the helicopter in place until Mahannah could finish getting Drinkard ready to be transported.

And all of this took place in a rising crescendo of Chinese shelling, and the helicopter pilot was mad and was cursing everybody out. Of course, neither Holmberg nor his men could actually hear what the pilot inside the buzzing helicopter was trying to tell them because of all the shelling noise and the noisy chopper itself. But the pilot was gesticulating wildly, and there were middle fingers being extended, and all kinds of nasty visual things were going on. At long last, Mahannah was finished, and he had Drinkard ready to go. Drinkard was gently lifted onto the outside stretcher and strapped in, and then, and only then, Holmberg's men let go of the helicopter; and, *chunk-chunk-chunk*, it lifted up, and the patient and pilot skedaddled out without being hit. It was a miracle! They got Drinkard out, and Drinkard survived, I am happy to say. We heard later that the helicopter pilot, because he had volunteered to go one mile forward of the main line of resistance to evacuate a casualty, had been awarded the Navy Cross, which, I am sure, he deserved. But he certainly had received a lot of help from all the marines in Holmberg's platoon.

The fourth day Holmberg's platoon went to the OPLR, they moved up the old tank road, as I had done the two days I was up there. When they reached the ridge line at the beginning of the Hundred-Yard Dash, suddenly, the whole OPLR ridge line opened up on them. And Holmberg did what Wozencraft had done the first day we had gone out there. He called in a whole lot of artillery fire. But the enemy continued shooting, and as one of the troopers in my outfit had said once before, "I don't think they want to give it back to us today."

And so a crazy thing developed. Remember, we were occupying the hill in the daytime, and the Chinese occupied it at night. There was a great confab down at the division headquarters, and it was finally decided that since the OPLR was so far in front of our main line of resistance, it really wasn't supportable if the enemy wanted to hang on to it.

So Holmberg brought his platoon back, and we left the hill in the hands of the Chinese. Although it was not a great loss, it was a little depressing to all of us. When the war finally ended, the Demilitarized Zone became a band across Korea, bounded on the north by the farthest advance of the North Koreans and the Chinese, and on the south by our farthest positions. Our boundary of the Demilitarized Zone during the time I was there never changed, but there were some adjustments made in a couple of big battles toward the end of the war, after I had returned home. It hurt to think that we were giving up the one hill we felt was rightfully ours, and so it was decided to make the Chinese pay a price for having broken the protocol, such as it was, of the daily exchanges of this hill. We called in a tremendous amount of artillery onto that hill during the next day, and we also set up a new sniper position. It was an almost-mile-long shot from our lines, or at least fourteen or fifteen hundred yards, but you could still make out human bodies from that position.

Our air liaison officer wanted to try to get an air strike on the hill. At that stage of the war, aviation assets were committed and were under the control of the U.S. Air Force. While the marines had close air support from squadrons in Korea, which were normally assigned to us, we still had to request them through the air force. Well, it so happened that on the particular day when the Chinese decided to keep the OPLR, the air force had committed all our marine close support air squadrons to an army battle farther to the east, and they told our officer that they did not have anything to spare. Our air controller was, of course, furious and climbed all over them. So in the end, the air force called him back and told him that they did have a flight of four P-51s from South Africa, whose pilots had been in Korea for over a month. "We have never been able to give them a mission," our officer was told. "Would you accept them to fly your mission?" Our liaison officer, by that time, would have accepted World War I planes, if necessary, and so he said, "We'll accept them, and I'll guide them in."

Word came down from the company command post over our company communications net that we were finally getting air support against the Chinese newly entrenched on the OPLR. We learned that the South African Air Force was going to support us with a four-plane strike on the OPLR. Our air liaison officer, whom I eventually got to know pretty well, later loved to tell the story of this particular air support mission because, at least in retrospect, it was so funny.

At the time of the mission, our air liaison officer was on a very high-powered radio net with all these South African folks, tuned in to the flight commander of the four P-51 Mustangs. Now the P-51 Mustang was a very hot fighter plane, developed near the end of World War II. It was not a jet, it was a propeller plane, but was pretty fast. It had a water-cooled engine, was quite maneuverable, and was built as a fighter plane. It could do close support by dropping bombs, and it could fire machine guns as well. Our air liaison officer, having established communication with the commander of the air squadron, tried to explain the location of the target. The pilot, though, was so excited about finally being engaged in a combat mission that he whooped and hollered and yelled and screamed back and forth to the other three pilots in the air, who returned his enthusiasm in kind, and our air liaison, who was supposed to control the flight and tell the pilots exactly what to drop, and where, seemed unable to break through their noisy and jubilant conversation.

Finally, our air controller was told that one of the planes had napalm, and, "Great!" our guy exclaimed, and immediately tried to describe the place where he wanted the napalm to be dropped and to tell the pilot how to make the run. The standing order for close air support missions in those days in Korea, and **the marine and navy pilots** invariably observed this, was to always make the approach to the target parallel to and along the enemy lines. That took a little guts because every Chinese soldier from there to Beijing would be shooting at them with his rifle or machine gun or whatever else he might have handy. But if the pilot made his attack along the Chinese line, and if he missed his target, at least he would do some damage by hitting something else along the enemy line.

Apparently, that word had not reached the South Africans, because the first plane came over on its napalm run, and the plane came roaring in from the south, and we could see him coming, and he flew right over my platoon, and then he banked to the right. About three hundred yards in front of my platoon, right over the rice paddy in front of us and about nine hundred to a thousand yards from the target, he let go of that napalm. And this huge napalm bomb comes down, right in the middle of the rice paddy, and there is a tremendous jelly gas explosion, burning a large amount of debris in the process. And it does not do a bit of harm to the enemy.

The next pilot had a thousand-pound fuse-delay bomb. Now a fuse-delay bomb was a big, big bomb, which, instead of going off above the ground, would first bury itself in the ground and then go off, digging out a large crater in the process. It was designed to break through the tops of large bunkers and fortified positions and explode within, doing maximum damage. My third squad was the right flank of my platoon, and they occupied a nose around the front of a rather large hill along our main positions. The nose came right down to the main road along which the North Koreans had attacked in 1950.

And our second South African fighter plane started flying roughly in a northerly direction attacking the target from way back behind our lines. You could see him diving down from the heavens at right angles to the front line, which, of course, is exactly the wrong way to make a run. He came in, and we were all watching this plane because it came from our rear, and I kept my eye on it, and just as it got up to the ridge line where we were dug in, I suddenly saw a huge bomb leaving the plane, and it began its descent, and I looked over at the ground, estimating where it was going to land, and I could see that it would be landing just about where my third squad was positioned.

Fortunately, my troops in the third squad were also watching the plane, and as they saw the bomb leaving the plane and starting down toward them, they all dove into bunkers and trench lines, finding any protective cover they could. The bomb came roaring in, and it came down just forward of our trench line, which, at that point, was built up over a sort of cliff on a steep hill, and right at the bottom of that hill was the highway.

Well, that bomb did clear the trench line and landed squarely on the road, raising an enormous cloud of dust and debris, enough so that all my troops lying in the trench lines not more than fifty feet from where the bomb had landed were all buried in two or three inches of dirt. And for the rest of the time we were in this position, we had, right there in front of my third squad, as a memento, a gigantic crater. The hole was as wide as the road, and it must have been twenty feet deep.

Taking on the Burden of History

The bomb, needless to say, had missed the enemy position by exactly one mile, although it had almost wiped out my third squad. If that bomb had landed just fifty feet to the south, it would have produced multiple casualties in my platoon. And that was bomb number two.

Planes number three and four were loaded with 250-pound bombs. Marine close support planes used to carefully plant those bombs so that every one counted. But not the South Africans. Each one of the planes had, I think, eight of these bombs, and each one of them came in and dumped their entire load at once. They released all eight bombs simultaneously, and none of them closer than about five hundred yards to the target. They were quite successful in rearranging a number of rice paddies, knocking down some trees, and flattening out some hills, which were in no way associated with the enemy. And that does not take into account their big bomb, which had almost wiped out my squad.

By this time, our air controller, our guy who was charged with guiding the aviators, was practically hysterical on the radio, yelling and screaming, "My god! What the hell are you doing?" as the mission was turning into a total fiasco.

With a last "Tallyho, chaps!" the South Africans prepared to leave the scene of disaster. Our controller radioed back, "Hey! Aren't you going to strafe the position?" And since that got through, somehow, one of the P-51s turned around, came back, and shot up some more landscape in the general area of North Korea.

The air controller told us afterward that the pilots had talked to each other incessantly and that he could never break into their conversations long enough to guide them through. They regularly cheered each other on with their "Tallyho" and "Cheerio, old chaps!" And they were obviously having a good old blast, while doing absolutely no damage to the enemy. They, then, flew off into the sunset, and that's the last we saw of them, but I would bet that those guys went home and entertained many friends in the pubs with great stories about how they had gone up and bombed the daylights out of the enemy in support of the U.S. Marines in Korea.

With the new setup, and not having to go to the OPLR, we began a program of aggressive patrolling in front of our positions. Each night one of the platoons would be assigned a patrol, usually squad-sized, to investigate the various hill masses in front of us. And things settled down into a routine for a while. We abandoned the OPLR on about the eighteenth or nineteenth of May. To get from my platoon headquarters over to Griff's headquarters bunker for our daily afternoon meeting involved quite a hike, because I had to climb up over our hill and down the reverse slope of that hill, up a road that ran parallel to our lines, and then climb up on the hill to Griff's command and observation post. We would meet, and Griff would give us our assignments and our various responsibilities, and then we would play Twenty Questions with the password and return to our own headquarters for a meeting with our squad leaders to deliver the password and issue any special orders for the night.

During my first tour online from early May until the fifteenth of June, it was still legal for men online to buy beer. They bought it a case at a time, but the beer had to

Presuming to be a United States Marine

be under the control of the platoon commander, and it was issued to the men who had purchased it, two cans at a time, per day. Now the logistics of delivering these beer rations were sometimes rather extensive. The beer had to be paid for with cash before it was moved up to each platoon. But it is interesting to note that there never seemed to be a problem with beer delivery. There were always good and upright marines who were ready to work in order to transport beer at any given time.

At the six o'clock meeting with my squad leaders, I would dispense the two cans of beer to each man in each squad who had purchased it. Some of the men, of course, did not drink beer, or did not drink at all. Those guys were particularly popular if they agreed to buy their two cans on behalf of other marines who gave them money for the purchase, and who would subsequently end up with four cans for themselves. Of course, I don't know how much of that went on because the beer consumption was pretty carefully controlled, and I never had any episodes of troopers having too much beer to drink. We had just purchased our ration, and I must have had forty-eight or fifty cases of beer for my platoon at the grand new command post we had constructed, with its big, deep rooms. Outside the bunker, in the trench line and with a kind of big wall of dirt and sand bags around it, I had built a little cubbyhole where I kept the beer rations. I could keep strict control of the stash there.

We got word that the portion of my platoon that was near my new command post bunker was going to have to pull back from our positions, because the First Tank Battalion had some targets, which intelligence had identified between the OPLR in front of us, and Kumgok, the mountain to the left front of us. In that little area between the OPLR and Kumgok, the Chinese were building fortifications, and there was a lot of other activity going on as well. Word was that the tanks were to come and shoot at some of these fortifications with their 90 mm guns. These guns were long and very accurate and powerful. A platoon of five tanks came up and distributed themselves along the top of the upper slopes of the hill on the main line of resistance, where my platoon was, and the tankers began firing at the targets they had pre-selected. The reason the platoon had been evacuated from the area was because tanks always attracted an enormous amount of return fire. The Chinese were in the habit, if they ever spotted a tank out in the open, of firing anything and everything they possessed at it. While the Chinese were not overly blessed with antitank weapons, they did have some antitank shells in some of their bigger howitzers, and so they would fire anything just on the off chance that, maybe, they would get a lucky hit on some vulnerable part of the tank, like its sighting mechanisms or part of its exhaust mechanism or the engine cover. Troops had to be evacuated when tanks came up on a shoot like this, because the whole area where the tanks were would become inundated with enemy fire of all sorts. In fact, I think the Chinese even used to shoot rifles at tanks.

We pulled back on the reverse slope, and we could hear the tanks banging away and could hear the Chinese banging away in response. Then, finally, our tanks went rumbling off to the rear where their headquarters was, and we moved back up to our positions. As we approached my command post, we saw a tank track leading up and stopping right on top of my command post bunker. You will remember that this bunker was so beautifully and completely camouflaged that if you were outside and walking on the hillside, you would never even know you were standing on top of it. It was perfectly flush with the ground. A tank had obviously fired its whole mission right from the top of my bunker, and it is certainly a tribute to the skill with which that bunker had been constructed that it did not collapse under the enormous weight. Had it collapsed, the tank would have fallen through and been stuck. While the outside of the bunker had held fast, the vibrations from the tank's guns, as they were shooting, had shaken free every bit of loose dust and dirt present and filtered it down from the roof into the inside of the bunker, so that everything inside was covered with a thick patina of dirt.

But that was not the only thing that struck me as I approached my command post. An unmistakable smell of beer assaulted my nose, and when I rounded the corner of the trench line, I was confronted with visible evidence of a real tragedy. The enemy counterfire, while it had not been successful in damaging the tank, had achieved a direct hit on the platoon's beer rations. The smell was awful! About half of the cans were destroyed, and the ground all around the trench line had become saturated with beer. The bad news traveled through the platoon with lightning speed, and I got on the telephone right away to see if we could make arrangements for a replacement ration of beer lost in combat.

Another interesting thing happened during this time period, and I am reminded of it because one of the targets the tanks were shooting at about a mile from us showed clear evidence of relatively heavy construction by the Chinese on the little saddle that used to connect our sniper position with the OPLR. This was the same little valley in which I had fired my very first shots in the war in support of our sniper detail my first morning in combat.

I had been watching this area through my binoculars carefully, and it was clear that there was something major being built there. I reported this up the chain of command and suggested that we try to see if we could get a precision artillery mission for that target. The tanks had come up and blown things away, but that did not seem to have curtailed all Chinese activity. I talked to our artillery forward observer. As I told you, the FO who had been with the company when I first joined it was First Lieutenant Calvin Killeen, a Naval Academy graduate and a fine officer, who eventually retired as a major general. Cal, as I think I described on my very first day of combat, had fired a precision mission while he himself had been the target of a Chinese precision mission, and I thought then, and still do, that this was pretty heroic of Cal. He was a fine man and a very knowledgeable artillery officer. But he had been pulled back into the artillery battalion to take command of a battery, and so we had a new forward observer, a guy whose name I cannot remember. You will understand why that is just as well, in a minute.

Whenever I would see our new FO, I would say, "Man, you know, I have this target, why don't you try to get a precision mission on it?" Finally, he said he thought it would be a good idea, and, "I'll see if I can get it," he told me. He called me up one morning, and this must have been in early June, and said, "Hey, I've got an army eight-inch howitzer," which was the weapon of choice for precision missions. It was a very accurate weapon, and the army artillery men were very skilled with these howitzers. And the new artillery FO told me that the precision mission was scheduled for that morning at ten o'clock.

Now, I have explained how a precision mission works, and the technique of this, at least as was taught in artillery school, is that you should be able to hit any target with an eight-inch howitzer with no more than fifteen rounds. These rounds were called sensing rounds, and you would be "sensing" through your binoculars whether the rounds landed over or under, and then keep splitting the difference between the "splashes," as the exploding shells were called.

Our FO now said, "I'll tell you what. Why don't you sense the rounds, Lieutenant Van Sant, and I'll just patch your "senses" on through back to the artillery piece." And the more he talked, the more I began to suspect that he might be afraid to come out to my command post. I had planned to suggest that the precision mission could be done from my CP position because we had a good visual shot at whatever the Chinese were constructing from there. From the forward slope, I was looking right at the enemy. But that, of course, also meant that the observer was quite exposed.

"Of course," I told him, "I would be glad to do that." I felt an excitement about being able to call a precision mission. He made the necessary communications connection with his fire direction center, and I started sensing the rounds. Unfortunately, the Chinese structure was tucked into a fairly vertical slope of a hill, so that it was a little difficult to tell, but I guided them up, and back, and up, and back. You can imagine that this kind of a job, because you are constantly looking through your binoculars, takes a tremendous amount of concentration. The artillery FO had sent his radioman down to me so that I was working with this man, sending back information on where the splashes were hitting ground. And the splashes were getting closer and closer and closer and, finally, bingo! An eight-inch howitzer shell, 236 pounds of high explosives, is a big son of a gun. And such a shell went right down through the roof of the construction, whatever it was. There was a tremendous secondary explosion, and some of my guys who were watching thought that they saw a couple of bodies flying through the air. We had scored a direct hit. At that moment, I felt triumphant. Then I realized, when he cleared his throat, that a distinguished-looking marine, wearing colonel's eagles, had been standing behind me, observing.

"Good shooting, Lieutenant! What battery are you in?" he asked me. On the forward slope of the main line of resistance, you do not salute. Since you are under probable enemy observation, you do not want to reveal the presence of a high-ranking officer. And this colonel turned out to be the artillery regimental commander. He apparently had been driving along and heard a precision mission being executed. Because the single rounds come at a certain rate, with about thirty to forty-five seconds between them while the FO radios back the location of the sensor round and the guys on the gun make the adjustments to have the next round fall either shorter or longer, these precision missions have a certain distinctive sound to them.

Taking on the Burden of History

"Sir," I said, "I am actually Lieutenant Van Sant from Fox Company, First Marines." He became very disturbed and said, "Well, what are you doing calling a precision mission? What's your forward observer's name?" I told him, and the colonel turned around and stomped off, and that's the last we saw of that particular artillery forward observer. The thought of letting an infantry officer call a precious precision mission, and they were hard to get because they had to be obtained from the army, was more than the colonel could stomach. Fortunately, I did not get into any trouble. And we had hit the target, after all.

Here are a couple of little vignettes about checking lines during this period when I was platoon commander. As I explained, checking lines took time because I had to climb up and down hills, and walk along in the dark in a trench line, getting challenged all the time. I would visit a fighting position with two men, one of them always asleep, but invariably had somebody to talk to, and I had a number of very interesting conversations with some of my men on those tours.

One of them was Private First Class Davis, a very big man, an African American from Mississippi. He had already established an excellent reputation, not only in our platoon, but throughout our company. Davis was a BAR man, he had a Browning automatic rifle, which he would detail-strip on a daily basis. That means that he took every piece of his rifle apart and cleaned it and oiled it and lubricated all the moving parts every single day, without fail, rain or shine. People would tell him, "Davis, you clean that BAR more than anybody else in the Marine Corps." And he would say, "I want to be sure it works." And Davis was a brave man, as we will subsequently see. I think the guy who shared his hole with him must have slept every night for most of the night, because I found Davis always on watch. Every time I approached his position, it was always Davis who challenged me, and Davis always challenged. Most of the guys, when you came upon about ten feet from their position, would shout, "Halt! Who goes there?" And I would say, "Friend," and they would ask for the password, and I would give it, and then they would give the countersign, and they would tell me, "Okay, advance."

Davis would halt me no less than twenty yards away from his position. He had uncanny hearing. "Halt!" And then we would go through our routine. I remember his early challenges, and I remember Davis's position. I can still see it in my mind's eye. It was a good position; he had worked on it hard. People were always improving their fighting positions, but his was really luxurious.

Another reason why I remember Davis's position is that the next position to his was a machine gun position, and the guy in that position had a pistol. The number one gunner on a machine gun, as I knew from my machine gunner days, carried a .45 caliber pistol as his assigned weapon. I would have just finished with Davis, having been scared to death by his challenge, which seemed to come earlier and earlier as I was creeping along, and Davis would invariably surprise me. After calming down from the encounter with Davis, I would approach the next guy in the machine gun position, and that particular guy, in my opinion, had a very bad habit. He would hear me crawling along in the trench line. The trench line made a ninety-degree turn right before his position, and this darn guy would stand just behind that turn, and he would shove his pistol right into my stomach as I came around it. First he would shove his pistol, and then he would yell, "Halt!" It always worried me that he might have an accidental discharge at some time, and I could almost feel that .45 shell tearing up my insides.

A couple of times, I sat with Davis and talked with him for a long time. Davis told me, "You know, Lieutenant, I am a Negro. I love the Marine Corps because it is the first place where I have been treated like a man." Then he added, "You know what worries me, Lieutenant? When I go back to my hometown in Mississippi, and I walk down the street, and you've got to understand, Lieutenant, in my town, if a white man is coming down the street on the sidewalk, and you are on that sidewalk going in the opposite direction, you have to get off the sidewalk to let him pass." And he added, "I am not sure I will be able to do that anymore, Lieutenant."

Well, Davis did such a fine job that before I left Fox Company months later, I had him meritoriously promoted to corporal, and my successor got him promoted to sergeant; and in a couple of subsequent stories, you will hear more about Davis.

I have been recounting stories of checking lines at night, going around and visiting the troops, as we were required to do by division order. But it was also an interesting and congenial occupation and, with apologies to Shakespeare, "a little touch of Harry in the night."

My platoon occupied the position I have described from about the twelfth or thirteenth of May 1952 until the fifteenth of June, so that we actually spent over a month there, improving it; patrolling from it; and, as we will see, conducting several operations from it.

My platoon was really spread out. To its left, where we were tied in with the Seventh Marines, was a fairly large hill mass stretching across the front with a couple of little fingers and ridges. But right in the middle of my platoon's line position was a very long, wide rice paddy coming south way up into the hill mass that constituted our whole company front line. We had a trench dug all the way across the paddy, but the ground was so wet that you could not really dig any positions, and the paddy was at least 250 yards wide at that point. The trench line that had been dug across the paddy was only about four to five feet deep; if it had been dug any deeper, water would have appeared in the bottom of it. This area really constituted something of a weak spot in our whole company position. The paddy eventually became narrower and narrower up the ravine behind the trench line, and up at the head of that ravine was a big fighting position. Since the Chinese forward positions were only, maybe, four or five hundred yards away from this trench line, we were always concerned about the security of it. For that reason, we had very powerful machine gun positions and several riflemen on both ends of where the trench line crossed the paddy, in order to cover the gap. On the other side of the paddy from my headquarters, I had a whole squad reinforced on the next hill mass along our lines, beyond the paddy. It was this squad that had almost been hit by the South African thousand-pound bomb.

One misty, moonlit night, when the light was bright but visibility was shrouded, after I had checked the machine gun position on the western end of the rice paddy trench, I began creeping along across the paddy, when, my god! Right in the middle of it, I saw a Chinese soldier crouched down. I immediately dropped into the prone position at the bottom of the trench, got my carbine cocked, put a round in the chamber, and lay there quietly, never losing sight of the Chinese as he stood, bent over, frozen, stock-still, unmoving.

And I did not move, either. I watched him constantly to see what he might do. I did not think he had seen me. I hoped he had not seen me. I was lying there, every muscle tensed, every nerve on edge, just waiting. I waited, and waited, and waited, eyes fixed on this guy; a good ten minutes must have gone by, without any movement from either one of us. Finally, I told myself that I was going to get that son of a gun, and I started to spring to my feet, keeping the guy under constant observation, and he still had not moved, and my carbine was at the ready—ready to open fire on him at any time.

And then I realized that it was a bush. He was a bush! But it was the most Chinese-soldier-looking bush you could ever hope to meet under that misty visibility, and there was no question that I had instantly been fully prepared to do battle with that bush. I continued on my way, feeling just a little sheepish, across the paddy, to check my squad on the other side of it.

The paddy figured in another story. After the usual meeting of all the other officers of the company with Lieutenant Moody at five o'clock one day, we had obtained our password and countersign. When I returned to my command post, I called all my squad leaders together, distributed the beer ration, and passed on all the latest information, including the password and countersign so that it could be disseminated down to all the troops before it turned dark. The same password was used across the entire United Nations front, from the North China Sea clear to the North Japanese Sea on the other coast of Korea. The password always took effect at six o'clock in the evening, or 1800 hours, and lasted through that night; and the reason why we had the same password all the way across Korea was that sometimes patrols might go out through the lines of one unit and come back through another unit, so that the use of a universal password became very necessary.

And on that particular night, I distributed the password to my squad leaders who, in turn, gave it to all their troops. The long trench line across the paddy where I had my Chinese soldier/bush encounter was, as I have said, anchored by two machine gun positions. One of the machine gunners in the position on my side of the paddy was a fellow by the name of Leedy. Now, Leedy was a little bit crazy. For one thing, Leedy liked to pretend he was a truck, and he would either walk very fast or run along, making noises like a truck: "*Brrrrummm, brrrrummm.*" And he would "shift gears" going up a hill. I think that he had been a truck driver in civilian life. Leedy had the machine gun on my side of the paddy, and his buddy had the machine gun position on the other side. That night, as darkness was beginning to fall, I was approaching Leedy's position when the guy at the gun position on the other side of the paddy, yelled, "Hey, Leedy, what's the password?" I was just coming up on Leedy's position and heard the question, "What's the password?" And was about to shout, "Leedy, don't yell the password, you idiot," when

Presuming to be a United States Marine

Leedy shouted it out, with the countersign, even. He yelled out the entire Eighth Army password-countersign in the dusk, when sound carries as clearly as a bell.

We knew the Chinese had a listening post right across the little paddy valley in front of us, and I was sure they had heard everything. That listening post would figure in an adventure a couple of weeks later. I now had to go through the embarrassment of reporting the incident back to the company, which reported it to the battalion, which reported it to the division, which reported it to the First Corps, which reported it to the Eighth Army, and the entire Eighth Army's password had to be changed at about seven o'clock that night, and all because of Leedy. What a disaster! Now, maybe the Chinese had not heard the password, although I don't see how they could have helped hearing it, because Leedy shouted it out loud enough to carry clear across that paddy. If you took the same distance at another angle, you would have been right inside the Chinese listening post, and even if the Chinese did not have an English language specialist at that listening post, we certainly couldn't take any chances in combat. And that was good ole Leedy, the noisy truck driver.

Throughout the month of May, we performed fairly routine tasks. We sent out patrols occasionally; usually they were reconnaissance patrols. A reconnaissance patrol tries to remain concealed without giving itself away to the enemy, as opposed to a combat patrol, which patrols out until it meets the enemy and then engages him. Most of our patrols were for the purpose of reconnaissance. We mainly occupied our listening posts and outposts and patrolled in front of our positions, settling into a kind of routine.

I think it was during this quiet period in late May, when I was still a relatively new platoon commander, that I faced an unusual leadership challenge. One day, during daylight hours, I was walking my line and checking in with my troops to see how they were and if there were any problems. As I entered one bunker fighting hole, I noticed that the rifleman who occupied it was hunkered over, concentrating on what was obviously a very absorbing task. He had laid all his clips of M1 rifle ammunition on a shelf dug into the dirt on the side of his hole. He had a big smooth rock propped up at about knee level, and he was using a sharpened KA-BAR knife on the tips of each bullet. He was cutting the tip off the bullet and then notching it.

I quickly realized that he was making dum-dums, a type of ammunition explicitly and specifically outlawed by the Geneva Convention. In Basic School, we had been well drilled on this provision. A rather tense conversation ensued between us. "Private, what are you doing?"

"I am making dum-dums, sir," he said.

"You know they're illegal?"

"Well, . . . ah . . . ah . . . ah, no, sir."

"Well, they are," I said. I picked up all the dum-dums he had already made. "We'll forget about this for now, but if I ever catch you making dum-dums again, you are going to see the man. This is a hell of a war, but there are some rules, and by God, we are going to play by those rules." I could see that he was dismayed, if not defiant, and I almost surprised myself with my insistence on the strict application of the rules of the Convention.

Taking on the Burden of History

I have already mentioned that during this period, our company was conducting extensive patrolling. Each of our three platoons was patrolling in front of our positions every few nights. In accordance with a division order, each patrol was required to have three means of communication with the MLR. The usual setup was that a patrol would carry an SCR-300, a large and powerful radio; have a wireman with a "wire pack"; and carry flares to be fired from a rifle. When on patrol, we mainly relied on the sound power wire communication because we could hook this in on the company net and keep up with everything happening back on the line, and the folks on the line could keep up with everything happening, observations, and so on with the patrol. It was customary, after a patrol had reached its FPOA (farthest point of advance), and as the patrol turned around and made some progress back toward the lines, for the wireman carrying the wire pack to disconnect the phone receiver from the wire as we hurried back to the lines. As will be seen, this practice created a problem that resulted in a change in the whole communications SOP. And my platoon discovered it.

One evening, around 2000 hours (8:00 p.m.), I was sitting in my palatial platoon headquarters when a couple of 60 mm or 82 mm mortar shells landed right on top of and just to the side of my bunker. My platoon guide was monitoring the company sound power net and he said he had heard the distinctive sound of a mortar shell being dropped in the tube. He passed me the receiver, and I too heard *chunk, chunk, chunk*—the unmistakable sound of mortar shells being dropped in the tube. A few moments later, three more shells landed right on top of our bunker.

I don't believe I have introduced our company 60 mm mortar officer. He was Lieutenant Philip Dooley, USMC, a regular officer who went on to a distinguished career in the marines. Lieutenant Holmberg, also a regular officer, had nicknamed Dooley, "Defilade Dooley." Anyway, when I heard the chunks of the mortars, followed by the explosions of the shells, I was convinced that our own 60s were shelling me. With some exasperation, I called our 60s and said, "This is Lieutenant Van Sant, let me speak to Lieutenant Dooley." The man on watch in our 60 mm mortar position immediately responded and said, "Here is Lieutenant Dooley."

I said, "Hey, Phil, have you guys gone nuts? You are shelling my CP."

"Van, I haven't fired a mission in over an hour. It's not me," replied a similarly irate Lieutenant Dooley.

"Well, who the hell is it? I can hear the rounds dropping in the tubes, and it sounds just like what we hear when you are firing a mission," I replied.

"I tell you, it's not me." And then, somebody on one of the other phones on our company net said, "I'll bet the Chinese have plugged into a cut-off wire left by one of our patrols."

One had to admire the Chinese for their deviousness. It resulted in a battalion order that all wiremen on patrols forward of the main line of resistance were to cut off their wires behind the MLR when returning from a patrol. The enemy had obviously attached a receiver to one of our wires and carelessly left it alive near one of their mortar positions. If they had not made this mistake, we would never have known.

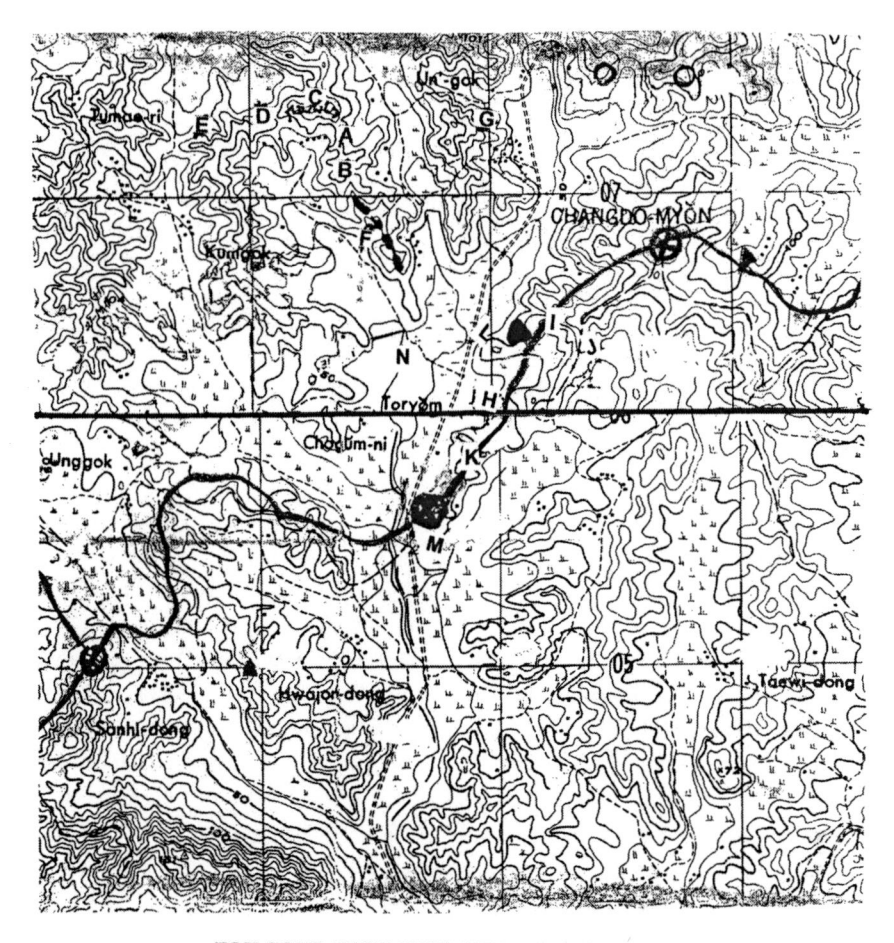

FOX COMPANY'S SITUATION IN MAY OF 1952

Legend

A The "Hundred Yard Dash"
   A saddle between two ridges
B Ridgeline south of Dash.
   Where I first came under fire.
C Trench on OPLR. Site of O.P.
   Enemy on ridgeline 150 yds north.
D Our sniper position on north
   face of Kumgok hill mass.
E My furthest advance west on face of
   Kumgok my first day
F Tank Road leading up to ridge
   line and 100 yard dash.
G Twin tip hill mass we called OP 3.
   Objective of ill-fated May 28 action.
H Middle of wide paddy where I
   confronted Chinese "soldier."
I Main Fox Company observation post.
   Black triangle = right boundary 2nd Plat.
J Fox Company Command Post
   bunker.
K My 2nd Platoon Command Post. Built
   on a cave.
L Where South Africans 1000 lb
   Bomb landed in front of squad
M Boundary between my platoon and
   7th Marine Regiment.
N Where South African napalm
   bomb landed. Target was C

Heavy black line running from southwest to northeast is main line of resistance (MLR) trench line. Circles with X in middle are boundary markers between units.

Chapter 10

TWO ENGAGEMENTS, THINGS HEAT UP (1952)

On about the twenty-third or twenty-fourth of May, I went back to one of our company commander's daily meetings, and Griff Moody advised us that there was a fairly large operation planned for the morning of the twenty-eighth of May. Now, as I have said, the left flank of our company, Fox Company, was tied into the right flank of the Seventh Regiment, and they had the rest of the division front all the way across to the Panmunjom area and, finally, tied in with the Korean Marine Corps, down to the mouth of the Imjin River, which was the west coast anchor of the whole UN line. The Seventh Marines occupied a position just across a main road from us, which was the north-south road leading to Seoul. This road had been the main line of attack when the North Koreans invaded South Korea, and one of the reasons the Marine Corps had been moved over to the west coast in March was to defend that corridor. Just to the west and north of the highway was a hill mass called 104. Like our OPLR, it was a hill we had occupied when we first arrived in March, but since then, the Chinese had dug in on it. The Seventh Marines were going to launch a massive company- or battalion-sized attack on 104, and our company just to the east of them, was assigned the mission of launching what was called a supporting attack. The supporting attack was normally used to mislead the enemy as to our real intentions. This was to be a very coordinated operation, and both attacks were to jump off at seven o'clock in the morning on the twenty-eighth of May—a day which shall live in infamy.

Griff told us that ours was to be a platoon-sized attack; in other words, one of our three platoons would attack up the hill called OP-3, which looked like a twin topped pyramid in front of the right (eastern) portion of our company front. There was considerable evidence that the Chinese were beginning to occupy that hill since they could come in behind it well screened from our fire or observation. Our attack would be supported by a section from the battalion heavy machine gun platoon. The heavy machine gun platoon was the platoon I had hoped to get when I first reported in, if the reader will remember.

There we sat, the three platoon commanders, listening to our instructions. The first platoon was commanded by a man whom I shall call Lieutenant Z, the longest-serving platoon commander in the company. This was the end of May, and he'd had the platoon since February. I had the second platoon and was the newest and most inexperienced rifle platoon commander, and the third platoon was commanded by a man who is still a close friend, Bill Holmberg.

I had already come to know Holmberg fairly well because he had come back from the OPLR to the platoon sector to my right where we tied in together. A couple of times, we had sat for some time together at the boundary of our two platoons, talking about our lives. Bill Holmberg had married, gone to his wedding reception, had a one-hour honeymoon in a hotel, and then boarded a plane for Korea. He talked a lot about his marriage to Mary, whom he obviously deeply loved, and whom I later came to know too. These conversations were very serious and formed the basis of a friendship that, I am happy to say, continues to this day.

Now Griff asked for a volunteer to lead a platoon-sized assault on OP-3. He looked at Holmberg, and Holmberg kind of shrugged. Then he looked at me, and I am thinking about all the advice I was given when I first entered the service, to not ever volunteer for anything. And while Holmberg and Lieutenant Z had both been on OP-3 and knew the terrain, I had never been up there myself. I shrugged my shoulders too.

Next, Griff looked at Lieutenant Z, whose response could not have been more impressive if he had been acting in a war movie. He casually lit a cigarette and drawled, "I'll do it." At that moment, my admiration for Z's courage knew no bounds. I was really impressed with this man, who so clearly demonstrated his willingness to perform a dangerous task with a puff on his cigarette. And that was that. From this point on, Griff and the people back in battalion operations worked with Z. As we will find out, Z, unfortunately, never had a plan. Instead, he perhaps imagined that he would walk up that hill with his platoon and take it by casually waving his cigarette about.

It was the beginning of one of the two worst debacles I witnessed in Korea. As daylight approached on May 28, Griff repositioned Holmberg's and my platoons, so that we were stretched out pretty thinly. Our two platoons were to man the whole company-sized line of resistance and free up Z's platoon to take OP-3. In the middle of the night, at about three o'clock, I had my platoon extended and moved to the right, or the east, and Holmberg had moved his platoon in to occupy all of Z's platoon's position. The upshot was that I inherited Holmberg's command post (CP). I had never seen his CP before. It was a sort of sandbag palace, quite high, and built above ground. It was not protected by any natural features of the earth or any little hillocks. It was pretty shaky-looking, actually. The walls were only a couple of rows of sandbags, and there were places where you could see daylight through the walls, and it had a layer of logs and a layer of sandbags on top to protect it from falling shells. Holmberg, at the time, was making a fetish of how cool and relaxed his platoon was. As I have said, Holmberg was a Naval Academy graduate and a very brave and squared-away marine, but in combat mode, he made quite a point of showing his whole platoon was imperturbable, cool, and nonchalant.

In my platoon headquarters, I had an assistant platoon commander, Master Sergeant Smith, and a platoon sergeant, Staff Sergeant Crawford. In addition, I had a platoon

Taking on the Burden of History

guide, Sergeant Ray, and a runner, who was also a radioman. For most of May and into June, I had another noncommissioned officer, Gunnery Sergeant Garrison.

We all moved into the third platoon command post to oversee the defense of the lines. One of the problems with Holmberg's command post position in the company was that his visibility forward was not as good as it was from my area.

As seven o'clock approached, there was a burst of preplanned artillery and mortar fire, and the entire front in our area opened up, and we started blowing the hell out of OP-3 and the supporting hills behind it.

Z's platoon jumped off at precisely 7:00 a.m. They crossed the road in front of our positions, crossed a sloping paddy, which turned out to be a minefield, and started up the hill. At five minutes after seven, word came through on our radio that there was a problem with the Seventh Marines and that they had postponed H-hour until 8:00 a.m. Griff reported back to them that we had already jumped off and that Z and his people had started up the hill. The activity in our sector was the only big thing happening on the entire front, and every artillery piece from China opened up on us, and we began receiving an enormous amount of incoming fire, not only on Z's platoon, as they were trying to get up the face of OP-3, but on us, as we were supporting them.

Of course, the whole purpose of our supporting attack had been lost when the Seventh Marines delayed their jump-off by one hour, because now the Chinese commanders were not faced with deciding which one of the two was the main attack. In combat, men can lose their lives because of lateness and delays, and this debacle painfully taught me to try to always be on time, even in civilian life.

The route Lieutenant Z had selected to lead his troops up the hill led right through a minefield. *Boom!* Within a couple of minutes, two or three of his men had been wounded by mines. When the guy ahead of one of the first platoon marines hit a mine, he, as is proper, hit the deck to protect himself. He threw himself off the path; and as he made contact with the ground, his helmet set off another mine, which utterly decapitated him. There was nothing left of his head.

And that was only the beginning of the disasters. Z, apparently, was shaken, but kept on going, and plugged on up the hill, and the heavy machine guns kept on going up too. These machine guns were commanded by a staff sergeant named Raykus, whom I came to know much better, and with whom I served many years after the Korean War. He was a fine man. Raykus got the tripods of his heavy machine guns up to the top of the hill at OP-3 and killed a couple of Chinese in order to do it, but when he got his machine guns set up and looked around, there was no infantry to protect him. And there he was, sitting on top of OP-3 with two heavy machine guns and no protection. Of course, the Chinese were pretty stunned at first, and were not immediately threatening, although eventually they attacked, wounding Raykus pretty badly.

Sergeant Raykus looked around and encountered some of Z's troopers who had made it up the hill, and all were asking, "Where in hell is Lieutenant Z?" And all of this was gradually coming through, as I listened in on the company sound power phone system and on the radio. We suddenly realized that we faced a chaotic situation

Presuming to be a United States Marine

on the slope of OP-3. We had a number of marine casualties, we'd already had some men killed, and nobody seemed to be in charge. Holmberg, bless his heart, occupied a position right at the forward slope in front of OP-3, and he took some men to get the casualties evacuated. And throughout all this activity, everybody continued asking, "Where is Lieutenant Z?" Now, Lieutenant Z had a radioman who had tried to stay with him, carrying the backpack radio, which in those days was very big and very heavy. And that poor radioman ran all over the hill, from the top to the bottom, looking for the lieutenant, until he himself was killed by the Chinese.

In the meantime, Griff, in the company observation post, could see most of the front and OP-3 and what was developing there. Suddenly, Griff sensed a movement behind him, turned around, and there stood Lieutenant Z. Lieutenant Z had taken off his gold bars and was holding them in his hand. He held them out to Griff, saying, "I can't do this!"

It fell to Holmberg, mostly, to clean up, and I got a squad to help, and we managed to get all the people who were left from the heavy machine gun platoon and the guns back, and all the casualties and the dead evacuated, and we were able to get them all off the hill. This happened between seven and eight o'clock, when the Seventh Marines finally jumped off on the attack; but in the meantime, we had taken an enormous amount of incoming fire. Fortunately, I had no wounded in my platoon, although Holmberg had a couple. Of course, the people in Z's platoon had suffered the most casualties, with several either wounded or killed. And the tragedy was that, had they had a leader, their mission would have been accomplished, because many of the troopers had reached the top of the hill and had dug in.

I was not present when Lieutenant Z confronted Griff, and I don't think that Griff and I ever talked about it in later years, but apparently, Griff simply gave Z's gold bars back to him and told him to get out of there. The next time we heard of him, Lieutenant Z had got himself a job back in regiment as an assistant regimental operations officer. And nobody ever cared to talk about that incident much. I must say that my feelings about Z plummeted from absolute, unabashed admiration, even near adoration for the coolness with which he had volunteered for the job, to almost total disgust. I encountered Lieutenant Z a couple of times later while I was in Korea, and he always appeared to be disconcerted to see me. He remained in the Marine Corps Reserves for some time, and I saw him again several times years later, but our meetings invariably produced uncomfortable feelings between us.

When the Seventh Marines finally jumped off at 0800 hours on that day, they found themselves engaged in a real battle to which we, just off to the east, had front-row seats. They were able to take 104 with four or five tanks, dealing the Chinese a hell of a blow. But they lost a lot of men in the process, and in the end, it was decided, as it had been decided with our OPLR, that the position was too far out and too close to the Chinese to consider occupying it as our outpost again. And that was the great battle of the twenty-eighth of May.

Now, to switch gears for a minute, I had started telling about the members of my platoon command party. Master Sergeant Smith was assistant platoon leader, and this came as a result of the fact that by late 1951 and early 1952, the Marine Corps had realized it had an abundance of senior noncommissioned officers, master sergeants, gunnery sergeants, and staff sergeants who had not been to Korea. They were all career marines, and the Marine Corps wanted to be sure that all of them had an opportunity to go to Korea. For the early months that I was there, our units were top-heavy with staff noncommissioned officers, and we had more than our complement. Master Sergeant Smith was actually appointed assistant platoon leader, and as my assistant, he stayed with me, advised me, and helped me all the time. Master Sergeant Smith was a man who must at the time have been forty years old, and very mature. He was a good marine, a wonderful man, who had fought all the way through four or five campaigns in the Pacific. He was an interesting-looking man, almost a spitting image of the handsome and masculine-looking actor Gregory Peck. He was tall and slender, and he was lean and mean.

My platoon sergeant was a staff sergeant with the wonderful name of Fayette Delbert Crawford. I figured that Fayette Delbert Crawford had spent his entire life overcoming the name that he so unfortunately had been saddled with. The name "Fayette Delbert" just seems to conjure up a little boy in a blue velvet suit with a fluffy, lacy collar and cuffs, but Fayette Delbert was anything but a cream puff—he was one of the toughest men I have ever known. The reader may remember the Johnny Cash song, "A Boy Named Sue," and Sue became super tough in order to overcome his name. Fayette too, was hard-nosed, and although he demanded everything of the troops, he never demanded anything he would not do himself. He was a picture postcard of a noncommissioned officer, a well-built, muscular man, about six feet one. He had grown a beautiful handlebar moustache in Korea, which he waxed very carefully. He was a colorful-looking figure, tough as hell. There were some novels written after World War II that used the expression "war lover." Crawford was not exactly a war lover, but Crawford was probably among those closest to that type of a personality I have ever encountered. Later on, when we got into some hot action, he would exclaim, "God, isn't this wonderful, Lieutenant?"

Crawford, as I say, had fought all the way through World War II, but he was actually embarrassed by his previous service. He had been put on sea duty out of boot camp, had spent the entire war aboard battleships and aircraft carriers as part of the Marine detachment, and had seen a lot of battles. He had seen the Battle of the Philippine Sea, he was at Okinawa, and I think he even participated in the earlier battles of Savo and Guadalcanal. But although he had been bombed, he never felt that he had really fought as a marine in the war. He considered that he had been "safe" on ships because he had slept between sheets every night. He thought that he had not really roughed it like his fellow marines. He, in fact, had an inferiority complex about his past service.

And man, was he glad to get down in the mud with the troops in Korea. He loved it! And he ran a tight ship. It is mostly due to Crawford, and not to the power and influence of Platoon Commander Van Sant, that the second platoon was the most squared-away platoon in the company. Crawford simply made it that way.

Presuming to be a United States Marine

I learned, within days after taking over the platoon, not to inquire too carefully into why I occasionally saw members of the platoon turning up with red marks on their faces or, in one case, a black eye. While by 1952, the Marine Corps was transitioning into a service that really did not countenance that kind of a physical leadership, Crawford was from the old school. Crawford was the type of sergeant who did not strive to be popular with the troops; he wanted to be respected. And that he was! I think everybody in the platoon was terrified of Crawford. But since no punitive activity on his part was ever officially brought to my attention, I never made an issue of it. Crawford was an absolutely ideal platoon sergeant in the sense that he knew his job, he knew what to do, was very conscientious, and possessed all the qualities you would want to see in your platoon sergeant.

Sergeant Ray was my platoon guide the entire time I had the platoon. The responsibility for our logistics was a job for the senior buck sergeant in the platoon. He made sure we had ammunition, food, and water; and this assignment as platoon guide was normally given to a sergeant in the platoon who had already had a squad for a while. The designation "guide" was given as a kind of reward. A platoon guide would not be leading patrols, as the squad leader did, so that his was a little safer job, and Sergeant Ray certainly deserved it. He was from Louisiana, as I recall, and had a slow Louisiana drawl. There was one thing about Sergeant Ray. He was afraid of snakes; in a subsequent story, we will hear about an encounter between Sergeant Ray and a serpent.

I have already told you about the medical corpsman assigned to our platoon—Mahannah, a brilliant man who was utterly conscientious and professional. I talked with Mahannah on several occasions and found out that his goal was to get through the war, get out of the Marine Corps, and go to medical school. He was an absolutely superb corpsman who knew his job in and out. When Mahannah arrived to take care of wounded marines, you could just see that they were immediately reassured by his presence alone.

After the somewhat abortive attack on OP-3 on the twenty-eighth of May, we resumed our routine with rather more aggressive patrolling. My platoon ran several fairly lengthy patrols, including one all the way up on the old hill mass of Kumgok.

On about the fifth of June, word came through that the division and regimental intelligence officers needed the kind of intelligence you could only get from a prisoner and that, therefore, we were required to obtain some prisoners. In Fox Company, we liked to think of ourselves as something of the regimental star company, because it was the company that had voluntarily stayed online the longest, acquiring a fighting reputation in the process. Fox Company was chosen to execute a company-sized raid on the Chinese, for the purposes of determining the layout of their battle positions there and taking prisoners for interrogation on what units we were fighting.

At about that time, and I always associate it with the raid, word came that the division had set up a kind of an incentive program. Any marine who captured a Chinese prisoner would get a free case of beer, and five days' R & R in Japan. Griff gave

Taking on the Burden of History

us, you might say, a warning order that we were going to be asked to do a night raid, and D-Day was tentatively set for the night of the twelfth and thirteenth of June. Griff also told us that if, in the meantime, we could manage to "schnocker" off a prisoner, then maybe the raid would be called off by regiment and division, but that, since the intelligence people were desperately short of information, prisoners would still have to be obtained in one way or another.

I began organizing a patrol. On the left front of my position, on a ridge coming down from Kumgok, were the ruins of a village marked on the map as the village of Chogum-ni. There were foundations of some buildings and huts left, but the buildings had all been obliterated, probably at the beginning of the war, when the North Koreans marched through. The village had a rather attractive cemetery with headstones, although cemeteries tend to become rather spooky places on night patrol.

Chogum-ni was at the south end of the north-south portion of the Kumgok ridge line. The Chinese were now well dug in on Kumgok, and we strongly suspected that they had either a listening post or an outpost in Chogum-ni, and so I organized a five-man snatch party. We were going to go to the village, and if that listening post existed, we were going to find it, though we had never spotted it at all, because the Chinese were good at concealment. But if it was there, and if we could latch on to a prisoner, we would be on easy street. Griff had already indicated that the next operation was going to be a company-sized raid, so that there would be two assault platoons and a reserve platoon involved and, since the first platoon had been shot up on OP-3 on the twenty-eighth of May, it was clear that these assault platoons would consist of my platoon, the second platoon, and Holmberg's platoon, the third platoon.

We started planning for the raid right away and decided that Holmberg was going to go around OP-3 and behind it, because aerial photos had shown that the Chinese had dug a kind of a network of trenches from a hill behind OP-3 up to the reverse slope of OP-3, and that they were really loading up on that particular hill mass. I was to conduct a supporting attack to the west of OP-3 on the old tank road, which led up to the Hundred-Yard Dash and the OPLR. I was quite familiar with that terrain. As we planned it, Holmberg's platoon would try to get in behind the Chinese and try to capture the prisoners, and I would be creating a diversion and set up a base of fire to help cover Holmberg.

In the meantime, I worked on my Chogum-ni patrol. I was to lead it, I think, on the night of the eighth of June. I woke up in the morning of that day, with the whole right side of my face swollen. This had all come about after my last line check at 0300 hours. I had a really terrible toothache and what seemed to be an abscessed tooth. Of course, everybody in the platoon knew that I was taking the patrol out; I'd had the platoon for almost four weeks by now and knew the men pretty well, and they knew me.

Suddenly I found myself facing the prospect of leading the most important patrol of my service so far, and I had a bad tooth! I went back to Griff, got the company jeep, and took it back to battalion headquarters. Battalion headquarters had two medical doctors, the battalion surgeons. There were always two per battalion. I went in to see the battalion surgeon, whom I had met before, and he looked at my face and inside my mouth, and he said, "Hell, I can see the tooth. You are going to have to go back to the division dental company and have it extracted. That tooth has got to come out."

And I asked, "Well, how long will that take?" And he said, "Oh, you'll be away for two or three days." And I said, "I can't do that. I am supposed to take a patrol out tonight. I can't go away for two or three days. That would just be a disgrace!"

The doctor thought about that and told me, "Well, look, I am not a dentist, I can't give you Novocain, because I don't have any, but," he added, "I think I can take that tooth out." And I bravely said, "Take it out!"

I sat down in a chair, and he got a pair of pliers, wiggled and jiggled the affected tooth a couple of times, and *choonk*. Out it came. I probably have experienced pain that bad a couple of times in my life, but may never have experienced worse pain. My gum started bleeding immediately, but the doctor knew what to do about that and gave me a pack of cotton to put on it and a couple of prescription drugs for the pain.

"That's a first one for me. I have never taken out a tooth before," the doctor told me quite happily, proud of his accomplishment. I mumbled, "Well, it's the first for me too. I have never had a tooth taken out without Novocain."

So I wadded up my gum with some more cotton pads, climbed into the company jeep, and returned to Fox Company. My gum hurt for the rest of the day and through the night, but I did not pay any more attention to it. It is amazing that when you are under tension and stress, you do not pay any attention to physical pain, because you have other things on your mind, not the least of which is the ever-present possibility of losing your life.

As soon as it got dark, our patrol took off, and although the moon was not yet full, we could see reasonably well. We crept across the paddy in front of Chogum-ni and entered the little village. We poked around quietly, hoping to sneak up on a Chinese listening post. One of my troopers was carrying a carbine, and the carbine had a magazine that fit up into it with a release mechanism that was clicked up. The carbine was not too well designed in those days because the magazine-release catch was right next to the safety catch. Whenever you were sneaking along on a patrol, you kept the safety on, because you did not want the carbine to fire accidentally, but whenever you got to a point when you thought you might be encountering an enemy, you took the safety off.

As we were prowling along silently, instead of hitting the safety catch, my trooper hit the magazine release, and as luck would have it, the magazine dropped out of his carbine, hit a stone, and produced a big clanking noise. Before we could do anything about it, we heard *tshoom, tshoom, tshoom*, as a lone Chinese took off at high speed, back toward Kumgok. We did not see him, but he had certainly heard us approaching, and we certainly heard him running off, and so our opportunity to schnocker off a Chinese prisoner was foiled.

We probed around a little bit longer, finding some evidence of where the Chinese listening post had been. A single man had clearly been hiding in the ruins of the village

Taking on the Burden of History

but was long gone by the time we arrived on the spot, and we returned empty-handed and resigned to a company raid, unless Holmberg, who had also gone out with a patrol from his platoon that night, had been more successful.

Holmberg took his patrol out from the lines at a point about seven hundred yards to the east of where I had been and also came back empty-handed, although he managed to clear some mines and open up the way for his platoon to go right underneath the Chinese positions, and so he did accomplish something on his patrol that would help facilitate the success of the future raid.

Word came down that we were going to execute the raid on the night of the twelfth of June. In order to make the raid possible, Fox Company was removed from its positions on the afternoon of the eleventh; and leaving most of our gear behind, we took our fighting materials, our ammunition and weapons, and pulled back about a mile or two behind the line we had occupied, and were replaced by E Company, Second Battalion, Fifth Marines.

I subsequently learned that the reason for having a company from the Fifth Marine replace us was that on June 15-16, E Company, Fifth Marines, was scheduled to relieve Fox Company, First Marines, in our positions. It was felt that this would give the E Company troopers a preliminary reconnaissance of the positions they would be assuming in a few days.

As luck would have it, my old friend, George Morrison, had managed to get himself assigned as the company commander of E Company, Second Battalion, Fifth Marines. He was one of two first lieutenant company commanders (Griff was the other) and, subsequently, the only first lieutenant company commander in the division, after Griff was promoted to captain later in June.

George was making a reconnaissance before bringing his company up. When he came to my platoon, we had a big and joyful reunion, and I introduced him to Griff. George had not seen any combat yet because the Fifth Marines had been in division reserve, having cocktail parties and generally enjoying a good time, while we were roughing it online. I was really happy to see George but could not resist telling him in vivid detail about all the action I had seen up on the OPLR and on patrols. After all, I was now the old and experienced vet, while he had been sipping drinks on easy street, and you can be sure that I rubbed that in liberally. Griff too formed a fast friendship with George, although it never had much chance to flourish, but there was a lot of immediate respect between the two of them, and I later regaled Griff with many stories about George and our escapades in California.

The afternoon of the eleventh of June, we pulled off our positions online and marched back to the rear to an area the operations office had selected, somewhat similar to what we were going to encounter on our raid. That night we conducted a practice, after which we were fed a really substantial hot dinner and were afforded the luxury of sleeping through the night. The 50 percent watch online has already been described, so that at any given moment one-half of the Fox Company was asleep, although the platoon commanders had to be out twice each night, checking their troops. But now to have the opportunity to go to the rear, curl up and snooze all night with a hot dinner in the belly would have been even more of a boost, had we not been mindful of the fact that we were being fattened up for the kill.

The next day, we did a lot of rehearsing and going over plans on how we would conduct the raid. I had, I think, a very good plan, and after we had thoroughly practiced it, my troops all knew the tactical plan. We were going to put two squads up on the old tank road, right next to the Chinese position in front of our old OPLR, pour fire into it, and seal off that whole area so that Holmberg could take his platoon in behind the OP-3, siphon off some prisoners, and get out. My mission was not to take prisoners, my mission was to get up to my position and fire. We worked out a route to reach the tank road across a paddy and across a minefield, and several of the men in my platoon, as well as I, pretty well knew the route. I was going to position my two squads with machine guns on the tank road, with my third squad in reserve. Sergeant Ray, the platoon guide was put in charge of this reserve and was to occupy a little knob behind the tank road to support and help us if need be.

And so we rested up all that day. Late in the afternoon, our battalion chaplain, McCabe, passed the word that he was going to hold a communion service at six o'clock. It was still quite light at that time of the evening, and almost the entire company came, including many Catholic boys. There was a good deal of joshing between them, and as they prepared to attend the Protestant service, I heard a couple of them talking, "Well, this service is the best thing we have going for us here, so we'd better grab it."

And we were sitting on a little hillside, with the altar set up down on the bottom of the hill. Just as the service began getting under way, across a field and down the road in the distance, we could see a cloud of dust, and here came a jeep with the Catholic chaplain. He came roaring up and announced that there would be a Catholic Mass with Communion, and so we lost about one-third of our congregation. But Chaplain McCabe carried on, unruffled, and Holmberg and I, who had really become good friends by this time, went up and took Communion together all by ourselves before our troops came up. After this spiritual refreshment, we walked back up to our temporary positions to make last-minute preparations. We were given face paint to darken our wrists and our faces. We applied the camouflage paint liberally all over our faces so that in the dark, we would not show up at all. My attached machine gun sergeant was Staff Sergeant Nethery, who went by the name of "Ricochet." Ricochet was a grizzled veteran marine who had been in the Corps since 1936. He had been on the ship's Marine detachment on the USS *Vincennes* when that ship was sunk at the beginning of WWII. He had gone from there to Guadalcanal, back to Parris Island as a drill instructor, and was sent over to the Iwo Jima battle. Ricochet had acquired his nickname at Iwo when a bullet had penetrated his helmet and was deflected by his helmet liner in such a way that it completely circumnavigated his head, plowing up the flesh along the way. This had given him a very distinctive scar. He was cue-ball bald, and his scar, resembling a halo, wound all around his head. Ricochet had the reputation of being something of a maverick. In his sixteen-year career, he had been up and down the rank ladder

Taking on the Burden of History

several times. He tended to be a heavy drinker, and some of the troops were a little leery of him. They thought he was "shaky." But on this particular night of our raid, Ricochet was to perform admirably.

As we were applying the camouflage paint to our faces, Sergeant Ricochet Nethery saw fit to loosen up the tension in our platoon with a joke. We smeared the paint on each other's faces, and Ricochet was busy camouflaging me, and I was applying the face paint to him. Suddenly, he yelled out, "Quick! Tell the quartermaster to send off for another tube of paint. I am doing the lieutenant's nose." In the words of the theater, this brought down the house.

It was now completely dark. Holmberg's third platoon fell in first, in a column on either side of the road. My second platoon came next, and Lieutenant Smythe, who had been sent up and assigned to take over Lieutenant Z's platoon, the first platoon, fell in the rear. The first platoon was to be the reserve force for this raid. Lieutenant Smythe seemed to be a good fellow. He was from Southern California and had a little bit of the beach boy outlook on life, but he had impressed most of us as by being a good platoon commander.

We took off in that three, two, one order, and as we were hiking down the road in the dark, I suddenly realized that clomping along in the back of my platoon was Chaplain McCabe. One of my sergeants, Master Sergeant Smith, said, "Lieutenant, he really wants to go along, and I am going to hang with him to make sure he doesn't get into any trouble." Then Holmberg's platoon peeled off to the right and went up to their staging position, from where they were going to jump off. I went down through the lines, right where my positions had been, and at precisely eleven o'clock, two things happened.

First, the full moon rose over the horizon, and our two platoons crossed the line of departure, which, in this case, was the road that ran down across the front of our company positions, and we plunged into the rice paddy.

Ricochet, was with the point man, working his way through the rice paddy, because Ricochet knew where the mines were. After we had gone about 100 to 150 yards in this paddy, we had to make a right turn down a path leading to the little knoll that marked the southern end of the old tank road. Ricochet did not know that path too well, but he came back to tell me he thought it was all right. And so we moved along the path, with the point man from my second squad ahead, Ricochet behind him, and me behind Ricochet. Behind me was the corporal, acting squad leader of the second squad, and he was a good man.

Now a second thing happened. As we proceeded along the path, the point man passed it, Ricochet passed it, I passed it, and we had apparently all missed stepping on a foot-activated box mine. But the corporal behind me was not so fortunate. He stepped on the mine, and *VARROOM!* It went off. Of course, everybody hit the ground because when a mine goes off, at first you don't know whether it is a mine or a shell, but we immediately figured it out because the corporal had yelled out. The war was over for him. I think the surgeons saved his foot, but he had lost a lot of pieces of it.

Presuming to be a United States Marine

We had to appoint the next senior man in the squad as the squad leader, and that was a little bit hairy under the circumstances because we had to pull him out of the two assault squads. In addition, of course, the mine going off had alerted the Chinese. They immediately began firing up and down the front. We moved on and reached the little hill that led up to the tank road, and we were all right at first. And then all hell broke loose. My god!

First of all, Holmberg's platoon had stepped into it. We could hear them off to the right. There were grenades and machine guns and rifles and all kinds of mortars being fired. Next, the Chinese opened up on my platoon. And there were tracers everywhere from Chinese machine guns, and we were pinned down at the bottom of the hill just south of the tank road.

After the whole raid was over, Master Sergeant Smith told me a funny story about Chaplain McCabe that happened about this time when all hell broke loose after my squad leader had stepped on the mine and the whole Chinese line opened up on us. From our rest and practice area about a mile behind the lines, when I led the second platoon back up to pass through the main line and jump off on the raid, Sergeant Smith walked with me until we reached the main trench line. There, by prearrangement, he stopped off and checked each one of our men through with a supportive word of encouragement. This was not unappreciated by the troops. He commanded a great deal of respect. We had arranged that he would stay back on the line to ensure that we got whatever support we needed as we assaulted the enemy.

As the last member of our platoon filed past him, Sergeant Smith was surprised to see an additional figure plowing along. Smith stopped him, and it turned out to be Chaplain McCabe. The following conversation ensued. "Sir, where are you going?" asked Sergeant Smith.

"I want to go with the troops," said McCabe.

"Sir, I'm sorry. We may need you later, but these troops are going to assault the enemy. They can't be worried about you."

Sergeant Smith said the chaplain was very reluctant, but Smith pulled him into the trench line and resolved to keep an eye on him.

When the mine went off and the Chinese lines began laying down a hail of fire on my platoon as well as Holmberg's to the east, Sergeant Smith said that Chaplain McCabe instinctively jumped out of the trench line and began to move forward to where we were being fired at some four or five hundred yards forward of the line. As luck would have it, Sergeant Smith said, the Chinese machine gun fire was passing over us out there in front of them on the main line, and the rounds were landing in bunches right where Sergeant Smith and the chaplain were watching the action. Sergeant Smith had to jump out of the trench line and grab the chaplain and pull him back into it. He said the chaplain was bewildered by the whole thing but that instinctively, he wanted to be with us out there being fired at.

I realized that there were a few Chinese at the top of the hill on the little knoll, but there did not seem to be very many of them. It was a small outpost, I thought. I picked up my handheld radio, the old 536, a piece of junk that never worked very well. I also had a wireman with me, who had been carrying a wire that uncoiled from a pack on his back, so that I had wire communications with the command post as well. I also had a larger radio for communication with the company, strapped to the back of my runner. I called back to Griff, using code words, and told him that we had been pinned down. He said that from where he was, at the company observation post, he could see that. And I said to him, "We are going to move ahead."

And telling you this is a little bit emotional because it was another defining moment for me. I threw down that dumb 536 radio and never found it again. As I put it down, I became aware of myself, as if I were outside of myself and watching myself. I knew what I had to do. I had told Griff over the radio that I was moving ahead. When I call this a defining moment, it was as if, in that instant, I had become two people, and the two were struggling with each other to see who would prevail. One Van Sant was very comfortable lying there on the ground at the bottom of the hill. It had become a warm, cozy, and safe place. I could feel the blades of grass against my cheek. Powerful forces within me were telling me that I had done my job, I'd gotten my people this far. Why risk further danger? But the other Van Sant insisted, *You told Griff you were going on up that hill!* Which Van Sant would prevail?

The few Chinese on top of the knoll at the south end of the tank road were shooting at us. The main Chinese position behind them was firing at us with everything they had. These positions were set up at the other end of the Tank Road on the same little ridge line, on the slope of which I'd had my very first experience under fire the first day I had gone to the OPLR. There I had watched that first blossom on the end of a Chinese rifle. Now the small Chinese outpost was right above us, and all of them were shooting those same blossoms at us.

Sergeant Ray had dropped off with a squad and had occupied a little knoll west of us. I had the remaining thirty-five men—riflemen and machine gunners—with me. From the main Chinese position, we were pinned down by at least three machine guns, so that everybody was on the ground. But somehow, duty prevailed, and I pushed myself off from the ground, stood up, and yelled, very loudly, "Come on, let's go!" And, all glory to the Marine Corps and its training, every single man stood up behind me as one man. And we swept up over that Chinese outpost knoll like a small tidal wave. For the first and the last time in my life, I was actually leading a real charge.

As soon as we got to the top and I was one of the first, if not the first to reach the top of the knoll from which the tank road led on up to the OPLR, and from which the men in the Chinese outpost who had been out there were running away north up the tank road, and I could see one of them very clearly, because the moon was now full and bright, and I could see them running back toward their main line positions. I got my carbine up and cranked off two rounds at him, and then the carbine jammed.

The reason the carbine jammed was because the experienced old salt I thought I was had taped two thirty-round magazines together head-to-head with black tape, thinking that I would carry with me, right in my weapon, a full sixty rounds of ammunition. A carbine had two kinds of magazines. One was a straight and rectangular magazine, holding fifteen carbine rounds. The bigger magazine held thirty rounds and had to be curved, because the base of any cartridge is always slightly larger than the tip of it. In theory, you could slip the thirty-round magazines, taped together head-to-head, into your carbine and fire off the first thirty rounds, then take the magazine out, turn it around, slip the other end in, and fire thirty more rounds. That was the theory. If I had ever explored this method more thoroughly, or listened to anybody's advice, I would have learned that sixty rounds of carbine ammunition, because of that curve, pulled down and back on the shells as they were going up and out of the magazine into the chamber of the weapon, and would jam the weapon after two rounds because the shell simply could not get up into the chamber. And so I don't think I killed any Chinese on that occasion. I might have winged one, but by the time I got myself together to clear the jam in my carbine, they had all disappeared.

We had practiced so much, and I had preassigned the positions for the machine guns several hundred yards toward the Chinese positions on the tank road. We laid those guns right in, and they were completely covering the main Chinese line in the One-Hundred-Yard Dash / OPLR area with machine gun fire. We opened fire heavily on the Chinese; and of course, our supporting arms, our artillery and mortars, were just lambasting the enemy. We could tell that there were some fires and secondary explosions in the Chinese positions; the Chinese, only about fifty yards away from us, were dimly illuminated, and we could see them running around as their volume of fire diminished somewhat.

But unfortunately, something happened then that Lieutenant Holmberg and I are still arguing about, and may go to our graves arguing about. One of the prearranged signals we had was a green star cluster grenade fired off the end of a rifle, and it meant "cease fire." It would, of course, be addressed to our friendly forces, because we could hardly signal to the Chinese to stop their fire.

Let me tell you a little bit about Holmberg on this raid, as near as I can reconstruct it, having talked to many of his men, and to Bill himself. Holmberg's platoon got all the way around across the front of OP-3 and came clear around to the back of it. They then cut in toward the trench lines that connected the Chinese positions on the reverse slope of OP-3 back with their main line. Our intelligence thought that OP-3 probably held either a couple of reinforced enemy squads, or maybe a platoon, and that the area behind was probably a Chinese company headquarters of some sort.

Holmberg got into this trench network between OP-3 and the Chinese main line and there found not a platoon, but an entire company. Holmberg had dropped off one of his squads as a blocking position and then had charged into the trench network with two squads. And the trench network was not just made up of ordinary trenches. The Chinese had underground mess halls there, and all kinds of little cubicles of rooms in a really elaborate and complicated layout.

Taking on the Burden of History

Holmberg realized that, with about twenty or twenty-five of his men, he had surrounded about ninety. As he always said later, "Fleetingly, I had a wonderful vision that I was going to be the Sergeant York of the Korean War." Because apparently, many Chinese threw down their weapons, ready to surrender, and Bill was momentarily in hog heaven, thinking that he held the world by the tail. Unfortunately, though, the Chinese commander had different ideas, because his remaining troops almost immediately launched a tremendous counterattack. In the positions in front of my platoon, there were some Chinese machine guns down near the eastern end of the ridge line we were attacking, and those guns fired over into the area behind OP-3, where Holmberg and his platoon now found themselves.

Somehow Holmberg got the idea that these Chinese guns firing at him were my guns. I have gone over the events with him on a map. I showed him exactly where my guns were and where they were firing, and I have got him to finally admit that no, it had to have been Chinese guns firing at him. But even so, I have the feeling that in his heart of hearts, he still believes it was our guns shooting at him. And war is confusion. War is chaos. But now Holmberg signaled cease fire with the green star cluster, and I got word back from our company—"cease fire, cease fire"—and I told Griff what we were doing, and I think he understood.

In the meantime, things had really gone bad for Holmberg. The counterattack was in full swing, as more Chinese swept in.

Although Holmberg's troops managed to pick up some prisoners, they also kept losing some of them, either because the prisoners had become casualties, or because they had run off. In spite of these great odds, in the end, Holmberg managed to bring back two Chinese prisoners. Right at the height of this melee, Holmberg himself got wounded in the stomach by a hand grenade. He sized up the situation. At that point, he had his prisoners and had reached his objective. He ordered his men to start pulling out.

From all I have gathered in talking to the survivors, the situation was pretty chaotic, and by this time, seven or eight of Holmberg's men had been killed. He was so outnumbered that there was no way the survivors could drag our marine bodies back, and that was very unfortunate. Although it is a long-standing tradition of the Marine Corps that we always take out our dead, in a raid this deep into Chinese territory, there was simply no way it could be accomplished. And that was sad. At least eighteen of Holmberg's troops were wounded, including himself.

Bleeding heavily from his stomach, Bill organized the evacuation and organized the prisoner detail. He bled so much that when his troopers got him back to our lines, his boots were filled with his own blood. Holmberg and his surviving troops got out of the trench line, and they reached the blocking position in the road where the other troops were, and at about that time, Holmberg fainted and was carried back by two of his troops. Bill received for his brave action the Navy Cross, and that was richly deserved. He had almost lost his life in the raid.

Presuming to be a United States Marine

In that melee and after, I finally had convinced Griff that we were not involved in the shooting of our own marines and that we had plenty of Chinese to shoot at, and because by this time, the Chinese were shooting at us with everything they had—mortars and machine guns and small arms fire—we were allowed to open fire again. And we did and settled down into a real knock-down, drag-out firefight.

And Griff says, "I want you to stay out there until we can get Bill's whole platoon back." And that must have been about midnight, and I was lying on the ground, and our machine guns were shooting, and the Chinese were shooting back at us. Periodically, I moved around on the old tank road hill, checking on people. We had good positions. We were not dug in, but my men had cover and could fire. Generally, in a situation like this, I stayed with one squad, and Staff Sergeant Fayette Delbert Crawford remained with the other squad. Once, as we met in the center of the platoon, Crawford called out to me, "Isn't this wonderful, Lieutenant?" I couldn't quite agree with him that it was wonderful, but I could see that he was finally overcoming the frustrating four years of World War II when he had watched all the action from aboard a ship.

The Chinese artillery and mortar shells continued to pound us. In training, we were told that in combat, we should get up on high ground. The tank road ran right along the top of a ridge line, so that we were mostly directly on top of it. The great majority of the shells fell either on the one slope or on the other below us. Including the man who had stepped on the mine I had just stepped over, I only had three wounded and nobody killed during the raid, which was miraculous, considering the volume of fire we took. I turned in a report afterward that I thought we had killed at least twenty Chinese in their positions, judging by the fire we had poured in and the resulting confusion we observed.

But we were slugging it out on the old tank road, and the Chinese MLR position fired at us. You could hear Holmberg's platoon off to the right, withdrawing and disengaging, and the volume of fire over there finally subsided to practically nothing. And then something that will always haunt me happened. There was a valley to the east of us, the valley between us and OP-3, and the hill mass area where Holmberg was. From way down in that valley and across, at least several hundred yards away from any one of our people, we heard a man crying out, and it was clearly a marine. He gave his name, and he shouted, "I can't move, I can't move!"

I reported back to Griff that there was somebody down there who must have become separated from the rest of Holmberg's platoon and was wounded. I wanted to take a detail, or have Sergeant Crawford take a detail to try to get the wounded marine back, but Griff vetoed that because the man was, clearly, too far away from us. Griff also told me that he had dispatched a relief column, which would be coming out and up the road. I described where the voice was coming from as best I could in the dark, and Griff relayed that information to the relief column.

The relief column was Lieutenant Smythe's first platoon, in reserve. But the man who turned out to be actually leading it was Gunnery Sergeant John Francis Kelly,

Taking on the Burden of History

whom I have mentioned before. You will remember him as the gunnery sergeant who had been wounded by the Chinese with his own booby trap. We subsequently found out that John Francis had heard about the raid while he was on the hospital ship down in Inchon harbor. He managed to get ashore, going AWOL from the hospital ship, hitched a ride somehow, and reported in to Griff. Because John Francis was familiar with the terrain, he went out with Lieutenant Smythe on the cleanup detail, pulling all of Holmberg's wounded off, as well as Holmberg himself.

I was still in my position, covering this relief detail because, by this time, they were all behind me. The shelling and shooting by the Chinese continued as we kept up our fire, and soon my guys were running low on ammunition. It must have been about two or two thirty in the morning, and we had been out there for almost three hours. I called back to Griff, who was well aware of the fact that we had MIA, the marines missing in action, who actually were dead by then, as well as the one lone marine whom I had heard calling out. The relief column had looked for him but had been unable to find him. What undoubtedly happened was that when the Chinese heard him calling out to us, they located him and picked him up. We checked very carefully at the end of the war and found out that none of the seven men who ended up missing from Holmberg's platoon, not one of the seven, had been repatriated as a prisoner. So we are reasonably sure that they were all killed or died of wounds later.

What I was using to communicate with Griff was an SCR 300 radio, the big backpack radio, which my runner carried. And I asked Griff, "How are things going with the third platoon?" And he answered, "Fine. We are pretty well cleaned up." I asked, "Have you got any plans for bringing us back yet?" And Griff said, "No, I want you to stay out there a bit longer."

And then I said something that subsequently became a joke throughout the First Marine Division. I said, "Griff, we can't stay out here all f—ing night!" And as soon as the words, or that one word in particular, had left my lips, all the hours and hours of communications training came back to me, when we were told that under no circumstances, absolutely never, were we ever to use profanity of any sort over the radios in the system. So now I had said this word, so I followed it up with, "Whoops, I am sorry, I didn't mean to say f—ing." What I did not know, as I uttered these words, was that every radio in the entire First Division, clear back to the commanding general, was cued in on our frequency because we were the biggest event happening in the Korean War that night, and everybody was listening to the radio. Apparently, after my "Whoops, I am sorry, I didn't mean to say f—ing," one of the people at division headquarters said, "You could hear the shells exploding, you could hear the machine gun fire, and here is this lieutenant apologizing for breaking communications training. He's a well-trained marine!" I was told later that the division command post just cracked up over this, and about fifteen or twenty minutes later, Griff sent word that I could bring my men on back.

Presuming to be a United States Marine

The little knob behind us was what I had selected for the reserve squad's position to back us up. Sergeant Ray, the other member of my headquarters team, had remained there with the reserve squad, and a couple of amusing things happened to them while they were back there. I had mentioned that Sergeant Ray had, to say the least, a huge aversion to snakes. As luck would have it, in the full moonlight, as Ray climbed around on the little knob, he inadvertently stepped on the biggest snake he had ever seen. He told me later, "I was scared to death because of the war, but when I stepped on that snake, it got even worse!" And of course, this encounter could have had tragic consequences, but fortunately, the snake did him no harm, so that he was able to successfully avoid evacuation for being "wounded in action by a Korean snake."

Davis from Mississippi, who was then still a private first class, was back on that little hill with Sergeant Ray. In the course of the battle, the Chinese laid a lot of mortar shells on their position without hurting anybody. And Davis became a hero to everybody. There were quite a few spider holes dug on that hill—deep, circular holes, fairly small in diameter. Once, when the shelling got pretty bad, all the troops in the squad took cover in these spider holes. But one of the holes was a great, big hole, and about thirty seconds after Davis had jumped into it, a Chinese mortar shell dropped into that same hole right behind him. Apparently, the shell had a fuse delay. It must have landed at an angle, hitting the side of the hole with Davis way in the bottom of it. The shell exploded in the hole, and immediately, everybody became concerned about Davis, "Oh my god! Poor Davis." And they rushed out to help him. When they reached the hole, they saw that it was filled with the dirt the shell had blown loose. And this is how one of the troops described what happened next.

"Suddenly," he said, "the dirt begins to shake, and move, and out of the dirt rises Davis, cursing, spitting, mad as hell, and without even a scratch on him." That mortar shell had buried all its fragments in the dirt, and Davis must have been far enough down, so that the only thing that had hit him was the stirred-up dirt. But was he angry! He materialized, fuming that the so-and-so Chinese had almost got him.

When we received word to pull out, I passed it on to everybody. We picked up the machine guns, folded them up, and started out. It was an interesting moment, because a couple of things happened as we were pulling off. I got all my machine gunners out, and all my riflemen out, and suddenly, one of the squad leaders came and said, "Lieutenant, Private First Class Thomas is missing."

"What?"

"Yes, sir," he said.

I asked, "Where was he?"

And he said, "He was right up over there, Lieutenant." And he pointed down the road, toward the Chinese area.

"My god!" I said and told him to take the rest of the squad, while I went back and crawled across the tank road.

If the Chinese saw any movement on the tank road in the moonlight, they would immediately start firing machine guns, so that crossing the road back and forth was always tricky. But I managed to get across to the other side, where Thomas was said to be, and by golly, there he was, just off the skyline, and I could see him clearly, I could see his helmet, and I called out to him, in as muted a way as was possible, "Hey, Thomas!"

And here I encountered a scene that would have made every marksmanship instructor in the Marine Corps happy and proud. Thomas had found himself a nice really well-covered and concealed position. He was a rifleman, and he had his M1 rifle, and from where he was sitting, he had a good view of the whole trench line the Chinese had dug on the top of their main position. There were a couple of fires burning, which illuminated the Chinese position, and you could see figures moving around.

But Thomas was just lying there, totally concentrating, and he had never even heard the word to pull out. He was hiding, lying on his stomach, just as he had been taught to do on the range, squeezing the rounds off as a sniper would, and I have the feeling that he did a lot of damage in the process.

I told him, "Hey, Thomas, we are going home."

"Oh, thanks, Lieutenant," he said, rushing up to me. He had been so focused on his task that nothing had broken his concentration, not even the call to pull off. And so we pulled over together, got across the road to a little accompaniment of Chinese machine gun fire, and then safely came off the hill.

On the trip back, we had to cross the minefield again. I had Sergeant Crawford take half the platoon on one route, because we wanted to get back quickly, and I took the other half with me. Crawford who, as you know, rightly prided himself on being a squared-away marine, accidentally set off a flare that had been planted on the trail he had taken. And that big flare went off and illuminated him and the whole detail of the platoon with him, which, of course, immediately attracted a good deal of Chinese fire. When we finally got back to the lines and I ran into Crawford, he was just mad as hell at himself. "How did I ever trip that flare?" he asked. "I am so stupid!" And this near-perfect marine was really down on himself.

As I was coming back, I did not know yet what had happened to Holmberg. All I knew was that I had heard a lot of firing and confusion and the lone marine yelling for help, but I had no conception of the magnitude of what had transpired. From my point of view, my platoon had done a fantastic job: I had only three men wounded and nobody killed. And I had the feeling that we had really hit the Chinese hard.

It was a beautiful moonlit night, and as we were pulling off, some of the level of fire began to subside, although the Chinese were still throwing a good deal of mortars, but at least the small arms and artillery were not firing. As we were coming across the paddy to get back to our lines, and not yet knowing about the horrors that had transpired on that night, I thought, like Crawford, *By golly, this is really good*. That was the only moment in my year in Korea when I actually felt a little bit exultant.

But I was soon to be dashed down from that crazy high. I returned to the old company position from which we had jumped off, and which was now temporarily occupied by Easy Company, Fifth Marines. Wozencraft, the company exec, met me and gave me a complete report on all that had happened. And what he told me was pretty depressing. They would not let me see Bill Holmberg, as he was about to be evacuated in an ambulance, but I gathered at that point that most of the people who had seen him thought he would not pull through, and that was just an awful prospect to contemplate. And a lot of Bill's men were wounded, although they had made it back. In addition, of course, the seven marines from his platoon who had been killed were still out there somewhere, deep in the Chinese positions. And I would say that we did not return to a happy campground.

The battalion intelligence officer got hold of me right away, took me to a bunker, and debriefed me. He could not debrief Holmberg because he was on his way to the hospital. But he debriefed me, and I told him everything I knew, what we had done, what had happened, and what my estimates were of our opponents. When all that was over, I marched with the rest of my platoon back to the rear again for one more night back to the place where we had camped the night before during our practices.

We were given a big breakfast, and then we went back up to resume our old positions on the line, relieving Easy Company of the Fifth Marines. By this time, we still had not had much sleep. It was the thirteenth by now, and we reassumed our positions on the line sometime late that afternoon, although as soon as we got back online, the good news came that we were going to be relieved by the Fifth Marines on the fifteenth, just two days away, and Easy Company was going to take up Fox Company's positions. And I must say, having been online for a little over a month and having experienced as much as we had, the word that we were going off-line on the fifteenth was certainly welcome news to all of us.

I will tell the story about being relieved online and what that involved in a minute, but a couple of things happened on the fourteenth, the one full day we spent online between the time we got back up from the raid position and when we were finally taken off for good. The First Marine Division, as well as the Korean Marine Corps, and I hasten to give them full credit because they were a great outfit, were the western anchor of the entire Eighth Army line on the whole front in Korea. And as I mentioned before, we were stretched all the way from the sea to the mouth of the Imjin River, roughly along the 38th Parallel, and across the main highway and corridor from North Korea leading down to Seoul.

Just to our east, or to our right, was the British Commonwealth Division, who were obviously very highly thought of, and rightly so. As we will see in later stories, the British Commonwealth Division was a fine outfit. The English regiments, the

Taking on the Burden of History

Australian regiment, and the Ghurkas from India were all fine battalions and regiments lumped together under the British Commonwealth Division. It must be said that the British fought their wars in a little more genteel fashion than we did. The Fox Company raid, the battle I have just described, had been the big battle of the day, with everybody's attention focused on it, and everybody, if they could get the frequency, had listened in. Our British friends, just to our right, had a quartermaster who made the pronouncement, as I learned later, that, "We must help those poor chaps out, you know. After all, they have been through hell!" I got up on the morning of the fourteenth in my old command post bunker after a fitful sleep, and one of my squad leaders called to say that we had a problem. The problem turned out to be a truck the British quartermaster had sent over, loaded with booze. But not just any kind of booze, mind you. Most of it was fine scotch and cognac. He had parked the truck at the bottom of the friendly side of the hill behind where my platoon was. Any good news travels fast through the trench lines of marines, and word had spread that there was booze for sale. No doubt, this was a congenial gesture from our British friends, and as I recall, they did not charge exorbitant prices for high-quality cognac and scotch, but as my sergeant had told me, almost everybody in my platoon had managed to sneak out in order to buy himself a bottle or two.

As you know, at this point in the Korean War, the troops were allowed to have two cans of beer per day, which was strictly rationed out, but no hard liquor of any sort was allowed online. To jump ahead in my story, when we got back online the next time, the Women's Christian Temperance Union back home had heard about the two beers per diem and had them knocked out, so that for the rest of the time I was in Korea, there was no booze online of any kind, not even beer. But at this moment, thanks to our thoughtful Englishmen, why, there suddenly was a quantity of not only booze, but high-class high-proof booze to be had. There was nothing for me to do but to start out walking at one end of my platoon, which was now spread out in the old positions along the long trench line of over a thousand winding yards, snaking over hills and through paddies, and approach each man individually.

I asked, "Have you got booze?" And then added, "I know it is around, so you might as well tell the truth."

Most of the men said, "Yes, sir."

And I told them, "Now look. That's wonderful, and I know you certainly deserve it. But I am giving you this order. I want to see you putting it in your pack, NOW. Even if you've had a drink, I want the bottle in your pack, and it is not coming out until we go off-line tomorrow. Is that understood?"

And I must say that the majority of the men, being the well-disciplined marines they were, obeyed the order, which was being personally transmitted by me to each and every man in the platoon. Unfortunately, though, this process of approaching each man separately took some considerable time to complete, and by the time I met with my right flank, I could see that my men were getting progressively more drunk.

Presuming to be a United States Marine

In fact, there was one fighting position, and it was the riflemen who were associated with Leedy, the machine gunner who had broadcast our password, where one of the guys had really had a snootful by the time I arrived. I found out that some of the guys had run out of their positions to grab him, because after a couple or three stiff drinks, he picked up his rifle and helmet and headed north to take on the whole Chinese army all by himself and settle this thing once and for all, single-handedly. In a way, it was good that this had happened because it sobered everybody else up, and they all stopped drinking. We had dodged a bullet, and there were no subsequent problems. With as much vigor as was polite, since they were our allies after all, I went back and chewed out the British soldiers and told them to kindly get the hell out of our vicinity, which they duly did, having been able to conduct a brisk business for a while. But remember, now I was stuck with a platoon in which almost every man had in his pack at least one bottle of scotch or cognac.

The morning of the fifteenth dawned, and here came good old Easy Company, Fifth Marines, our helpful friends who had taken over our positions when we went on the raid, and I saw George Morrison again and, as always, found it to be a pleasure.

Relief on lines is a pretty complicated matter. The unit coming in has to take each position and bring the right weapons to the right position, and each position is relieved, one at a time. My men would pass my command post and get back over the hill to safety, and we formed up behind the hill in preparation for marching off. In the type of war we were fighting then, in these sorts of fixed positions, one had a tendency to accumulate a good deal of gear and memorabilia, and this and that. We were equipped at that time with what was called a packboard, and this was a pretty neat invention. It was something that northern explorers and mountain climbers carried on their expeditions. It had canvas webbing and a rigid board to which a waterproof bag was tied. When I had broken down my possessions in Kobe, I retained enough extra clothing and gear to keep myself well equipped and also kept some books, including a prayerbook and Bible. My fairly full waterproof bag was lashed to my packboard, and, together with my weapons, ammunition, a sleeping bag, and all my gear, I was carrying a load of about eighty pounds.

Word was that we were going to pull off our main line positions, gather on the road that led up to them, collect about one mile behind the company, return to the positions we had held when we rehearsed the raid, and be met by trucks to take us back to the rear.

As I have already said, the Marine Corps kept two regiments online, and one regiment in reserve. The standard cycle was that a regiment would spend from sixty to seventy-five days online, and then go into reserve for thirty to forty-five days, with some variation, so that the Chinese would not get too used to the schedule.

Taking on the Burden of History

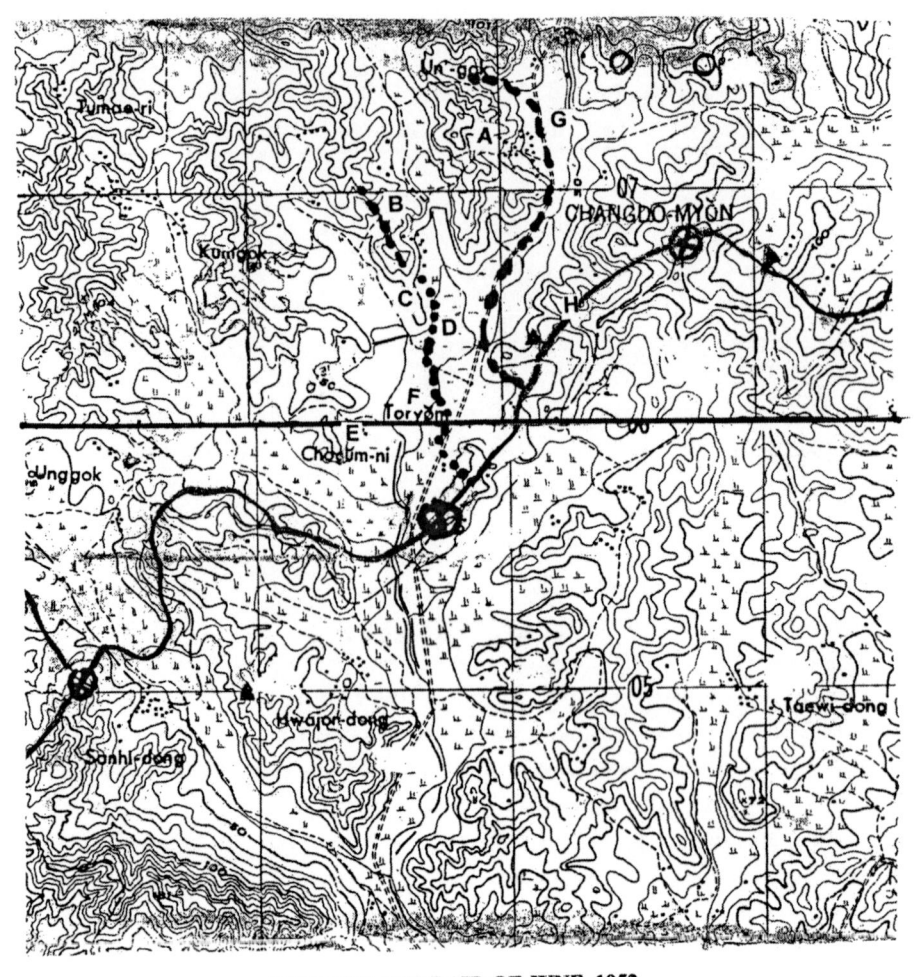

PATROLS AND RAID OF JUNE, 1952

Legend

- A OP 3. Valley behind, north, of it was Holmberg's raid objective.
- B Old Tank Road. My platoon got to north end in raid.
- C Chinese outpost which pinned us down and which we took
- D Spot my squad leader stepped on the mine
- E Where my trooper dropped his magazine on pre-raid patrol.
- F ●●●●●●●●●●●● My platoon's raid route.
- G ▬▬▬▬▬▬▬ Holmberg's platoon raid route.
- H Fox Company Observation Post (OP).

The regiment in the rear was located south of the Imjin River, and there were some pretty nice camps there, and you got hot meals, and you slept on a cot. You trained, and the training was rigid and quite onerous, but not too bad and specifically

300

oriented to preparing troops for whatever conditions we were dealing with in Korea at that time.

The division had three battalion-sized reserve camps, so that the whole regiment was not put in one place but was divided between three camps. In the course of my year in Korea, I actually ended up by staying in all three of the division's rear camps. The first one we went to was affectionately known as the Rock Pile, and that described it well. But the camp was a pleasant enough place and the food was good, and we certainly felt a wonderful relief after what we had been through.

The Rock Pile, from our positions online, was probably, as the crow flies, about eight or nine miles from where we had been online, but the road network ran through very hilly and mountainous terrain, so that the actual distance was probably closer to twelve to fifteen miles. And we marched away from the main line of resistance (Line Jamestown) on this June morning to get to the trucks. But there were no trucks in sight.

We were first told the trucks would be to the rear of the line where we had camped before the raid, so we walked there. No trucks. Then we hiked on back to the battalion headquarters. Still no trucks. And so we just kept on marching. It was a really hot day, and we were all very much loaded down, and some of my troops, in addition to all of their other gear, were loaded down with several bottles of booze they had obtained from our friends, the Brits.

We walked along, and walked along, and I could see my troops beginning to fade. It was a blistering day, and we had not expected this enforced march, and everybody was moaning and griping about where the trucks were. But we kept on walking, finally got back to the Imjin River. By this time, as the road took us, we were probably five or six miles from the lines, and that made us all feel better because we knew that we were probably out of mortar and all but the largest artillery range. We were safer now.

We took a break in our march every few miles, and eventually, I began to realize that very surreptitiously, some of my troops had begun dipping into their English-provided refreshments, the most notable among them being Staff Sergeant Nethery, or Ricochet. As I have told you, I came to learn that Ricochet, poor fellow, had a real alcohol problem, and how he survived online I will never know. Ricochet, by now, was beginning to stagger a little bit.

As we marched on along the river to get to a bridge that crossed over it to the south side where our reserve or rest camp was located, we ultimately saw a cloud of dust in the distance, and from that cloud emerged our trucks. We climbed aboard and rode the last 20 percent of our trip in style.

Chapter 11

IN DIVISION RESERVE (1952)

We arrived at our battalion-sized reserve camp, affectionately known as the Rock Pile, on the fifteenth of June, and we left it on the twenty-seventh of July. It was, overall, a pleasant place; we slept in tents, on cots shrouded with mosquito netting; and we were able to enjoy many amenities of civilized living, which had been denied to us up on the lines.

The Marine Corps and our organization, I thought, showed a good deal of sense in easing us into our reserve life. Although I had not been with them the entire time, my company, Fox Company, had gone online in March, so that by this time, many of the men had been online for over three months and had not even been in regimental reserve.

When you are online, you actually don't bathe, and even brushing your teeth can be a problem. For the first day or two after we got off-line, we went back to the shower unit and washed and scrubbed and cleaned. We were issued a whole new set of clean clothes to drape over our spotless bodies, and that was nice. We had good meals, and the food was plentiful and hot and tasted delicious. For the first couple of days, there wasn't much harassment, either, with only a morning formation, just to check the roll and pass out the mail.

Near the center of our company's camp was a high hill, and scattered along the bottom of this hill were the tents in which our troops were housed. At the end of the company street sat a great big tent occupied by the staff noncommissioned officers.

There were steps carved into the hill that rose above this area, and the officers' tent was at the top of this hill. At that time, there were seven officers in the company, and we all slept in one large tent, including the company commander. It was customary the entire time I was in Korea to select an officer from each battalion scheduled to go into reserve or rest camp and provide him with orders to fly to Japan. And before that officer left for Japan, everybody put in their orders for liquor and paid him in advance. The designated officer would gather up the orders from all the other officers in the battalion and fly to Japan to make his purchase from the military liquor store. He would then have to arrange for transportation on an airplane to get the liquor back to Korea, and for a truck to be sent down by the battalion to bring the supplies back to the reserve camp. It was an efficient method, and the task of purchasing the liquor was usually given to an officer who had already spent a good deal of time in Korea.

The problem these officers encountered, once they reached Japan, was that their order was often large enough to fill an entire plane, and they would have a hard time requisitioning an airplane just to fly the order back. In addition, there was often a lurking suspicion that the officers managed to create problems obtaining a plane, in order to extend their stay in Japan to enjoy the fruits of liberty there.

One of the ironies was that Bill Holmberg had been selected to be the Second Battalion, First Marines, booze officer to go to Japan just before the raid came up. I had not realized, until many years later when he told me, that Bill had been given the choice by Colonel Quilici to take the liquor run. If Bill had accepted it, another officer in Fox Company would lead his platoon in the main assault. That other officer would have been me.

Bill, obviously, did the right thing by choosing to lead the raid, and an officer from one of the other companies was assigned to go to Japan. When we returned to reserve camp, the booze had not arrived there yet. As it turned out, I became the person who was able to solve the problem, at least for the officers in Fox Company. I'd had a Basic School classmate, a fellow named Cox, who was a pretty good friend. We had been in the same platoon all the way through Officer Candidate Screening and Basic School. Cox had been in the Second Battalion, First Marines, for some months, but had volunteered to be an aerial observer. This meant that he would fly over enemy lines in a little Piper Cub and call in artillery fire. The day I had arrived at the reserve/rest camp, Cox had come up to visit me, and he told me, "If you ever need any booze, we have plenty of it back where I am, just let me know." He flew out of a little airstrip just behind division headquarters.

So that first night in our camp, I got on the telephone and got hold of him, and he told me that he had plenty of booze and invited me to come on down to pick it up. The problem, though, was how to reach his little airstrip. Unbeknownst to me, one of the other officers in the company called up the battalion motorpool and ordered the Fox Company jeep to be sent around for Lieutenant Van Sant. And this was at about nine o'clock in the evening, and five minutes later, up drives the company jeep. Griff was off someplace, fortunately, because if he had ever found out about our little diversion, he would have been pretty upset. I think it was Lieutenant Wozencraft who came with me. We got in with the driver and took off.

In a combat zone, for good reason, there are no road or street signs. In case the enemy breaks through, you don't want to give him any guideposts as to his location. You just have to rely on a map in order to get around. By the time Wooz and I finally took off, it was really dark outside. The only place I had ever been in Korea was Inchon, where I had landed and boarded the train for Seoul and thence on to Munsan-ni and then been taken by truck to the lines, and that was all I'd ever seen of the First Marine Division sector. I certainly did not know where anything else was, and as it turned out, our driver did not either. But we took off in the darkness toward a largely unknown destination.

Once we passed a certain line, roughly across the Imjin River, we had to black out the vehicle. There were rectangular-shaped glows on the front of the vehicle so that, up close, the vehicle could be seen. But while these lights would not shine very far into the distance to make it difficult for the enemy to spot the vehicle, they also did not illuminate much of the scenery for the driver. I had a vague idea of where Cox's airstrip was, but Wozencraft had taken it upon himself to give directions to the driver. Suddenly, we were crossing the river again going north, which alarmed me a bit.

"Wooz," I said, "I think that strip is down well south of the Imjin. So why are we going north again?"

And Wooz replied calmly, "Don't worry about it, I know where we are." We reached a road that had the appearance of being the widest and best-maintained road in the whole division sector, and we were plowing along on it, making pretty good time, even though we were still blacked out.

Quite suddenly, a large installation loomed ahead of us. The driver slowed down and stopped. Two very nattily dressed army MPs with polished helmets came up to the jeep and looked down on us. We asked them, "Where are we?"

They answered, "This is the checkpoint. You are on the road to Panmunjom." And that, as you know, was where the truce talks were taking place in a large one-thousand-meter circle between the enemy lines and our lines. We realized that we had gone in precisely the wrong direction. We had been headed north, instead of south, where we should have been going.

The MPs saw that we were officers, and so they were reasonably respectful in a disdainful sort of way. They were familiar with the airstrip and gave us good directions to it. We had to turn around, go back across the river, and south, where we finally found the airstrip at around eleven o'clock that night, along with my buddy, Lieutenant Cox. He wanted to give us the booze, but we felt we could not accept such a generous gesture and insisted on paying for it. It was, of course, quite cheap at that time, maybe $2 or $3 a bottle, and we bought about four bottles from him. And that, we figured, would be enough to tide us over until our booze officer returned from Japan.

It was nice to see Cox again, and he was clearly enjoying his work and having a good time. We jumped into our jeep, found our way back to the camp, and returned in glory as the conquering booze heroes. It was close to midnight by the time we got back to camp. We decided to have a nightcap and save the rest for a party the next night. And so we did.

On about the second or third day, we were in reserve; we had a change of command. Our battalion commander up to that point had been Colonel Quilici, in front of whose tent I had sat when I got assigned to Fox Company after my arrival in Korea. Lieutenant Colonel Quilici's tour was up, and he was being replaced by Lieutenant Colonel Roy Batterton. Roy Batterton was one of the finest marine officers I have ever known. He was a veteran of Guadalcanal, had subsequently been in one of the raider battalions, had participated in a number of different raiding operations in the Pacific, and was now a lieutenant colonel. He was from Virginia, originally, and a great horseman. He had grown up on horseback, I think. Colonel Batterton was an inspiring leader, and in the light of what we were facing over the next few months, it was a good thing we had him as our commander.

Batterton took over the battalion in a small ceremony and then called all the officers together, told us a little bit about himself, and announced that he was going to insist on a sharp, squared-away unit that accomplished its missions. He pointed out to us that "by now, you must have realized that 80 to 90 percent of your actual combat operations take place at night. From now on, this battalion is going to reverse the clock." He said, "We will relax, eat, and sleep during the daytime, and we will train at night." And by golly, that is what we did.

Batterton was a hands-on leader. Many of our troops had the experience, when they were out at night, say, practicing patrolling or climbing through underbrush, of suddenly seeing a shape materializing before them. They would challenge that shape, and it would turn out to be Colonel Batterton making his rounds. Word got around among the troops pretty quickly that the colonel was a guy who was out there with his troops, and for his troops.

The first week or so in reserve camp, we settled into a fairly nice pattern. One of the platoons, the third platoon, which was the one that had suffered so many casualties in the raid, Holmberg's old platoon, had a new platoon commander. He was ordered to take the platoon out to the Widgeon bridge across the Imjin River, east of our camp. The Imjin turns south in that area, and so it was much closer to the camp than it was due north of us. Guard duty at the Widgeon Bridge was something of a reward and a chance for the lieutenant to get to know his platoon, but as we will see later, some problems arose out there.

The rest of the company settled into a training routine at night, and a party with a few drinks, beginning at about four or five in the morning after we had finished training. We were off on weekends and ate, relaxed, and wrote letters home.

On about the fourth or fifth day, word came through that First Lieutenant Moody had been promoted to captain. It was customary in the Marine Corps that when an officer was promoted, it was his responsibility to "wet down the rank insignia," whether it be captain's bars or major's leaves, the newly promoted officer was responsible for giving a wetting-down party. And so Captain Moody, who by this time, I must tell you, was worshipped by everybody in the company, from the officers on down to the lowest private, gave a party. The troops wanted to honor him, and so he had a little beer party with the troops. Then he gave a wingding up in the officers' tent. We actually fixed it up and got some extra refreshments and goodies, and we had a really nice wetting-down party for Captain Moody.

The party was held on a weekend, so that we did not have to worry about training. Griff had invited all the staff noncommissioned officers to the party as well, and we ended up being just a happy-go-lucky collection of drunks. I was probably one of the more sober people, which turned out to be a good thing.

Taking on the Burden of History

Gunnery Sergeant John Francis Kelly, you will remember, had been seriously wounded by the booby trap the Chinese had set for him and had gone AWOL from the hospital ship without ever being medically discharged. He had really led, with Lieutenant Smythe, the relief expedition that extracted Holmberg and his wounded the night of the raid. And now John Francis happily participated in the celebration of Captain Moody's promotion. I have always felt that he was, at that point, probably more susceptible to the effects of alcohol than the rest of us, because he had not yet completely recovered from his serious wound, and John Francis passed out cold in the officers' tent, giving me the opportunity to achieve a measure of immortality in Fox Company.

After he had collapsed, I picked up old John Francis, who was not a very big man, in my arms like a baby. I gathered him up, and the Lord must be with drunks and fools, because I made it all the way down the hundred or so steps, down the side of that rocky hill, carrying poor unconscious John Francis, tenderly draped across my two arms. I hauled him down and put him to bed in his tent. Many of the troops in the company saw this, and I later heard surreptitious whispers that I looked like Frankenstein's monster coming down the hill with Gunnery Sergeant Kelly in my arms.

We partied into the night, and all the staff NCOs made it down the hill, still conscious, or at least semiconscious, and all the officers made it back into their mosquito nets and cots. But we had a storm that night—a bad rainstorm with strong winds hit us. Whenever that happened, we had to put down the side flaps, which were usually kept rolled up so that the air could circulate through the tent. The side flaps in our tent were put down, but when I woke up the next morning in my cot, picked up the flap in my tent, and looked out down the hill into the gray and rainy world, I saw that the staff NCO tent below us, at the bottom of the hill, had blown over during the night.

Pretty soon, I could see some movement underneath the canvas, and then out from the tent canvas lying on the ground came an arm. It turned out to be Ricochet's arm. His cot was in the place that had become exposed to the elements. This arm coming out from underneath the edge of the tent flap began extending its hand and grabbed the tent like a blanket like a cover and pulled it over his body so that it would not get wet in the rainstorm. It was clear that Captain Moody had managed to get his rank insignia well wetted down, in every sense of the word.

After we had been in reserve camp for about ten days, word came down from the regiment that Fox Company, because of our long period online and the large raid we had conducted, had been selected to represent the regiment, and therefore the division, in the 1st Corps Honor Guard. The First Marine Division, the British Commonwealth Division, two army divisions, and three South Korean divisions made up what was called the 1st Corps.

The 1st Corps was a formidable force. It must have had a couple of hundred-thousand men and was one of three operating corps in the Eighth Army. The 1st Corps was commanded by an army lieutenant general, and its headquarters was in a town called Uijongbu.

Presuming to be a United States Marine

There was a change of command ceremony because Lieutenant General "Iron Mike" O'Daniel, who had been the 1st Corps commander for quite a long time, was being relieved by another lieutenant general. An interesting foot note is that General O'Daniel, when he was relieved of command of the 1st Corps, and this was probably in late June of 1952, did not immediately return to the United States. He went on to Saigon and established the first office of the Military Assistance Command in Vietnam. He founded that group and was its first general. Of course, the French were still in Vietnam then, but this became the first move we made to assist the French and, ultimately, the South Vietnamese; and Iron Mike was in at the very beginning.

The honor guard was composed of platoons from each of the operating divisions of the 1st Corps, and that meant that the Commonwealth Division and the First Marine Division each had a platoon in the guard, and each of the army divisions had a platoon, and each of the South Korean divisions had a platoon. In addition to these platoons representing divisions, each member of the United Nations, who had a unit of any size in Korea, was entitled to a platoon in the honor guard. I think we had battalions or regiments from Brazil, the Philippines, and Turkey in the 1st Corps, each represented by a platoon, so that the honor guard consisted of about ten or eleven platoons, each platoon with forty-five men.

Our instructions were that out of all the men in Fox Company, we were to create one honor guard platoon. The idea was that this provisional honor platoon would have a gunnery sergeant in charge and that sergeant, obviously, was to be Gunnery Sergeant John Francis Kelly, who had spent years on the drill field at Parris Island. He was a very sharp marine, who knew how to drill troops and how to train them. Because, thanks to the vagaries of combat, I was now the senior lieutenant in the company in terms of service, I was given the job of commanding the honor guard platoon.

It immediately became clear that Griff took this honor guard thing pretty seriously. He told me, "You realize that we are going to be competing with all those other army units, and the Commonwealth, and they are all going to put their best foot forward. We have really got to be sharp!"

Under John Francis Kelly's drill instructor leadership, we selected forty-five of the best-looking, most squared-away, and sharpest men we had in Fox Company. We selected the cream of the crop, and we drilled, and drilled, and drilled, and drilled them. Sergeant Kelly did most of the drilling, but occasionally, he turned the men over to me because I would have to give the men some commands when we actually got to the honor guard. It was an interesting exercise. Griff went to great lengths to get good uniforms for us. The uniform for this guard was to be the standard field uniform, which we called utilities or dungarees in those days. Griff did a little scrounging around and found some people back in division headquarters who were able to obtain starched utilities for us. We all had to scrub our leggings white. We wore, of course, the standard marine helmets but were given brand-new, clean camouflage covers for them. Everybody's rifle was oiled, and the stocks were polished; and, I mean to tell you, we really looked good.

Taking on the Burden of History

The great day for the ceremony came, and we piled into open six-by-six trucks, and damned if it did not rain! Our starched uniforms got a bit of a washout, but we thought that, all in all, we still looked pretty good. The trip to Uijongbu was an interesting experience for me because it was the first time I had traveled any distance in Korea. The farther we got away from the lines, it seemed, there was a much greater variety and multiplicity in the organizations we saw in the camps we passed. I swear I think we even saw something called a mess kit repair platoon back there. There are expressions in the military, "in the rear with the gear," and the one that was common in Korea was "rear echelon pogue," which described somebody back in the rear with the gear, helping to support the front.

As a front-line marine, I briefly felt a little bit jealous to see these guys sleeping on cots, living in nice tents, and having lovely hot meals every day. It certainly was an eye-opener, and I began to realize that a modern fighting force formed a very thin and narrow blade at the front, with a thicker and thicker blade reaching deeper and deeper into the rear. But be that as it may, I realized that I would not have traded places with any of them.

Uijongbu had a nice parade ground in its center, surrounded by various buildings and Quonset huts from the 1st Corps Headquarters. The Korean city had not been as shot up as the villages in the area where we were fighting had been. The flat valley bottom, on which the parade ground was sited, was completely surrounded by mountains—360 degrees of steep, sheer cliffs all the way around. It was almost like being in the bottom of a saucepan on the stove, although there were, obviously, passes leading through the mountains.

The time came, and the platoons, representing the various divisions of the 1st Corps, were lined up in the order of the seniority of the commanding general of each division. As it turned out, the senior general of the Corps was the Commonwealth Division's commander, so they formed the right-hand post of honor in the front of the honor guard. Our general, General Selden (remember him from the 1st Battalion/stacking arms incident at Camp Lejeune), was second in seniority, so that we were placed next to the Commonwealth Division.

The army divisions were represented by platoons from their ranks, and as I have said, platoons from the other members of the United Nations who were fighting with us were represented. Most of the army divisions were represented by platoons of military policemen with their polished helmets and their shiny brass, and they had not made any attempt to look like field soldiers.

The Commonwealth Division was made up of representatives of the various organizations fighting in it. It was a very colorful assemblage of troops, but not very uniform. There were members of the Scottish Black Watch, there were Ghurkas and another Indian unit, there were Australians, and representatives of the British home regiments. This ceremonial platoon was commanded by what looked like an old senior first lieutenant, who must have come up through the ranks. He was a huge mustachioed man possessed of a huge voice.

Presuming to be a United States Marine

And the Commonwealth Division came sashaying onto the field, marching away, and the British, by the way, march in a very distinctive fashion, quite different from our method, and the British lieutenant was shouting commands that caused the mountains to tremble. And I took my platoon out with as much flourish as I could muster, and the two platoons lined up, and the other platoons lined up to our left. The commander of the honor guard, who was an army officer, probably a major or lieutenant colonel, would shout a command, and each platoon commander would repeat the command and order his platoon to execute various maneuvers of the manual of arms, prepare for inspection, and so on.

Our guys did well—they performed beautifully, and they were feeling really competitive, particularly with the Commonwealth Division to our right. When we finished all our military maneuvers, there was the change-of-command ceremony, and the colors of the 1st Corps were passed on by Lieutenant General O'Daniel. Back in the rear, where all the ordinance outfits and mess kit repair platoons were, we saw signs everywhere proclaiming the motto of the 1st Corps: "Sharpen your bayonets!" There was a bayonet depicted on the sign, the symbol of Iron Mike's leadership.

After the change of command had been completed, the new Corps commander asked General O'Daniel if he wanted to say anything to the honor guard. The general got up, stepped to the microphone of the big public address system, and gave a very rough-tough and inspiring speech, which concluded with "Keep 'em sharp, boys." After he finished and we were dismissed from the honor guard, I had Sergeant Kelly come out and march the platoon off the field, because he deserved the recognition. We looked good, and I was proud of us.

But as we were loading aboard the trucks, a couple of the men came up to me and said, "Lieutenant, you did a great job, but you know, that Limey officer gave louder commands than you did!" They added, "Don't get us wrong, sir, we could understand everything you said, but he was just louder." And it was true, his voice had bounced and rumbled off those mountains, and, thinking I had let my troops down by not being as thunderous as my British counterpart, I felt chagrined. As we will see, though, I was to get a chance for redemption and revenge.

All the roads in Korea were terrible—they were made of nothing but dirt, and we sat on not-very-comfortable springs in open trucks that never proceeded at more than fifteen or twenty miles an hour. The air was usually permeated with dust, but of course, on this day, we were driving through mud. Mud or dust, even a ten- or fifteen-mile trip contributed to an ordeal, but we reached our barracks and settled back down into our training routine.

This was a pleasant time of catching up with correspondence, and I had a chance to write home and do some reading. I remember a few amusing stories from that time. Lieutenant Wozencraft's cot stood in the middle of our squad-sized tent. Several of us had positioned our cots right along the walls of the tent, but Wooz had set his squarely in the center. Now, Wooz enjoyed his booze. He drank a good deal. He was unmarried, but when he left the United States, he had been very heavily engaged to a young woman whom he had met at the Naval Academy. You will remember that Wooz had been in Korea a good deal longer than I had, as he had arrived there in February. In June, Wooz had received a Dear John letter from his fiancee, whose heart had obviously not grown fonder in his absence. Instead, she had grown fonder of someone else. That threw Wooz for a loop, and he became pretty depressed for some time.

One night, I remember, Wooz had been out with some friends from one of the other outfits. Wooz preferred to drink scotch. He had purchased his whole ration of booze in scotch. He had taken his bottle along with him, and when he returned to our tent, he put it on the dirt ground right by his cot, without troubling to put the cork back in. He then climbed under his mosquito netting and went to sleep.

As luck would have it, we had a generator in these camps that produced enough electricity for a lightbulb in the center of each tent, and it so happened that Wooz had positioned his open bottle directly under our single lightbulb. Anyone who has ever come near a lightbulb in the summertime knows that it attracts bugs. And since ours was a bare lightbulb without any shade, why, a multitude of bugs circled around the light, from time to time knocking into the hot bulb, where they would get fried and drop straight down. Wooz had forgotten to turn the bulb off when he came stumbling in and left the light on all night.

I woke up the next morning, probably one of the first people to awaken, lifted up the flap of my mosquito netting, and saw Wooz's bottle on the floor right beside his cot. While I watched, very slowly, a hand stretched out from under Wooz's mosquito netting, reached down, felt around on the deck, and found and grabbed the bottle by its neck.

I had realized, as I was looking at Wooz's bottle, that the scotch in it was topped off with at least an inch, and maybe two, of dead bugs that had dropped down from the naked lightbulb. I was fascinated, I was frozen, as the hand pulled the bottle inside the mosquito netting, and I knew it was being tilted up.

"Ah, Wooz, hold it!" I prepared to shout, but I was too late. Suddenly Wooz came roaring out of that mosquito netting, spitting and coughing up bugs. Instead of a big slug of scotch, he had ingested a big slug of bugs. Oh, he was mad, and I told him, "Wooz, I was trying to warn you, but I did not get it out in time," neglecting to share with him the fact that I had become totally fascinated by my observation of the bugs in the bottle. But Wooz was a good fellow, a good man.

Another thing happened at about the same time, during the earlier portion of reserve camp. We received a lot of mail, which was nice, and one day, I received a very official letter from the Hyattsville, Maryland, Draft Board. When I had been discharged from the Marine Corps in 1946, after returning from China, all discharged service personnel had to register with their draft board again as to the service they had already completed so that they could remain on the draft records. You may remember my telling you that I had dutifully registered with the Hyattsville Draft Board after my discharge.

The letter I now held in my hand had originally been postmarked in the summer of 1950. It was now the summer of 1952. On the envelope of the letter was displayed the story of my life, as it had been forwarded to all the places where I had ever lived over the last few years. Literally. First, it had been sent to Annapolis. From Annapolis it had been forwarded to New York City, then back to Annapolis. It had next been forwarded to Camp Lejeune, and, finally, it had been sent on to me in Korea.

When I opened the letter, I saw that it contained a very stern, now-two-year-old, message. It explained to me that the draft rules, effective during the Korean War, stipulated that if I had served eighteen months or more during World War II, I was exempt from the draft. If, on the other hand, I had less than eighteen months of service (and it turned out that I had just less than eighteen months of service in World War II) I was eligible for the draft. This notice, further, ordered me to appear for induction at such and such a place, at such and such a time. I had a great time with this no-nonsense missive. I sat down and composed a very carefully worded letter to the draft board to inform them that their threatening letter had caught up with me on the front lines in Korea, where I was enjoying life as a lieutenant in the United States Marine Corps. But to give credit where credit is due, and that is to the U.S. Postal Service, the draft board's letter had tracked me down in the end.

At some point in that five-week period between the fifteenth of June and the twenty-sixth of July, the whole battalion got formed up and organized for an amphibious landing. Our training out in the boondocks was interrupted, and we were all assigned to various boat teams and were moved, first by truck, to Munsan-ni, and then on the train to Seoul, and then to Inchon, where we were outloaded back aboard ship. The amphibious fleet then sailed north.

Right off the west coast of the Korean peninsula were a number of islands, and one of these islands was Tokchokto. This was actually an uninhabited island. Even though Tokchokto was beautiful, it wasn't actually big enough to support farming. It was very mountainous and rugged, and probably volcanic. We used Tokchokto as a training exercise ground. Since the island was really offshore from an area claimed by both Koreas, another purpose was to remind the North Koreans that it was our island and not theirs. From the shore, they could probably see our fleet coming in and landing on it. But basically, this was an amphibious training exercise for our troops.

I was still second platoon commander at this point. We went ashore in landing craft, stumbled up on the beach, shooting blanks and giving the invisible enemy hell. At the right flank of the beach was an almost needle-like extremely steep hill, with some vegetation sprouting from it. There was a space about the size of a card table at the top of this needle. My platoon's objective was to take the top of that hill.

And I went charging across the beach, dropping off a couple of squads to defend the hill by completely encircling it. I took one squad, and we charged all the way up the steep hill together and reached the top, completely exhausted. I tapped into the radio, and after reporting the accomplishment of our mission, Griff began talking to me personally from his end.

He said, "I want you to be very careful and very quiet about this, but what I want you to do now is to simulate that you have been hit by a stray bullet or shell, and I want you to look unconscious. Don't move a muscle. Don't say a word. I want to see what your platoon does and how they respond to this problem. Just put down the radio right now, and sink down, with your eyes shut."

I did as I was told. The radio was still hissing, which meant that I had not checked out, and I lay, quite rigidly, and with my eyes shut. I had my platoon guide and my platoon sergeant and my runner there with me, and a couple of other guys were scattered among the edges of the card-table-sized mountaintop.

It seemed to me that I had been lying still for an eternity, without anybody noticing anything. Finally, I heard one of the guys saying, "Hey! What's the matter with the lieutenant?"

And somebody else was saying, "Lieutenant Van Sant, Lieutenant Van Sant!" And I was still lying there, still as a stick.

Finally, somebody said, "Gee, there must be something wrong with him!" And Platoon Sergeant Crawford's voice said, "Well, damn it, we have to get him down from here."

We did not have a stretcher with us, and it did take them a while to catch on, but they finally hacked down a couple of sapling trees and brought them up, got out some shelter half and poncho material, and fashioned a makeshift stretcher. They got me on it and strapped me to it and began the descent from this precipitous needle. It was hilarious, or at least it is hilarious now that I can look back on it.

They only dropped me two or three times on paths that were just barely clinging to the hill in places. I remained at all times "unconscious," and the men eventually managed to evacuate me all the way down to the bottom of the needle and took me, limp and with my eyes firmly closed, to sick bay, where Griff met us with, "Well, what's the matter with Lieutenant Van Sant?"

Sergeant Crawford said, "Sir, I don't know, he just isn't talking. He won't respond, sir, and he won't open his eyes." And then Griff explained the whole brilliant exercise to him and to the rest of the men, and allowed me to open my eyes again.

Griff frequently made inspection tours of the third platoon, enjoying life out at the Widgeon Bridge. The new lieutenant, a perfectly decent and fine officer, was, at the end of June and by the beginning of July, still inexperienced. About half of the men in his platoon were veterans of the great raid in which Holmberg had been wounded, and the other half were newly arrived replacements. The lieutenant did not have the full platoon; I think he had about two squads, plus a machine gun section. But Griff was concerned because they were three miles from the nearest Marine Corps installation, and the lieutenant was really on independent duty, so to speak, and not subject to the oversight and control of anybody else at that point.

There was a further peculiarity. The Widgeon Bridge across the Imjin was placed where the river formed a tremendous loop south, and as the sectors were divided, the First Marine Division sector adjoined the Commonwealth Division. The Widgeon Bridge was actually the responsibility of the Marine Corps, in its rear position, but the only people who used it much were the British because it was one of their main routes for crossing the Imjin. The Widgeon Bridge was a pontoon bridge and had to be guarded twenty-four hours a day. The new lieutenant was not, as I say, very experienced, and the third platoon, which he had taken over, had, as you know, been badly shot up. Several of the men were missing, and we knew they were dead, but we had been unable to retrieve their bodies because they had penetrated so far into the Chinese position. In addition, half of the rest of the platoon had been wounded in the raid. We had many wonderful noncommissioned officers, but the platoon sergeant of the 3rd platoon was perhaps not the greatest leader, so that at this point, the situation of a young officer taking over was a little awkward.

And the lieutenant made an unfortunate mistake. The guard detail at Widgeon Bridge had a couple of squad-sized tents that would hold about twenty men in each. He decided to live in the squad tent with the troops, and, even in a combat zone, that is not a desirable thing to do because it is too easy for the officer to become "one of the guys."

Griff went to the Widgeon Bridge for an inspection and found that people were out of uniform, that there was no guard posted at the bridge, and that the area had not been policed up. The sleeping bags had not been rolled up, and if this sounds rather unimportant, it is, nevertheless, a little touch of housekeeping that needs to be watched over. I think the lieutenant had never been an enlisted man but had gone straight through Officer Candidate School, had received his commission, progressed through Basic School, and had then gone to Korea to take over this shot-up platoon. It was a tough challenge for him. Griff was pretty disgusted with what he had seen the second time he had gone out to the Widgeon Bridge. He realized that he had to get that lieutenant back under his observation on a daily basis, and so he pulled the third platoon off the Widgeon Bridge, even though that duty had been given to the men because they had suffered so much in the raid. The next platoon from the raid was, of course, mine, and so I was now given the responsibility of guarding the bridge.

Of the five-plus weeks we spent back in the rear during that summer of 1952, I spent about fifteen days guarding it. Griff had shared with me some of his observations, so that when I went out, I made sure things were done right. I found a bunker a fair distance away from the troops' squad tent, established my command post, and lived there by myself. I gathered up the troops' beer rations, passed out two cans a night, and we began functioning on the Widgeon Bridge just as if we were online. Of course, back of the bridge, particularly in what was, essentially, a British sector, I was sure those of my troops who were resourceful could obtain their booze needs from the ever-obliging English. I immediately established a plan for the day, issued a set of orders, and we had everybody standing relays of watches on the bridge at night.

In the daytime, we organized working parties and built fortifications on each end of the bridge, as there was some possibility that the Chinese might try to break through, and if that ever happened, there would have to be a way to dig in to defend the bridge. No fighting positions had been constructed there in the past. We had a morning formation, we had drill, and then everybody went off on either work detail, or fortification improvements. Everything went by the book and by the numbers. None of the troops had to stand more than two hours' watch at night, but we guarded the bridge all night. We had drills for breaking out and getting into the prepared fighting positions we had created. Everything proceeded almost as if we were on garrison duty in the States. As one will always find in the Marine Corps, when things are done in a strict fashion, the troops respond and love it, because they are challenged to be real marines, and not just guys with a lot of leisure time and no set tasks.

Immediately west of the bridge, there was a beach on the Imjin, with a beautiful place to swim, and every afternoon, we had recreational swimming for two hours. This was a period when we played and relaxed. During that time, I fraternized with the troops, jumped right into the water with them, and we played tag and all kinds of water games. Of course, we all had inflatable air mattresses, and someone found some inner tubes somewhere, and we floated around in them and had a lot of fun. It was a good time and a great preparation for what was to come. Thank the Lord that we knew little about what we were about to face soon. The platoon pulled together, and morale was very high. It was a great experience for me. When the day's work was done and the evening meal of C-rations had been eaten, I withdrew into my command post to read, without further associating with the troops. We were on the Widgeon Bridge on the fourth of July 1952. I telephoned back to our base and arranged to get the mess hall to send us out a hot meal for the holiday. We had our hot meal and a formal ceremonial observance of Independence Day. Then we had an additional recreational period, and for that, I had managed to scrounge from the people back at our camp two pairs of boxing gloves. You will remember that boxing in the Marine Corps was considered to be recreation. Ricochet was with us as the machine gun section leader, and Ricochet was in good shape at that time. He'd had his big party when he got off-line and wasn't drinking heavily now. He was working hard and being what Ricochet could be when he was in good shape—a tough marine.

I pulled the boxing gloves out, and guys of approximately the same weight were lining up for matches with each other. We improvised a little ring in an area behind the bridge, and Ricochet came up to me and said, "The men would really like to see you box, Lieutenant. They want me to box you." Ricochet was a pretty big man, very broad-shouldered and very thick, not fat, but big and almost apelike. But he could not have been taller than six feet one, but he probably weighed as much as I did, if not more. And Ricochet, who, as you may remember, liked to make jokes about my nose, said, "Lieutenant, I would be happy to go to it, and I will be careful not to hit your nose." I told him that would be fine.

Among all the boxing matches, the one between Ricochet and me was far and away the featured match of the entire boxing show. Various troops had been thrashing each other when, finally, the eagerly awaited heavyweight match of the Lieutenant vs. Ricochet was announced. It must have looked pretty comical. Nobody got hurt, and I don't remember that either one of us got knocked down. But Ricochet's arms were not very long, and I found that if I extended my right arm all the way out and put my

Presuming to be a United States Marine

boxing glove on Ricochet's forehead, he could not reach me. I would push him away, as Ricochet started flailing away at me with both fists, and his fists whistled right past my stomach and my chest, but he would be unable to administer a punch. Of course, he soon started protesting, and I stopped holding him off, but we must have looked quite funny because the troops obviously had a wonderful time watching us. We then banged away at each other a few times, and that was the end of the featured match. It turned out to be a great way to celebrate the Fourth. After the boxing matches, we all went swimming again to cool down.

Griff came out to check on me. He would appear about every three or four days, and I guess he was pleased with what he saw because he never made any criticisms. When he found out my living arrangements, and that I had set myself up a little private room in a bunker, he thoroughly approved of that, and of the kind of discipline I was asserting over the beer and the fact that everything went by the clock—the day was planned, and the bridge was being guarded.

Because the Widgeon Bridge was in the British sector, I met a number of Englishmen walking by on foot, or driving by in jeeps. It took some getting used to, but I finally became accustomed to the English method of saluting, which is quite different from ours. Their hands are on a ninety-degree angle to the ground, and they shake the saluting hand up and down. The first time I saw an English salute, I thought that the man giving it was either having a fit of apoplexy or swatting at a fly. A new officer, Tom Jannelle, had checked into our company. Griff decided that the best thing for Jannelle would be to come out and keep me company. He passed word to me that Jannelle seemed to be a good officer, but without any experience, and Griff wanted me to pass on to him any tidbits of information I had acquired based on my experience.

It is interesting to note, as an aside, that when I first joined Fox Company, our company exec, Lieutenant Wozencraft, had been a tail gunner on a torpedo bomber in World War II, where he saw a lot of action; Bill Holmberg had enlisted experience; and Lieutenant Dooley, the Boston Irishman who was our mortar officer, had acquired some reserve time before going through NROTC training. Our machine gun officer, the Princeton graduate, had been the only relatively inexperienced officer. In the years since Korea, he has had a very distinguished career as publisher of the *Military History Quarterly*. There was also another man, whom I have called Lieutenant Z, who had enlisted experience at the end of World War II. Every single one of the officers, when I first joined, had significant experience either as an enlisted man or with a lot of officer preparation. The officers who later replaced our casualties were Lieutenant Smythe, the California beach boy, and two new just-out-of-college second lieutenants with no prior military experience at all, so that the drop in the level of experience in officer material was significant. Jannelle was also a just-out-of-college officer. He was a fine young man. The company jeep brought him up to me late one afternoon, with a letter from Captain Moody explaining what I was expected to do with Jannelle. He moved into the bunker with me, and I had plenty of room for his sleeping bag. We lived together companionably for about a week or ten days guarding the bridge, as I worked him into some duties as my assistant. It was nice to have him.

At night, a sentry was posted at each end of the bridge at all times, and a third sentry walked back and forth across the bridge, with orders to look for anything suspicious in the water. In order to keep my troops on their toes, I used to make rounds at night to check on them and to make sure they were manning their posts in the proper manner. After Lieutenant Jannelle's arrival, I began using him for half of these inspections. He would share the checking of the watches at night, which enabled me to get a little more sleep.

As we were thrown together in close proximity, we would talk about a million things. You get to know somebody pretty well under these circumstances. In spite of his lack of experience, Jannelle was really with the program. He loved the Marine Corps and expressed several times to me, "I just can't wait till we get up online and I can get to fighting."

I tried to counsel him with, "You know, Tom, it really isn't good form to be too gung-ho and too aggressive because that makes you look pretty foolish. Remember that most marines are respectful of the enemy and the dangers they encounter in combat, and it sounds corny for you to start talking this way. Believe me, when that first round gets fired at you, you will begin to see the world from a different perspective." I think I got through to him, and as we will see, he did a fine job under rather difficult circumstances as they came up in the future.

At some point later in July, we received word that there was going to be another honor guard. The same crack provisional platoon that had been trained by Sergeant Kelly was broken out, and we trained some more and drilled, and drilled, and got all sharpened up again to go to Uijongbu. We climbed aboard trucks and drove down the same dusty road, and fortunately, the weather was nice this time around. The British Commonwealth Division had just installed a new division commander junior to General Selden, our own division commander. That meant that this time, we were the lead platoon of the honor guard. The occasion was the first inspection tour of the Far East command by the famous and legendary General Mark Clark. General Ridgeway replaced General MacArthur when the latter was relieved in the spring of 1951. Mark Clark was sent over in the summer of 1952 to relieve General Ridgeway as our representative in Japan and the commanding general of all the Far Eastern forces. General Clark was famous from World War II as the Allied commander in Italy. The procedure this time was not a change-of-command ceremony, but it was General Clark's first inspection tour of Korea. He was to inspect the honor guard, and my marine platoon was the first platoon to be inspected by him. This procedure gave us the opportunity to shout out a number of other commands. In the meantime, I had been doing a little practicing and was prepared to project my voice to hurl off the mountains mightily. The same great big old British lieutenant was there, but in the end, I could tell the Limey knew he had been beaten. As I marched the platoon off the field, one of the troops whispered approvingly, "Nice going, Lieutenant, you were really loud!" In addition, a supremely ignominious thing had happened to the British platoon. One of the Ghurkas dropped his rifle, and it made a clanking noise everybody could hear. The marine honor guard, in contrast, came through with flying colors. The whole exercise was an unforgettable experience. The troops all opened ranks, lined up for inspection, and I aligned them properly and then went out to stand in front of the platoon. General Clark, leading his accompanying party including the Corps commander and a number of colonels came up to me, and I saluted him sharply and said crisply, "Marine honor guard prepared for inspection, sir!"

He said, "Thank you, Lieutenant." He asked me how long I had been in Korea and displayed, in general, a very gentlemanly and pleasant manner. He talked to me for a minute and then walked on down toward the Commonwealth platoon, although he did not actually inspect the troops. It was a gratifying experience for me to exchange a few words with a legend. We went back that time feeling a lot better about ourselves because our troops had looked good, and made to look even better when one of the Ghurkas had dropped his rifle during the manual of arms, which was not only unfortunate, but unforgivable. In addition, the volume contest in giving commands had this time been won by the marines, hands down.

The entire Widgeon Bridge experience was good for my platoon. We had a chance to accomplish a mission in a "squared-away Marine Corps fashion," yet we also had a lot of fun. In view of what we were to face afterward, and the fact that for far too many of my men it was the last fun they would ever have, the guarding of the Widgeon Bridge stands out as a golden moment in our collective Korean experience.

Many months later, I became aware of an additional aspect of the Widgeon Bridge experience that I had been totally unaware of at the time. Sometime in December, on some occasion, I ran into one of the few old second platooners still in Korea. By this time, I was back on the battalion staff. I can't remember who reminisced with me about our glorious days guarding the Widgeon Bridge, but he let drop something about the "comfort girl." I must have looked puzzled because he suddenly became very upset and said, "Oh my gosh, Lieutenant, just forget what I said." I was not going to let him get away without further explanation, and after pressing him pretty strongly, he finally said, "Well, Lieutenant, I guess it won't make any difference now. Almost everybody involved is either dead or rotated back to the States. You know, we really had a good thing going out there at the bridge, but I realize you never knew anything about it." He then proceeded to unfold the most amazing story. Our camp at the bridge was on the southern side of the Imjin River, and because the river makes a huge loop to the south in that sector, our camp was only about half a mile north of the no-cross line. Established much earlier in the static war, this was the line north of which no nonmilitary personnel were permitted to move. It was one of the reasons why I had never laid eyes on a female between my arrival in Korea in May and my R & R in late November. I now learned that my troops took advantage of my strictness and squared-away operation at the Bridge to establish for themselves an additional fringe benefit. Someone had made contact with a, shall we say, courtesan, back at the no-cross line and had invited her to come up to our unit. With the tremendous esprit and unit spirit I had fostered in my platoon, they all worked together to establish this "debutante of the pike" in a beautifully furnished and decorated cave about fifty yards behind our camp at the bridge. She "serviced" the entire platoon. In fact, because I had organized things in such a squared-away Marine Corps fashion, the visits of my troops to this lady of the night were scheduled to come after they came off their night watches on the bridge.

My informant further unloaded the story about the great argument that arose among the men in my platoon. Apparently, there were two schools of thought about what they should do. One party, which never achieved a majority, said, "The lieutenant is a nice guy and a former enlisted man. He will understand, and we ought to tell him about our special fringe benefit." The other party said, "Sure, he is a nice guy, but he would never agree to such a setup that is clearly in violation of Marine Corps regulations. He does things by the book." As this amazing story unfolded, I was grateful that I never had to face a decision about the fringe benefit. But all good things must come to an end. We were finally relieved by another unit on the Widgeon Bridge guard and went back to the rest of the company at the reserve area to begin preparations for our return online. After leaving the bridge on about the twenty-third or twenty-fourth of July, we were slated to relieve the Seventh Marines on the night of the twenty-seventh to the twenty-eighth of July. People had either been training for five or six weeks, or guarding the bridge.

After my return to battalion headquarters shortly before going back online, I was having dinner one night with the battalion surgeon, the same guy who had so proudly taken out my abscessed tooth. He casually said, "Oh, that's right, you were on the bridge, weren't you?" And he added, "The river is beautiful there, isn't it? But of course you didn't swim in it, did you?"

When I asked why, he looked at me, alarmed, and shouted, "Oh my god, you did not swim in the Imjin River, did you? Tell me you did not swim in that river!"

I had to admit that not only had I swum in it, my whole platoon swam in it every day. He again exclaimed, "Oh my god!" And then he proceeded to list every type of disease and fever-causing bacterium present in the river, at the same time expressing complete disbelief that we were all still alive. I knew that there was a pretty horrible disease people got, including some guys from Fox Company, called hemorrhagic fever. Still, as it turned out, too many of the men who swam in the river with me did not live long enough to suffer any ill effects from the water. Instead, they suffered the ill effects of the war. But I was not to know that until later. The surgeon explained in some detail the problems of sanitation at that time in a country like Korea. He said that because the Korean farmers used human excrement to fertilize their fields, many dangerous bacteria were introduced to which the Koreans themselves had developed an immunity. We Westerners, on the other hand, lacked any kind of protection and were certainly at high risk. Especially harmful was the runoff from the fields into the drinking water.

Presuming to be a United States Marine

On the night of July 27-28, we were hauled up in trucks to the main line of resistance to relieve the Seventh Marine Regiment. We were assigned the company position on the very right flank of our regiment. And my second platoon was put on the very right flank of the company. This had the effect of linking my new platoon position to the leftmost platoon of the Fifth Marines, who were occupying my old platoon position before we went off-line on June 15. As a consequence, I was on very familiar ground. Whereas in May and June I had looked out onto the front and right side of Chogum-ni, I now looked out on the front and left side of the ruined village.

CHAPTER 12

STROMBOLI

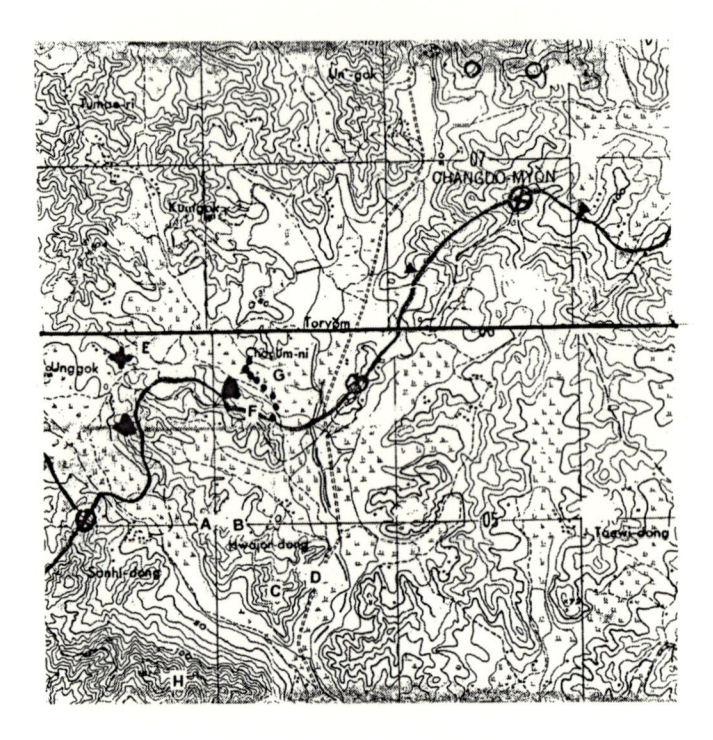

FOX COMPANY'S POSITION JULY 27 - AUGUST 20, 1952

This company position marked by X in circles is the company front just to the left (west) of the company's position in May and June. Black triangles are platoon boundaries.

Legend

A Company headquarters bunker

B Company observation post. My location during Stromboli.

C Artillery/mortars observation post.

D Company supply point. Home of SSgt Richardson's water.

E Stromboli. Company outpost. Scene of battle of August 13.

F My 2nd Platoon headquarters bunker.

G • • • • • • Route of my mine-clearing and patrol.

H Hill 181, dominant terrain feature in whole sector.

Presuming to be a United States Marine

It was reassuring to go back to a position with which I was fairly familiar. We prepared to go back online with some new equipment, and it was at that point that the officers had their carbines taken away and were armed with .45 caliber pistols instead. The pistol was a lot lighter and not nearly as bulky and did not get in the way and knock into things as our carbines were apt to do, so that was fine with us. My memories of breaking camp from reserve and going back online are grim in one respect. The day before, on the twenty-sixth, it started raining, and for the next seven days, it rained in a way that I had never seen it raining in the United States, not even at Camp Pendleton, other than in occasional brief downpours when the heavens seem to open up. But during the monsoon season in Korea, the downpour lasts for days and days. Subsequently, I have noticed in the news every year that the last few days in July and the first few days in August invariably bring floods to Korea. It is an annual phenomenon.

In my correspondence with my parents, I learned that their train had got trapped in the same monsoon some thirty years earlier, as they were traveling through Korea in 1922 on the way to their missionary posts in China. At that point, they had known each other only as members of a large group of young adults. Their train had become trapped in the same sector where I was now located, because the bridges had washed out, both in front of it and behind it. On that trapped train, my mother wrote to me now, she had first begun noticing my father because he had been so strong in the crisis. She implied that this was the beginning of her feelings that culminated, two and a half years later, in their being married in China. So my very existence might be considered the result of the annual Korea monsoon.

And now it had rained for about twenty-four hours without interruption. By the time we reached our position on the line, we were sodden. A new first sergeant, just off the boat to join us, became lost in the rain. Griff could not find him, and nobody knew where he was. As it turned out, he had almost wandered off into no-man's-land in front of the lines before one of our troopers finally found him. As I remember, he was soaked to the bone and really ticked off. This episode became the talk of the company for several days. I found my new command post and my line positions, but everything was encased in mud. I had never seen mud so dense, and never want to again. We had no choice but to put up with it as we took over for the Seventh Marine unit. They happily skedaddled back to their well-deserved rest in the rear, while we settled into their positions. The rain was so heavy that there was no visibility, particularly at night. The downpour simply turned everything pitch black.

The company had one outpost, at that time code-named Stromboli, about two hundred yards in front of us. The name gave it a kind of exotic and beautiful aura, but Stromboli was anything but exotic and beautiful. We manned this outpost with a very heavily reinforced squad. I think we had a couple of machine guns and maybe fifteen men, and perhaps a rocket launcher out there. Stromboli was not a very big hill. In my sector, there was some high ground overlooking the village of Chogum-ni to the east, which, you will remember, I had patrolled just before the raid. We kept an eye on it, because we would occasionally spot the Chinese coming down off the hill mass of Kumgok to Chogum-ni.

Although we were separated by quite a distance across a flat rice paddy, we used to exchange fire with them. We settled down as best we could into this rain-drenched, muddy place. My command post was on top of the hill, just a bit over on the reverse slope in a pretty nice bunker. We were a little worried about incoming messages that bunkers up and down the First Division front were getting completely saturated with water, causing some to collapse. When you have a mound of sandbags and huge twelve-by-twelve timbers coming down on you while you are inside a bunker, you don't stand much of a chance. A number of marines were killed in bunker collapses during that monsoon season.

We put out some listening posts in front of our positions and set up a routine of patrolling in front of our Stromboli outpost. On about the second or third of August, the rain stopped almost as suddenly as it had started. My platoon was in great shape then, and morale was still high from our Widgeon Bridge experience. I knew every man in the platoon intimately, and this gave me a great feeling.

There was a vertical trench line dug forward of my command post, which ran down the forward-facing slope of hill, although, of course, it did not run straight down. A vertical trench line is never dug to run straight. It always runs in a zigzag pattern, providing covered access down to the main line trench. Our vertical trench line intersected the main line of resistance trench line halfway down the hill. The MLR trench line, the main trench, the same line which snaked continuously, all the way across Korea. The front slope of that particular hill, down to which the vertical trench was dug, was pretty steep. At the height of the rainy period, I happened to walk out one day to check on something with the squads down on the main line. Emerging from my command post just behind the top of the hill, I started down the vertical trench when I suddenly realized that the vast quantities of moisture had created vast quantities of slick-as-grease mud. I lost my footing on a particularly steep spot, fell backward, and began racing down the trench line on my back, gathering speed down the slope of the hill like an out-of-control, crazed bobsled or toboggan, feet first, rolling over in the curves and completely covering myself with mud in the process. There was absolutely nothing to hold on to or grab as I went hurtling down, faster and faster, until the vertical trench line ended in a *T* at its intersection with the MLR trench line. I must have been moving at a snappy clip of fifteen to twenty miles per hour, and *bam!* I ran right into the MLR trench line. By that time, I had rotated completely three or four times and had managed to shroud myself in mud from head to toe. My face and body were completely frosted with mud. About three or four of my troopers had seen the last ten or fifteen yards of my mad bobsled ride and were, understandably, doubled over with laughter. They did not recognize me until I stood up, but to give credit where credit is due, they immediately began a desperate struggle to assume a more respectful appearance from the one they had heretofore displayed. I must have looked hilarious. I rose with as much decorum as I could muster, tried to find some cloth to wipe off the mud on my face and in my eyes and my nose, and, in general, to restore at least some shreds of my badly damaged dignity.

In this disreputable state, I started down the MLR trench line. Rounding the bend, I encountered my old friend, Davis, the BAR man who, in the pouring rainstorm and in all that mud, had very carefully laid out his poncho, with his Browning automatic rifle completely stripped down. He told me, "Lieutenant, I am putting a lot of extra oil on everything because of all this rain." In spite of adverse circumstances, he persevered in taking excellent care of his weapon.

Several things happened once the rain stopped. First of all, the Chinese began to get very much more aggressive, as we will see, in that first week in August. They were aggressive to the point where they must have known what I personally did not find out until a couple of weeks later, and that was that the monsoon had washed out almost all the bridges across the Imjin River behind us, including the Widgeon Bridge. Only one bridge survived, the Freedom Bridge, which had been constructed very high above the river with the best of modern engineering knowledge and technology. Now the whole division deployed across the Imjin River had to depend on that one bridge for all its supplies. The Chinese had some pretty long-range artillery, but the Freedom Bridge was located very far behind the lines at that point. Although the Chinese did, every once in a while, attempt to hit it, they were never successful in destroying it. I was to learn later that supplies were at a critical low for us during that time in August, and in fact, there came some days when the only commodity allowed to cross the bridge was ammunition. No food and no water were allowed, just our most essential supply at that point, ammunition. The Chinese were trying to take advantage of our rather depleted resources, making the flood work in their favor.

Two squads of my platoon were on the same hill mass as my command post. Beyond the right flank of my second squad, the hill dipped to a low spot down which ran a road, generally north and south, flanked by small paddies between my hill mass and the hills of our old company position to the east. These paddies extended north and widened out to surround the good old village of Chogum-ni. This road marked the boundary between the two online regiments of the entire division. The road ran south clear to the Imjin River and on to Seoul. It had been one of the main axes of advance when the North Korean force first invaded South Korea on June 25, 1950. The vulnerability of this particular avenue, coupled with the sensitivity about the area around Panmunjom, had been the main reason why the Eighth Army Command had moved the First Marine Division and the Korean Marine Corps from the east coast of the peninsula to the west coast in March of 1952 before I arrived.

Standard Marine Corps tactical doctrine dictates that any natural boundary such as a road, stream, or wall must be clearly in the Zone of Responsibility of a single unit. This meant that the left flank, or western regiment, of the division had to have positions on both sides of the road, and that put my third squad across the road and dug in on the hill rising up from the road and some narrow paddies. This squad tied in with the left flank of the Fifth Marine Regiment. I had been used to this arrangement during May and June when we were the left flank platoon of the right regiment. At that time, the Seventh Marine Regiment to our left always kept a squad on the hill at the left flank of my platoon.

My squad on this little hill was my third squad. They had machine guns attached to them as well as Weapons Company antitank personnel. Such a tailor-made task force required a more senior noncommissioned officer, and I had assigned Gunnery Sergeant Garrison this task. Gunny Garrison was the last of the surplus senior noncommissioned officers left in my platoon. Sergeant Smith had been elevated to company gunnery sergeant during our time off-line. Garrison was a colorful old marine who had enlisted in the middle of the Depression, fought all the way through World War II, and spent many years as a drill instructor at Parris Island. He had led one of our late May patrols and done a good job. He was reliable, not imaginative or creative, but reliable. The final member of this task force was one of my two platoon medical corpsmen, Hospitalman Third Class Richard Payne. Payne had joined us when we were in the rear in June and was a very competent and dedicated hospital corpsman. I felt that because the task force was somewhat detached from the rest of us, they should have their own corpsman. As a result, HN Payne became the centerpiece of an interesting story.

On the front lines, it was customary to dig what we may euphemistically call an excrement hole for a small unit. Usually we tried to place at least a small sandbag "seat" around such a hole. If conditions permitted, we might even place a standard issue wooden seat adapted to this function over the hole, which wooden seat could later be reused. Now Gunny Garrison had determined that his old excrement hole had been filled up by the previous Seventh Marine outfit and that his task force needed a new hole. For some reason, Gunny had determined, that since field sanitation was a function of the medical services, the medical corpsman should dig the hole. He therefore called Payne to his command post and ordered him to find a new site and dig a new excrement hole.

Hospitalman Richard Payne was an intelligent and, as we will see, a brave and dedicated corpsman. He was also a conscientious objector, who had volunteered to serve with the marines. If the gunny had asked him as just one of the troops on the position to dig the hole, he would have probably complied cheerfully. But since the gunny asked him because he was a member of the medical service, HN Payne took the view that his medical status did not include digging holes. A titanic struggle ensued, the result of which was that Gunny Garrison "ran Payne up" to me, the next link in the chain of command. He sent Payne across the narrow paddies and road alone, which was a little hairy since we did not like to make the crossing in daylight under observation by the enemy. As Payne was making his way to my command post, Gunny called me and gave me his version of what had happened.

Before Payne even arrived, I had come to the conclusion that Garrison's order was a bit out of line. But unfortunately, by the time Payne arrived, he was defiantly angry and was ready to take on any second lieutenant. It was a difficult confrontation for me. Payne's rebellious anger made it impossible for me to tell him that I thought he was right. What followed was that I carefully explained to him what an order was and, since he was displaying it, what silent contempt was. After discussing these things for a while, he calmed down, and I called Gunny back and suggested that since he was the medical expert, Payne should pick out the spot and help one of the other marines in the task force to dig the hole. In the end, this solution satisfied both Gunny and Payne.

On August 3 or 4, 1952, I was told by Captain Moody that there had been so much suspected enemy activity in the village of Chogum-ni that we were going to have to patrol the area and the village itself again. This was a dangerous prospect to contemplate because the village snuggled right up under the Chinese stronghold of Kumgok. Moody told me, "Since this is in your sector, I expect you to take the patrol." He added, "But you have a problem. That paddy between you and Chogum-ni on all the maps is marked as a minefield."

"Can't we get the engineers up here to clear the mines?" I asked him.

Griff went through the channels, but word came back that the division engineers would only clear mines behind the MLR, not in front of it, and if we wanted those mines to be cleared out, we would just have to clear them out ourselves.

So I told Griff, "I am not going to send anybody out into a minefield! I'll do it myself." Once again, my respect for the Marine Corps rose. The Corps had provided me with enough training in detecting and disarming mines that I felt equal to the task. It was not something I would attempt to do on a cloudy and black night, but fortuitously, the time approached when the moon would be bright, so that I would be able to see the minefield quite clearly. On the map, and physically on the ground, I doped out a route across the paddy. A paddy has wet beds where the rice is planted, and those areas are surrounded by dikes used by Korean farmers to walk on without getting their feet wet and, more importantly, without uprooting their rice plants. The dikes, in fact, form their paths. But the paddies here had not been planted for a couple of years, and it was well known that the mines were concealed mainly on the dikes.

I talked to a couple of the old sergeants and got some advice on what I might expect. It turned out that I would be dealing primarily with two kinds of mines, both antipersonnel mines, not antivehicle mines, most likely box mines and bouncing Betties. A box mine was about one-half the size of an ordinary shoe box and rectangular in shape. If you stepped on it, it would go off, but would ordinarily not be fatal. It will be remembered that on the raid, I stepped over one, and the corporal behind me had stepped directly on it, and although his foot was badly mangled, he had survived. The more serious kinds of mines would be the bouncing Betties, and these were buried with three prongs sticking up above the ground, but carefully hidden among the grass or other vegetation. If stepped on, a prong would activate a charge, sending a cylinder about four to five inches long and about two and a half inches in diameter, filled with high explosives, up about four or five feet in the air, where the mine would explode. Bouncing Betties could also be activated by a trip wire. Many times, they were set with both the prongs and a trip wire. Bouncing Betties were lethal. It was a bouncing Betty, it will be remembered, that had almost done in Gunnery Sergeant John Frances

Taking on the Burden of History

Kelly in May. If they went off in the air, everybody within a five- or ten-foot radius was going to be hit by fragments and either be very badly wounded or killed. The way to detect a bouncing Betty was to find the trip wire or to feel the three prongs. The way to detect a box mine, on the other hand, was to take a bayonet, knife, or stiff wire, and jab it in the ground.

I devised a tool. Taking a long pole, I placed a piece of the metal banding tape used to hold together large wooden crates on one end of it. I bent the metal tape in such a way that the edge would scrape across the ground in a vertical position. Pushed along the ground in a sweeping motion five or ten feet in front of me, if it hit the prong of a bouncing Betty, I would be able to feel it. The detonation of a box mine depended on heavy pressure over the area under which it was buried, like the bottom of a foot, so that a different method had to be used. I would get down on my hands and knees and poke my bayonet well ahead of my knees vertically into the ground, covering the same area I had just explored for the Betties. This, as you can imagine, was a very tedious business. I had to get across a paddy of close to two hundred yards, feeling for Betties with my tool, then getting down on my hands and knees to search for the box mines. I realized, even before I started, that this operation would take 100 percent of my attention, and I would, therefore, need a couple of men to go along with me for protection. I clearly could not be concerned about looking out for the enemy because I had to remain completely focused on my task. There were two guys with fine records, who had been in the platoon a lot longer than I. But they now appeared to have become afflicted with what we used to call in Korea, and I think this was true in Vietnam as well, a "short-timer's attitude." They knew their chores were almost over, and as a matter of fact, both men were rotated home about two weeks later. The closer the time of their departure approached, the more of their nerve they seemed to lose. Not surprisingly, Staff Sergeant Crawford was down on both of them. I told these two men, "We are going to go on a patrol to Chogum-ni in a few days, but before we do that, we have to clear the minefield first. If you will go with me on a mine-clearing expedition to protect me, I will make sure you don't have to go on the patrol itself." That seemed like a good tradeoff because these guys were experienced. Besides, a couple of people who by now might be a little extra scared would be useful to me because of their sharpened desire for survival. These two guys assured me that they would be glad to accompany me, and I gave them their instructions. They were to stand at least ten yards behind me, because in case I accidentally exploded a mine, I did not want them to get hit too. I wanted them to divide up the terrain around us into sectors, and I wanted them to be constantly on the lookout for Chinese, particularly after we crossed the rice paddy in our approach to Chogum-ni at the other side of it.

As I began the operation, I literally forgot about the men, and that is the proper thing to do when you are clearing mines. I soon found two box mines and marked them with flags and tape after poking with my bayonet around the outline of each mine. I also found one bouncing Betty buried in the dike fairly late into the operation, but a second Betty became a bigger story.

Presuming to be a United States Marine

At some point earlier in the war, somebody, and who knows whether it was our side or the other side, had laid a whole lot of barbed wire in this paddy. Some of it tangled along or across the dikes, but much of it was spread out down into the wet paddy itself. In some places, I found a fairly substantial snarl of a multitude of wires—straight, taut wires, tangled wires, and wire coils. Crawling along a portion of the dike away from our positions, I had worked my way to a point about halfway across the paddy when I encountered a large metal barbed wire stake pole driven into the ground at a point where the dikes all came together at right angles from four different directions. Strands of taut barbed wire, as well as randomly tangled wire, ran in all directions from that pole, and some of the taut wire was under very high tension. This made for a real obstacle, and I realized that in order to pass through this point with a patrol, I would need to determine how to get around, or through, this snarl and barrier of wires. I was armed with all kinds of tools, including very heavy wire cutters. Moving around in the bright moonlight, I determined to cut through the wire fence tangle so that the patrol could make a right-angle turn at this dike junction.

Squatting at the big steel pole with my wire cutters, I began to cut a number of the wires and had soon worked my way through the tangle to a heavy wire stretched very tightly. Although I am left-handed, the only way I could reach this wire was with my right hand. I placed the wire cutters into my right hand and reached out to cut the wire. Just as I was going to clamp down, something brushed across the back of my right hand. I was suddenly on 125 percent alert. When you are clearing mines, your life depends on you being supersensitive. What the hell was that? I pulled the wire cutters back to see what had brushed the back of my hand and saw a fine loose trip wire attached to the wire under tension that I had been about to cut. Feeling along the trip wire with my fingers, I traced it as it went down to the right of my squatting body into the side of the dike under my feet. As I progressed along the wire with my fingers to the dirt side of the dike, I felt the familiar fuse mechanism of a bouncing Betty buried in the side of the dike, angled up. This particular Betty would have been activated by the trip wire. Had I cut the barbed wire under tension, as I had been fully prepared to do, it would have quickly coiled up away from the stake, and I would not be in a position to tell this story. That Betty would certainly have blown up right beside me as it came up out of the dike. It had clearly been buried there to destroy anybody who attempted to cut the barbed wire under tension. With as steady a hand as I could muster, I disarmed the Betty by very carefully unscrewing its fuse. Next, I checked all the other wires leading up to the post until I was sure that there were no other trip wires or any other suspicious wires of any kind. Then I cut through all wires, so that when I returned with the patrol, we could proceed down the new section of dike unhindered.

I found another Betty buried in the ground on the dike and activated by its pressure points. I marked everything so that the troops would know exactly where the mines were. In this process, which demanded such deep concentration, focusing, and making sure that my every sense was alert to the possibility of other mines, I had worked my way across fairly close to Chogum-ni. As I approached the ruined village, I allowed myself to pause, remembering my two guys riding shotgun with me and turned around to look for them. Instead of ten yards, they were about thirty-five yards behind me. I realized that the deeper I had progressed across that paddy, the slower their own movements had become. I found myself only about ten yards away from where the low hill started up toward Chogum-ni. According to our maps, Chogum-ni itself was not mined, although, as we will see later, the maps were wrong. I decided that I had gone quite far enough, and this was confirmed by the fact that I suddenly heard a shuffling noise. Standing up from my kneeling position, I looked in the direction of the sound. Thick long reeds with a lot of undergrowth grew at the edge of where the paddy ended and the ground rose up toward Chogum-ni. I could see that some of the reeds were mashed down in the shape of a human body. It did not take me long to guess who that might have been. And it was at this moment that I had turned around to see my shotgun marines not nearly close enough to me. The man in the reeds must have observed me doing my work. He probably watched and waited for me to approach his position so that he could grab me. I took my special tool, with the steel banding on a nice long pole, and planted it right in the soft soil of the dike to mark how far I had reached with the mine clearing. I turned around and rather quickly moved back toward our lines, picking up my two troopers along the way, and remonstrating with them a little for getting so far away from me. They apologized, particularly when I told them that I thought a Chinese had been lying in the reeds, waiting to pounce on me if I got any closer.

But we had, at least, accomplished our mission, and two nights later, I took the patrol out to Chogum-ni. On the patrol, we found a lot of evidence that the Chinese were not occupying it permanently. The village was much too exposed for them as well. The fronts were not parallel there, because our line folded in so that when the Chinese were in the village, we could see them from both sides and in the front. It was clear that they were covertly entering the village at times, and so I patrolled the area with a squad and put observers and listening posts there. That charming cemetery in Chogum-ni turned out to be filled with mines and booby traps, and the ground was laced with trip wires. Our patrol left rather quickly and, fortunately, before any of the men had tripped any of the wires. The next night, my platoon sergeant, Crawford, who was always hot for leading patrols, took a patrol with another one of my squads, this time out in front of Stromboli toward 104, where the Seventh Marines had attacked on the infamous operation on May 28. This area was farther to the west of our platoon position. It was a sad night. As aggressive as Crawford was, he charged right into a Chinese position with only about six men. Three of them, including Sergeant Crawford, were wounded, although no one was killed, while the little group of marines did a lot of damage to the Chinese.

There was one of my troopers, who had been in the platoon as long as I had been in it, a nice young man somewhere from the Midwest, who was the only enlisted man in my platoon with a year of college under his belt. He was an intelligent, fine, articulate guy. When Crawford had led the men into the Chinese trench line position, this young marine had been creeping along behind Crawford. Unexpectedly, the ground under him started to feel higher, softer, and lumpier. He realized that he was creeping along on top of the body of a Chinese soldier, and that the body was very much alive. The Chinese lay absolutely still, playing possum. Afterward, the trooper told me that he had reacted completely instinctively as he had been trained to do, by jabbing his bayonet into the body under his feet and dispatching the poor Chinese. But his bayonet had got stuck, and he had a hard time getting it out. To kill the Chinese with his bayonet upset the marine greatly. It bothered him for the rest of his time in Korea, although he may not have shared his distress with anybody else. I found this to be proof that human sensitivities do not necessarily disappear in war.

The patrol was a big success, but at the price of a disaster. On the one hand, Crawford and his men had found a Chinese position we did not know existed and had killed several Chinese soldiers in addition to the wretched bayoneted fellow. On the other hand, one of the Chinese succeeded in hosing Crawford down with the submachine gun we called a burp gun. Crawford, of course, had been wearing a flak jacket, and so he had not sustained any wounds to his torso. But he was hit in both arms and both legs. One of the bullets had whacked him right around the knee. We kept track of him after he was evacuated and learned that he was eventually sent back to the United States. The doctors managed to save his leg, but it ended up being about three inches shorter than the other. Crawford had to get out of the Marine Corps, which must have nearly killed him because he loved it so much.

During this early August period, Chaplain McCabe, who had accompanied us on the raid, bless his dear Presbyterian heart, visited us and held a service, which had a profound effect on my own religious faith. He did his utmost to bring his Christian message to the front lines. He always carried a big back pack, filled with U.S. Navy combined hymnal and prayerbooks. Every time he could gather a few people around him, the chaplain would hold a church service. He would pass out his little prayer and hymnbooks and hold a service for whomever he had gathered. One day, when we were still in the position where I had to clear out the minefield in front of us, McCabe came up. By that time, he knew me pretty well, and he said, "Lieutenant Van Sant, could I hold a church service for your platoon?"

"Oh, that would be wonderful," I told him and passed the word on over our sound power phone system to announce that we would hold church.

And McCabe asked me, "Where do you think I could hold the service?"

Our platoon was dug in on a ridge line, with several deep ravines behind it on the reverse slope of the hill and away from the enemy. One of these ravines, right behind my command post bunker, seemed a good place to hold a service. About thirty of my troops managed to break away and come back over the hill, quite far down into the bottom of the ravine. There we thought that we were pretty well protected and out of sight of the enemy. Chaplain McCabe passed out his hymnal/prayer books and began. About five minutes into the service, a Chinese mortar shell came banging in fifty yards or so behind us. It was clear that it had overshot us. But then we heard another shell landing to the left of us, and another to the right of us. I observed where the mortar shells were landing. The closest one was still more than forty yards away, but I was thinking that some Chinese mortar man must know that there was something going on. I prepared to suggest that we break off the service and get the men dispersed.

Although he did not say anything, I felt that Chaplain McCabe could read my mind. He gazed at me with a look of complete confidence, as if to say, *There is nothing to worry about, nothing to worry about at all! We are all in the hands of a Higher Power.* And he kept right on with his service, and that Chinese mortar man kept right on with his shelling, never getting closer to us than, eventually, about thirty-five yards away. I counted the thumps and realized that we had thirteen mortar shells landing around us during that church service. But none of the shells hit anybody, just as Chaplain McCabe had promised with his eyes.

My life was to undergo a big change on about the eighth of August. I got a call from Griff, who told me that Lieutenant Wozencraft was being rotated back to the States. He said, "I'd like you to be our executive officer." It was hard to believe that it had only been three months earlier when I had gravely pronounced to Griff that I was actually senior to Lieutenant Wozencraft, as if I should have been appointed executive officer right then and there. I must confess that I was pleased and honored, although I was sorry to leave my platoon. But Lieutenant Garner, who had joined us in June, had been groomed to take it over, although, as we will see, he only kept the platoon for a few days. In the lot of new lieutenants we received, Lieutenant Garner impressed me as being the savviest. Jannelle, who had been my guest at the Widgeon Bridge, was also doing a great job with the mortar section. I now gathered up my gear, was relieved by Lieutenant Garner, and made my way back to the company command post. While our platoon hill was in a good position, we came under enemy observation each time we had to go back to the company command post. It was a hard position to get in and out of. As a result, we had a rule that every squad would bring out two five-gallon water cans a day, and that was all the water we could live on for that day. It was just too risky to keep walking back and forth across the field behind the platoon. I managed to successfully traverse the space to the command post, reported back to Griff, and took over as the company XO. That began a period of a new kind of work that was most interesting and, as we will see, soon became most exciting.

I became responsible for the administration of the company. That meant making sure that the supply sergeant was doing what he was supposed to do, and that the first sergeant and the company clerk were keeping the company records straight. In combat, online, not many records are kept, but some accounts are maintained even under these circumstances. One of the most miserable aspects of my new job was taking inventory of the personal effects of the men who had been killed or wounded. Even at that point, we had casualties from some of our patrols. As company exec, I immediately began sifting through their personal possessions, a part of the job I never got used to. After completion of the inventory, the items were boxed up and returned to the next of kin.

Presuming to be a United States Marine

There were not-yet-mailed letters written by the marines, and among them, letters to be delivered in case of their death. These letters were sacred. We did not open them. The personal effects of the wounded were boxed up and sent to the hospitals. Several of the troopers possessed fairly extensive collections of pornography, and there was an unwritten rule that any such material would be censored out and not returned to Mother. Of course, compared to the kind of pornography we have become accustomed to in high-tech America, this was all pretty crude and simple stuff. I also assisted Griff in whatever way I could in overseeing the supply and administration, making sure that the mortar platoon had ammunition and mortar shells, and that the water was being brought up properly, and therein lies a tale.

We had one character whom I have not mentioned yet. He was the company supply sergeant, Staff Sergeant Richardson. Staff Sergeant Richardson had come to Korea at the end of the Chosen Reservoir battle. He had joined Fox Company, First Marines, had spent all of calendar year 1951 in Korea, and was rotated home the following December. Richardson had been in the large operation in early 1951 called Operation Killer and had been involved in the battle for Hill 749 up on the east coast in September of 1951. Richardson got married after his return home in December, although the marriage may not have worked out very well. He was a little bit what we then called in the Marine Corps, "Asiatic." He wanted nothing more than to get back to Korea, pulling many strings and wires to get himself returned in the Twentieth Replacement Draft, the same one I had come over with. I remembered seeing him a couple of times, even though there were about four thousand people in the draft, and one certainly did not get to know everybody. But we came over to Korea together, Richardson on his second tour. He had been assigned to a rear echelon outfit, but because he considered Fox Company to be his home, he continued raising hell with the division adjutant in order to be sent back to us. Somebody down in division who knew Griff called him and forewarned him, saying "This fellow is a good marine. He does his duty and is a hard worker, and he is kind of famous around here, but he has seen too much action already."

When Richardson checked in with Griff after having successfully pulled all the strings he could reach, Griff told him, "Sergeant Richardson, you are just the man we need! I don't have a good supply sergeant, and you know how things operate around here." Griff had powers of persuasion. He was charismatic, and Richardson was so impressed with Griff and with Griff's confidence in him that, yes, he said, he would set out to be the very best supply sergeant in the entire Marine Corps, because Fox Company was the very best company in the entire Marine Corps. And Richardson predictably did a great job. Richardson was a master of "the scrounge." He could work deals and get things nobody even remotely believed could be found anywhere on the face of the earth.

Sometime after I had been heavily prepped by the battalion surgeon about the dangers of drinking water from the rice paddies, and about two days after I took over as company XO, I had to return to our Battalion Headquarters from the line. Griff had let me take a company jeep with a driver, and our route to headquarters went right by Richardson's supply point in the rear of the company, behind our company CP. I told my driver to pull in so that I could check on how Staff Sergeant Richardson was getting along. He came out to see me because he regarded me as a great buddy since we had come over in the same draft together. He fell all over me, and knowing we were on C-rations, offered some special foods he had been able to scrounge up.

"Oh, Lieutenant," he said, "how would you like to drink a nice cup of clear, cool water? I have found this pump," he said, and I don't know whether he had bought, stolen, or traded it, but, "I have scrounged up a pump," he told me, and it turned out to be one of those old hand pumps with a long pipe, for use in a well. Up on a bank on the hill, Richardson had engaged some troops to dig a well, and he had put the pump in and covered the well over. The ground water in the area was probably coming off the top of the mountain called 181. Probably. But that mountain began rising only about twenty yards above a rice paddy, and you will remember what kind of fertilizer I was told was being used on these paddies. Richardson pumped out a canteen cup of water and handed it to me with a dazzling smile. I looked at the well pretty carefully and asked, "Where did this water come from, Sergeant?" I was thinking of the purified water carried up to us in water trailers called buffaloes.

He said, "Oh, Lieutenant, this water is clean and clear, just taste it, it's very refreshing!"

I contemplated the surgeon's pronouncements about human waste and bacteria and said, "Sergeant, you are not distributing this water to the troops, are you?"

And the sergeant says, "Sometimes I do, Lieutenant." And I am thinking that the whole company will be coming down with something unspeakable from Richardson's polluted water, and I am getting ready to really launch into Richardson for his negligence, when the other company jeep drives up with Captain Griff Moody in it. Griff hops out of the jeep with, "Sergeant Richardson, let me have some of that refreshing water of yours." Talk about having your feet cut out from under you. Sergeant Richardson looked at me with an expression of, *Well, Lieutenant, what are you going to say to me now?* But discretion was the better part of valor at that moment. And none of us ever got sick from the sergeant's "good, clean water."

DIGRESSIVE SKETCH OF GRIFF MOODY

The reader has already been provided with digressive sketches of Chesty Puller, Bill Boatsman, and George Morrison. I have added these sketches because these three, along with Griff Moody, were the four people who had the most profound influence on me as a marine. I have already recounted that I think Griff was not too impressed with me at first: my appeal to seniority when I first joined Fox Company and my skulking in the trench line because of the sniper my second day on the OPLR. But as my weeks in Fox Company passed, I think I was able to redeem myself in his eyes.

Griff was an only child. His parents, whom I got to know quite well in subsequent years, were a lovely, genteel couple from old Georgia families. The sun rose and set on

Presuming to be a United States Marine

Griff as far as his mother and father were concerned, and they worshipped the ground Griff walked on. Griff had been a good son. He had done well at the Naval Academy and had been a football star there. After Jimmy Carter was elected governor of Georgia, Griff told me that he had come to know his fellow Georgian, Carter, who was a year or two behind him at the academy. Griff graduated from the academy in 1945, too late to get into the Pacific war. He immediately began to create an outstanding service reputation. The Marine Corps has always been small, and there are some officers of whom it is said, relatively early on in their careers, that they will be a general someday. This was the prediction for Griff's future. He was immediately in demand as a general's aide, and when I went through Officer Candidate Screening and Basic School, Griff was the aide to General Hart, the commander at Quantico. The only thing lacking in his credentials was a wife. Griff was now twenty-eight years old, but there have been a few unmarried Marine Corps generals in the past, and we have even had a commandant who did not get married until he was fifty-five years old, but he did finally marry.

While we were in Korea, about once a week without fail, a box filled with the tastiest home-baked pastries and delicacies of every conceivable sweet sort, which could be expected to survive the trip across the Pacific, was delivered to our command post. Wozencraft had mentioned a couple of times that it was sure nice living with Griff because he was always very generous in sharing these goodies from Mama.

In the narrative pages that follow, there will be more Griff stories as I recount the events of August and September 1952, but here I should like to look into the future from that time. After the month I spent as Griff's executive officer, we became fast friends. When I returned from Korea, Griff was the inspector-instructor for the Reserve Battalion in Pittsburgh. On my way to Cincinnati in early May of 1953, I stopped off to visit him, and we went to see Shirley's grave together. After I had arrived in Cincinnati, I proposed to Peggy, my old girlfriend from the days before Shirley, who was working there. Peggy and I were married in September of 1953 in Trenton, New Jersey, and Griff was one of my ushers, and we used his sword to cut the wedding cake. Griff remained close to Peggy and me for the rest of his life and became godfather of our second child, Mary. We visited back and forth as his career in the Marine Corps continued to flourish. In 1961 and 1962, after tours at Quantico, the Naval Academy, and jump school at Fort Benning, Griff returned to Quantico as an instructor. I was a professor at Mary Washington College in Fredericksburg by then, and Peggy and I introduced him to an attractive young single English professor. The four of us double-dated for a year, which ended with Griff proposing to the professor. At this time, he was promoted to lieutenant colonel and given orders to report to Saigon to become the senior adviser to the Vietnamese Marine Corps. Griff did not think it would be fair to marry anyone under these circumstances. He took off for overseas still single and, because his tour was extended, lost the English professor to another man. This was as close as Griff ever got to marrying.

Griff spent almost a year and a half in Vietnam, from the summer of 1962 until the end of 1963, well before the heavy American involvement. He was on the way home through Australia when Kennedy was assassinated. When he reported in to Headquarters, Marine Corps, in early 1964, he was told that the commandant, General Wallace Greene, wanted to see him. For some years, the Marine Corps had been trying to get a marine officer assigned to the Office of the National Security Adviser in the White House. The position was finally established in early 1964 just as Lyndon Johnson was setting up his administration. The commandant offered the job to Griff, and he took it. This was the same billet that became famous twenty years later when it was occupied by Lieutenant Colonel Oliver North. Griff loved working in the White House and saw the president frequently. I think he made himself indispensable to the national security advisor and was often involved in innermost circle policy meetings in the times when the Johnson administration was grappling with the decision to send combat troops in to Vietnam. We saw him often, but he could not tell us much of what was going on.

In the spring of 1965, disaster struck. While on duty at the White House, Griff had a heart attack of the disturbed heartbeat variety. He was rushed to the Bethesda Naval Hospital, and doctors tried to catheterize his heart through his arm. Griff's muscles were so well developed that the surgeons did serious nerve damage to his hand, his arm, and his back during the operation. The catheterization did not really work, and he was forced to spend a couple of months in the hospital recovering. After a convalescent leave during which he visited Peggy and me in the late summer of 1965 in Puerto Rico, Griff returned to the White House for some months but was eventually transferred back to Headquarters, Marine Corps.

Sometime in 1969, Griff was ordered overseas and, having been promoted to colonel in 1968, was slated to command a regiment in Vietnam. On the way, in Okinawa, he had another heart episode. He was sent back to the States and hospitalized. By this time, he was carrying on a running battle with the U.S. Navy Bureau of Medicine, who wanted to retire him on disability. He kept barely passing physicals but managed to stay on active duty. Sometime in late 1970, he was detached from the Department of Defense to the State Department. During the next two years, he represented the Marine Corps and the United States as a (finally *the*) senior Department of Defense representative on the extended and lengthy negotiations between Japan and the United States. Out of these negotiations came the final peace treaty between the two nations, and the U. S.-Japan Status of Forces Agreement. This assignment required the use of all his talents, but as always, Griff did an outstanding job.

As I got to know Griff better, I realized how intelligent he was. In fact, he was the smartest person I ever encountered in the Marine Corps. He was a true Southern gentleman, always diplomatic, yet projecting a firmness and strength that compelled obedience. At the same time, he had what is called the common touch. Whenever he talked to anybody, be it a private or a general, Griff made that person feel special and important. By the time I became company executive officer on August 8 or 9, 1952, I understood that every officer and man in Fox Company worshipped this man. Hell, I worshipped him.

Presuming to be a United States Marine

The Navy Bureau of Medicine eventually prevailed, and early in 1973, Griff was retired from the Marine Corps on disability. He had had an apartment in Crystal Towers in Arlington ever since he had come back from Vietnam in 1964. His parents began dividing their time between Georgia and his place in Washington. He bought a beach cottage in Topsail Beach, North Carolina, where he often relaxed. During the time period between 1972 and 1975, my wife, Peggy, was in the throes of her final illness, so that most of my contact with Griff at that time was by phone. I had a long talk with him on the phone in the late spring of 1975. Soon after that, Peggy died, and we had one last brief phone conversation then. His heart problems continued to plague him.

In October of 1975, Griff decided to drive down to his North Carolina beach cottage for a long weekend alone. When he did not return by Monday, his parents called his cottage. Receiving no answer, they contacted the North Carolina county sheriff's department. The sheriff drove out to the cottage and found Griff dead from his fourth heart attack. An autopsy disclosed that he had probably died late Saturday or early Sunday. Griff was such a gregarious and sociable individual that it is hard to think of him facing death alone. Although he never found a lifelong partner, he loved the troops, the Marine Corps, and his enormous circle of friends.

I have already told about my lunches with Chesty Puller during the sixties. When Chesty found out I had served with Griff, he immediately expressed his admiration for Griff, saying, "He's one of the good ones." It was during one of these lunches that I had the sad duty of reporting Griff's heart troubles, and Chesty was most distressed. As the reader will soon see, Griff was one of the great warriors. The last few weeks of August 1952 were his greatest moments.

This will be my last digressive sketch. All honor and glory to Private Boatsman, Lieutenant General Puller, First Lieutenant Morrison, and Colonel Moody—good marines all, my mentors—all now on duty guarding heaven's streets.

—end of digressive sketch—

During that second week of August, we were patrolling aggressively in front of our company position and manning the outpost Stromboli, which was not much of a hill but would give some early warning protection to our main line. On the eleventh of August, to the west of us, Easy Company was the first marine company to become involved in the Chinese offensive that lasted for a number of weeks and ultimately became known under the general heading of Battle of Bunker Hill. Easy Company had an outpost called Siberia, and Dog Company, or Delta Company as it is now known, was positioned between us and Easy Company. The Chinese moved in one night, completely surrounding Siberia. They began to blow the hell out of it, and just about wiped out everybody on it with the exception of a couple of guys who managed to straggle back. Our battalion commander, Lieutenant Colonel Batterton, was pretty upset about losing Siberia. Taking some people out of the battalion headquarters, he organized a counterattack right away. The company commander of the Headquarters

Taking on the Burden of History

and Service Company of the battalion was a marvelous character from Ohio named Lieutenant Vince Pomocky. In his relatively safe and cushy job, Pomocky was a gourmet cook and high-liver of every sort, but Pomocky had guts. Pomocky was designated as the commander of this counterattack. He gathered up a group of volunteers, typists, clerks, and messmen from the battalion headquarters; charged back up with them; and retook Siberia. He took it and held on to it for about six to eight hours, but damn if the Chinese did not take it back from him. Batterton and his operations officer, a wonderful man and experienced veteran of World War II, Major Dermott McDonnell, realized that the way Siberia was set up, it would be almost impossible to hold it. The Chinese had a fairly gentle slope from their side of the hill up to it, but on our side, it was it was almost a sheer cliff. It was simply very hard to reinforce from our side. Just to the west of Siberia was another position, Hill 122. It was located in the midst of no-man's-land, although we strongly suspected that the Chinese spent a lot of time on it. Later, that hill became known as Bunker Hill. Bunker Hill lay halfway between a huge mountain, Tae-dok-san, 236 meters high to the north and our positions on Hill 201, which was directly south of Bunker Hill. These two hills, plus 229 to the southwest of 201, dominated the whole area.

On the twelfth of August, the First Battalion was in reserve, and we, the Second, along with the Third Battalion were online. A company from the First Battalion, B Company, was ordered up from the rear reserve. They charged off the forward slope of 201. Hill 201 was pretty sheer in front, with wonderful observation posts from which you could see all over the Chinese hinterland. B Company jumped off from that hill and took 122. On the next night, the thirteenth, the Chinese decided to reclaim 122 with an enormous force.

We were a couple of miles to the east, in our Stromboli position. Our lines were in front of still another dominating hill, called Hill 181, behind us. This was the hill from which I fervently hoped clean water had trickled into Richardson's well. The Chinese attacked Stromboli and our main line, but this turned out to be only their supporting attack. Their main attack was on Bunker. That whole battle, with many sub-battles, raged on for thirty-six hours and took place on the thirteenth and fourteenth of August 1952. Our position and role in it seemed to us anything but secondary, except that we soon realized the enormous noise of the fighting two miles west of us at Bunker Hill. Subsequently, various estimates were made of the size and strength of the Chinese attack force. I know that our company alone was attacked by at least a Chinese battalion. The company at Bunker Hill was probably attacked by a regiment. Because I was not a participant in that Bunker Hill battle, I will only mention briefly that B Company was completely shot up and decimated. A company from our Third Battalion, I Company, went up, fought bravely and with distinction, and held on to Bunker Hill against everything the Chinese threw out at them.

Meanwhile, back at our Stromboli ranch, we were having our own problems. My memories of that event remain distinct and clear, almost minute by minute. Griff and I were sitting in our command post just before the Chinese attack on Bunker. As I recall, we were nibbling away on some goodies from Georgia shortly after midnight when our company radioman, who always monitored the radio at night, heard "Psst . . . psst . . . psst"—somebody hissing over the radio. In a very low voice, Staff Sergeant Bill Chain, from the first platoon, who was in command on Stromboli that night, whispered to our radioman, "Could I speak to the captain or the lieutenant?"

The radioman handed me the radio, and I said, "Yes, Sergeant Chain, what's up?" And he whispered back, "They are all around us. We are completely surrounded." We had something we called box-me-in fires, preregistered by all five of our 60 mm mortars. These concentrations put down a mantle of mortar fire in a sort of box around Stromboli, so that if Stromboli were attacked, they could be automatically fired at anybody trying to climb the hill.

I asked Chain, "Do you want us to fire the box-me-in?" And Chain whispered back, "No, sir, not yet."

Then, while I was talking with Chain over the radio, I suddenly heard all hell breaking loose. I heard machine gun fire, grenades going off, and the worst thing was that Chain himself was hit while he talked with me. He called out that he had been hit by a hand grenade and couldn't see. But Chain, wounded and blinded, kept his cool. Chain had no more than fifteen or twenty men, but he kept them in their perimeter, and those marines never lost Stromboli. Almost all of them were either wounded or killed, but those still alive continued firing and successfully held off the Chinese.

And now the whole front before us erupted with Chinese fire, especially directed at the first platoon in the center and the third platoon on the left of our company sector. The Chinese fire included small arms, grenades, mortar shells, and artillery. An enormous amount of fire came our way. Griff suddenly threw on his flak jacket and helmet, saying to me, "Van, you have now got the company!"

Several days later, he gave me the whole background leading up to his decision. On the night of the raid, June 13, when Holmberg had stepped into it out on OP-3, Griff had told the then battalion and regimental commanders that he was going to go out to bring Bill and his platoon back. But the regimental commander, Colonel Flournoy, had given Griff a very explicit order, "Under no circumstances, Captain Moody, are you to go forward of the main line of resistance, not under any circumstances. You will remain where you are, and you are not to move. Is that understood?"

Griff now told me, "They kept me from getting Holmberg, but by golly, they are not going to do that to me again!" What I did not realize at the time was that there was a standing division order, which absolutely forbid any company commander to go forward of the main line of resistance. Griff knew of this order, but having been exec for only a few days, I knew nothing about it. Griff now gave me his direct order. "You have the company." And that was that.

Our company observation post, the company OP, was on the highest hill, other than 181, in our sector. A good company OP, it enabled one to see the entire company front, and although it was not very high, our OP did afford a sweeping view of everything happening across the company front. I will never forget climbing up into that OP, with my radioman and with a couple of telephones wired in. To get there, I had to pass Lieutenant Jannelle's mortar section down about thirty yards from the OP. His men were already pouring out 60 mm mortar fire to box in Stromboli. Griff took off for the junction between our third platoon and the first platoon. There was a cut at this junction section of the main line that had to be passed through in order to reach Stromboli.

I suddenly felt the full weight of responsibility for all the 265 marines in our reinforced rifle company. I was to lead this group in a situation that already looked totally chaotic. Shells were exploding everywhere—small arms fire, grenades, and rockets produced a horrible symphony of sound. I was as scared as I ever was in Korea, and a thought passed fleetingly through my mind. It was Harry Truman's famous statement when he was asked how he felt when told of President Roosevelt's death: "I felt like the moon, the stars, and all the planets had fallen on me."

The third platoon had the most advanced positions on our line, at least with respect to where the Chinese were presently hitting us. Griff had a radio and a radioman, and I had a radio and a radioman, and he and I remained in constant touch. But I was also responsible for all the communication with the supporting arms, and with battalion and regiment. Colonel Batterton got on the radio, and I told him what I knew—that Stromboli was surrounded but that the men were still fighting, and we were still holding on. My old platoon, the second platoon, was off on our right flank and was not too heavily engaged in the battle. Before Griff left, we had called Lieutenant Garner and told him to take a squad out to reinforce Stromboli. As directed, Lieutenant Garner gathered a squad, pulled them off their platoon positions, and went around behind and up between the third and first platoons to the cut through the hill. They advanced through the cut, and Garner almost reached Stromboli. That cut was to become a famous location for many months to come. But the Chinese had Stromboli completely surrounded, and Garner got himself into an enormous fight with obviously superior Chinese forces. Almost all of his men were wounded, and a couple of them were killed. Garner himself was badly wounded.

The Chinese continued heavily shelling our lines, especially the first and third platoon positions. Lieutenant Smythe, the California beach boy, got hit so seriously that he had to be evacuated. The third platoon, which had been so badly shot up on the raid, controlled the area around the cut, the critical defensive position against this particular Chinese attack. The third platoon lieutenant was also gravely wounded within the first five minutes of the action. The situation was grim. But Griff, of course, had told me that he was not going to be denied doing what he felt he had to do this time around. At the company OP, I had wire communications to battalion and to regiment, 4.2 Heavy Mortars, division artillery, and especially our own battalion 81 mm mortar forward observer, Sergeant Chuck Lundeen, and his capable assistant, Jerry Dudding. This capable duo provided us excellent support, not only on this night, but subsequently. (I should add that the battlefront maps in this book were supplied by Sergeant Lundeen.) Most of the wire communications to our rifle platoons was soon interrupted when the wires were cut by incoming fire, so that I had to rely on radios for intracompany communication. But all this time, I had a grandstand seat to the battle as it unfolded before and slightly below me. I could look down on most of the action and think of Robert E. Lee's remark about the "awful beauty of war." The battle had started in the early morning hours of the thirteenth of August. At the height of it, the entire company front was lit up with illuminating shells, and a great many marines in Fox Company were shooting, and a great many Chinese were returning fire, and shells were exploding all around us all the time. The scene became an enormous panoply of light, color, sounds, and odors, with smoke draped over it all. And I was sitting in the observation post, as if presiding over it all, or so it felt to me, briefly.

Griff's radioman had been wounded, and Griff called back to me to say, "Van, Garner has been shot up, and the lieutenant here is badly wounded, and I hear Lieutenant Smythe is badly wounded too." He added, "What I am going to do is to get a squad from the third platoon and see if I can get out to Stromboli. Under no circumstances are we to fire on Stromboli itself, because our people are still fighting there." And I could see all of that myself from where I was. I called in what artillery I could get, unaware that the attack on Stromboli was a Chinese supporting attack, and that the main effort of the Chinese was to throw at least a regiment against Bunker Hill. When I called for artillery, I was told that all the artillery was tied up fighting the battle of Bunker Hill. I stressed to the people back in battalion and regiment that we had quite a fight on our hands too. Finally, our artillery support that night came from the Korean Marine Corps, just to the left of our division. They turned their guns around about ninety degrees and fired in support of us and did a good job in the process. (Over fifty years after this night, my wife and I took a Korean revisit trip in September 2002. We were treated royally by the South Koreans, and we extended our trip to Beijing. A distinguished physician, Dr. Robert S. Peters, from California, made both the Korea and China portions of the trip. While in China, we began talking about our Korea experiences. It turned out that young Lieutenant Bob Peters had been an advisor to the Korean Marine Corps artillery in 1952. He turned out to be the one responsible for getting the whole Korean battalion to turn their howitzer trails ninety degrees to the east so they could support the beleaguered marine company holding on to Stromboli. Needless to say I fell all over him with gratitude and was filled with wonder at the smallness of our world.)

Our battalion 81 mm mortars were supporting us too, as were our own company 60 mm mortars, under Lieutenant Jannelle. In fact, his mortar section set a record that night for the expenditure of 60 mm mortar ammunition. For about three and a half hours, they steadily fired the box-me-in fires. I think they fired over 2,800 rounds, which meant that we had to call back for truckfuls of 60 mm mortar ammunition in order to resupply Jannelle's mortar position. As his position was hard to reach from the road, that became a logistic nightmare. But in the end, it was accomplished, and Jannelle's troops fell to and performed a magnificent job. By the next morning, Jannelle had four 60 mm mortars left. From the impact of the mortar shells dropping into the tubes, exploding, and then pooping out, the base plates had been driven completely into the ground. Only about six inches of the mortar tubes protruded above ground from the incessant firing. The mortar and base plate had driven themselves right in to the ground and had to be dug out. But our troops held on.

Within an hour, Colonel Batterton had become aware of the fact that Fox Company was involved in a big battle. He got on the telephone with me, and I had a couple of sharp conversations with him. First of all, Batterton had the idea that since the Chinese had surrounded and by this time probably overrun Stromboli, we should fire artillery with variable time fuses over it. A variable time fuse is a shell with a sensor in its nose. After it is fired, and as it approaches the ground, at about twenty feet, the sensor explodes the shell, and the fragments rain down over a wide area. This was the ammunition Wozencraft had called for when we were stopped my first day of combat on the OPLR.

I told Batterton, "Sir, we have men alive out there who are still fighting." And he said, "You could not possibly have men alive there." But I assured him that we had. He became impatient with me, but I held on and went to the mat with him over the issue, and in the end, he did not give the command to commence fire on our own positions. It is a measure of the man that several days later, he thanked me for holding out. Earlier I had told him that we had no rifle platoon commanders left. Not much more than an hour later, two lieutenants reported in to me, and they turned out to be two of the finest people I would ever know—Lieutenant Robert Burhans and Lieutenant Robert Haebel. Burhans had gone through Officer Candidate Screening with me, and we had started Basic School together. But during the fifth week of Basic School, Burhans had broken his leg in an exercise. He had to be held back and had graduated with another Basic School class behind us. Haebel had been two Basic School classes behind me, so that I was senior to both of them. Haebel, incidentally, retired as a major general. I assigned Haebel to take over my old platoon, since the second platoon had lost Lieutenant Garner, and Burhans took over Holmberg's old platoon, the third. They reported in, got their assignments, and took off. Both of them found Captain Moody, who was still organizing his counterattack. The leadership of our platoons was now in good shape again, or at least for the second and third platoons.

Lieutenant Smythe's first platoon had a very fine master sergeant, who took it over for about a day or so. We had taken significant casualties both on Stromboli, from which we had not yet been able to evacuate our wounded, and from Garner's force, as well as from the people on our main line of resistance who remained heavily engaged with the Chinese. Soon a steady stream of ambulances began lining up to carry the wounded back.

Griff checked back with me for a report of everything I had done with respect to the fires and said that he was preparing to take off through the cut. The Chinese had set up a Maxim gun to fire right into the cut toward us, making it almost impossible to get through, but not only did Griff and his whole detail somehow manage to avoid the fire from the Maxim gun, but Griff was eventually able to knock the gun out completely. His detail then charged the Chinese, who took off, so that Griff reached Stromboli unhindered, chasing the Chinese off from there as well. Naturally, his detail sustained several additional casualties in the process. On Stromboli, about seventeen or eighteen marines were found, many of them still alive, although almost all were wounded. Three of my old second platooners with Garner had been killed, and at least five or six were wounded. But the Chinese withdrew, accompanied by a sound pounding from us. Eventually we recovered all of our wounded. In all, thirteen men had been killed, and forty-seven were wounded.

As they were being evacuated, a couple of the men who remained alive on Stromboli told Griff that Sergeant Chain, although blinded at the very beginning of the battle, had constantly moved around, encouraging his troopers and telling them not to give up. As the Chinese were working their way through his positions, he kept asking people how much ammunition they had left. If somebody was running out, he would get some and crawl over to the trooper with fresh supplies. Because almost everybody on Stromboli, if not killed, was wounded we only had verbal statements about Chain's unusual valor. Sergeant Chain was written up by Griff and by Gunnery Sergeant John Francis Kelly for the Congressional Medal of Honor.

The recommendation reached the White House during the first weeks of the Eisenhower administration. I don't know what military aide to the president was handling those things at the time, but Chain's Congressional Medal of Honor got bumped back to the Navy Cross. The word Griff received was that had Chain died, he would have undoubtedly been awarded the Congressional. We were always distressed about that, feeling that Chain had been shortchanged for his bravery.

Kelly and I and a couple of others, wrote up Griff, and he too subsequently was awarded the Navy Cross. It is hard for me to imagine in my old age how difficult it is to write somebody up for a medal during the chaotic conditions of war when, for the moment, you have a million other concerns on your mind, all of them far more serious than medals. In both of these cases, Griff's and Chain's, the heroism was so palpable and tangible that all the troops insisted Moody and Chain be written up at once.

After the dust had cleared for the next few days, I was doing inventories of personal effects of the evacuated dead and wounded and writing letters to the families of all the troopers from my old platoon who had been killed. This is always an excruciatingly sad duty, but in a couple of cases, we received some very moving responses to our letters from members of their families. The forty-seven wounded were "wounded-evac'ed." That meant that they were in the hospital, and it meant that they had been more than nicked. The miracle was that Griff himself, with all his exposure, sustained not even a scratch, and we thought then that he led a charmed life.

After the battle in the night of the thirteenth of August 1952 we received reinforcements to replace some of our casualties. The Chinese had hurled everything they had at Bunker Hill to our left, but its marine defenders had fought them off in a massive battle. The marine units involved were B Company, I Company, and G Company from our First Regiment, as well as a company from the Seventh Marines that had

Taking on the Burden of History

been pulled up out of division reserve. In both battles, Bunker Hill and Stromboli, the Marine Corps had suffered very serious casualties.

The First Regiment had been organized in 1901 in the Philippines. The worst day the Regiment had ever experienced in its entire history in terms of killed and wounded was a day at Pelelieu during World War II. The second worst day now became August 13, 1952. The losses were enormous. The First Marines had suffered many casualties during the Inchon landing, the Reservoir, and all those famous battles earlier in the Korean War, but they suffered more casualties on the night of the thirteenth of August 1952 on Bunker Hill and Stromboli. While it was a victory for us in the sense that the Chinese had not gained an inch of ground in either place, the First Regiment had become badly depleted by the loss of many officers and men in the process of defending that ground.

Burhans, a former motor transport officer, and Haebel, a former amphibious tractor lieutenant, had both volunteered to be pulled out of their units and sent to us as rifle platoon leaders. They were outstanding officers who took to their new jobs right away, and I will have more stories to tell about both of them in subsequent accounts. Beginning on the fifteenth of August, and from then until the twenty-second, we settled back and absorbed our forty or so replacement troopers. Lieutenant Kimbrough, who had come over in July and had been our machine gun platoon leader, was assigned to take over Lieutenant Smythe's first platoon, and another officer, Lieutenant Bob Murphy, was sent to us and took over our machine gun platoon. So we inched up closer, although not quite back to full strength, as we began the task of reorganizing. One of our mortar tubes had completely worn out, several machine guns had been damaged badly, and all of these had to be replaced. We stayed in the same online positions, and we put men on the outpost every night and continued patrolling, but we were able to settle into a kind of routine.

Chapter 13

BUNKER HILL I

To our west, the Chinese kept up steady pressure on Bunker Hill. They were not pleased that the marines had taken the hill away from them and did everything they could to retake it. And so began a kind of a war of attrition on both sides. The Chinese themselves had suffered enormous casualties on the night of the thirteenth, but they continued keeping up the pressure on us.

The regiment began rotating companies through Bunker Hill. A company would be pulled up out of regimental reserve, put on Bunker Hill where it would last for three or four days, and be pulled off. On the twenty-first of August, we were given a warning order that Fox Company would be replaced by one of the other companies in the regiment. It seemed to us that our new regimental commander, Colonel Walter Layer, shuffled companies like chessmen, moving them back and forth across the regimental front. We were alerted that we were going to be pulled off-line and sent back to our battalion command post to be completely fitted up in one day. Then came the shock. We were going to take over Bunker Hill. Fox Company was going to Bunker Hill next. The men took the news well. As always, the unspoken feeling that Fox Company was the best company in the regiment prevailed. In fact, our company sign read, "Fighting Fox Company, Finest of the First." It was as if the higher powers had finally decided to put the first string into the Bunker Hill battle, or so we thought. We had accomplished our mission on the raid and had done a fine job holding Stromboli. We still had a good nucleus of experienced marines. And now we were going to the big time.

Let me say a little about the regiment. In May, when I first reported into Korea, Colonel Flournoy was regimental commander. Flournoy is an old Virginia name. I only saw the colonel a couple of times, but he struck me as a very distinguished-looking gentleman, who appeared to be riding on horseback even while walking on his own two legs. At the same time, Lieutenant Colonel Batterton replaced Lieutenant Colonel Quilici as our battalion commander, Colonel Flournoy was replaced by Colonel Walt Layer. Layer was a pretty good officer with the unique aspect of being a reserve. He had come up through the ranks to colonel as a reserve officer. He had fought all through World War II, had returned to civilian life, and had been called up in 1950. As far as I know, he was the only reserve officer in the history of the Marine Corps who ever commanded an infantry regiment in combat. As a reserve myself, I recognize that this was quite a distinguished assignment. There is no question that Colonel Layer knew what he was doing, but he was somewhat irascible by nature. And now Colonel Layer was shuffling companies around like chessmen as he was trying to cope with the enormous Chinese attacks on Bunker Hill. We were pulled out of line at about one o'clock on the morning of the twenty-second. We pulled back behind the biggest hill mass in our battalion front, the hill called 181, where we were scheduled to be picked up by trucks and taken back to the battalion command post to be checked out and refitted. As was usual, we waited, and waited, but the trucks never came. Finally, we gave up waiting, and in the dark marched to the battalion command post on foot through territory with which we were completely unfamiliar. Nevertheless, we managed to find our way, arriving at the battalion command post at about 0400 hours.

The troops were allowed to get a little nap and a much-appreciated hot breakfast, the first hot meal they'd had since the twenty-seventh of July. But another bombshell was dropped on us. All the men who had been in the Thirteenth Replacement Draft since August of 1951 were not to accompany us to Bunker Hill. It so happened that there were a lot of men in Fox Company from the Thirteenth Replacement Draft, because the company had sustained so many casualties in the summer of '51. Suddenly we realized that we were going to go on Bunker Hill without about twenty of these experienced people who were to be rotated back to the United States. We had mixed feelings about this. Understandably, we were very upset to lose these valuable troops because we knew how much we would need them. On the other hand, we were happy for them because these guys had been fighting in Korea for a year, and it was glorious and grand and well deserved for them to go home. They themselves had mixed feelings, and some were downright upset, but no one more so than Gunnery Sergeant John Francis Kelly, who would now be unable to go to Bunker Hill with us.

An enormous number of personnel, administrative, and logistics problems faced me. Without any sleep after our arrival at the battalion command post, I went back and forth between personnel, operations, and the supply bunker. A group of guys from a 90 mm antiaircraft group, way back in the rear, were "volunteered" and sent up to us as replacements. I greeted them and tried to get them matched up with the veterans in our company so that they would have someone to take care of them when they went out on Bunker Hill. They appeared to be pretty bewildered. These were men not trained as infantry soldiers; they were just bodies who could carry a rifle. I felt sorry for them, but will quickly add that they proved themselves and performed well. The First Marine Division, and especially the First Marine Regiment, was, of course, in a very critical position because of the many casualties it had sustained, although the marines, as always, continued to fight bravely. After I integrated the new guys into their various platoons, most of the troops had a whole day to rest and to enjoy hot meals. They had cots set up in tents and got their gear and equipment ready. It was a moment of relaxation for them, but for the officers, it was a day of hard work. I kept

Presuming to be a United States Marine

running around from supply to the ordnance shop and to the personnel office, trying to get matters organized. I remember that I spent the entire day on my feet.

By the twenty-second of August, the rains had finally stopped, and so at least we did not have to deal with any downpours, although as I recall, the day was cloudy and dim and not very pleasant. I remember thinking that I had to finish all my tasks for Fox Company and felt the weight of the whole world on my shoulders. We could not leave without everybody having everything they were required to have, and have it up to snuff. Staff Sergeant Richardson was of great help that day for our people. He went running around himself, scrounging up things, stealing things, even causing things to materialize out of thin air like he was some magician. Lieutenants Burhans and Haebel, who had joined us the night of Stromboli, and Lieutenants Kimbrough and Murphy, spent the day working with their sergeants and platoon members. These four officers, plus Griff and Jannelle, all went up to the division observation post on 201 to make a reconnaissance of Bunker Hill. Because I was entirely wrapped up in logistics and administrative problems, I was unable to go along with them, which was too bad. In the entire First Marine Division front at that time, this particular observation post offered the broadest panorama of the total division sector. A hill of 201 meters (approximately 700 feet) may not sound like a very high hill until you remember that at its bottom, this hill—as well as 229, 181, and Tae-dok-san—were all close to sea level.

Lieutenant Kimbrough, who subsequently got a PhD in English Lit from Harvard and taught at the University of Wisconsin all his life, gave the most graphic description of what they had seen. He said, "There is a long hill in a straight line, and at either end of it is a horseshoe-shaped hill, one on the left, and one on the right. Then there is a little ridge line trailing off from the left horseshoe. One slope of the hill faces our lines, and the other slope of the hill tilts toward the Chinese." And he added, "The marine positions on this hill look like a man with outstretched fingers, barely hanging on to the side of a cliff. From the division OP, you can also see a fair amount of the Chinese trench lines, and they are in the same position on the other side, so that both appear like two clawing hands trying to clench each other." I suppose it was enlightening to have this literary metaphorical view of the situation facing us.

The battalion staff officers filled me in on what we had to look forward to. The arrangement was that after another hot meal and a nap, we were going to be loaded aboard trucks at about two o'clock in the morning of the twenty-third and taken to a point behind our main line on Hill 201, supporting Bunker Hill. There we were going to transfer to tracked vehicles, either Amtracks or weapons carriers. Because of the July and August rains, the road network on the main line behind Bunker Hill was so badly chewed up that a truck could not drive up Hill 201. Even though the rain had stopped, the roads remained muddy and slick. It turned out to be quite a trip. We got the whole company massed into twenty trucks, went forward again, drove up, got out of the trucks, got into the tracked vehicles, climbed up Hill 201, and finally arrived just behind the main trench line on top of 201. We then proceeded down the forward face of 201 to Bunker Hill on foot. The trip from our main line out to Bunker Hill was one of the most difficult hikes I have ever taken. Hill 201 was very steep on its forward slope. An old, rocky streambed ran down the face of this dreadfully precipitous hill, and we had to climb down this streambed to get down into a little valley. We crossed a paddy, went around a hill, behind another hill, and then at long last arrived on Bunker.

Fox Company had been down from 221 men to probably 160, but the reinforcements from Weapons Company and others must have brought the total up to 200 men. As it turned out, the next day, we received another platoon from H Company of the regiment. The company we were relieving after five or six days on Bunker Hill, Charlie Company, had been steadily probed but had not been involved in a big battle. When a company in the Marine Corps makes a tactical movement of position, it is led by the company commander, with the company executive officer as the last man in the column. Our relief action was complicated, because Bunker Hill was complicated. My section of our single file had to climb down the rocky streambed to reach the valley behind Bunker Hill, and then we had to climb back up onto it.

Morning had dawned by the time I arrived, with the last platoon of the company, in the streambed at the bottom of 201. We were under enemy observation for this portion of the trip from there until we actually arrived on Bunker Hill itself. As I was getting bathed in increasingly brighter sunlight, I began sending the message up through the ranks, "Tell the people up front to speed up!" Everybody crept along, trying to make as little noise as possible. We began passing the Charlie Company people on their return trip to the main line, away from danger, and heard several of them stage-whispering to us the good old Marine Corps greeting, "You'll be sooorry!" Fortunately, the last detail of men in my company, including me, got up on the hill before the Chinese spotted us, or if they had spotted us, they decided not to waste any ammunition on us. Bringing up the rear, I managed to get there without coming to any harm. Griff gave me a quick rundown. He had put Lieutenant Kimbrough with the first platoon out on the right flank, which was actually the most critical part of the hill. The first platoon, over the time I had been in Fox Company, had received the fewest casualties of any of the three platoons. Haebel with the second platoon had the straight ridge line between the two horseshoes, and the third platoon had our horseshoe, and I say "our" because we had put the company command post in that horseshoe with a little ridge line curving off to the left. Even now it is hard for me to say this, but for the first time since I had met Griff, I detected a note of despair in his voice. I asked him where our command post was going to be, and he told me, thereby revealing the source of his despair, "There is a cave here, and Charlie Company was using it. Take a look at it." I went into the cave on the nose of the hill that was the right side of the horseshoe. I climbed in and saw that it was lit up brightly by Coleman lanterns. The cave was deep underground, but there was a foot of water on the floor.

Griff said, "When I got here, Captain"—and I forget the name of the commanding officer of C Company—"was actually sitting in the water." And Griff added, "Van, we can't live in there!" And the note of resignation I heard in his voice really touched me.

Presuming to be a United States Marine

I told him, "You're damn right we can't live in there." The reader must know by now my own enormous admiration for Griff, and he was universally admired and respected in the company. But suddenly he looked vulnerable, and I had absolutely never seen that look before. I assured him that "Griff, we will build a new command post." Fortunately, the marines who had first taken Bunker Hill on the eleventh, twelve days earlier, had made, with the help of the Korean Service Corps, an enormous effort to bring in fortification materials. We had corrugated steel, and there were sandbags, logs, and all kinds of other materials just lying around, all hauled out by supply trains. I found a location very near the cave, snug under an overhanging hill, a good spot almost in the center of the company. My runner, Griff's runner, and I, and our artillery FO, a wonderful man named Glen Allen, who was with his radioman, and a couple of other headquarters people—all of us turned to and began digging dirt and bagging sandbags. In two hours, we had built a new command post. We found a number of logs to put on top of it, and on top of that, we put some more sandbags. While we could not stand up in it but had to squat to move around, it would hold four or five people comfortably. It had thick walls of sandbags and dirt, and we had dug into the hillside a little bit. We moved in and subsequently found that it was a good thing we had built it so well, because it got hit a couple of times, and that story is coming up.

On the first night, the night of the twenty-third and twenty-fourth, we were told that a patrol from one of the other companies in the regiment was to make contact with us and then patrol in front of the right-flank horseshoe to check out the Chinese positions there. At about eight or nine o'clock that night, a very earnest and idealistic-looking young lieutenant arrived. His name was Valentine, and he was from Virginia. Griff had me brief Valentine on our situation—where our troops were deployed, and how we were dug in. Lieutenant Valentine had a staff sergeant with him and a squad of thirteen men. They took off behind Lieutenant Haebel and out to the position of Lieutenant Kimbrough. They checked in with him and climbed around in front of the forward slope of the hill. Naturally, they had headed right for the Chinese and brought down a hell of a fight on themselves. Miraculously, only about four or five men were wounded, but one man was killed. That one man was Lieutenant Valentine. He was given a posthumous decoration for his valor. His staff sergeant said of him that he had been an aggressive young officer. Getting that squad extracted and pulled back and the casualties evacuated consumed a good deal of that night, but nothing else happened on our first night on Bunker Hill. We put out a few patrols on the second night, the night of the twenty-fourth and twenty-fifth, off to the flanks. We knew where the enemy was. He was dug in on one slope of the hill, the north side; we were dug in on the other slope, the south side; and the top of the hill was up for grabs. As it turned out for months to come, this would be the perpetual situation on Bunker Hill. We didn't really need to send out combat patrols unless we wanted to destroy something. That night was fairly calm. Nothing much happened. All was quiet.

And then came the twenty-fifth. The Chinese all-out attack on Bunker, along with the supporting attack on Stromboli on the night of the thirteenth of August having

Taking on the Burden of History

failed, a Chinese general must have decided that, on the night of the twenty-fifth, his troops were going to retake that hill without fail. It was an interesting night. Because one stretch of the route out to us was constantly under observation, we only resupplied at night. As soon as darkness fell, and it did not get dark until fairly late in August, the Korean Service Corps supply trains began to roll. And the Korean Service Corps guys were really good. By this time, we must have had the support of fifty or sixty Korean volunteers. They would load up with all kinds of supplies—ammunition, water, and food—and there would always be some marines coming along with them. Lieutenant Jannelle was back on the line with his 60 mm mortars, and Sergeant Richardson was with Jannelle. If they got their hands on any goodies, they would try to send some out to us on the supply train. On the evening of the twenty-fifth, a great big supply train arrived with food, ammunition, and an enormous amount of mail. We had not received any mail in a long time. I remember this particular occasion so well because at that time, I was corresponding with three different young ladies back in America. One was a young woman, Peggy, to whom I had been engaged at one time before I married Shirley. Peggy and I had begun writing to each other again by the time I went to Korea. I was still corresponding with Lorraine, my friend from Los Angeles. In addition, Archer had introduced me to a young woman, whom I had seen a few times in Richmond in the last couple of months before going out to the West Coast. As has already been reported, I later married Peggy, who bore me two wonderful children and who, too, died too young. That one night, I received letters from all three of these women, in addition to a couple of letters from my parents, and I found this bonanza of mail really exciting. I remember, though, having an eerie thought that there might be some sort of significance to this windfall, and that this might be the last mail I would ever be reading in Korea.

I might as well tell the story now. For the six months I was with Fox Company, we had fifty-six men killed. When I inventoried their personal effects, I found that in surprisingly many of the cases, one of the killed marine's buddies—or somebody in his unit or somebody who shared the foxhole with him—would tell us that the same day, perhaps only hours before his death, the marine had mentioned to one of these friends that he knew his number was up. I am a skeptic about premonitions, and I don't really believe that anyone knows when his or her number is up. All the same, whenever the thought of my number being up came to my mind, I would immediately suppress and submerge it and shove it away into as deep and murky a recess as I could find in my memory. At the time, I never, ever, talked about this, but a number of the guys who had died apparently had voiced their feelings of impending death to someone close to them, and that person later remembered what their buddy had said. I have discussed this phenomenon with other skeptics since the war, and it was rightly pointed out to me that I should keep in mind the probably much greater number of men who had voiced some premonition of their impending death but who, in fact, remained very much alive and thus did not get computed into the data.

The evening continued to be fairly quiet although Haebel's platoon, which had set up patrols closer to the forward slope, came back to report that there seemed to

Presuming to be a United States Marine

be an awful lot of activity at the bottom of their side in the Chinese area. The time was about one o'clock in the morning. Griff and I and Glen Allen, the artillery FO, were all seated comfortably in our command post. We had our maps out and all of our communications equipment ready to go. Griff and I each had a runner who, if we wanted to move, could also carry a radio. Suddenly, all hell broke loose. There came pounding Chinese artillery, which turned into one of the heaviest artillery barrages ever fired by the Chinese during the war. We were getting incoming rounds at a rate of something like three or four thousand an hour right on our positions on Bunker Hill. In the distance, we heard a bugle. And then they came.

In the daylight, a day earlier, I had tried to climb up a few paces to the top of the hill above our CP to look down the forward or at the northern slope. As soon as I reached the crest, some damn Chinese sniper with an automatic weapon saw me and did not miss me by much. I pulled back quickly. Now Haebel climbed up to the top of the hill in the darkness and reported back, "My god! There's a sea of human beings charging up the hill." Haebel was a good man. He told his troops not to fire until they clearly saw the enemy. I could hear him giving instructions on our sound power network, which, of course, got wiped out so quickly that we had to rely exclusively on the radio. Most of the Chinese charging up the hill were equipped with what we used to call burp guns, which were a little smaller than the Thompson automatic submachine gun, or the Tommy gun. They all fired at once as they rushed along, and you could have cut the curtain of bullets with a knife. The muzzle on an automatic weapon as it is fires tends to rise particularly if the gunman is excited. I am sure the Chinese were excited, so none of the bullets were hitting anywhere near any of our people. Instead, all the bullets from these burp guns sailed up in the air, way over us, and we could hear them like a steady stream of locusts—*tchuk-tchuk-tchuk*—flying over our heads. Haebel's platoon returned fire, and Glen Allen, who had registered a lot of artillery concentrations the day before, now called them in on that forward slope location. The first Chinese attack was clobbered. Unfortunately, farther to our right, Lieutenant Kimbrough was not faring so well.

When all hell had first broken loose, I had called all three of our platoons on the radio. I got Lieutenant Haebel and Lieutenant Burhans right away. Finally I got through to Sergeant Wally Cunningham in the first platoon, and he was reporting to me on the ferocity of the Chinese attack when he was badly hit by a mortar round. His arm and right side were so badly mangled that he was discharged from the Marine Corps on disability. In subsequent years, I have had a chance to reminisce with both Sergeant Cunningham and Sergeant Chain, and they have both concluded that talking with Lieutenant Van Sant on the radio in combat was a very dangerous thing, since both were very badly wounded while doing so. The fact is, the first platoon was almost completely overrun. The Chinese had swept over all their positions, and the next morning, there were only five people from this platoon left. The others were either wounded-evacuated or killed. The Chinese also hit our second and third platoons hard.

Taking on the Burden of History

Once again, as we have seen, my old platoon, the second platoon, did a great job. I like to think that the wonderful time we'd experienced at the Widgeon Bridge had built a lot of esprit in the unit among those who were left.

Finally, I had sent my runner, PFC Kolka, to find out from Lieutenant Kimbrough in the first platoon what he needed. Kolka, a brave and dedicated marine, went out and returned about thirty minutes later. I was squatting down outside our bunker, out in the open. Kolka squatted down facing me and reported, "Sir, there's nothing but Chinese out there. The lieutenant, I think, is sealed up in his bunker." He said that he had helped a couple of wounded marines back and that things did not look good. While he was making this report to me, a large Chinese mortar shell landed right behind him. It did not kill him, but he took a lot of fragments in the back, particularly to the back of his arm and hand. As I was saying good-bye to Kolka being carried off on a stretcher, I thought that if he had not been squatting in front of me, I would have taken those fragments in my face and chest. And I have always felt a little guilty that it had been Kolka, who shielded me, and not I who was wounded from that shell. By this time, after the enormous first barrage, we were taking heavy casualties. As I have already said, Master Sergeant Smith, my former assistant platoon leader, had been promoted to company gunnery sergeant, which meant that he was the number two enlisted man in the company. Only First Sergeant Alsop was senior to him. Master Sergeant Smith was back with us by our command post, and he did a wonderful job that night. On this night, in Fox Company, we had 18 killed and 112 badly wounded marines. Smith throughout that night organized all the stretcher bearers and the corpsmen, of whom a couple were badly hit. Corpsman Dick Payne, who had worked on the tie-in position with the Fifth Marines and had starred in the excrement pit confrontation, had his jaw almost shot away. As we were being shelled incessantly, Smith presided over the abattoir, which was the only way to describe it, with enormous courage. After we got Kolka evacuated, I crawled back to the bunker to tell Griff what I had found out about the first platoon. He had been talking to the lieutenant over the telephone, and they had reached the same conclusion. The Chinese, in fact, were holding the horseshoe now, and the lieutenant, sealed up in his bunker, was totally out of touch with any of his men or the situation, but he hung on in his bunker until the battle was over.

Lieutenant Murphy, who had just reported in to us after the Stromboli battle of the thirteenth, was our machine gun officer. The machine gun officer of a rifle company, when it is in combat, really does not have much to do. He has three sections of machine guns, but each section is assigned out to a rifle platoon, so that at this point, he loses his entire command because once the sections are assigned to a rifle platoon, the rifle platoon commander becomes their boss. At that point, Murphy, who I think was a Boston Irishman, was just a spare lieutenant. He had learned about our situation on the right flank and came crawling into our bunker to help out. Griff had him take a squad from our relatively unengaged third platoon under Burhans, sitting at that moment on the left flank of the company, to try to rescue the sealed-up lieutenant.

Presuming to be a United States Marine

Murphy took off. We had many more than the standard allotment of six machine guns, because the companies that had been there before us had piled in as many machine guns as they could get their hands on. The first day at Bunker Hill, we had taken count and found that we had seventeen machine guns. By about three o'clock in the morning of August 26, I think that only two of our machine guns were still undamaged and functioning. Murphy found another working gun that had a badly damaged tripod. Damned if Murphy did not pick up that light machine gun, which still weighed about forty pounds with the ammunition, and carry it along with him. Murphy, of course, was familiar with machine guns, and he knew that the barrel and air-cooled jacket would get hot from firing. So he removed an empty ammunition belt from another gun and wrapped it around the barrel of his gun so that it would not burn his hand. Thus armed, Murphy stomped out with his handheld machine gun like some sort of Rambo to hose down the Chinese and drive them off. And to his everlasting credit, his operation was successful. I was sorry that I did not get to know him better because he was surely an unusually brave man. Unfortunately, Murphy was pretty badly wounded by a shell, which peeled off a flap of his skin on one side so that it hung over his cartridge belt in a grisly manner. He had to be evacuated to the hospital. Murphy received the Silver Star for helping to reestablish our positions.

The engagement of our First Marine Division artillery and mortars and the army's artillery were the biggest event in Korea that night, and we received a lot of support as we clobbered the enemy. In fact, the aerial observers in their little Piper Cubs noted that the Chinese did not finish evacuating their casualties until three o'clock the next afternoon. It had been a titanic struggle, but we had managed to hold on.

Portions of that night are a jumble in my memory. A Chinese soldier on our right flank got back behind the second platoon and almost reached our company CP before somebody shot him; and the chaos, the noise, the odors, and the smoke of war were again very much in evidence. The night of the twenty-fifth and twenty-sixth of August came to be known, among us First Marine Regiment members, as the second big battle of Bunker Hill, the first one having taken place on the thirteenth of August. Easy Company, or E Company, was to fight the third big battle in early September.

As I look back through my memories of that night, a number of other things stand out. One of them is a memory of Lieutenant Bob Haebel, whom I overheard on the radio talking to one of his men. This marine's closest pal had been killed, and he wanted to make sure that the body would be evacuated. Having a dead buddy so close is always difficult. Unfortunately, it was at the height of one of the Chinese charges, and Haebel was gently trying to calm down the man and get him to join the firefight with the promise that he personally would see to it that the body of his friend was evacuated. The carnage of that night is almost inconceivable. Our entire company position was approximately the size of two football fields laid end to end. Some staff man in the division OP on top of 201 behind us had been charged with counting the incoming rounds that landed on our positions on Bunker Hill. He reported that at least ten thousand rounds had been fired by the Chinese on those two football fields. We probably fired twice as many rounds back at them. Looking at the hill in subsequent days, I became more and more struck by the miracle that any of us survived. There was not a blade of vegetation left on the surface of the hill by the end of the battle. Although a lot of the greenery had been blown off in previous shellings, there had been some left when we had come out two days before. Now there was none. The hill had turned into a stark and forbidding moonscape.

Another memory is the smell. In previous combats, I had always noticed the gunpowder and cordite smell, immediately recognizable in any battle. But on Bunker Hill that night, we also smelled blood. So much of it had been spilled that it had soaked the ground, and its scent hung heavily over the hill with its sweet, oppressive odor. The smell of human blood is so pronounced that it pierces the soul with the awareness of the sacrifice of the buddies who had recently stood so close.

A final memory is the result of some conversations I have had almost fifty years after the battle with some of the troops who shared the experience with me. The battalion 81 mm mortar forward observer, Sergeant Chuck Lundeen, whom we have already met, had been set up right beside our CP bunker. With his usual competence and efficiency, he had come in several times during the night to report to us and to get his instructions. He has told me recently that as the noise, confusion, and bloodshed were rising during the night, a number of the troops were beginning to wonder if we would be able to hold on. But then, he said, he saw Captain Moody and me come out to check on some things, and we seemed so calm and businesslike that they all took heart. I must confess that there were times during that night, especially when our first platoon was overrun, when I wondered if any of us would make it through.

In the approaching light of the dawn, we found ourselves with one machine gun. Counting the people from the other company who had come in, we had about eighty effective people left. Lieutenant Kimbrough returned to the CP, and he and Griff conferred privately for a while. He appeared to be close to a nervous breakdown but wanted to carry on. Finally he and Griff agreed that he should be evacuated. It had been an unspeakably horrible experience for him. With the help of Lieutenants Haebel and Murphy, we had prevailed, and Lieutenant Glen Allen, our artillery forward observer had persevered and earned our undying appreciation for his skilful work that night. He had been our observer the night of Stromboli too, and he had called in the Korean Marine Corps artillery. But poor Lieutenant Allen became obsessed with the idea of being an aerial forward observer, riding as a passenger in a Piper Cub and calling in artillery fire. He got himself transferred to this duty in the fall of 1952, and after a number of successful missions, his plane was shot down. No parachutes were observed to bail out from the plane, and he was listed as missing in action. His name is now inscribed on the wall in the Punch Bowl in Honolulu as "Missing, presumed dead."

Presuming to be a United States Marine

During the battle of Bunker Hill, Chinese artillery or mortar shells scored direct hits on top of our hastily built bunker twice. In both cases, sandbags were blown away, causing sand and dirt to filter through the logs on top of us. I remember that in the light of our Coleman lantern, we looked up from our maps at each other with some relief that our bunker was holding up. Outside our bunker, Sergeant Smith was organizing people and doing a hell of a job before he was hit in the back. Our wire communication back to battalion had been knocked out during the night, but we got it back in by morning. Major McDonnell, the battalion operations officer, called us up and spoke to me. He asked, "How are you all doing?"

And I said something like, "Well, sir, we have been pretty beat up." I remember that Griff, whose imperturbability and calmness, thank God, had returned, grabbed my arm abruptly and said, "Fox Company is NEVER beat up!" This was a second instance of "if looks could kill . . . ," and I thought it likely then that Griff, momentarily, may have considered choking me by the throat. In some sense, this was a relief as I reflected on his return to what was for him normalcy. We had got all 112 of the wounded men taken off the hill and evacuated to the hospitals in the rear before the morning, but the dead were laid out behind our command post. We had pulled them back there and covered them up, making sure their dog tags were out and showing. They did not get evacuated until later in the morning. Under any circumstances, a stack of eighteen dead bodies of men is too many bodies to live with. After talking to us over the telephone and having me assure him that, after all, we were "not at all beat up, sir," Major McDonnell himself turned up on Bunker Hill. He crawled right into the bunker with us, reached into his back pocket, pulled out a flask of brandy, and let each of us take a slug. To my knowledge, in the entire evolution of that war, McDonnell was the only Marine Corps major ever to go out on to Bunker Hill. Bunker Hill was an outpost, and although it was supported by several companies behind it on the main line, it never had more than a company on it. A company is commanded by a captain, so that there were lots of captains on Bunker Hill, but I don't think a major had ever come out to cheer anyone up before except for Major McDonnell, and that was on the morning of the twenty-sixth. Eventually, a still higher-ranking officer would spend some time on Bunker Hill, but that was later. Right after Major McDonnell came out to us, he and Griff had a moment of silence, standing together solemnly and looking at our dead marines. Afterward, the major gave us the welcome news that in the early morning of the twenty-seventh, we were being relieved by G Company. We were obviously so shot up that there was no way we could hold the hill with eighty effective people against another massive attack by the Chinese.

We spent that day trying to catnap as much as possible. I realized that I had not slept much in over eighty hours. It was the only time I ever observed a certain phenomenon in all the troops, and saw it in Griff, and he saw it in me. Being as fatigued and fought-out as we were had a strange effect on our eyes. Our eyelids pulled back above and below the cornea, and the whites of the eye became much

Taking on the Burden of History

more prominent. Everybody's eyes looked white and seemed to be bulging, giving us all an eerie appearance.

At two o'clock in the morning, the first elements of G Company began arriving, while what was left of our troops began pulling off. We had to make our way back up that same precipitous, rocky streambed on the face of the 201 "mountain." As exhausted as we were, it became one of the hardest climbs imaginable for all of us. But we managed to reach the top of the "mountain." Sergeant Richardson was there; and Lieutenant Jannelle and all the mortar men who had supported us on the big hill greeted us solemnly. The rest of the men from company headquarters, First Sergeant Alsop, the company clerk, and the supply clerk were all lined up on the main line trench intersection to welcome us back. I believe Chaplain McCabe was there also.

Sergeant Richardson handed each man, as he went by, a carton of cigarettes with a quiet word of encouragement. Nobody asked him just where he had been able to obtain all those cigarettes. We walked down the reverse slope of the big Hill 201, where for once the trucks were waiting for us. The motor transport people, bless their hearts, had originally sent twenty trucks to take us up to Bunker Hill. Naturally, they sent twenty trucks back to take us off again. Our men, with their hollow-eyed look, filed out, each man clutching his carton of cigarettes. We filled up the first four or five trucks, and the big convoy was ready to move out. Fifteen trucks filled with marines when we had gone up to the line now rumbled back empty. It was one of the most heart-rending scenes I saw in Korea.

We did not go south of the Imjin this time. Instead, we went back to a position for the reserve battalion of the line regiment. We arrived at the camp. It was a nice camp, not too large. Fox Company and a few troops from an assortment of other companies from the First Marines, who had been shuffled in and out of Bunker Hill, were all living at this camp. We were far enough to the rear so that we were allowed a drink, although we had to scrounge for the booze. We had, of course, not been able to spare a lieutenant to send off to Japan to get it. My recollection is that thanks to our two new lieutenants, Haebel and Burhans, who both had good connections back at the division rear, we were well taken care of. As we arrived at the company street, a very nice street with squad tents up and down in two rows, the men climbed off their trucks. Some were clutching pieces of personal gear, which had helped them to survive Bunker Hill, their cartons of cigarettes still held firmly in their grip. Captain Moody had Sergeant Smith, who had been wounded but not evacuated, fall the company out in company formation. Miraculously, we still had the second and third platoon leaders, Haebel and Burhans. But the first platoon had nobody, except for five men. The second platoon had maybe twenty, and the third platoon had maybe twenty-five or thirty men left. The machine gun platoon had sustained terrible casualties on Bunker, and even the mortar section back on 201 had some men wounded. We were a grand total of I would say eighty or eighty-five men. We were lined up as if we were a whole company, only with many clearly conspicuous gaps in it. Sergeant Smith took a report from the senior noncommissioned officer in each platoon, about-faced, and reported the company to the company commander. This would have been a normal morning formation routine. But Sergeant Smith had compiled the statistics for each platoon of so many men killed, so many men wounded and evacuated, and so many men evacuated for other reasons. He read off all this data, and how he did it without breaking down, I'll never know. As the company executive officer, I stood just to the rear of the last person in the second platoon, right in the middle of the company, facing the company commander. And that was a good position for me because it allowed me to weep freely. I stood back, bawling my head off, and Griff ordered, "PRESENT ARMS!" Which means that the officers hand-salute, and the troopers all present arms with their rifles. We had an eternal terrible two minutes of silence for the men who had left the gaps in our formation.

I stood behind my decimated old platoon, the second, and grieved for all the men I had taken up online just a month before who were no longer with us. Griff, Jannelle, and I were the only remaining officers. It was a deeply solemn moment. We were dismissed, and by this time, it must have been about ten o'clock in the morning. Word came that we were to fall out for a hot lunch in the mess tent. Griff and I went up to the battalion command post, which had moved back there also. Our battalion was now almost completely off-line. At battalion headquarters, we were told by Colonel Batterton that we would remain at the camp for about ten days and that more replacements would be sent up to flesh out our depleted ranks. He said that while there, we would engage in some training, but for the first day, we were just to eat and sleep, and if we were able to have a drink, that would be fine with him. We took him at his word. At this point, we were joined by a new lieutenant, Lieutenant Hill, who came to take over Lieutenant Kimbrough's job. He was another volunteer lieutenant from motor transport, a trucking officer. Lieutenant Hill very much liked motor transport, and we detected that he was not entirely happy about being given a rifle platoon.

There was no big battalion affair for us; instead, each platoon had their own party, and we Fox Company officers all assembled in our squad tent. I remember that we had a wonderful time playing a great variety of gambling games. We played poker for a while, but then decided that this did not offer enough fast action and switched to blackjack. None of us had much of any real money, and we were all drinking pretty heavily. We ended up by playing for matches, with each match worth a dollar. I had one of the worst nights of gambling I had ever had, and although I was probably among the most sober men in the group, if not the most sober, I was just dealt terrible cards. Griff, on the other hand, was lucky as hell. It must have been about three in the morning when we finally collapsed. We totaled up everybody's winnings and losses with these matches, and I had enough "money" to pay off most of my losses, except that I still owed Griff $150. This was mortifying, because I simply did not have it. After he was rotated home, I sent a letter to my father, who handled all my money, instructing him to make out a check and send it to Captain Clarence Griffith Moody in payment of an honorable debt.

Taking on the Burden of History

We were a very congenial group. Haebel and Burhans were fine men; the new lieutenant, Lieutenant Hill was good; and Tom Jannelle was an old salt with the company by now. We were missing a machine gun officer because Lieutenant Murphy's heroism had dispatched him directly to the hospital.

You will remember Chaplain McCabe, who had been involved in the entire operation at Bunker Hill. He had come back with us to produce another Chaplain McCabe story. That first party night, the chaplain had been partying somewhere with another group. The next morning, when what was left of our company walked on a dike past a rice paddy to the mess tent for a hot breakfast, somebody happened to look down. There, lying in one of the rows in the paddy was our good Chaplain McCabe, peacefully snoring away. En route to his tent, he must have somehow wobbled off the dike, landing right in the paddy. The company filed past him while he continued snoozing like a baby. It was clear to us that this courageous man of God, too, had felt the need to unwind after the Bunker Hill battle and just never found his way back to his tent. And nobody ever criticized him for it either.

We immediately began getting replacement troops, whom we welcomed and billeted right away. Naturally, we first tried to get them oriented to what a wonderful company Fox Company was with its unusual spirit, and so we all began training together. The training was designed by our brandy-bearing Major McDonnell, who visited us the morning after Bunker Hill. He was a man who had spent a lot of time in reconnaissance companies. He had been taught many specialties, like night-vision techniques (we had no night-vision technology then, of course) and hand-to-hand combat. As a matter of fact, he left our battalion six weeks later and became the commanding officer of the division reconnaissance company. McDonnell was a scholarly man. He devised an excellent training program, and to this day, I practice techniques I learned from him to improve my vision at night. He and the staff of the operations and training office found a section of terrain near our camp where we were required to spot certain things at night. He personally showed us how to do it effectively, and we were tested to determine that we were doing what we were supposed to do. Everybody, both the troops and the lieutenants, profited from this exercise. The technique was not to look straight at any object. It takes the eye about two minutes to adapt to darkness, but it will adapt, and the pupil will open wide and take in much more light than if the surroundings were illuminated. We were taught to close our eyes whenever we encountered any light source so that we could keep our so-called night vision. It was an interesting exercise.

We also reviewed some techniques in patrolling and scouting and had a generally useful ten days at the camp, snapping in the new people, getting them adjusted, and filling out our ranks. Every night the regimental reserve camp had to send up a platoon, called the clutch platoon, which took up a position on 201 behind Bunker Hill and was maintained in readiness. If the Chinese attacked the hill, the platoon was to report immediately to the person in charge in order to reinforce the men on the hill, and to replace the casualties that inevitably would be sustained in such a battle.

Presuming to be a United States Marine

You will remember that a platoon from H Company came out and joined us in our own battle of Bunker Hill. But the Chinese gave G Company, who had relieved us, a break. They had some patrolling activity and a few shellings, but nothing very serious until the night of the fifth of September.

One night before that, around the first of September, Fox Company was assigned to provide the clutch platoon. Griff decided that since every other officer in Fox Company had already been through Bunker, Lieutenant Hill should take the clutch platoon up into the reserve position behind Bunker. We constructed a kind of composite platoon because almost all of Lieutenant Hill's first platoon had been shot up on Bunker. But Hill took the surviving five experienced Marines from his old platoon, as well as a smattering of people from the other two platoons, to make up a new composite platoon. Hill was to leave right after dinner at about seven o'clock in the evening. When we returned from our meal, Hill was getting his combat gear on and buckling on his pistol, while one of the sergeants fell out the platoon in the company street. Hill reached under his bunk, pulled out a bottle of whisky, and took an enormous draft from the bottle. The possible effect of the alcohol on him worried me because Hill was a short slender man with not much bulk on him. He took off and spent the night behind Bunker Hill with this composite platoon. He returned without having been called upon that night, so that he gained some experience without any of the adventures some of the others of us had lived through up there. In a few short weeks, Hill turned into a good, solid officer. On his first night, we could plainly see that he was scared to death. Little did he know that the rest of us were also scared to death. We were scared all the time. I, having been in combat for four months, knew my fears had become overlaid with numbness. I was frightened all the time, but I got used to being frightened all the time, and I simply accommodated fear into my life.

Training was finally completed, and although we were not back to full strength yet, we were now close to 180 men. We were short one officer, but we were ready to go. Battalion and regiment had decided that we would go back to the company front on 201 behind Bunker Hill, and that Bunker Hill would become a platoon-sized outpost to be manned by our company. Interestingly enough, the third big battle on Bunker Hill took place while we were in the rear camp on the night of September 5 and 6. Easy, or E Company, had relieved G Company and had the whole company deployed on the hill, when the Chinese hit them probably as hard as they had hit us. We could hear the incessant shelling from where we were. Easy Company had a rather startling experience in all this. The entire company, including the company command post, was overrun. The Chinese penetrated everywhere on the hill, even into the command post positions.

E Company's executive officer was my good friend Vernon Vick, who had reported in along with me. As you may remember, he had been allowed to select Easy Company in order to "get to know" his platoon. Vick's career had almost mirrored mine. He'd had a platoon for three or four months, and then became the company executive officer. The company commander, who shall remain nameless, and Lieutenant Vick were in their company command post on Bunker Hill together during that last big battle. The world was coming to an end, and the Chinese were swarming everywhere. The company commander turned to Vick and said, "My god! What are we going to do? Maybe we should surrender!" And I may be the only person to whom Vick ever confided this story, because the two of them were alone in the bunker and nobody else had heard these words. Vick did not hesitate. He simply knocked the company commander out cold. Vick climbed out of the bunker, rounded up some marines, and chased the Chinese off, taking some prisoners in the process. E Company's job on this defense was outstanding, but Vick found himself in a peculiar position. He certainly could never tell anybody what had happened. E Company's commander got a decoration for bravery, but then no one knew that he had been unconscious the entire time the Chinese were being repulsed under Vick's leadership. Vick ended up by getting a Bronze Star for something he did as an executive officer but could, of course, never be written up for bravery as the temporary company commander. He certainly could not come clean about his assault on a superior officer. Thank the Lord for marines like Vernon Vick, the tough and quick-thinking Texas marine. After E Company took prisoners and chased off the Chinese, everything came up smelling of roses. A corpsman with E Company was awarded the Medal of Honor for sacrificing his life by killing two Chinese who threatened three wounded marines he was treating. And all that happened on the fifth of September. After the battles on August 13 and 25 and this battle, marines never again fought a battle of that magnitude on Bunker Hill, although we continued to man it as an outpost for the rest of the war. Even though the Chinese gave up their large attacks on Bunker Hill, they continued to dig in and try to move forward toward the marine positions. The First Regiment had been so shot up from the Bunker Hill activity that the powers that be decided to maintain a platoon-sized outpost on the right-hand horseshoe, the portion of Bunker Hill most vulnerable and closest to the enemy. And guess what company was assigned to provide this outpost as well as man 201 behind the bunker? Why, of course, Fighting Fox Company, Finest of the First! After ten wonderful days in regimental reserve, on September 6, Fox Company was ordered to establish the platoon-sized outpost on Bunker and also man the main line of resistance on Hill 201.

In addition, we were told that within a week or two, we should initiate another outpost on a hill higher than Bunker, located in the front of our company position on Hill 201. That meant that we would now have two outposts, as well as the main line to defend, although regiment readjusted the company frontages to give us a shorter company front. The company to our left took up about nine hundred yards extending across the front slope of a huge hill called 229. Hill 229 was somewhat to the rear, and before it stretched a big fairly level plain all the way to Panmunjom. It was clear that the Chinese were not going to be able to attack 229. We now had a platoon on Bunker Hill, about a platoon and a half on the main line, and about one-half of a platoon was to be established on the left outpost.

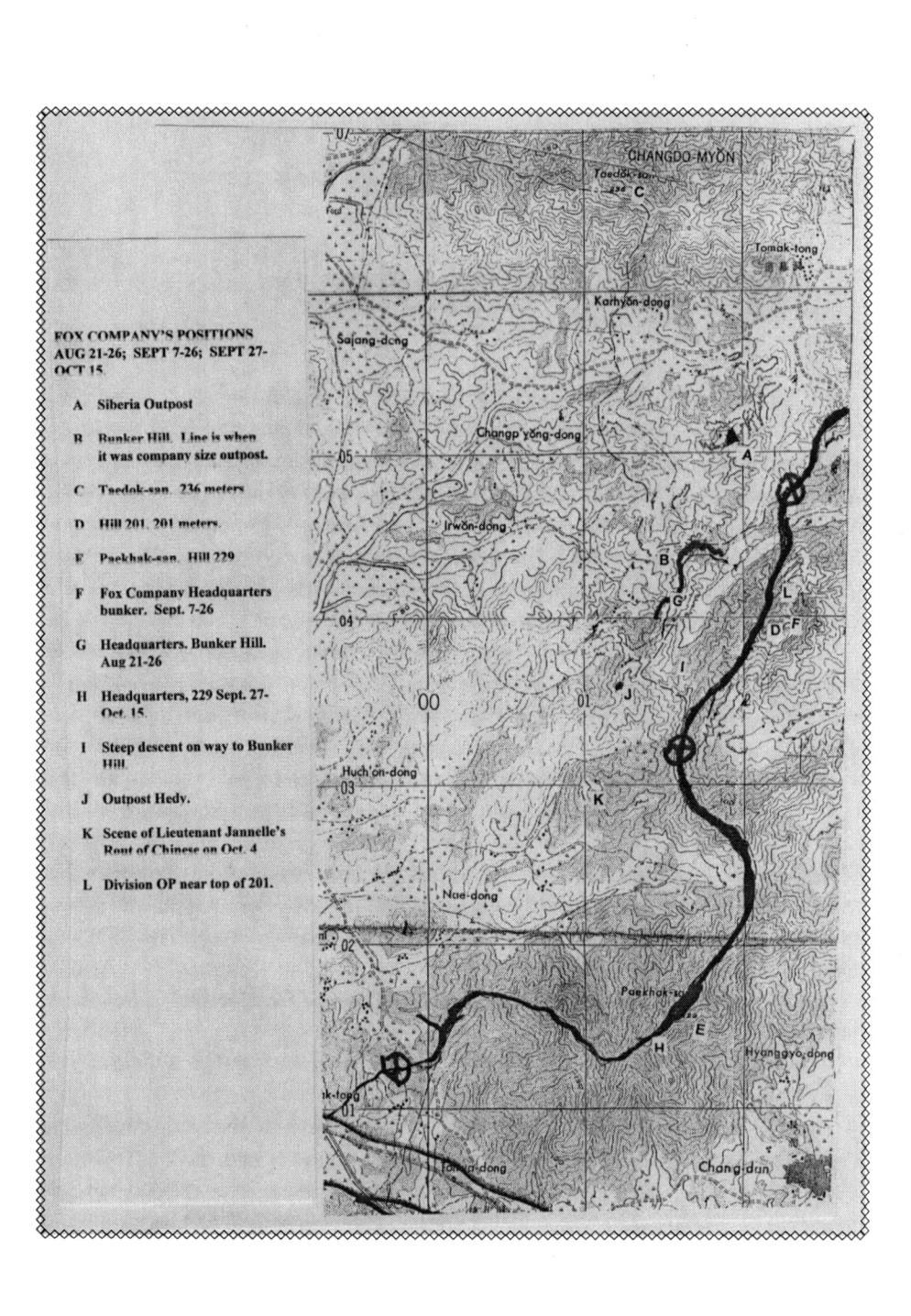

**FOX COMPANY'S POSITIONS
AUG 21-26; SEPT 7-26; SEPT 27-
OCT 15**

A Siberia Outpost

B Bunker Hill. Line is when it was company size outpost.

C Taedok-san, 236 meters

D Hill 201, 201 meters.

E Paekhak-san, Hill 229

F Fox Company Headquarters bunker. Sept. 7-26

G Headquarters. Bunker Hill. Aug 21-26

H Headquarters, 229 Sept. 27-Oct. 15.

I Steep descent on way to Bunker Hill.

J Outpost Hedy.

K Scene of Lieutenant Jannelle's Rout of Chinese on Oct. 4

L Division OP near top of 201.

Chapter 14

BUNKER HILL II

We had received orders to move the company up on the seventh of September. Because Hill 201 was so massive, and because it held the division observation post, the company command post bunker on 201 was more magnificent than any I had ever lived in. Griff and I moved in, got our troops all deployed, and got the Bunker Hill outpost established. At the beginning, Haebel ran the horseshoe with his second platoon, and did a good job. Of course, the Chinese continued to probe; there were lots of small actions resulting in two or three marines wounded per night. Haebel was out there for about a week. After that time, Burhans took over with the third platoon.

In the meantime, an absolutely cataclysmic event took place. We got back online on the seventh of September, and after settling in, Griff and I started to plan how to establish the new outpost. I made the first of several one-man patrols into the boondocks of the area to scout the position for the new outpost. It was first named Yellow and later came to be known as Hedy. Looking back, I see that going out by myself into this largely unexplored area was a pretty dumb thing to do. The terrain was surrounded by the Chinese.

On our second day back, there was a message from battalion headquarters that Griff was to report to regimental headquarters immediately. Wondering why he was being summoned, Griff took off in the company jeep. About an hour and a half later, the telephone rang, and it was Griff.

He said, "Van, you are now the commanding officer of Fox Company. I have been relieved of command."

Stunned and deeply disturbed, I said, "What? What in the hell? What are you talking about?"

You will remember that right after the battle of Stromboli, the troops had come to me as the executive officer, insisting that Captain Moody's valor had to be written up. A citation and many letters were written, with statements by these troops, by Gunnery Sergeant John Francis Kelly, and by me, about what Griff had accomplished that night. We had put him up for the Navy Cross and forwarded the papers on to Colonel Batterton. Batterton, who also thought the world of Griff, passed the citation on with a very strong endorsement. On about the eighth of September, the Navy Cross recommendation arrived on the desk of the First Marine regimental commander, Colonel Layer. There was, of course, the standing division order that company commanders were not ever to go forward of the MLR. Obviously, exceptions to that order were already being made when company commanders took their companies out to Bunker Hill, but under normal circumstances, the order stood. Colonel Layer fully approved the Navy Cross. He took the position, however, that he had no choice but to relieve Captain Moody of command for disobeying a division order expressly prohibiting company commanders to go forward of the main line of resistance. And now you know why my opinion of Layer is slanted. A ton of bricks seemed to drop on me, not only for the loss of the much-respected and much-loved Moody, but for my sudden emergence as company commander behind Bunker Hill. It was a tremendous responsibility. Batterton, who was pretty unhappy about Moody, had to accept the order from his CO, Colonel Layer. He called me and said, "I have complete confidence in you, Van. No problem, no problem." But he added, "Division is sending another captain up here to take over the company from you. He will probably arrive tomorrow or the next day, but the company is yours to keep for now."

And so I was given the exciting experience of commanding a company as a second lieutenant behind Bunker Hill. It is hard to describe what an awesome feeling of responsibility that was. I realized that for months, I had been privileged to serve, and I think most people who knew him would agree with me, under an all-time great marine, in whom everybody had complete confidence. I wondered how the troops were going to be affected when they found out that their solid father figure, Captain Moody, was gone. But there was nothing to do except to dig in and fall to.

One very amusing experience happened during my time as a company commander. From May 5, 1952, when I arrived in Korea until I took over the company, I had not laid eyes on a female of any nationality. Indeed, I had almost forgotten what a woman looked like. Lieutenant Haebel had just had a pretty strong probe by the Chinese. Lieutenant Burhans was patrolling in the area where we were going to establish the new outpost. Colonel Batterton had told me, "Look, don't do the outpost until you have your new company commander and until you yourself have looked it over. Then we will establish it." Our patrol had run into some Chinese. That night I found myself with two different battles in two different parts of the company front. Needless to say, I was kept up all night calling in supporting fires and getting casualties evacuated. It was around seven in the morning when I was finally able to go to sleep after that very rough night.

As I was snoring away in our palace of a command post, the famous woman war correspondent and photographer Marguerite Higgins suddenly arrived. By that time in the Korean War, nothing got into the news much, but the Bunker Hill battles had made *Time* magazine. When I read the article later, it described Walt Layer's boys on Bunker Hill. Marguerite Higgins talked her superiors into letting her come on an assignment, I think, for *Life* magazine. Once she was in Korea, she persuaded the division commander into letting her go up to the lines and had wangled permission to proceed all the way up to our division observation post on 201. She had been given a colonel as her escort, and these two arrived at our company command post in a First Division jeep. Not that I knew any of this was happening, mind you, because I was sound asleep inside my sleeping bag on my sandbag bunk. The colonel came up to the CP, and good old Sergeant Smith, with First Sergeant Alsop, met him. The colonel wished to speak to the company commander.

Sergeant Smith told him, "Well, sir, yes, you may see him, I'll let you look at him, but he had a rough night last night, sir!"

In fact, Sergeant Smith flatly refused to wake me up. So the colonel from division brought Marguerite Higgins inside so that she would be able to see what the inside of a front line command post looked like. She looked around, and Smith told me later that she came up to me as I lay there all wrapped up in my sleeping bag, gazed down on me tenderly, and commented, "He does look a little tired, doesn't he? The poor boy."

What a shame! A woman had stood in the closest, even vaguely intimate, proximity to me, and yet I never even saw her. I slumbered soundly through her visit and never heard a thing. Smith and Alsop had a big time telling me the story later, laughing. Escorted by Sergeant Smith, the colonel and Marguerite Higgins now took off from our post to the division observation post. They would have to climb on a trail up to a switchback on the top of Hill 201, cut back around a hairpin turn in the trail up the hill, and enter a long sandbag tunnel to reach the OP. Many months prior to Marguerite Higgins's visit, a one-holer head (or john) had been dug right at the hairpin and most visible point of the switchback trail, just at the rise of the trail. It was a deep pit, with sandbags all around it, and on top of all that sat a wooden seat suitable for going to the bathroom. As Marguerite Higgins was climbing up the trail with her escort party, they suddenly beheld one of our more colorful sergeants squatting on the throne, dreamily gazing into the distance, with his trousers around his ankles, spread-eagled on the seat so that he faced down the trail. Suddenly he snapped out of his daydream and beheld the last sight he had ever expected to see—a woman. He yelled out in panic. But there she was, unmistakably looking right up at him. The poor sergeant was so shocked that he just jumped up and took off, with his trousers still around his ankles. He stopped for a brief moment to pull them up and disappeared with lightning speed over a nearby hillock. The escort colonel mumbled an apology to Marguerite, but it probably was not the first time she had come upon such a scene in her colorful life.

I received a call from battalion to advise me that Captain Tom Barrow was on his way up to take over Fox Company from me. I awaited his arrival with much anticipation and a little bit of dread. Tom Barrow turned out to be a completely different man from Griff, but I must say that he turned out to be a very fine man, and I will try to explain why. Captain Barrow was a called-back reserve. He'd had extensive experience in World War II, mostly as an enlisted man. He had received a battlefield commission near the end of the war for the work he had done during World War II as a combat photographer. He became a lieutenant in combat photography and subsequently received his promotions to captain, but his training in infantry had all been in a reserve company in one of the

Presuming to be a United States Marine

New England states between World War II and Korea. He had never been an infantry officer in combat. Tom Barrow was a down-to-earth, salt-of-the-earth guy. His feet were firmly planted on the ground, and while he was not a brilliant warrior like Griff Moody, he turned out to be a gutsy guy. He was older than Griff, and quite sensitive. I don't know what kind of briefing Colonel Batterton had given him back in battalion headquarters, but Barrow told me, "You understand, Van, that you are well thought of. And I am not very experienced at all this. I have seen a lot of combat, but it was behind a camera. Keep on running the company for now, and what I am going to do is to go out and meet with all the men, the noncommissioned officers, and the officers. At the same time, I will also familiarize myself with the terrain." He had just arrived in Korea a few days before, and he added, "I will familiarize myself with everything, and I am going to ask you a lot of questions. And when I feel that I have a firm grasp of the whole situation, I will tell you that Fox Company is now mine."

I can't say enough about how reassuring that was for me to hear. Marines sometimes get so imbued with the Marine Corps spirit that they feel they can do anything, that they can immediately take over and do any job better than anyone else. But that was not Barrow's way. We spent a lot of time together. I briefed him on everything I knew about every man still left in the company from the original troopers. We climbed all over the place to learn the terrain. The first thing he brought up was the establishment of the outpost, which Colonel Batterton had discussed with him, and this time I took a couple of people with me and went out to make another thorough reconnaissance. We decided to situate our outpost about 250-300 yards in front of our main trench line on the peak of a hill connected back to the main line by two big saddles. We christened it Outpost Hedy (after the glamorous movie star Hedy Lamarr). It was a fairly easy place to reinforce. The front slope of this hill fell in an almost sheer precipice down into a valley, and one of the reasons why it made such a good outpost was that it would have been very hard for the Chinese to assault it up that cliff-like hill.

I later followed the progress of that outpost, which I had established, with some interest. It is discussed in great detail in *The Last Parallel*, a book written by Martin Russ, who served in the First Marines and had come to Korea in December long after my time on Hedy. There was not much space on the peak of the hill, so that we could not put many men into the outpost at any given time, but the observation was excellent. From Hedy, we could see parts of the reverse slope of Bunker held by the Chinese, and we were sometimes able to call in fire on them. Hedy looked out on the valley toward some other Chinese outposts, and at night, we could see the Panmunjom searchlights off in the distance. Once we had dug in, the Chinese immediately started zapping us with artillery and mortar fire, and eventually, as we will see, they even tried to probe it a few times, although never successfully.

Three nights after we established Hedy, and about four or five nights after Captain Barrow had reported in, battalion operations office called, and Major McDonnell said, "You ought to send a very small patrol of two or three guys down to the front slope of Hedy and see how close to it the Chinese have dug." So we sent a patrol out, and the patrol got down to the bottom of the hill in front of Hedy when, by God! The Chinese hit them. One of the guys was wounded, and the other two got up but could not carry the wounded man because of the steep hill. The Chinese, apparently, had also broken off and disengaged. They were not dug in; they were just sneaking around themselves.

Captain Barrow was following all this on the radio, and Barrow says, "You mean we have a marine out there, wounded, and we can't get him back?" And he told me, "Remember now, you still have the company." And damn if he did not walk out the door. He went out to Hedy and climbed down the slope, reached the wounded Marine, and carried him back up that cliff. And I never had any occasion to question his courage after that, nor did the troops. A couple of them came back to me and said, "Captain Barrow ought to really get something for his action." I agreed and wrote him up for a Silver Star, which got bumped back to a Bronze Star. But I had become smart enough to write him up in such a way as not to reveal that Barrow had been forward of the main line of resistance, and that was quite a feat since, by the time he picked up the wounded man, he was about four hundred yards forward of it. His brave action made an enormous impression on me, as well as on all the men.

About a day or so after that, Barrow concluded that he had familiarized himself with every aspect of the outposts and the company sector, and he said, "Okay, Van, I am going to take over the company now. You have just become the executive officer again." We formed a very strong friendship in Korea, which, I am sorry to say, we did not pursue once we returned to the States. But Barrow was a good man, a good marine. Since Griff had been relieved on Sept. 8, all this must have taken place about September 15.

Soon after I returned to the position of exec, I got a strange call from Regimental Operations. They informed me that a rear admiral of the USN Medical Corps would be reporting in to our command post. The admiral—was the commander of the whole structure of Navy Hospital Corpsmen. He was intensely interested in the process of how the wounded were treated and evacuated. Regiment informed me that I was to arrange for the admiral to go out to the Bunker Hill outpost as soon as it was dark, escorted by two of my best men. Regiment made the rather macabre observation that Fox Company, of all the companies in the division, was the most likely to have a casualty that night.

Early that evening, the admiral arrived. He was most genial and gung-ho. He told me he wanted to be in a place where it was likely that someone would be hit, and he wanted to observe how the wounded were treated, how they were evacuated, and how they were handled by the collecting and clearing company (the Navy/Marine Corps equivalent of the Army's MASH). In fact, if possible, he was going to stay with the wounded man clear back to the hospital ship or the hospital in Japan. I was awestruck by his eagerness as well as his naiveté. By this time, I was beginning to experience some emotional numbness. I was a little callous and probably a little cynical. Also, I felt responsible for the safety of this fellow who voluntarily wanted to go out to Bunker

Presuming to be a United States Marine

Hill. The thought occurred to me that there was no guarantee he might not turn out to be a casualty himself. My face must have betrayed that I thought he was nuts, because he assured me rather sternly that he was serious about his request. I arranged for him to go out with the first Korean Service Corps supply train to Lieutenant Haebel's position on Bunker. Having warned Haebel, I asked him to fully inform his troops about their visitor's purpose. Needless to say, the Fox Company grapevine was in fine shape, and by the time the admiral arrived on Bunker Hill, every man in the company knew about it. The good admiral climbed down the rocky streambed on the face of 201 and went out to Bunker Hill to observe a casualty. Haebel told me later that he settled in to Haebel's tiny command hole to wait for the blood to flow. He waited and waited and waited, but on that night, Haebel had no casualties. Our company had at least one man wounded every night from September 7 until September 28, the three weeks we occupied this outpost position, except for the night the admiral came. He returned with the last supply train, pretty disgruntled and muttering that the severity of our situation was overrated. Alas, the troops were distraught. They wanted him to stay with them every night as a good-luck charm.

Sometime around September 19 and soon after Captain Barrow took over the company, I sat down one day and began to count marines. Since we had returned to this position on September 7, we had been suffering a steady rate of casualties, mostly wounded, thank goodness, but still lost to us in the hospital. We had come back up to the lines with close to 180 men, and we were now down to a little over 100. On about the eighteenth of September, Haebel came off the Bunker Hill outpost, and Burhans took over the new Bunker Hill outpost with his third platoon. The first night Burhans was there, he got hit fairly heavily by a Chinese probe. Haebel returned to the main line and, with about sixteen or so men from his platoon, immediately took over Hedy.

As my company exec status had been restored, I began keeping track of the men we had on Hedy. Burhans had sixty men on Bunker Hill, including the reinforcements from Weapons Company and heavy machine gunners, and we had eighteen to twenty men on Hedy. I suddenly realized that in addition to myself, Lieutenant Jannelle, Lieutenant Hill, the first sergeant, the gunnery sergeant, and the company corpsman, we had eight marines manning the main line of resistance with all the rest of our marines deployed forward of it. I reviewed this situation with Captain Barrow and told him, "You know, sir, we have almost eight hundred yards of company front trench line on the main line of resistance. We have eight bona fide infantrymen manning this front. Sir, with your permission," I said, and I was always respectful with Captain Barrow, for he had earned my respect, "let me go back to battalion and see what I can do about getting us some replacements."

I obtained a company jeep, drove back to battalion headquarters, and explained our need to my friend the adjutant. But the adjutant said, "Van, we just don't have any troops. There is nothing in the pipeline, there is simply nothing I can give you." But then he added, "Oh, wait a minute, you are getting one man back!" That one man turned out to be Sergeant Drinkard. Sergeant Drinkard, you will remember, was the

365

man who, in May, had been very badly wounded on the OPLR and had to be evacuated by helicopter under enemy fire. The helicopter had to be held down and the pilot made to wait for the corpsman to finish treating Drinkard. Drinkard had gone back to the hospital ship, then to a hospital in Japan, where he had been repaired and sent back to Fox Company after a convalescence of four months. I got hold of Sergeant Drinkard and welcomed him. He did not remember me, because he had not been in my platoon, but I refreshed his memory and reminded him of some guys he knew, and so we had a kind of reunion.

Before driving off, I went up to his tent and saw Colonel Batterton, who asked how Captain Barrow was getting along. I could gladly tell him that he was getting along excellently and gave him an expurgated version of Barrow's pulling the wounded trooper back on Hedy. Since Colonel Batterton had been burnt with Moody, I believe he now conspired with me to make sure that the write-up of Barrow's actions did not violate division orders.

In a deep lament, I said to Colonel Batterton, "You have assigned us two outposts, sir, and we have about eight hundred yards of company front. After I get my two outposts manned, I have got eight people to guard that entire company front. If the Chinese ever break through the outposts, we are finished."

And he responded, "Well, Van, I am sorry. You know, even the general is upset about this, but we just don't have any more men to send you. Headquarters has cleaned out all of the antiaircraft battalions in the rear, they have cleaned out all the supply people in the rear, and they have swept up every warm marine body and sent them up to us, and that is just all we have for now. We will be getting a replacement draft in a week or two, though." Our considerable mutual respect allowed me to keep on arguing for more men. We had walked to the other end of his tent where the flaps were pulled open and we could gaze out on a beautiful little valley, a pretty vista with some trees left in it. I will never forget this moment. He put his hand on my shoulder and said, "Van, as I think you know, I saw a lot of combat in World War II, and I have seen a lot of it over here too. There is one lesson I have learned in all that combat experience." He paused. "Things are never as bad as they look!" With these stirring words of reassurance and a pat on the shoulder, he sent me back, with my one single replacement, Sergeant Drinkard.

We set out on the long jeep ride back from the battalion command post to our own command post on top of Hill 201. About halfway back up to the lines, a Chinese shell landed on the road about fifty yards in front of the jeep. The driver slammed on the brakes, but, "Keep going," I told him. It was a good thing we did because about fifteen seconds later, a great big shell landed right behind us, and had we not moved, it would certainly have smashed into the jeep. The Chinese were not able to observe this fire because we were way behind the reverse slope of a high hill, but Sergeant Drinkard, who sat in the backseat next to me, began to shake. God, I felt sorry for him! We finally reached the company command post, and the first sergeant came out and asked me, "Did you get any replacements, sir?"

"No, but I got Sergeant Drinkard," I told him.

The second platoon, Haebel's platoon, needed some people, and so we assigned Sergeant Drinkard to Haebel, who immediately had to send him out to Hedy. And this is a very difficult story to tell. Drinkard went out, good man, and that night, the Chinese hit Hedy as hard as they had hit it since we first established it. They probed with an infantry probe that tried to climb up the spine of the ridge lines spreading out from Hedy, not on the sheer front side of it, but around it. They shelled it intensively, and they fired a white phosphorus shell. That kind of shell is normally used to create a smoke screen in order to protect or conceal a unit. It burns with enormous intensity, giving off huge clouds of white smoke. That Chinese white phosphorus shell scored a direct hit on Sergeant Drinkard and incinerated him instantly. We had to send the company corpsman out with a body bag. The guys had reported back that Drinkard's entire body had turned to white ash, although even in his shriveled-up state, he was still recognizable as a human being until the corpsman touched him. Then he disintegrated. That ash was reverently and lovingly gathered up and placed inside the bag. Let us consider this. Drinkard had been almost killed on the outpost line in May. With some considerable degree of difficulty, he was evacuated, treated, and had finally recuperated. He was sent back to the front lines, where he did not last more than six hours. Besides Sergeant Smith and me, there were not too many people left in the company who even remembered when Drinkard had been hit the first time. War is hell, and all honor and glory to Sergeant Drinkard, who probably should have been sent back home after his first serious wound.

Hedy was never lost. It was an impregnable outpost, and the Chinese never found a way to take it. Lieutenant Haebel continued to be a rock, constantly improving our positions on the new outpost. He also initiated a number of short patrols to ensure Hedy's safety and integrity. On about September 20, another disaster struck. Leading a patrol off the right flank of Hedy that night, Lieutenant Haebel's patrol ran into some Chinese. A brief firefight ensued, and Haebel was wounded by a hand grenade. He came back holding his forearm and wrist and tried to get the corpsman to just bandage him up so he could stay with his troops. But the corpsman took a careful look and realized that Haebel's forearm was shattered and his wrist a mangled mess. And so we lost Lieutenant Haebel. He faced several surgeries before his hand and wrist were completely restored, I think. Our paths crossed a number of times in subsequent years, and I regard him as one of the finest marines I ever knew.

The same night Haebel was wounded, Burhans's platoon on Bunker Hill was hit also. One of his troopers was evacuated by the ever-loyal Korean Service Corps stretcher bearers, and readers by now will recognize the evacuation route as an odyssey. The stretcher had to be handed up that rocky almost-vertical streambed on the face of 201. The KSCs were performing their usual gentle and careful job and had just lifted Burhans's man up the hill. They crossed the main trench line when I arrived to meet Haebel, who was also walking up the streambed. There must have been an illuminating flare in the air, because I could see the face of the man on the stretcher in one of the

Taking on the Burden of History

most poignant moments of my Korea experience. The man had propped himself up on both his elbows. He stared intently with a horrified expression at the foot of the stretcher. I turned away from his face, which had drawn my attention first. When I looked at the foot of the stretcher I saw why he was so shocked. I could see his waist, his thighs, and his knees under a blanket, but somewhere around his calves, the bottom of both legs, including the feet, had been completely obliterated. The lower part of the blanket just flapped over the end of the stretcher. I touched his shoulder and wished him well, saying, "Thanks!"

Meanwhile, Burhans was out on Bunker Hill, raking in the Purple Hearts. He got one soon after he joined the company, when he took out a patrol in front of Stromboli, engaged the enemy, and got a flesh wound in his arm. He had received another wound on the night of the twenty-fifth on Bunker Hill for a second Purple Heart, and somewhere inside that month, he was hit by shell fragments and was awarded his third Purple Heart. The second night Burhans was out on Bunker, he sneaked a little patrol out over the crown of the hill to the Chinese side and made a very careful visual reconnaissance. He saw that they had modified an enormous existing concrete bunker. Burhans speculated that it was very probably a bunker the South Koreans had built initially on the forward slope of the hill facing north because this portion of Bunker Hill was located just south of the 38th Parallel. Whatever fortifications the South Koreans had made before the war started would have been erected in that area. Of course, the Chinese had it on a reverse slope now, as we were on the slope on the other side of the hill. The Chinese had a Maxim gun inside the bunker, and Burhans had a great idea, which involved using shaped charges. A shaped charge is a special kind of an explosive charge. The explosive is contained in a ten-inch-diameter metal cylinder about two feet long, with the explosive hollowed-out at one end in an internal conical shape. This cylinder of explosive is mounted vertically on a stand, with the hollow cone in the explosive pointing downward. When it goes off, the shield around the charge directs all the explosives down in a very concentrated manner. A shaped charge like that could blow a hole in a bunker with concrete walls two or three feet thick, and it could even blow a hole in steel. I immediately ordered a couple of shaped charges for Burhans, the crazy, gung-ho nut. He was going to take the shaped charge out and put it on top of the Chinese bunker only about twenty yards from his own bunker, and he planned on doing this by himself. We received the shaped charges the next day, and the KSC supply train took them out to Burhans. He got one of them primed up with a fuse and put the other one behind his command post bunker.

That night Burhans surreptitiously climbed out in front of his position, crept over the top of the hill and down the other side, and managed to get away with it unscathed. He crept all the way to the bunker, placed the charge on top of it, and set the time fuse off. Just when he thought he had been able to sneak away, the Chinese spotted him, and their machine gun opened up on him from inside the bunker. From the tracers, Burhans realized that the machine gun was firing in a fixed, preplanned pattern or concentration. This pattern was aimed down a draw, which would have

Presuming to be a United States Marine

been a very likely avenue of approach were we to probe the Chinese. Unfortunately, when he was spotted, Burhans was still on the other side of the machine gun's pattern of bullets, which was clearly outlined by tracers. He realized that he had to somehow get through a hale of bullets in order to reach his own positions on the other side of the top of the hill. Lying perfectly still, he tried to conceal himself as best he could in a little depression in the ground. The thought came to him that he was trapped and would either be killed or taken prisoner. Just then, the fuse reached the shaped charge, and it went off with an enormous *boom!* Immediately, a number of things happened, almost all of them good for Burhans. First, the shaped charge effectively shattered the bunker. Second, the machine gun that had Burhans pinned down had been firing from inside the bunker and was knocked out by the shaped charge. Third, the place where Burhans was huddled was so oriented that the blast from the shaped charge blew him right through the machine gun pattern, over the top of the hill, and almost back to his own bunker. He lost consciousness momentarily, and when he came to, he was sprawled out right in front of his own position. The only adversity he suffered was a pretty bad gash in the arm, either from a fragment of the shaped charge or possibly from a Chinese grenade. Burhans had a corpsman with him, who immediately phoned back that the lieutenant had been wounded.

From the medical channel in the First Division, it was unveiled that this would bring Burhans his fourth Purple Heart. That got reported quickly back down through the medical chain of command and then back up the military chain. Word quickly came to the battalion headquarters that Colonel Layer had ordered Lieutenant Burhans off the hill the minute this order reached him. Colonel Batterton called up Captain Barrow to explain the order. We were quite joyous at the news that Burhans had merely been wounded, because we had heard the shaped charge going off and had feared the worst. Burhans himself came on the telephone to tell us, "I think I really got the bunker!" But he admitted that he was hurt, as he put it modestly, "a little bit." When Colonel Batterton told Captain Barrow of Colonel Layer's order, Barrow replied, "I am down a few officers already, sir. I just lost Lieutenant Haebel last night." And Batterton said, "You've still got Van Sant. I want Van Sant out there." And Colonel Batterton himself thanked me for taking the job and stressed the importance of holding the position. He pointed out that there had been considerable discussion at regiment and division about the wisdom of changing Bunker Hill from a company-sized outpost to a platoon-sized outpost. He implied that the personnel shortages in the division had forced the decision upon them. He then blew a little smoke up my rear, so to speak, by saying, "You are the most experienced lieutenant in the battalion."

I thought to myself, *Whoopee-do!* but said, "You know, sir, losing both Burhans and Haebel in two days is really hurting us, but I see your arguments." And it was true. Burhans and Haebel were two of the finest, most hard-charging lieutenants I ever knew in the Marine Corps. We had only had their services for thirty-seven days in Haebel's case and thirty-eight days for Burhans. And so after my first delightful tour in the second big battle of Bunker Hill, I found myself going out to it once again on the night of

Taking on the Burden of History

the twentieth of September. I hooked up with the last train of KSCs for that night and climbed down the familiar rocky streambed on the forward slope of Hill 201. Passing our old now-unoccupied command post, I walked on to what on the twenty-fifth of August had been Kimbrough's horseshoe-shaped line on the right flank. Burhans gave me a very thorough rundown of what was there and who was there, although as company exec, I already knew who the guys were, and they knew who I was. Burhans's troops clearly admired him, but a couple of the guys knocked me out when they said, "We were sure glad to hear it was you coming out." And that made me feel good as I watched Burhans taking off with the last KSC supply train.

We all made first lieutenant that November, and Burhans was made company commander of the regimental Weapons Company. This was a pretty nice job, and probably safe enough for him not to acquire any more Purple Hearts. We stayed in close touch then, and I saw him after the war a couple of times too.

And so I found myself back on Bunker Hill. I crept around that first night, before it got too light, and checked in with many of my troops. Burhans had arrived there with sixty troopers five days earlier. He had already lost at least ten men, and I would have thirty-nine men left when I came off on the twenty-fifth or twenty-sixth. But although we had sustained twenty-one casualties over a period of about eight or nine days, not a single one of the men was killed. After some of the carnage we had experienced, not having to mourn any deaths among our men was a welcome relief.

I settled into the job of platoon commander again and, with the approaching daylight, introduced myself to each man, fully aware that we were all just clinging to this position by our fingernails. While I was confident of the men, I faced a serious problem. I had no noncommissioned officers. The senior man left in the platoon was a private first class. Fortunately, he was a good man and became my platoon sergeant. I did not forget him after I left Bunker. He was promoted to corporal as soon as we got off-line.

I shared a little fighting position with the platoon corpsman, HM Birkenstock, someone I already knew well and one of the finest men I have ever known. He was absolutely fearless and would go anywhere in any situation to take care of a wounded man. He also was a conscientious objector and absolutely opposed to taking up arms and hurting anybody. Our position, which I inherited from Burhans, consisted of a small covered bunker with thick sandbag walls. These walls were probably about four to five feet high, so that we could not really stand up inside. If both of us were in the position at the same time, we would just fit, but with no room to spare. The cover for the bunker consisted of a layer of six-inch timbers covered with a couple of layers of sandbags. Outside the entrance was an open firing position with a big sandbag wall facing in the direction of the enemy. This firing position was stocked with a Browning automatic rifle, two M1 rifles, and a stack of five crates of hand grenades. The interesting aspect of this position, as I realized immediately after my initial reconnaissance on my arrival, was that it was not only the command post for the platoon but also one of the most advanced fighting positions in our perimeter. It filled a gap between a marine to the right of us, who covered a little cut that made our whole position vulnerable, and a man to the left who helped cover another possible approach into our positions. My platoon's horseshoe-shaped position had very strong fighting positions placed about ten or twenty yards apart all around just off the top of our side of the slope. The Chinese were dug in similarly on the other side of the slope, just below the top on their side, creating a very cozy arrangement. They did not completely encircle us. In fact, from the aerial photos I had seen, the closest Chinese trench line was the one right in front of my fighting position. But their trenches were located all the way across the upper loop of the horseshoe, and a little way down its sides. Burhans had warned me about another ravine down into the Chinese-occupied side, which also reached up into our positions. I saw for myself that it was the most vulnerable part of our perimeter, and as a result, both Haebel, during his tour, and Burhans had placed at the head of the ravine a large fighting position of a little sandbag castle in which was positioned a machine gun. In addition, a flamethrower team from Weapons Company had a flamethrower built into this bunker, and it was sandbagged so that it was aimed to fill the whole ravine with fiery napalm if the Chinese ever tried to come up that way.

And therein lies another tale. As I walked (and crawled) around on my first full day, meeting all of my men and checking on their positions, I made each one of them tell me what their plan was if anything happened and how they were going to deal with possible contingencies. I was shocked to find that, because of the casualties, the large bunker and flamethrower position was occupied by a single man, our flamethrower expert. It turned out that his partner had been wounded the night before I came out, and he assumed he would also man the machine gun, since the original machine gunner had also been wounded. As I began to question him, I was soon struck with terror. This man was a great big nice-looking guy, a brand-new replacement. He had just come overseas, had been assigned to Weapons Company of the Second Battalion, and had been sent out to support Fox Company.

I asked him, somewhat skeptically, "You are our flamethrower man. Have you ever fired a flamethrower?"

"Well, no, sir. I never have."

Then I asked him, "Are you getting your bottles every night?"

And he looked at me with a blank expression, "Bottles, sir? What bottles?"

Then I explained to him the very elaborate system that Haebel, and then Burhans and I, together with the supply people, had worked out. A flamethrower operated with a reservoir of gasoline and napalm, carried in two big tanks. But nestled between the two big tanks was a small quart-sized steel jar filled with compressed air, and it was this compressed air that provided the pressure to spew the gasoline and the napalm out of the tanks. Once fully charged and compressed, an air bottle for a flamethrower should last for forty-eight hours, and we had set it up so that a brand-new charged bottle was to be sent out every night. This assured us that we always had a fully operational flamethrower with a fresh bottle in it. Unfortunately, since our new man was replacing a casualty, this requirement had not been passed on to him. Moreover,

Taking on the Burden of History

he had arrived in the replacement draft as a flamethrower operator's assistant, and Weapons Company had assumed that his operator would give him on-the-job training. This poor fellow did not even know the function of the bottle and, in fact, knew very little about flamethrowers in general because the trained operator had been wounded only hours after our new guy's arrival. Right then and there, on a very forward position on Bunker Hill, I set up a little training class on how to arm and fire a flamethrower. The marine was a good young man and a very willing student, and I showed him how to put the bottle in and how to connect it. A fresh bottle had come up with me the night before, and we put it in together. The flamethrower had two triggers, one to light the match and the other one to release the compressed air and to send the fuel through it. By the time I had finished my instruction, our new flamethrowing man had become fully checked out. I realized with some dismay, though, that for at least the last twenty-four hours, and probably for forty-eight hours, our secret weapon to fill the ravine with flame and cook the enemy had been inoperable. "Bottle? What bottle?" our "expert" had asked in bewilderment.

I mentioned my platoon sergeant, the PFC, and he was a good man, very reliable, and I am sorry I cannot remember his name. I had, in fact, remembered only a handful of these men's names from Burhans's old platoon. I am glad to say that since the war, I have had some very poignant reunions with several of them who remembered me and my hasty trip out to replace Burhans. My PFC platoon sergeant had a lot of initiative and constantly brought different matters to my attention. Another PFC worked right under him, and I was glad I had him too, because the platoon sergeant was wounded a day or two after I took over in a terrible, and intensely human incident. I had sent word to him to come over to my CP. His position was on the right-hand side of the horseshoe, and I was clear up to the head of the horseshoe, a little bit to the left. To come see me, he had to climb out of his position, descend into the ravine on his side, proceed through the bottom of the ravine, and climb up to my position. I was standing on the hillside overlooking the ravine when I saw him approaching. He reached the bottom of the ravine and was starting on his way up when a mortar shell landed right in front of him. It hit between us, and I heard some fragments flying past me, without finding a target. But the shell badly wounded my PFC platoon sergeant. When the dirt, dust, and smoke cleared, he was lying on the ground, still conscious but with the whole lower part of his abdomen bloodied. I yelled for Birkenstock, the corpsman. Birkenstock had heard the shell and came running out with his kit to the wounded marine. The man was still lying on his back, but he had propped himself up on his elbows, and he was staring down at the bleeding extending from his lower abdomen all the way into his crotch. He was examining himself with an intensely worried stare. Birkenstock, who had taken care of many wounded by that time, instantly realized the problem, whipped out his scissors, cut the wounded man's trousers open, and looked at the man's most important treasure, which was at that moment clearly the object of the marine's fullest concern.

Presuming to be a United States Marine

Birkenstock raised his hand, put his thumb and forefinger together, and said, "It's okay, buddy, everything is fine down there." After receiving this good and welcome news, the poor guy permitted himself to faint dead away. Birkenstock gave him the standard treatment of the time, sprinkling antibiotics over the wound, putting a dressing over it, and working to stop the profuse bleeding. It was about ten or eleven o'clock in the morning, when we did not like to engage in any traffic between the main line and our outpost because portions of the route were under enemy observation.

I asked Birkenstock, "Do you think he will be okay until tonight when we can safely evacuate him?" Birkenstock looked at me and said very forcefully, "No! This man has got to be seen by a doctor immediately." So I called back to the company command post and explained the situation, and volunteers from the Korean Service Corps worked their way out to us with a stretcher, picked up the acting platoon sergeant, and took him back. As much as you hear people talking about "hating your enemy," the Chinese did not shoot the litter party, perhaps only because it presented no threat to them. But I honor them for their humanity. As the stretcher party made its way back from Bunker Hill, I had my binoculars trained on our marine. He was carried back on the exposed path that snaked up to the bottom of Hill 201 and then bumped up the rocky streambed. This time around, as always, the stretcher bearers completed an almost impossible task. And while I do not recall the wounded marine's name, his facial expression just before he fainted remains vividly etched in my memory.

We kept dreadfully busy, but I was able to spend some time talking with Birkenstock and got to know him better. I think he had gone to college for about a year in Ohio somewhere. He told me the complete story about his feelings when his draft number had come up. He maintained his conscientious objector status but volunteered for the Navy Medical Corps. As I have already mentioned, several of our corpsmen were conscientious objectors, and every last one of them was a brave man. Since my service in Korea, whenever I hear people criticizing conscientious objectors, I tell them what those guys taught me about courage.

And then came the night of the twenty-second and twenty-third of September, which was when the Chinese, finally, succeeded in getting me. By that time, I felt pretty confident about my platoon's position. We had sustained several casualties already, but our positions were well supplied, well structured, and well organized, and we mutually supported each other all the way around the perimeter. Thanks to Burhans's daring raid on the bunker not too far from my fighting position, I thought that the Chinese had, perhaps, become a little bit discouraged from attacking us. High up on Hill 201 behind us and just below the big division OP, we had the support of a very ingeniously placed and well-camouflaged sniper position. The sniper did not use a rifle; he had a .50 caliber machine gun. This fairly large small arm was the most accurate small arms weapon there was. A telescopic sight was welded onto the top cover of the machine gun, and the sniper could sit up in his position, crank the wheels of the machine gun around, and zero in on his sight with such accuracy that he could hit a pie plate at a thousand yards with the rig. The sniper spent most of his time looking down from his high angle over the top of the hill among our positions, often catching glimpses of Chinese soldiers on the other side. Although the sniper's .50 caliber bullets were clearing right over our heads by not more than a few feet, they really sounded good to us. We knew from observers at the OP that the sniper took a steady toll on those people opposite us who were always raising trouble for us. I almost felt sorry for them because every time they moved, *bang!* Our sniper would hit them. He was exceedingly accurate.

While I can't say that I was arrogantly confident, I felt that we were in good control at this point, and that thanks to Burhans's raid, the continuing work of the sniper, and the fact that our positions were well established, the initiative was on our side on Bunker Hill. But on the night of the twenty-second and twenty-third, any complacency on my part came to an abrupt end. Birkenstock and I always switched off on our nighttime watches. He would sleep while I stood watch out in the fighting position, and then I'd go to sleep while he stood watch.

In the very early morning hours of the twenty-third, I was asleep in the little bunker, and Birkenstock was outside with his eyes riveted on the potential appearance of the enemy. At this point, I was no longer thoroughly checking the lines on the outpost very carefully each night. As we were on such cozy terms with the enemy, the men were invariably wide awake. They knew that if we wanted to continue staying alive, it behooved us to stay awake at all times.

Suddenly, Birkenstock grabbed my shoulder, shaking me awake. "Lieutenant, Lieutenant, get up! You have to come out here now. This is your kind of war. I don't do this!" I climbed out and up into the fighting position with its sandbag wall to find myself looking, not twenty yards away, at about four or five black shapes, who graced me with a vision of those brilliant little flowers growing from the ends of rifles aimed at me.

And Birkenstock said, "They are coming! And it looks like they are coming right at us." I grabbed an M1 and fired a couple of rounds at the enemy, but that did not seem to be doing any good. So I started throwing hand grenades. I must have thrown a couple, and because we were so close to the enemy, I could sense I was causing some confusion. But the advancing shadows were undeterred, and they began to throw grenades back. Then a Chinese grenade exploded just a little left of center in front of my face, and probably not more than two feet away from me, with a huge and blinding light.

My first thought when I saw that blinding light was, *My god, this is it!* Slowly I felt myself losing consciousness. The last thing I was aware of, as I sank down and before I became unconscious, was a sense of deep disappointment with what little I had managed to accomplish in my life. I was permeated by a very painful and profound feeling of sorrow as I hit the ground. I don't think I was unconscious for more than ten or fifteen seconds. Then I opened my eyes with a fresh realization of, *My god! I am not dead!* I stirred and felt some stinging around my ankles and my left knee, but I was alive, I was all right, I was okay!

Presuming to be a United States Marine

The Chinese hand grenade was what we called a potato masher. It was grasped by a wooden handle, and with that wooden handle, the grenade could be thrown a good deal farther than our own pineapple hand grenades. At the end of the wooden handle was a metal casing filled with picric acid explosive. This made a very powerful grenade, which, when it exploded, blew the metal casing into thousands of small fragments, and that was what I had felt around my ankles. The explosion itself was enormously powerful, almost equivalent to what we called in the United States Armed Forces a concussion grenade. It did not kill by fragments, it killed by its blast. The metal casing on our grenades was much heavier. Ours would explode into many fewer very sharp fragments, each one of them big enough to cause some damage on impact.

Not until the dust cleared did I realize what had happened to me in the wounding, but I gratefully recognized that I was all right. Jumping up, I turned into what the guy in the position just to the left of me, PFC John H. Armstrong, later described as a "whirling dervish." I emptied a whole case of twenty-four or twenty-five grenades in, I bet you, not more than a minute and a half. I was pulling pins—pull pin, *thwack!* pull pin, *thwack!* pull pin, throw. I laid down a curtain of hand grenades in front of our position and saw that it caused so much consternation in the enemy ranks that they decided to pull off, leaving us as quickly as they had approached us. Birkenstock, sitting in the doorway of our little bunker, had watched the whole dispatch of the Chinese probe. When it was over, he clapped his hands and said, "Man, Lieutenant, that was pretty great!" The guys to my right and the guys to my left were also shooting in support, but the main detail of the Chinese who had been trying to break into our perimeter had come straight at our fighting hole. After they pulled off, I called back to battalion and was able to get Major McDonnell, our wonderful operations officer. I told him exactly what had happened. He asked me to estimate the number of Chinese and the number of their casualties. I restrained myself with some effort, claiming only a half dozen Chinese casualties. I had received the gift of a couple of tiny holes in my ankle, and while I have not checked it in years, a piece of gristle eventually grew around one of the pieces of debris that had lodged in the ankle. There was a large scrape on my knee, which Birkenstock dressed. I did not at first realize it, but I would be deaf in my left ear for a couple of weeks from the blast of the explosion. But I was supremely fortunate. Had circumstances been different by just a fraction, I might not be sitting here writing my story. The potato masher was a good grenade and easy to throw, but the wooden handle acted as a kind of buffer, so that the fragments from the explosion of this type of a hand grenade tended to form a wide cone. The potato masher aimed at me flew through the air, rotating, as it exploded fairly close to my face. If, as it tipped over in its travels, the grenade had oriented itself so that the main thrust of that cone of explosives and fragments had been aimed at my face, it quite possibly could have blown my head off. I am lucky that the Chinese happened to throw it in such a way that most of the force of the explosion and the fragments were directed straight downward. Birkenstock filled out a form to write me up for a Purple Heart, dressed my little wounds, and that was it. We both decided that the wound was WIA non-evac,

Taking on the Burden of History

which meant, wounded in action, not evacuated. I felt very fortunate even though I had for one terrible moment thought that my number had been called.

At the height of this incident, when I had turned into a grenade-tossing whirling dervish, the noise from our little battle had been suddenly punctuated by an enormous explosion, which literally caused the ground to shake. I thought, *My god, what are the Chinese shooting at us now? It must be the end of the world!* When I surveyed the damage the next morning, I realized what had caused the blast. It will be remembered that Burhans had planted a shaped charge on top of the Chinese bunker and had badly damaged it. But we had sent Burhans two shaped charges, and without my knowledge, he had stored the spare shaped charge behind our little bunker command post. A Chinese mortar shell had scored a direct hit on the shaped charge, setting it off and creating a huge cavity behind our bunker only a minute or two after I had thought I had been killed.

The entire experience was to have a profound and lasting effect on my life. The memory of my feeling of disappointment with myself as I was losing consciousness made me resolve not to waste the rest of a life that had been so miraculously preserved. The day after this terrible night, an incident occurred that brought home to me once again the importance of humanity. In the days of the Korean War, a C-ration consisted of a dry unit and a wet unit. The dry unit had chocolate, crackers, sugar, powdered cream, instant coffee, jam, and cookies. But it also contained a pack of cigarettes. Back in the days when cigarettes were helping to win two wars, World War II and Korea, they were an absolute essential for the front line marine and soldier. On the day after I had been wounded, I was opening a dry unit with great anticipation for the cigarettes. In about one of every twenty-five C-rations, we would find a pack of Kools. In those days, I would smoke Camels, Luckies, Philip Morris, and, if necessary, Chesterfields or Pall Malls, but no self-respecting marine smoked filter cigarettes, except in the most dire circumstances. And then there were Kools. Kools were not only filtered, but, horror of horrors, they were mentholated. It was a direct insult to get a pack of Kools.

After I ripped open my C-ration and found the Kools in it, I was so incensed that I took the pack and flung it in the general direction of the Chinese over the flat top of the hill. This was actually the exact position from which the previous night's attack had come. Not too far below the crest, I knew there was a big Chinese trench line that led down from the bunker Burhans had damaged. *Here*, I thought to myself, *you can have the damned Kools!* About a minute or two later, I heard a small thump outside our fighting position. I investigated and found a small packet of papers and a booklet. The packet consisted of an abbreviated history of the Korean War, from the point of view of the North Koreans and the Chinese, printed in booklet form on very cheap paper. Also included in the packet was a little certificate, which, when presented to any Chinese or North Korean soldier, would entitle one to be immediately taken prisoner without being harmed in any way. There was, further, a kind of propaganda leaflet, and all was printed in very crude English. Clearly, this material had been prepared by the psychological operations people on the other side. The pamphlet on the history of the war was particularly interesting. It consisted of about one hundred pages in English with some crude photographs, and I immediately began reading this version of the story of the Korean War with interest. It seems that the war started because the fascist forces of Syngman Rhee had attacked north across the 38th Parallel on the twenty-fifth of June 1950. There, they were immediately stopped and hurled back by the glorious North Korean Army, which then devoted itself to working for the unification of Korea. The writers of the pamphlet had to dance a little bit around the Inchon landing, but it was clear that the real heroes were their Chinese friends, who had so unselfishly and loyally volunteered to come to the aid of their North Korean comrades in November of 1950. I found this perspective on the same war in which I was fighting to be very interesting, if perplexing. The pamphlet remained one of my most prized possessions for some time, although I regret to say that in all the hustle, bustle, and shuffle of my return back home, I lost it—or what is more likely, some friendly fellow marine liberated it from my possession as a historic souvenir.

With this Chinese gift, I was again reminded that the enemy on the other side of the hill consisted of other human beings, and that all of us had common traits. The man who had tossed the grenade that got me may very well have been the same man who later tossed the gift of the propaganda packet to me, thus reciprocating my "gift" to him of the cigarettes. And here we all were thrown together, although we would all have been much better off and happier to have remained apart.

After the raid in June, and before we had come back online on July 27, the battalion personnel officer had informed me that the Marine Corps was undertaking the integration into the regular officer corps of certain reserve officers. He pointed out to me that the Corps planned to integrate approximately 20 percent of its reserve lieutenant strength.

He said, "The Marine Corps, because of your class standing in Basic School, offers you a regular commission without any further screening." I truthfully replied that I was rather torn, but that I certainly loved the Marine Corps and thought he should go ahead and prepare the paperwork. He told me that he would get me a regular commission certificate, and next time I came off-line, the colonel would want to have a little ceremony to celebrate my becoming a regular officer. And that was the way we left it. I had not formally accepted the commission, but the paperwork to obtain it was being put through.

The next night, after all the excitement surrounding my skirmish, the wounding, and the grenade throwing, the KSC supply train brought me several goodies. One was an envelope from Lieutenant Jannelle, now commander of the second platoon. He had found my pinup of Marilyn Monroe in the company CP and took the time to send it out with an encouraging note, because word of my wounding had filtered back to company headquarters. I think the very sexy pinup of Marilyn was initially sent to me by my friend Lorraine from California.

A second message that came out with the supply train was from the battalion adjutant, informing me that my regular commission certificate had arrived, and the colonel wanted to present it at my convenience. I immediately put up the Marilyn Monroe photograph on the interior of our bunker. A few weeks later, I wrote a fan letter to Marilyn in which I told her that I thought I had placed her pinup in a position closer to enemy positions than any other of her pinups in the entire Korean theater. I stressed in my letter how important looking at her was to my morale. I also mentioned that I had not seen a female of any kind since leaving Japan on May 5. Alas, my fan letter never produced any response at all.

The news about the arrival of the regular commission created some soul-searching on my part. After I was wounded, I had given a regular commission much deliberation and thought. I eventually realized that although I would fight for my country when it was my duty to do so, to devote my entire life to this kind of work was something else altogether. My final decision was to return to the States and go to graduate school. Within twenty-four hours of reaching this conclusion, I resolved to become a college professor. As difficult as this decision making proved to be, I could never escape the terrible memory of losing consciousness, amid a strong feeling that my achievements up to that point did not present a pleasing picture. Certainly, part of this very negative view of my life was the loss of Shirley, for whom I continued to mourn.

Poor old Fox Company with its ups and downs had been online since July 27. It had been shot up badly on the night of August 13, and on the twenty-fifth and twenty-sixth of August, on Bunker Hill. We had practically been wiped out. We still occupied two outposts, Hedy and Bunker, as well as eight hundred yards of the main line of resistance, but we had suffered a steady stream of casualties (and you will remember my telling you of the night we were down to 108 people to cover that entire area, with the two outposts using up almost all of those men). Because of these circumstances, the battalion and regiment finally decided that Fox Company would be pulled out of this tough position.

Colonel Batterton called me up personally on September 25 and told me that we were going to be relieved on the following night. He gave me an order, which produced quite a tale. Bunker Hill was first occupied on August 11 by B Company, and then I Company of the First Regiment. From the time marines first went out on the hill, there had been a tremendous buildup of all different kinds of supplies and ammunition brought in by the Korean Service Corps. We had sandbags and timbers by the tons. We had steel plates. We had ammunition of every conceivable variety. My new PFC platoon sergeant did a little inventory just on our perimeter, and he told me, "Sir, we have enough machine gun ammunition here to defend the regiment." We had piles and piles of 3.5 inch rockets. We had piles and piles of .30 caliber rifle ammunition. Vast quantities of building materials were stacked up to the west, or left end, of the hill, where our company command post had been in the other horseshoe on the 25th-26th of August.

Colonel Batterton now ordered, "Van, as you bring your platoon off, I want you to clean up that hill and have every man bring a full load of gear."

By that time, I was down to thirty-nine men from the original sixty-five taken out by Burhans. I asked my PFC platoon sergeant what he thought our largest surplus was.

Presuming to be a United States Marine

He replied that it would be the machine gun ammo, without any doubt. I therefore issued the order that every man in the platoon was to carry four boxes of machine gun ammo. Each ammo box weighed twenty pounds. This meant that in addition to his weapon, his pack, and everything else, every man had to carry an additional eighty extra pounds. Even as I issued that order, I thought the task to be almost sacrificial. Four times 39 is 156. My men would carry a total of 156 boxes of machine gun ammo. As we were relieved, making sure that every single man had his four boxes, I carried my eighty pounds too. Stumbling up that rocky streambed with all our gear and ammo, we presented a less-than-sharp picture, but we managed to get up to the top and from there to our main line. By the time we arrived there, the rest of Fox Company, with Captain Barrow, had long since been relieved and gone on to their new positions. Two six-by-six trucks were parked by the company command post waiting for all the gear that my thirty-nine men were to haul off the mountain. The men stacked all their boxes on about one-half of the floor bed of one single six-by-six truck, and the two trucks rumbled back to battalion. I gathered my troops, and we climbed on some other trucks to take us up to the top of Hill 229, the largest mountain in the division sector overlooking Panmunjom. As I have already indicated, no-man's-land was wide in front of 229, and it was being vigorously patrolled, but fifty men could have held that impregnable mountain. Although we were still online, we almost felt as if we were on R & R, rest and rehabilitation.

One of the interesting aspects of driving up this very steep mountain was that the engine of the six-by-six truck that carried us up there would get so hot that the entire engine block turned red hot, and part of the engine became white hot from the stress of the sharp climb. Division motor transport had a standing order that no truck could make more than a total of four trips there without having its brakes relined. Much later, during a night when I was in the battalion command post behind 229, I heard a six-by-six truck, a noisy vehicle under the best of circumstances, hurtling down with a great deal of increasing noise. It was clear that the poor driver was desperately trying to keep his vehicle on the very narrow, winding, steep dirt road. We heard the truck banging along, in the next moment, an awful smash, and after that an ominous silence. We learned that the driver had been killed because the brakes on his vehicle had failed.

But it was delightful up on 229. Captain Barrow greeted me as I was turned back into the company executive officer. Poor old Tom Jannelle finally got the second platoon. He had the 60 mm mortar section all through our battles but had continued to agitate with Captain Barrow about getting a rifle platoon. We still had Lieutenant Hill in the first platoon, and a new lieutenant came up and took over the third platoon from me. In the beautiful command bunker on top of the mountain, I had my own little room with my air mattress and sleeping bag on a little bunk carved, like a shelf, from the wall. Even with a dirt floor, it was really elegant. We had lots of good food supplements, and so we thought that it was just glorious to be on 229. It had taken us most of the night to get off Bunker and to get the machine gun ammo stacked on the

Taking on the Burden of History

truck, and it must have been about nine o'clock in the morning by the time I was able to fall into bed and into a deep, exhausted sleep. I was awakened by the telephone at about 1600 hours.

It was Colonel Batterton. "I want to speak to Lieutenant Van Sant!"

I got on the telephone, and Colonel Batterton said, "Lieutenant, I am really disappointed in you."

I asked in dismay, "Sir, why?"

He answered, "I sent two six-by-six trucks for your platoon to clean off Bunker Hill and bring everything back with you, but only one of the trucks came back, and it wasn't even full!"

"Well, sir . . . ," And I tried to explain to him that this represented, in addition to each man's personal gear and weapons, eighty pounds of weight per man, but Colonel Batterton was not letting me say very much.

Batterton said, "I'll tell you what I am going to do. You get two marine volunteers from Fox Company, and they do not have to be from the platoon you brought out, because those guys are tired, I know. But I have arranged with the Korean Service Corps for sixty additional Korean Service Corps bearers, and I am going to put you in charge, and I am going to send you back out to Bunker with the sixty KSCs, and I'll tell you what, you will probably need four marines, just use volunteers from other platoons, and I want you to clean up that hill! Is that understood?"

"Yes, sir," I replied, because what do you say? What can you say?

So without a full night of sleep, back into a truck I got, and back over to Bunker Hill I rumbled, finding the ever-faithful Korean Service Corps guys there. Fortunately, we had a couple of Korean sergeants who were good interpreters, and I pulled everybody together and explained to them what we had to do. I had four marine volunteers from Fox Company to ride shotgun and protect the KSCs. We divided the group into two different details, rotating them, so that we always had one moving back from the hill loaded down and one going out to the hill empty-handed. I must give credit to the bearers. If you tried to explain to them as much as possible what was needed, they would really fall to. We loaded up four six-by-six trucks of building materials, ammunition, and anything else that had been left out there in one night of work.

Ah! But that's not even the beginning of the story. The Chinese realized that there had been a change of units in the troops they were opposing out on Bunker, and man, they really hit the new outfit on the outpost pretty hard that night. And so I found myself sitting down in the old command post section on the now unoccupied left, or western, end of Bunker Hill, all by myself most of the time, while one Korean Service Corps bearer detail left and the other one had not arrived back yet.

A gunnery sergeant from another outfit, who had been patrolling out in front of the unoccupied left end of Bunker, came through our position with his patrol. He hung around and hung around with me. I finally asked him why he kept on staying and whether he was not supposed to be out patrolling. He said, "Well, yes, sir." And took off again around the left end of Bunker in the direction of Hedy. We worked steadily all night, and I don't remember ever working so hard in my life. I was helping to load these guys up and moving things around to be ready when the next KSC bearers came back.

All this time, a big battle was raging about one hundred yards away on the section of the hill I had just left, which was now our outpost. Some rather excited marines appeared to tell me that they needed stretcher bearers. So I reassigned a dozen of my Koreans to stretcher-bearing duty. The platoon that had relieved me was engaged in a violent fight and had obviously already taken quite a few casualties. We could hear lots of small arms fire, grenades, and plenty of shelling, and it was all happening just about one hundred yards away from where I was sitting.

I will pause for a minute now, draw back a bit, and talk about some personal responses to war and to combat. Fear is always prevalent in war, and this bears repeating. The entire time I was in Korea, I had an ever-present "little friend" down in the pit of my stomach. It was a knot of fear. I was always afraid, and by this time, it was near the end of September, and I had seen almost five months of carnage, blood, dirt, and smoke. War is a cruel experience. On the night I was cleaning up Bunker Hill, I had an encounter that brought home to me just how numb and dehumanized I had become. I was forcibly reminded of my increasingly callous outlook by one of my most ghastly experiences in the war.

After I had assigned the Korean Service Corps men as stretcher bearers, they carried eight or ten killed or wounded marines back just in that one night. They were taking the casualties right past the location where I was organizing the building materials and the ammunition to be taken back to the lines. I observed one of the stretchers with a marine lying on it facedown. There was not a mark on him, not even the slightest indication of a wound. The thought came to me that the guy might be a malingerer, trying to get out of combat by pretending to be a casualty. I speculated that the Koreans, not being English-speaking, may have been fooled by this man who had climbed onto the stretcher feigning a wound—an obvious dereliction of duty. I motioned to the bearers to stop, and I walked over to the stretcher. With a good deal of officiousness, I grabbed the marine roughly by his shoulder and said to him, "What in hell is wrong with you, marine?" I pulled up and back on his shoulder so that his head came up.

The head had no face. The entire front of the marine's head was gone. His face was gone. Death had left its mark only on his front, leaving his back untouched. The sight of that bloody scene pierced me like an arrow. *God, how low you have sunk,* I told myself with some disgust. *How abysmally low you have sunk!* When I could find the time to think, I continued to reflect on my tour and the battle of Fox Company on the twenty-fifth and twenty-sixth, and my six days with the third platoon as platoon commander, and my one day out on the cleanup detail. Later, I learned that I had spent more time on Bunker Hill than all but one other officer in the Marine Corps during that August-September period when the fighting was so heavy. That other officer was an officer in Charlie Company who had spent sixteen or seventeen days on Bunker Hill. Counting my third cleanup duty, I had spent a total of eleven days there.

Chapter 15

FINAL DAYS WITH FOX COMPANY, INTO RESERVE

A very exhausted Van Sant the next morning after the cleanup managed to make his way back up to 229 and collapsed. The following evening, the telephone rang. It was Colonel Batterton again asking to talk to Lieutenant Van Sant.

He said, "Van, I want to apologize." And I think you will understand now why I admired him so much. He had, apparently, talked to somebody in the supply department, who pointed out to him the enormous load of machine gun ammunition my marine platoon had brought off in their greatly fatigued condition.

"I apologize," he said. "I should have known better." By this time, he had seen the enormous quantities of material my Korean Service Corps detail had brought back from Bunker Hill. I don't know of many marine lieutenant colonels who would so abjectly apologize to a second lieutenant, but Colonel Batterton once again showed himself to be a good man and a great leader.

I settled into 229, again enjoying my role as company executive officer. It meant that I did not have to go out on patrols, although we did a lot of patrolling from 229. Even so, I have two patrol stories; one interesting and humorous, and the other, inevitably, tragic.

We are now up to the night of the twenty-ninth and thirtieth of September, and we had only about two more weeks left online. The turnover in the company of both enlisted men and officers was so great that it is hard to keep track of some of the people because so many of them did not last very long. The new lieutenant, whose name I cannot now remember, took a patrol out. His task was to go out parallel to the Panmunjom corridor just to the east of the road that came out from the main line to Panmumjom, and just outside a no-fire zone twenty-five yards on either side of the road. No weapon could be fired either into the corridor, out of it, or over it. There was a one-thousand-meter circle around Panmunjom itself, with a searchlight in its center pointing straight into the air, shining at all times and clearly marking the periphery of the circle. On the other side of that circle was a corridor, which led back to the North Korean town of Kaesong. Obviously, no weapons could be fired over, into, or out of Panmumjom at the very center of the circle itself. From the time the peace talks began in the summer of 1951 until the final truce was signed, those restrictions were pretty scrupulously followed by both sides, and neither side ever gratuitously broke that agreement. The corridors existed to provide free access to the negotiators and their support people. There was a very strict restriction on the number of combat troops allowed into the circle at Panmunjom, limited to security troops only. At our main line of resistance, we always maintained an up-to-strength snatch team with new and high-powered vehicles and crack marine troops prepared for any contingency. If a whistle blew, the snatch team was to move out from our lines on the no-fire corridor to Panmumjom, rapidly gather up all United Nations and South Korean negotiators, and carry them with the greatest possible speed back to the safety of our lines. Fortunately, although the snatch team was alerted a couple of times, it never had to be used during the entire negotiation process. It is eerie to think that we fought each other tooth-and-claw not more than a mile away, yet scrupulously observed the negotiation process.

One night, our new lieutenant took his patrol out into no-man's-land in front of 229 to the east of the circle with the task of spotting any Chinese in that area. In the middle of no-man's-land, he passed a Chinese patrol, although he did not immediately realize it. The Chinese patrol, equally unknowingly, passed our patrol in the dark of the night. Creeping by each other, the last people on both patrols suddenly realized each other's presence, and an enormous firefight ensued. Both details were approximately the same size of about twelve to fifteen men. Everybody dropped down to the ground and began banging away at each other, and both sides took casualties. When they finally broke off firing, our lieutenant, with two wounded men, moved to the west and into the corridor on the road that connected Panmunjom with our lines, and the Chinese did the same thing. The only problem was that the Chinese found themselves to be closer to our lines while our marines were closer to the Panmunjom circle and the Chinese lines. The two patrols, both needing to return to their respective friendly positions, had to pass each other again on the corridor road, this time inside the no-fire zone. Both groups were carrying casualties, and both very scrupulously obeyed the restrictions imposed on them by the rules of the no-fire zone, neither patrol now firing at the other. During most of this episode, I was on the radio with our lieutenant, talking him through it, and I remember his saying, "My god! I am now walking down the corridor back to our positions, and we are coming down one side of the road, and the Chinese are coming in the opposite direction, down the other side of the road, and we are just looking at each other in passing." It must have presented a very strange scene.

The other story is not so funny. On the very right flank of the company position on 229, the trench line came down off the hill onto lower ground, then started up Hill 201 to our recent company position behind Bunker Hill. Lieutenant Hill's first platoon, our right-flank platoon, covered from the lower eastern slope of 229 down and up onto the western end of hill 201. Out in front of this platoon position was a hill in no-man's-land. From time to time, the Marine Corps had kept an outpost on that hill. Since it was not really dominating territory, and once we had established the outpost on Hedy farther to the east, this hill became superfluous to have as an outpost. If, on the other hand, the Chinese had occupied it, their outpost would have become a real threat to the spot where our company and the company to our right on Hill 201 joined. We were therefore always concerned about this hill in front of our positions. Tom Jannelle, who remained a gung-ho marine, had taken over my old second platoon. When we were told by battalion that we better start patrolling that hill, Jannelle was ordered to take out a squad-sized combat patrol with a corpsman and a radioman, to go out, reconnoiter, and attempt to make contact with the enemy in that sector. Since the days when we had been roommates guarding the Widgeon Bridge, Tom and I had become good friends, and he worked very closely with me in the planning of his patrol. We decided to run it fairly late at night; I think that he jumped off at about three o'clock in the morning. Just before he left, he said, "You know, I have been issued these good binoculars, which I am not going to need. Could I leave them with you?"

"Sure," I said, and so he did.

Tom jumped off and went out through Lieutenant Hill's platoon, which manned the main line in that area. He worked his way out to the hill, which stood out there in no-man's-land, looking at us. His patrol had just climbed up over the top of the hill when they realized that their patrol had landed in the midst of a relatively large Chinese force. Both sides immediately began shooting. Jannelle managed to pull his patrol back over the top of the hill without any injuries to his men and set up a perimeter there. Jannelle next climbed back to a place on top of the hill where he could look down. What became apparent was that under cover of darkness, and completely concealed from our observation, the Chinese had moved forward a substantial force, probably a company, and had dug in on the far side of the hill. Clearly, their intentions were to stay there all day and then jump off the next night and hit the somewhat weak spot in the little draw where our company joined the company now occupying 201, Hedy, and Bunker. Not realizing this Chinese maneuver, Jannelle probably seriously underestimated the numbers of the enemy. He came back down to his troops and told them, "Come on, we are going to sneak back up to the top of the hill, and when I give the word, we are going to charge, and we are going to get those bastards!" Tom's troops had a lot of confidence in him. They did as they were told and, cresting the hill, yelled all manner of blood-curdling yells, including the rebel yell, laying down an enormous blast of fire.

While Tom had gravely underestimated the Chinese strength, Tom's charge was so impressive that the Chinese began to pull out and retreat right away. By this time, it was beginning to get light. We had observers strategically placed at points along the line, and we obtained a pretty good visual count of the Chinese force. Even after Tom's patrol had killed a number of Chinese, we counted about 150 Chinese pulling off, running pell-mell, turning tail, fleeing north to the Chinese main line positions well behind the hill, all as a result of the assault of Tom's thirteen-man patrol. It was one of the most unevenly matched battles during my time in Korea. That small patrol killed or chased off an entire Chinese company, stopping what could have been a pretty nasty attack on us if the Chinese had been able to carry off the surprise. But the cost was high. Tom was killed. A Chinese burp gun stitched him up and down. A very richly deserved Silver Star was given to Lieutenant Jannelle posthumously.

Lieutenant Hill went out with his platoon, but by the time he arrived, the Chinese had bugged out, and his marines were left with the sad task of carrying back the casualties. In addition to Tom, a couple more of his men were dead, and three or four were wounded. Lieutenant Hill, the former motor transport officer, was a good man and did his job well. He had an acerbic wit, and I remember that when he returned with the casualties, he told me, "You know, Van, I am getting tired of cleaning up all these messes!"

For the rest of my time on 229, my duties as company exec were not too onerous. I remember writing some letters and being able to read a little. The worst aspect about being on 229 was traveling to battalion in the company jeep down that infamous mountain and then climbing back up it again. One wanted to keep these trips down to a bare minimum because that road, in its narrowness with its curves overlooking cliffs on all sides, was simply heart-stopping. The last story to tell from this tour deals with the spectacle we were able to view from the front-row seat we had on Hill 229. The next large hill mass to the west of us was where we were tied in with the Korean Marine Corps. The Korean Marine Corps had been founded in 1946, and from the outset had been advised by the U.S. Marine Corps and trained by the U.S. Marine Corps. They had adopted most of the traditions of the U.S. Marine Corps, including fighting tough. They were a brigade covering a whole regimental front, the western anchor of the entire United Nations line in Korea. Their positions went all the way west to where the Imjin joined the Han River coming up from Seoul and then flowed into the sea.

Out in front of their main line was 151, a large hill outpost. The second week of October, the Chinese made an enormous all-out effort to take 151 away from the KMCs. On about the eighth or ninth of October, they eventually managed to take it. On 229, we were sitting much higher and not more than a mile or so east of 151, so that we could see the battle fairly well from our front-row seat. The Chinese took the hill by throwing, probably, fifty thousand rounds of artillery; they pounded away and charged up at night and finally got it. American bombers came in the next day, and I never saw so much visible aerial bombardment and artillery shelling at any time during the war. The next night, the Korean Marines went charging up, took the hill back, and never gave it up again. It was a good introduction into how well the Korean marines fought and how organized they were, and this knowledge served me in good stead when I worked with them a few weeks later.

Memorial Service
in honor of
U.S. Marine Corps and U.S. Navy
personnel who served with the
First Marine Regiment of the First Marine Division F.M.F.

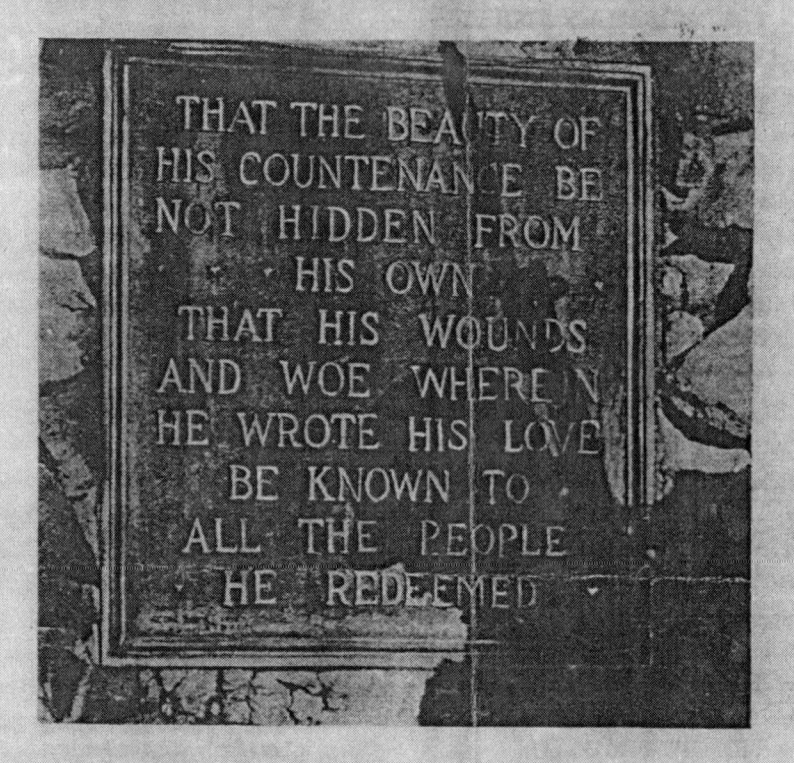

> THAT THE BEAUTY OF
> HIS COUNTENANCE BE
> NOT HIDDEN FROM
> HIS OWN
> THAT HIS WOUNDS
> AND WOE WHEREIN
> HE WROTE HIS LOVE
> BE KNOWN TO
> ALL THE PEOPLE
> HE REDEEMED

In The Field   Korea   26. October 1952

The program for the Memorial Service held by the 1st Marine Regiment on October 26, 1952. The service honored the 169 officers and men from the regiment who were killed on the line tour from July 27 to Oct. 15, 1952. 75 of the dead were from our 2nd Battalion.

MEMORIAL SERVICE

CHURCH CALL — Bugler

THE NATIONAL ANTHEM — Division Band

THE INVOCATION — Catholic Chaplain Patrick Adams

INTRODUCTION OF THE COMMANDING GENERAL — Colonel Walter F. Layer

THE MEMORIAL ADDRESS — Major General E. A. Pollock

THE MARINE HYMN — Division Band

*** HONORS ***

ROLL CALL OF THE DEAD

1stBn, 1st Marines	LtCol M. A. LaGrone
2ndBn, 1st Marines	LtCol C. E. Warren
3rdBn, 1st Marines	LtCol S. J. Altman
AT-Co, 1st Marines	1stLt B. C. Kearns
3rdBn, 11th Marines	LtCol C. O. Rogers
"C"Co, 1st Tank Bn	Capt. G. M. McCain

MINUTE OF SILENT TRIBUTE — Assembly

THE MEMORIAL PRAYER — Protestant Chaplain Oscar Weber

RIFLE SALUTE — Honor Guard

TAPS — Bugler

THE BENEDICTION — Jewish Chaplain Samuel Sobel

```
************************************************
            THE ROLL OF THE DEAD
         26 July 1952 to 12 October 1952

              ✝         🌎         ✡

               First Battalion, First Marines
```

Allen G. Stenerson	Donald Bailey
Willie Ray Deason	Jasper V. Russel
Henry B. Machado	Herbert W. Balboni
Ruben Cruz	Daniel J. Duggan
Richard W. Arndt	Earl W. Lester
Donald A. Fatica	Thomas G. Dier
Hubert J. LeBlanc	Amous L. Amey
Francis P. Soucie	James B. Pickworth
Daniel F. Belles	Gene R. Burkman
James V. Cullen	William K. Baker
Fred M. Allen	Louis D. Drazey
Daniel C. Barcak	Gilbert P. Mantey
John B. Powe	Robert L. Aldridge
Johnny Kilburn	Joe H. Turner
James D. Baker	Harold E. Upmeyer
Gerald Bradley	Edward W. Baumgard
Ernest J. Garnier	Robert J. Carroll
Robert T. Alilovich	Charles W. Parrish
John P. Borseti	Atnory Laboy-Collazo
Ervin Lemaster Jr.	Kenneth J. Jack
Joseph R. Kennel	Mario A. Desantis
John F. Popp	Bennie Bennitt Jr.
Junior R. Collins	Howard F. Chase Jr.
Richard M. Islas	Loren E. Anderson
Jimmie D. Young	Charles A. Fjaer
Herbert W. Smith	Regis E. Krug
John F. Bagwell III	Eugene Cota
Larry E. Miller	Robert J. Betz
Richard H. Eldam	

```
************************************************
```

Second Battalion, First Marines

Wilfred E. Hall	Raymond L. Hergert
Robert E. Stafford	Phillip N. Hobson Jr.
Joseph L. Francomano	Alber E. Drummond Jr.
Billy Seals	Warren E. Christian
Donald A. Sorrentino	George M. Matthews
Vernon Mahan	E. Pomales-Santiago
Bobby Canterberry	Roger L. Desclos
Donald C. Trausch	John M. Juilien Jr.
Olie J. Belt	Carl M. Burke
Arthur G. Choquette	Sidney M. White
Edward R. Belardi Jr.	James W. Buddenberg
G. Cruhigger-Rodriguez	Earl D. Stoll
James J. Carlson	John J. Dopazo
Floyd F. Cox	Alefandro Gonzales
James A. Naour	William R. Haralson
Robert M. Ellars	George R. King
Owen A. Norton	Edward W. Breutzmann
Larry D. Turner	Donald R. Jackson
Thomas R. Cook	Thomas A. Janelle
Roy L. Griffin	Harold L. Piesik
Merlyn Johnson	James L. Gillam
French Mounts Jr.	William W. Lewis
John J. Boyle	Brian B. Thornton
Donald D. Miner	Donald L. Fish
Henry V. Camire	John T. Hoenes
Juan B. Cordova	Edward Schmitt
Arnold R. Tobias	Frank W. Halley
Harold E. Reins	Floyd Cooper Jr.
Jose M. Linares-Ortiz	Horace Hayes
David E. Halverson	Edward C. Benfold
Alfredo P. Charles	Richard C. Willmann
William A. McGinnis	Cecil A. Snodgrass
Mason C. Hazard	Gerald L. Haerr
Kenreth F. Wolf	Richard W. Kountz
Bill E. Johnson	Vincent Calvanico

****

Second Battalion (continued)

Henry V. Flores
Raymond C. Chapman
Ernest W. Schooley
Robert F. Miconi
Charles H. Hines

Third Battalion, First Marines

Melvin H. Weiss
Frank Harris
Merlin M. Mc Keever
Cornelius F. Harney
Ray A. Mc Claskey
Andrew J. Morgan
Earl L. Valentine Jr.
Fredrick W. Miner
Herbert L. Golding
Carol C. Prejean
Allan J. Bouquin
Richard Y. Kono
Robert A. Muth
Freddie L. Bradshaw
Robert L. Epperson
Charles E. Skinner
Leocadio Rivera

Stanley T. O'Banion
Robert King
John J. Hughes
Romolo A. Bucci
Tommy J. Neves
Leo A. Biross
Clarence C. Ferrell
Spurgeon Wright
Edward Goodman
Kermit M. Ferrell
John E. Finn
Antonia Jaime
John E. Lammers
Manuel G. Alvaredo
Marion Ray King
Daniel L. Blubaugh

ATCo First Marines

John C. Holley
John P. Langwell

Third Battalion, Eleventh Marines
Cornelius J. Baker Jr.

"C" Company, First Tank Battalion
John R. Hannigan

****

Presuming to be a United States Marine

After our company's third platoon, under my command, had been relieved on the outpost on Bunker Hill, activity on that outpost tapered off. The big probe on the night after I was relieved and sent back out to clean up was the last significant action on the outpost we had established on the east end of Bunker Hill. The Chinese seemed to have lost interest in that position. A few weeks later, the decision was made to move the outpost left to the western horseshoe instead of manning the eastern horseshoe. This new location of the outpost was the position where our company CP had been when we were on Bunker Hill in August, and was also the place where I had organized the cleanup of the hill with the KSC. The old abandoned position on the right came to be called Old Bunker, and the new position on the left became New Bunker. New Bunker remained an outpost of the First Division until the end of the war, I believe. While the Chinese could influence what happened on Old Bunker, because they could dig their way around it almost completely, they could never dig their way all around New Bunker. New Bunker Hill is also described in some detail by Martin Russ in his book *The Last Parallel*, which I have already mentioned.

Apart from the heavy patrolling, 229 was a fairly restful place to be, and I could almost look upon it as a rest cure. Lieutenant Jannelle was killed on October 7, and on about October 10, we received word that we were going to be relieved by the Fifth Marines and go into reserve. On the next day, we got new word that the First Regiment and the Fifth Marines were going to make history on the fifteenth of October, because the entire relief of lines was to be accomplished by helicopter. This meant that the Fifth Marines would be deployed by helicopter and flown up to landing zones just behind the main line of resistance. Next, the First Marines, who were going to be relieved, would load up the helicopters and be flown to their reserve positions in the rear. In October of 1952, the helicopters the Marine Corps had were not nearly as efficient or as large as the follow-on models of the late fifties and early sixties, especially in terms of their capacity to carry troops. The standard closed helicopter of the time would hold a pilot, a copilot, and maybe five, but usually four, fully armed and loaded passengers. Even though we were considerably under strength, we were, with replacements, probably back up to 160 men by this time, so that in order to extract our company, some forty helicopter-loads of four men each would be required. In order to relieve a whole regiment, swarms of helicopters would have to be deployed. But the powers that be intended to try a phased airborne operation, and this made sense. When one regiment relieves another regiment online, it is not done instantly with any mode of transportation. The procedure takes a long time to complete because each position has to be relieved individually. One of my main duties as company executive officer was to plan for any kind of embarkation or flight by organizing the company accordingly. I drafted up an order, broke the company down into helicopter teams of four men each, and got the word down to each platoon how they were to break down and who was going to fly in what helicopter.

The eagerly anticipated, by us at any rate, date arrived. Looking back from the top of 229, we saw coming north across the Imjin River clouds of helicopters carrying the

Taking on the Burden of History

Fifth Marines. They came roaring up, and when they began landing behind 229, we started to get the relief parties ready. As the new Fifth Marine platoons arrived and took up positions, our Fox Company rifle platoons were filing back up over the mountain to the helicopter landing zones. I was zealously running around, getting everybody organized. When I approached the landing zone, one of the helicopter officers told me, "Lieutenant, I am sorry, but it is pretty warm today. We can only take three men at one time because helicopters lose lift when the weather gets warm." On the spot, I had to reduce and reorganize each unit and its helicopter load breakdown. The idea was that these helicopters were to be loaded and deployed in such a way that when they landed, each unit retained its fighting integrity, and the people from the same unit would land in the same place.

In addition to this screwup, I also found out that we would not be immediately taken to the rest camp, but instead to something affectionately known as the Kansas Line. The Kansas Line behind the Imjin River was a very carefully prepared second line behind the main line, or Line Jamestown. The Kansas Line was entrenched and fitted with well-prepared fighting positions. Its purpose was to allow us to fall back south of the Imjin River in case of an overwhelming enemy attack. The Kansas Line was on good, high ground dominating the river. It had been worked on and improved ever since the marines had moved to the western Korean front in March of 1952. Even if the enemy had managed to get across the river, they would have had to frontally attack this well-prepared line with very little opportunity to retake Seoul.

By October 15, 1952, our company was pretty tired. It is sad to contemplate that of the 221 men and 7 officers who went online on July 27, I was the only officer left from the original company, along with 19 enlisted men. Several dozen men from the Thirteenth Draft, who had gone up on July 27, had been rotated back to the States, but the overwhelming number of our missing had been killed or were in hospitals. Now we landed in our helicopters at the Kansas Line, deployed smartly to the prepared positions, and waited for the next move. Fortunately, a blessed convoy of trucks appeared, so that this time around, we did not have to walk. We were headed for the battalion-sized reserve campsite closest to the division's command post, way back "in the rear with the gear." The terrain was rather rugged, but it was a nice and comfortable place, and I still look back upon it fondly. Further adventures awaited us there, with which I will regale you in a moment.

First things first, of course, and that was the essential whisky ration. The booze run had been made, and the battalion's ration was waiting for us this time around. But perhaps the biggest news for me was that Major McDonnell, the battalion operations officer, called me into his office and asked me, "Van, how long have you been here?" I told him it had been since May 5, and he said, "You have been with Fox Company the whole time, right? Well, I have talked to Colonel Batterton about this, and we would like you to be the new assistant battalion operations officer." The assistant battalion operations officer in a battalion is normally either a captain or a senior first lieutenant. It was something of an honor to be given the job, although I was going to be made a first lieutenant the following month, so that I would be a bit better ranked for the job. Once again, I was filled with conflicting emotions, not unlike those I had experienced when Groucho Marx tried to pick up my date back in Los Angeles. I knew that the job of an assistant operations officer was interesting and challenging, although I did not yet know that it would become even more interesting than I had anticipated. With this new job, I would also be the battalion liaison officer, and that meant that I would be the first person the battalion would send to any other sector at any time when there was a possibility of a deployment of the battalion to some new location. On the other hand, it meant leaving Fox Company. And that would be hard. Since it was the kind of job offer that I did not have to accept or reject right away, I talked to Captain Barrow about it. He encouraged me to take the job, reminding me how lucky I was to have survived. After I had become Major McDonnell's assistant, several humorous aspects to this new job evolved as time went by. I packed my gear at Fox Company and moved into a squad tent with the Headquarters and Service Company officers, some of whom subsequently became very close friends. Two of these officers were Lt. Pomocky, the hero of Siberia and still the commanding officer of the Headquarters and Service Company, and Lieutenant Tom Palmer, the battalion intelligence officer. Before I could leave Fox Company officially, there were two important ceremonies in which I had to participate. The first was a memorial ceremony similar to the one held back in the middle of June when we came off-line after the raid. As impressive as the June ceremony had been, it did not have the magnitude of the October memorial observance. In June we had honored fifteen Fox Company marines who had made the supreme sacrifice. In October it was forty-one.

The traditional Marine Memorial ceremony is always held in the field as soon after the deaths as feasible. The company is lined up at attention, platoons online, company online—the most formal formation troops can be placed in. The colors are presented and honored. The chaplain makes an invocation and says a few words. After this, one by one the names of the dead from the unit are read. As each man's name is read, a buddy of his comes forward with a bayoneted rifle. The bayonet is jammed into a sandbag in a straight line of sandbags, so that the rifle stands up vertically upside down. The buddy then places his helmet on the butt of the rifle and, for the remainder of the ceremony, stands there at attention, holding the butt of the rifle. Forty-one names took a long time to read, honor, and mourn. The memory of those forty-one bayoneted rifles, each with a marine standing by it, is still enormously moving to me. When all of our dead had been named, Captain Barrow said a few words, taps was played, and a firing squad fired a three-round salute. One of the most wrenching aspects of this ceremony was that some of our dead, particularly those killed in early August, no longer had any surviving buddies in the company—those buddies too had been either killed, wounded, or rotated. Some of the ceremonial bayonet and helmet holders had to stand in for dead men whom they did not know.

A second ceremony for Fox Company was a mass Purple Heart decoration ceremony. All the men out of the hospital and back with the company, as well as all men who

Taking on the Burden of History

had been wounded in action but non-evacuated, received Purple Hearts in a massive ceremony. I lined up for one last time as company XO. In a ceremony like this, the company once again is in platoons online, company online, across a wide front. The command is given by the first sergeant. "PERSONS TO BE DECORATED FRONT AND CENTER." On this occasion, over half of the company advanced to be decorated. For the smattering of men left behind, most of whom were new replacements, one can only imagine how exciting and frightening this occasion must have been for them. Captain Barrow pinned on my Purple Heart and said some nice things.

I had the comforting thought that when times were at their worst and most critical for me (the period from July 27 to October 15, 1952), my immediate superiors (Moody and Barrow), and the superior one rank above them (Batterton), had been outstanding. This fortunate condition becomes supremely important in war, as we will see.

My first task as assistant operations officer was to write up a battalion order in preparation for a change in command ceremony. Lieutenant Colonel Batterton was being relieved as battalion commander by Charles E. Warren, Lieutenant Colonel, U.S. Marine Corps. I don't quite know how I am going to deal with my subsequent disenchantment with him, because Colonel Warren had many virtues. He was experienced and one of the best supply officers in the Marine Corps.

He had taken over the supply battalion at Guadalcanal and had done a good job there. Warren was an expert on how to get hold of gear and how to distribute it. Although Colonel Warren had probably not been associated with an infantry outfit since prior to World War II, he had always had a hankering for the job of an infantry battalion commander, and in the end, the Marine Corps had succumbed to this request.

I must say that, for the job he was trying to do, he was the worst officer under whom I ever served in the Marine Corps. There is simply no way of getting around my eventual disdain for him, and it will not take me long to give ample and concrete evidence, beginning as early as the change-of-command ceremony.

The entire battalion was massed for the ceremony. As you looked across the battalion front, you saw lined up three-deep the first platoon, Dog Company, with the second platoon behind them, and the third platoon behind them, and the machine gun platoon behind them. Coming across the battalion front was Easy Company, Fox Company, Weapons Company, and Headquarters and Service Company, all lined up on our nice big parade field. We prepared all the troops for inspection. A new battalion commander is given the privilege of inspecting his new command by either walking up and down the lines, or by taking the weapon from each man to inspect his rifle. Major McDonnell, I, and the logistics officers, with the battalion staff in a small formation at the very front, prepared for inspection. The troops opened ranks, and the inspecting party of Colonel Batterton and Colonel Warren proceeded down the ranks to inspect the battalion.

Colonel Warren walked up to the first man in the first squad of the first platoon of Dog Company. That man was, of course, a sergeant, so that the colonel would not take his weapon. But the next man had a rifle, and Colonel Warren reached for it.

Presuming to be a United States Marine

Instantly, it became abundantly clear that he must not have inspected any rifles since, probably, Basic School. The colonel looked as if he did not quite know what to do with the weapon and handed it back to the trooper. A trooper holds the rifle at port arms, with his right hand on the butt of the rifle held low. His left hand is halfway down the barrel of the rifle, so that the rifle is held high at a forty-five-degree angle across the front of his body. The inspecting officer takes the rifle in that way and hands it back at that angle. Not Colonel Warren. He handed it back with the butt of the rifle down to the left and the muzzle up to the right. And God bless that trooper from Dog Company. He stood frozen like a statue and would not accept his rifle back. In due time, we came to realize that Colonel Warren had a way of covering over any embarrassing situation by growling. "GrrgrrrAuck" he now muttered, inspecting the rifle again and handing it back in the proper fashion, so unnerved, however, that he did not take any more rifles from the rest of the battalion. He walked down the ranks, still mumbling and growling under his breath. Roy Batterton must have known Colonel Warren, and I can only imagine what his feelings must have been to be turning his precious battalion over to somebody who did not even know how to inspect a rifle. As would become obvious in the future, the things Colonel Warren did not know about running an infantry battalion could fill volumes. After we managed to limp through the change of command, the orders were published, and the battalion colors were passed by Colonel Batterton to Colonel Warren in the usual colorful ceremony. Being off-line in a rest camp presented a good opportunity to give the troops a little pomp and circumstance, as well as a little spit and polish after all the muck and mud and the horrors they had experienced online. Whenever there is a change of command in a battalion, all the officers who remain get a fitness report from the outgoing colonel. My fitness report from Colonel Batterton was "superb."

With Colonel Warren, we got Major McNeill as the battalion executive officer. Major McNeill was a good man, and thank God we had him. Had we not had Major McNeill to temper Colonel Warren's foolishness at least to some extent, I don't know what would have happened to us. Even so, enough bad things came to pass in the future.

Major McDonnell, our brandy bearer on the morning after the Bunker Hill battle, was a real character. He sang in a strong, pleasant voice. He loved to sing the good old songs. He must have known the words and melody to every men's chorus song written up to that point in time. It turned out that Lieutenant Pomocky, the H & S Company hero of Siberia, was a singer too, along with a couple of recently arrived company commanders. Eventually, I got hooked on it as well. Major McDonnell shared a fairly commodious tent with another major, who was going to eventually relieve him. We would gather in the center of this tent, all the while partaking of liquid refreshments to keep our voices properly oiled. Under McDonnell's leadership, I learned many songs in those frequent songfests. Although we never became a barbershop quartet, as time went on, we tried to harmonize some of the songs. One night, during the ubiquitous rain, the top layer of the ground had gradually turned into the usual mucky soup. Major McDonnell's tent was on one side of a very steep, sharp rise, while our Headquarters and Service Company officers' tent sat on the other side of the same hill. The fastest way to get from Major McDonnell's tent back to our tent was to walk straight up over the top of the hill, where a helicopter landing pad similar to the one shown in the popular television series *M*A*S*H* had been constructed. After our songfest, I started out back to my tent in the pitch darkness, reaching the helicopter pad without any difficulty. Given that my whistle had been well oiled back in Major McDonnell's tent, I may have been a little bit unsteady on my pins. It was my plan to cut off to the right about halfway down the hill back to our tent when I was precipitously compelled to do a reprise of my famous mud toboggan slide online during the rainy season. My feet suddenly flew out from under me, and I went swooshing down the road in the slippery mud. When I reached the bottom of the hill, I slammed into a tent, like a crazed missile, understandably causing some consternation among its occupants. Somewhat lamely, I struggled back to my own tent once again, covered from head to toe with prime Korean mud, as well as a good measure of embarrassment.

Another time, our group of officers who shared the H & S Company officers' tent had some kind of a card game going, probably poker, or maybe blackjack. We were wrapped up in our game and enjoying it when Major McDonnell came in to invite us for an evening of song. It was getting late, and we did not feel like climbing around to the major's tent, and so we said, "No, Major, not tonight," trying to put him off his idea. But since he had probably partaken of some after-dinner refreshments himself, and since all of us were only lieutenants or, at most, captains, and he was a major, this did not sit very well with him at all. He continued walking around us, shoving playfully against some of us, urging, "Come on, come on, let's go sing. You don't want to play cards anymore. Let's go sing instead!" Respectful of his rank, we told him, "No, sir, we would really like to finish this game." But he seemed to be in the kind of mood in which he was not going to take "no" for an answer. Major McDonnell and I had developed a very nice close and friendly working relationship. Nevertheless, I now managed to do one of the dumbest things of my life. I stood up, saying, "Oh, come on, Major, it's just too late." I grabbed his arm in what I thought was an affable way. What I did not realize was that the back of his legs were against one of the cots, which caused him to lose his balance. In the most ignominious way, he tumbled backward over that cot, landing in a heap on the floor and leaving me aghast. He stood up; dusted himself off; and, without uttering one single word, stormed out of our tent. While I had about ten witnesses to the fact that I had not made any kind of gesture against him at all, except for holding on to his arm, I must confess to having a wild hope that he had feigned his fall, as basketball players sometimes do when they "take a charge." Naturally, all the guys immediately and obligingly pointed out the trouble I was in, without any doubt. "Back to Fox Company for you," they told me, along with all manner of other reassuring and helpful predictions on the demise of my future in the Corps.

Getting up in the morning and slinking down to the officers' mess tent, I attempted to make myself look smaller. I did not encounter Major McDonnell. Close to eight o'clock, I crept into the operations office tent with its field desks and drawing tables.

Presuming to be a United States Marine

Major McDonnell sat hunched over his little desk, writing away at something. "Sir, Lieutenant Van Sant requests permission to speak to the major," I said in the most formal yet humble way I could muster.

"What do you want?"

Sweating profusely, I said, "Sir, I want to apologize for what happened last night, and I want to assure the major that I was in no way attempting to knock him down."

He said, "Van, I don't want to talk about it. Forget it!" And that was that. The incident was never mentioned between us again, and we remained good friends.

During the last two weeks in October and the first couple of weeks in November, we had several other adventures in rest camp. Ted Williams, the famous baseball player, had been called back to active duty at the beginning of the Korean War. Ted had been an aviator in World War II, went to be retrained in jets, and had flown a number of missions in Korea. While piloting his jet in an attack mission in North Korea, a lucky Chinese machine gunner had hit his engine badly enough to disable it. Apparently Ted retained some control over the plane, managed to get it back over the lines to friendly territory, and crash-landed it on a field outside our camp. It is interesting to note how, even in a combat zone, word can pass in a flash. I would say that within no more than ten minutes after Ted Williams had climbed out of his plane safely, every man in the battalion knew that he had landed. There was a mass exodus with rank being no object. All of us lieutenants, captains, majors, privates, everybody, ran out the gate to see Ted Williams and his plane. I arrived at just about the time the division military police were putting up yellow tape all around the jet to keep everybody off and swatting down all the marines who were swarming over the plane like locusts, trying to get souvenirs of a piece of Ted Williams's plane to take home. Even though by the time I arrived Ted Williams himself had already left, I could at least console myself by getting a good look at his plane. It was an exciting experience to have one of the all-time great baseball players landing close by. We admired him for being able to control his plane so brilliantly.

My first experience as a liaison officer came on the fifth of November, and that was an adventure in itself. Up on Hill 229, we had had a front seat as the Chinese took Hill 151, before the Korean Marines took it back and held it. On the night of November 5, the Chinese made an all-out effort to annihilate the Korean Marine Corps. Their plan clearly was to drive all the way to the Imjin River and unhook the left flank of the entire UN line in Korea from the sea. As we subsequently learned, the Chinese threw at least one, and possibly two, divisions into this effort. Even though the Korean Marines put up a tremendous battle, our division headquarters was concerned about the magnitude of this Chinese attack. I would venture to say that their effort was bigger than anything thrown at us at Bunker and probably constituted one of the largest Chinese attacks in the last two years of the war. This time the attack was being launched against Koreans.

Division headquarters determined that in case of any threat of a Chinese breakthrough, our battalion, Second Battalion, First Marines, one of the three First

Taking on the Burden of History

Regiment battalions in reserve for the whole division would be the first deployed by the U.S. Marine Corps in support of the Koreans. That meant that our battalion had to send a representative to the Korean Marines. The task of battalion liaison officer to the U.S. Marine advisory group with the Korean Marines now fell to me. After reporting to the head of that group, a colonel, I had to keep abreast of all developments so that if our battalion had to be deployed in support, I would have all the information on where we were to go and what we were expected to do.

In our operations section, we had a wonderful character, Sergeant Sullivan, a mapmaker with whom I became close friends. There was also Corporal O'Brien, a sharp young man full of Irish blarney, who had been to some college before he came into the Marine Corps. I was given O'Brien to take with me as a driver, and off we went to the Korean Marines headquarters.

The Korean Marine Corps was organized into a large brigade structure. Their brigade headquarters was a large underground bunker with at least four or five rooms for the different operating branches. It was reminiscent of a beehive and filled with feverishly working staff people. The trip in the jeep to the headquarters had been pretty exciting. The enormous battlefield was being saturated with massive amounts of incoming artillery fire. There were guns firing, flares going off, and ambulances driving around everywhere, evacuating the wounded. From what I could observe, the Chinese were strongly menacing. They had not retaken Hill 151 but were threatening to go around it. The firefights taking place at the front lines were unusually visible from the brigade headquarters.

I was briefed by the USMC colonel adviser, and he suggested that I observe the battle from the operations office. It will not come as a surprise at this time that, even in 1952, our forces had the capability of intercepting radio transmissions from the other side and translating them immediately, although when I was released in 1953, I swore an oath that I would not give that information to anybody. The intelligence office adjacent to the operations office was clearly receiving a steady stream of current information everywhere across this fairly broad front of five or six miles. Every single artillery piece in the entire First Marine Division was being fired. The Korean Marines were firing in support of their own front lines, and we were getting support from some big army guns located in that western sector.

The senior marine advisor recommended to the Korean general commanding the brigade that he should try to get what we used to call rocket ripples, since the Marine Corps artillery corps was equipped with rocket batteries. A rocket ripple was a big holder with sixty-four very large rockets fired off in rapid succession. The problem with the rocket ripple, though, was that it had to be deployed forward. That meant that the rocket launchers had to be brought close in to the enemy before they could be fired. The technique was that once a rocket ripple was fired, the launchers had to be immediately pulled out. The rockets, as they blasted off, raised so much smoke, dust, and dirt that the enemy was immediately made aware of the launcher's location and could target it with counterfire.

Presuming to be a United States Marine

The First Marine Division brought up our whole rocket battery for this big battle in Korea that night. For several hours, the battle swayed back and forth with the outcome in doubt. Then the Chinese general commanding the entire operation decided to commit his reserve division. To accomplish this mission, he had to move his men across a bridge over the Sa-chon River just north of the battlefield. We intercepted word that he was bringing his reserves in at just about the time the rocket ripple arrived from the U.S. Marine artillery regiment. That rocket ripple was zeroed in on the area just at the north end of the bridge across the Sa-chon River, and it went off at the critical point where and when the Chinese sought access to the bridge. Having been laid in very accurately, it introduced sheer chaos. Over the radio we heard the Chinese generals in various states of extreme upset. Having probably lost hundreds of men, the commanding general could be heard weeping. The Chinese had accompanied the launching of their attack by a great number of bugles. We now started hearing the bugles again, only now they were playing a different tune. The survivors of the entire attack force of the Chinese turned around and withdrew. They simply melted away. The Korean Marines had achieved an enormous victory. To this day, November 5, 1952 is celebrated by the Korean Marine Corps as their day of honor.

In that impressive bunker, there were probably a dozen U.S. Marines of various ranks up to colonel, about fifty Korean Marine officers, and probably about fifty Korean Marine enlisted men, who were sticking pins in maps, drawing arrows, and briefing people back and forth. Much of the work was carried out on large flat tables covered with maps, manuals, and books.

While I could not understand the language of the victory statement the Korean general issued, the gist became visibly clear when spontaneously all the Korean Marines jumped up on the tables and began singing their national anthem. It was a most inspiring moment even for me as a spectator. I believe that much of the present Korean Marine Corps esprit dates back to their victory in that battle. They had suffered horrible casualties, although the Chinese casualties were even greater. My recollection is that the Korean Marines lost over three hundred men, killed, and certainly a thousand wounded. I would bet that the very heavy Korean regiment may have lost almost one-third of its strength in that single night.

November 10, of course, is always our Marine Corps Birthday. As we were in reserve, we were able to plan a full-blown Marine Corps Birthday party with all the pomp and circumstance. I look back upon the stirring experience fondly now, although some of us were destined to experience a major glitch. The mess hall put out word to all the troops that there was going to be a turkey dinner in honor of the Marine Corps Birthday celebration. After the ceremony on the parade ground, the troops filed into the mess hall, filled with expectations of a mouth-watering turkey dinner. Unfortunately, the mess sergeant in the troops' dining hall had made the tragic mistake of miscalculating the head count.

The troops were regularly rotated through the mess hall by companies. One week it would be Dog, Easy, Fox, Weapons; the next week Weapons, Easy, Fox, Dog; and the next week Fox, Easy, Dog, so that during the four weeks we were in reserve, each of the three rifle companies and the Weapons Company would get to eat first, and a different company would eat last. Dog Company had drawn the sad lot of eating last on this occasion. About one-half of the company got their turkey and sat down with it contentedly. But after that, the turkey ran out, sending the mess sergeant into a deep panic. There was clearly nothing to be done in this awful situation but to break out the old standby—Spam. What happened after the troopers looked down on their so-called celebratory turkey dinners constituted the only possible and logical conclusion to such a disaster. They immediately began bombarding each other freely with the Spam, banging their metal mess kits on the tables, and generally engaging in a bloody revolution.

The battalion officer of the day, Lieutenant Broujos also of Dog Company, was called to the mess hall. By the time he got there, things had deteriorated into utter chaos. Standing in the Spam-laced, deafeningly noisy atmosphere, Broujos did what I had seen another officer of the day do back in Camp Lejeune. Broujos took out his pistol and shot up in the air. This tactic never fails to get people's attention, and it proved itself true again in this instance. Broujos told the troops that nothing was going to happen to anybody, as long as everybody calmed down at once. And because Broujos was a good officer whom they knew well, they obeyed him, and the riot subsided. One might say it turned out a humdinger of a Marine Corps Birthday party, and raucous too.

About this time, Major McDonnell received orders for a job he had sought for a long time, commander of the Division Reconnaissance Company. He was relieved by Major Bob Dominick, another fine officer. A physics major in college, Dominick was assigned to work on guided missiles after World War II and in time received orders to ship to Korea as operations officer for an infantry battalion. He was a good and very smart man. He recognized that in terms of in-country experience, along with Lieutenant Vick in Easy Company, I was the most experienced officer in the battalion. Dominick did a wonderful job in Korea. He retired as a colonel also, and we now live close to each other in the Northern Neck of Virginia. When Bob took over, we reorganized the operations office together. Word came on about the sixteenth of November that we were to go back up online again to relieve the Seventh Marines. The first and third battalions were made the frontline battalions for the First Regiment, and our battalion was to be put in regimental reserve, which meant hot chow for us. We found ourselves back in the same camp where our battalion had been billeted when I first reported in the previous May. It was the beautiful big camp at Sangkorangpo on the big bend of the Imjin River, and we happily remained there for a good, long time.

As soon as we arrived back online, Major Dominick was given word by the regiment that we were expected to prepare something called recoil plans for the whole regiment. A recoil plan was a nice way to describe retreat and counterattack in case of enemy breakthrough. We were expected to prepare such a plan particularly for our battalion, the reserve battalion of the regiment. But once prepared, the plan was to remain in place so that any battalion could use the same plan. Major Dominick and I had a lot of fun fantasizing about various wild operations we were going to perform under our recoil plan. One I remember on our list of so-called contingencies was Recoil Plan E, which, in case of breakthrough by the Chinese, called for all men to inflate their mattresses and float on them across the Imjin River. We also visualized having the Marine Corps reinstitute cavalry to use as a counterattack force. Nevertheless, of course, we took our job very seriously and worked very hard on these plans, which are probably still stashed away gathering dust in some ancient archive.

And now we are up to November 20. After dinner that night, I went back to the operations tent to work on a plan to be carried out by a reinforced platoon from Dog Company two or three days later, when my field telephone rang. I picked it up and heard the voice of good old Pomocky, captain and commander of the Headquarters and Service Company.

"Hey, Van," he said, "could you come back up to our tent for a minute?" I let him know that I was busy working on something, but he insisted that I come because there was someone there who wanted to see me. Cursing gently to myself, I set aside whatever I had been working on and walked the fifty yards or so from the operations tent back to the tent where I lived. The tent was all closed up but lit up from the inside. As I opened the door, many voices yelled, "Surprise!" to remind me that it was my birthday.

All the officers in the battalion had come to help me celebrate, and Colonel Warren had had a birthday cake baked, which was certainly nice of him. Everybody cheered me and thanked me, and I was speechless. With his supply connections, only Colonel Warren could have produced a birthday cake in that position north of the Imjin. As the former commander of the First Service Battalion, he knew bakers in the rear. I have been the fortunate recipient of three really spectacular surprise birthday parties in my life, but this was the first one, and certainly the most moving. A couple of speeches were made, and the colonel asked me to come forward. He handed me a set of orders to report to division headquarters at six on the following morning. I must say that the colonel's eager participation in this wonderful surprise for me was much appreciated. He could be an awfully decent man in spite of his incompetence as an infantry battalion commander.

It was probably nine in the evening by then, with the party just getting started. I did not mind that division headquarters was miles away in the rear, because my birthday present was to pick up the November 21 contingent for R & R in Japan. The three or four other officers who had already been sent off had joined the battalion months and months after I had, and I had given up on ever being sent on R & R myself. What a nice and welcome birthday present this was!

The party continued with many toasts until I was finally able to get everybody out of the tent to snatch some sleep. Early in the morning, I made my way to division headquarters to start the process of R & R. I picked up my orders on the way to ASCOM City, the main depot for division supplies just behind Inchon. In order to go back to Japan for R & R I had to have a good uniform. At ASCOM City, my footlocker was brought out of storage so that I could get my gear. After that we continued on to Kimpo, the big airfield outside Seoul to catch the plane that would take us to Japan.

Taking on the Burden of History

According to division policy, each day, one officer and forty-five enlisted men were sent on R & R to Japan. The officer was in charge of the men, which meant that I had to muster them when I picked them up although, of course, I did not have to worry about any kind of disciplinary problems on that particular leg of the trip. Clearly, all forty-five men were more than eager to go. The problem would be at the other end after the five days of R & R, when I had to muster them again to get them back to Korea.

I mustered the men, and not surprisingly, they were all present and accounted for. We went out on the tarmac at Kimpo and climbed aboard a DC-54, a big, fat four-engine prop Marine Corps transport plane holding about sixty people and their luggage. Twice before our trip in November 1952, during the Korean War, Air Force planes carrying troops on R & R had crashed on their flight between Korea and Japan. Inevitably, the thought of these accidents crossed my mind, although I immediately reassured myself that we were in a Marine Corps plane, which would under no circumstance go down. No chance at all.

We took off and reached our altitude. A master sergeant aviator type came to ask me invitingly, "Would the lieutenant like a cup of coffee?" When I advised him that I would enjoy one, he said, "Well, Lieutenant, come with me." I noticed that this plane had some amenities I was not prepared for. The troop seats in the cabin were crammed in very much as they are in a modern jetliner. But through a doorway forward of the cabin was the crew chief's domain, boasting elegant and plush furniture and his own coffeepot, and I enjoyed meeting the pilot, copilot, and navigator in the cockpit later on. But I had not been in the fellow's care for very long when I realized that he did not just want to share with me a cup of coffee.

He told me, "Lieutenant, do you realize that we are now five thousand hours past one of our routine inspections and two weeks past another routine inspection? Lieutenant, they are flying us too far, too often, too much. We are just not being inspected enough." And he clearly felt that he had found a shoulder to cry on, because he continued in his litany of complaints. This airplane, this air crew, had not had a rest for three weeks. In that time span, they had flown to Europe and back, and flown a couple of times across the Pacific, and not only were they absolutely worn out, but all the important and vital mechanical checks on the airplane had not been carried out. That, as you may imagine, was not necessarily a reassuring fact for me to absorb. As I sat there sipping my coffee and remembering those two previous R & R plane crashes, I thought, *Oh God, please get me through this in one piece.* I don't believe I have ever been happier to see terra firma come up than at the end of that particular flight.

We landed in Kyoto, that beautiful city I had visited briefly on my way to Korea. Before checking into the bachelor officers' quarters for my first night, I bid the troops farewell and told them to meet me at the same spot five days hence for our flight back to Korea. After that, they were out of my control.

The bachelor officers' quarters were all set up for our R & R operation. As soon as I checked in, I was given my footlocker, and some boys took my dress shirts and uniform to clean and press in one hour so that I could go on liberty without disgracing the

402

Presuming to be a United States Marine

Marine Corps. The officers' club in Kyoto was a lovely place. It had a beautiful dining room, an orchestra playing dance music, and it was so elegant that I decided to stay where I was for the rest of the day before moving on and exploring elsewhere.

There was a message waiting for me at the front desk from Durante, a corpsman who had been with our first platoon in Fox Company. He is remembered as the man who had encountered a Chinese soldier in a trench line on top of OP-3 and, not being a conscientious objector, had whipped out his pistol and emptied the magazine without ever hitting the Chinese. Eventually, he had conked the enemy on the head with his empty pistol. He had been wounded, I think, back in June, and was evacuated back to the hospital in Japan, where he had a fairly long recovery period. Since the Naval Hospital in Kyoto had a shortage of corpsmen, Durante had been reassigned into that hospital. I am sure that this had been a welcome reassignment because Durante was living a life of luxury when I caught up with him.

In his job, he had access to the rosters of all R & R parties and had noticed my name. When I called him back, he invited me to a party the next night. He explained that he was living with a Japanese lady in an apartment in the civilian sector of Kyoto and that he and a circle of his fellow-corpsman friends socialized and had parties pretty regularly. He told me on the telephone, "I think you will enjoy yourself, Lieutenant, because we try to do everything in the Japanese manner." And this sounded very interesting to me. But for this night, having decided to hole up in the BOQ, I went downstairs to the dining room, ate a delicious steak dinner, and put it away with some cocktails.

There was a kind of a dance hall at the club, with a small orchestra of Japanese musicians playing dance music. All the men, of course, were officers, mostly marines. Most of the women were Japanese, but there were a few American nurses and civil servants present. The place was jumping, to put it mildly. As I walked in after dinner, I saw our former regimental commander, Colonel Layer, in full uniform, sitting in a corner with a very beautiful Japanese babe on his knee.

Let me share with you now my theory of leadership in combat. Up and down the chain of command, one can survive one lemon, and one can even survive two lemons provided they are not in a row, that is, one superior lemon and one inferior lemon, in terms of their rank and position. But when there are three lemons in a row, one is in deep trouble. Our regimental commander, when I checked into Korea, was Colonel Flournoy, a wonderful man and a great colonel. Colonel Quilici, the battalion commander who had originally assigned me, was a good man. And of course, Griff Moody, my company commander for almost all my first two line tours in Korea, was outstanding. Quilici was relieved by Batterton, and Batterton was a good man. But above all of them was Colonel Layer, who had relieved Colonel Flournoy. Colonel Layer had many good attributes. He was the only reserve officer who served as a regimental commander in the entire Korean War, and that is to his credit. He quite possibly was something of a publicity hound. The battle of Bunker Hill received a good deal of attention in publications like *Time* and *Life*, where we were repeatedly called "Colonel Layer's Boys." To the best of my knowledge, Colonel Layer came up

Taking on the Burden of History

to the division observation post on Hill 201 a couple of times at best, and without in my opinion ever achieving the status of a particularly heroic regimental commander. In all fairness, I must add that I really had it in for him since he had relieved Griff of command, summarily ordering him off lines for disobedience of orders. Colonel Layer had recommended him and allowed Griff to receive the Navy Cross, but he had relieved Griff of duty.

And now here was Colonel Layer in Kyoto, obviously drunk as a skunk, pawing over a cute Japanese woman on his knee and presenting as disgusting a sight as I had ever seen. As soon as I saw him in the little room off the dance floor, I turned around to leave. But Colonel Layer knew me, and he had recognized me, thanks again to all of my seventy-seven inches.

"Hey there!" he called across the room. "You are one of my boys! Come over here and meet . . . ," And he mentioned her name, and I had to go through the embarrassment of this full colonel's making a really big ass of himself. As soon as I saw a few officers whom I recognized from other outfits in Korea, I beat a hasty retreat. One of these officers was still recovering from his wounds, and I realized that by this time, he was beginning to anticipate his recovery and return to Korea to fight some more. I spent the night at the BOQ and the next day sightseeing in Kyoto. I think that most people who have visited Japan find Kyoto to be a most beautiful city.

In the evening, I set out to find Durante. The party turned out to be one of my great experiences, although I did not cover myself with glory at all times. The house was a traditional Japanese house with paper walls and padded flooring, something like raffia matting, so that it gave a little bit. As is customary in Japan, I took off my shoes before entering. Durante's apartment was on the second floor. Durante's "wif-oo" was cooking a Japanese dinner in the small kitchen. There were three other couples in attendance. In addition, my hosts had gone to the trouble of lining up a young woman to be my dinner companion.

It was a very festive party occasion in this completely Japanese environment. At least initially, I felt a little bit awkward about the rule that officers and enlisted men do not fraternize socially. But these men were corpsmen who made me feel welcome, and so I allowed myself to enjoy this interesting experience, the delicious meal, and copious amounts of sake. We sat cross-legged on the floor, Japanese-style, and the corpsmen were very much at ease in their Japanese clothing. We reminisced about our experiences online in Korea and talked at great length about Griff Moody. Durante had not heard the story of Moody's relief but knew that Colonel Layer was leaving the next day for the States. I must have witnessed the colonel's last fling in Japan.

But what would my Japanese visit have been like without an embarrassing episode? As lovely as the house was, unfortunately, there was only one restroom facility. In a native Japanese house, restrooms were quite different from ours. They consisted of a long, narrow trench over which one would squat or, if you were a man, stand over and aim. The restroom had a very inauspicious location on the first floor. The stairway from the second floor, where Durante's apartment was located, had almost at the bottom a ninety-degree turn with a little platform, from which the stairs cut down with a very sharp turn to the right into a little hallway. The restroom was actually behind the stairway.

Necessity and the potent nature of sake in due time prescribed that it was time to visit the restroom. I came lurching down the dimly lit staircase in my stockinged feet, unable to properly negotiate the right-hand turn to the little platform. Instead I proceeded to go straight, falling down about three steps, and finding a shortcut to the front hall by breaking through the wall. That wall, before I wiped it out, had hidden the staircase from the front entrance into the house. This experience sobered me up quickly. I apologized profusely all around and offered money for repairs. But my friends assured me that such a thing had happened before and would happen again and that, while the inside partitions could be easily destroyed, they could just as easily be replaced.

In spite of my temporary loss of dignity as an officer when I tumbled through that wall, the evening had turned out to be very agreeable. The young woman whom they had provided to sit with me and to entertain me, did just that. She was not there to provide sex, but rather, to offer me a relaxing time. I appreciated Durante's hospitality in providing me with such a pleasant dinner companion.

Back in my BOQ room, I determined that I was going to take off from Kyoto the next day for Osaka. Osaka has been called the Chicago of Japan. When I was growing up, Chicago was the second biggest city in America, the Number Two City, and everybody accepted it as such. Osaka was, and still is, after Tokyo the Number Two City in Japan. It is a large manufacturing center with an enormous population, many theaters, clubs, and all kinds of entertainment. I was told that Osaka was a neat place to go to, and so I made my way down there by myself. One of the failures of the R & R system was that only one officer from the division went on it each day. Unless you found an old buddy somewhere, you were completely on your own.

Once I arrived in Osaka, I checked into a luxurious brand-new international hotel and began exploring the town. The occupation of Japan inaugurated by General MacArthur was still ongoing. Many U.S. agencies had offices scattered all over the country, but especially in Osaka because it was such an important economic center. Somehow I fell in with a crowd of women who were civil service employees of one of the U.S. government agencies there. I separated one of the women out and was chasing her a little bit around the backseat of a car. She invited me into her apartment, and we were sitting on her couch when, suddenly, she turned to me, grabbed me by the shoulders, and asked very earnestly, "You are on R & R, aren't you?"

I admitted that I was. She said, "When do you have to go back?" And since this was my third night, I only had two more nights to call my own. She told me, "I like you, and I would like to go out with you, but I have to tell you that I have had it up to here dating guys who are on R & R. So get out!" And that was that. I was back outside alone in the cold and cruel world. In spite of my disappointment, I must say that I could fully understand that young woman's feelings. She was clearly looking for a relationship

Taking on the Burden of History

that would last longer than a couple of days. And if some of her colleagues in the civil service had not reached this conclusion, they must have begun losing some of their self-esteem from the brief affairs they had with guys who were arriving from and returning to Korea. I thought it was to that young woman's credit that she was so direct and firm about her feelings with me.

The next night, I went out to explore the nightlife of Osaka. This was a time of rebuilding in Japan, and I discovered a new nightclub with something resembling a bullring inside, and tiers of tables in a circle around the dance floor. The dance floor was pivoted in the center and rotated the dancers on it slowly around. The club was mostly frequented by the Japanese, and I found myself among no more than about a dozen Americans in attendance. Sitting in my seat at a table on one of the tiers, I enjoyed myself observing the scene on the dance floor. The Japanese men of that era could really drink hard, and from time to time, one of the men would lose his balance, staggering all the way across the floor and collapsing in a heap on the other side, where the floor sat still. But possibly the most thrilling aspect of R & R was being able to take a bath at least once a day, getting all clean, and feeling like a civilized human being again.

On the evening of my last night, after returning to Kyoto, I was sitting in the bar of the club well before dinnertime. The telephone rang behind the bar, and the Japanese bartender called out for Lieutenant Jones. Lieutenant Jones picked up the receiver and said, "Hello, Mom! How are you doing?" And he proceeded to have a three- or four-minute conversation with his mother, his father, at least one of his siblings, as well as his girlfriend. After he had hung up, I could tell that he was high as a kite from this conversation. This was my last night in Kyoto, and I jumped on the lieutenant, "You were talking to somebody in the States, weren't you?" And he explained to me that if you called a certain number, the Japanese overseas operator would put in your call and add it to the running inventory, and tell you, almost to the hour, how long it was going to take for your call to come up to the head of the line to be placed anywhere in the United States; and after you were given the time, you had to give them a telephone number where you could be reached.

I immediately called the Japanese operator and asked how long the wait for a call to the United States would be. Very politely, the lady told me, "We are really swamped now, and so it will probably be about twenty hours."

Since it was now about five in the afternoon, and since I had to leave the next morning for Korea, there were no twenty hours left in my R & R. And while I must say I had been really well taken care of otherwise, nobody had told me about being able to make a telephone call home with a prior reservation. And that was too bad.

The next morning, I was driven out to the airfield in Kyoto, my roster in hand of the rest of the forty-five troopers from the First Marine Division who were going to fly back to Korea. The plane was to leave at some time around nine o'clock in the morning. At ten minutes before nine, forty-four men were present. No doubt about it; there was one missing. I talked to some of the aviation officers and asked them what would happen if my last man did not appear. Well, in those days, as had been explained to the troops beforehand, to miss the connection back to Korea constituted what in the military is called missing a movement, and missing a movement is punishable by up to a special court-martial. It is a particularly severe form of absence without leave. It will be remembered that when I was a young private in Pearl Harbor bound for China, had I missed my ship after it sailed, I would have been in very deep trouble. I would, in fact, have missed a movement.

My watch showed five minutes before nine o'clock, and the young lad had not arrived yet. We started loading onto the plane when, in a cloud of dust, a Japanese taxicab came roaring in. Our worried marine ran for his life across the tarmac and just barely made it in. I was so glad to see him because he would have been in deep trouble had he arrived even a few seconds later.

After five days of civilized living, the ride from Japan back to Korea was pretty grim, although as soon as we got on the plane, we all desperately clung to a festive atmosphere as the troops were all swapping sea stories about the adventures they'd had in Japan. And never mind that many of these adventures were possibly outright lies. At the same time, and you could see it in the troopers' eyes, the awful thought of having to go back to the lines was clearly at the back of everybody's mind. It was another instance of mixed feelings created by circumstances beyond our control. I remember being anxious to get back because the great Dog Company raid had taken place in my absence, and I was eager to find out what had happened. In ASCOM, I placed my footlocker and all my nice uniforms back into storage, had myself reequipped for combat, bounced back to division in a truck, then out to my regiment, and finally out to my battalion, where I arrived around suppertime.

As soon as I walked into the operations tent, I asked Major Dominick how the Dog Company had fared with their raid. He gave me a rather ambiguous look and said, "Not too well." It seems that something we had done in preparation for the raid had tipped off the Chinese. As soon as we had jumped off, they immediately reacted by subjecting our men to a counterattack before they even reached their objective. We took a great number of casualties in the enormous Chinese artillery and mortar fire. As Dominick told me, within five minutes of the beginning of the action, sixty men had been wounded and several killed. Lieutenant Broujos covered himself with glory, not for the first time or for the last, by managing to keep organized and by getting the wounded and the killed back to the main line. To put it bluntly, the raid was a failure and never even managed to get off the ground. This was very sad to hear, although one rather interesting story emerged.

We always had in the Second Battalion, First Marines, headquarters two surgeons, both navy lieutenants senior grade. These were medical officers who had completed their internships. The service of surgeons in combat qualified, in part, as their residency so that they tended to be rather young men. The two we had at that time were two of the greatest characters I have ever known. Dr. Marsky was actually a pediatrician, who used to comment about not being very well equipped for dealing with all the wounded men he was called upon to treat. The other surgeon was Dr. Pernokas, a doctor of Greek extraction from Baltimore. Pernokas was, undoubtedly, one of the best combat surgeons the navy had. After his tour of duty as a battalion surgeon, he went back to what we call in the navy and Marine Corps collecting and clearing companies, and these were the same as the army's MASH, or Mobile Surgical Hospitals. In the Collecting and Clearing Company, after an action some months later, I heard that Pernokas had operated for twenty-eight hours straight, and that all his patients had survived. I came to know Pernokas quite well, because we later shared a tent for a time.

When Dog Company's unsuccessful raid quickly began producing casualties, Marsky and Pernokas went right up to the lines to take care of them. As a pediatrician, Marsky was very careful and methodical, and therefore slow. He competently took care of and evacuated five of the sixty wounded. Pernokas took care of and evacuated the remaining fifty-five. The two doctors with their different backgrounds accomplished their tasks in equal time.

After my restorative R & R, the first blow I received was the news of the raid debacle. The second blow was even harder. Tom Palmer, our battalion intelligence officer, called me over and said, "I know you were a friend of George Morrison's." Tom had been a Basic School classmate of George's and knew him well also. And Tom said, "I have some bad news for you. George was killed." Subsequently, I learned the full story about what happened to George. When we arrived in Korea in May of 1952, George was already a first lieutenant. He was given Easy Company, Second Battalion, Fifth Marines. Our paths had crossed when George's company came up and took our positions while we went on the raid in June. George kept the company, and all through the summer and fall of '52, he was Easy Company's commander. He was the only first lieutenant company commander in the entire First Marine Division, because the rank of captain is the table of organization rank for this position. The assignment simply came as a recognition of his leadership skills. I was given a clue of these skills when one of George's officers talked to me about Lieutenant Morrison at the Widgeon Bridge. His troops, I thought, had the same feelings about him as our troops had about Griff Moody. George's company had manned the same section of the line where we had been during the Stromboli action in early August. Marines still maintained an outpost on Stromboli and still patrolled forward of that, just as we had done during the summer.

It was now late November, and George had ordered a patrol from his Easy Company to go out to the same general area where my staff sergeant, Crawford, had been badly hit. The patrol stepped into a fairly large firefight with the Chinese. Many marines were wounded. George had put on a flak jacket and, strapping the radio on his own back, had gone down to oversee and supervise the cleanup and evacuation of the wounded. Unfortunately, his action echoed Griff's. Like Griff, George got in trouble for moving forward of the main line through the famous cut leading to Stromboli. But George's troubles were of a catastrophic nature.

Presuming to be a United States Marine

George carried one of the rear corners of a stretcher bringing in the last wounded man. George, who, as you will remember, was big and beefy, never zipped up his flak jacket in the front. Now the weight of the radio he was carrying on his back pulled the unzipped flak jacket farther apart, exposing his chest. A large Chinese mortar shell, probably an 82 mm, landed directly on the stretcher. It killed the wounded man and all the stretcher bearers, including George.

But the legendary George Morrison went down in history. After the shell had landed and he was only barely alive with a big piece of shrapnel lodged in his chest, George got his handset from his radio and reported in to his battalion commander that all the wounded had been evacuated. Next, George reported five more deaths, KIAs—killed in action, under the code name of Schlitz.

"Five more Schlitz," George reported, "including Easy Six." Easy Six was George Morrison's own code name. George had reported his own death.

Tom Palmer, my good friend, told me this story. Coupled with the problems the Dog Company raid had experienced, all this was a sharp contrast to my surprise birthday party and my orders for R & R.

Chapter 16

Winter and Back Online

I soon got back to work. It was now the end of November and the beginning of December, and we began to experience what people often associate with Korea, namely the Korean winter. Much of what you may have heard about the Korean winter is true. Korean winters are tough, very tough. Soon after I returned from R & R, we had our first storm, which deposited about five or six inches of snow on the ground. Major Dominick told me that regiment was unclear as to the exact map locations of what we called blocking positions across the regimental front, and that we had no real up-to-date overlay of all these positions. He gave me whatever information we had, and Sergeant Sullivan, the draftsman in our operations section, and I loaded up with water and rations and took off at predawn, because the days were pretty short by now. We walked the total regimental front of about ten very hilly miles just behind the trench line front, and we sketched out and mapped and put down the coordinates of every one of the so-called blocking positions for the entire regiment. We walked uphill and down, and we walked the whole length one way and back, double-checking all our observations in the process. The task of getting the raw data, then copying the data and the coordinates down on the rough overlays took us from dawn to dusk.

When we returned, we found out that the temperature had never climbed above about fifteen degrees Fahrenheit, which is closer to zero than one might think. By that time, we had been issued what in the Marine Corps were called Mickey Mouse boots. Mickey Mouse boots had a layer of fiberglass insulation between two layers of rubber, like a fiberglass insulation sandwich, and were enormously effective. In fact, the boot may have been too effective. I will never forget pouring probably a pint of perspiration out of each one of my boots at the end of that long day and, about a week later, being blessed with immersion (or trench) foot brought about by that one day of walking in my sweat inside the Mickey Mouse boots. But I should not complain; my feet were never cold but remained nice and toasty. Sullivan and I went over all the data we had gathered, and Sullivan, the good draftsman with a little bit of artistry thrown in, turned out an excellent product. Regiment was very happy with our work. I had taken a camera along on that trip, and I snapped a picture of Sergeant Sullivan standing on the 38th Parallel. Of course, our good maps and compasses helped us to calculate its exact location.

In December the weather settled down to being really cold. We had one day I remember well, when the temperature went down to eight degrees below zero. This was the day when I had another painful but, in retrospect, rather humorous misfortune. As the weather turned progressively colder, I began operating on a schedule that would take me to the toilet in the heat of the day between noon and one in the afternoon. It was simply too cold to do a bowel movement at any other time of the day. We were still in regimental reserve then and had a so-called four-holer, a wooden structure with four seats cut into it and a deep pit under it, the contents of which were covered daily with lime. Our four-holer was surrounded by a wall of canvas, so that we had some privacy on the sides. There was no roof.

On that very cold day when the temperature dipped to eight degrees below zero, I suddenly became very busy around noon on some project, and so I kept postponing what I knew would be my inevitable journey. Something else kept coming up—I got yanked out to go back to regiment in the jeep, and as the sun was going down by five o'clock, I had still not made my daily pilgrimage. I decided that I was just going to have to wait until the next day. But as the evening wore on, Mother Nature sent me stronger and stronger signals, giving me to understand that I was not going to make it to the next day. At about eleven that night, I finally succumbed and struggled to the four-holer in the dark.

I have mentioned the Mickey Mouse boots. But to the everlasting credit of the Marine Corps, our whole bodies were kept warm by layered clothing consisting of long underwear, with a regular work uniform on top of that and over it another layer of fleece-lined, water-repellent gear, topped off with a parka. The fact was that except for the hands, which could not fire a rifle if covered with mittens, this costume was so efficient that our bodies were constantly covered with a thin patina of perspiration.

And so, obeying Mother Nature, I dropped my trousers and sat down on one of the four available holes, and oh, that wood was cold! But I dutifully answered the call. When it came time to clean up, I reached for the paper and started to rise but quickly realized that I was stuck to the seat. I was frozen to the seat. I was frozen hard to the seat, and I realized that when part of my body was exposed to the elements and joined to that cold seat, the patina of moisture on it had frozen to ice. I simply could not move. I did what you should never do in circumstances like this. I panicked and hurled myself off, but not without leaving a thin circle of myself bonded to the seat. The part of me that got away remained rather sore for several days on the rounded outline of the seat quite clearly marked on my buttocks. This, I thought, was life at its lowest ebb. It was really tough.

In early December, we were alerted to the fact that President-elect Eisenhower was going to be visiting the First Marine Division. During his campaign against Adlai Stevenson, the Korean War had become a campaign issue, and Ike had promised that "win or lose," after the election, he was "going to Korea." Adlai Stevenson had made the same promise. And so we braced ourselves for the visits. During the months of August, September, and October, when I had been company executive officer, I had also been the company voting officer. This meant that each man who voted by absentee ballot had to have his sealed ballot notarized by me, and I was responsible for forwarding it back to the troopers' local election board. The reader will remember that during that period, we had lots of other things on our mind, and so not many men had voted. I think only eight had managed to do so, and at least one of the eight was killed long before the election. In fulfilling this duty, I was very scrupulous not to express any interest in how the men had voted, but every single one of them felt compelled to tell me. Ike carried Fox Company seven to one. I myself was unable to vote. Had I voted, it would have been for Adlai, although I have always admired Eisenhower too. But my father was a classmate of Adlai Stevenson's at Princeton, and they had known each other there.

We were informed that Ike was at division headquarters. He never came forward of that position, and this caused some amusement among the more knowledgeable troops. The First Marine Division headquarters was so far south of the Imjin to the rear of our front lines that it was immune to enemy fire. The papers at the time reported that Ike had gotten to within artillery range of the enemy. We all commented that if the Chinese had taken their largest artillery piece, towed it forward to their most advanced and southernmost outpost, and loaded it with the maximum number of powder charges, they might have been able to reach the First Marine Division headquarters with a shell. Thus, Ike had not been in much danger.

A couple of weeks later, after we had gone up to the lines, word came through that Adlai Stevenson would be in the division sector. Then we heard from the main line of resistance where the word had spread like wildfire all the way across Korea that Adlai had visited the Hook. Now the Hook on the extreme right flank of the division had been the scene of several great battles and was now in the hands of the British Commonwealth Division. Not only did Adlai visit the Hook, but while he was there, the Chinese threw in a ten- or fifteen-round mortar concentration right on the position he was visiting. He had to take cover, and his escorts were in quite a tizzy over it. But the news spread quickly across the entire Eighth Army front that Adlai Stevenson had been under fire. The contrast with Ike's brave advance up to the First Marine Division's headquarters two weeks before could not have been greater. I think that if the election had been held just in our sector that day, Adlai would have scored a stunning victory.

While our battalion was in regimental reserve, our right-flank battalion on the MLR was tied in with the British Commonwealth Division. The lines had been readjusted in the fall of 1952, so that everybody had moved left, or west, by one company front because it was realized that the First Marine Division was covering about twice as much front line as any other division in Korea. Therefore, we needed to consolidate our positions, and that meant that the British took over the Hook. In early November, while we were still in division reserve, the Seventh Marines had fought a very tough battle on the Hook, but had held it. The Hook was the largest position on what was then the right flank of the First Division. It got its name from the way the terrain looked on the map, curled around like a hook.

The Black Watch, the very famous Scots regiment, came with the British Commonwealth Division to the Hook. It was not as large as our regiment, but they occupied the same zone we had formerly occupied with a rifle company. The British clearly did not spare their troops when they were digging in. In December, and this culminated a number of attacks by the Chinese on the British, the Chinese made an all-out attempt to take the Hook. Even though the British had a real defense in depth behind the Hook, the Black Watch found itself embroiled in a tough battle, which got all the way down to hand-to-hand combat. But the Black Watch prevailed in this fairly decisive fight.

Because we were the reserve battalion near regimental headquarters, every day Colonel Warren would take me as the battalion liaison officer back to regimental headquarters to a briefing at about 6:00 p.m., or 1800 hours. I dreaded these trips for a number of reasons. For one thing, it meant being in a jeep with Colonel Warren, for whom by this time, I had no use. He was such a sham, talking tough, growling, "Van Sant this," and "Van Sant that." He had become a really distasteful individual to me. As if this were not bad enough, our vehicle was fitted out with side curtains that enclosed it, and a part of the backseat had been taken out to insert a heater. Because the body of the jeep was made of canvas, the designers, figuring that enough heat would have to be generated for the prevailing frosty conditions, installed heaters powerful enough to heat an entire house. As was customary, the senior officer sat next to the driver in the front seat. I as the junior officer sat in the back right next to the heater.

I would get all bundled up to walk to the colonel's tent in about 10 degrees or 15 degrees above zero, or on many a night, right at zero. Next, I would climb into the jeep where the temperature had to be 130 degrees or 140 degrees. The ride from our battalion command post to regimental headquarters was not too long, but it was over a bumpy road, and I would suffer all the way there. The regimental briefings were interesting and entertaining and tended to confirm the view my friend Captain Moody held, that people back at the regimental headquarters have no idea what takes place up at the front lines. Having been a front-line trooper myself, it was interesting for me to see how matters looked from the rear. It is quite simply a different war, back at regimental headquarters.

We would often get briefings from the Commonwealth Division's liaison officer, as it was customary to keep everybody across the front informed of what was happening in adjacent sectors. I must say that one of the most entertaining of these briefings came after the big Commonwealth Division's Battle of the Hook, where the Black Watch had distinguished itself. Their liaison officer gave a beautiful battle briefing on the Chinese breakthrough and how the Black Watch counterattacked and threw the enemy out, and all the bloody fighting and the considerable casualties the Black Watch had suffered. The Chinese had suffered many more casualties, of course, and one of the reasons for this was the tremendous artillery support the British had given to their troops in the battle.

And I shall, for the rest of my life, remember the wonderment on the part of our marine officers when the liaison officer casually stated that, "I think you people call them box-me-in fires, but we call it battlefield isolation. We fired battlefield isolation around the Hook on the enemy side." One of the more senior marine officers asked what volume was fired, and the Black Watch liaison calmly answered, "Oh, we fired about sixty or seventy thousand rounds of three-pounders."

"Sixty or seventy THOUSAND rounds!" several senior marine officers exclaimed in amazement.

One of the best-kept secrets in the Korean War was that we were on a kind of ammunition rationing. For normal day-to-day operations, when we were just manning our lines, patrolling, and sending out outposts, we were only allowed to fire so many rounds of mortar of a certain caliber and so many rounds of artillery. That was simply all we had. I will say that the rationing was removed during such times as when we were surrounded and almost overrun at Stromboli, and also on Bunker Hill in August. In cases like these, whatever ammunition was needed to do the job could be fired. But at no time in any of these battles, or in any of the subsequent battles, did we ever fire anything approaching that many rounds. Our marine officers became increasingly more upset and horrified about the wasteful "Limeys" expending all that ammunition, and perhaps somewhat enviously wondered how in the heck they got away with it. The British liaison officer, then, gave a very good and quite interesting explanation.

The British standard regular light artillery piece, which corresponded to what we called our 105 howitzer, was a gun they called a three-pounder. The three pounds referred to the amount of the explosive that was actually in the shell, and the piece was standard all through World War II for the British, just as the 105 was for us. At the beginning of World War II, and before Japan had attacked Pearl Harbor and had declared war on Britain, the British had sent a convoy of supplies and equipment to Hong Kong to be redistributed throughout the Orient to the various British units stationed out there. One of these ammunition ships, completely loaded with three-pounder ammunition, was sunk at Hong Kong, but the ammunition did not explode because it was very tightly sealed up in containers. The fatal damage to the British cargo ship had been nowhere near the cargo hold, so that throughout the war, on the bottom of Hong Kong harbor sat a ship filled with three-pounder ammunition.

After the war, a British salvage organization was able to bring up all of the ammunition in its waterproof containers and set it out on a dock in Hong Kong. The British ordnance people wanted to send it back to England. But more senior English authorities concluded that because the ammunition, although sealed up, was at least six years old by the time it was salvaged, it could not be returned to the home island. After cutting through some British red tape, the Commonwealth Division obtained permission to shoot up the ammunition in Korea. And so a whole shipload of three-pounder ammunition was sent to Korea and arrived there from Hong Kong at just about the time of the Battle of the Hook. The orders were to shoot it up, so the British unloaded on the poor Chinese thousands and thousands of rounds of artillery fished up from Hong Kong harbor. It was a good explanation, and we understood it, and whatever jealousy there may have been on our part went unspoken, and there was a little bit of twentieth-century history in it too.

The British artillery was a fascinating subject. The actual cannon in an artillery organization was usually somewhat behind the lines. Artillery men didn't normally engage in ground combat. There were certainly many exceptions to that, particularly in a breakthrough. All artillery men were trained in what was called direct-fire techniques. As the enemy closed in on an artillery position, the guns were lowered and fired directly at them with a big blast. But the normal way of shooting artillery was by so-called indirect fire when the men shooting the cannons don't see the target. They were connected by radio, or in some cases by telephone, with a forward observer who called in the rounds from the gun. The gun was fired by lining up the barrel on an aiming stake, which gave the lateral, from side-to-side motion. The altitude of the barrel was measured on a vertical scale plate, which had a bubble mechanism, much like a carpenter's level. The bubble would be leveled at a certain altitude. The other variable was the number of charges put behind the shell. Theoretically, with all these variables, one could fire a cannon and hit a target on the nose. Artillery usually covered an area of fires in what was called a concentration, and most of the time, they were fired by a whole battery. There could be several batteries of twelve to sixteen guns, all firing at once. Sometimes, particularly in a big battle, as the observer adjusted his fire, the gun crews would fire continuously.

I have discussed my own story of a precision mission, when a bigger gun would be hitting a point target on the ground. A precision mission could be fired with a three-pounder or a 105, but the gun itself would not be very accurate. About the time I was taking the steam-bath jeep rides back to the regimental briefings, a friend of mine was in an outfit that tied in with the Black Watch behind the Hook near a large observation post the forward observers used for a panoramic view of the battlefield. A British artillery officer was in the OP one day trying to hit a point target in front of the Black Watch on the Hook with a precision mission using a single three-pounder gun. The target was a hole situated on a very steep hill, almost a cliff, which meant that the target presented itself literally as a point target. The poor old British officer would fire a round, and it would be too far, and he'd drop it, and it would be too short. Then he would fire over and get off to the side a couple of times. My friend, who was watching up in the OP, said that the British officer was getting more and more frustrated. He was beginning to expend ammunition although, as we found out later, the British did not have to worry about that since they were blessed with an almost infinite supply. But this precision mission was taking much time and effort. In great exasperation after missing his target for about the fortieth time, the British officer, according to my friend, exclaimed, "By God, I am going to stay here until I hit that fellow, even if I have to miss tea!" I am happy to say that many years later, when I was touring Edinburgh,

Taking on the Burden of History

Scotland, I saw, in Edinburgh Castle, a shrine to the Black Watch, and incorporated into the shrine was the regimental history with detailed descriptions of the Battle of the Hook, and of all the British officers who were involved in it.

We finally got word on about December 7 or 8 that we were going to go up to what was the left battalion position in that regimental front. It turned out to be the same battalion lineage that we'd had when I first joined the unit in May, but moved one company front to the west. Fox Company was put back on the old position behind Stromboli. There were, of course, very few people left in Fox Company in December who could remember being there in August. Sergeant Smith was still there, bless his heart, and continuing to do a good job.

For a front-line command post, the battalion command post for that left battalion was quite good. It was positioned not very far behind the lines, and if something was going on along the lines, we felt a part of it. The main feature of this command post was its commodious operations bunker, although it was not of the size of the Korean Marines Regimental Headquarters bunker I described earlier. We lived in tents scattered around a horseshoe-shaped road surrounding a paddy. On the higher ground around the paddy were nice tent sites. We lived and slept in tents but worked in the big bunker. The troops had a big tent, and we even had a little mess tent. Online a battalion headquarters just has a small number of enlisted and officer staff, because all the troops from the rifle companies and from Weapons Company are up on the line.

We remained there until we went off-line on the sixteenth or seventeenth of January, a total of about five weeks for me. It was the dead of an extremely cold winter, and we had to make many adjustments because of the very low temperatures. But we settled in, and Major Dominick and I developed a routine. He lived in a tent with the battalion executive officer, Major O'Neill. Colonel Warren, our golden boy commanding officer, had a tent of his own. I shared a staff tent with three other officers. Fortunately, for most of the time we were there, we were not too heavily engaged, except for one ghastly episode.

Operating an infantry battalion in combat generates an enormous amount of record keeping and work and a great deal of communication. The bunker was equipped with radios and phone lines to everybody. We worked hard. I awoke at noon every day, went to the mess tent, and ate what was being served at that time, namely lunch, and that was my first meal of the day. I then worked all afternoon in the bunker until dinner, after which I would return to work. Most of our combat patrols and our small raids, and most of the Chinese activity began at about 8:00 or 9:00 p.m. and continued through the night. This was a nighttime war, no question about it. Major Dominick would be operations officer an hour or so before midnight. He would then return to his tent, and I would take over. From then until five o'clock in the morning, I was the operations officer for the battalion. Running the battalion gave me a great feeling. Periodically I would check with the company commanders to arrange for artillery or mortar fire and to make preparations for air raids in the morning if necessary. It was a very fulfilling job, and I like to think that the company commanders came to rely on me, because

Presuming to be a United States Marine

I was usually on watch when anything happened. Dominick, who was an early riser, would often have a cup of coffee and early breakfast and drift in at about six o'clock or seven o'clock. We did not really have anybody on watch from five o'clock to seven o'clock or eight o'clock, but then nothing much happened during those hours.

When I was off my watch, I would return to my tent. Climbing into a cold sleeping bag in a cold tent at five in the morning is an experience I would not wish on anyone. God, it was cold! But there were a few compensations. Peggy, the lady whom I married after the war and who became the mother of my children, had sent me a lovely package sometime in November. She had come across a small lifesaver. It was a flat little metal bottle filled with cotton. By pouring lighter fluid into it, lighting it, and closing it up it would turn into a very small heater. I could defrost my hands on it, or I could stick it down into my sleeping bag to warm at least a small portion of myself. On arrival in my ice cold tent, I would gratefully light up this thing, warm my hands first, then stick it down into the general area of my feet inside my sleeping bag. At 5:00 a.m. each day, I allowed myself one single shot from a bottle of Old Fitzgerald, the finest bourbon ever made, to warm up my interior before sliding down into my bag, feeling around for Peggy's warmer with my toes, and going to sleep. *Bang!* I would be asleep just after 5:00 a.m. every morning and wake up at noon to start another day. And this routine worked out very well.

The operations bunker held the intelligence section, the operations section, and the logistics section. Intelligence and logistics would have an enlisted man, and either one of their sergeants or one of their clerks on duty all night. Sometimes Tom Palmer, the intelligence officer, would stay up too, but as operations officer, I was in charge of the entire bunker. In the hours before midnight, all the more senior officers, usually the battalion exec and Colonel Warren, would come into the bunker to get caught up on what was happening, look at the maps, try to figure out what was to be done next, and ask questions.

It was in these long evenings in December that I was able to form a pretty clear appraisal of Colonel Warren's inadequacies as a battalion commander. I will give him credit for asking questions occasionally. On the other hand, his questions were so elementary that I would be shaken by the thought that my life was in the hands of this man who often pretended that he knew the answers to everything. It soon became clear that Colonel Warren was not really much interested in fighting a war now that he had his battalion and could add that experience to his resume. He was happy, I think, that he had commanded an infantry battalion in combat. Colonel Warren was in the habit of bringing in a little folding camp stool and setting it up along the middle of a long table with intelligence on one side and operations on the other. We soon realized, to our dismay, that the colonel was reading comic books. He would sit there all evening, deeply immersed. Occasionally, something would amuse him, and he would chuckle to himself. I thought about all my idealistic views on the heroic commander in combat, a view certainly reinforced by Colonel Batterton, the great combat commander who was always on the job and always working, and found them dashed by this new man leading us by reading comic books. Colonel Warren, in fact, had nothing to contribute. He almost always let his staff and his subordinates solve a problem, although I must add that I would come to wish he had invariably done that.

Tom Palmer worked well with the aviation people, and about every four or five days, we would get an aerial photo run of our front. The photographs were taken in what was called stereo pairs to be viewed through a pair of lenses on a little rack. The photo pair was taken in such a way that they would pop up three-dimensionally when viewed through the lenses. Two pictures were required to achieve this effect, one taken slightly ahead of the other. It was the same principle as the stereopticon used at the turn of the nineteenth century before we had movies. These old-fashioned stereopticon lenses were just like the ones we used.

One night Colonel Warren was reading his funny books while we were all working away busily. Tom had just received a good new run of photos of our front, and they were all set out on a part of the intelligence section table close to the colonel. He grabbed one of the lenses used to obtain a three-dimensional image of these photo pairs and began moving the lenses around on one single photograph, muttering under his breath. Finally, he threw down the lenses and said, "Goddamn it, I never could get those pictures to pop up." No wonder he could not, as there is no way anyone could get them to pop up with only one picture. Again, I thought with some dismay that he was my commanding officer.

After I had gone to bed, as usual at 5:00 a.m., on Christmas Day, about an hour later, when it had become daylight, I heard a lot of our people yelling and talking. It turned out that all across our front forward of our positions, the Chinese had crept up and erected decorated Christmas trees directly opposite our troops. That shook up everybody because, after all, the Chinese had managed to trim some of these trees in areas fairly close to our positions. Especially during this time of winter when sound travels well, the Chinese used to do a lot of propaganda broadcasting over loudspeakers directed at our troops. It was quite clear that they'd had a field day with their Christmas setup. The general theme of their broadcasts was something like this, "Aren't you sorry you are over here?" they blared at us. "We the Chinese Peoples' Army volunteers are trying our best to make you feel at home and to wish you a happy Christmas. Why don't you just stop fighting, come over to us, and surrender?" This was followed up by beautiful recorded Christmas carols wafting all across the front. Understandably, we did not drop our weapons and run to meet our comrades of the Chinese Peoples' volunteers, even though they had clearly gone to a lot of trouble on our behalf with their decorated front-line Christmas trees and Christmas carols.

After my interrupted sleep that morning, I sank back into more sleep and got up, as usual, at noon. When I arrived at the mess tent, some of my fellow officers were sitting around a wooden picnic table with a lovely woman. Colonel Warren sat at the head table with a civilian man who looked somewhat familiar. It turned out to be the movie actor Rory Calhoun. Rory Calhoun at that time was married to a Mexican film star, Lita Barone, who never made it in American films. She was a beautiful dark-haired woman.

Presuming to be a United States Marine

Rory Calhoun eventually made a famous horror movie in which he played the manager of a hotel, although before his visit to Korea, he had mainly done cowboy movies.

I must pay some tribute to these two actors here. Most of the Hollywood stars who came over to raise morale probably never got farther forward than division, or they were back in the rear entertaining the aviators. But this couple had managed to snake their way all the way up to the command post of an infantry battalion online. I am sure that other than the photographer Marguerite Higgins, Lita Barone must have been one of a very few women that close to the lines in that entire area and era of the Korean War. Rory was sitting with the senior officers—Major McNeill, Major Dominick, and the colonel—but the attractive young woman sat with us lieutenants and captains, and what a lift that was! We really appreciated their visit.

After lunch, Colonel Warren, who could be very, very tough-sounding, said, "Now, gentlemen, we want to take our guests on a tour of the battalion command post here, after lunch." So we all filed out of the mess tent, which was some distance behind the operations bunker, and walked around the horseshoe-shaped roadway on a dike around the big paddy. As we were walking around the horseshoe, the Chinese threw three mortar shells right into the middle of the paddy. Naturally, everybody hit the deck, and I would bet that in years to come, those mortar shells would become embellished by the time those two actors returned to Hollywood and told the stories of their visit to Korea. But they would have had every right to embellish as they had certainly been under fire. We quickly escorted them into the big bunker, where Colonel Warren asked Tom Palmer to explain his job, and Major Dominick and me to explain our operations and the general situation of our battalion. We were online and actively engaging the enemy, although at the moment, we were still somewhat sheepishly cleaning up the Christmas decorations, which the Chinese had so very kindly put up for us.

I gave a brief presentation on how the entire bunker operated on a day-to-day basis. The two Hollywood folks were very attentive and were, I think, reasonably impressed by what it was like to be working in an operations bunker of a front-line marine battalion. They asked some questions and showed themselves to be two very pleasant people. Since Lita Barone made most of her movies in Mexico, I was never able to see her on the silver screen, but Rory Calhoun, who in 1952 was a fairly dashing-looking individual, continued as a cowboy actor for some years.

When they departed in a jeep back to division, Colonel Warren called me aside in that inimitable tough manner of his and, talking through the side of his mouth, said, "Lieutenant Van Sant, your moustache is disgraceful. Shave it off immediately!"

As I had reached a certain age in Korea, I began to realize that the hair on my upper lip really grew pretty well, and sporting a moustache seemed an innocent-enough sideline to take. I think I had started growing it sometime after I returned from R & R in Japan, so that unfortunately, when Colonel Warren made me shave it off, it had become quite luxurious. It was typical of what Colonel Warren liked to do; he liked to throw his weight around periodically, just to let us know that he was in charge.

Taking on the Burden of History

And now we come to the great raid on Kumgok, the hill I had met my first day on the outpost line of resistance back in May. At that time, I had walked all around the northern face of it, probably the last American to have done that, as the Chinese soon dug in on the forward slope, facing us.

Although not huge, Kumgok was a substantial hill. Facing the Chinese, it was very broad, almost like the top of a *T*. The body of the hill pointed down to the old village of Chogum-ni. A road went through a gap, and that had been the main North Korean and Chinese avenue of approach in their two previous offensives to Seoul. It was a gateway to Seoul, and Kumgok looked like an arrow pointed at that gateway.

We had pretty good intelligence about it from the air and from patrols and from my reconnaissance patrol up onto the forward face of Kumgok in May. It was clear to us what the Chinese had done. They had heavily fortified the top of the *T* parallel to the front, and that was clearly their main line. They had run trench lines down the body of the *T*, pointing toward Chogum-ni, and had dug in all along the top of the hill until it reached the end of the ridge line. There, facing us, was a sort of a heavily fortified knoll, clearly a Chinese outpost. From all we could see, it might have been possible to cut off that outpost with a skillful raid, isolate it with box-me-in fires, hit it directly, perhaps taking prisoners to get some idea of the Chinese strength and even of their plans regarding the outpost. After all, the outpost heavily fortified the front end of Kumgok, and south of that Chogum-ni, where the Chinese had obviously been keeping listening posts for a long time. It was a good target for a raid, and word came down sometime in late November or early December that our battalion was to plan a platoon-sized raid on the outpost in front of Kumgok. Major Dominick was completely unfamiliar with the terrain, whereas I knew it intimately. Consequently, I had a lot to do with planning this raid. We estimated the number of troops needed and roughed-out an approach for them. As is customary in the Marine Corps, the details are always left to the unit commander leading the raid, or to his company commander. Colonel Warren was excited about the raid. Since the raid he had tried to pull off with D Company, when I was on R & R, had been a fiasco, he was eager to be more successful this time. The tentative date set was December 27.

Kumgok was predominantly located in Easy Company's sector, which of course was the sector where Fox Company had been when I had first joined them in May. Now my old outfit was just to the left, in the same position we had been when we occupied Stromboli. But Kumgok was closer to Easy Company. The raid was assigned to them, along with the responsibility for planning it. Tom Palmer had obtained a lot of very useful information for us about the locations of the Chinese and their trench lines. Major Dominick and I put all of this together and prepared a very detailed plan for the raid.

Even now, I am overwhelmed with a deep and abiding sadness when I think of that raid. For the raid back in June, Holmberg and I had started planning many days ahead, but Easy Company had never designated the platoon to carry out their raid. Easy Company was still commanded by the same captain who had been undeservedly decorated for his great victory on Bunker Hill. Colonel Warren now intervened and informed us, and the company commander of E Company, that he thought Lieutenant Burrus ought to lead the raid. He made this pronouncement on Christmas Day, two days before the raid, just as Lieutenant Burrus was arriving back from Japan. Lieutenant Burrus had been graced with that wonderful duty bestowed on select lieutenants to fetch booze from Japan in the unofficial capacity as battalion booze officer although the official title was something like special services. We were scheduled to be relieved and leave for the rear around the fifteenth of January. Colonel Warren, by the fifteenth of December, wanted everything to be squared away as far as the booze was concerned, and Lieutenant Burrus, who had been with Easy Company for about four or five months, had been selected for the plum assignment of booze officer. It turned out that the volume of booze orders from our officers was enormous. After purchasing the booze, Lieutenant Burrus had to negotiate with the people in aviation for space to fly the booty back to Korea in a cargo plane. On this occasion, our battalion had somehow managed to order almost a planeload of booze, and this sheer volume got Burrus hung up in Japan for several extra days while he tried to negotiate for airspace to get all the orders back to Korea.

I subsequently heard from my old friend Lieutenant Vick, company exec for Easy Company, that Burrus knocked himself out trying to accomplish his assigned task. Colonel Warren, who perhaps suspected everyone else's motives because he knew his own, was ticked off at Burrus for spending so much time in Japan. Around the time we were showing off our stuff to the Hollywood stars, the colonel told us, "I think we should send Lieutenant Burrus. He has been sitting in Japan now for six or seven days having a ball." As Vick told me, this assessment was completely unfair.

Burrus was handed the plan, without any opportunity for rehearsal, without any chance even to meet with his sergeants to discuss the raid at any length. The raid was timed to jump off at 4:00 a.m. on the twenty-eighth. Burrus was to take his platoon out to Chogum-ni and work around the right side of the outpost at the south end of Kumgok, which was the best avenue of approach. They were to work their way up and sweep through the outpost in front of Kumgok just as it was getting light at that time of year, probably seven o'clock in the morning. The raid, presumably, would be over by the time the sun came up. Since there was about a foot of snow on the ground, Burrus's troops were issued white uniform covers to blend in.

Burrus had no choice in this matter. His battalion commander had told him to lead this mission. Had I been Burrus's company commander, I would have at least protested in order to protect my officer. Giving a young officer virtually no time to prepare for an extremely delicate and complicated raiding mission was simply outrageous.

The secret to the success of this raid was going to be our supporting arms. We had a lot of support from a number of artillery and heavy mortar outfits. Once shooting began, the entire battle area was to be sealed off with artillery and mortar fire around the outpost, so that the Chinese would not be able to get anybody through. In fact, the supporting fire plan was one of the most carefully prepared plans I had ever seen, and

Taking on the Burden of History

we thought we could pull this raid off. Major Dominick and I began having misgivings, though, when we found out about the colonel's insistence that the unprepared Burrus lead the platoon.

Troops were moved forward at three o'clock in the morning. Because this was to be a big operation, Colonel Warren resolved to go up to the Easy Company command post and control things from up there, and Major Dominick decided that as operations officer, he should be on duty in the bunker at the same time. So instead of my usual operations watch from twelve midnight to five, I went to bed at one that morning, just as things were starting to get under way. Although I had been intimately involved in the planning of this raid, it was out of my hands now. It was up to Lieutenant Burrus and his troops to execute.

Before I went to bed, it began snowing, starting at about one o'clock in the morning. It snowed, and it snowed, and it snowed. The blizzard developed into the biggest snowstorm of that winter and dumped at least two feet of snow on us. The wind blew, and even by the time I went to bed, I could not see my hand in front of my face. There were almost complete whiteout conditions.

At three o'clock in the morning, the troops began moving out to get to Chogum-ni to jump off. Major Dominick called the Easy Company command post and strongly advised Colonel Warren that because of the blizzard conditions, and because of the almost whiteout, which would surely make command and control of the troops impossible, he thought the raid ought to be called off. Major McNeill, the executive officer, concurred in this opinion. Several months later, my friend Lieutenant Vick told me that our new regimental commander, Colonel Hewitt Adams, USMC, had called down to our battalion headquarters for Lieutenant Colonel Warren and had been forwarded by the switchboard to the Easy Company CP. Colonel Adams had been connected with Colonel Warren and had said, "The weather is pretty bad, are you sure you want to go through with this?" Vick, who was a witness to what happened, next told me that the regimental commander told the colonel, "I don't think it is a good idea to run this thing. The snow is so bad that those troops are not going to be able to find their way around. They have to cross a minefield to get to Chogum-ni."

And Colonel "Tough-guy John Wayne" Warren, replied, "Hell, we can do it! Second Battalion can do it, we can do it! We are going to go ahead with it." Vick could not hear the regimental commander's reply but came away with the impression that the commander felt he could not order Colonel Warren to cancel the raid, but that he nevertheless expressed his opinion that it would be wiser not to proceed with it. How many men in history have unwisely assumed a tough-guy image, the "we are going to forge ahead and do it" sentiment? And so Warren gave the order to jump off.

Completely unfamiliar with the terrain, Lieutenant Burrus took off in the blinding snowstorm, leading a raid of troopers who had moved to that area only a few days before he had taken off for Japan. Lieutenant Burrus reached Chogum-ni under ever-worsening weather conditions. When he arrived there, he told his platoon sergeant, "You stay here with the second and third squad. I am going to take the first squad, and

Presuming to be a United States Marine

we will try to go up the route we are supposed to go on and see what we can see." The gunnery sergeant said simply, "Be careful, sir." And Burrus took off.

We had not planned to conduct the raid in a blizzard. It had been planned for normal weather conditions. As soon as fire opened, the assault element led by Lieutenant Burrus was to have been protected by box-me-in fires, the isolation fires.

Up until the time Burrus and his thirteen men left the sergeant and the rest of the platoon at Chogum-ni, there had been no contact with the enemy at all. There was no sound, all was quiet and muffled by the snow on the ground. After Lieutenant Burrus had been gone for some time and still no sound was heard, the sergeant began to worry. He tried to raise the lieutenant on the radio but could not get through, although Burrus may have been observing radio silence because he was so close to the enemy.

Suddenly, some small arms fire broke out. That was our signal to commence battlefield isolation, and we threw everything we had at Kumgok and the Chinese. But there was not much small arms fire, and after we debriefed everybody the following day, we thought it possible that a Chinese might have detected Burrus. In any case, the Chinese got nervous and began shooting with poor fire discipline. Once they started firing, we responded vigorously, and they must have thought they were engaged in a real battle. For some time, there was an enormous amount of fire. But neither friend nor foe was able to shoot at any specific target because of the blinding weather conditions.

I was fitfully trying to sleep in my tent, but when I heard the sound of fire, I went over to the operations bunker. I found a pretty upset Major Dominick. He said, "We have no idea where Burrus is. We are in touch with the sergeant, and he is in a holding mode. There is absolutely no sign of Burrus." Apparently, the sergeant wanted to gather up some men and go looking for his lieutenant, but Colonel Warren thought that was a bad idea and vetoed that. And so the sergeant eventually returned.

It stopped snowing at about ten or eleven o'clock in the morning. Around noon, several of us went up near the platoon command post, which I had helped dig many months before. We hoped a good view of Kumgok and Chogum-ni would enable us to figure out what had happened.

From the command post, we saw a horrifying sight. Lieutenant Burrus had pressed forward. He had pressed forward *clear around and well beyond* the outpost. He had climbed up the main body of Kumgok almost to the main Chinese positions, far deeper than he was expected to go. But without the technology we have now, and in the heavy snowstorm, he could not have known his position. There is no question that he and all of his troops were killed by our own isolation fires, which we had so carefully planned for the destruction of the Chinese positions. We could see the bodies. They were scattered right up the hill in a straight line, as if still charging forward.

What had happened was unmistakable. It was clear. Our intelligence officer, Palmer, looked at the scene and came back silently. I looked, and Major Dominick looked. We said nothing at first. Colonel Warren, with all my reservations about him, at least expressed a good marine attitude. "My god!" he said. "We can't let those bodies just stay out there. We have got to get them back." This, under normal circumstances, would have made a lot of sense. Unfortunately, we would have had to unleash a battalion-sized attack on the main Chinese positions in order to reach the place where the bodies needed to be picked up. Although it had stopped snowing, the drifts of freshly fallen snow were about two or three feet deep in places.

In the early afternoon, we had a meeting of the staff with the colonel after we all realized what had happened. "We'll get them back," said Colonel Warren assertively. "We will ask Fox Company to send some men and stretcher bearers out to pick up the bodies." I remember that Major Dominick and I looked at each other. Did the colonel think that the Chinese were going to let the troops and bearers walk right into their positions and wait for them to gather up the bodies and carry them back?

Although it could have been purely my impression, I think I detected an attitude in Colonel Warren implying that since his staff did not seem to be able to plan things right, he would just have to take charge himself. And so he set about planning the retrieval operation.

In the preparation for this mission, we went through almost a carbon copy of what had happened the night before, when everyone was trying to get the colonel to postpone the mission. Any officer who had any clout with the colonel tried to reason with him. Although as a mere first lieutenant I had no clout at all, I probably knew the terrain better than anybody. We asked the colonel how many men he was going to send out. We figured that in the snow, it would take four men to carry each stretcher, and that meant fifty-two stretcher bearers. They would not be able to fight, of course, and so we would need to engage the whole company for this particular rescue mission.

"Well," the colonel growled out of the corner of his mouth, "we can't do that. They'll just have to drag them through the snow." And we felt with some dismay that he was getting in deeper and deeper in order to maintain his tough-guy image. He came up with a plan. Lieutenant Shelton, a Fox Company officer from Virginia and a close friend of Tom Palmer's, was to take eight men and approach the outpost from Fox Company's side of Kumgok. They were to engage the outpost while twelve men from the lieutenant's platoon under their sergeant were to run around the end of the hill with twelve stretchers and pull the bodies back as best they could.

The forward nose of the Kumgok outpost on the Fox Company side was just a sheer wall, but Colonel Warren would not listen to anybody's concern. He issued his order. For me this was one of the most upsetting situations I had ever encountered in the Marine Corps. I knew that my boss, Major Dominick, understood the folly of this mission, as did the battalion executive officer and the regimental commander. The Fox Company commander, a newly joined captain, understood, and the poor lieutenant who was expected to carry this mission out with twenty men—eight to take the outpost and twelve to pick up thirteen men with twelve stretchers—understood all too well. The bodies, after all, were clearly visible in the snow on the forward slope of the main Chinese positions.

The entire operation was scheduled to jump off around 8:00 p.m., or 2000 hours. I had permission from Major Dominick to take Corporal O'Brien from our operations office, and we drove in the deep snow up to what had been my platoon position at one time, looking out onto Kumgok. We took a radio and stayed in touch with Major Dominick back at battalion headquarters. Again, I had a front-row seat for this next action without having any idea whether there was anything I could do to help. I felt so upset that I simply had to be present in some way.

Another idea of Colonel Warren's had been that, "we wanna be able to see what's going on, so we'll illuminate the battlefield." The artillery had the capacity to fire flares, which would descend in parachutes and could illuminate an area of one square mile for an hour or two, almost like a football field is illuminated with floodlights.

Most of the time, at least in Fox Company with Captain Moody, we did not like to illuminate battlefields, feeling that it would be better to sneak around under cover of darkness. But there had been occasions when we did use illumination, for example, at the end of the Stromboli action when we fired up some illumination for the evacuation.

And now Colonel Warren had his illuminated battlefield, so that Corporal O'Brien and I clearly saw everything that went on in this evacuation action. All honor and glory to the Fox Company lieutenant and his eight men. They set off across to Chogum-ni and sneaked around, so that we momentarily could not see them very well, then emerged walking up, while the detail of stretcher bearers behind them slid around to their right in order to get to the front of the Chinese outpost and so to the bodies. The lieutenant reached the bottom of the sheer side of Kumgok. The Chinese, who had obviously been observing them advancing all the way up in the almost-daylight brightness, suddenly opened up fire. The fire was directed not only against the lieutenant but also against the line position where the corporal and I were sitting. We scrambled around looking for cover in our front seats to the firefight, which unexpectedly began to include us.

I am sorry to say that the lieutenant and several of his men were killed, and most of the rest were wounded. To their everlasting glory, the twelve stretcher bearers, who never got around the front of the outpost because there was simply no way they could get around there, returned with the body of the lieutenant and the other casualties caused by the action on this misbegotten retrieval operation. But no one was ever able to get to Lieutenant Burrus's raiding party high up on Kumgok and much deeper into Chinese-controlled territory; there was simply no way that could be accomplished.

At a reunion of our battalion in 2001, I was able to talk with John Armstrong, a man who was wounded during the retrieval operation. I had first met John when he joined Fox Company in early September of 1952 as a transfer from an antiaircraft battery. He had been in the third platoon and had been out on Bunker Hill in late September with me. In fact, he was in the next fighting position to mine when the Chinese had attacked my position and when I threw the grenades after being wounded. It was he who had said that I looked like a whirling dervish, and he retold that story to our comrades forty-nine years later in New Orleans.

Armstrong had been with Lieutenant Shelton on the futile assault on the Chinese outpost in front of Kumgok. He was badly wounded and evacuated back to the States. He said that from the lieutenant on down, there was a clear understanding that the operation was extremely difficult, if not impossible to carry out. Yet marines follow orders.

More men had been killed needlessly in this second fiasco. I don't remember ever being so mad in my life. When we were sure that all the Fox Company casualties had been safely evacuated, O'Brien and I got into our jeep and drove back to battalion headquarters. What happened next constitutes a miracle that my career as a marine officer continued. Colonel Warren was sitting in the big operations bunker back in headquarters listening to the Fox Company commander's information. I remember walking up and saying, "Well, Colonel, I hope you are happy!" And these may have been the most insubordinate words I have ever uttered in the Marine Corps. "I hope you are happy. You got eight more people killed. For what?" And I turned around and walked away. He sat in stunned silence. The enormous ramifications of what he had ordered may have finally crept into his consciousness.

Fortunately, we got the twelve stretcher bearers back, although several were wounded. The poor guys who went after that outpost and tried to fight their way up a steep incline found the Chinese not only shooting but rolling grenades down at them. The entire scene had been illuminated like a theater to better enable us as spectators to clearly see the senseless slaughter. Even though half a century has gone by, it is hard for me to relive the absurdity of this action in my memory.

The regimental commander who had sent up his own people to observe informed Colonel Warren it was clear to him that despite our precious traditions of honor, glory, and never leaving anybody behind, those Marine bodies were irretrievable. Unless we were to open up a whole new regimental or division-sized spring offensive to take Kumgok, we would have to list them as missing, presumed dead. And that concluded that action.

We stayed in that same beautiful operations bunker online for another two weeks or so after the retrieval debacle. For the remainder of that period online, the battalion ran regular patrols. The Chinese probed our lines several times during the first two weeks in January. There was still a lot of snow on the ground, and it continued being very, very cold.

D, or Dog Company, had conducted a brave but largely unsuccessful raid in November. Easy Company had experienced Lieutenant Burrus's misfortunes next. Fox Company had had the disastrous attempt to retrieve the bodies after that. Understandably, we did not look back on that particular tour online from the fifteenth of November to the fifteenth of January with much pride. We had not had many significant successes against the enemy, certainly nothing that could compare to what we had been able to accomplish in the spring, summer and early fall.

One January night around 2:00 a.m., while I was on my midnight-to-five duty watch, I heard two booms in the otherwise quiet night. It sounded like grenades exploding—*bang! bang!*—followed by a deep and absolute silence. The telephone from D Company rang about two minutes later. D Company had just been taken over online by Captain Rocky Eldracker, a real character. He was a hard-charging, whisky-

Presuming to be a United States Marine

drinking, poker-playing marine. But Captain Eldracker had a pretty highly exposed panic button. He was now yelling over the telephone, "Van Sant, I want you to alert division artillery. Next, I want you to go back to the Eighth Army eight-inchers, and I want you to get aviation alerted. The Chinese are all around Reno!"

Reno was an outpost in front of the Dog Company positions. Reno and two other hills named for Nevada towns formed a kind of triangle, which later in March would become known as the famous hill battles of Reno, Carson, and Vegas. Reno was the westernmost hill just to the right of the Easy Company positions. It was an interesting hill, almost perfectly cone-shaped. It had fairly steep sides, but artillery and mortar fire had leveled off the top of the cone to some degree. American forces maintained anywhere from two squads to a reinforced platoon outpost on Reno. It was a hill big enough to hold that many people. The structure of the Reno fortifications was almost symmetrical. A trench line completely encircled it down from the crest of the hill, and this ringlike trench about ten or fifteen yards down from the crest constituted the main battle position. The trench on the back side of the hill led to a trench that came on down the hill and across a little valley back up to the main line.

On the forward slope and sides of Reno, we had what we called one-man listening posts in spider holes. These spider holes were positioned at the end of thin trenches, connecting with the ring trench on the upper side of the hill. There were about five or six spider holes scattered all the way around the forward and side slopes of Reno. It was customary to position a single marine in a spider hole with the task of detecting any enemy movement approaching Reno at night. The marine had a sound power phone to reach the main battle position with an alert if he detected any enemy activity.

Because of the state of alertness these marines had to constantly maintain, most outfits manning Reno would relieve the spider hole occupants at least every two hours. A trooper would go down the hole listening carefully every single minute of his watch and would be relieved by a rested and alert replacement, often after just one hour.

Now, in Captain Eldracker's opinion, we were faced with an all-out Chinese assault. "They have Reno surrounded," he yelled, and he wanted every bit of supporting arms available, seemingly reading to me a laundry list right out of his Basic School notebook about what I was supposed to get for him, admonishing me to be prepared and on call.

He hung up with, "I've got to go, I'll be back to you in a minute."

I called the artillery regiment, but expressed myself very carefully to them. Eldracker had sounded tremendously excited, and yet I had heard nothing since the two booms ten or fifteen minutes ago. So I told the artillery regiment, "I will put you on a low-level alert, there may be something happening on Reno. You might want to get out your concentrations for that area, get a couple of batteries keyed in."

In the complete stillness of the night, I waited, and waited, and waited for Captain Eldracker's next call. It was about 2:30 a.m. by this time. I waited until about 2:45 a.m. without ever hearing from Captain Eldracker again. Not even one solitary sound could be heard from the front lines. Finally I called Captain Eldracker's command post myself, and a young marine communicator answered the phone. I said "This is Lieutenant Van Sant from Battalion Three. Is Captain Eldracker there?"

He said, "Oh no, sir. He is asleep."

And I told him, "Well, young man, please go and wake him up."

When Eldracker got on the line, I informed him, exaggerating a little bit, of all the supporting arms I had laid in for him. I said, "Captain, I have the whole artillery regiment on full alert, I have the 4.2 mortars ready to go for you, what's happening?"

And if you can imagine a person sounding very sheepish over the telephone, then you can imagine how the captain sounded.

"Weeell, upon further investigation, we found . . . ," And he somewhat reluctantly detailed the story of the origin of the two bangs in the night.

It turned out that one of the D Company marines had just been relieved from his spider hole and was starting up the trench line back up to the ring trench. Off to his left, he heard some unexpected movement and, being a well-trained marine, unhesitatingly threw a grenade. But what he had heard was the marine from the next spider hole proceeding up his vertical trench to the ring. Fortunately, the grenade did not hit the second trooper, although when he heard the bang, and being no slouch himself, our second guy instinctively threw one back. That accounted for the two bangs in the night.

All of this information, mind you, came at the end of a rather exhaustive investigation. If either one of the marines had actually got his grenade into the trench, it would have been disastrous. But make no mistake, poor old Eldracker had been ready to fight World War III at least for a brief moment.

As the first and second weeks in January passed and we finally finished our November, December, and January tour online, I must say it was with some real glee that we came off-line. This time we returned to the battalion camp known as the Rock Pile, the camp we had been sent to in the summer after the raid.

Chapter 17

BACK TO RESERVE AND BACK TO THE LINES

The Rock Pile camp turned out to have been improved considerably since summer. Among other things, it now boasted some Quonset huts. Within a few days, word came down that we were going to get a new battalion commander, within a couple of weeks. Although the Marine Corps got Colonel Warren out of his position as our battalion commander, he would be able to say for the rest of his life that he had commanded an infantry battalion in Korea. That, I feel compelled to say again, was a job for which he was not well qualified.

Particularly for the last week or ten days under Colonel Warren's command, it was inescapably apparent that he had become thoroughly disliked by everybody. It seemed to me that he began to withdraw into a shell from which he did not often emerge, although he never stopped talking tough. Even though we did not see much of him, both Lieutenant Palmer and I managed to have a run-in with the colonel.

Tom Palmer; Pernokas and Marsky, the two battalion surgeons whom I have already described; Pomocky, the hero of Siberia; a couple of other battalion staff officers; and I all lived in a very large squad tent with a very-much-needed stove to warm us through the icy cold time of year. Koreans use terraces on hills everywhere in order to increase space for growing food, and our tent stood on a terraced hillside. The terrace just below ours held the colonel's tent.

It must have been the second or third evening after we had settled into reserve. Tom Palmer, usually a very genial and sociable fellow, had withdrawn into a corner and was deeply engaged in some sort of a writing project. We were off duty at this time of the night, but Tom had launched on his writing project right after we had returned from our evening meal. I noticed that every few minutes, Tom would take a slug of whisky, after which he returned to his writing.

Earlier in the day, Tom had told me that the Fox Company lieutenant killed on the recovery fiasco when he went out with the stretcher bearers to retrieve the bodies from Kumgok had not only been a classmate of his in Basic School, but that they had first met back in Virginia at the College of William and Mary. Tom knew the lieutenant's parents well. After the lieutenant's mother had been officially notified of her son's death, Tom had received a letter from her. Distraught, she conveyed to Tom that she would appreciate knowing any of the circumstances surrounding her son's death. That deep concentration of Tom's in his corner laced with slugs of whisky occurred while he was responding to her letter. And the more Tom wrote, the madder he got. He never showed the finished letter to anybody. Tom sealed and addressed the envelope and walked out of the tent to the little mailbox near the adjutant's tent. On his way there he would pass above Colonel Warren's tent.

First, Tom mailed his letter. But during his walk back to our tent, this normally cool and placid man had become increasingly agitated. He reached the terrace right above the colonel's tent. The effects of coffee for supper and the whisky he had consumed to calm his nerves having had time to combine and bear down on him, he experienced a need to relieve himself. In his deep anger, he stood on top of the terrace and aimed right down on top of the colonel's tent. *Prrrr.* The sounds of such relief falling on canvas are unmistakable. The colonel in his tent began yelling, "Hey, what's going on out there?" And Tom said something to the effect of, "You deserve this," calling the colonel some unprintable name. The colonel came storming out of his tent, but by that time, Tom had finished his revenge and had disappeared so that the colonel never knew who had peed all over his tent. And when I see Tom next, I will have to ask him what he had said as accompaniment to his magnificent wet and smelly gesture of disdain.

Once we had returned to the reserve position, we launched an intensive training program, soon made much more intensive by our new battalion commander. Operations and training had already laid out a number of plans. Our office was responsible for setting up, coordinating, and assigning training areas and missions, as well as types of training to be conducted. I had been hard at work on these projects even before we got back to reserve camp, and once there, I worked on them all the time. We had all our companies jumping. In the area around the camp, we set up different kinds of ranges for practicing different kinds of operations. We had several weapons ranges where machine gunners, flamethrowers, and mortars could practice; we had maneuver areas; and we had places where people could practice scouting, patrolling, and compass marches. We conducted a wide variety of training while in reserve.

The same rule we had in China applied for heating our tents in Korea. We were not permitted to run the stove during the night. We would light it in the morning, swathed in our thermal underwear inside our sleeping bags, and shake and tremble until the tent warmed up a bit and we could get up. We would fall out of the tent and go down to the officers' mess tent, where big boilers of coffee were bubbling every morning.

In the field, we provided our own utensils. We had our own coffee cup, which fit around the canteen; our own fork, knife, and spoon; and our own mess tray, which would fit in the pack. My coffee cup had a heavy rim around it, which would get very hot once the coffee was poured into it. The first thing I did each morning was to fill my cup up to the brim with boiling hot coffee and drink deeply in the hope of warming

Presuming to be a United States Marine

myself up a little. One morning, it was even colder than usual. I was shaking inside my parka with the hood up and a mountain hat underneath it, gulping down my first cup of coffee. Because I shivered in the cold, and because my cup was so full, a little stream of coffee dribbled down the front seam of my parka. I quickly wiped it off, without paying any further attention to it.

After breakfast, I went to work in the operations tent. We had five units to be concerned with—the Weapons Company, the three rifle companies, and the Headquarters Company, whom we were forcing to do some field work too. Almost everybody in the battalion was out in the widely scattered training areas, some maybe several miles away. As I was working at my desk later that morning, I received a call from a sergeant at the adjutant's office. He had just had a call from the main gate that General Pollock, the new First Marine Division commanding general, was entering the area.

"Better call the colonel," I said.

"I have tried that, and the colonel is back at regiment," the sergeant told me.

"And where is the exec?" I asked.

"Well, the exec is away too," the sergeant said.

Going down the totem pole, I asked, "Where is the adjutant?" But he was out as well. We had after all just come off-line and had to catch up on many administrative matters. It turned out that all five companies were out in the field with their commanders and their next senior officers. The sergeant told me, "I think, Lieutenant, that you are the senior officer aboard." And so I pulled on my parka, ran out, and got down to the road below our operations tent at just about the time the general's jeep pulled up.

I had met General Pollock a couple of times already. One of the great marine generals, he retired with the rank of major general. He had been a battalion commander at Guadalcanal. Later I came to know his son, also a marine officer, quite well.

Swooping down to the general's jeep, I snapped off a crisp salute and said, "Lieutenant Van Sant reporting. Second Battalion, First Marines, all in the field, training, sir." I gave the regrets of the battalion commander, and he said, "That's fine, Lieutenant Van Sant, that's fine. I just wanted to see what kind of training the people in your battalion are doing. Do you think you can show me?" I said, "Of course I can, sir." And the general put me in the backseat, as they always do.

We had to climb all around as there were many places where the troops were training that we could not reach by jeep. Because I had set up the entire training program, I knew where everybody was and what they were doing. I would guess that we must have spent some four hours clambering about, visiting. It was great for a general to come out and for the troops to see that he was interested in their training program. It was clear that he was quite genuinely interested and knowledgeable. He was thoroughly briefed, and when we were finished, I saluted him again and bid him farewell. He thanked me and said, "Lieutenant, this was an excellent job. The state of your training program seems to be very good." And he threw out a few more compliments, saluted, and took off. He had met all the captain company commanders in the different training locations, but he had spent most of the time with a lowly first lieutenant.

431

Taking on the Burden of History

That evening in the officers' mess after our dinner, Colonel Warren bellowed from his head table, "Van Sant!"

"Yes, sir." I got up from my table and approached him.

He said, "I got some words down the chain of command about you. General Pollock called up the regimental commander and told him all about the tour you had given him."

"Yes sir?" I said.

"He told the regimental commander you had done an outstanding job. But then he also said"—and I braced myself because I could see the glee on Colonel Warren's face—"tell Lieutenant Van Sant he should be a little more careful with his personal appearance. There was a big stain on the front of his parka."

Oh God! I was embarrassed! Can you imagine coming down from the division commander to the regimental commander to the battalion commander and finally to me, the word that I had been found with a coffee stain on my parka?

As always, when there is a change of command, the outgoing battalion commander, Colonel Warren, had to write a fitness report on every officer in the battalion. In those days, the report had to be signed by the marine on whom it was written as an indication that he had read it. At some periods in Marine Corps history, the fitness reports were simply sent to Headquarters, Marine Corps, and if you wanted to read your fitness report, you just had to go all the way to Marine Corps Headquarters to examine it, but in early 1953, we were allowed to look at them.

I will never forget going to the battalion adjutant's office to sign my fitness report. Colonel Warren's last blow was that he gave all officers in the battalion mediocre fitness reports. Almost all officers were rated "average" or "above average." Later, Major Dominick said, "Well, Van, as one 'above average' officer to another . . ." But that was by no means Colonel Warren's last shot. It was clear that he was still trying to forge a tough-guy reputation for himself.

It will be remembered that when we were relieved off-line in October, we had been flown in helicopters to take up positions on the Kansas Line, the backup defensive line. The Kansas Line was being worked on all the time, and one of its main strongholds was at the great bend of the Imjin River at a very heavily fortified large mountain mass. The division had made up a fire plan overlay for this part of the Kansas Line, and marked on this overlay was every machine gun position, every antitank gun position, every flamethrower position, the positions for recoilless rifles, and all mortars and artillery. All positions were marked on an overlay on transparent paper, which, when laid on an area map, would show all the fortifications when they were occupied. The fire plan for the Kansas Line assumed that the positions were to be occupied by at least a battalion, if not a regiment. The document, of course, was *top secret*. If it fell into enemy hands, it would instantly show them all the weapons positions for the entire division's main backup position.

The division sent Colonel Warren, as a battalion commander, a copy of this overlay, and he never shared it even with his own operations officer, Major Dominick. He kept

Presuming to be a United States Marine

it in his sole possession at all times. He may have wanted to impress his superiors when he managed to deal himself into taking General Pollock on a tour of the Kansas Line, but he took the overlay with him. I don't know if Warren ever showed the general the overlay on a map because I am not sure that Warren knew how to put an overlay on a map, but he had the overlay on his person. He later recollected folding it up and placing it in the pocket of his parka. A day or two later, orders relieving him of command and returning him to the States came through. He had, in fact, been the draft commander for our Twentieth Replacement Daft in April 1952 when I had come over. Now he was going back to the States in January, and I thought to myself that it must be nice to be a lieutenant colonel. I still had almost three more months to serve in this place.

Our battalion adjutant was our classified material control officer. He had seen and logged in the top-secret overlay addressed to Colonel Warren when it arrived. Even a colonel has to check out of all battalion offices, including the supply office, the adjutant's office, and the classified material control office. When Colonel Warren came to check out with classified material control, the question arose, "Where is the overlay?"

"Oh my god!" said Colonel Warren. "I don't have it."

So Warren went back and tore apart his bunk, his tent, and all his personal gear, but he could not find it. He returned to the adjutant and told him that he could not find the overlay. The adjutant replied, "You were charged out with it, Colonel, I can't release you without it." And the adjutant went off to see Major Dominick to tell him about this dilemma while I listened in on their conversation. God, were we doomed to have this man staying with us forever?

With the colonel's approval, the adjutant gathered a working detail of marines to go through every pocket in every parka in the supply tent pile of turned-in parkas in order to find the overlay. This was done, but no overlay. It simply did not turn up in the search. It was gone. He had lost it somewhere else. But where? This was pretty serious, and the colonel himself was beginning to panic. In desperation, I finally came up with an idea. You will remember the wonderful Lieutenant Burhans, who had joined Fox Company the night of Stromboli, whom I had to relieve as third platoon commander after he had received his fourth Purple Heart. Burhans had been placed in command of the regimental Weapons Company, and while that job called for a captain, a senior first lieutenant could carry it also.

I firmly believed that all of us wanted to get Colonel Warren off the hook and back to the States, if not for his sake, then for ours. But if we could not come up with that top-secret overlay, we might be looking at an indefinite delay in his departure. And so I called on my old friend Bob Burhans. I went by his headquarters and asked him if he had a copy of that particular top-secret overlay. He said, "Yes, as a matter of fact, I do." I explained our situation, and Bob, who knew Colonel Warren by reputation, realized how anxious we were to get a copy of the overlay. Bob generously gave me his copy of the overlay to take back to our operations shop with our incomparable draftsman Sergeant Sullivan. Bless Sullivan, who was able to produce a beautiful replica of the overlay with all the correct paraphernalia on it, even the top-secret markings. Sullivan did a magnificent copying job under the circumstances. I quickly returned Burhans's copy of the document and triumphantly delivered the copy of the overlay to Colonel Warren, who by this time was very much relieved to receive it, no questions asked.

This entire episode raises some interesting moral questions, of course. For one thing, we broke a number of regulations in bailing out Colonel Warren. And yet it might be understandable that we were willing to do almost anything to get him home. While the overlay was probably legitimately called Top Secret, I do wonder how much it would have jeopardized any defenders of the Kansas Line had the enemy obtained a copy of it showing all the weapons and their positions. If a copy of that overlay had fallen into Chinese or North Korean hands, it could have been damaging. But the scale of the battle that would have had to have been fought in order to push us back to the Kansas Line at that point of the war was inconceivable. Somewhere in Korea, perhaps buried in the bottom of an old trash barrel, might still be a copy of a top secret-overlay charged out to Lieutenant Colonel Charles E. Warren.

We did not get our new battalion commander until almost immediately before we went back online. He was a character named Gililland, with the nickname of Cotton. This nickname originated in the head of very fluffy blond hair he possessed. Lieutenant Colonel Cotton Gililland was certainly a far better commander than Warren. He was a very knowledgeable infantry unit leader and a brave man. In my Valhalla of battalion commanders, Lieutenant Colonel Roy Batterton will always be first, but Quilici and Gililland were close seconds. While his charisma may have been slightly contrived, a more serious problem was his occasionally almost uncontrollable temper.

Two illustrations of why Gililland's charisma may have been slightly contrived. Soon after his arrival, he met with all the officers. He stood in front of us and put us at ease. He told us that his nickname was Cotton, taking his hat off to show why, and that appeared a bit theatrical. He went through exactly the same routine with the troops when we were all in formation so that we officers had the honor of hearing the presentation twice.

The next thing he told us, and we heard that twice too, was that as a major, he had been the executive officer of a battalion of the Twenty-eighth Marines on Iwo Jima. We knew that the commander of that battalion had been killed after the landing and before the beginning of the battle for Mount Suribachi. Gililland told us that he had taken over the battalion as executive officer while still a major. That meant that he had been the commander of the marines who took Mount Suribachi, made famous by the photograph and the statue of the flag raising. I subsequently saw the colonel under pressure and had no doubt about his courage. While I always felt that it would have been nicer for the Suribachi story to have come out through the very efficient troopers' grapevine rather than from the man himself, I developed a very good relationship with Colonel Gililland.

As had been true of Batterton, Gililland had very tough ideas about training. For the last couple of weeks we were in reserve under Gililland, he instituted an even more rigorous training program in the sense that we practiced specific drills in anticipation of specific situations we might have to deal with after our return to the lines. Colonel Gililland had an obsession with specific training on assaulting fortified positions. In our circumstances just behind the lines of combat, we could practice many things we would not have been able to get away with in a regular training program back in the States. Gililland sat down with Major Dominick, the other members of operations and training office, and me and laid out to us exactly what he wanted. And what he wanted was for every man in the battalion to have the experience of throwing a satchel charge into the aperture of a fortified bunker position, while machine gun fire aimed into the aperture was passing right beside and over the marine. He wanted every man to familiarize himself with the distraction of covering machine gun fire landing nearby while he was engaged in throwing a charge. He also wanted every man to experience the heat of a flamethrower as it was fired into the same aperture. I searched the terrain around our camp until I found a place where we could run this problem, and we processed almost every man in our battalion through it. Each man had to crawl out under live machine gun fire and get up into a position. Although not everyone had to fire a flamethrower, every man had to experience working under its heat. And everyone had to throw a small charge through the aperture of the bunker we had built.

After we had designed everything to meet Colonel Gililland's rigorous specifications, he reviewed it all and made some changes. Every man in the battalion had to go through a regular routine, and while we were just off the line of combat, we began feeling as if we had returned to battle. We did not have all the safety devices used back in the U.S. training installations either. We simply had real machine guns stacked up, fired real bullets into a hole, and each one of us had to go up to that hole and throw a satchel charge in. In this way, we gained the experience of throwing a satchel charge under live fire, including flamethrowers. Needless to say, Gililland immediately gained the reputation among the troops as being a pretty tough guy, something to which Warren had so desperately aspired and had never achieved. I remember being concerned at the time about the enormous number of satchel charges expended in these exercises, thinking that they might have been better used against the enemy, but the troops certainly gained excellent training.

That particular tour on the old Rock Pile through the second half of January and first half of February was time spent hard at work but it, too, had some pleasant aspects with some laughs thrown in. I lived with some wonderful characters in the officers' tent. One of those was Doc Pernokas, whom I have already introduced to you. Before he became battalion surgeon, Pernokas had been with the Collecting and Clearing Company, the navy's and Marine Corps' equivalent of the army's MASH unit. He already had a decoration from the Bunker Hill battles in recognition of his surgeries on casualties for a solid twenty-eight hours without interruption.

He was a hail-fellow-well-met, a little bit loud, and as proud of his Greek ancestry as had been my friend George Morrison. He was deeply dedicated to his profession. Everybody I ever knew in the medical line of work during my time in Korea, as

Taking on the Burden of History

well as some civilians in subsequent years, was aware of Pernokas's reputation as an exceptionally skilled surgeon. Many of us would tell him, "You know, Doc, if anything ever happens to me, don't let anybody else touch me. I want you, and nobody else, to take care of me!" It was a reassuring thought for all of us.

And Doc Pernokas liked to drink and play poker and tell stories. In our officers' tent, we got into the habit of getting a pretty good game going from time to time. I enjoyed playing poker, particularly in a genial group. Often, officers from the rifle companies would join us for some pretty big games, and when I was not playing, I used to kibitz a lot. One of the regulars was Captain Rocky Eldracker, whom you will remember as the commanding officer of D Company. Now Eldracker was the type of guy who would pretend to be more drunk than he was just to lull people into a false sense of security with regard to his ability to play the game. To give credit where credit is due, he was a good poker player.

One particular night, there must have been about six or seven of us, the maximum number able to comfortably play draw poker with one deck of cards. We were playing straight draw poker, nothing wild, no fancies, just the pure game on this particular hand. We also played seven-card stud and five-card stud and many variations—high, low, and so on—that night, but what I will describe now was absolutely straight poker.

I picked up my five cards and squeezed them off, and lo, I had been dealt four Jacks, four natural Jacks, four of a kind. And that, next to a royal flush, is the best hand you can have in poker, particularly when there is nothing wild. Naturally, I very studiously contained my joy, took the odd card, and threw it in, asking for another card, which I did not need so that people would think I was trying to fill out a flush or a straight. It was one of those rare moments in a poker game when several people are dealt good hands, and all of them think they have this one licked. Usually we would bet $1 or $2, and sometimes $5. As the stakes got higher, a couple of people dropped out of the game, but at least four of us, including Eldracker and me, stayed in. Bets had gone up to $20, and somebody said, "I'll see your twenty and raise you five." And the next guy raised it by ten, and so on.

As luck would have it, the other people dropped out one by one. It was now between Eldracker and me betting against each other and raising each other each time. I was running out of cash, but it so happened that I had just received a check in the amount of $150 for some reimbursement the Marine Corps owed me. I threw it in, and that meant that I was seeing Eldracker's last bet and raising it by at least $50 to $75. By this time, there was nearly $1,000 in the pot. Although we had the tradition that you could pull money out of the pot and owe it, I never liked doing that and did not like to play with people who regularly did it. After my toss of the check into the pot with the big raise, Eldracker matched the raise in order to see me. At that point, I felt in supreme command of the moment as I looked at the pot, which now included my $150 check. With a confident flourish, I laid down my handful of natural Jacks.

Rocky Eldracker, who had consumed some quantities of alcohol, looked me in the eye and said, "Oh, thash not good enough, no way!"

Presuming to be a United States Marine

"What?" I said. And Rocky laid down his hand of four natural kings. Ah! Life at its lowest ebb once again!

Eldracker started sweeping up all the money, and I endorsed my check over to him, "Pay to the order of Captain Eldracker," signed, George M. Van Sant.

But then I swept through my pockets, found a few more dollars, and kept on playing. It was getting late. The game began petering out, and people were quitting, but Eldracker and I continued head-to-head. Slowly I managed to win back nearly $75. Eldracker and I started playing a new game, two-person blackjack, which not many people in their right mind would ever play. By this time, my one goal in life was to get some of my money back from Eldracker. I managed to win back several hundred dollars, including my check, which Eldracker had to endorse back over to me. "Pay to the order of Lieutenant George M. Van Sant," and signed "Captain Eldracker."

It will be remembered that I had given my father power of attorney in order to pay off all my debts that had accrued from my late wife Shirley's long sanatorium stay. He wrote me a letter after he had taken the check down to our bank, telling me that the endorsements on the back of the check had caused a lot of amusement at the Alexandria National Bank and asking me to tell him the story behind the check. I wrote him a humorous explanation of the poker game and how I had emotionally risen to the highest heights and plummeted to the deepest depths on the roller coaster of the poker game.

The other highlight of this period in division reserve was another amphibious landing on Tokchokto by the battalion. It will be remembered that the previous summer, when I was still a platoon commander, we had landed on this little island off the coast. This time I was assistant battalion operations officer, responsible for a great deal of the planning and preparation of the operations plan for the whole operation. We made the landing sometime in early February. For the week or so before it, I was busy in the operations tent in the Rock Pile.

As before, we rode by truck to Munsan-ni, and then by train through Seoul to Inchon. This trip was made memorable by the fact that I was suffering from the worst case of diarrhea in my entire year in Korea. In my memory, the trip was filled with the eternal quest for suitable heads (johns, toilets). My trots, as they were called then, were accompanied by very sharp cramps. In short, the trip was miserable and only got worse after we boarded the small landing craft (LCVP) for the ferry out to the ship. A strong wind roughed up the North China Sea, creating choppy waters and slowing down the entire transfer operation. Soon our boat was traveling in a circle off the starboard side of the ship with about eight other boats going round and round in the same big circle. Within a short time, most of the marine passengers on our boat were seasick. Once again, I was grateful for my apparent immunity to that condition, as the churning in my bowels from the diarrhea was bad enough. While we circled and circled for what seemed like hours, I had an opportunity to figure out how the navy was conducting the operation. Our destination ship had five cargo nets hanging over the starboard side, one near the stern, about three midship, and one fairly close to the bow. What was striking about these nets was the variation in their lengths. The stern net was short—people only had to climb up ten or twelve feet to the deck. The three midship nets were somewhat longer, maybe twenty feet to reach to the deck. But the one net up at the bow looked to be about four stories high. This particular ship had a very high forecastle.

As our circle of landing craft rotated around, a control officer aboard ship would signal a particular boat to come to a certain net. Because of the high seas, the process of unloading a boat took an extraordinarily long time. Several men fell off the net because even the ship was rolling a lot, and the landing craft were jumping up and down on pogo sticks. It was very slow going especially for the boats called in to the net near the bow. As I watched and calculated, it soon became apparent that we were destined for the bow net. And lo, I was right. We eventually slipped up under it and began the long, long climb up the side of the rolling ship after jumping out of our cockleshell, weighted down with a full pack and weapon. Climbing up a cargo net under the best of conditions can be a harrowing experience. Considerably weakened by my intestinal problems, I literally prayed my way up that net. I threw myself over the rail onto the deck with the last ounce of strength I still possessed and lay crumpled in a helpless heap until a sailor bent over me.

"Take me to sick bay," I uttered feebly and was soon carried off. A doctor examined me, gave me two prescriptions, one of which was for paregoric and assured me that I should soon be fine. Still somewhat weak, I gathered my stuff, found my stateroom, and reported to Major Dominick.

He informed me that after the evening meal, all staff officers and commanders were to report to the mess for a meeting with the commodore in overall command of the landing. He also informed me that I was to be the tactical-logistical (TAC-LOG) officer for the landing. This meant that I was the liaison from the commander of the landing force, our battalion commander Gililland, to the commodore. It also meant that I would not be billeted on the APA or troopship but would be stationed on the destroyer, the designated control vessel for the whole operation. Since the entire task force had now lifted anchor and was under way for Tokchockto, I had to gather my gear, report to the ship's landing ladder, and speed through the choppy seas in the captain's gig to the destroyer steaming ahead several hundred yards off our port bow. Under normal circumstances, this would have been an exciting adventure, but with the condition of my nether regions and my continued weakness, it only added to the day's ordeal. It must have been about 2200 hours (10:00 p.m.) when I finally climbed aboard the destroyer, was warmly welcomed aboard, and immediately conducted to a fine private stateroom. I fell into the bunk and, despite the heavy seas and the great speed with which we were plowing through those seas, slept soundly, awaking the next morning refreshed and ready to go. After a delicious U.S. Navy breakfast, I reported to the commodore and explained my role. I had a radioman from our operations section with me, who was on our battalion operations net. All requests, queries, and reports from the colonel were made through me, and I passed them on to the proper

Presuming to be a United States Marine

staff section in our amphibious task force headquarters. The destroyer was fitted for special operations. It had additional radar and extra spaces for setting up control operations. It was used for landing reconnaissance details of marines, a designation of what later became the SEALs. As we neared our objective and deployed for the landing operation, I spent most of my time on the bridge with the skipper and the commodore. Often I had to duck behind the bridge to the operations center to pass on or obtain information in my role as supporter of the battalion being landed. A TAC-LOG officer has responsibilities for relaying and responding to tactical inquiries and also logistic matters. He is required to phase in the shipment ashore of supplies, equipment, ammunition, etc. in an amphibious landing.

From the ship's bridge, I had a box-seat view of the whole operation. The amphibious tractors and the landing craft executed their missions with ballet-like precision, and the landing went off well. I was fascinated by the radar, which by today's standards would certainly be considered primitive. From the operations center, we could observe each boat and each tractor as it made its way to the beach. If any got out of line, word could immediately be passed to the coxswain to straighten up.

We had landed over half our landing waves when a sailor manning an antiaircraft radar sang out with some urgency, "Enemy MIG 30 miles out at thirty thousand feet, closing fast." General Quarters (all weapons manned and crew deployed for battle) had already been sounded for the landing operations, but all the gun crews were now ordered to man their guns. It was very exciting to see the smooth teamwork these sailors exhibited as they manned their guns. The commodore now turned to me and asked me if I was going to relay information about the hostile aircraft ashore to Colonel Gililland. We had a short discussion. By now several sailors with binoculars had spotted the single plane extremely high up in an almost cloudless sky. The commodore speculated that the plane couldn't be very hostile from that height, and since it was a single plane, it was probably reconnoitering and taking long-range photos of our operation.

As a result, I did not relay the information ashore. The landing was going very well, and the problem we had worked out for the troops once ashore was going off smoothly. I was afraid Colonel Gililland might overreact if informed of a possible attack from the air. Meanwhile, the plane never descended to a lower altitude. It passed all the way over our task force, turned around, and flew back to North Korea. After the completion of the exercise, the troops were loaded back aboard the ship, and we turned around and steamed back to Inchon. My couple of days spent on this very comfortable destroyer were marred by the fact that it had been rather snugly constructed during World War II. Overhead beams were only about six feet and one inch above the deck, and the overhead itself was only six feet and three inches above the deck. With my two extra inches in height, I was never able to stand up straight when indoors. Despite my constant and watchful attention, I whacked my head at least three times on this ship, and whacked it hard. I believe that to this day, traces of that particular tour can be felt on my scalp.

After our amphibious exercise, we trained, worked, and played poker in the Rock Pile until about the fifteenth of February when it came time for the First Marines to go back to Line Jamestown (the main line of resistance) again. This time we were assigned to the left regimental sector, the same sector to which we had been assigned for the Bunker Hill operations during the previous late summer.

Our battalion headquarters in this sector was at the bottom of the reverse slope of 229, the huge hill mass F Company had occupied in late September and early October. This command post was not bad. The battalion headquarters had some interesting new responsibilities in this particular sector. The left flank of the battalion tied in with the Korean Marines, and on this same left-flank tie-in position was stationed the snatch team prepared to go out the famous corridor that led from the railhead at Munsan-ni out to Panmunjom. Our battalion had the responsibility for overseeing that corridor and making sure that it remained absolutely sacrosanct.

Furthermore, we maintained a full company at an outpost called OP-2 just outside the no-fire Panmunjom circle nestled into the corner where the corridor from the south entered into the big one-thousand-meter-in-radius circle around Panmunjom. As long as we did not fire across the circle or across the corridor, we were permitted to fire out in an easterly direction from the outpost. The Chinese too could fire at us in that outpost as long as they did not fire into the Panmunjom circle, or into the corridor. The layout on the map and the ground was rather interesting. An exit from the corridor lead out to OP-2 where we had a whole rifle company, and I visited there several times during that February and March period in 1953.

My friend and fine officer, Captain Tom Barrow, had been relieved as Fox Company commander before Christmas and was now the logistics officer (S-4) for the battalion. At one time, Tom and I were in an observation post on the forward slope of our company position in this little corner of OP-2, half surrounded by fighting territory, and half surrounded by neutral territory for the peace talks. The OP looked into the circle and at Chinese positions that were being dug around just east of it; we could also look off to the east on a plain.

The Chinese who had dug around the circle toward our OP-2 corner had their own observation post about 150 yards from ours. Both these observation posts were sitting in what would be called fire-zone territory; one could fire from them, but only in certain directions, and one could not fire from either one at the other. The Chinese observation post nudged up against the circle of the Panmunjom truce talks, and ours was up against the no-fire corridor.

Barrow and I walked out to the OP on that fine day, equipped with binoculars and looking across at the Chinese observation post. We saw there some unmistakably Caucasian-looking gentlemen who simultaneously had their binoculars trained on us. It was clear that these were Russian officers. We continued looking at the Russian officers with some Chinese officers standing behind them, and they all carried on with their careful observation of us. We were all watching each other from a distance of 150 yards. Down in the bottom of the trench line of our OP, there happened to be a loose length of pipe about three inches in diameter and at least ten feet long, with its purpose unknown to us. Barrow, on a whim, picked up this pipe, carefully positioned it over the parapet of the trench, got behind it, sighted through it, and aimed it directly at the Chinese and Russian officers in their observation post. Immediately, all hell broke loose on the enemy OP. You could see them picking up radios and picking up telephones in a flurry of activity. We figured they must have assumed that we had a secret weapon of some sort that could fire at great distances and have its shell drop to the ground.

Having been in Korea for about ten months, I must say that I was beginning to feel a bit put-upon. As I have explained, the rotation rate for officers was variable. The tours, of course, were beginning to stretch out because of the number of casualties we were sustaining. But officers who had come over one and two months before I did were home by Christmas. For me it was not to be.

Major Dominick, a man for whom I developed a tremendous respect and affection, proved himself to be a fine marine officer. We were concerned about the conditions on the forward slope of Hill 229, where Tom Jannelle had been killed back in October, and Dominick wanted to take a look at the terrain there. One day he and I entered the MLR trench line from the old observation post behind Bunker Hill. We walked west along the trench line on the top of 201, clear down from that hill across a little valley, staying in the trench line as it continued across the forward slope of 229. It was probably late February or early March. The weather was beginning to warm up a bit, and the snow was melting off the ground, although we were still bundled up. The hillside was bare and barren.

As we were walking along the face of the lower slopes of 229, we heard a bang from the Chinese lines, followed by a whistling sound and another bang much closer to us. By that time, I had developed an acute ability to judge the size and caliber of a shell by the sound it carried. First came the resonance of the gun being fired, then the *whoosh* of the approaching shell, and finally the magnitude of the explosion. I knew that this particular shell had come from a 76 mm gun, a long-barreled and very accurate gun the Soviet Army had developed and their Chinese friends had copied and adapted to their own use. With certain types of ammunition, the 76 mm was a good antitank gun. It was modeled on a slightly larger-caliber weapon made famous by the German army in World War II, the 88 mm gun. The shells of the 76 mm had tremendous velocity, and that is why we always knew when being shot at by the 76 mm. Dominick and I now looked toward the Chinese-held land and saw a puff of smoke. The Chinese were obviously sniping at us with a 76 mm. We continued hastily along the trench line across the slope, and—*phhsstt, BANG! phhsstt, BANG! phhssttt, BANG!* The Chinese 76 mm gun sniper continued trying to hit us. Thanking God that the sniper was unsuccessful, I began to empathize with the duck in a shooting gallery if, indeed, it feels anything as it crosses in front of the people banging away at it. We continued creeping along, bent over and trying to expose as little of ourselves as possible until we reached a deeper trench line connecting with trench lines that took us away from the sniper, and we found ourselves still alive.

While still in battalion headquarters behind 229, I received a letter one day in March. The upper left-hand corner of the envelope showed the return address to be

Taking on the Burden of History

"the White House, Washington DC." I knew immediately that the letter was from my good friend Steve Benedict. Steve had been a classmate of mine at St. John's. We had been good friends in college and had often double-dated after we first started dating vigorously in 1944 and 1945. For some medical reason, Steve was classified 4-F and had never been in the service. He seemed to feel that it was his patriotic duty to keep up the morale of Van Sant in Korea and became a faithful correspondent sending highly interesting letters.

During my stint in Korea in 1952, Steve had begun working with General Dwight Eisenhower. Steve's family was friends of the Eisenhower family, and after Ike decided to make the run for the presidency, he hired Steve as a speechwriter for his campaign. After Ike's nomination and at the beginning of his campaign, Steve became one of many speechwriters on Eisenhower's staff. Steve retained a great respect and admiration for Dwight Eisenhower, and the friendship lasted until Ike's death.

Steve had been sending me blow-by-blow descriptions of his life, which I, stuck as I was in the mud, the freezing cold, and the ever-present dangers to my life in Korea, found most interesting and entertaining. First of all, he described Ike's travels as he was seeking the Republican nomination. In the summer of 1952, while I was on Bunker Hill, Steve wrote about the convention. Finally, he regaled me with stories about riding along on the campaign trail. After Ike had won the election, Steve, who was then still a young man, was placed on the White House staff as assistant to Ike's economic adviser, Gabriel Hauge. This put Steve in close proximity to an unlimited supply of White House stationery.

The White House envelope addressed to Van Sant arrived when we were in the headquarters behind 229. After dinner on that day, Major Reifel, the new battalion executive officer, came over and said, "Van, the colonel would like to see you after dinner."

"Yes, sir." I went up to Colonel Gililland's tent, knocking on the tent pole with, "Lieutenant Van Sant reporting, as ordered, sir."

"Oh, come in, come in, Van, sit down," said the colonel genially and motioned me toward a camp stool. Mind you, this seemed a little strange to me, because Colonel Gililland took military protocol very seriously. He was not ordinarily known to engage in hail-fellow-well-met banter with a lowly lieutenant, and I wondered what I had done to merit the friendly attention suddenly showered upon me.

But I said "Yes, sir" as I sat down. He began talking about our recent operations and the weather, clearly beating around the bush. Finally he stopped his prattle and said, "Van, is there something about you I should know?" I was totally mystified by his question.

"No, sir," I floundered. And he danced around whatever aspect of my life he wanted me to clarify without my being any more enlightened on the subject.

Inevitably, he had to speak straight out and get to the point. "It's come to my attention, Lieutenant, that you have received a letter today from the White House. Do you have a relationship with the president?"

Presuming to be a United States Marine

I have no doubt that it cost him something to ask this question. While mail received from overseas in a combat zone becomes something of a public property, and who sent what to whom often becomes common knowledge in an outfit, mail should still remain a completely personal and private matter. As I subsequently found out, the battalion mail clerk had seen the envelope with the White House address on it and had spread the news all around the command post that Lieutenant Van Sant had received a letter from the president. A variety of stories about the letter began cropping up and reached the colonel, stimulating his interest. Of course, at the same time, he knew full well that it was none of his business whether or not Van Sant received a letter from the White House, and he also knew that I knew this, which was why he had so strenuously beaten around the bush.

And then I made two big mistakes. First, I should have kept him sweating and squirming much longer, and next I should have implied modestly that I did have a great deal of influence in the White House. Instead, I told him the truth. As soon as Gililland realized that, really, I had no important connections, his whole demeanor changed. The next thing I knew, I was out of his tent, having been dismissed perfunctorily. And that was the end of my illustrious presumed connection with the president of the United States of America.

My duties in the operations office spanned from sometime around the seventeenth of October when we went into reserve after Bunker Hill until I left Korea in April of 1953. My boss for the longest period of that time was Major Robert Dominick, who retired from the regular Marine Corps as a colonel. As operations officer, Bob was the third senior officer in the battalion. The battalion commander was a lieutenant colonel, the battalion exec was a senior major, and then there was Bob. Our senior enlisted man, who was either a master sergeant or a gunnery sergeant, was called operations chief. There was a lot of turnover in the chief's position during my five and one half months in operations as we had at least four different operations chiefs. These men did a good job overseeing the troops in their section and making sure that things went along smoothly.

Among the characters I remember best was Sergeant Sullivan, whom we have already met. Sullivan's main job was to be our draftsman and artist. He was skillful and conscientious at his job, and he produced beautiful overlays. His other job was to make coffee for the section, and that is a story in itself.

We had in the operations section a marvelous kettle. Sergeant Sullivan had inherited this kettle from his predecessor along with a story. The kettle had made the original landing in Inchon with the marines. For the subsequent two and a half years, it had remained the property of the operations section of the Second Battalion of the First Marines, and it had even survived the Reservoir, although its lid had been lost over time. This large metal kettle was a work of art and a piece of history, and so was the recipe for making coffee straight from the United States. Sergeant Sullivan's father had worked on the railroad and had prepared what he had called railroad coffee. The way Sergeant Sullivan made his father's railroad coffee was to fill the kettle with cold water,

Taking on the Burden of History

set it on top of a stove, and bring the water to a vigorous boil. Sullivan would pour approximately one cup of ground coffee into the boiling water and take the kettle off the stove. Slowly, after the water stopped boiling, the coffee grounds would settle at the bottom of the kettle. The kettle would go back on the stove, but the water would not be allowed to boil again. Periodically, Sullivan would rinse the inside of the kettle and throw away the used grounds. This method of making coffee in the same kettle over a period of two and a half years produced an interior coating about one-fourth-inch thick, which only enhanced the flavor of the coffee. That coffee was nothing short of superb, and all through that winter's bitter cold, we could always count on a nice steaming hot cup of it.

There was another interesting aspect to Sergeant Sullivan. Before he arrived in Korea from the West Coast about a month or two ahead of me, he had become involved in some kind of altercation with another marine on his last liberty. This marine had hit him squarely on his mouth, knocking out the sergeant's two front teeth. As this had happened close to his departure for Korea, he had to sail on toothless. There was a Christmas song about that time in American popular music, in which the singer mournfully declared,—"All I want for Chrithmath ith my two front teef,/my two front teef, my two front teef,"—punctuating the last word with a whistle, presumably through the gap created by the loss of those teeth. Our Sergeant Sullivan, who even with his front teeth intact certainly would not have taken any prizes for good looks, sang that song quite effortlessly, and often.

We seem to have run toward Irish staff people in the section. The clerk/typist's name was Corporal O'Brien. O'Brien was from New York State. He was one of several enlisted men in Korea who had gone to college before coming into the Corps. O'Brien had gone to Rensselaer Polytechnic Institute. He was a bright young man and a very skillful typist. In those days, all our orders and all our operations plans were done on mimeograph. Battalion headquarters had a mimeograph machine, and O'Brien was a genius typing mimeo stencils. He could finagle them and correct them and move them around. He was very skilled in the proper Marine Corps layout for an operations plan or an operations order, and he knew all about annexes and about all the structural elements that go into the kind of paperwork that had to be done. O'Brien was a very competent young man with a wonderful sense of humor. When he was not typing, he sometimes helped Sullivan with overlays, as he was a fairly good draftsman too, and he generally made himself useful.

A third man we had was a driver/messenger/communications man. We were constantly exchanging plans, orders, documents, overlays, and code books with the rifle companies online, and we kept our driver busy pretty much all day. Since we moved fairly frequently, we had a jeep with a trailer, and all our field desks, all of our drafting tables, and all of the equipment that went along with our operations office fit very neatly into that one jeep with its trailer. We became very skilled in packing everything up, loading it up, and unloading it all again as we moved into the various different headquarters.

Presuming to be a United States Marine

Corporal O'Brien had an older brother who was a captain in the Army Transportation Corps stationed at Inchon. One day O'Brien's brother called on the field telephone with an invitation to visit him at Inchon. We were the reserve battalion online at the time, and so our Corporal O'Brien asked Major Dominick if he could get liberty. Major Dominick, who was very appreciative of Corporal O'Brien's work went to Colonel Gililland, and they managed to finagle some kind of order for O'Brien. He could, of course, not get liberty but he got a set of orders from division "detaching Corporal O'Brien from First Marine Division for temporary duty with the Army Transportation Corps for four days in Inchon." They next arranged for Corporal O'Brien to catch a ride in the jeep to the railhead at Munsan-ni some miles behind us, from where he could travel on the supply train to Seoul and on west to Inchon.

O'Brien returned from his trip bursting with stories. He regaled the section for days on end with his adventures in Inchon. O'Brien's brother was probably about twenty-six or twenty-seven years old and, being in the supply corps, had connections with everybody. It seems that he was sort of the port commander at Inchon. There was an Army MASH unit with nurses on the little base, and anchored right off the coast of Inchon was a navy hospital ship, with more nurses aboard, ready to come ashore when off duty.

In honor of his little brother, Captain O'Brien had planned a big party. The problem was that the party was to be held in the small Inchon Officers' Club. All the captain's friends, as well as the nurses, were officers, while our O'Brien was a corporal. But he told his brother, "Hell, a corporal in the Marine Corps is the equivalent of a lieutenant in the army anytime." And he borrowed some second lieutenant bars from somebody. For the four days he was in Inchon, Corporal O'Brien morphed into a lieutenant. He described the parties with the nurses to us, and, I mean, they really sounded magnificent. Even if some of the stories may not have been strictly true, they were highly entertaining. The entire time he was at Inchon, the focus of his attention was turned on one particular U.S. Army nurse. Before too long, they became so wrapped up in each other that when his time at Inchon came to an end, she kept asking him for his address in order to keep in touch with him. O'Brien, of course, worried about her mailing a letter addressed to "Lieutenant O'Brien" at our battalion headquarters. He found it very difficult to tell her the truth and waited until the last possible moment before telling her. "This may make a lot of difference to your feelings for me, but I am a marine corporal, not a lieutenant."

And bless her heart, she told him firmly, "That does not make any difference to me." For the rest of his time in Korea, Corporal O'Brien carried on a passionate correspondence with his nurse back at Inchon. I've often wondered if they got together after the war.

These were the men with whom I worked, and I believe that together we were able to accomplish many good things. Every time we took up a new battalion position on the First Division front, and I was in a total of three different battalion fronts, we examined all the operations orders and plans in effect. Operation Recoil, which I have already described, was the First Division's name for our blocking and counterattack plan. The plan envisaged a recoil, or orderly movement backward (that is, retreat to a blocking position), and then a mighty spring forward like the recoil of a large artillery piece.

Most of the division battalion fronts we occupied either did not have a recoil plan, or if they had one, it was not considered by our commanders to be very good. Therefore, when we had nothing else to do, we would prepare recoil plans. This meant that we had to go out and make reconnaissance of the ground, find the best blocking positions, whom we could call upon to block an enemy penetration, what resources we had to mobilize a counterattack, and from where that counterattack could be launched. These were really interesting tasks. As a result of all our work, by the spring of 1953, the basic counterattack plans for three of the four online battalion fronts in the entire First Marine Division sector were authored by Major Dominick and Lieutenant Van Sant.

Then somebody had the bright idea that we ought to have what was called a command post exercise, or CPX. Even though we were online, we were always trying to exercise the communications sections and the staff people to get them to understand how to operate more effectively together. Our battalion staff did a CPX with the Korean Marine Corps, and that was an interesting experience.

Every Marine Corps staff has four sections—(1) personnel, (2) intelligence, (3) operations, and (4) logistics. But instead of having the staff section heads perform this exercise, the second in command, the company execs, whether officers or enlisted men, were chosen for the duty. That, of course, meant that I became operations officer, and this was thrilling to me. The hypothetical situation presented to us in the CPX exercise was that the Chinese had penetrated a certain position, and we were now operating with a blocking position and counterattack on the ground behind the lines where the two units linked together, which put us in the KMC (Korean Marine Corps) area.

In the midst of this hypothetical situation, by the way, I was able to observe a Korean Marine Corps unit, uninvolved in our exercise, performing a gun drill with a .50 caliber machine gun. To a civilian, that probably does not sound like anything very spectacular. But a .50 caliber machine gun is very heavy, and the U.S. Marine Corps only performed gun drill with .30 caliber machine guns. The often small-boned Korean Marines in their drill not only toted the great, big, heavy barrel of the .50 caliber machine gun and the great, big, heavy gun cradle, and the great, big, heavy tripod, each of which weighed at least seventy pounds, but they ran up a hill with these gun parts, assembling them as they reached the top and starting to fire them in the same manner we did in our training with the .30 caliber machine gun. The pieces of gun these guys were carrying were quite often bigger than them. Although I was awestruck by this display, I prudently held back any suggestion to the U.S. Marine Corps that it ought to try gun drill with a .50 caliber. It was a very impressive exercise to watch, particularly as performed by somebody else.

Our own exercise began. I took my communications people and my Sergeant Sullivan with his overlays and his drafting set, and we took off. I conferred with all the number two staff men participating in the exercise and the KMCs, and together we devised a counterattack plan involving slipping a tank company around a little hill and hitting the enemy by surprise. We formulated the plan, wrote it up, and the exercise was declared ended. After that we had to submit the plan to the section chiefs and to the colonel to see what they thought of it.

One of my proudest moments came when Colonel Gililland, having looked at the plan, having listened to my explanations in further detail on the map, and having stepped out on a kind of observation post from where he could see the terrain, said, "Van Sant, that's outstanding. That's exactly what I would have done." The highest compliment, indeed. I was amazed, because I was well aware of Gililland's tendency to be hypercritical.

Chapter 18

GOING HOME (1953)

Time was marching on into March. The rotation differed for enlisted men and officers. At that time, enlisted men returned home about one month earlier than the officers because of the loss the previous summer and fall of so many officers. In March, as a matter of fact, the Fifth Marines to our right were engaged in several heavy battles of Reno, Carson, and Vegas. Vegas, particularly, was a battle fully as engaging and as big as Bunker Hill, so that the division was taking considerable casualties. Still, I allowed myself to feel some excitement, thinking that I might be able to go home in March. All through that month, I was keeping my ear in the office of the adjutant to hear what the word was about the rotation home. Finally, near the end of March, the good news came that, yes, I was going home. I had my orders that in one week I was to detach from the First Marine Division and report to ASCOM City near Inchon to be processed, then go aboard ship to sail back to San Francisco.

Vernon Vick, who had come over to Korea with me, was being rotated home too. He had stayed in Easy Company during his entire tour from May until April. He was still executive officer and had a good new company commander. Easy Company was on that hairy place, OP-2, near Panmunjom, and so his company commander sent Vick back to battalion headquarters to be relieved a few days early. Major Dominick relieved me of some of my duties also, and since I had a tent to myself, Vick moved in with me. This gave us the opportunity to reminisce, to grieve, and to relax together for a few days. It was during one of these visits that Vick told me the true story of what had happened September 5 on Bunker Hill.

One night I went to bed fairly early while Vick had gone off with some of his other buddies at battalion headquarters for a few drinks. Because we were way down at the foot of 229, and the reverse slope was safe, we were afforded the luxury of electric lights from a generator. When Vick returned, he apparently turned on the light hanging from a cord on the center pole of the tent. I was sound asleep at the time and had not heard him coming in. Soon Vick fell into his bunk and into a sound sleep without, however, having turned off the light. He had, furthermore, made the mistake of leaving the tent-flap entrance open.

Presuming to be a United States Marine

Colonel Gililland, as mentioned earlier, had a huge temper. I was suddenly awakened from my sound sleep by a noise. Looking up, I beheld Colonel Gililland, bayonet in hand, hacking away at the electric cord to the lightbulb and mad as hell. His face was white from anger, and I contemplated the fact that his apparition was as scary as almost anything I had seen in the war.

Gililland kept slashing away at the cord until his bayonet broke through. He yanked off the lightbulb in its fixture and took it with him. All the time he was engaged in this activity, I never let on that I saw him. After he left, I whispered, "Hey, Vick! Did you see that?" Vick had seen it too and had also decided that discretion—that is, remaining asleep—was the better part of valor.

The next morning, Major Reifel, the battalion executive officer, came up to me at breakfast and said, "The colonel is mad as hell at you, you left your light on last night and the tent flap open." And I told him I had not left anything on or open and that I had been sound asleep. At this point, Vick, bless his heart, came up and confessed to being the culprit. And Reifel said a little sheepishly, "Well, here is your light." He handed us the piece of the electric cord with the fixture and bulb dangling from it and added that the colonel had been pretty mad but had later reconsidered his punishment.

On my arrival in Korea, I had been issued a pair of binoculars by battalion supply. As I was checking out to leave Korea, I had to turn in my pistol, my binoculars, and some of my cold-weather clothing. I gathered it all up and went over to the supply tent to check everything back in. The supply sergeant asked me to give him the serial number of the binoculars I was returning, and I gave it to him.

If you will remember, as Lieutenant Jannelle was leaving on that last patrol on which he was killed, he had handed me his binoculars for safekeeping, not wanting to leave them in the foxhole or take them along, so that I had been carrying his binoculars, as well as mine, with me ever since. When I read off to the sergeant the serial number on the binoculars, he said, "Sir, those are not your binoculars." He looked over his list and said, "Lieutenant, I am really sorry you gave me that number. My records show that those binoculars were checked out to Lieutenant Jannelle, and they are officially listed as 'expended in combat.' If you had turned in your own binoculars first, you could have kept those for the rest of your life, and nobody would have ever known the difference." And he added, "Now that I know what happened, I am going to have to ask you for both sets." And there, through the efficiency of the Marine Corps, went a free pair of binoculars down the tubes.

Vick and I, having arrived in Korea at the same time, now left together. Vincello, the third V who had come in May, had been rotated back several months earlier because his obligated service as a reserve officer had expired.

I climbed into a waiting jeep, officially said good-bye to everybody, including Bob Dominick and Tom Barrow, both of whom I had come to admire and respect greatly, and then we headed to the rear for the Munsan-ni railhead. This was a very emotional time. I was delighted to be leaving but sad too, and amidst these conflicting emotions,

Taking on the Burden of History

an interesting phenomenon occurred. As the jeep drove farther and farther away from the noise of the guns and all the other noises associated with the war, as we left the lines behind us and those staccato sounds began to fade, I gradually felt my little friend down in my stomach disappearing.

Who was this little friend? This little friend, as I have mentioned before, was a heavy ball in the pit of my stomach. I had first encountered him on that night I landed in Korea, and he had made his home inside me ever since. I can't say that I had any regrets about bidding farewell to him, because he represented my constant fear. That fear had never left me for an instant until this moment of departure from the war.

We arrived in Munsan-ni, boarded the train, and checked into ASCOM City to go through an interesting kind of processing. Our footlockers—left behind in Kobe, Japan, on the way over—had by now been shipped to ASCOM City, so that I was once again reunited with my footlocker. I inventoried everything and got my uniforms out and squared away. We were given medical processing and a physical exam. I had weighed 213 pounds when I arrived in Korea. As I was leaving, I weighed 177 pounds, and it showed.

We were deloused, which, as one can imagine, was not a thrilling experience. The delousing was done with a bellows-like mechanism filled with white powder, which was squirted all over our utility uniform, down our trousers, and into our boots, as well as all over our hair.

We must have stayed in ASCOM City for several days because in addition to the physical, getting our gear back, and the delousing, I also remember going to church on April 5, the day before my departure from Korea, for Easter services. It struck me at the time that Easter formed a pair of bookends for my Korean tour. I have already described the Hollywood Bowl sunrise service Lorraine and I attended before I sailed over to Korea. I also thought back to Easter in the English church in Tianjin, China, in 1946 when I turned at the communion rail to find my company commander Lieutenant McCulloch kneeling beside me.

In ASCOM City, I renewed my acquaintance with my old friend, the alcoholic captain company commander in the draft coming over. He had managed to get himself a cushy job as Headquarters Company commander for ASCOM City. He had little to do but was close to a source of supply for satisfying his favorite hobby. He had seen my name on the outgoing draft roster and sent a message to me the first night to come by his hut for a drink. I visited him and had a couple of drinks with him. He was happy as a clam—had a girlfriend available, unlimited whisky, and very little to do. Although he was eligible for rotation back to the States, he had voluntarily extended his tour and settled in to the good life. As he explained to me, he was geographically separated from the next lieutenant colonel up the chain of command, and he could stay mildly and pleasantly drunk most of the time. I'll bet he stayed over there until the truce.

While we were still in ASCOM City preparing to go on board ship, we received word that General Pollock was coming down and wanted to say good-bye to the officers personally. We were all lined up, 28 of us being rotated home from the First Marine

Presuming to be a United States Marine

Division. There had been exactly 128 officers when we had come over to Korea with the Twentieth Draft. The great bulk of these men had probably been rotated home because they were wounded, but some had been killed, and a few, such as Lieutenant Vincello, had already completed their obligated service. We now represented a small group of survivors assembled for the general.

General Pollock went down the line and shook hands. He spent a few minutes talking with each one of us and asking our name if he did not know it. Of course, he knew me not only from my outstanding tour of our battalion's training program, but also from the coffee stains on my uniform.

I have mentioned that as much as I loved the Marine Corps, and still do, I wanted to do something different with my life. From Korea, I had applied for, and had been admitted into, the University of Virginia's doctoral program in philosophy. General Pollock had obviously gone over the names of the men recommended for regular Marine Corps commissions, and when he came to me, he said, "Lieutenant Van Sant, I am sorry that you decided not to take a regular commission."

"Sir," I said, "I love the Marine Corps, but I am going to graduate school."

"Where are you going?" he asked.

"Sir, to the University of Virginia." And he brightened up at that bit of news. General Pollock was a Southerner, and as the University of Virginia enjoys a high reputation among Southern gentlemen, he was visibly pleased that I was going there. Then he asked, "Well, what are you going to study there, Lieutenant Van Sant?"

"Philosophy, sir," I replied. His face went blank.

He said, "Oh," turned, and went on to the next officer. I had the distinct feeling that, overall, the general was not really too keen on my postwar plans. I think General Pollock may have had some idea that he might become commandant, and he did get a third star after the Korean War. But in 1959 came the announcement of General Shoup's appointment to commandant. I heard from an officer who witnessed it that General Pollock, who was sitting at his desk when the announcement came through, got up, gathered up his briefcase, and walked out of his office. He got into his official lieutenant general's command car and asked to be taken to his quarters. When he arrived there, he picked up the telephone, called Washington, and retired from the Marine Corps. I gather that General Pollock was not overly keen on serving under General Shoup.

At Inchon harbor, I kept my eyes open for Corporal O'Brien's brother, but without seeing him, I rode out on a landing craft and climbed aboard ship for the sail back to San Francisco. I believe it was the morning of April 6, 1953.

We experienced a relatively quick crossing of the North China Sea over to the west coast of Japan to a city called Sasebo on the southernmost island of Japan. As we have seen, for the first part of the war, troopships engaged in carrying replacement drafts over to Korea used to dock at Kobe to unload. After ASCOM City was built near Inchon, the draft going to Korea went all the way through from San Diego to Inchon, off-loaded its new replacements, took on people being rotated back to the States, and returned to Sasebo for supplies.

Taking on the Burden of History

We arrived in Sasebo late in the afternoon and heard the very welcome announcement that we were going to get liberty that night. The port of Sasebo is probably one of the most beautiful ports in the world, with a very large basin of water, the bay, which ships entered through a narrow portal with high rocky promontories sliding down into the water on either side. The bay was surrounded by some of the most beautiful terraced farms and the most beautiful landscaping with little pagodas I have ever seen. On that spring day in 1953, everything looked green and lush and beautiful. Sailing through the narrow portal into the bay was like entering paradise.

The port city of Sasebo was on the innermost edge of the bay, so that we had to sail all the way in. Because it is such a good deep-water port, it had big wharves, and the ship could tie right up at the wharf. I heard later that Sasebo had been one of the main Japanese submarine bases during the war because of the deep nature of its harbor opening right into the South China Sea, close to all of the supply lines that supplied Japan, and close to the routes to the Philippines and the East Indies. In addition, it was not too far to the southern seas where American war ships were beginning to patrol as the war progressed. All of this would have contributed to the suitability of Sasebo as a good location for a submarine base. During the war, the entrance to the harbor had been very heavily fortified, and sailing through the portal, we could see fortifications on the hillside.

As soon as I had found my compartment, shared with about a dozen lieutenants, I went to the officers' mess, where I reunited with some of my old friends who had come over to Korea with me but had been in different units and in different parts of the battlefront. One of those was my good friend, Hildebrandt, who had been my roommate at the BOQ at Camp Pendleton, the man from whom I had borrowed a car on the foggy night of the famous George Morrison / Van Sant expedition to San Diego. Hildebrandt was a fellow whose company I always enjoyed. He was bright and well educated, well read, and interested in everything. He had been in the Seventh Marines the entire time in Korea, and we realized that a couple of times, our paths had almost crossed. We decided to go on liberty together that night to explore the city of Sasebo. I could think of nothing more delightful than to go on liberty in that beautiful harbor town with Hildebrandt.

We got ourselves as slicked up as we could in our Marine Corps uniforms that had been sitting in Kobe and ASCOM City for a year, except for a brief reprieve to Kyoto during R & R, and went into Sasebo. Imagine a shipload of young enlisted marines, as well as twenty-eight young officers being turned loose on a not-very-big city and joining the human contents of some navy vessels docked there, to boot. The pace of social life in the honky-tonks, the dance halls, and the bars picked up considerably. By 1953, places like these in Japan had lots of neon signs, lots of noise, and lots of hoop-de-la, and Hildebrandt and I just wandered around for a while, noting that Sasebo's greatest beauty was to be found in the rural areas surrounding the city and the bay.

We thought it would be good to have a nice dinner and see what we could see. And suddenly, a serendipitous thing happened to us as we turned away from the brightly lit streets with mobs of noisy marines and sailors milling about. We happened upon a little place with an entrance cutting across a corner at a forty-five-degree angle. It had a large plate-glass window facing both streets, and in one of the windows hung a sign with some Japanese writing on it. I can't remember the exact name of the establishment, but it seems to me that it was something the equivalent of "the Teeny-Weensy Cafe." We looked inside, and it was empty. It only seemed to have one or two tables and a very small dance floor.

As we were looking in, we saw a Japanese man wearing a white apron, and he saw us also and motioned us in. In very broken English, he explained to us what he could do for us. He and his wife would cook dinner for us, and we would be served sake. We would be served by his two daughters, whom he introduced to us as they were standing shyly nearby in their beautiful geisha-like kimonos with a pad on the back. And if we would do him the honor of providing our patronage, he would close his place up for us, pull down the shades, and we would be entertained for the entire evening. The manner in which he told us this was very appealing. He had, correctly, gathered that we had just arrived from Korea. He told us the price for our dinners and explained that the price he had quoted included everything—dinner, sake, dancing with his daughters, and tip; and my recollection is that the entire evening's entertainment for both of us cost something like $30.

The dinner was done in Japanese style. We had taken our shoes off and sat on the floor. The table was beautiful, and the entire place had a simple elegance about it. The two daughters were both lovely young women, probably in their early twenties at most. From the kitchen, we could hear the mother and the father busily working away on the dinner.

The sake was heated properly, and the Japanese ritual about pouring it was being observed. Warm sake goes straight to one's head and stops at one's heart on its way up. The dinner was magnificent and consisted of many courses, each one of which was beautifully served with the plates laid out in perfect symmetry. Hildebrandt, who had grown up on the West Coast, knew how to use chopsticks, and I had learned to use them as well. I remember a soup, a magnificent clear soup of some kind. The sake was poured throughout dinner and was followed by some kind of brandy. Our Japanese host had what was in 1953 a state-of-the-art stereo system, and he began playing some Japanese music on it for his daughters to dance an elegant Japanese dance for us.

After this performance, our host put on some western music, and the two lovely young women indicated that they would dance with us. They were excellent dancers, and we enjoyed ourselves immensely. The entire evening stands out in my memory as wonderful, and the words "exquisite" and "elegant" come up first and foremost. And what about sex, you may ask? That, clearly, was not in the picture at all, as it had not been at Durante's party in Kyoto. Fortunately, both of us had the grace to understand that as we remained in our best and most polite behavior. Also, Mama and Papa were watching us, kindly but firmly, at all times.

The Japanese nation, of course, supported our Korean war effort very strongly, and our little family somehow communicated to us that they appreciated what we had done and wanted us to feel relaxed and rewarded. It turned out to be one of the most delightful, serendipitous experiences of my life, and Hildebrandt and I were lucky to have just simply stumbled upon it. I think we must have stayed in that little restaurant until at least eleven o'clock that night. We never got drunk, we just glowed pleasantly. Once we got back out on the street, we were enveloped by a maelstrom of military police with whistles and sirens blowing—in other words, the usual crowds and noises on a liberty night in any port. We made our way back to our ship. There were guys being dragged, and MP trucks were arriving to dump drunk marines off at the ship. One had the feeling, though, that even the MPs knew and appreciated the fact that we were just emerging from Korea, and they went out of their way to show some leniency, wherever possible.

Since the ship had sailed from America to Korea, and then on to Japan, it had to be provisioned. For most of the next morning, new provisions and supplies were loaded on board. It must have been around noon when we sailed out of that beautiful harbor, and I have ever since held a soft spot for Sasebo.

Now the trip from Japan back to San Francisco took a little under two weeks, as I recall. We sailed straight through without stopping at Pearl Harbor. A few of the officers had some duties and responsibilities to oversee troop compartments, but fortunately, I had no such responsibilities. I was left with nothing to do except sleeping and eating, and I have to say that of the four Pacific crossings I made on troopships in my Marine Corps career, the food on this ship was by far the best. It was, in fact, outstanding, and the portions were generous. I told you that I weighed 177 pounds when I was given my last physical in Korea. I think that by the time I reached home in Alexandria, I was close to being back to 190 pounds, all put on while sailing back home. I found myself suddenly without any pressure, without any tension, and without any responsibility.

The wardroom aboard the ship was pleasant, inviting, and comfortable. Because of the attrition in the number of officers, we were not jammed in as we had been on the way over to Korea, although in Japan, the ship picked up about twenty army officers and some navy doctors who were being rotated home.

As one might expect, these pleasant conditions precipitated one of the most intense bridge-playing binges in which I had ever participated. We played an enormous amount of bridge on the way back. In fact, I would say that other than eating, taking a turn around the deck each day for exercise, and sleeping, the rest of my time was taken up by playing bridge and drinking vast amounts of coffee.

Early on in the trip, maybe the second or third day, I met a navy doctor, a lieutenant senior grade, the equivalent of a captain in the Marine Corps. He had been a battalion surgeon with the First Battalion of the First Marines and was an old friend of my old friend, our great battalion surgeon, Pernokas, whom he had known even before going to Korea. And since this man was not only a friend but also a great admirer of Pernokas and, moreover, was a good bridge player, we developed a close bridge partnership.

While the army and Marine Corps officers got on really well, and there were never any interservice conflicts of any sorts, there may have developed a slightly competitive spirit between us. My doctor friend and I began developing a reputation for being absolutely invincible bridge partners. Naturally, we got into the habit of gladly accommodating anyone who wished to play with us, and we would then just wax them. Only two or three days from San Francisco, an army officer said, "You know, we ought to organize a bridge tournament." And my partner and I thought this was just a great idea. We asked what the prize was going to be.

Bridge tournaments are usually duplicate bridge, which means that one is not subjected to the problems that arise when one gets bad hands, and everybody gets a chance to play hands of all varieties. Our friends from the army, though, may not have been up to speed on how to organize such a tournament. What they told us was, "In the first round, everybody will enter as a pair, as a partnership. Then we will make up a schedule, and in the first round, the partners will play one rubber of bridge, and the winner will advance, and the loser will drop out." This was a sort of elimination approach with quarterfinals and semifinals, leading up to the finals.

My partner and I were really excited to hear about this tournament and thought that we had it all locked in, no doubt about that. What we did not appreciate was that the first rubber would be all-critical and important. I was dealt my first hand and saw that I had two points in the point-counting system. I learned later that my partner had, I think, three or four points of his own. Our two opponents in this first rubber were army officers, and it became clear from the conversation between them and with us that it was highly unlikely they had ever played bridge before they set foot on board ship. They asked us very rudimentary questions about the game.

The first hand they were dealt was overwhelming for the two of them, while we had nothing. With a great deal of stumbling, they bid a game in spades and made a little slam, and we took one trick. But they had won the first game in a rubber. We then dealt another hand, and damned, if the same thing did not happen in the second hand. We had nothing, absolutely nothing. I had the worst bridge hands I had ever held, two in a row. And darn if these two army officers were not dealt magnificent hands again, and while they screwed up the bidding, fortunately for them, they stumbled into bidding a game and, of course, made a game and another slam. They should have bid it, but they won the rubber anyway and advanced to the second round, where they were creamed. Many people in the wardroom had been saying, "Man, Van Sant and his partner are going to take it. They can't be beat." But we were out in the first round. And I was rarely more disappointed in my life while being reminded of beginner's luck and of "pride goeth before the fall."

Between lots of sleep and lots of food and lots of bridge, that trip across the Pacific has a warm feeling in my memory. The only blemish, the only flaw—and this brings up an interesting aspect of combat and postcombat—was that in our officers' stateroom, one of the guys, and I can't remember which regiment he had been in, had horrible nightmares. He talked and yelled out in his sleep, reliving recent war episodes, and his occasional blood-curdling screams woke everybody in the stateroom. We felt sorry for the poor guy, whose appalling dreams occurred about every second or third night.

Taking on the Burden of History

We would eventually manage to wake him up from his nightmare in an effort to stop his suffering. But we were on edge trying to settle down to sleep every night, half expecting his terrible screams to awaken us. I remembered a marine in my machine gun platoon in China who occasionally would become violent in his sleep, screaming, jumping out of his bed, and throwing objects, although it must be said that he had never been in any combat, and so this may have been a reflection of some traumatic experience he had suffered somewhere else. I wonder if my stateroom mate's post-traumatic experience has persisted after he returned to the United States, or whether he eventually stopped having his nightmares. I have always thanked the good Lord for giving me peaceful sleeps without any post-combat flashbacks or trauma.

The trip passed quickly, and I think it was the morning of April 21, at about six o'clock, when the loudspeaker system all over the ship announced, "Now hear this! Now hear this! All passengers are advised that it is a beautiful day outside, and if you hurry up and get up on deck, you will be able to see the sunrise over the Golden Gate Bridge." Although we did not have to get to breakfast until seven o'clock, at least half of us got dressed to go topside. In our officer country, there was a little deck space with a good view from the front of the superstructure of the ship.

And it was a beautiful sight! It was an exquisite April day, and we were coming eastward from the Pacific toward the Golden Gate Bridge just at dawn. When I reached the deck, the sun was just peeping over the horizon behind the bridge, which appeared tiny in the distance. As we advanced toward the bridge, the sun rose quickly through a bank of lovely clouds that reminded me of my epiphany on the way to China eight years earlier. Remembering that other sunrise, I had a rush of feeling, but this one was filled with gratitude toward God for having brought me home safe.

And as we sailed toward that famous bridge, I pondered what the future might hold for me. I could hardly be expected to know that after getting my PhD in philosophy from the University of Virginia, I would become a college professor for the rest of my life. I could hardly be expected to know that I would meet, fall in love with, and marry three more wonderful women, two of whom were to be taken from me by untimely deaths, just as Shirley had been. I could not be expected to know that, despite these tragic deaths, I would be blessed with two wonderful children and four stepchildren, as well as many grandchildren, and remain close to a loving large, extended family of in-laws.

Finally, I could not know then, on that April morning, that I would have twenty-four more years in a very active reserve career in the Marine Corps that ended with my retirement as a colonel.

In spite of tragic losses, this life to which I was reborn after returning from Korea has been a wonderful life. I trace that rebirth back to that moment on Bunker Hill as I began to lose consciousness from the hand grenade. But as we slid peacefully under the Golden Gate Bridge on that golden April day, all of that wonderful life lay ahead and is another story.

THE END

POSTSCRIPT

In Spring of 1954, a number of officers from the 2nd Battalion had a small reunion at the Officers' Club at Quantico, Virginia. Many are mentioned in this book. Standing L to R: Major "Locker Box' Jones, 1st Lt. Gorton Cook, Captain Tom Palmer, Major Dominick, a guest, 1st Lt. Van Sant, 1st Lt. Bill Russ, 1st Lt. Ralph Shugart. Kneeling in Foreground L to R: Captain Esmond Harper, Captain Rocky Eldracker, Lt. Col "Cotton" Gilliland, and 1st Lt. Ralph Quinn.

In 1995, after many delays, a memorial on the mall in Washington DC was finally dedicated, honoring the veterans of the Korean War. With thousands of other veterans of that "forgotten war," I spent about four days in Washington attending various events. Thanks to some enterprising work by some veterans of my era in Korea from D Company, Second Battalion, First Marines, a bunch of us were notified about a banquet in a hotel in Arlington of old 2/1 members. At the banquet, I ran into a few guys from

Taking on the Burden of History

Fox Company and Weapons Company. We all decided to form an organization and plan other reunions. I got my name on their mailing list but never attended any of the reunions between 1996 and 2000.

But then several things happened. First was the explosion of the Internet, and suddenly I was in contact with a number of my old friends. Then my son discovered the Korean War Project on the Internet, and I registered on it. In 2000 and 2001, I was in contact with a whole lot more of my old troopers. In addition, an active-duty U.S. Army officer stationed in Korea, who was a relative of Lieutenant Burrus, found my name as the author of an after-action report on Burrus's ill-fated Kumgok raid. I wrote up an account of that, and one thing led to another.

First was this memoir; second, my wife and I resolved to go to the next Second Battalion, First Marines, reunion, which happened to be held in New Orleans in late May of 2001. I was a little apprehensive about meeting all my old troops, hoping that they still thought well of me. As soon as we registered for the reunion, about a half a dozen people crowded around me, and everybody talked at once. No need for apprehensions. But I still did not know what they had planned.

The last night of the reunion, after a banquet dinner, there was a program. Several notables were introduced. Then the battalion chaplain who relieved Chaplain McCabe, Chaplain Kuhn, gave a very eloquent speech about the Korean War, its significance, and the importance of our sacrifices. It was truly a beautiful speech. Then the emcee called forward John Armstrong, the man who had the next fighting position to mine on Bunker Hill when I was wounded. John launched into words of high praise about an unidentified fellow marine he had fought with in Korea. I was really impressed with this anonymous fellow who did these miraculous things. Then suddenly he called me forward and presented me with a certificate, a facsimile of which follows.

Those rascals who signed this had been planning on this presentation for over a year. Needless to say, when I went up to receive the certificate, I could barely speak. I think the reader will understand how overwhelming the sentiments expressed on it were for me. In the full and adventurous life I have led since that April 1953 morning sliding under the Golden Gate Bridge, I can modestly say I have received numerous recognitions. I have been active in academia, in my church, in my community, and in politics. From all these quarters, I have received awards, commendations, testimonials, honorary memberships, etc. But I hope the reader of this memoir can understand that the impacts of all these recognitions pale beside the pride I feel in the attached certificate.

LETTER OF RECOGNITION AND APPRECIATION

We, former members of Fox Company, 2nd Battalion, 1st Marine Regiment, 1st Marine Division and associated units, present this Letter of Recognition and Appreciation to GEORGE VAN SANT for his efforts while serving in Korea as Platoon Commander and Executive Officer of Fox Company in the Summer and Fall of 1952. We do not know if you were officially recognized by the Marine Corps at that time, but we want you to know that we believe your courage, your spirit, and your leadership is deserving of recognition. It may be too late for medals, but we want you to know that your efforts were and are appreciated.

After almost fifty years whenever Fox Company members meet you are remembered as their memories are shared. Your deeds of action were an inspiration to many of us. You are commended for your leadership while taking care of your men. You are remembered as an outstanding Marine officer. We are proud of our association with you, and we appreciate all you did for us.

Semper Fidelis

Presented at the 2001 2nd Battalion, 1st Marine Regiment, 1st Marine Division Reunion in New Orleans, Louisiana.

Richard Payne, HN 2 PLT, Fox Co.
Wally Cunningha, Sgt Fox Co
Humberto Marquez, Cpl. Fox Co.
RON REGAN FOX CO.
John H Armstrong Fox Co
Robert Ford Fox Co
Al J Baron 2d Plt Fox Co
James Bourgeois, Fox Co.
Ray S. Norton Fox Co.
Jerry L. Dedding Wpn
Chuck Lundeen W-2-1

INDEX

A

Adams, Hewitt, 422
Alsop (first sergeant), 350, 354, 362
anecdotes
    banana shipment, 154
    beer can pyramid, 180
    Chinese soldier/bush, 273
    Colonel Buse's rifle platoon
        inspection, 170
    Cooper and his picture, 169
    dead commander's casket
        on board ship, 151
    Great Drinking Contest, the, 103
    hitchhiking adventures, 175
    Lieutenant Mason's foot/shoe
        inspection, 132
    lost overlay, 432
    porcupine, 112
    South African Forces'
        four-plane strike, 266
    White Russian girl, 133
    Wozencraft and the bugs, 310
Armstrong, John, 375, 425, 458
army. *See* U.S. Army
Autoport, 13, 14

B

Baker Company, 175, 178, 179, 180, 209
Barone, Lita, 418, 419
Barr, Stringfellow, 162
Barrow, Tom, 362, 363, 364, 365, 366, 369, 379, 393, 394, 440, 449
Bartell (corporal), 23, 44
Basic School, 140, 188, 190, 193, 194, 198, 208, 211, 244, 248, 275, 303, 313, 333, 340, 377, 408, 427, 429, *See also* Quantico
    graduation and class ranking, 193
Batterton, Roy, 304, 305, 335, 338, 340, 343, 355, 360, 361, 363, 366, 369, 378, 380, 382, 392, 394, 395, 403, 417, 434

Beidaihe Beach, 109, 126, 127, 129
Beidaihe Junction, 106, 109, 127
Beijing, 66, 95, 126, 143, 144, 339
Bianco, Joseph, 116, 118
Birkenstock (platoon corpsman), 370, 372, 373, 375
Boats, 89, 93, 102, 103, 114, 118, 123, 168, 335
Boatsman, Bill. *See* Boats
Boatsman, William. *See* Boats
Bolgiano, Margaret, 16, 18, 62, 63, 147, 148, 162
Bonin, Louis A., 23, 24, 25, 27, 28, 32, 44, 52, 56
boot camp, 11, 14, 19, 20, 21, 22,
    See also Parris Island
    boondockers, 23, 34
    boxing, 41, 42
    graduation, 55
    hand grenades, 52, 55
    laundry, 40
    piss-cutters, 23, 48
    Platoon 467, 24, 25, 26, 28, 37, 52, 60
    punishments, 32, 33, 34, 35, 43, 105
    rifle training, 30, 39, 42, 43, 45, 49, 50, 51, 52, 55
    swimming, 33
boot leave, 43, 55, 56, 60, 61, 62
booze, 61, 103, 120, 221, 298, 301, 303, 304, 309, 313, 354, 392, 421
    Great Drinking Contest, the, 103
box-me-in fires, 337, 339, 414, 420, 423
boxing, 57, 119, 121, 122, 123, 314, 315
    boot camp, 41, 42
Boyer (private), 33, 34
British forces, 99, 246, 298, 299, 308, 312, 414, 415, 416
    British Commonwealth Division, 297, 306, 316, 412, 413
Brokaw, Tom
    Greatest Generation, The, 11
Bronze Star, 358, 364
Broujos (lieutenant), 400, 407

Browning automatic rifle (BAR), 51, 52, 124, 258, 260, 272, 323, 370
Buchanan, Scott, 162
Bunker Hill (Korean War), 335, 336, 339, 341, 342, 381, 383, 391, 414, 425, 440, 441, 448, 456
  battles in, 343, 360
Burhans, Robert, 340, 342, 345, 349, 350, 354, 356, 360, 361, 365, 367, 368, 369, 370, 371, 372, 373, 376, 378, 433, 434
Burrus (lieutenant), 421, 422, 423, 425, 426, 458
Buse, Robert, 168, 170, 171
Butler (lieutenant), 203

C

Calhoun, Rory, 418, 419
Camp Geiger, 69
  Camp Geiger Infantry Training Unit, 173
Camp Lejeune, 15, 19, 34, 43, 60, 61, 73, 74, 158, 166
  Tent Camp, 19, 20
Camp Pendleton, 118, 207, 208, 209, 210, 213, 214, 215, 217, 219, 321
Chain, Bill, 337, 341, 349
Chaplain McCabe. *See* McCabe (chaplain)
Charlie Company, 88, 94, 95, 96, 98, 119, 123, 125, 152, 153, 346
Chiang Kai-shek, 90, 97, 144
China, 14, 62, 63, 66, 71, 74, 79, 81, 84, 87, 88, 118, 151, 162, 166, 168, 172, 178, 192, 195, 203, 246, 321, 339, 430, 450, 456
Chinese communists, 90, 97, 245, 246, 247, 251, 253, 254, 255, 256, 257, 258, 259, 260, 263, 264, 265, 266, 269, 270, 271, 273, 276, 278, 280, 281, 283, 284, 289, 290, 291, 292, 293, 294, 295, 296, 306, 313, 336, 383, 384, 385, 397, 398, 399, 412, 413, 415, 416, 423, 425, 426, 440, 441, *See also under* Bunker Hill; Stromboli
  listening posts, 275, 284, 285
Chinese funeral, 115
Chinese Nationalists, 90, 126, 129, 142
Chinese New Year, 114
Chogum-ni, 284, 285, 319, 321, 323, 325, 326, 328, 420, 421, 422, 423, 425
Chongqing, 62
Chosin Reservoir, 67, 69, 70, 173, 246, 331
Clark, Mark, 248, 316, 317
combat zone, 303, 313, 397, 443
Congressional Medal of Honor, 67, 209, 341
Cooper (rifleman), 169

Crawford, Fayette Delbert, 279, 282, 283, 293, 296, 312, 326, 328, 329, 408
Cunningham, Wally, 349

D

Daskalakis (first lieutenant), 199, 200
Del Valle, Pedro, 36, 49, 56
Delta Company. *See* Dog Company
Diamond, Lou, 22
Doc Mahannah. *See* Mahannah (corpsman)
Dog Company, 248, 335, 394, 395, 400, 401, 407, 408, 409, 420, 426, 427, 428, 436, 457
Dominick, Bob. *See* Dominick, Robert
Dominick, Robert, 400, 407, 410, 416, 419, 420, 422, 423, 424, 425, 432, 433, 435, 438, 441, 443, 445, 446, 448, 449
Dooley, Philip, 276, 315
Drinkard (sergeant), 264, 265, 365, 366, 367
Dudding, Jerry, 338
Durante (corpsman), 403, 404

E

Easy Company, 248, 286, 297, 299, 351, 357, 394, 400, 408, 421
Eisenhower, Dwight, 411, 412, 442
  administration, 341
Eldracker, Rocky, 426, 427, 428, 436
Etheridge, Marion, 244, 248

F

Fifth Marine Division, 89, 286, *See also* Fifth Marines
Fifth Marine Regiment, 171, 245, 323, *See also* Fifth Marines
Fifth Marines, 88, 106, 248, 297, 299, 319, 350, 391, 448
  Second Battalion, 286, 408
fire-zone territory, 440
First Corps, 275, 306, 307, 308, 309
First Marine Division, 66, 67, 89, 92, 106, 119, 122, 137, 195, 244, 246, 247, 249, 294, 297, 303, 306, 312, 323, 344, 345, 351, 398, 399, 406, 408, 411, 412, 446, 448, 451, *See also* First Marines
First Marine Regiment, 67, 86, 88, 105, 119, 130, 144, 259, 351, *See also* First Marines
First Marines, 105, 131, 244, 248, 257, 259, 286, 331, 342, 354, 363, 391, 439, *See also* First Marine Division; First Marine Regiment

First Battalion, 123, 139, 454
Second Battalion, 244, 303, 397, 407, 431, 443, 457
First Marines Club, 103, 104
First U.S. Corps Honor Guard, 306, 307, 308, 309, 316
fitness report, 395, 432
Flournoy (colonel), 337, 343, 403
Foot (nickname), 116, 121, 137
Fox Company, 168, 171, 180, 255, 259, 260, 264, 272, 278, 283, 286, 302, 306, 307, 315, 318, 331, 343, 346, 348, 350, 358, 364, 379, 380, 394
Fredericksburg, Virginia, 19, 63, 66, 70, 181, 333

G

G Company, 341, 353, 354, 357
Garner (lieutenant), 330, 338, 340
Garrison (gunnery sergeant), 280, 324
German, Ken, 95, 96, 124
Ghurkas, 298, 308, 317
Gililland, Cotton, 434, 435, 438, 439, 442, 443, 445, 447, 449
Goldstein (corporal), 180, 181
Greatest Generation, The (Brokaw), 11
Greene, Wallace, 71, 334

H

H Company, 346, 357
Haebel, Robert, 340, 342, 345, 346, 347, 348, 349, 351, 352, 354, 356, 360, 361, 365, 367, 369, 371
Headquarters and Service Company, 101, 336, 393, 394, 396, 401
Hedy, 360, 363, 365, 366, 367, 378, 380, 384
Higgins, Marguerite, 361, 362, 419
Hildebrandt, Bill, 215, 223, 452, 453, 454
Hill (lieutenant), 355, 356, 357, 365, 379, 384, 385
Hill 122, 336
Hill 151, 385, 397, 398
Hill 181, 332, 336, 337, 344, 345
Hill 201, 336, 345, 346, 351, 354, 356, 357, 358, 360, 362, 365, 366, 367, 370, 373, 383, 384, 404, 441
Hill 229, 336, 345, 358, 379, 382, 383, 385, 391, 397, 440, 441, 442, 448
Hill 749, 331
Ho Chi Minh, 90
Hodes, Hiram, 101, 102
Hollingshead, Byron, 251
Holmberg, Bill, 250, 252, 262, 263, 264, 265, 276, 279, 280, 281, 284, 286, 287, 288, 289, 291, 292, 293, 294, 296, 297, 303, 305, 306, 312, 315, 337, 340, 420
honor guard. *See* First U.S. Corps Honor Guard
Hook, the, 412, 413, 414, 415, 416
Hungnam, 246, 247

I

I Company, 336, 341
Imjin River, 245, 248, 278, 297, 300, 301, 304, 305, 312, 314, 317, 318, 323, 354, 385, 391, 392, 397, 400, 401, 412, 432
Inchon, 67, 224, 243, 244, 246, 294, 303, 311, 342, 377, 401, 437, 439, 443, 445, 448, 451
Iwo Jima, 15, 28, 67, 84, 102, 118, 119, 120, 122, 123, 146, 287, 434

J

Jannelle, Tom, 315, 330, 338, 339, 345, 348, 354, 355, 365, 377, 379, 384, 385, 391, 441, 449
Japan, 16, 43, 44, 48, 84, 85, 89, 94, 119, 135, 218, 220, 221, 222, 223, 243, 245, 302, 303, 316, 354, 366, 378, 404, 407, 414, 421, 422, 452, 454
negotiations with USA, 334
R & R in, 283, 317, 401, 402, 403, 405, 406, 452
Japanese encephalitis, 137
Japanese forces, 15, 48, 66, 89, 90, 93, 94, 97, 100, 119, 124, 133, 134

K

Kansas Line, 392, 432, 433, 434
Kelly, John Francis, 263, 264, 293, 294, 306, 307, 341, 344, 360
Killeen, Calvin, 251, 255, 256, 257, 258, 270
Kimbrough (lieutenant), 342, 345
Kobe, 220, 222, 224, 299, 450
Kolka (PFC), 350
Korea, 168, 173, 188, 193, 195, 198, 209, 212, 218, 219, 220, 224, 344, 351, 363, 397, 399, 400, 402, 404, 407, 408, 412, 414, 441, 442, 451, 456
Korean Demilitarized Zone, 265
Korean Marine Corps, 247, 278, 297, 323, 339, 352, 385, 397, 398, 399, 440, 446
Korean Service Corps (KSC), 261, 347, 348, 365, 367, 373, 378, 380, 381, 382

Korean War, 11, 34, 56, 91, 172, 204, 208, 219, 245, 247, 280, 294, 298, 311, 342, 361, 376, 377, 397, 402, 403, 411, 414, 419, 451
   buildup, 182
Korean War Memorial, 141
Korean War Project, 458
Kuhn (chaplain), 458
Kumgok, 251, 255, 256, 269, 283, 284, 285, 322, 325, 420, 421, 423, 424, 425, 426, 429, 458
Kyoto, 223, 402, 403, 404, 405, 406, 452, 453

L

landing zones, 391
Last Parallel, The (Russ), 363, 391
Layer, Walter, 343, 344, 361, 369, 403, 404
Leedy (machine gunner), 274, 275
liberty, 65, 73, 74, 99, 101, 102, 105, 109, 110, 114, 115, 120, 123, 125, 132, 133, 136, 154, 155, 156, 157, 169, 171, 174, 175, 178, 179, 205, 209, 210, 215, 218, 220, 222, 303, 402, 444, 445, 452, 454
   base liberty, 79, 82, 84
Lieutenant T, 139, 140, 146
Lieutenant Z, 279, 280, 281
Lindsay (private), 254
Line Jamestown. *See* MLR (main line of resistance)
Lorraine, 207
Los Angeles, 204, 207, 210, 211, 214
Lundeen, Chuck, 338, 352

M

M1 rifle, 43, 50, 51, 86, 92, 139, 178, 179, 275, 296, 370, 374
MacArthur, Douglas, 48, 316, 405
Mahannah (corpsman), 264, 265, 283
main line of resistance. *See* MLR (main line of resistance)
Manchuria, 44, 89, 96, 97, 102, 126, 127, 133
Manthey (gunnery sergeant), 178, 179
Marine Corps, 11, 14, 194, 195, 202, 204, 207, 213, 219, 244, 245, 247, 252, 282, 283, 290, 299, 302, 314, 333, 346, 377, 384, 391, 394, 411, 449, *See also all related topics*
   corporal, position of, 124
   customs and traditions, 19, 187, 292, 305, 420
   drill instructors, 46
   enlistment/recruitment, 16, 17, 63
   fielding competitive base teams, 198
   four sections of MC staff, 446
   Marine Corps Birthday, 69, 72, 73, 199, 399, 400

Table of Organization, 167
treatment of athletes, 199
views on religion and church, 39
Marine Corps Reserve, 16, 67, 68, 69, 70, 118, 162, 164, 166, 168, 173, 248, 391
   battalion reserve, 354, 398, 400, 445
   division reserve, 412, 437
   regimental reserve, 245, 343, 356, 358, 400, 411, 412
Marshall, George C., 91
Marsky (pediatrician), 407, 408, 429
Marx, Groucho, 212
Mary Washington College, 70, 72, 333
Mason, A. T., 130, 131, 132
Matson (staff sergeant), 180
McCabe (chaplain), 287, 288, 289, 329, 330, 354, 356
McCulloch, Bill, 122, 124, 131, 138, 139, 141, 142, 147, 450
McDonnell, Dermott, 336, 353, 356, 363, 375, 392, 394, 395, 396, 400
McNeill (major), 395, 419, 422
McNulty (captain), 170, 171
Mickey Mouse boots, 410
mines, 85, 86, 108, 245, 248, 280, 286, 287, 288, 289, 293, 296, 325, 327, 328, 329, 422
   bouncing Betties, 263, 325, 326, 327
   box mines, 288, 325, 326
Missar (colonel), 196, 197, 198, 199, 200
MLR (main line of resistance), 249, 251, 259, 276, 293, 301, 322, 323, 325, 361, 392, 412, 440, 441
Moody, Clarence Griffith. *See* Moody, Griff
Moody, Griff, 71, 252, 258, 259, 268, 278, 279, 280, 281, 283, 284, 286, 290, 292, 293, 294, 303, 305, 307, 311, 312, 313, 315, 321, 325, 330, 331, 332, 335, 336, 337, 338, 339, 340, 341, 345, 346, 347, 349, 350, 352, 353, 355, 357, 360, 362, 363, 403, 404, 408
Morrison, George, 172, 208, 213, 214, 215, 216, 217, 218, 220, 286, 299, 408, 409, 435
Munsan-ni, 244, 303, 311, 437, 440, 445, 449
Murphy, Bob, 342, 345, 350, 351, 352, 356

N

Naktong River, 245
navy. *See* U.S. Navy
Navy Cross, 66, 265, 292, 341, 360, 404
Nelson (corporal), 56, 57, 59
Nethery, Ricochet. *See* Ricochet
Neustadt, Jack, 162
Nicoletti, Francis Xavier, 116, 117, 118

464

Nimitz, Chester, 48
no-fire zone, 382, 383
Norfolk, 74, 75, 157
North China Sea, 84, 85, 86, 152, 224, 274, 437, 451, 452
North Korea, 164
North Koreans, 245, 246, 247, 265, 267, 278, 284, 311, 323, 376, 377, 434
North Vietnam, 90

O

O'Brien (corporal), 398, 424, 425, 426, 444, 445
O'Daniel, Iron Mike, 307
Officer Candidate School, 72, 147, 165, 172, 173, 178, 180, 182, 184, 186, 244, 248, 303, 313, 333, 340, *See also* Quantico
Okinawa, 14, 15, 67, 84, 120, 123, 124, 131, 146, 168, 282
One-Hundred-Yard Dash, 253, 254, 264, 291
OP-2 (Outpost 2), 440, 448
OP-3 (Outpost 3), 251, 278, 279, 280, 281, 283, 284, 287, 291, 292, 293, 337, 403
Operation Recoil, 445
OPLR (outpost line of resistance), 251, 252, 253, 254, 256, 257, 258, 259, 262, 263, 264, 265, 266, 268, 269, 270, 278, 279, 281, 284, 286, 287, 290, 291, 332, 340, 366, 420
Osaka, 405, 406
outpost line of resistance. *See* OPLR

P

Palmer, Tom, 393, 408, 409, 417, 418, 419, 420, 423, 424, 429
Panama Canal, 79, 80, 152, 154, 157
Panmunjom, 247, 248, 278, 304, 323, 358, 363, 379, 382, 383, 440, 448
Parris Island, 11, 12, 14, 19, 20, 21, 22, 24, 26, 27, 28, 29, 30, 35, 36, 40, 43, 44, 48, 52, 53, 54, 56, 58, 63, 64, 65, 72, 162, 179, 184, 198, 287, 307, 324, *See also* boot camp
  basketball, 57, 58, 197
  cat fever, 52
  dental dispensary, 37
  mess halls, 47
  V-J Day, 48
  weather, 30, 31
password and countersign, 250, 260, 268, 272, 274, 275
Payne, Richard, 324, 325
Pearl Harbor, 13, 81, 82, 83, 84, 134, 414
Peck (general), 106, 108, 109, 120
Peleliu, 67, 169

Pernokas (surgeon), 408, 429, 435, 436, 454
Peters, Robert S, 339
Poe, Harvey, 164
Pollock (general), 431, 432, 433, 450, 451
Pomocky, Vince, 336, 393, 395, 401, 429
Porter (boxing partner), 41, 42
Port Royal, South Carolina, 20, 33, 61
Posey (Great Drinking Contest), 103
precision missions, 256, 270, 271, 272, 415
Puller, Chesty, 65, 66, 73, 123, 131, 335
Puller, Lewis. *See* Puller, Chesty
Puller, Lewis Jr., 72
Puller, Martha, 70, 71, 72
Purple Heart, 368, 369, 375, 393, 433
Pyongyang, 246

Q

Qinhuangdao, 95, 96, 97, 106, 108, 109, 134
Quantico, Marine Corps Base, 65, 72, 124, 158, 172, 173, 180, 181, 182, *See also* Basic School; Officer Candidate School
Quilici (lieutenant colonel), 248, 249, 303, 304, 343, 403, 434
Quirk (platoon leader), 170, 171

R

R & R, 283, 317, 401, 402, 403, 405, 406, 408, 410, 419, 420, 452
Raykus (staff sergeant), 280
Ray (runner, radioman), 280, 283, 287, 290, 295
Reifel (major), 442, 449
replacement drafts, 44, 103, 106, 118, 119, 173, 220, 244, 366
  Ninety-fourth Replacement Draft, 74
  Thirteenth Replacement Draft, 344, 392
  Twentieth Replacement Draft, 207, 208, 219, 331
  Republic of Korea Army. *See* South Korean army
Richardson (sergeant), 331
Ricochet, 287, 288, 301
Ridenhour (machine gunner), 257, 258, 259
Ridgeway (general), 316
Rivers, L. Mendel, 49
Rockey (general), 94, 135
Rock Pile, the, 301, 302, 428, 429, 435, 437, 439
Russ, Martin
  Last Parallel, The, 363, 391

S

Sangkorangpo, 245, 248, 400
San Francisco, 448, 451, 454, 455
Sasebo, 451, 452, 454
Schools Demonstration Troops (SDT), 194, 195, 196, 197, 198, 199, 202
Sclavas, John, 170
Scottish Black Watch, 308, 413, 414, 415
Second Marine Division, 89, 171
Seoul, 67, 89, 164, 244, 245, 246, 247, 278, 297, 303, 311, 323, 385, 392, 401, 420, 437, 445
Seventh Marines, 108, 126, 127, 129, 139, 246, 248, 259, 273, 280, 281, 318, 328, 341, 400, 412
Seventh Marine Regiment, 66, 108, 278, 324
shaped charges, 368, 369, 376
Shepherd, Dee-Dee, 221
Shepherd, Lemuel, 86, 221
Silver Star, 351, 364, 385
Sixth Marine Division, 86, 89, *See also* Sixth Marines
Sixth Marine Regiment, 171, *See also* Sixth Marines
Sixth Marines, 168, 173, 179, 209
  First Battalion, 174
  Sixth Marines Club, 179
Skyrm, David, 120
Smith (master sergeant), 279, 281, 288, 289, 324, 350, 353, 354, 362, 367, 416
Smith, Winfrey, 164
Smythe (lieutenant), 288, 293, 306, 315, 338, 339, 340, 342
South African Air Force, 266, 267, 268
South Korea, 89, 164, 245, 246, 247, 278, 323
South Korean army, 245, 246, 247
St. John's College (Annapolis, Maryland), 13, 15, 43, 56, 58, 62, 162, 163, 164, 165, 172, 206, 250
St. John's College (New York), 56
State College, Pennsylvania, 13, 14
Stearns, Dan, 14, 19, 20, 21, 172
Stevenson, Adlai, 411, 412
Stromboli (Korean War), 345, 347, 350, 352, 360, 368, 408, 414, 416, 420, 425
  battle of, 320
Sullivan (major), 196, 198, 199
Sullivan (sergeant, draftsman), 398, 410, 433, 443, 444, 446

T

TaeDocSan, 256
Tenth Corps, 246
Tianjin, 86, 88, 89, 90, 91, 94, 95, 96, 97, 98, 99, 100, 101, 102, 104, 106, 108, 109, 110, 112, 114, 115, 120, 126, 129, 130, 132, 134, 135, 136, 137, 140, 141, 142, 143, 144, 147, 153, 159, 450
Tokchokto, 311
trench lines, 249, 255, 256, 257, 258, 259, 261, 263, 267, 269, 270, 272, 273, 274, 289, 291, 292, 296, 298, 322, 323, 329, 332, 345, 363, 365, 367, 371, 376, 383, 403, 410, 420, 427, 428, 440, 441
Basic School training, 189, 213
Tumae-ri, 256, 258
Tun Tavern, 35, 73

U

U.S. Army, 31, 63, 75, 174, 202, 244, 247, 256, 266, 272, 307, 308, 351
  Army Transportation Corps, 445
  Eighth Army, 246, 275, 297, 306, 323, 412, 427
  Tenth Army Corps, 89, 246
U.S. Coast Guard, 77, 78, 80, 85
U.S. Navy, 31, 35, 85, 95, 150, 151, 196, 205, 221, 252, 256, 437
  Navy Medical Corps, 95, 373
Uijongbu, 306, 316
United States Marine Corps (USMC). *See* Marine Corps
United States Marine Corps Reserve (USMCR). *See* Marine Corps Reserve
USS *General J. C. Breckinridge*, 149, 150, 152, 156, 157
USS *Missouri*, 48
USS *Wakefield*, 74, 77, 101, 119, 149, 157

V

Van Sant, Peggy (fiancee, later second wife), 333, 334, 335, 348, 417
Van Sant, Peggy (sister), 192
Van Sant, Shirley (first wife), 163, 164, 166, 167, 169, 170, 172, 173, 174, 175, 178, 181, 183, 191, 193, 194, 195, 203, 204, 244, 254, 333, 348, 378, 456
Vandegrift, Alexander, 36, 49
Vick, Vernon, 244, 248, 249, 357, 358, 400, 421, 422, 448, 449

Vietnam, 71, 193, 307, 326, 333, 334
Vincello (lieutenant), 244, 248, 449, 451
Virgil, 125, 126, 128

W

Warren, Charles E., 394, 395, 401, 413, 416, 417, 418, 419, 420, 421, 422, 423, 424, 425, 426, 429, 430, 432, 433, 434, 435
Washington DC, 16, 61, 102, 161, 192, 202
Weapons Company, 196, 198, 248, 259, 324, 346, 365, 370, 371, 394, 400, 416, 431, 433, 458
Widgeon Bridge, 305, 312, 313, 314, 315, 317, 322, 323, 330, 350, 384, 408

Wozencraft, Clark, 251, 252, 253, 254, 255, 256, 257, 258, 259, 260, 262, 265, 297, 303, 304, 309, 315, 330, 333, 340

Y

Yalu River, 246
Yemassee, South Carolina, 20, 61

Z

zone of responsibility, 323